JOURNAL FOR THE STUDY OF THE NEW TESTAMENT
SUPPLEMENT SERIES

257

The Message of Acts in Codex Bezae

A Comparison with the Alexandrian Tradition

VOLUME 1

Acts 1.1–5.42: Jerusalem

Josep Rius-Camps and
Jenny Read-Heimerdinger

A Continuum imprint

Published by T&T Clark International
The Tower Building, 11 York Road, London SE1 7NX
15 East 26th Street, Suite 1703, New York, NY 10010

www.tandtclark.com

British Library Cataloguing-in-Publication Data
A catalogue record for this book is available from the British Library

Library of Congress Cataloging-in-Publication Data
A catalogue record for this book is available from the Library of Congress

Typeset by CA Typesetting, Sheffield
Printed on acid-free paper in Great Britain by The Cromwell Press, Trowbridge, Wiltshire

ISBN 0-8264-7000-9 (hardback)

CONTENTS

Preface ix
Abbreviations xi

GENERAL INTRODUCTION 1

PROLEGOMENA 1.1–14 45
Overview 45
Translation 47
Critical Apparatus 49
Commentary 57
Excursus 1: The Restoration of Israel: Two Conflicting Plans 79
Commentary (cont.) 88
Excursus 2: The Ascension of Jesus and the Parallel of Elijah 93
Commentary (cont.) 98

I. THE REPLACEMENT OF THE TWELFTH APOSTLE: 1.15–26 107
Overview 107
Translation 108
Critical Apparatus 109
Commentary 115
Excursus 3: The Replacement of Judas and its Consequences 136

II. THE OUTPOURING OF THE HOLY SPIRIT: 2.1-47 140
General Overview 140
[A] 2.1–4: The First Outpouring of the Holy Spirit 140
Overview 140
Translation 141
Critical Apparatus 141
Commentary 143

[B] 2.5–13: The Reaction of the People in Jerusalem to the Manifestation of the Spirit 152
Overview 152
Translation 153
Critical Apparatus 153
Commentary 158
[B′] 2.14–40: Peter's Two-Part Response and its Outcome 165
Overview 165
Translation 165
Critical Apparatus 167
Commentary 178
[A′] 2.41–47: The First Summary: The Way of Life of the Jerusalem Church 193
Overview 193
Translation 195
Critical Apparatus 195
Commentary 198

III THE SIGN OF THE LAME MAN'S HEALING: 3.1–4.35 202
General Overview 202
[A] 3.1–10: The Healing of the Lame Man 203
Overview 203
Translation 204
Critical Apparatus 205
Commentary 209
[B] 3.11–26: Peter's Speech in Solomon's Porch 217
Overview 217
Translation 217
Critical Apparatus 219
Commentary 226
[C] 4.1–4: The Imprisonment of Peter and John 239
Overview 239
Translation 240
Critical Apparatus 240
Commentary 242
[B′] 4.5–22: The Meeting of the Sanhedrin 244
Overview 244
Translation 246
Critical Apparatus 247
Commentary 255

[A′] 4.23–31: The Release of the Jesus-Believing Community 267
Overview 267
Translation 269
Critical Apparatus 270
Commentary 272
4.32–35: Bridging (Second) Summary: The Community Ideal 281
Overview 281
Translation 282
Critical Apparatus 283
Commentary 285
Excursus 4: Similarities and Differences between the First and Second Summaries 287

IV THE JERUSALEM CHURCH: 4.36–5.42 289
General Overview 289
[A] 4.36–5.11: The Selling of a Field 290
Overview 290
Translation 292
Critical Apparatus 293
Commentary 298
Excursus 5: Joseph Barnabas and Joseph the Son of Jacob 308
Excursus 6: The Symbol of the Field 311
[B] 5.12–42: The Testimony of the Apostles 314
General Overview 314
[BA] 5.12–16: Signs and Wonders through the Hands of the Apostles 315
Overview 315
Translation 316
Critical Apparatus 317
Commentary 319
Excursus 7: Luke's Adaptation of Mk 6.53–56 324
[BB] 5.17–21a: The Jealousy of the High Priest 325
Overview 325
Translation 326
Critical Apparatus 326
Commentary 327
[BC] 5.21b–26: Preparations for the Sanhedrin Meeting 331
Overview 331
Translation 332

Critical Apparatus 333
Commentary 335
[BC′] 5.27–33: The Sanhedrin Meeting 337
Overview 337
Translation 338
Critical Apparatus 338
Commentary 341
[BB′] 5.34–40: Gamaliel's Intervention 345
Overview 345
Translation 346
Critical Apparatus 346
Commentary 350
[BA′] 5.41–42: The Liberation of the Apostles 355
Overview 355
Translation 355
Critical Apparatus 356
Commentary 357
Excursus 8: The Re-enactment of the Exodus 358
Excursus 9: The Parallel Roles of Gamaliel and Judas Iscariot 363

Bibliography 366

PREFACE

This study of the the Acts of the Apostles had its origin in a chance meeting between the two authors at the International Colloque on Codex Bezae held in Lunel, France, 1994. For some years previously, we had each been working independently on the text of Acts unaware that, using quite different approaches, we had arrived at similar conclusions. These concerned not only the authentic status of Codex Bezae but also its clear theological message, and were in opposition to the usual view that the manuscript transmits a secondary text. As we discovered how close was the agreement between the separate results of our research and how complementary were our respective interests, we decided there and then in Lunel to prepare for publication in English a systematic examination of the text of Acts which would bring out the different messages and aims of the two principal manuscript traditions. We would use as a basis the commentary of Acts being produced in Catalan by Rius-Camps, altering, amplifying and updating it as our understanding of the text of Acts developed or was enhanced by the other's contribution. This series of volumes is the fruit of that collaboration.

Josep Rius-Camps has been engaged in work on Acts since the mid-1970's. As a lecturer in Patristics at the Pontifical Institute in Rome, he was conducting research into the prophetic texts of the pre-Nicene Fathers when he was led to examine the records in Acts of the prophetic manifestations within the first Christian communities. He was struck by an underlying tension between, on the one hand, the insistent exhortations with which the prophets transmitted the guidance of the Holy Spirit and, on the other, the slowness or unwillingness on the part of some of the Christian leaders, notably Paul, to heed the prophetic messages. He saw that the tension was considerably increased when the account of Acts was set against the sayings and works of Jesus as presented in the Gospel of Luke. This turned out to be the starting point for a fresh look at the relationship of the book of Acts to Luke's Gospel and the author's purpose in writing it, and how that purpose was expressed in manuscripts other than the ones on which the familiar text of Acts was based. Following the publication in Catalan and in Spanish of monographs and articles on the subject, Rius-Camps launched the first volume of a full-scale commentary of Acts in Catalan in 1991, subsequent volumes having appeared since then (details are given in the Bibliography).

Jenny Read-Heimerdinger, for her part, was drawn to the text of Acts through a dual interest, firstly in the directions being taken by studies in first-century Judaism, and secondly in Discourse Analysis as a linguistic discipline. While studying textual criticism in France in 1982, she had begun to detect variant readings in the so-called 'Western' text of Acts which she identified as encapsulating traditions and perspectives that were typically Jewish. Subsequently, while studying discourse analysis, she observed that many of the elements identified by linguists as playing a significant role in the telling of stories were among the features frequently affected by variant readings in the manuscripts of Acts. She went on to carry out a linguistic comparison of Codex Bezae and Codex Vaticanus using the tools of discourse analysis to evaluate the variant readings and published the results in 2002 (see Bibliography).

In our individual research, we had already each adopted a method for our study of Acts which we have continued to follow in our joint work. This method consists in regarding as the most important part of research an accurate analysis of the text (what might be termed 'micro-analysis'), giving preference to arguments depending on internal considerations and leaving on one side in the first instance the many, and often contradictory, opinions that may have accumulated in the course of the exegetical history of a given problem. That is not to say that we ignore the vast amount of scholarship relating to Acts, but that we seek to base our conclusions on an understanding of the text rather than on an evaluation of published material.

We have set out in a *General Introduction* to the series the details of our methodology and explanations of the basic notions underlying the analyses. The comments on particular verses and passages will consequently be clearer and more readily comprehensible if the *General Introduction* has been read beforehand.

Our warmest thanks are due to Jean-Marc Heimerdinger and Enric Muñarch for their assistance in preparing this first volume.

Josep Rius-Camps and Jenny Read-Heimerdinger

Abbreviations of Journals

Bib	*Biblica*
BJRL	*Bulletin of the John Rylands Library*
BZ	*Biblische Zeitschrift*
CBQ	*Catholic Biblical Quarterly*
ET	*Evangelische Theologie*
ExpT	*Expository Times*
FN	*Filología Neotestamentaria*
JBL	*Journal of Biblical Literature*
NTS	*New Testament Studies*
NovT	*Novum Testamentum*
RB	*Revue Biblique*
RBén	*Revue Bénédictine*
RCatT	*Revista Catalana de Teologia*
RevThom	*Revue Thomiste*
RHPR	*Revue d'histoire et de philosophie religieuses*
RTP	*Revue de théologie et de philosophie*
SBL	*Society of Biblical Literature*
SE	*Studia Evangelica*
ST	*Studia Theologica*
TR	*Theologische Rundschau*
TLZ	*Theologische Literaturzeitung*
ZNW	*Zeitschrift für die neutestamentliche Wissenschaft*

TEXT-Critical Signs and Abrreviations

The following conventional signs and abbreviations are used:

cj.	conjectured reading
lac.	lacuna
MS, MSS	manuscript, manuscripts
vl, vll	variant reading, variant readings

After a manuscript letter or number, in superscript:

*	original hand
2	second hand
corr	corrector (followed by the letter assigned to successive correctors of the manuscripts only)
ms, mss	one or several manuscripts only

Principal manuscripts cited

א01	Codex Sinaiticus
B03	Codex Vaticanus
D05	Codex Bezae Cantabrigiensis: Greek pages
d05	Codex Bezae Cantabrigiensis: Latin pages

General Introduction

The story of the book of Acts is a familiar one: how the apostles – the Twelve and later Paul – took the good news of Jesus to the people of Jerusalem, Judaea and Samaria, and the ends of the earth; and how, under the guidance of God, through Jesus and the empowerment of the Holy Spirit, the Church was founded. So it comes as a surprise to discover that in one MS, although the familiar events and characters are all there, the story is told somewhat differently. In Codex Bezae, the successive events and the divine interventions are a framework that the narrator uses to present the inner journey of the apostles as they leave behind their traditional Jewish teachings and expectations and, with considerable difficulty, finally come to understand and accept the message of Jesus. So it is the story of their failures, mistakes, misunderstandings and even disobedience, as well as their achievements and joy, as they struggle to match the teaching of Jesus – especially with regard to Israel and the nations – with the Jewish Scriptures and the interpretations of them they are familiar with.

The shift from the mentality the apostles are used to, with all its hopes of a restored Israel under the rule of the Messiah, to the new way of thinking required by the death and resurrection of Jesus, is a radical one with immense implications for Jewish self-identity and the privileged position of Israel as the people of God. Just as in Luke's Gospel the disciples are seen to be slow to grasp what Jesus means and to alter their ways of thinking, so too, in the Bezan text of Acts the apostles, not least Paul, start off with ideas that are firmly rooted in Jewish Messianic, eschatological traditions but gradually, as they observe how God acts, they learn to modify their ideas and attitudes until they are completely free from the old religious order. [1]

1. J. Rius-Camps has described this interpretation of the book of Acts in *El camino de Pablo a la misión de los paganos* (Madrid: Cristiandad, 1984); *De Jerusalén a Antioquía. Génesis de la iglesia cristiana* (Córdoba: El Almendro, 1989). These two works are a summary of his four-volume commentary on which the present work is based, *ibid.., Comentari als Fets dels Apòstols* (4 vols.; Barcelona: Facultat de Teolo-

Although the presentation of the apostles in Codex Bezae is critical it is no hostile account of a bitter outsider, out to attack the foundations of the Church or to scorn the religion from which it emerged. For the story is told with detailed and authoritative, first-hand knowledge of Judaism, evident in the intricate web of Jewish allusions and resonances that abound in the Bezan form of the text.[2] Its narrator is thus capable of a remarkable understanding of what his characters go through and his purpose appears to be to inform his audience (even Theophilus himself, who could have once been a high priest, cf. §X below) of the truth of what they, observing from their Jewish standpoint, have been questioning and puzzling over. The characters are real people, with outstanding qualities such as determination and courage, certainly, but coupled with human weaknesses that prevented them from becoming instant supernatural heroes because they had to learn faithfulness to Jesus' teaching the hard way, through experience.

The message of Acts according to Codex Bezae, coherently and systematically maintained, is primarily a theological one, not a historical one as it is in the more usual story. There is no disguising which version we prefer. The difference between the two texts (the Alexandrian and the Bezan text) can be likened to the difference between a photograph in black and white and another in colour; or between a painting and a 3-D model; or again between a series of still photographs and a moving film. The Bezan text was not, however, the form in which the book of Acts was the most widely copied and handed down in the Church. It is perhaps the critical stance, together with the Jewish perspective, that accounts for the creation of a parallel account of the beginnings of Christianity more

gia de Catalunya – Editorial Herder, 1991–2000). A series of detailed textual notes is also being published in *Filología Neotestamentaria,* see *Bibliography*.

2. For suggestions concerning Jewish features in the Bezan text of Luke-Acts, see the articles by J. (Read-)Heimerdinger: 'Acts 8:37: A Textual and Exegetical Study', *The Bulletin of the Institute for Reformation Biblical Studies* 2 (1991), pp. 8–13; 'Unintentional Sins in Peter's Speech: Acts 3:12–26', *RCatT* 20 (1995), pp. 269–76; 'The Seven Steps of Codex Bezae: A Prophetic Interpretation of Acts 12', in D.C. Parker and C.-B. Amphoux (eds.), *Codex Bezae: Studies from the Lunel Colloquium. June 1994* (Leiden: E.J. Brill, 1996), pp. 303–10; 'La Tradition Targumique et Le Codex de Bèze. Ac 1:15–26', in A. Borrell, A. de la Fuente and A. Puig (eds.), *La Bíblia i el Mediterrani* (2 vols.; Montserrat, Barcelona: Publicacions de l'Abadia de Montserrat, 1997), II, pp. 171–80; 'Barnabas in Acts: A Study of his Role in the Text of Codex Bezae', *JSNT* 72 (1998), pp. 23–66; and with J. Rius-Camps, 'Emmaous or Oulammaous? Luke's Use of the Jewish Scriptures in the Text of Luke 24 in Codex Bezae', *RCatT* 27 (2002), pp. 23–42.

acceptable to Christians unaccustomed to thinking in Jewish terms about their faith in God.

What seems to have happened during the course of the transmission of the text of Acts is that the form of the Greek text reproduced in Codex Bezae has been fossilized: the language and the religious perspective have not been updated but remain fixed in their early form. The extant MSS suggest that it was scarcely reproduced in Greek although the earliest translations into other languages appear to have had access to something similar to it. The characteristics of the 'fossilized' text become most evident when a comparison is made with the more familiar form of the text.

Codex Bezae is a well-known manuscript whose text of Acts has been studied many times before but rarely as an entire document standing in its own right. It is the detailed and exhaustive examination of the Bezan text that has yielded the new findings and in these volumes, we will be setting out the arguments on which our deductions concerning the primary nature of the text and its theological message are based. By comparing the two main forms of Acts, we will seek to show that if the Bezan form of text were used as the documentary basis for study instead of the usual text, then the results of the diverse examinations of Acts would not only be different but surprisingly informative. No claim is being made that Codex Bezae transmits the original autograph of Luke; the contention is more simply that its text predates that of the Alexandrian tradition and is closer to the language and thought of the third evangelist.

First of all, some further introduction is needed. In the sections that follow we will present the basic tools with which we work and the methods we use; we will also explain the chief principles that govern our interpretation of the text and that underlie the exegetical commentary.

I. *The Text of Acts*

One of the most interesting and fruitful areas for investigation, among all the issues concerning the formation of the New Testament, is the text of the Acts of the Apostles. This is partly because the differences between the manuscript traditions are so great, and partly because there are still so many unresolved questions to do with the transmission of the text of Acts. It is true that for the purposes of printing editions of the Greek New Testament, a text has been reconstructed but there are nevertheless many places of variant reading where uncertainty remains over which is the best reading to print.[3] Even where there was unanimous agreement among the

3. The current editions of the Greek New Testament are the 27th edition of Nestle-

editorial committee of the current editions (a body of five textual critics), there are many other scholars who have continued to disagree with their choice, in particular instances or in the text overall, on a variety of grounds.[4] The large amount of unexplained variation between the manuscripts of Acts holds a fascination for textual critics and provoked several studies in the early part of the 20th century which became reference points for the debate.[5] In the final decades of the century, the question of the text of Acts was opened up again for fresh examination and a number of new contributions to the debate were published.[6] An outline of the textual

Aland, *Novum Testamentum Graece* (N-A[27]) and the 4th edition of the United Bible Societies, *The Greek New Testament* (UBS[4]). They share the same text (which reproduces that of the previous edition) but have a different critical apparatus, as is explained in the introductions to each edition. The companion volume to the UBS[4] edition by Metzger (*Commentary*, pp. 222–445) explains the editorial committee's reasoning behind a good number of the variants cited in the UBS apparatus of Acts. In his monograph, *The Problem of the Text of Acts* (Cambridge: Cambridge University Press, 1992), W.A. Strange expresses reservations about the committee's methods of establishing the text, see especially pp. 23–25. For a more general discussion of the merits of the current editions, see J.K. Elliott, 'A Comparison of Two Recent Greek New Testaments', *ExpT* 107 (1996), pp. 105–106; and for a briefer examination, see M. Silva, 'Modern Critical Editions and Apparatuses of the Greek New Testament', in B.D. Ehrman and M.W. Holmes (eds.), *The Text of the New Testament in Contemporary Research* (Grand Rapids, Michigan: Eerdmans, 1995), pp. 283–96.

4. The collection of articles edited by Ehrman and Holmes, *Contemporary Research*, discussing developments in New Testament textual criticism in the second half of the 20th century, is helpful for understanding the disagreement with the present choice of the New Testament text; see especially J.K. Elliott, 'Thoroughgoing Eclecticism in New Testament Textual Criticism', pp. 321–35; and M.W. Holmes, 'Reasoned Eclecticism in New Testament Textual Criticism', pp. 336–60.

5. The starting point for the 20th century debate was, in many ways, the theory published by F. Blass, *Acta Apostolorum sive Lucae ad Theophilum liber alter: Editio philologica apparatu critico* (Göttingen: Vandenhoeck & Ruprecht, 1895), positing that both of the main forms of the text were the work of the same author. His ideas attracted a serious response notably from Ropes (*Text*) and Clark (*Acts*).

6. The colloquium held in Lille, France in 2000, on the history of the New Testament text up to 200 CE is evidence of the ongoing debate on the early form of the text. Papers on Acts may be consulted in C.-B. Amphoux and J.K. Elliott (eds.), *The New Testament Text in Early Christianity: Proceedings of the Lille Colloquium, July 2000* (forthcoming).

An examination of the work carried out on the text of Acts up to 1969 is provided by A.J. Klijn, *A Survey of the Researches into the Western Text of the Gospels and Acts*, Part I (Utrecht: Kemink, 1949); Part II (Leiden: E.J. Brill, 1969). The situation at the beginning of the 1990's was described by C.D. Osburn, 'The Search for the situation of Acts will be helpful for seeing where Codex Bezae comes into the debate and for clarifying our own position.

It is common to think of the witnesses to the text of Acts as falling into two distinct text-types, the Alexandrian and the Western. The real situation is, as might be expected, rather more complicated than that. Certainly it is true that among the earliest witnesses (the papyri, the other Greek MSS, the versions and the Patristic quotations) there is a large number that transmit a broadly similar text, known as the Alexandrian text (AT). This is the text found in most of the Greek majuscules of which the best known are Codex Sinaiticus (ℵ01) and Codex Vaticanus (B03).[7] Likewise, it is that read by the majority of papyri, notably by the well-preserved P^{74}, and by all but a few minuscules. The works of the Greek Fathers most commonly cite the AT and it formed the basis of the standardized texts of the early versions (the Latin Vulgate and the Syriac Peshitta, for example).

Difficulties arise when it comes to determining another group among the remaining witnesses and defining it as 'Western'. In the first place, it is now well-recognized that the label 'Western' is a misnomer because the witnesses to which it is given by no means all come from the West; it was originally used because many of the witnesses initially identified as having a form of text distinct from the AT were associated with Rome. The greater problem, not so widely acknowledged, is that the MSS and quotations of Acts that are classified as 'Western' do not share a common text. Their chief characteristic is that they differ from the AT. Their other distinguishing feature is that they differ among themselves. It is essential to recognize that the 'Western' text is therefore not a text-type but a group

Original Text of Acts: the International Project on the Text of Acts', *JSNT* 44 (1991), pp. 39–55. Useful summaries are also given by Barrett, I, pp. 22–26; Metzger, *Commentary*, pp. 223–35; Strange, *The Problem*, pp. 1–34; P. Tavardon, *Le texte alexandrin et le texte occidental des Actes des Apôtres. Doublets et variantes de structure* (Paris: J. Gabalda, 1997), pp. 1–41. Cf. Klijn's article 'In Search of the Original Text of Acts', in L.E. Keck and J.L. Martyn (eds.), *Studies in Luke-Acts* (London: SPCK, 1968), pp. 103–10; of more recent interest is G.D. Kilpatrick's 'The Two Texts of Acts', in W. Schrage (ed.), *Studien zum Text und zur Ethik des Neuen Testaments* (Berlin: Walter de Gruyter, 1986), pp. 188–99.

7. Reference to majuscule MSS by a letter and a number is in accordance with the new Gregory system of numbering the MSS (see L. Vaganay and C.-B. Amphoux, *An Introduction to New Testament Textual Criticism* [Cambridge: Cambridge University Press, 1992], p. 63). We have adopted this practice for the sake of greater visual clarity in technical discussion.

of types.[8] Because we have no illusions about the feasibility of altering a label which has become so firmly established, we will continue to use the term 'Western' but will always place it in inverted commas.

Among the variety of 'Western' witnesses, one MS stands out from the rest because it is the only one in Greek to have a text that consistently differs from the AT. It is Codex Bezae (D05-d05) mentioned above, a bilingual Greek-Latin majuscule MS copied around 400 CE and containing in its present state the four Gospels and Acts.[9] There are important lacunae in the book of Acts (Greek: 8.29–10.14; 21.2–10; 22.10–20; 22.30 to the end of the book),[10] which have arisen because of the loss of certain leaves. The Latin translation (d05) is on pages facing the Greek and imitates the division of the text into sense-lines; it is made, however, from a different Greek exemplar than that of the Greek side and it is closer, though it by no means belongs, to the Alexandrian tradition.[11] Not only is there no other Greek witness like Codex Bezae, but more strikingly it has a large number of readings that are unattested anywhere else in the manuscript tradition, not even in its own Latin text. Having said that, it does have some measure of support from three of the earliest papyri fragments (P^{38}, c. 300; P^{45}, third century; P^{50}, fourth to fifth century)[12] and occasion-

8. D.C. Parker, *Codex Bezae: An Early Christian Manuscript* (Cambridge: Cambridge University Press, 1994), p. 284; B.M. Metzger, *The Text of the New Testament* (Oxford: Clarendon Press, 1964), p. 213; Vaganay and Amphoux, *Introduction*, p. 110.

9. There exists a facsimile edition of Codex Bezae edited by F.H. Scrivener, *Bezae Codex Cantabrigiensis* (Pittsburgh, Pennsylvania: Pickwick Press, repr. 1978) that is largely accurate for Acts; its Greek text was reproduced by A. Ammassari, *Bezae Codex Cantabrigiensis* (Città del Vaticano: Libreria Editrice Vaticana, 1996). The presentation of the manuscript by Parker in *An Early Christian Manuscript* is an excellent source of information on the manuscript itself. The book also examines the questions of the origins of the manuscript and discusses the text, providing the debates on both issues with new contributions which are important but with which we do not always agree. A recent international collection of essays covering a range of aspects of Codex Bezae is D.C. Parker and C.-B. Amphoux (eds.), *Codex Bezae: Studies from the Lunel Colloquium June 1994* (Leiden: E.J. Brill, 1996).

10. The bottom of another page has been torn (21.16–18) but the text had already been noted by an early copyist of the MS, see Scrivener, *Bezae Codex*, p. 446.

11. See J. Rius-Camps, 'Le substrat grec de la version latine des Actes dans le Codex de Bèze', in Parker and Amphoux (eds.), *Lunel Colloquium*, pp. 271–95.

12. For full details of the support for D05 in the papyri, see B. Aland, 'Entstehung, Charakter und Herkunft des sog. westlichen Textes untersucht an der Apostelgeschichte', *EThL* 62 (1986), pp. 5–65, and see J.K. Elliott, 'Codex Bezae and the Earliest Greek Papyri', in Parker and Amphoux (eds.), *Lunel Colloquium*, pp. 161–82, esp. pp. 178–81.

ally a few of the minuscules (614, 1175, 1518, 2412). There is one other majuscule manuscript, the Latin-Greek Codex Laudianus (e08-E08), which transmits in a good number of places the approximate contents of Codex Bezae though not in an identical form.[13]

The bulk of support for Codex Bezae comes from witnesses in other languages: the earliest Latin Fathers (Irenaeus, Tertullian and Cyprian) and the Latin, Syriac and Egyptian versions in their pre-recensional form. In Latin, the chief manuscripts with a 'Western' text are gig (Codex Gigas) and h (the fragmentary Fleury palimpsest). In Syriac, support for the Bezan text of Acts is found in the readings from the Harclean version that appear in the text marked with two asterisks (sy^{h**}) or that are given in the margin (sy^{hmg}); and with remarkable closeness, in the small number of verses that have been preserved in fragments in Christo (or Syro)-Palestinian, an Aramaic dialect (sy^{pal}).[14] One more manuscript, in Middle Egyptian (Codex Glazier, mae or G^{67}), tallies very closely with the Bezan text of Acts for the extant chapters 1–15. The discovery of these two last mentioned MSS is relatively recent and has brought to light support for readings previously thought only to exist in Codex Bezae.[15]

All of these witnesses that give partial support to Codex Bezae – the few Greek MSS, the quotations of the Fathers and the early versions – have further readings of their own that distance them from the AT. The different forms of the text that they display have none of the homogeneity of a recension but the question of how they came into being is one that has not been answered although various hypotheses have been posited, as noted throughout in the course of this section. The only attempt to construct a full critical apparatus of the text of Acts was published in 1984 by two French scholars, M.-É. Boismard and A. Lamouille, whose names have since become familiar with anyone working on the text of Acts.[16]

13. It is suggested that the Greek E08 is a retroversion of a (now lost) Latin text that shared some readings of the exemplar of D05, see Boismard and Lamouille, I, p. 24.

14. The Christo-Palestinian MS is presented by C. Perrot, 'Un fragment christo-palestinien découvert à Khirbet-Mird', *RB* 70 (1963), pp. 506–55.

15. The text of Codex Glazier is still unpublished but is presented by T.C. Petersen, 'An Early Coptic Manuscript of Acts: An Unrevised Version of the Ancient So-Called Western Text', *CBQ* 26 (1964), pp. 225–41; see E.J. Epp, 'Coptic Manuscript G^{67} and the Role of Codex Bezae as a Western Witness in Acts', *JBL* 85 (1966), pp. 197–212. Some unconvincing arguments were put forward to challenge the early date assigned to the text of G^{67} by E. Haenchen and P. Weigandt, 'The Original Text of Acts?', *NTS* 14 (1968), pp. 469–81.

16. Boismard and Lamouille's critical apparatus, together with their reconstruction

The information provided by the Boismard and Lamouille edition with regard to the variant readings and their support is invaluable because it is the most complete available and is generally reliable. Our own work on the text does not back up, however, their particular reconstruction of the 'Western' text which is an eclectic one, and on many occasions we will have reason to disagree with their identification of successive layers of the text.[17] For further details of critical editions of Acts, see §III below.

A number of interesting investigations into specific aspects of the 'Western' text have been carried out with conclusions that look promising because they show that there is a wealth of material among the non-AT witnesses that cannot simply be rejected as later scribal emendation. Individual studies have usually focused either on the language of the 'Western' text (style, Semitisms, Lukanisms)[18] or on the contents (theological tendencies)[19]. Although their results have naturally been debated, it is significant that they have repeatedly tended to provide evidence for the

of the 'Western' text and stylistic analyses was first published as *Le texte occidental des Actes des Apôtres: Reconstitution et réhabilitation* in 1984. A new edition was brought out as *Le texte occidental des Actes des Apôtres: Édition nouvelle entièrement refondue* (EBib, NS, 40; Paris: J. Gabalda, 2000).

17. Boismard and Lamouille justified their reconstruction in a series of volumes which form a commentary on Acts from different points of view: *Les Actes des deux Apôtres*, I. *Le texte*; II. *Le sens des récits*; III. *Analyses littéraires* (3 vols., EBib, NS, 12–14; Paris: J. Gabalda, 1990). The series was completed by a historical study by J. Taylor as part of the same commentary: IV–VI. *Commentaire historique* (3 vols., EBib, NS, 23, 30, 41; Paris: J. Gabalda, 1994, 1996, 2000). Cf. the review of vol. V by Read-Heimerdinger, *JTS* 47 (1996), pp. 239–45.

18. For a summary of the linguistic studies, see Strange, *The Problem*, pp. 27–32. Two authors who offer perceptive insights into the nature of the language of the 'Western' text are Delebecque, *Les deux Actes,* and M. Wilcox, *The Semitisms of Acts* (Oxford: Clarendon Press, 1965).

19. E.J. Epp (*The Theological Tendency of Codex Bezae Cantabrigiensis in Acts* [Cambridge: Cambridge University Press, 1966]) aimed to show that there was an anti-Judaic bias in Codex Bezae which demonstrated that it was the work of Christians belonging to the established church. His thesis was contested by C.K. Barrett, 'Is there a Theological Tendency in Codex Bezae?', in E. Best and R. McL. Wilson (eds.), *Text and Interpretation* (Cambridge: Cambridge University Press, 1979), pp. 15–27, who argued that the opposition to Judaism as well as other supposed characteristics of Codex Bezae were already tendencies of Luke in the firm text of his work. Despite the cogency of Barrett's reply, Epp's monograph has been influential in informing popular opinion of Codex Bezae and has never been challenged with an exhaustive examination of the Bezan text that counters his claims. Our own analysis does not substantiate the interpretation of the anti-Judaic bias of Bezan Acts as a later Christian revision.

conclusion that the 'Western' text is consistent with both Lukan language and thought such as can be established from the firm text of his writings.[20]

For all the interest of these works, the conclusions fail in the end to lead to definite solutions that provide an overall explanation for the variants in both textual traditions. They have had, in addition, to contend with the esteem with which the AT is traditionally regarded and the preference given to the MSS Sinaiticus and Vaticanus by the editors of the Greek text since Westcott and Hort. The prevailing opinion is that the 'Western' text of Acts is by and large to be rejected as secondary, and the common view of Codex Bezae in particular is that where it is not simply a compilation of errors it is the fanciful work of a wayward scribe, or the end product of a long development of modification.[21]

The efforts to give serious consideration to the worth of the 'Western' text are hampered by a problem of methodology. By treating the 'Western' text as one to be reconstituted from the diverse witnesses, there has been a failure to notice the inner coherence of both language and contents throughout the text of Acts in the one extensive representative of the 'Western' text in Greek, that is Codex Bezae.[22] There is hope for change,

20. The recent examination of the text of Acts by Strange (*The Problem*) seeks to draw together the strands of language and contents and concludes that the 'Western' variants as well as the AT represent two separate posthumous editions of Luke's text, the 'Western' taking into account his own marginal notes. This solution is reminiscent of that proposed by Blass in *Acta Apostolorum*.

21. J.D.G. Dunn (*The Partings of the Ways Between Christianity and Judaism and their Significance for the Character of Christianity* [London: SCM Press, 1991, repr. 1996]) describes the 'Western' text as 'a form which consistently seeks to clarify and smooth the earlier text by numerous elaborations' (p. xi). Cf. Haenchen, pp. 47–53, who concludes that the readings of the 'Western' text are nowhere to be regarded as original. Throughout Metzger's *Commentary*, there are references to the work of the copyist of Codex Bezae who 'enhanced', 'emphasized', 'expanded' or 'embroidered', but without any attempt to consider all the various Bezan modifications as part of a cohesive whole. The view of K. Aland is that the text of Codex Bezae is the end product, 'ein Höhepunkt', of a series of texts which sought to provide a paraphrase of a previous version, see *Text und Textwert der griechischen Handschriften des Neuen Testaments*. III. *Apostelgeschichte* (2 vols., ANTF, 20–21; Berlin: Walter de Gruyter, 1993), I, pp. 710–19; and see B. Aland ('Entstehung, Charakter und Herkunft') who likewise assigns to D05 a position at the end of a period of development. Boismard and Lamouille (I, p. 11) regard Codex Bezae as a 'témoin très abâtardi [du texte occidental]'; Parker (*An Early Christian Manuscript*, and see 'Professor Amphoux's History of the New Testament Text: A Response', *New Testament Update* 4 [1996], pp. 41–45) likewise deems it to be made up of successive layers of emendation and error.

22. This is a problem with Epp's work for, despite its title (*The Theological Ten-*

however, in the increasingly insistent call to regard this witness as a separate document in its own right. This has come notably from the French textual critic C.-B. Amphoux[23] but the independent exegetical analyses of É. Delebecque, primarily a classical scholar, also draw attention to the consistency of the Bezan text of Acts, on the level of language as well as of narrative perspective.[24]

Our own analyses confirm the self-contained nature of the Bezan Acts and likewise the close correspondance between it and the writings of Luke overall, especially with respect to its theological message but also the linguistic form in which that message is expressed. This will become clear in the course of the commentary but it is worth saying at the outset that the similarities between the Bezan form of the text and characteristic features of Lukan writing are much too subtle and complex to be the work of a later imitator of Luke's style, as has been suggested.[25] It is principally on the grounds of internal criticism that we believe the Bezan text of Acts to represent a form of text that predates the AT and that can take us back to at least the first half of the second century. This is not to say that there are no scribal errors in Codex Bezae but these can be fairly easily detected

dency of Codex Bezae Cantabrigiensis), he draws on MSS other than Codex Bezae when this MS does not support his claims.

23. Amphoux has frequently argued that Codex Bezae in its entirety represents a coherent text, see, e.g., 'Schéma d'histoire du texte grec du Nouveau Testament', *New Testament Update* 3 (1995), pp. 41–46, and his work on the Gospel of Matthew, *L'Évangile selon Matthieu. Codex de Bèze* (L'Isle-sur-la-Sorgue: Le Bois d'Orion, 1996). Whilst we would disagree with his particular reconstruction of the history of the text of the Gospels and Acts (Vaganay and Amphoux, *Introduction*, p. 98; see extended treatment of the subject in *La Parole qui devient Évangile* [Paris: Seuil, 1993]), we applaud his endeavours to make Codex Bezae known as a MS with a consistent text.

24. In addition to his full-scale comparative translation of the two texts of Acts (*Les deux Actes*), Delebecque published a number of exegetical articles which defend the carefulness of the Bezan scribe and which point to a coherence of meaning in the Bezan text (gathered together in *Études sur le grec du Nouveau Testament* [Aix-en-Provence: Publications de l'Université de Provence, 1995]). Despite the confusing similarity of the title of the later volumes by Boismard and Lamouille (*Les Actes des deux Apôtres*), Delebecque's work has little in common with their series.

25. Barrett asks 'whether it would not be natural for an editor or a copyist, working with a text with which he had long been respectfully familiar and introducing occasional additions and paraphrases, to do so in the style of the author whose work he believed he was restoring to its proper form' (I, p. 28). The difficulty with this suggestion is that the form of the text peculiar to Codex Bezae represents very much more than 'occasional additions and paraphrases'.

and put to one side. Attention will be drawn throughout the *Critical Apparatus* to the process of eliminating accidental errors of copying.

There are, of course, considerable implications in accepting that the Bezan text transmits an earlier form of the text than the AT; the deference shown to the weight of historical tradition makes it enormously difficult to consider such a move. Despite the opposition that will inevitably be aroused, we nevertheless believe that when the text of Codex Bezae is examined as a whole and as a form standing in its own right (rather than as a string of variant readings, or as part of an eclectic 'pick and mix' text), there is ample evidence in terms of both language and content that such a move ought to be made.

Important questions are naturally raised as a consequence, not least about why the original text should have been modified to produce an alternative form, and why it should be the secondary form of the text that came to be regarded as authentic. Possible reasons were hinted at above but, rather than develop the discussion as this stage, it is preferable to deal with issues of this nature within the *Commentary*. We anticipate looking at these questions again in the final volume where the factors that have been emerging in the course of the analysis can be drawn together.

II. *Studies of Acts*

In parallel with the renewed interest in the text of Acts, there has been a wealth of new research carried out in recent years in a diversity of other domains where the book of Acts has been the focus of attention.[26] On the one hand, Acts has been taken in conjunction with the Gospel of Luke in an examination of Lukan thought, style and contents, and the contribution it makes to a spectrum of themes has been valued by those seeking to define characteristics of the third evangelist. Although such works may be seen as relating primarily to the Gospel, their relevance for an understanding of Acts should not be ignored.[27] On the other hand, Acts has been studied as a book in its own right for the light it sheds on the emergence and life of a religious group in the first century, the earliest Christian

26. A comprehensive examination of the exegetical criticism of Acts up to the 1970's is to be found in W.W. Gasque, *A History of the Criticism of the Acts of the Apostles* (Tübingen: J.C.B. Mohr [Paul Siebeck], 1975); see the later study by Gasque, 'A Fruitful Field. Recent Study of the Acts of the Apostles', *Interpretation* 42 (1988), pp. 117–31.

27. A selective bibliography of representative works, including those dealing with Luke-Acts, is provided in the commentary on Acts by Johnson, pp. 18–21. This is initially more helpful than the longer bibliographies cited by Johnson.

Church.[28] It has been the object of historical studies covering a range of perspectives, including sociological ones.[29] It is one of the chief documents to which reference is made in the contemporary search to define and explain the separation of Christianity from its Jewish roots.[30] In a comparison with other writings of antiquity, it has been assessed as a literary document.[31]

It is a curious thing that in all of this immensely detailed scholarship, the text of Acts is almost universally treated either as settled, or as sufficiently settled not to interfere with an examination of its contents. Even in the latest spate of commentaries on Acts that have appeared in English since 1992, only passing acknowledgment of the existence of variant readings is made in most instances and little new insight into the exegetical significance of alternative readings is provided.[32] In textual studies, in contrast, some of the contributions have recognized the link between textual and exegetical, historical or sociological issues for example, and invite collaboration from scholars in other disciplines.[33] Indeed, when the

28. The collection of essays edited by B. Witherington, *History, Literature and Society in the Book of Acts* (Cambridge: Cambridge University Press, 1996), provides a useful insight into the kinds of domains investigated in recent years, and has ample bibliographical notes.

29. Of particular note is the detailed study by C.J. Hemer, *The Book of Acts in the Setting of Hellenistic History* (ed. C.H. Gempf; Tübingen: J.C.B. Mohr, 1989) and the series of volumes of historical essays edited by B. Winter, *The Book of Acts in its First Century Setting* (6 vols.; Grand Rapids: Eerdmans, 1994–98).

30. See Dunn, *The Partings of the Ways* and the works that he presents in this context; J.T. Sanders, *Schismatics, Sectarians, Dissidents, Deviants. The First One Hundred Years of Jewish-Christian Relations* (London: SCM Press, 1993); G.N. Stanton and G.G. Strousma (eds.), *Tolerance and its Limits in Early Judaism and Christianity* (Cambridge: Cambridge University Press, 1998); J.B. Tyson, *Images of Judaism in Luke-Acts* (Colombia, S. Carolina: University of South Carolina Press, 1992).

31. Cf. Witherington (ed.), *History, Literature and Society*, Preface, pp. xii–xiv.

32. Although some of the most recent commentaries on Acts in English refer to variant readings in the course of discussion of particular verses, they appear to be hardly aware of the extent of the ongoing research into the text of Acts, see, e.g., Barrett who nevertheless provides an introduction to the textual witnesses and the main textual theories (I, pp. 2–29) though the sketch of the history of the text promised for his second volume does not reflect the ongoing debate (II, p. xxi). The consideration accorded to textual questions in the latest commentary on Acts in French by P. Bossuyt and J. Radermakers, *Témoins de la parole de la grâce: Lecture des Actes des Apôtres* (2 vols.; Brussels: Institut d'Études Théologiques, 1995) is similarly disappointing.

33. Cf. comments on the desirability of inter-disciplinary exchange in the review by

problems concerning the text of Acts are tackled head on, they open up paths to be explored by exegetes, historians, theologians, sociologists, linguists *et alia*, and every interested reader should be given access to the riches to which they lead.

III. *The Critical Apparatus*

In order to avoid the distortions that are created by comparing the textual traditions of Acts – Alexandrian and 'Western' – we have preferred to compare specific Greek MSS, forms of the text that actually existed and that were *the* text of Acts for one community or another.[34] As a representative of the AT with which to compare Codex Bezae, Codex Vaticanus has been selected and every instance of variation examined; additional variation with Codex Sinaiticus has also been noted.

The practice has been to regard every variant reading as potentially significant. Only spelling differences that are due to known phonetic confusion are ignored. No variants are dismissed as grammatical errors unless there is clear evidence that they constitute nonsense or impossible Greek; the criteria appealed to in deciding about 'grammatical error' are discussed in the following section (§IV) on language. The *Critical Apparatus* is thus considerably fuller than that of the current editions of the Greek New Testament. Although the restricted apparatus of the N-A^{27}/UBS^{4} editions has advantages for general purposes where a compact volume is required, the grounds on which variants were selected for inclusion are disputable since the editorial committee tended to treat each instance of variation as more or less independent and to disregard anything deemed to be insignificant.[35] It will be seen that, in fact, most of the time the readings work together within their own text, not just with those in close proximity but across the verses and the chapters.[36] This makes it

J. Read-Heimerdinger of Ehrman and Holmes (eds.), *Contemporary Research*, in *NovT* 38 (1996), pp. 300–304.

34. There is a particular difficulty in comparing the AT with the 'Western' text since most of the witnesses of the latter are not in Greek. By taking Codex Bezae as an MS in its own right, a thorough and precise comparison of language is possible in a way that it is not with any other representative of the 'Western' text.

35. The criteria that guided the editorial decisions are explained in Metzger's *Commentary*, pp. xxiv–xxviii and in the Introduction to N-A^{27}, pp. 6–9.

36. E.C. Colwell, *Studies in Methodology in Textual Criticism of the New Testament* (Leiden: E.J. Brill, 1969), discussed the extent of a variation unit, which he defined as 'those elements of expression in the Greek text which regularly go together' (pp. 97–99). Cf. E.J. Epp, ('Textual Criticism: New Testament', *ABD*, VI, pp. 412–35

all the more imperative to consider them exhaustively if an accurate picture of the MSS is to be obtained.

In the *Critical Apparatus*, the reading of B03 is given first, with a list of the supporting witnesses in brackets; these are followed, after a single vertical line, by any related readings together with their textual support. A double vertical line precedes the reading of D05, which is likewise followed by a list of supporting witnesses and any related readings. After the textual evidence has been given in each instance, the significance of the variant is discussed.

The attestation of the Greek MSS is taken from the *Horizontal Line Synopsis* of R. Swanson who sets out the evidence of each variant reading in full.[37] For the readings of the versions and Church Fathers, the critical apparatus of Boismard and Lamouille was used (see §I above).[38] For ease of recognition of the witnesses, the sigla adopted by N-A^{27} have been used throughout.

The support of the Greek text by the Latin side of Codex Bezae, d05, is of especial value since it derives from a different exemplar. In the places where the Greek text is missing, it is the Latin text, where it is extant, that is taken as the text for comparison with B03. Where the Latin and the Greek pages of Codex Bezae are lacunary, other 'Western' witnesses that are known to share D05 readings elsewhere (notably the Old Latin MS h

[414]), 'A "variation unit" is that determinate quantity or segment of text, constituting a normal and proper grammatical combination, where our mss present at least two variant readings and where (after insignificant readings have been excluded) each of these variant readings has the support of at least two mss.' The difficulty with both of these definitions is that it is clear from recent developments in linguistics that there are strong bonds between elements on a much larger scale than was previously thought and it can no longer be maintained that only elements within the traditional 'normal and proper grammatical combination', 'go together'. In practice, each individual case of variation tends to be treated by textual critics as independent of one another even though they occur in close proximity. When, on the contrary, the narrative of Acts is regarded as a cohesive discourse, it becomes apparent that variant readings frequently depend upon one another at least within the same speech or episode, and not uncommonly within the book as a whole.

37. R. Swanson, *New Testament Greek Manuscripts. Variant Readings Arranged in Horizontal Lines against Codex Vaticanus. The Acts of the Apostles* (Sheffield: Sheffield Academic Press, 1998).

38. The critical analysis of K. Aland, *Text und Textwert der griechischen Handschriften des Neuen Testaments*. III. *Apostelgeschichte,* is less useful for a detailed comparison of MSS, for it groups together readings in such a way as to mask a high proportion of variants.

and the Middle Egyptian, mae) are used. There are two problems with having to fall back on other witnesses. First, since they are chiefly versions, a linguistic comparison with the AT is inevitably restricted for many discourse features of Greek do not show up in translation (word order, links between sentences, the article, for example). The degree of exegetical precision is affected in consequence. Secondly, so many of D05's readings are singular that it is quite possible that in the lacunary passages, none of the other 'Western' witnesses reproduce even the content, let alone the form, of the text exactly as it was in D05. Once more, this causes the detail of the exegesis to be affected and the interpretation of the text is necessarily tentative. A particular difficulty concerns the portrait of Paul, for the picture that emerges in the extant chapters of Codex Bezae is so different from that of other manuscripts that it may be legitimately supposed that other differences existed in ch. 9 and chs 23–28 of which all trace has been lost. If ever the missing pages of Codex Bezae come to light, they may well bring some surprises! Meanwhile, we will avoid attempting to re-construct the text of Codex Bezae or even a 'Western' text where the Bezan text is missing. The most we can do is to refer to readings of 'Western' witnesses, meaning that they are not Alexandrian.

The variant readings between the Codex Bezae and the AT are numerous, affecting over 25% of the total length of extant Bezan text. The figures in the Table 1 are derived specifically from a comparison of the extant text of D05 with the corresponding portions of B03.[39] (A comparison with א01 produces almost identical results because there are 92 places where D05 agrees with B03 against א01, and 115 places where D05 agrees with א01 against B03.) The variation can be classified into four types: material that is present in D05 but not in B03; conversely, material that is absent from D05 but present in B03; material that is present in both texts but in differing forms (lexical or grammatical); finally, material that is again present in both texts but with a differing order of words.

Table 1: *Types of Variation between D05 and B03*

	Number of words affected
1. Words present in D05 and absent in B03	1,448
2. Words absent in D05 and present in B03	579
3. Readings present in both texts but with grammatical or lexical differences	1,352

39. The figures in the table were arrived at by a personal count of the text of D05 by Read-Heimerdinger; for fuller details, see *The Bezan Text*, pp. 2–21.

4. Readings present in both texts but with differences in word order	263
Total number of variant words	3,642
Total number of words in B03	13,036

It is very rare for a variant reading to involve more than one type of variation at the same time. The category that involves the greatest amount of variation is the first, whence the description of the 'Western' text as the 'long text'. However, it should be noted that there is even more variation to do with alternative forms of words (category 3) – either grammatical (tense, case, number and so on) or lexical (synonyms) – and the order of words (category 4). Furthermore, account must also be taken of the material absent in D05 but present in B03. When the figures for the first two categories are put together, it emerges that Codex Bezae is only 6.6% longer than Codex Vaticanus rather than the 10% that is sometimes quoted.[40]

IV. *Linguistic Analysis*

Where variation involves grammatical differences, the standard grammars are referred to and are cited as appropriate; for lexical items, the available dictionaries of New Testament and classical Greek have been consulted, including the new dictionary by J.P. Louw and E.A. Nida which groups words according to semantic domains.[41] Grammars and dictionaries, however, cannot present a fully objective analysis since the account given of some of the finer points especially (precisely the kind that are affected by a high proportion of the variation existing between the MSS) may well be dependent on the editor's or author's choice of text and on his understanding of the text. Reference works cannot, in consequence, be regarded as infallible, however useful they are, but at the places where we do not accept an opinion we aim to give a justification for our disagreement.

In some respects, the older works are being complemented by fresh research arising from developments in linguistics which are casting new light on grammatical and semantic analysis. There are many features of New Testament Greek whose variation has traditionally been attributed to

40. This is the figure given by Metzger, *Commentary*, p. 223, having rounded up calculations made by comparing Clark's text with that of Westcott and Hort. Cf. Strange, *The Problem*, p. 213, n. 18.

41. For details of the dictionary by Louw and Nida, see *Bibliography* I.

an author's style, or a scribe's personal preference where variation is found between MSS. Regional differences and developments in the language over time have also been considered as influences affecting the choice of one form instead of another. These are the factors that are generally taken into consideration when evaluating variation in details of language that seem to reflect a difference not in intended meaning but in linguistic habit. It is common, accordingly, for variant readings to be evaluated on the basis of how they compare with an author's 'usual' practice, where 'usual' is calculated according to statistical frequency.[42]

Progress in the understanding of how Koine Greek (and indeed language generally) functions on a broader level than that of the customary level of the sentence has brought a new awareness of the real factors governing the selection of some of the most common variables. On the one hand, these factors have to do with pragmatic matters outside the discourse itself, such as the purpose of the author in communicating their message, their relationship with their addressees or how they view their subject matter. On the other hand, within the discourse an author's choice is affected more specifically by the nature of the writing (narrative or reasoned discourse, for example), the different stages in the discourse, the ways in which the paragraphs are fitted together, the need to draw attention to some element or the relative intrinsic importance of a topic for the overall subject matter. These are just some of the aspects of language for which rules are now being drawn up, and it has been found that in some respects each language has its own rules. It could be said that, overall, the concern of the linguists who study language in this way is to see how a text (whether oral or written) holds together; in their examination of the text, they find themselves looking at the relationships between the different levels from the smallest (the choice of words) to the largest (the context of the discourse). This kind of linguistic analysis is referred to, in a very general way, as Discourse Analysis and has enabled many aspects of Greek grammar to be explained where previously there has been confusion or a lack of understanding.[43]

42. See, for example, the evaluation of specific variants in J.K. Elliott, *Essays and Studies in New Testament Textual Criticism* (Córdoba: El Almendro, 1992); see G.D. Kilpatrick's essays, *The Principles and Practice of New Testament Textual Criticism* (Leuven: Leuven University Press, 1990).

43. A clear introduction to the discipline is presented by S.E. Porter, 'Discourse Analysis and New Testament Studies: An Introductory Survey', in S.E. Porter and D.A. Carson (eds.), *Discourse Analysis and Other Topics in Biblical Greek* (JSNTSup, 113; Sheffield: Sheffield Academic Press, 1995), pp. 14–35. For a more detailed

For the actual formation of the text, there are many particular variables that play a part in reflecting the interests described above and that contribute to the overall purpose of the discourse or, alternatively, that are governed by that purpose. The kinds of variation that are consequently of interest to Discourse Analysis recur with frequency as variation between the texts of Acts, although they are by no means all cited in the current editions because their significance has been assessed by the editors on the grounds of traditional grammar. That such a situation exists is not so much a reproach as simply a reflection of the recent nature of the fairly rapid changes that have been taking place in linguistics. It is time, nonetheless, for textual criticism to make use of the modern developments in linguistics and to reassess old judgments.[44] That is one of the things we hope to be doing.

As noted above, certain differences between the texts of Acts can be seen to derive from pragmatic factors that operate outside the text and the topics mentioned in this respect are addressed in the course of the *Commentary*. Concurrently, within the text, differences occur at various levels of discourse. Without intending the list to be exhaustive, attention is drawn to the following elements that are typically affected by variation:

1. Lexical items: choice of vocabulary, use of synonyms, compound verbs; compound nouns
2. In the structure of the verb: aspect, tense and number; participles
3. In the structure of the sentence: word order; case and prepositions
4. In the structure of the paragraph: conjunctions; other connecting devices
5. In the tracking of characters: the article; names, pronouns and zero-reference

presentation of the basic concepts, see G. Brown and G. Yule, *Discourse Analysis* (Cambridge: Cambridge University Press, 1983). A useful introduction to the subject can also be found in D. Black and S.H. Levinsohn, *Linguistics and New Testament Interpretation* (Nashville, TN: Broadman Press, 1992), a cross-section of essays that apply Discourse Analysis to particular problems. Three recent New Testament Greek grammars that apply modern linguistic principles to the study of the language are: S.H. Levinsohn, *Discourse Features of New Testament Greek* (Dallas: Summer Institute of Linguistics, 1992); S.E. Porter, *Idioms of New Testament Greek* (Biblical Languages: Greek, 2; Sheffield: JSOT Press, 1992); R.A. Young, *Intermediate New Testament Greek* (Nashville, TN: Broadman & Holman, 1994).

44. The usefulness of Discourse Analysis for textual criticism is the focus of Read-Heimerdinger, *The Bezan Text*, on whose findings we draw for the linguistic analysis of variants.

Some of these aspects of New Testament Greek have been thoroughly researched; others are still under investigation. Results of research already carried out will be taken into account and where the conclusions of ongoing research are accessible these will also be discussed.

V. *Literary Devices in Luke's Writing*

A literary analysis goes hand in hand with a linguistic analysis; in other words, there must be a consideration of the way in which Luke uses language in order to construct his narrative and thereby express his meaning. He is generally recognized as a masterful writer whose skill in the composition of Acts goes far beyond the straightforward telling of the story of the early Church. On the one hand, he adapts the language of his narrative to correspond to the situation he is relating and knows how to give it the appropriate colour to suit the character or setting of an episode – Semitic, Roman, legal, nautical, or whatever else is applicable. On the other hand, he manipulates with considerable artistry a collection of literary devices. These function in combination to reinforce and support each other; they serve as guides and markers to make known Luke's own thoughts as narrator at the same time as they signal the intended meaning of his account, without the authorial comments and intentions needing to be spelt out explicitly. In so doing, they operate as a kind of code, and yet it is not a code that conceals the meaning of his text as if he were writing a secret document for initiated followers but rather it is a code that opens up the meaning of his text, that gives it a depth and completeness. If explicit statements were used, they would make the account both lengthy and cumbersome. To some extent, literary devices are used to serve the purpose of later marks of punctuation of which the early MSS are almost totally devoid. That Acts was written to be heard read aloud plays without doubt no small part in their usefulness.

It is difficult to determine to what extent Luke draws on a traditional stock of devices. A number of them are known from secular Greek authors; others are devices characteristic of Jewish methods of interpreting Scripture as described in the Rabbinical writings. Some are commonly recognized and discussed in works on Luke's writing, although reference tends to be made to them more often by scholars dealing with the Gospel than with Acts.[45]

45. A recognition of Luke's narrative craft undergirds the analysis of Acts by D. Marguerat (see *The First Christian Historian. Writing the 'Acts of the Apostles'* [trans. K. McKinney, G.J. Laughery and R. Bauckham; SNTS, 121; Cambridge:

Specific examples of Luke's literary techniques, and the variations in their functioning in the different forms of the text, will be pointed out throughout the *Commentary* but a summary of the chief devices can be given here.

V.1. *Literary Structures*

They form a diversity of figures that can be symmetrical (of the type a b // b′ a′, for example), or concentric (in some such form as a b c b′ a′). Such structures are familiar patterns of classical poetry and rhetoric, although in Luke's narrative their function is by no means simply to create aesthetic or dramatic effect but principally to communicate meaning.[46] As formal structures, they build a framework for the narrative and give it shape. By the mirroring of concepts, characters and events, they articulate implicit statements or comments that the author does not otherwise express in explicit terms. They can occur on a large scale across several chapters (see §VIII below) or on a smaller scale within episodes or within speeches. They are determined by objective reference to the contents, but more especially by paying careful attention to the language and by observing the repetition or opposition of lexical items and syntactical features.

In the *Commentary*, the text of Acts has been analyzed according to its structure, working from the Bezan text where a formal pattern is usually more apparent. On the highest level, the narrative can be seen as falling into parts, which represent the successive steps in the spread of the gospel and which determine the organization of the *Commentary* into its four volumes (see §XII below). Within each part, *sections* are identified and labelled with Roman numerals (I, II, III etc.); these group together a series of episodes that is introduced by such phrases as 'In those days' (for further details, see §VIII below), and often concludes with a summary

Cambridge University Press, 2002]) which makes many interesting observations about the implicit techniques used by Luke.

46. For a discussion of two such structures in Luke's Gospel, see J. Rius-Camps, 'Lc 10,25–18,30: Una perfecta estructura concèntrica dins la Secció del Viatge (9,51–19,46)', *RCatT* 8 (1983), pp. 283–358, and 'Estructura i funció significativa del tercer cicle o Secció de les Recognicions (Lc 6,12–9,50)', *RCatT* 9 (1984), pp. 269–329. A helpful presentation of the research carried out into the literary structures in the New Testament is to be found in K.E. Bailey, *Poet and Peasant* (Grand Rapids: Eerdmans, combined edn, 1983), pp. 44–75, and *Through Peasant Eyes*, 'Introduction' (Grand Rapids: Eerdmans, combined edn, 1983), pp. xvii–xx. Cf. W.S. Kurz, *Reading Luke–Acts: Dynamics of Biblical Narrative* (Louisville, KY: Westminster/John Knox Press, 1993).

statement; all but the shorter sections sub-divide into *sequences*, indicated by A, B, C etc., that contain a single event or development within an episode. The smallest unit of structure is termed an *element* for the purposes of the *Commentary*, usually consisting of a single main verb together with its associated dependent clauses. Exceptions occur where two main verbs conjoined by καί refer to two aspects of the same action, which have been treated as one element; similarly, a clause introduced by γάρ has been viewed as belonging to the preceding element unless it is a separate narrator's aside.

V.2. *'Head–Tail' Linking of Structural Divisions*

The beginnings and ends of episodes are specifically constructed so as to show the relation between them, using such devices as anaphoric references to time, or character, or situation in order to create analogies, make comparisons or draw contrasts. Many of the phrases that open new sections or sequences (see §V.1 above) come to resemble formulae by their frequent occurrence – they are more than simple quirks of Lukan style and close attention needs to be paid to them.[47]

V.3. *Repetition in Two- or Three-Fold Patterns*

In the case of some events, similar or identical occurrences are reported. The three accounts of Paul's conversion are a striking example, but such repetition occurs quite frequently. At least part of its purpose is to allow implicit comments to be made through the differences between the accounts.

Likewise, characters are sometimes presented in groups of two or three where the interrelationships serve to transmit information relating to themes in a wider context: Joseph Barnabas, Ananias and Sapphira in Acts 4–5, for example, not only carry significance on account of their own actions but are also used to make further implicit comments through the way in which they interrelate, both in real life and in the scheme of the narrative.

V.4. *Parallel Accounts*

According to this device, two (occasionally more) people or groups of people operate in parallel within the same sentence or paragraph. What Luke does is begin by naming the persons or groups, and follow the presentation immediately with as many verbs or phrases. These verbs or phrases

47. For an analysis of the devices used by Luke in Acts to link episodes, see Levinsohn, *Textual Connections*, pp. 1–82 *passim*.

do not apply to all the characters at once, but each one corresponds to only one character according to the order of occurrence. The same feature is found in the addresses of some of the speeches. An early example in Acts is found in the response of Peter to the two-fold questioning of the onlookers at the Pentecost outpouring of the Spirit (2.14). The key to understanding the device is to recognize that when two names are mentioned, for example, the first verb/phrase that follows goes with the first-named person and the second verb/phrase with the second-named person.

V.5. *Equivalent Terms*

Terms affected are lexical synonyms, grammatical alternatives or orthographical variations of names, where a specific and distinctive meaning is conferred on each one. It is usually the case that one term has a neutral, ordinary sense and that the parallel term has a stronger, theological sense. This dual system, which runs throughout the two volumes of Luke's work, constitutes a vehicle of communication that is used with careful and deliberate precision and whose value for the formulation of Luke's message cannot be easily overstated. Instances will be pointed out as they occur but an example that can be usefully explained here relates to the spelling of the city of Jerusalem. When Luke refers (or has a character refer) to the town as a geographical place, devoid of religious significance, he uses the Hellenistic spelling (Ἱεροσόλυμα). When, in contrast, he refers (or has a character refer) to the city as the seat of Jewish authority, the centre of the Jewish religion, he uses the Hebrew-derived spelling (Ἰερουσαλήμ).[48] The distinction between a neutral and a religious sense has been rejected by some exegetes and textual critics as too simplistic. It will be seen that the clarity of the distinction depends firstly, on which text is followed and secondly, on the interpretation given to the passages in which the name of Jerusalem occurs. It should be noted that when necessary the distinction is shown in the *Commentary* by the terms 'Hierosoluma' (neutral sense) and 'Ierousalem' (religious sense). The dualism of the spelling, as of other equivalent terms, is maintained with greatest regularity in Codex Bezae and concords perfectly with the point of view of the narrator expressed in that text.[49]

48. The importance of Jerusalem in Second Temple Judaism is discussed in several of the articles in M. Poorthuis and C. Safrai (eds.), *The Centrality of Jerusalem* (Kampen: Kok Pharos, 1996). See also Read-Heimerdinger, *The Bezan Text*, pp. 311–44.

49. Cf. a comparable study of Jerusalem in the Gospel of John by J. Rius-Camps, 'The Spelling of Jerusalem in the Gospel of John: The Significance of Two Forms in Codex Bezae', *NTS* 48 (2002), pp. 84–94.

V.6. *Representative Characters*
They are often introduced with 'a certain...' (τις). They are not so much characters in their own right as representatives of a class or a group, though that is not to deny their historical existence, and indeed, Luke frequently confers realism on them by the mention of their name and other factual details. They function as corporate characters who represent groups such as the lame, the demonized, the Roman pro-consuls or the leaders of the synagogue. The symbolic nature of these characters is not always readily apparent but attention will be drawn to it in the course of the *Commentary*.

V.7. *Names of People and Places*
The importance accorded to names by Luke is apparent from the many occasions when they contain clues as to his underlying message. Some of these names contain or create play on words with part of the pun (for example, the first biblical occurrence of the name, or a particular meaning conferred on it) not infrequently having its origin in the Jewish Scriptures or in contemporary Jewish tradition.[50]

V.8. *Numbers*
Numbers are important in a similar way. Some numbers recur and have their Lukan origin in the Gospel (seven, twelve), with earlier reference still to events in the history of Israel. Sometimes, markers (the comparatives καθώς/ὡς/ὡσεί/ὥσπερ to which specific value is accorded by Luke) indicate when a number is to be taken literally, or metaphorically, or as a reference to a parallel figure in the Scriptures.

V.9. *Key Expressions*
Certain phrases are repeated and come to have the value of technical terms. In addition to some of the names and numbers which could be included in this category, there are other phrases that are brought into Luke's writing (notably from Jewish oral or scriptural tradition) having already acquired a certain fixed meaning.[51] There are others still which it must be supposed (for want of evidence for their prior existence as fixed

50. For a detailed analysis of the importance of a place name in Luke's Gospel, see J. Read-Heimerdinger and J. Rius-Camps, 'Emmaous or Oulammaous? Luke's Use of the Jewish Scriptures in the Text of Luke 24 in Codex Bezae', *RCatT* 27 (2002), pp. 23–42.

51. Cf. Jacobs, *The Midrashic Process*, pp. 3–4, for discussion of the presence of a comparable device in Jewish interpretation of Scripture.

expressions) Luke himself invests with a characteristic meaning for the purposes of his narratives (Gospel and Acts).

V.10. *Jewish Exegetical Techniques*

A major problem in identifying techniques as typical of Jewish exegesis in particular is that the early written accounts of interpretative systems date from no earlier than the second century when the Rabbis began to systematize and normalize the methods to be employed. Pre-rabbinical exegesis, and the features that distinguish it from the later systems, is still very much a matter under investigation.[52] The oral nature of much of early Jewish teaching poses an obvious difficulty in determining exactly how it was formulated at any given date before it was actually written down. The information that can be deduced, however, from the intertestamental books of Scripture, the targums, the reconstructed synagogue lectionary cycles, the Qumran documents, Jewish legends and stories, and the writings of various kinds by Jewish authors, is tending to show that the writers of the New Testament drew, in varying measure, on a body of traditional material.[53] In fact, the writings of the New Testament can even serve as

52. Interesting and perceptive articles are increasingly being published by Jewish scholars as well as by those investigating the New Testament. Among the works that seek to define the methods employed, note may be made in particular of those by B. Barc, 'Le texte de la Torah a-t-il été récrit?', in M. Tardieu (ed.), *Les règles de l'interprétation* (Paris: Cerf, 1987), pp. 69–88, and *Les arpenteurs du temps: Essai sur l'histoire religieuse de la Judée à la période héllenistique* (Lausanne: Éditions du Zèbre, 2000); M. Fishbane, *Biblical Interpretation in Ancient Israel* (Oxford: Clarendon Press, 1987); D. Instone Brewer, *Techniques and Assumptions in Jewish Exegesis before 70 CE* (Tübingen: J.C.B. Mohr, 1992), where the author has gathered together a useful list of devices and establishes a distinction between the methods of the scribes and those employed in contemporary Jewish literature, although his claim that New Testament authors followed scribal exegesis rather than other types is debatable; I. Jacobs, *The Midrashic Process* (Cambridge: Cambridge University Press, 1995); J.L. Kugel, *In Potiphar's House: The Interpretative Life of Biblical Texts* (Cambridge, MA.: Harvard University Press, 2nd edn, 1994), which defines a method that can be followed by scholars wishing to carry out their own detective work into scriptural traditions.

53. Research carried out over the last 30 years or so into the intertestamental and traditional Jewish material is invaluable. In addition to the authors mentioned in the previous note, special reference is made to D.R.G. Beattie and M.J. McNamara, *The Aramaic Bible: Targums in their Historical Context* (JSOTSup, 166; Sheffield: Sheffield Academic Press, 1994); B.D. Chilton, *The Glory of Israel: The Theology and Provenience of the Isaiah Targum* (JSOTSup, 23; Sheffield: JSOT Press, 1982); R. Le Déaut, especially *Liturgie juive et Nouveau Testament* (Rome: Biblical Institute Press,

primary data for an enquiry into the procedures followed for interpreting the Jewish Scriptures in the first century, and Acts is an important document for this enquiry.

The use of traditional exegetical methods applied from an insider Jewish perspective, together with the application of other literary techniques, is much more clearly apparent in the text of Codex Bezae than in the AT; although they are by no means absent from the more familiar text, they are neither as visible nor as sustained. There are now more than a few independent investigations that have been published showing that traces of some targumic or legendary material can be detected in specific passages in the text of Acts. When the Bezan text of the passage is examined, rather than the AT on which the initial investigation was based, it emerges in most cases that the traces of traditional material are more abundant and more cohesive in Codex Bezae and demonstrate sustained rather than spasmodic use.

The Bezan text not only displays more complete and more complex allusions to the Scriptures but furthermore uses the ancient event in a typically Jewish way as a paradigm to interpret the recent developments in the history of Israel. Underlying its message is a basic principle concerning the Jewish understanding of the life of Israel, namely that all of history is contained in the Torah.[54]

People or events are portrayed as familiar people or events from the Scriptures. Sometimes it is the name of the person that gives the clue that Luke is activating a scriptural paradigm, but more often than not the clues are contained in subtle and apparently insignificant details that are easily missed if the allusions are not recognized. Recognition is rendered the more tricky by the fact that details included in Luke's portrayal (especially in the Bezan text) derive not only from written tradition (principally the Septuagint version but by no means uniformly) but more tellingly from legends and teachings that became associated with the original scriptural account and that were regarded to some degree as authoritative. By his application of this device, Luke causes characters and events in the early Church to be seen as re-enactments of the earlier history of Israel

1965); M. McNamara, *New Testament and Palestinian Targum to the Pentateuch* (Rome: Biblical Institute Press, 1966); J. Mann, *The Bible as Read and Preached in the Old Synagogue*. I (New York: KTAV, 1940); II (ed. I. Sonne; Ohio: Hebrew Union College, 1966); C. Perrot, *La lecture de la Bible* (Hildesheim: Verlag Dr. H.A. Gerstenberg, 1973).

54. On the Jewish concept of history, see J. Sacks, *Crisis and Covenant* (Manchester: Manchester University Press, 1992), pp. 208–46.

(cf. §XI below). The work of the contemporary historian consists in bringing to light the ancient models that lie behind present events and that give them coherence and meaning. Since, in the case of a Jewish audience, the writer could suppose that they knew the biblical stories already, it was sufficient to make a single reference to the model for the allusion to be clear. While such a reference could be by explicit quotation it was more frequent in early Jewish literature to slip in a simple word or phrase from the text the historian wished to allude to as a means of identifying it. Such words or phrases served as keys to the biblical paradigm. What needs to be borne in mind today is that the original biblical stories underwent development in the way they were interpreted, and the form alluded to is likely to be that expanded or otherwise modified by tradition. Overall, Luke's scheme of writing is a complex and sophisticated system in which every detail is significant. Rules applied to the Jewish Scriptures in pre-Rabbinic exegesis could be said to be in operation in the Bezan form of the third Gospel and Acts, too: nothing is superfluous, nothing is contradictory.[55] Further comments are made on this aspect of Luke's writing in §X below.

VI. *The Gospel of Luke and the Book of Acts*

It is especially on the basis of a comparison of the vocabulary, literary devices and rhetorical structure in the Gospel and Acts that we adopt without reservation the hypothesis that the third Gospel and the Acts of the Apostles are to be regarded as the work of the same person, traditionally known as Luke. Concerning the identity of Luke, however, the arguments that have been put forward for identifying this person with Luke who is the doctor and companion of Paul (cf. Col. 4.4; 2 Tim. 4.11; Phlm 24) are unsound.[56] In particular, one of the most popular features appealed to, the presence of the 'we' passages, cannot count as evidence if, as we believe, it should be considered as a quintessentially Lukan literary procedure rather than a literal matter of fact.[57] Nevertheless, it is clear that the

55. The explanation of 'Western' variants by Barrett, seeking to account for the different wording, echoes the popular view: 'any words will do provided that they represent the sense of the text with reasonable accuracy; if they express that sense with greater vividness and give the narrative a greater connectedness, so much the better' (II, p. xxi). The comment 'any words will do' totally misses the point of the sophistication and intricacy of the narrator's craft in the Bezan text.

56. The traditional identification of Luke was examined in the classic work by J. Cadbury, *The Making of Luke-Acts* (London: SPCK, repr. 1968), pp. 351–60.

57. See J. Rius-Camps, 'L'aparició/desaparició del "nosaltres" en el llibre dels Fets: un simple procediment teològico-literari?', *RCatT* 6 (1981), pp. 35–75.

author of the book of Acts was familiar with details of Paul's life and ministry that could not be gleaned from his letters. Furthermore, he also reveals some aspects of Paul's personality and theology that do not come through in his writing. His knowledge does not necessarily imply, though, that he accompanied Paul during his missionary activity nor does the possibility that he acquired his information second-hand detract from its reliability. Since the question of the author's real identity remains unanswered, we will follow the usual convention of calling him 'Luke'.

Luke's work consists of one book in two volumes, the first (Τὸν μὲν πρῶτον λόγον, Acts 1.1) being the Gospel and the second the Acts of the Apostles.[58] As discussed in §VIII below, the prologue of the Gospel is to be considered as an introduction to the whole work, the complexity of the relations between the two parts suggesting that when the Gospel was being written, the second volume was already in mind.

It is to be supposed that the two parts of Luke's writing became separated at a fairly early date, probably when the various gospels were grouped together for which the earliest evidence dates from the middle of the second century in Tatian's *Diatessaron*. There are no Greek MSS that place the Gospel of Luke and Acts in consecutive order, although some Syriac MSS retain this order as do certain of the Patristic catalogues.[59] By the end of the second century, according to the *Muratorian Canon*, the second volume was circulating as 'The Acts of the Apostles'. The fact that this name was given to it is an indication of how by this time the purpose of the work was construed as being that of a historical narrative although this interpretation seems to have been founded on a misunderstanding of its original purpose, as explained in the following section. Consequently, neither the title given to Luke's second volume nor its place after John's Gospel corresponds to Luke's intention. The precision of the tools now available for exegesis is such that the two books can once more be presented as belonging to a single work and as enhancing and complementing one another. Even though this understanding of Luke's writing is now

58. The grounds on which the unity of Luke-Acts is to be maintained (despite the theories put forward against it by M.C. Parsons and R.I. Pervo, *Rethinking the Unity of Luke and Acts* [Minneapolis: Augsburg, 1993]) concern essentially a) the anticipation in the Gospel of the narrative of Acts, b) the constant echoing and development in Acts of themes and terms used in the Gospel and c) the holding over to Acts of elements of Mark's Gospel not used in Luke's own Gospel.

59. See B.M. Metzger, *The Canon of the New Testament* (Oxford: Clarendon Press, 1987), Appendix II. See also J.K. Elliott, 'The Manuscript Heritage of the Book of Acts', in Amphoux and Elliott (eds.), *Lille Colloquium*, forthcoming.

found in scholarly works, which refer to 'the two-fold work of Luke', there is not yet any clear demand for the two books to be put back together in the way that they were intended. Such is the timidity with which the errors of Church tradition are customarily approached.

VII. *The Purpose of Acts*

The aim of Luke in writing the second part of his work is to be understood on the grounds of its inseparable link with the first part. Rius-Camps' earlier studies of Luke's work led him to formulate a precise account of the relationship between the two parts which he is to be explained in the following way.[60] In the Gospel, Luke presents the sayings and deeds of Jesus (cf. Lk. 1.1–2; Acts 1.1–2), with Jesus acting as the model for his message. In Acts, Luke broadens the setting to show step by step how the message was lived out within actual communities who strove to imitate the model. This 'incarnation' of the message, as it could be called, was achieved with varying degrees of success which Luke points out and comments on. It is when all the obstacles to the implementation of Jesus' teaching, set up by the disciples and Paul in particular, have been removed, that Luke finally brings his work to a close (ἀκωλύτως, Acts 28.31). Thus, Acts is a kind of extension of the gospel genre (cf. §XI below). The first book acts as a touchstone to check if the words and deeds of the disciples were right, that is, if they were in line with the words and deeds of Jesus, the perfect model.

Pointing out parallels between Jesus and characters in Acts, or between incidents in the Gospel and episodes in Acts, is nothing new, but what is strange is that it is scarcely ever suggested that this parallelism could be contrastive or antagonistic, and not necessarily have positive connotations. It has to be asked, for example, if it is sufficient that Luke describes the trial of Paul in Jerusalem and Caesarea in parallel with that of Jesus for that parallel to be necessarily a straightforward one? Is there not, in theory at least, the possibility that Luke may have wanted to use the Gospel paradigm as a backcloth in order to bring out features of Paul's behaviour that characterize it as a deviation from the model? In order for such a theory to be entertained, Paul (and the other Christian leaders) will have to be allowed to have committed errors, even serious ones, without that causing his apostolic calling and ministry to be denied.

60. See *El camino de Pablo a la misión de los paganos* (Madrid: Cristiandad, 1984); *De Jerusalén a Antioquía: Génesis de la iglesia cristiana* (Córdoba: El Almendro, 1989).

According to this analysis of Luke's purpose, which is particularly upheld by the Bezan form of the text, the intention in the first part of Acts (chs 1–12) is to relate, from both a negative and a positive point of view, the problems encountered by the two principal churches of Jerusalem and Antioch, both in their establishment and their public functioning. Already in the Gospel, Luke makes a comparison between the message, election, sending out and return of the Twelve (Lk. 5.1–11; 6.13–16; 9.1–6, 9–10) and the message, appointment, sending out and joyful return of the Seventy (Lk. 9.57–62; 10.1a, 1b–16, 17–24). In Acts, the same comparison is repeated in describing the two churches. The former (Acts 1.15–5.42) was founded on the basis of the 'Twelve' and was made up of what we will term Jewish 'Jesus-believers'. It was regarded, and regarded itself, as a kind of Judaism (cf. §X below) and became referred to at some stage as the 'sect of the Nazorenes' (24.5, 14; 28.22). The latter (6.1–12.25) was formed on the basis of the 'Seven' Hellenist disciples (cf. 6.1–6) and was made up largely of people who were not formerly Jews. It was regarded, at least from the outside, as 'Christian' (cf. 11.26). The figure of Peter, acting as spokesman of the apostolic group, played a leading role in the setting up of the Jerusalem church and also in the consolidation of the one in Antioch. The first part of Acts closes with Peter being released from a whole way of thinking and understanding that was holding him back from making his own personal exodus out of Israel towards the Gentiles.[61]

In the second part of the book (chs 13–28), the subject is the mission to the Gentiles. Traditionally, this mission has been regarded as operating around Paul's four apostolic journeys but Luke's aim, certainly as far as the Bezan text is concerned, has a different focus. Although Paul is undoubtedly the main protagonist, the centre of the narrative is not the person of Paul as such but rather it is the plan communicated through the Holy Spirit, namely that the mission of the Gentiles was to be entrusted to the best representatives of the Antioch community, Barnabas (a prophet) and Saul (a teacher), and in that order (13.2). The mission consists of four stages, with the Jerusalem Council separating the first one from the other three:

1. First stage of the mission: Cyprus, Pisidia, Lycaonia, and Pamphilia (13.4–14.27)

   The Jerusalem Council (14.28–15.40)

61. The portrait of the apostles in the Bezan text of Acts is the subject of J. Read-Heimerdinger, 'The Apostles in the Bezan Text of Acts', in Nicklas and Tilly (eds.), *Apostelgeschichte als Kirchengeschichte. Text, Traditionen und Antike Auslegungen* (BZNW, 122; Berlin-New York: Walter de Gruyter, 2003), pp. 263–80.

2. Second stage of the mission: Macedonia and Greece (15.41–18.23)
3. Third stage of the mission: Asia (18.24–20.3)
4. Fourth stage of the mission: Paul's trial and the road to Rome (20.4–28.31)

The second part of the book of Acts closes precisely at the point at which Paul, having appealed to Caesar in Rome and thereby reversing his decision to go to Jerusalem, acknowledged that the Holy Spirit was right with respect to the blindness and stubbornness of the people of Israel and with respect to the openness of the Gentiles (28.25–28). Accordingly, Luke expresses a certain critical view of the way in which the mission progressed, as he examines in a somewhat stylized way the various troubles, successes and failures of the great missionary, Paul.[62] This understanding of the purpose of Luke means that the ending to Acts is not abrupt or left up in the air, as it is often felt to be;[63] the book takes leave of Paul at the point when, finally, he is carrying out the mission entrusted to him by Jesus at the time of his conversion and re-iterated by the Holy Spirit among the Jesus-believing community at Antioch.

The preoccupations of Luke in writing his two-volume work indicate a concern not so much with Christianity but more especially with the distinctively new elements of the kind of Judaism that was Christianity. In seeking to identify the implied reader for whom Luke was writing (for this in turn sheds light on his purpose), it is necessary to bear in mind the wealth of minute and complex detail to do with Jewish ways of thinking that are included in the narrative, and that are much more subtle in the text of Codex Bezae (cf. §X below).

VIII. *The Organization of the Narrative of Acts*

There are parallels between the narrative structure of Acts and the Gospel of Luke that confirm this interpretation of Luke's purpose.[64] The prologue

62. Cf. J. Rius-Camps, 'The Gradual Awakening of Paul's Awareness of his Mission to the Gentiles', in Nicklas and Tilly (eds.), *Apostelgeschichte als Kirchengeschichte*, pp. 281–96. In the AT, the picture of Paul is more idealized than in the Bezan text, an embellishing that explains some of the contradictions between the account of Acts and the letters of Paul (see J.C. Lentz, *Luke's Portrait of Paul* [Cambridge: Cambridge University Press, 1993]); others are due to Luke's critical perception of Paul's mission.

63. See W.F. Brosend, 'The Means of Absent Ends', in Witherington (ed.), *History, Literature and Society*, pp. 348–62, for an examination of some of the suggestions put forward for the ending of Acts.

64. R.C. Tannehill (*The Narrative Unity of Luke-Acts. A Literary Interpretation*, I. *Luke*; II. *Acts* [Philadelphia: Fortress Press, 1986, 1990]) has made a careful study of many of these parallels.

to the second volume serves first of all to establish the unity of his work. Like a spine that binds the parts of a book together, it acts as a kind of hinge. The initial sequence of Acts re-states in summary form the same themes that had been dealt with in the earlier volume; it also takes the final episode of the Gospel (Luke 24) and opens it up to present an expanded and complementary version for the start of the new volume (see *Commentary*, 1.1–5).

In addition to the insertion of the hinge sequence to link his two volumes, Luke applies a common basic plan to the early sections of both the Gospel and Acts which presents the two key characters – individual or collective – who will intervene subsequently in the development of the mission.[65] In the Gospel, the parallel presentation of the two characters weaves together the separate stories of their conception and their birth:

I. *John the Baptist*
A Conception (Lk. 1.5–25)
B Gestation: visit of Mary (Galilee) to Elizabeth (Judaea); the filling of Elizabeth and the baby with the Holy Spirit (1.39–56)
C Birth (1.57–58)
D Circumcision/naming (1.59–79)
E Colophon (1.80)

II. *Jesus*
A′ Conception (1.26–38)
B′ Gestation: journey from Nazareth (Galilee) to Bethlehem (Judaea) because of the census (2.1–5)
C′ Birth (2.6–20)
D′ Circumcision/naming (2.21–39)
E′ Double colophon (2.40–52)

In the first part of the book of Acts, this structure is applied to two collective units in such a way that the first is compared with John the Baptist while the second is aligned with Jesus:[66]

I. *The Jesus-believing Church in Jerusalem*
A Reconstitution of the ‘Twelve’ (Acts 1.15–26)
B Gestation: outpouring of the Holy Spirit and the first summary (2.11–47)
C Public manifestation to Israel and second summary (3.1–4.35)
D Persecution/separation of the church from the Temple (4.36–5.42)
E Colophon (6.7)

65. For a fuller presentation of this parallel see Rius-Camps, *De Jerusalén a Antioquía*, Appendix I: ‘Estructuración de Lc 1–2 // Hch 1-12’, pp. 341–46.
66. Rius-Camps, *De Jerusalén a Antioquía*, pp. 309–11.

II. *The Christian Church in Antioch*

- A′ Constitution of the Hellenist group (the 'Seven') (6.1–6; 6.8–8.1a)
- B′ Gestation: dispersion throughout Judaea and Samaria and a three-fold series of conversions (8.1b–11.26)
- C′ Public manifestation (11.27–30)
- D′ Persecution/separation of the church from Israel (12.1–23)
- E′ Colophon (12.24–25)

Once the two characters have been established on the scene in the Gospel, the story of their mission follows on immediately: first, in a condensed form, that of John the Baptist and secondly, that of Jesus. Similarly, once the two main churches have been introduced in Acts, the narrative continues by developing the story of the mission of the Antioch church. This mission, entrusted as it was to Barnabas and Saul as representatives of the Antioch community, corresponds in broad outline to the mission of Jesus (investiture, speeches and activities that follow a set pattern, successive phases of the mission, journey to Jerusalem and final outcome). Although exact or consistent parallels cannot be maintained between the two, nevertheless a relationship between them can be established which, contrary to what readers of Acts have come to expect, is one of antithesis. As for the correspondance with the preparatory mission of John the Baptist, Luke has interwoven it with the presentation of the two churches, aligning it with the missionary activity of the apostolic community.

Another structure acts as a kind of backbone for this Gospel framework consisting, as is commonly recognized, of the geographical expansion of the testimony to Jesus. The command to the 'Eleven and all those who were with them' (Lk. 24.33) to take the good news to all the Gentile nations (εἰς [ὡς ἐπὶ D05] πάντα τὰ ἔθνη, Lk. 24.47), beginning in the religious centre of Jerusalem, was initially reproduced at the end of the Gospel and is repeated in a more explicit form at the beginning of Acts. 'The apostles' (cf. Acts 1.2) are to witness to Jesus first in Jerusalem as the religious centre of Judaism; then 'in all Judaea (orthodox Jewish territory) and Samaria (non-orthodox territory)' which will come about as a result of the persecution that will cause them to be scattered, although still within the boundaries of Palestine; finally, 'to the ends of the earth', signifying the opening up of the mission to the Gentile nations (1.8).

IX. *The Speeches in Acts*

The debate concerning the origin of the contents of the speeches of Acts is well summarized in the major commentaries; there are numerous contributions that continue to be added to the discussion from a wide variety of angles.[67] How faithfully do the speeches transmit the words actually spoken? Where did Luke get his information from? Did he compose them from scratch himself? Did he use kerygmatic statements from earlier sources? Were some of his sources in Aramaic? On the question of Luke's use of earlier material in the composition of the speeches, we will refer only indirectly in the *Commentary* to possible clues; in fact, each speech needs to be examined separately, for there is no overall answer, and too much rests on speculation and hypothesis to draw firm conclusions.

Leaving aside the matter of exact sources, where there is general agreement today is that all the speeches as they now stand in Acts have been written by Luke,[68] and we have no difficulty in following the consensus of opinion. What we challenge is the assumption commonly associated with this view, namely that Luke expresses through the apostolic and missionary speeches his own theological thought. In other words, what he puts into the words of the various Christian characters is thought to correspond without qualification to his own understanding. In his earlier study of the purpose of Luke, Rius-Camps arrived at the opposite conviction, namely that Luke does not identify with the positions adopted by the individual characters in the varied situations in which they pronounce their speeches. The reasons for his view are based on the following grounds.

In the first place, scholars who tackle the subject make a distinction (even though not always explicitly) between speakers who are believers, and those who are not believers. As far as the speeches of the latter are concerned, no-one thinks of imposing full responsibility for the ideas they express on Luke. Indeed, the very fact that they are not believers makes it likely that Luke distances himself from them to a greater or lesser degree. This is the case for both speakers who are sympathetic towards the believers (such as Gamaliel addressing the Jerusalem Council, 5.35–39), and speakers who are hostile (such as Demetrius speaking to the silversmiths at Ephesus, 19.25–27).

67. A contribution to the debate that concentrates on the preaching contents of the speeches is by R. Bauckham, 'Kerygmatic Summaries in the Speeches of Acts', in Witherington (ed.), *History, Literature and Society*, pp. 185–217.

68. The older position was that Luke had compiled them from his different sources without writing them as such. This view has changed progressively, particularly since the publication of the thesis argued by M. Dibelius, 'The Speeches in Acts and Ancient Historiography', in *idem*, *Studies in the Acts of the Apostles* (London: SCM Press, 1956), pp. 165–66, according to which all the speeches are of Luke's composition, based on contemporary preaching traditions. Cf. J. Kilgallen, *The Stephen Speech* (Rome: Biblical Institute Press, 1976), p. 121; R.F. O'Toole, *The Christological Climax of Paul's Defense (Ac 22:1–26:32)* (Rome: Biblical Institute Press, 1978), p. 156.

When it comes to the believers, it is assumed that Luke identifies with their thoughts and teachings and includes the contents of their speeches, evangelistic or apologetic, in his account of the early Church in order to transmit authoritative doctrine or to demonstrate how Christians should conduct themselves. By virtue of their being apostles or disciples, tradition has been allowed to place a halo around them and to endow their words with an infallibility that few question.[69] This happens even in the instances where there are some very obvious contradictions in the positions adopted by the different speakers. It is true that a willingness among scholars to accept that there were important disagreements between sections of the early Church has become apparent. Nevertheless, more generally, when confronted by contradictions between speakers, blame is laid on Luke who is said to sometimes contradict himself or to be afraid of altering the inconsistencies of his sources. All of these explanations may work in accounting for contradictions between opposing positions of different speakers but there are also instances in the speeches pronounced by the same character where the ideas expressed on separate occasions contradict each other. Inevitably the solution is to attribute the contradictions and other inconsistencies to Luke, who is made to bear responsibility for them as the author of the narrative.

This is something of a blind alley and in order to find a way out of it, we need to go back to look at the infallibility conferred by Church tradition on the apostles and disciples. This way of treating the Christian leaders in Acts has its dangers. It obscures the process of the gradual conversion of Jesus' disciples because they are seen as fully in agreement with Jesus' message right from the beginning. Although it is readily accepted that during the time of their master's life his followers misunderstood him or resisted some of his teachings, once the ascension has taken place in Acts 1.9 they are suddenly considered to be entirely in harmony with Jesus' vision of things. Yet no explanation is available to account for this profound change; not, that is, until Acts 2 when they receive the Holy Spirit. If, on the other hand, Acts can be read without the preconceived notions about the infallibility of the apostles, it becomes clear that even the early Christians, no less than later ones, had the freedom to choose to

69. Despite the statement by F.S. Spencer, 'Neglected Widows in Acts 6:1–7', *CBQ* 56 (1994), pp. 715–33, that most scholars recognize the fallibility of the apostolic speeches in contrast with the infallibility of the narrator (p. 719), in practice it is rare indeed to see the evangelistic speeches treated as anything other than representative of authoritative Christian doctrine. Spencer's article is one of those welcome exceptions whose method we would endorse though differing with some of his conclusions.

follow their own ideas rather than divine guidance and did so, especially when the latter appeared to be in contradiction with what they, as faithful Jews, had always received as the truth.

It is once more an accurate grasp of the purpose of Luke in writing Acts (and the Gospel) that will allow the role of the speeches and their contents to be properly understood, and the problem of the inconsistencies to be successfully resolved. If Luke can be seen to be critical of the way in which the message of the Gospel (the first volume) was lived out by individuals and communities in reality (the second volume), then by no means does he have to be regarded as necessarily endorsing what is said on every occasion in Acts. Rather he is transmitting in the speeches the kind of thing the characters could and would have said given their understanding and disposition at the time of speaking. There is nothing odd about Luke's allowing the facts to speak for themselves; it is a device inherent in the method that he uses throughout the whole of his work and that was already established in the composition of the Jewish Scriptures (see §V.10 above). In this way, he highlights, on the one hand, behaviour that is either partially or entirely in line with the deeds and thinking of Jesus and, on the other, he lays blame or censure on conduct that is not in agreement with the model proposed in the Gospel. It is essential for modern-day readers to interpret correctly this critical attitude on the part of the author, and to be clear that a critical attitude is not the same as hostile accusation and still less enmity.

One of the difficulties in discerning Luke's intentions accurately today lies in the fact that they are less clear in the AT which has been the one known to most exegetes since the third century. Whilst it is by no means impossible to interpret the AT according to the perspective outlined above (indeed, Rius-Camps had arrived at his broad understanding of Luke's work before reading the text of Codex Bezae and discovering how much it supported what he had already seen), Luke's original purpose tends to be partially obscured by the rendering in that text of both the speeches and the narrative. Codex Bezae stands out as an earlier text precisely because it offers a more nuanced account of the beginnings of Christianity and because it displays a spectrum of theological understanding among the first disciples which it would make little sense to invent and insert into the text at a later date. It is worth repeating that the way in which the author's perspective is conveyed by the text of Codex Bezae is so complex and dependent on so many minute details that it would not have been possible to introduce the alterations into an existing text. In contrast, to modify details of the Bezan text that were disturbing was a less complicated task, especially as it apparently did not need to be carried out completely to be effective.

The understanding of Luke's purpose proposed here naturally presupposes that it is possible to establish criteria whereby an objective distinction can be made between those places where Luke fully endorses the contents of a speech and those where, on the contrary, he simply seeks to convey the mentality of one person or another in a given situation. What criteria does Luke provide the reader with in order to evaluate the speeches and to discern if their contents are in accordance or not with the model established by Jesus?

The first criterion, and the basic one, is that which has already been mentioned, namely a reference to the presentation of the model in the Gospel. In principle, the parallelism between Acts and the author's gospel is well-recognized,[70] but in practice the explorations of the nature of the comparisons tend to be carried out with certain presuppositions in mind. In taking account, for example, of the comparisons that Luke establishes on occasions between Jesus and Peter, or Jesus and Paul, it is indispensable to draw on the information provided in the Gospel to evaluate the episodes of Acts in question. It will be seen time and again that not only are these parallels more apparent in the text of Codex Bezae but that they also retain a critical dimension in that manuscript which is all but absent from the other forms of text.

Once it has been accepted that the Gospel contains the paradigm to be used in deciding what is the narrator's point of view with respect to the individual speeches in the second volume, then a secondary set of criteria has to be taken into account. These have to do with indications that Luke gives within the surrounding context of the speech. Clues are given principally in his presentation of the speaker so far, in the tone of the narrative, and also within the speech itself where the vocabulary may be used to signal a parallel as either analogical or antithetical. In many cases, it will be a matter of paying attention to the smallest details and in this respect the question of the text is crucial: it is of critical importance in establishing the nature of intended parallels to know exactly what Luke wrote

70. A survey of studies of Lukan character parallels up to 1983 is to be found in S.M. Prader, 'Jesus–Paul, Peter–Paul, and Jesus–Peter Parallelisms in Luke-Acts: A History of Reader Response' (SBL Seminar Papers 1984, ed. K.H. Richards, Atlanta: Scholars Press, 1984), pp. 23–39; Prader's survey is discussed by J.B. Green, 'Internal Repetition in Luke-Acts: Contemporary Narratology and Lukan Historiography', in Witherington (ed.), *History, Literature and Society*, pp. 283–99.

because he makes so much use of lexical and syntactic mirroring to communicate his intentions.

Two examples may serve to illustrate ways in which the criteria can be applied. When Luke introduces Stephen with an account that establishes his excellent spiritual qualities, when he constantly underlines the fact that as he addresses his opponents he is full of the Holy Spirit, and when he further presents the opposition to Stephen in terms of opposition to a prophet, the audience of Acts knows that his speech represents authoritative teaching in line with the plan of God. In contrast are the apologetic discourses that Paul makes on three occasions. Already in Luke's Gospel, Jesus had twice warned his disciples not to fall back on apologetics as a substitute for prophecy (Lk. 21.12–16, cf. 12.11–12); the very terms that Jesus uses to issue this warning (ἀπολογέομαι –ἀπολογία) are found six times in the words of Paul (Acts 22.1; 24.10; 25.8; 26.1, 2, 24). If Paul was obliged to have recourse to apologetics to defend himself, it was in fact, as we saw earlier (§VII), because he followed his own resolution in going to Jerusalem against the instructions of the Holy Spirit, and thereby deprived himself of the divine assistance that Jesus promised. Not only does Luke not go along with the contents of Paul's lengthy and repeated defences, he links them furthermore with Peter's denial of Jesus.[71]

In this way then, the responsibility for the contents of the speeches lies not with Luke but with the characters who pronounce them and it is they who, in different sets of circumstances, can be found to make contradictory statements. It is clear that the correct reading of the speeches is all important to making sense of Luke's purpose. The recognition of Luke's role in the composition of the speeches acts as an interpretative key whose value will be seen from the beginning to the end of the *Commentary*.

X. *Acts in the Context of First Century Judaism*

Reference has been made on a number of occasions in the above sections to ways in which Luke draws on the written and oral traditions of the Jewish Scriptures and teachings. It is common for studies of Luke's work to set his writings against the background of Judaism and to see what evidence of this background can be found in his account of Jesus and the lives of his followers. It is, however, an unfortunate error of procedure to consider Judaism as a 'background' to either the third Gospel or the book of Acts. As far as the early Church is concerned, both the founder and the movement established by his followers belong to Judaism. They may

71. Rius-Camps, *El camino de Pablo*, pp. 253–57.

diverge from other types of Judaism in the first century but they do not initially represent anything other than Judaism.

It is chiefly in the Alexandrian form of the text of Acts that support can be found for the hypothesis that Luke was a Gentile.[72] In the text of Codex Bezae, the author displays an intimate knowledge of the subtleties of Jewish thinking and behaviour, not only in the objective portrayal of his characters but even in his personal manner of expression as narrator. The negative criticism of Jewish individuals and institutions that is intensified in Codex Bezae is conveyed in terms that were above all meaningful to Jews of the first century. This contradicts, of course, the popular notion that the scribe of Codex Bezae was further removed in time and thought from the days of Jesus and the earliest Christian communities than was the author of the alternative form of text. In contrast, it means that the author of the Bezan text communicates his message from an insider Jewish point of view. In other words, the book of Acts and more especially the Bezan text of the book, is 'hostile' to Jews in the same way that the biblical prophets are hostile to Jews (and it makes little sense to say that the vehemence and insistence of their denunciations were 'anti-Jewish'). Rather than speak, therefore, of the Jewish *background* to Acts which can give the impression that the Church in Acts is quite separate from Judaism, it is preferable to speak of the Jewish *context* to indicate how the Christian movement is viewed from within Judaism, and even from different points of view within Judaism.

It is being increasingly acknowledged that the first Jesus-believing communities defined themselves in relation to Judaism, and were defined in the same way by other Jews. Studies of the New Testament writings therefore derive great benefit from the recent interest and researches of Jewish scholars in the domain of first-century Judaism as distinct from Rabbinic Judaism of the second century. It is now well-known that in this period, the late period of the Second Temple before the Jewish religion was made normative by the reforms and stipulations of the later Rabbis, Judaism was far from being one, uniform religious movement and it was perfectly possible for the disciples of Jesus, like Jesus himself, to be considered as representing one kind of Judaism.[73]

72. For a discussion of the growing opinion that Luke was a Jew, see F. Bovon, 'Studies in Luke-Acts: Retrospect and Prospect', *HTR* 85 (1992), pp. 175–96.

73. Dunn (*The Partings of the Ways*) summarizes the progress made in the understanding of Judaism in the first century, underlining the part played by J. Neusner, among others, in bringing about the change (pp. 11–16).

This historical analysis is of the greatest importance for an accurate evaluation of the varying texts of Acts. There is a large number of Bezan readings that appear to be the result of a curious interest in irrelevant details and that are usually regarded as evidence of scribal meddling with the original text to make it more colourful and interesting.[74] When examined in the light of research into Second Temple Judaism, including studies of intertestamental literature and traditional teachings, it emerges on the contrary that many of these readings can be accounted for by the author's close familiarity with the writings and teachings of certain strands of Judaism in the first century. In addition to a thorough awareness of how these traditions were transmitted at the time, they translate an intimate knowledge of the debates that they provoked and that were current among the different Jewish groups. Furthermore, they depend for their relevance on the assumption that the addressees of the text will also understand the allusions to the debates, frequently made in a discreet and implicit manner. Unfortunately, knowledge today of the complexity of Jewish traditions in the first century is still imprecise and incomplete. This means that there are readings in the Bezan text that at present remain incomprehensible but that may well be understood in the future and that consequently should not be rejected prematurely as fanciful scribal invention. It is even possible that what can be uncovered through a minute examination of the earliest forms of New Testament texts, forms that were later pruned of references too specifically Jewish to be intelligible or acceptable to a wider Christian audience, can furnish information for the reconstruction of early Jewish tradition.

The plurality of Judaisms makes it easier to appreciate the lack of uniformity in the theological understanding among the first Jesus-believers, a disparity that manifests itself most clearly in the different positions held concerning the definition of Israel and the status of the Gentiles within it.[75] The ensuing conflicts and tensions between the different groups – which cannot be reduced to simply two factions, the Hellenists and the Hebrews – are clearly painted in the text of Codex Bezae and to some extent in the 'Western' text generally. The AT attenuates considerably the disagreements among the Jesus-believers. There were important differ-

74. This kind of statement is made throughout the discussion of the variant readings in Metzger's *Commentary* and is reproduced by commentators.

75. Attention is drawn to the different Christian positions on important aspects of the faith in B.D. Chilton and J. Neusner, *Judaism in the New Testament: Practices and Beliefs* (London: Routledge, 1995); see, e.g., pp. 98–128 on the opposing views expressed by John, Luke and Paul on Israel.

ences between Palestinian and Diaspora Judaism that need to be carefully weighed up when seeking to appreciate the Jewish perspective in Acts for, indeed, there is not just one Jewish point of view. On the other hand, it is as inaccurate to attribute divisions in Judaism solely to regional differences as it is to draw uniformly sharp distinctions according to geographical location.[76] Likewise, within the Church, the divisions are more complex than discussion on the possible existence of Hellenist and Hebrew parties usually allows for.[77] For a complete picture, however, it is essential to refer to the Bezan text for it is only there that the strength of the disagreements and their causes has been preserved. The AT presents a tableau of the early Church that is more harmonious and at the same time less nuanced, in keeping with its tendency to tone down the theological contents of Luke's narrative, as will be discussed in the following section.

Recognizing the Jewish context of Acts has certain consequences for identifying the addressee, Theophilus. The Jewish Scriptures, teachings and expectations are so much in focus in the Bezan account of Acts that it is difficult to see what sense it would have made to a Roman officer, such as the 'most excellent Theophilus' (κράτιστε Θεόφιλε, Lk. 1.3; cf. Acts 1.1) is often assumed to be. If, on the other hand, Luke's Theophilus were the only Jew known to have had this name, none other than the former high priest, son of Ananas I, who had served in office from 37–41 CE,[78] then he could well have found that the Bezan Acts was intelligible to him since it addressed him in terms that were familiar to him. His own involvement, as well as that of his family, in many of the events narrated in Acts would make the story particularly meaningful to him.

76. A nuanced approach to the differences between Palestinian and Hellenistic Judaism is expressed by, e.g., M. Hengel, *Jews, Greeks and Barbarians: Aspects of Judaism in the Pre-Christian Period* (London: SCM Press, 1980); L.H. Feldman, 'Palestinian and Diaspora Judaism in the First Century', in H. Shanks (ed.), *Christianity and Rabbinic Judaism* (London: SPCK, 1993), pp. 1–40. Sound, historical information can also be found in S. Safrai and M. Stern (eds.), *The Jewish People in the First Century* (2 vols.; I, Philadelphia: Fortress Press, 1974; II, Assen-Amsterdam: Van Gorcum, 1976), though sufficient distinction is not always made between the different types of Judaism in the first century.

77. The monograph by C.C. Hill, *Hellenists and Hebrews: Reappraising Division within the Earliest Church* (Minneapolis: Augsburg, 1992), has provided fresh input for the discussion on which comment is made at the relevant points of the *Commentary*.

78. R. Anderson, 'À la recherche de Théophile', in *Saint Luc, évangéliste et historien* (*Dossiers d'Archéologie* 279 [2002–3]), pp. 64–71.

XI. *The Genre of Acts*

There has been much debate over the literary category to which the narrative of Acts should be viewed as belonging.[79] It is in many respects the patterns and nature of the variant readings between the two main textual traditions that demonstrate that in the Bezan text the intention of the author was not to write a straightforward historical account of the beginnings of Christianity.

As the title given to the second volume of Luke's writing illustrates, it was seen from an early date as belonging to the historical genre and this perception of Acts continues to the present day in the description of Acts as one kind or another of historical monograph with various qualifications being given to that description. Luke, on the other hand, did not claim anything other for Acts than that it was the continuation of the Gospel, a genre that is primarily theological, with a historical reference point.

From the use which Luke consistently makes of Scripture, and from the way in which he situates the events of the narrative in relationship to events in the history of Israel, it is clear that he sees his writing as being in line with the Jewish Scriptures. His heavy reliance on Scripture to give meaning to his account is by no means a repetition of established teachings but is, on the contrary, richly creative as can be seen over and over again not least in the freedom – again greater in the Bezan text – with which he uses the Septuagint. The interpretations he gives to incidents that occurred during the early years of the Church, presenting them (as will be seen at appropriate points in the *Commentary*) as on an identical scale and of an identical nature as incidents recorded in the Scriptures, demonstrate an authority that cannot be not self-invested if it is to be credible, or indeed valid. Furthermore, Luke displays an awareness of fulfilling a prophetic role in writing not just Acts but Acts as the second part of a unified work. He reveals the divine thoughts and will with respect to the people of God, communicated through Jesus and the Holy Spirit. Luke can show that some of the happenings about which he writes are in fulfilment of promises and prophecies of the past; others, he indicates, are harder to come to terms with because they represent a change in the divine plan brought about by certain actions that were not anticipated in the Scriptures.

79. C.H. Talbert, *Literary Patterns, Theological Themes and the Genre of Luke-Acts* (Missoula: Scholars Press, 1974), is particularly notable for having proposed the genre of biography. Articles by Brosend ('The Means of Absent Ends', pp. 348–62) and Green ('Internal Repetition in Luke-Acts', pp. 283–99) in Witherington (ed.), *History, Literature and Society*, both give helpful, up to date surveys of the debate as well as bringing their own contribution to it.

To some extent, unforeseen changes in the divine plan continue to be made during the time-span covered by the narrative of Luke-Acts. It is these that are usually overlooked in studies on Acts, and as a matter of fact the references to them in the familiar text are very much toned down or even obliterated in comparison with the Bezan text. Yet changes in the will of God are already encountered in the Jewish Scriptures when God is revealed as modifying his plan in response to the free-will actions of Israel or some sections of Israel. It should not, therefore, be completely surprising that the manner in which John the Baptist and Jesus were received should bring about an alteration in the plan of God compared with the way things were foreseen in the writings of the Prophets. It is particularly with respect to the existence and identity of Israel that there is a fundamental change. Luke shows how this is brought about through events during the life of Jesus first of all, and secondly after his resurrection.

We would concur, in other words, with the growing recognition that Luke's purpose in his writing is to show how the plan of God was worked out in Jesus, with the qualification that when Acts is taken into account, his work shows in addition how it was *not* always worked out as it should have been because of human obstacles, even obstacles among his disciples. Luke is, in short, providing an authoritative and prophetic statement about the intervention of God among the people of Israel. It is a historical statement in so far as it relates to events and people in the real world, but it is history perceived in a peculiarly Jewish way. Three features may be described as characteristics of the Jewish view of history:

1. Israel as the people of God is the centre of the universe, the ultimate reality, and all events involving other peoples are perceived in relation to Israel.
2. The God of Israel is the major protagonist in events in the real world and understanding the significance of these events depends on a revelation of his purpose.
3. Events not only have a reality in the time span within which they actually occur (their present) but equally they derive substance from corresponding words and events of the past that are related in the Scriptures and interpreted by tradition. Reality in the present can sometimes be viewed as a fulfilment of the past in the sense that it was foreseen in prophecy; at other times, it can be viewed as a fulfilment of the past in the sense that it is a re-enactment of events that have previously taken place and are recorded as part of the history of Israel.

Much of this, as some scholars have been at pains to point out, is evident in the text of Acts that is customarily read.[80] When the AT, however, is compared with the Bezan text, it is evident that the AT transmits a less theological and more chronological view of history, and that it regularly removes indications of a Jewish or spiritual perspective in what can be described as a tendency to 'historicize' the text.

XII. *The Organization of this Work*

Our study of Acts is organized in four major parts:

I. Jerusalem: the formation of the church of Jesus-believers in Jerusalem (1.1–5.42)
II. Judaea and Samaria: the birth of the Christian church in Antioch (6.1–12.25)
III. To the ends of the earth: the first three stages of the mission to the Gentiles (13.1–20.3)
IV. Rome: the final stage of the mission (20.4–28.31)

Within each part, the book of Acts is divided into sections and then, except for the *Prolegomena* and the first section, into sequences; the identification of sections and sequences does not necessarily follow the chapter divisions but is determined by the narrative structure of the episodes (see §V.1 above for details of the structural analysis). Each sequence is approached in three ways: a translation, a critical apparatus and a commentary.

The *Translation* consists of a side by side English translation of the texts of Codex Bezae and Codex Vaticanus, set out according to the elements of the structure of the passage. It aims to provide an accurate rendering of the differences in meaning, including wherever possible subtle differences in shades of meaning. This aim will take precedence over an

80. J. Jervell has written at length on the subject of Jewish history in relation to Luke-Acts, most recently in 'The Future of the Past: Luke's Vision of Salvation History and its Bearing on his Writing of History', in Witherington (ed.), *History, Literature and Society*, pp. 104–26, though we differ from his interpretation of Luke's view of the Jewish people and the nation of Israel. Cf. C.A. Evans, 'Luke and the Rewritten Bible: Aspects of Lukan Hagiography', in J.H. Charlesworth and C.A. Evans (eds.), *The Pseudepigrapha and Early Biblical Interpretation* (Sheffield: Sheffield Academic Press, 1993), pp. 170–201; F. Hahn, 'Der gegenwärtige Stand der Erforschung der Apostelgeschichte: Kommentare und Aufsatzbände 1980–1985', *Theologische Revue* 82 (1986), pp. 180–200. More usually, attempts are made to compare Acts with Greek or Roman ways of viewing history but even the classical historians share some of the Jewish historical concepts which distance them from a twentieth-century outlook, see F.F. Bruce ('The Acts of the Apostles Today', *BJRL* 65 [1982], pp. 36–56) who quotes Hengel: 'Classical historians accepted history as the record of the interplay of superhuman forces which influenced human actions' (p. 55).

idiomatic English rendering, however much such a translation could be preferable for other purposes. Justification for the wording of the translation is occasionally given at the relevant place in the critical apparatus but more usually within the *Commentary*.

The *Critical Apparatus* sets out the readings of Codex Vaticanus and Codex Bezae, following the system explained in §III above.

The *Commentary* discusses the meaning of the passage, seeking to compare the message of the Bezan text with that of the AT. Interaction with relevant scholarly debate is placed in the footnotes, but it should be noted that repetition or discussion of previous commentaries is avoided except for the sake of making a particular point. The commentary will not dwell on matters of factual veracity related to local history, which have already received careful treatment, but will focus instead on the underlying message of the book.[81] Where a topic raises issues that require a more developed presentation, this is provided in an excursus. As far as possible, the exegetical discussion in the *Commentary* sections does not depend on a knowledge of Greek, hopefully making the work more accessible to a wide range of interested readers.

81. The question of the historical accuracy of Acts is well documented, see, e.g., Dibelius, *Studies in the Acts of the Apostles*; Hemer, *The Book of Acts in the Setting of Hellenistic History*; M. Hengel, *Acts and the History of Earliest Christianity* (London: SCM Press 1979); and the series edited by B. Winter, *The Book of Acts in its First Century Setting* (6 vols.; Grand Rapids: Eerdmans, 1994–98). See also the commentaries on Acts by F.F. Bruce and C.K. Barrett, in particular.

PROLEGOMENA
1.1–14

Overview

The introductory section of Acts functions in combination with the final chapter of Luke's Gospel to provide a hinge linking the two volumes, with Luke 24 and Acts 1.1–14 each representing one side of the hinge. The link between the Gospel and Acts is of critical importance because of the specific relationship of the one to the other, a relationship that needs to be understood from the outset of the second volume: in the Gospel, Jesus is established as a model or paradigm with whom the apostles are compared in the book of Acts. The comparison is always implicit but quite deliberate, for Luke creates an abundance of clues and signs throughout Acts that are intended to prompt the reader to consider the deeds and words of the early Church leaders in the light of those of Jesus. It is such inner connections between the two volumes that provide the evidence that the Gospel and Acts were meant to be viewed as connected parts of the same work.[1] However, the comparison should by no means be expected to be always positive; on the contrary, in the early stages of their ministry especially, the various apostles frequently stand in rather unfavourable contrast to their master but as the narrative progresses they are seen to grow in understanding and obedience. If this is not readily apparent in the AT, in Codex Bezae it is quite plain to see once the traditional reading of Acts has been laid aside.

Structure and Themes

The opening verses of Acts, in continuation with the Gospel, still have Jesus as the main character. They do not belong to the story proper of the second book; this starts at 1.15. Their purpose is to direct a spotlight on

1. The unity of the work of Luke, the Gospel and Acts, has been questioned by several scholars, most recently by M.C. Parsons and R.I. Pervo, *Rethinking the Unity of Luke and Acts* (Minneapolis: Fortress, 1993). The interpretation of Acts that emerges from our analysis requires, on the contrary, the existence of the Gospel as an earlier part of the same work, see *General Introduction,* §VI. It should also be noted that a consideration of the unity of Luke's work is inevitably dependent on the particular text examined.

the final instructions of Jesus before he leaves the disciples for the last time, and to draw attention at the same time to the disciples' ways of thinking which are somewhat at odds at this stage with Jesus' teaching.

The section is divided into two main parts (1.1–8; 1.9–14), with the second mirroring the structure of the first in a five-fold pattern:

[a] 1.1–2 The ministry of Jesus up to his final departure
[b] 1.3[2] Jesus' post-resurrection appearances, including his teaching concerning the kingdom of God
[c] 1.4–5 The final meal; the order not to leave Hierosoluma and the promise of the Holy Spirit
[d] 1.6 The expectations of the apostles
[e] 1.7–8 The universal commission of Jesus
[a′] 1.9 The ascension of Jesus
[b′] 1.10–11 The apparition of Moses and Elijah and their instruction concerning Jesus' return
[c′] 1.12 The return of the apostles to Ierousalem (religious centre)
[d′] 1.13 The list of the Eleven in the upper room
[e′] 1.14 The women (and children D05) and members of Jesus' family

Each of the elements identified above has its parallel in Luke 24:

[a] Lk. 24.51 The final departure of Jesus
[b] Lk. 24.13–40 The appearances of Jesus to the disciples at Emmaus and to the Eleven together with the other disciples;[3] Lk. 24.26–27; 24.44–47, his teaching
[c] Lk. 24.41–43 The final meal; Lk. 24.48, the Father's promise and the order to wait in the city
[d] No expectations are specified but Jesus' promises to the disciples before his death (Lk. 22.28–30) had built up their expectations concerning the restoration of the kingdom

2. Commentators vary in their division of the first verses of Acts with the function of 1.3 proving the most debatable point. UBS[4] makes a break after 1.2, leaving a gap between 1.2 and 1.3 in the printed text. N-A[27] makes a more definite break with a gap and a full stop.

3. The text of D05 presents the post-Easter appearance of Jesus to the disciples differently from that of the other MSS, paying particular attention to the difficulty the apostles had in realizing what had happened to their master and how it was a fulfilment of the Scriptures. See C.-A. Amphoux, 'Le chapitre 24 de Luc et l'origine de la tradition textuelle du Codex de Bèze (D.05 du NT)', *FN* 7 (1994), pp. 21–49; J. Read-Heimerdinger and J. Rius-Camps, 'Emmaous or Oulammaous? Luke's Use of the Jewish Scriptures in the Text of Luke 24 in Codex Bezae', *RCatT* 27 (2002), pp. 23–42.

[e] Lk. 24.47–48 The universal commission
[a′] Lk. 24.50–51 The departure (D05) / ascension (B03) of Jesus
[b′] Lk. 24.4–7 The apparition of Moses and Elijah and their instruction concerning Jesus
[c′] Lk. 24.52–53 The disciples return to Ierousalem
[d′] Lk. 24.33 The Eleven
[e′] Lk. 24.10 The women. Significantly, no mention is made of his family

The parallels between the two books demonstrate that the most important themes of the last chapter of Luke's Gospel are taken up again in this section, but this time with some new, complementary information. In particular, the scope of the commission entrusted by Jesus to his disciples is clarified. The commission is the final element in the first part of the episode and its realization will control the basic plan of the book of Acts. In the text of Codex Bezae, there is a clear narrative progression through the section 1.1–14: 1.1 to ἀνελήμφθη summarizes in one movement the whole of the Gospel book; ἐντειλάμενος to εὐαγγέλιον in 1.2 backtracks and goes over the Gospel again, summarizing the role of the apostles and their relationship with Jesus; the following clause beginning οἷς καί in 1.3 maintains the focus on the apostles and opens up the post-resurrection period of the Gospel so that instead of being presented as one day as in Luke 24 it is counted as a period of forty days. These forty days are then scrutinized more closely in 1.4–5, with 1.6–14 zooming in, so to speak, on the final day of the period. In the AT, there is the same narrative progression but the variant reading of 1.2 makes the initial steps less visible.

Translation

	Codex Bezae D05	*Codex Vaticanus B03*
[a]	**1.1** In the first book, O Theophilus, I dealt with all the things that Jesus did and taught from the beginning **2** up to the day when he was taken up, having given instructions to the apostles whom he had chosen through the Holy Spirit and to whom he had ordered to preach the gospel.	**1.1** In the first book, O Theophilus, I dealt with all the things that Jesus did and taught from the beginning **2** up to the day when, having given instruction to the apostles whom he had chosen through the Holy Spirit, he was taken up.
[b]	**3** It was to them that he presented himself as alive after his suffering, giving many proofs, for a period of forty days during which he appeared to them and told them things about the kingdom of God.	**3** It was to them that he presented himself as alive after his suffering, giving many proofs, over forty days when he appeared to them and told them things about the kingdom of God.

[c]	**4** While he was sharing a meal with them, he ordered them not to leave Hierosoluma but, on the contrary, to wait for the promise of the Father 'which you heard' —he said— 'from my mouth, **5** that "John baptized with water but you will be baptized with the Holy Spirit", and you are about to receive him not many days from now, by the end of Pentecost'.	**4** While he was sharing a meal, he ordered them not to go away from Hierosoluma but, on the contrary, to wait for the promise of the Father 'which you heard from me; **5** Because John baptized with water but you will be baptized in the Spirit, the Holy one, not many days from now'.
[d]	**6** So they got together and insistently questioned him, 'Lord, is this the time when you will restore to the kingdom of Israel ...?'	**6** So they got together and asked him, 'Lord, is this the time when you will restore the kingdom to Israel?'
[e]	**7** And he said to them, 'It is not for you to know times or seasons: the Father has placed them within his own authority. **8** Rather, you will receive power when the Holy Spirit comes upon you and you will be witnesses of me not only in Jerusalem and all Judaea and Samaria, but also to the ends of the earth.'	**7** He said to them, 'It is not for you to know times or seasons: the Father has placed them within his own authority. **8** Rather, you will receive power when the Holy Spirit comes upon you and you will be witnesses of me in Jerusalem, and in all Judaea and Samaria, and to the ends of the earth.'
[a′]	**9** And when he had said this, a cloud took him up and he was lifted away from their sight. **10** While they were staring into the sky as he was going, behold! two men dressed in white had come to stand beside them.	**9** And when he had said this, as they were watching he was lifted up and a cloud took him up from their sight. **10** While they were staring into the sky, watching him as he was going, behold! two men dressed in white had come to stand beside them.
[b′]	**11** Finally, they spoke: 'Men from Galilee, why are you standing gazing into the sky? Jesus himself, who has been taken up from you, will come in just the same way that you saw him going into the sky.'	**11** Finally, they spoke: 'Men from Galilee, why are you standing looking into the sky? Jesus himself, who has been taken up from you into the sky, will come in just the same way as you saw him going into the sky.'
[c′]	**12** So then they returned to Ierousalem from the mountain known as the Mount of Olives which is near Ierousalem, a sabbath day's journey away.	**12** So they then returned to Ierousalem from the mountain known as the Mount of Olives which is near Ierousalem, a sabbath day's journey away.
[d′]	**13** On entering, they went up into the upper room where they stayed waiting. There were: Peter and John, James and Andrew, Philip and Thomas, Bartholomew and Matthew; James the son	**13** On entering, they went into the upper room and there they stayed waiting. There were: Peter and John, and James and Andrew, Philip and Thomas, Batholomew and Matthew,

	of Alphaeus, Simon the Zealot and Judas son of James.	James son of Alphaeus and Simon the Zealot and Judas son of James.
[e′]	**14** All of these were continuing steadfastly together in prayer with their wives and children, in addition to Mary, mother of Jesus, and his brothers.	**14** All of these were continuing steadfastly together in prayer with some women, in addition to Mary, the mother of Jesus, and his brothers.

Critical Apparatus

Explanation of the Critical Apparatus

The critical apparatus displays the variant readings of Codex Vaticanus (B03) and Codex Bezae (D05), and lists the witnesses that support each of them. The readings of Codex Sinaiticus (א01) are also displayed where they differ from those of Codex Vaticanus because of the importance of this MS as a witness to the AT.

The abbreviations used to refer to MSS are those used by the Nestle-Aland 27th edition of the Greek New Testament. For versions and Church Fathers not cited by N-A^{27}, the abbreviations of Boismard and Lamouille's *Le texte occidental des Actes des Apôtres* (details in *Bibliography* I) have been adopted. In the discussion of readings in the *Critical Apparatus*, as in the *Commentary* proper, uncial MSS are referred to by their number and letter, but in the list of readings uncial MSS are cited by their letter alone in order to prevent the apparatus from becoming overcrowded.

1.1 Ἰησοῦς B D W || ὁ Ἰη. א 81 *rell.*

The general rule, according to which the first appearance of a character on the scene is anarthrous, is followed by both B03 and D05. See Heimerdinger and Levinsohn, 'The Use of the Definite Article before Names of People', pp. 15–44 (22–23).

1.2 (ἄχρι ἧς ἡμέρας) ἀνελήμφθη D d || *om.* B א *rell.*

All MSS except D05 d05 hold back the mention of the resurrection to the end of the verse.

(ἐξελέξατο) ἀνελήμφθη B א *rell* || καὶ ἐκέλευσε κηρύσσειν τὸ εὐαγγέλιον D d gig t* sy$^{(p).hmg}$ (sa mae); Barn Aug Vig Ephr.

D05 has a second sentence relating to the same antecedent as the previous one. The relative pronoun is not repeated, even though the second sentence strictly requires a dative instead of the accusative (οὕς). According to Delebecque, this is a typically Attic construction (Delebecque, 'Les deux prologues des Actes des Apôtres', pp. 628–34 [630]); it is employed elsewhere by Luke (Lk. 3.17; 6.49; 12.24; 13.4; 17.31).

The additional Bezan sentence cannot be intended as a clarification of the content of the instructions of Jesus already mentioned (ἐντειλάμενος), for that reference relates to the period preceding his ascension, whereas the order to preach the good news was given when Jesus sent out the Twelve on their mission to Israel (Lk. 9.2: ἀπέστειλεν αὐτοὺς κηρύσσειν τὴν βασιλείαν τοῦ θεοῦ, cf. 9.6 εὐαγγελιζόμενοι; cf. Mk 3.14–15 D05: ἵνα ἀποστέλλῃ αὐτοὺς κηρύσσειν τὸ εὐαγγέλιον). See also Rius-Camps, 'Las variantes, I', pp. 63–66.

The place of ἀνελήμφθη in the two texts can be displayed as follows:

B03	D05
ἄχρι ἧς ἡμέρας	ἄχρι ἧς ἡμέρας
	ἀνελήμφθη
ἐντειλάμενος τοῖς ἀποστόλοις	ἐντειλάμενος τοῖς ἀποστόλοις
διὰ πνεύματος ἁγίου οὓς ἐξελέξατο	διὰ πνεύματος ἁγίου οὓς ἐξελέξατο
	καὶ ἐκέλευσε κηρύσσειν τὸ εὐαγγέλιον
ἀνελήμφθη	

1.3 δι' ἡμερῶν τεσσεράκοντα B ℵ *rell, post dies quadraginta* d; Aug || τεσσ. ἡμ. D* | τεσσ. δι' ἡμ. D^{A}.

The genitive is sometimes found in place of the accusative to express duration of time (B-D-R, §186.2; cf. §161.2, n. 4, citing 2 Thess. 3.8 and Rev. 2.10 where the genitive and the accusative are interchanged in the *vll*).

1.4 συναλιζόμενος B ℵ A C E Y 049. 056. 33. 69. 88. 330. 618. 927. 945. 1175. 1646. 1739^{c}. 1828. 1837. 1891. 2344. 2412. 2495 it vg sy co arm aeth || συναλισκ– D* (–σγ– D^{H}) | συναυλ– H^{2} 36. 88. 181. 323^{s}. 383*. 467. 522. 614. 629. 915. 1108. 1241*. 1518. 1739^{s}*. 1838. 1898. 2401^{c}. 2492 *pm, simul convivens* d e gig p* t; Did Eus Epiph Chr Ps-Chr Aug Qu Vig.

The usual meaning of the verb συναλίζομαι read by B03 (not found elsewhere in the New Testament) is 'come together' (B-A-G), with Jesus apparently the subject here, as he is the subject of the aorist verb following. The strangeness of the participle in the singular could have given rise to the *vl* συναυλ– ('be with, stay with', B-A-G; cf. Zerwick and Grosvenor, *Analysis*, p. 349), but this verb is not normally used intransitively. συναλίζομαι has a rarer meaning, 'eat salt (i.e. a meal) with' (B-A-G), which is understood by most of the early versions. In view of the parallel between the present scene and the end of Luke's Gospel (Lk. 24.41–49) where Jesus eats with his disciples on his last day with them, this would seem to be the intended meaning here. It is difficult to see how the verb of either D05 (συναλίσκομαι, 'be taken captive with') or D^{H} (συναλίσγομαι, 'be sullied') can be appropriate in this situation. Ropes (*Text*, p. 2) suggests that it is a case of phonetic confusion.

μετ᾽ αὐτῶν D d e gig p* s t y sy co arm; Ephr Epiph Aug Qu Vig | αὐτοῖς E || *om.* B ℵ *rell.*

This reading, attested as it is by those early versions that also take the previous verb in the sense of 'eat a meal', adds support to that interpretation.

(ἀπὸ) Ἱεροσολύμων B D d *rell* || Ἰερουσαλήμ ℵ.

ℵ01 is alone in reading the Hebrew-derived spelling for Jerusalem which has a theological connotation in Luke's writing. The Hellenistic spelling, designating simply the location, is fully justified in this instance by the parallel καθίσατε ἐν τῇ πόλει in Lk. 24.49.

ἣν ἠκούσατέ μου B P$^{56vid.74vid}$ ℵ A C D$^{s.m.}$ E H^{2} Y 049. 056. 33. 81. 945. 1175. 1243. 1245. 1646. 2344 𝔐 || ἣν ἠκούσα<τε>, φησίν, διὰ τοῦ στόματός μου D*, *quam audistis de ore meo* d p vg^{cl} mae aeth; Hil Aug.

ἤκουσα in D05 is taken to be a scribal error for ἠκούσατε. The solemnity and the scriptural resonance of the formula 'from my mouth' (cf. Lk. 22.71 [ἀπό]; Acts 15.7 [διά]; 22.14 [ἐκ]) as well as the insertion of 'he said' after the start of the speech (cf. Lk. 7.40; Acts 2.38 ℵ01; 25.5, 22; 26.25) strongly suggest that they are not simply added to aid the transition from indirect to direct speech. Similar occurrences of transition from indirect to direct speech are found in Lk. 5.14; Acts 25.4–5.

The fact that there is no trace of such a saying attributed to Jesus in the Gospel before the resurrection passages (Lk. 24.49 refers to the same scene as Acts 1.5) could have caused the elimination of φησίν, διὰ τοῦ στόματος between ἠκούσατε and μου. As a result, the following ὅτι, which is recitative in D05, takes on a causal sense in B03.

1.5 ἐν πνεύματι βαπτισθήσεσθε ἁγίῳ B ℵ* 81. 915 *pc*; Did | βαπ. ἐν πν. ἁγ. P^{74vid} ℵ^{2} A C E H^{2} Y 049. 056 33. 81. 1175. 1739 𝔐 vg; Or Cyr || ἐν πν. ἁγ. βαπ. D d gig p* t; Aug^{pt} Vig.

The position of the adjective after the verb in B03 is not found in any other mention of the Holy Spirit (for a list of references to πνεῦμα ἅγιον in Acts, see Read-Heimerdinger, *The Bezan Text*, pp. 160–61). Its detachment from the noun has the effect of stressing the adjective. The D05 reading stresses rather the whole phrase in a chiastic structure (ἐβάπτισεν ὕδατι // ἐν πνεύματι ἁγίῳ βαπτισθήσεθε), appropriately enough since Jesus is contrasting the baptism of water with that of the Holy Spirit.

καὶ ὃ μέλλετε λαμβάνειν D* d gig s t y vg^{mss}; Ephr Hil (Chr) Ambrst Aug^{pt} Vig MaxTaur Cass || *om.* B ℵ D$^{s.m.}$ *rell.*

The construction of D05 is not impossible (cf. 20.9 D05; καὶ ὅσα 15.20 D05, 29 D05), although the construction ὃς καί is more typical of Luke (Matt. x 1; Mk x 1; [+ 2 ℵ01 B03 + 1 D05]; John x 1; Lk. x 4 [+ 1B*03 + 2D05]; Acts x 12 [+ 2 ℵ01 B03 + 2 ℵ01 + 1 ℵ*01 D05 + 4 D05] and seems to be better Greek (cf. Delebecque, *Les deux Actes*, p. 29). The order καὶ ὅς stresses the relative pronoun and can be compared to the construction of participle + καί + personal verb which frequently occurs in D05 (Read-Heimerdinger, *The Bezan Text*, pp. 206–10). In both cases, the relative pronoun has the function of a demonstrative pronoun (ὅ = τοῦτο, see B-D-R, §293, 3c). In the construction as it stands, καί serves to connect a saying, already known to the apostles, with its imminent actualization. After the auxiliary verb μέλλω, the present infinitive is normal in Luke (Lk. x 10; Acts x 27) and in the New Testament generally, to indicate the immediate future; Luke alone uses the future infinitive ἔσεσθαι, and that on three occasions, to indicate an unavoidable fact (Acts 11.28; 24.15; 27.10).

(ἡμέρας) ἕως τῆς πεντηκοστῆς D* d sa mae; Ephr (In Eph 4,10) Aug^pt Cass || *om.* B ℵ D^s.m. *rell.*

The detail included in D05 goes further than the litotes of B03 and links the time of waiting not to βαπτισθήσεσθε but to λαμβάνειν. It places a limit on the period, that is, not just in a few days time (so far there have been 40 days since the resurrection) but by Pentecost, which was due to take place fifty days after Passover, so around a week from when Jesus was speaking.

1.6 συνελθόντες (συνσυν– B*) B D d S01² *rell* || ἐλθόντες ℵ*.

ἠρώτων B ℵ A C 88. 915. 1175 *pc* || ἐπηρ. D d E H² Y 049. 056 33. 81 𝔐; Hipp.

The compound verb of D05 conveys the sense of insistent action and focuses attention on Jesus as the object (Moulton and Howard, p. 312). The compound has already been used in the parallel construction of Lk. 17.20: ἐπερωτηθεὶς δὲ ὑπὸ τῶν Φαρισαίων πότε ἔρχεται ἡ βασιλεία τοῦ θεοῦ.

ἀποκαθιστάνεις τὴν βασιλείαν τῷ Ἰσραήλ B ℵ *rell*, *restituere* (*-ues* d^G) *regnum istrahel* d* || ἀποκαταστάνεις εἰς τ. βασ. τοῦ Ἰσραήλ D*.

The B03 verb is a compound derived from –ιστανω; the D05 verb is from the form –στανω (Moulton I, p. 55, n. 2) as in Mk 9.12 (ℵ* D); Acts 17.15 (P⁴⁵ D*). The meaning is the same though the D05 form may have resonances of its use in the LXX (see below). Since the D05 sentence lacks a direct object, εἰς could be taken as a copyist's error of dittography (Delebecque, *Les deux Actes*, p. 29). However, it is possible to view the preposition as an essential element of the Bezan text: whereas all MSS except D05 have the apostles ask about the restoration of the kingdom (dir. obj.) to Israel (dat., τῷ Ἰσραήλ), D05 has them persistently ask about the restoration (of something which has to be supplied) into the kingdom (ind. obj.) of Israel (gen., τοῦ 'Ι.).

There are comparable instances in the LXX where εἰς is used with the verb ἀποκαταστάναι (that of D05 here in Acts) once without a dir. obj. at Jer. 29.6, and specifically in connection with the restoration of something into an aspect of Israel at 1 Esd. 1.29 (Jerusalem); 6.25 (the house in Jerusalem); Jer. 16.15; 23.8 and 24.6 (the Israelites to the land of Israel). Among the first-century expectations of the Jews concerning the restoration of Israel by the Messiah was the hope that the twelve tribes would be restored (see *Excursus* 1). In view of these factors, the text of D05 can be construed as presenting the disciples enquiring about the replacement of Judas as one of the Twelve chosen by Jesus (see on 1.24 below). The phrase ἡ βασιλεία τοῦ 'Ισραήλ stands in contrast to ἡ βασιλεία τοῦ Θεοῦ of 1.3.

1.7 εἶπεν πρὸς αὐτούς B* sy^{p} | εἶπ. οὖν πρ. αὐτ. B^{2} | εἶπ. δὲ πρ. αὐτ. ℵ A H^{2} Y 049. 056. 33. 614. 945. 1739^{s}. 2412. 2495 𝔐 vg sy^{h} || ὁ δὲ εἶπ. πρ. αὐτ. C^{vid} | ὁ δὲ ἀποκριθεὶς εἶπ. αὐτοῖς E || καὶ εἶπ. πρ. αὐτ. D d it.

The asyndeton of B03 is highly unusual within a speech exchange in Acts; it draws attention to the unexpected nature of Jesus' reply (Read-Heimerdinger, *The Bezan Text*, p. 247). δέ, the correlative to μὲν οὖν of 1.6 and read by ℵ01, would be the expected conjunction.

The conjunction καί in D05 shows that Jesus' response is viewed neither as the correlative of the μὲν οὖν clause nor as a new development in answer to the apostles' question (Levinsohn, *Textual Connections*, pp. 83–120). The use of καί to introduce a speaker response is unusual in a dialogue in Acts and can be understood as an indication that there is a lack of true exchange and that there are two lines of thought (the apostles' and Jesus') running in parallel. Furthermore, Jesus' remarks are introduced with the aorist εἶπεν, interrupting the imperfect ἐπηρώτων. On this interpretation, καί cuts into the apostles' insistent question which is left unfinished (if the MSS showed punctuation '...' would be found at the end of the interrogative sentence), thus accounting for the absence of the direct object.

1.8 ἐν πάσῃ τῇ 'Ιουδαίᾳ B P^{74} ℵ C^{3} E H^{2} Y 049. 056. 33. 69. 88. 226*. 547^{c}. 614. 1175. 1245. 1739. 2147. 2412. 2495 𝔐 lat; Cyr || πάσῃ τ. 'Ιουδ. D d A C* 81. 206. 226^{c}. 323. 522. 547*. 945. 1243. 1611 *pc* sa mae aeth geo; Or Hil Qu.

The use of three prepositions in B03 divides the regions of the apostles' mission into three separate groups: Jerusalem / Judaea and Samaria / the whole earth. In the D05 text, on the other hand, the grouping is a two-fold one: Jerusalem, Judaea and Samaria / the whole earth. The former marks the point of departure (ἐν) of the mission, which is within the frontiers of Israel, and the latter its limit (ἕως), which extends throughout the Gentile world. The singular reading of D05 at Lk. 24.47–48 already set up this pattern, showing quite clearly the universal scope intended for the mission as well as its point of departure: κηρυχθῆναι ... ὡς ἐπὶ πάντα τὰ ἔθνη ἀρξαμένων ἀπὸ Ἰερουσαλήμ. καὶ ὑμεῖς δὲ μάρτυρες τούτων, 'to preach ... to all nations indeed, starting in Jerusalem. You yourselves (will be) witnesses of these things'. For questions regarding the punctuation, the choice from among the different variants and the theoretical ambiguity of the verb which needs to be supplied, see Rius-Camps, *De Jerusalén a Antioquía,* pp. 29–30.

1.9 καὶ ταῦτα εἰπών B ℵ^{2} A C E H2 Y 049. 056. 33. 81. 945. 1739 𝔐, *et cum haec dixisset* d | κ. τ. εἰπόντων ℵ* || καὐτὰ εἰπόντος αὐτοῦ D.

The genitive absolute of D05 anticipates the switch of focus to νεφέλη as the subject of the active verb that follows immediately in this text.

αὐτῶν βλεπόντων ἐπήρθη B | βλεπ. αὐτ. ἐπ. ℵ A C E H^{2} Y 049. 056. 33. 81. 945. 1739. 2412. 2495 𝔐 || *om.* D d .

The comment in B03, that the disciples watched Jesus as he left them, derives its importance from the parallel with the ascension of Elijah. D05 also recognizes a parallel between the two ascension stories but attributes it more to the mentality of the disciples than to Luke's theology (see *Excursus* 2).

καὶ νεφέλη ὑπέλαβεν αὐτόν B ℵ *rell* || νεφ. ὑπέβαλεν (*pro* ὑπέλαβ.) αὐτόν D, *nubs suscepit eum* d.

In B03, the cloud is introduced as a second element in the disappearance of Jesus while it is the main one in D05, possibly to draw attention to the difference with the ascension of Elijah who was taken up by a whirlwind.

ἀπὸ τῶν ὀφθαλμῶν αὐτῶν B ℵ *rell* || καὶ ἀπήρθη (ἐπ– D^{B}) ἀπὸ ὀφθ. αὐτ. D*, *et levatus est ab oculis eorum* d.

The absence of the article in D05 is also seen in the expression of Lk. 19.42 and Acts 26.18.

1.11 ἐν ἐσθήσεσι λευκαῖς B P^{56c} ℵ A C* Y 81. 323. 945. 1175 *pc* lat; Eus || ἐν ἐσθῆτι λευκῇ D d P^{56*} C^{2} E H^{2} 049. 056. 33. 614. 1739. 2412. 2495 𝔐 e sy geo; Or Aug.

The dative plural (of the rare word ἔσθησις, see Bruce, *Text*, p. 72) in B03 could be due, as in Lk. 24.4 (A C [L] W Θ Ψ 070 f$^{1.13}$ 33 𝔐 sy^{h}), to the fact that there are two people (Boismard and Lamouille, II, p. 5). In the LXX, it is found in 2 Macc. 3.33 of the two young men who appear to Heliodor, and in *3 Macc.* 1.16 of the priests. In D05, the dative singular of ἐσθής is used, as in other witnesses of Lk. 24.4 (P^{75} ℵ B D lat sy$^{s.c.p}$; Or). ἐσθής is also found at Lk. 23.11 and Acts 10.30; 12.21, as well as at Jas 2.2

(x 2), 3; in the LXX, at 1 Esd. 8.68, 70; 2 Macc. 8.35 and 11.8 (ἐν λευκῇ ἐσθῆτι), always in the singular.

βλέποντες B ℵ* E 33. 81. 323. 945. 1241. 1270. 1739ˢ. 2495 *al*; Eus || ἐμβλ– D, *aspicientes* d P^{56} $ℵ^2$ A C H^2 Y 049. 056. 614. 1175. 2412 𝔐 vg^{ms} sy^p; Aug Qu.
(ἀφ' ὑμῶν) εἰς τὸν οὐρανόν B ℵ *rell* a e ph vg $sy^{p.h}$ sa bo arm geo || *om*. D d 33. 69*. 242. 323. 326*. 330. 1270. 1837. 2495 *pc* gig t* vg^{mss} bo^{mss}; Aug Vig.

The insistence of B03 on the detail εἰς τὸν οὐρανόν (four times in two verses) is suspect. On the other occasions when Luke uses the passive of ἀναλαμβάνω to refer to the ascension of Jesus to heaven, this detail is not included (cf. Acts 1.2, 22); on the other hand, when its absence could lead to confusion in speaking of the sheet with the animals (10.16; cf. 11.10), it is made explicit.

1.13 εἰσῆλθον B ℵ *rell, cum introissent* d || εἰσῆλθεν D.

The singular verb in D05 groups the apostles together as a single body.

εἰς τὸ ὑπερῷον ἀνέβησαν B A C 81. 1175 | εἰς τ. ὑπερ. ℵ* 88 || ἀν. εἰς τ. ὑπερ. D d $ℵ^2$ E H^2 Y 049. 056. 33. 323. 614. 945. 1241. 1245. 1505. 1739. 2344. 2412. 2495 𝔐.

B03 draws attention to the 'upper room' by the pre-verb position of the adverbial phrase. In D05 the word order links closely the action of 'entering' (Ierousalem) with the verb characteristically employed of 'going up' to Ierousalem and, more specifically, the Temple (cf. Lk. 2.42; 18.10, 31; 19.28; Acts 3.1; 11.2; 15.2; 18.22; 21.12, 15; 24.11; 25.1, 9).

᾿Ιωάνν(–ν– B)ης καὶ ᾿Ιάκωβος καὶ ᾿Ανδρέας B ℵ A C 81. 88. 104. 1175 | ᾿Ιάκ. κ. ᾿Ιω. κ. ᾿Ανδ. A H^2 056. 323. 614. 1241. 1245. 1505. 1739. 2344. 2492 || ᾿Ιωάνης, ᾿Ιάκ. καὶ ᾿Ανδ. D, *Iohannis, Iacobus et Andreas* d.

In this list of the Eleven, B03 closely ties together the first four names with τε ... καί ... καί ... καί, then separates two pairs, and finally links the last three names again with two successive καί; D05, on the other hand, organizes the list into four pairs of names linked with καί, except for the first pair which seems to be underlined by means of τε ... καί, and finishes the list with a group of three, of which the first two are juxtaposed and linked by καί to the last. The article before the first name applies to the whole group (Heimerdinger and Levinsohn, 'The Use of the Definite Article before Names of People', pp. 19, 29). In contrast to this list of Acts, that of Lk. 6.14–16 ($P^{4.75}$ ℵ [B] D L [W] *pm*) sets out equally all twelve names of the people chosen by Jesus (all coordinated with καί, as indeed in the later list of the seven Hellenists in Acts 6.5), and places Simon with his brother Andrew, while the other pair of brothers, James and John, comes afterwards. The change of position of John in the list of Acts 1 (but not in [Ψ] 33. [945.1704]. 1739^{s}. [1891] *pc* 𝔐 sy^{h}) where he is closely associated with Peter, particularly in D05, prepares for the emergence of the pair in their future leadership of the group (cf. 3.1, 3, 11; 4.13, 19; 8.14); it is their capacity as leaders (already hinted at in the Gospel, cf. Lk. 8.51; 9.28) that has dictated the order of the second list.

᾿Ιάκωβος ῾Αλφαίου B ℵ *rell* || ᾿Ιάκ. ὁ τοῦ ῾Αλφ. D 642. 808. 1505 sy^{h*} mae bo.

The presence of the two articles in D05 distinguishes this James more clearly from the brother of John. The same *vl* is found in the first list in Lk. 6.15 where D05 also reads two articles.

καὶ Σίμων ὁ (– ℵ* 2492) ζηλωτής B ℵ^{2} *rell* || Σίμων ὁ ζηλ. D d.

See comments above on the first *vll* of this verse.

1.14 (ἦσαν) προσκαρτηροῦντες ὁμοθυμαδόν B D d *rell* || ὁμ. προσκ. ℵ 945. 1828. 2495.

ℵ01 accentuates the unity of the apostles, B03 and D05 the action of persevering.

σὺν γυναιξίν B ℵ *rell* || σὺν ταῖς (– D$^{s.m.}$) γυν. καὶ τέκνοις D d (Donatisti).

According to B03, the mention of women, without the article and following the list of the Eleven, could either refer to the group of women who accompanied Jesus from Galilee (Bruce, *Text*, p. 74; Metzger, *Commentary*, p. 284) or to the wives of the apostles (Barrett, I, p. 89); cf. Zerwick and Grosvenor, *Analysis*, p. 351: σὺν γυναιξίν without the article, 'with (several) women' or as a set phrase, 'with their wives'. However, concerning the first possibility, on each occasion that the group of women is mentioned, there is either some kind of qualifying word (Lk. 8.2; 23.27, 49; 24.22) or else the anaphoric article (Lk. 23.55; 24.24). The D05 reading, on the other hand, by the fact of having the article and mentioning the 'children', can only mean the wives and children of the eleven apostles. An equivalent sentence is found at Acts 21.5: προπεμπόντων ἡμᾶς πάντων σὺν γυναιξὶ καὶ τέκνοις (without the article, indicating a general category); cf. Matt. 14.21: χωρὶς γυναικῶν καὶ παιδίων; 15.38; 18.25; 19.29 *vl*.

Μαριάμ B E 27. 29. 40. 61. 81. 96. 142. 323. 618. 945. 1837. 1891 *pc* sa aeth; Chr^{pt} || Μαρίᾳ D d ℵ A C H^{2} Y 049. 056. 33. 69. 88. 104. 547. 614. 1175. 1739^{s}. 2412. 2495 𝔐 co; Chr^{pt}.

The Hebrew form Μαριάμ is indeclinable and is the form mostly used in the AT of the Gospel to refer to the mother of Jesus (Lk. 1.27, 30, 34, 38, 39, 46, 56; 2.5, 16, 34); D05 uses it only once (1.27). The Hellenized form Μαρία is declinable; it is used sporadically by the AT in the Gospel (Lk. 1.41; 2.19, while D05 uses it on all occasions except at 1.27 (1.30, 34, 38, 39, 41, 46, 56; 2.5, 16, 19, 34). Although it has been argued that we should accept 'as original the more Semitic variant' (Elliott, *Essays and Studies,* p. 32), account needs to be taken of Luke's use of dual names in their Semitic and Hellenistic forms (see *General Introduction*, §V.5). It is indeed possible that he is employing this literary device here: 'Mariam', her original name, denotes her Hebrew past, whereas 'Maria', the Hellenized form, denotes her election as the mother of Jesus (see Rius-Camps, 'María, la madre de Jesús, en los Hechos de los Apóstoles', pp. 273–75).

τῇ μητρὶ Ἰησοῦ B03 P^{74vid} || τ. μητ. τοῦ Ἰη. ℵ D^{B} *rell* || μητ. τοῦ Ἰη. D*.

B03 is alone in retaining the article before μητρί and omitting it before Ἰησοῦ, thereby referring to Mary as the mother of Jesus in a capacity that is presumed known to the audience. The alternative reading of ℵ01, which retains both articles, treats Jesus equally as known, whereas that of D05 simply identifies Mary as the mother of Jesus, referring to Jesus as the known person.

καὶ σὺν (τοῖς ἀδελφοῖς αὐτοῦ) B C^{3} E H^{2} Y 049. 056. 33. 69. 81. 326. 614. 945. 1739. 2412. 2495 𝔐 || καί D d ℵ A C* 88. 104. 134. 241. 464^{c}. 468. 547. 876. 915. 1175. 1311. 1758. 1765. 1838 *a* lat sa bo arm.

The text of B03 presupposes the presence of three groups, linked by the double preposition σύν: the Eleven // the women and Mary, the mother of Jesus // his brothers. The repetition of the preposition serves the purpose of making clearer the distinction between this latter group and the women which, in turn, avoids the name of Jesus being linked in any way with the mention of his brothers. The text of D05, on the other hand, distinguishes quite clearly between two groups of those present, arranged in chiastic form: the Eleven (masc.) / with their wives (fem.) and children // Mary (fem.), the mother of Jesus (her child) / his brothers (masc.). At the two extremes of the structure (men / women-children // woman-child / men), two groups are set in opposition to each other: the Eleven apostles and the brothers of Jesus. The opposition between 'all these' (οὗτοι πάντες), that is, the Eleven mentioned by name in 1.13, and 'the brothers of him' (lit.) in 1.14, is made much more evident by their respective positions at either ends of the chiastic structure. It is reinforced by the use in D05 of 'disciples' rather than 'brethren' in the opening address of Peter's speech in the following verse.

Commentary

[a] 1.1–2 *The Ministry of Jesus up to his Final Departure*

The opening verses present a summary of the ministry of Jesus as related in the Gospel.

1.1–2 The series of verbal and thematic allusions to the prologue of Luke's Gospel (Lk. 1.1–4) is so striking that they strongly suggest that the Gospel prologue is intended to stand as a general prologue to the work overall. The following parallels (//) may be noted (translation of the Greek is literal):[4]

1. Ἐπειδήπερ πολλοὶ ἐπεχείρησαν ἀνατάξασθαι διήγησιν ... ἔδοξε κἀμοὶ παρηκολουθηκότι ἄνωθεν πᾶσιν ἀκριβῶς... ('Since many people have attempted to compile an account ... it seemed good to me also, having investigated everything exactly from the beginning...'): a presentation of earlier accounts, which could have covered the topics of all of Luke's work, not just the Gospel // Τὸν μὲν πρῶτον λόγον ('the first book'): a reference to the first treatise or volume[5]
2. καθεξῆς σοι γράψαι ('to write for you in an orderly sequence'): the order in which Luke was thinking about writing his entire work // Τὸν μὲν πρῶτον λόγον ἐποιησάμην ('I made the first book'): a reference to the part already written

4. The question of the function of the prologue to Luke's Gospel in relation to the book of Acts is one that has often been discussed with reference to the matter of the genre of Luke and/or Acts. See L.C.A. Alexander, *The Preface to Luke's Gospel* (Cambridge: Cambridge University Press, 1993) for a full examination of the topic.

5. Although the particle μέν is not followed by a correlative δέ and no explicit mention is made of a 'second book', note should be made of the four other cases in Acts, all in direct speech, where μέν is used *solitarium*; in each instance, there is no need to make the correlation explicit for it is quite apparent in the mind of the speaker: 1.1 (the second book); 3.21 (the imminent sending of the Messiah); 4.16 (the possibility that the clear sign given by the apostles in view of all the inhabitants of Jerusalem should spread among the people); 27.21 (the fact of having set sail disregarding the warnings of Paul, 27.9–11); 28.22 (the other point of view, that of Paul). Something similar can be observed in the dialogues where there is a combined μὲν οὖν without a correlative: 1.18 (narrator's clarifying parenthesis); 17.30 (the present time of deliverance); 23.22 (the resolution that has already been taken by the commander); 26.4 + 9 (the charges that prompted the self-defence). Cf. Levinsohn, *Textual Connections*, pp. 104–106, 143–50, although we would not agree with all the detail of his analysis. It is inaccurate to suggest that the 'contrasting clause is implied in the summary of the contents of Acts in v 8' (Barrett, I, p. 65) for this clause belongs to Jesus' speech and cannot therefore be set grammatically against the narrative clause of 1.1.

In fact, the action proper of the second book does not begin until 1.15, which D05 signals as a new development (see *Critical Apparatus*, 1.15). 1.3–14 meanwhile constitute an expansion of the final episode of the Gospel and are thus retrospective: they are introduced by a relative pronoun οἷς followed by an adverbial καί whose function is parenthetic (with respect to the apostles) and epexegetic (with respect to the absolute participle ἐντειλάμενος). The solemn formula with which the second book opens, Τὸν μὲν πρῶτον λόγον, thus remains hanging in the air for a considerable span of narrative.

3. κράτιστε Θεόφιλε ('most honourable Theophilus'): the character to whom the two volumes were addressed // ̓Ω Θεόφιλε ('O Theophilus'): a purposeful reminder
4. περὶ τῶν πεπληροφορημένων ἐν ἡμῖν πραγμάτων ('concerning the things that have been accomplished among us'): the overall theme of Luke's work which could well be intended to apply to both volumes // περὶ πάντων ... ὧν ἤρξατο ̓Ιησοῦς ποιεῖν τε καὶ διδάσκειν ἄχρι ... ἀνελήμφθη ('concerning all the things that Jesus began to do and teach up to the day when ... he was taken up...'): the contents of the first volume viewed in retrospect
5. οἱ ἀπ' ἀρχῆς αὐτόπται: 'those [who were] eye-witnesses from the beginning' // ὧν ἤρξατο ̓Ιησοῦς ('that Jesus began to do'): the beginning of Jesus' ministry
6. καὶ ὑπηρέται γενόμενοι τοῦ λόγου ('and ministers of the word'): the guarantors of the message of Jesus // ἐντειλάμενος τοῖς ἀποστόλοις ('he gave instruction to the apostles'): the apostles were charged with carrying out the order to 'preach the gospel', explicit only in the D05 text ([οἷς] καὶ ἐκέλευσε κηρύσσειν τὸ εὐαγγέλιον)

The effect of picking up the prologue to Luke's Gospel in this way is that the opening verses of Acts do not so much constitute a new prologue as make use of the formal prologue of Lk. 1.1–4. Indeed, it would appear from the various details in the Gospel that anticipate the narrative of Acts, as the *Commentary* will point out at the appropriate places, that Luke already had in mind the second volume when he began to write his Gospel.

The name 'Theophilus' occurs in both places. It is generally agreed that Luke's addressee was well-educated and of some social standing. The adjective κράτιστε used before his name in the Gospel prologue (Lk. 1.3) is an appropriate title for an official of high rank (cf. Felix, Acts 23.26; 24.3; Festus, 26.25) and the overall sophistication and detail of Luke's work points to someone with sufficient knowledge and intelligence to understand his narratives.[6] The consistently Jewish outlook of the Bezan text of Acts supposes that this person was himself Jewish and was thoroughly versed in the intricacies of Jewish law and the interpretation of the Scriptures. Oddly, a survey of the names of Jewish males in the first century, recorded in the various sources – Josephus, the New Testament, Rabbinic literature, as well as in papyri and inscriptions – reveals that Theophilus occurs only three times and each time referring to the same person, the high priest, son of Annas I (Lk. 3.2), who served from 37–41

6. B. Witherington, *The Acts of the Apostles: A Socio-Rhetorical Commentary* (Grand Rapids: Eerdmans/Carlisle: Paternoster, 1998), pp. 42; 106, n. 7.

CE.[7] His interest in the incidents and people recorded in Luke's Gospel and Acts would arise from his first hand knowledge of many of them, including such dramas as the stoning of Stephen or the conversion of Paul which may even have taken place while he was in office (cf. Acts 7.1, 58). His brother Annas II was responsible for the execution of James, the brother of Jesus in 62 CE and his son Matthias was high priest in the years leading up to the first Jewish revolt (65–67 CE), all circumstances that could well have prompted a searching to know the truth about the Jesus-believers. While a Roman catechumen may fit with the narrative of Acts in the AT, a Jewish high priest matches much better the perspective and focus of the Bezan text. That Theophilus means 'friend (or beloved) of God' would have no doubt been a happy coincidence to its author!

In an extremely condensed form, Luke summarizes the essential contents of the first[8] book. He focuses on the starting point (the messianic anointing of Jesus after his baptism in the Jordan, Lk. 3.22) and the end point (the ascension) of Jesus' ministry,[9] offsetting the deeds with the sayings at the same time as underlining the intimate connection between them (lit. 'as much what he did as what he taught'). Luke claims to have told in the first book '*everything* that Jesus did and taught' and he includes in this 'everything' not only Jesus' public life from the Jordan onwards (implicitly: cf. Lk. 3.23)[10] but even the period between the resurrection

7. For further details, see R. Anderson, 'À la recherche de Théophile', in *Saint Luc, évangéliste et historien (Dossiers d'Archéologie* 279 [2002–3]), pp. 64–71 (66).

8. πρῶτον, in accordance with Hellensitic usage (Zerwick, *Biblical Greek*, §151) is the equivalent of πρότερον.

9. The construction ὧν ἤρξατο ... ἄχρι ἧς ἡμέρας, as in 1.21–2 (ἀρξάμενος ... ἕως [ἄχρι ℵ A min.] τῆς ἡμέρας), has the purpose of establishing with some precision the beginning and the end of Jesus' Messianic ministry, thereby detaching the main part of the Gospel from the introductory chapters (Lk. 1.1–3.20). The preposition ἄχρι prevents the verb ἤρξατο from being taken as meaning that the terrestrial ministry of Jesus only represented the beginning of an ongoing process, the second part of which is narrated in the book of Acts. With the verb, Luke indicates the beginning of Jesus' mission and with the preposition, the end; in between, with περὶ πάντων he encompasses the period of his activity and teaching while he was physically present with his disciples, a period that also takes in the post-Easter appearances.

10. The reference to ἦν ἀρχόμενος in Lk. 3.23 takes on even more force if the punctuation suggested by J. Rius-Camps ('¿Constituye Lc 3, 21–38 un solo período? Propuesta de un cambio de puntuación', *Bib* 65 [1984], pp. 189–208) is adopted. According to this, Lk. 3.21–38 would constitute one single period, comprising the investiture of Jesus with the Holy Spirit as well as the supposition that he was descended from Joseph.

and the ascension (explicitly). The declaration underlines the fact that the pre- and post-resurrection Jesus is one and the same, and that Jesus' presence in the world before the resurrection complements his presence after the resurrection.

Within this concise summary of the activity of Jesus, considerable emphasis is conferred on the statement 'after giving instructions to the apostles'.[11] The mention of 'the apostles' and the reference to the 'instructions' given to them brings to the foreground the two elements that bring about a change in perspective of Luke's second book: the last wishes of Jesus and the community that is to carry them out. It will no longer be the activity of Jesus and his message that is at the centre of the narrative, but 'the apostles',[12] that is the disciples in their capacity as 'missionaries',

11. This is the only occurrence in the New Testament of ἐντειλάμενος used in an absolute sense. It refers to the instructions given by Jesus to the apostles during the period between the resurrection and the ascension. É. Delebecque ('Les deux prologues des Actes des Apôtres', *RevThom* 80 [1980], pp. 75–85) is of the opinion that it refers to the orders 'que Jésus avait données aux apôtres (...) après le choix des Douze' (p. 631); M.C. Parsons ('The Text of Acts 1:2 Reconsidered', *CBQ* 50 [1988], pp. 58–71) oscillates between this opinion and the idea that it refers to the teaching given by Jesus in the upper room before his arrest and crucifixion (pp. 68–69). From a grammatical point of view, both these interpretations are unlikely for the sequence of the aorist finite verb (ἀνελήμφθη) followed by the aorist participle (ἐντειλάμενος) normally indicates that the action of the main verb follows on directly from that of the participle. The content of these instructions is about to be explained (1.4; cf. Lk. 24.49b).

12. 'The apostles' supersedes the designation of the chosen disciples of Jesus as 'the Twelve' (last mention in Lk. 22.47, replaced by 'the Eleven' in Lk. 24.9, 33) as from the time that they lose their significance as representatives of Israel following the defection of Judas. The heavily emphasized reference (διὰ πνεύματος ἁγίου οὓς ἐξελέξατο, see below) to the moment of their election by Jesus (cf. Lk. 6.13: καὶ ἐκλεξάμενος ἀπ᾽ αὐτῶν δώδεκα, οὓς καὶ ἀποστόλους ὠνόμασεν) draws attention to the transition from one designation to the other. As is the case with other pairs of names (see *General Introduction*, §V.5), Luke uses them as alternatives in order to underline two meanings: thus, while the group of 'the Twelve' carries connotations of the tribes of Israel with an associated theocracy and national-religious identity, the designation 'the apostles' has a much wider scope, namely that of their mission which is not restricted to Israel (compare Lk. 9.1–2, 10 with Lk. 10.1, 17). Luke plays constantly with this dual designation, according to whether he wants to underline the quality of *Israel's* representatives (Lk. 6.13; 8.1; 9.1, 12; 18.31; 22.3, 30, 47; Acts 1.26; 6.2) or that of the *mission* envoys (Lk. 6.13; 9.10; 17.5; 22.14; 24.10; Acts 1.2 and *passim*). The choice of term changes as Luke varies the perspective from which he is telling his story (see on 1.26; 6.2 below).

distinguished from their previous designation as 'the Twelve' now that they have received the charge to proclaim the good news contained in the Gospel. The instructions to which Luke refers have already been alluded to at the end of the Gospel: 'In his name *will be preached* repentance for the forgiveness of sins to all nations. Beginning with Ierousalem, *you* (AT) / repentance and forgiveness of sins will be preached in his name to all nations, beginning in Ierousalem. *You* (D05)[13] *will be witnesses of all this*. And now I will send you the Promise of my Father; but you, *stay in the city* until you are clothed with power from on high' (Lk. 24.47–49). In the retrospective account given in the narrative of Acts (see on 1.4, 8 below), the commission will be repeated with differences that are both appreciable and intentional.

The statement that Jesus gave instructions to the apostles is qualified by further information, namely that he had chosen them 'through the Holy Spirit'.[14] In Luke's dense and concise style, nothing is superfluous. The detail that Jesus 'chose' the apostles inspired by the Holy Spirit not only harks back to the election of the Twelve apostles narrated in Lk. 6.13 but also spells out what is to be supposed from the Gospel account, namely that the reasons for the choice and the discernment necessary for carrying out the choice proceeded from the Holy Spirit. It is only later, in reading the account of the election of the replacement of Judas (1.15–26), that the full significance of this detail will become apparent. It is to be noted meanwhile that it is not 'the Twelve' that is used here but 'the apostles'. Indeed, the role conferred on the apostles as representatives of Israel ('the Twelve', Lk. 6.13; 8.1; 9.1, 12; 18.31; 22.3, 30, 47) has already come to an end by reason of the defection of Judas. The insistence on the number 'eleven' at the end of the Gospel (Lk. 24.9, 33) as also in the beginning of Acts (1.13 [eleven names], 26 [B03]; 2.14 [B03; cf. 'the ten apostles', D05]) serves to underline the anomaly of the situation. This point will be developed with reference to Acts 1.15–26.

A second detail concerning Jesus' instruction of the apostles is added in Codex Bezae: he ordered them to 'preach the good news'. This is a

13. See on Acts 1.8 below.

14. Although the position of διὰ πνεύματος ἁγίου means it could be attached to ἐντειλάμενος, 'having instructed', the phrase in fact belongs to οὓς ἐξελέξατο, 'whom he chose'. It is unusual for a relative clause to be placed after a qualifying phrase but other instances of such a construction occur in Luke's writings: e.g. Lk. 24.7; Acts 1.10; 3.19; 4.33; 5.13; 7.35; 9.14; 12.25; 16.14; 19.4, 20. Cf. Boismard and Lamouille, II, p. 3.

reference to his earlier instruction at the time the Twelve were first sent out on mission, as outlined in Lk. 9.1–2.[15] A statement of the greatest importance is being made in the Bezan text by means of the association of this detail with the mention of the Holy Spirit: the election and the mission of the apostles will develop according to the plan foreseen by Jesus *when and only when* they keep to the instructions that he has just given them. It is crucial for readers of Acts to bear in mind both of these two factors – the election by the Holy Spirit and the command to preach the gospel – for they will serve as criteria with which to judge the apostles and the members of their communities as Luke portrays them in the rest of the book. Firstly, the insistence on the election of the apostles by Jesus under the inspiration of the Holy Spirit is relevant for considering the way in which the election of Matthias will be carried out and for understanding the mentality of the apostles at the time. Secondly, the contents of the apostolic mission must be seen to consist in the preaching of the gospel, the central concern of the first book. 'The good news', which appears here (according to D05) for the first time, will constitute from now on the paradigm that will allow the form and the contents of the apostolic preaching to be evaluated.

Giving instructions to the apostles forms the last element of Jesus' activity. His ministry, which had begun with the descent of the Holy Spirit on him, closes with his being taken away. The divine passive 'was taken away'[16] refers to his ascension – Luke will explain later in 1.9 how this happened – but the accent here, just as in the corresponding clause in Lk. 24.51,[17] is on the physical separation of Jesus from his disciples so leaving the door open to other forms of divine presence.

15. The problems encountered by commentators in attempting to make sense of the 'Western' reading arise precisely because of their use of a hypothetically reconstructed 'Western' text (Barrett, I, p. 68; Bruce, *Text*, pp. 67–68). The text of D05 as it stands is perfectly comprehensible and concords with Luke's purpose of showing how the apostles did not always fulfil the mission entrusted to them by Jesus (see *General Introduction*, §VI).

16. ἀνελήμφθη designates the taking away of Jesus, as in 1.11, 22: it is a technical term used by the same writer in Lk. 9.51, with a very clear allusion to the taking up of Elijah (cf. 4 Kgdms 2.9, 10, 11 LXX). See J. Rius-Camps, *De Jerusalén a Antioquía: Génesis de la iglesia cristiana* (Córdoba: Ediciones El Almendro, 1989), p. 20, n. 8, and also J. Dupont, ' 'ΑΝΕΛΗΜΦΘΗ (Actes 1,2)', *NTS* 8 (1962), pp. 154–57.

17. Physical separation is especially implied by the shorter reading (א* D it sy^{s}) but even the longer reading suggests it.

[b] 1.3 *Jesus' Post-Resurrection Appearances*
The chief purpose of the appearances of Jesus to his disciples is identified as the giving of instructions concerning the kingdom of God. The action takes place between Galilee (according to 13.31 D05, see *Commentary*) and Hierosoluma (see *General Introduction,* §V.5 and *Commentary*, 1.4).

1.3 The focus of interest now begins to shift from Jesus to the apostles.[18] It is the notion of Jesus' departure that brings about the transition for the apostles are the ones left behind and in need of reassurance that his death, and therefore his apparent failure as the Messiah (cf. Lk. 24.7, 26, 46), were not final since he continues to be alive (cf. Lk. 24.5, 23) and in a recognisable form (cf. Lk. 24.39). The difficulty the apostles must have felt in accepting the death of Jesus should not be underestimated, for a crucified Messiah flew in the face of all the Jewish expectations of his glory and victory.

In the Gospel, all of Jesus' appearances were set by Luke within the symbolic space of a single day (cf. Lk. 24.1, 9, 13, 33, 36). The action goes from early in the morning (Lk. 24.1, 2) and progresses towards the evening (Lk. 24.29), so that when the moment of the ascension is finally reached (Lk. 24.51), this logically must take place at night. In Acts, in contrast, the appearances are spread over a period of forty days. Far from being contradictory, however, the two accounts are mutually complementary, with the single day of the Gospel underlining the unity of the period and 'forty' emphasizing its length and completeness.[19] The forty days of Acts have a number of scriptural parallels,[20] notably in the duration of the

18. The transition is indicated in the Greek by means of a relative pronoun, οἷς καί, 'to whom (he presented himself, etc.)', which acts as a kind of fulcrum by which attention is switched from Jesus to the apostles. The resulting relative clause functions in reality as a main clause, a construction considered by some to be a Latinism and by others a Semitism (Haenchen, p. 108, n. 5). On the other hand, Delebecque ('Les deux prologues', p. 629) considers that 'en tant qu'adverbe et non conjonction, [καί] a son sens plein parce que l'auteur se sert de lui pour introduire, par une relative juxtaposée – et non coordonnée – une notion supplémentaire importante'. This use of a sentence initial relative pronoun followed by adverbial καί is very frequent in Luke's writing (cf. Acts 1.3, 11; 7.45; 11.23 D05, 30; 12.4; 22.5b; 26.10, 12 *vl*; 28.10: see Rius-Camps, *De Jerusalén a Antioquía*, p. 23, n. 17). The construction signals a change of focus between previously mentioned participants while maintaining a close link with the preceding material.

19. The length of the period between the resurrection and the ascension is again alluded to in Acts 13.31: ἐπὶ ἡμέρας πλείους B03 / πλείονας D05.

20. Forty is one of the multiples of four, a number that has a symbolic value in the

journey undertaken by Elijah when, after being given nourishment by the angel of the Lord, he went to Mount Horeb to speak with God (1 Kgs 19.8). This parallel is significant for another comparison between Jesus and Elijah that Luke will establish later in his preface to Acts (see on 1.9 below).

The forty days at the end of Jesus' ministry have a more immediate parallel in the forty days of temptation in the desert at the beginning of his ministry. The identical time-span sets up a comparison between [a] a period of *testing* involving a full range of temptations (Lk. 4.1–13), and [a′] a period of *countertesting* involving 'numerous proofs'. Between the two, falls [b] the Jesus' ministry as the Messiah, treated by the Synoptic Gospel writers as a single progression of events occurring within a year.[21]

The topic of Jesus' speaking during the forty days was the kingdom of God. He had already taught the apostles on this subject during his life before his death (Lk. 9.22, 44; 18.31–33; 22.28–30). Further instruction was necessary on several grounds. For one thing, the understanding of the disciples was limited, still conditioned by their hope, in accordance with the teaching of the scribes (Lk. 20.41–44), that Jesus was a Davidic Messiah (cf. Lk. 18.38, 39, where the blind man is a figure of the disciples who understand nothing of what Jesus has just said to them). Their expectation was of a kingdom of God that was essentially the kingdom of Israel, and their awareness of the Messiahship of Jesus has so far been conditioned by such nationalistic aspirations.[22] Following the death of Jesus, which left them disheartened and disillusioned, they needed to know that

Gospels and Acts, in continuation with the Jewish Scriptures, see, e.g., the sojourn of Israel in Egypt (400 years), Acts 7.6, cf. Gen. 15.13; Moses' exile (40 years), Acts 7.30, cf. Exod. 2.15; the generation of the desert (40 years), Acts 7.36, cf. Num. 14.33–34; the period of Jesus' temptation in the desert (40 days), Lk. 4.2; the crowd in the second miraculous feeding (4,000), Matt. 15.38; Mk 8.9, 20; the four corners of the sheet in Peter's vision, Acts 10.11; 11.5.

21. A series of features of Acts 1.4–9 reinforce the parallel between the two periods of 'testing' and 'countertesting': 1) 'he ate nothing' // 'while they were eating together'; 'not of bread alone' // 'the promise of the Father', i.e. the word of Yahweh; 2) 'he showed him all the kingdoms of the world' // 'he told them things about the kingdom of God'; 'I will give you all this power' // 'the Father has placed them in his own authority'; 'all will be yours' // the universal commission; 3) 'he set him down on the pinnacle of the Temple' // 'he was taken up'; 'he left him' // 'a cloud took him from their sight'. At the end of his temptations, 'Jesus went back to Galilee' // at the end of the appearances, the disciples 'went back to Jerusalem'.

22. Our article 'Emmaous or Oulammaous?' examines in greater detail Luke's presentation of the disciples' expectations after the time of Jesus' resurrection.

all that had happened to him had been foreseen in the Scriptures, and the conformity of the suffering of Jesus with the Scriptures forms the core of the message of the post-resurrection teaching (cf. Lk. 24.25–27, 32, 44–46).[23]

Not only that, but events have moved on since the last overt mention in Luke's writing of the kingdom of God, which occurs at the meal Jesus took with his disciples before his death (Lk. 22.28–30). On that occasion, he had taught the apostles about their role in the kingdom where, he promised, they would sit as (twelve D05) judges over the (– D05) twelve tribes of Israel. In the narrative of Acts, particularly according to the Bezan text, the notion of the privileged position of the apostles as a group of twelve is seen to be superseded by an altogether broader idea of leadership that is no longer restricted either to Israel or to the number twelve (see *Excursus* 1). The causes of the change, a radical one with far-reaching consequences, will become apparent during the course of the first chapter of Acts. Meanwhile, it may be assumed that when Jesus is said to instruct the apostles concerning the kingdom of God he is attempting to make them see the nature and the extent of his Messiahship and, in consequence, the universal scope of the kingdom of God. The verses that follow will show how far they are at this point from modifying their expectations.

[c] 1.4–5 *The Final Meal*

The third element of the opening section develops in further detail the earlier reference (1.2) to Jesus' last instructions to the apostles. The scene takes place in Hierosoluma.

1.4 This episode of the preface to Acts corresponds to the scene portrayed at the end of the Gospel in which Jesus appears to the apostolic circle, and when reference is also made to his eating with them (Lk. 24.41–43). This meeting takes place, therefore, in a house in town, rather than on the Mount of Olives to where the action moves in 1.6. The insistence on a meal shared together can be seen as a veiled indication of an anti-docetic stance.

The audience appears to be limited to the apostles according to Acts although the Gospel suggests a wider group (cf. Lk. 24.33, 36) and in Acts, too, the presence of more people may well be implied, as becomes

23. In the D05 text, it is quite clear that the last chapter of Luke's Gospel describes a progressive revelation that reaches its most complete dimension in the final meeting with all the disciples in Jerusalem. For a full evaluation and discussion of the different texts of Luke 24, see Amphoux, 'Le chapitre 24 de Luc'; Read-Heimerdinger and Rius-Camps, 'Emmaous or Oulammaous?'.

clearer as the action progresses. Identical instructions are given in both scenes but, whereas the Gospel records the words spoken by Jesus, in Acts they are reported in indirect speech, with the contents of the promise following on in direct speech without a break.

The order given by Jesus is a strict command (implicit in the imperative of the Gospel and explicit in Acts), the importance of which has already been made clear by the reference to it in the opening verses to Acts as the last wishes of Jesus before his final departure (1.2). The account of Acts presents the order as having two contrasting parts, a negation followed by a contrary affirmation.

Taking first the order not to leave Hierosoluma, it is important to note the choice of the form of the name for the city. Throughout the Gospel and Acts, Luke deliberately makes use of the two Greek spellings for Jerusalem to distinguish between the religious centre on the one hand, for which he adopts the Hebrew-derived spelling, and the geographical place on the other, designated by the Greek form of the name. The former refers to the holy city, the seat of Jewish authority with the Temple and its religious rulers. The latter is a neutral designation for the city, devoid of religious significance.[24] The use of Hierosoluma here thus corresponds perfectly to Jesus' words 'stay in the city' in the Gospel account (Lk. 24.49). The choice of the neutral form attributed by Luke to Jesus at this point is full of significance for it indicates that Luke intends Jesus to be understood as telling the disciples that they should wait simply in Jerusalem as a town and that they should have nothing to do with the Jewish religious institution. In point of fact, Luke has already described Jesus as 'leading out' the disciples (Lk. 24.50, the verb being reinforced with the adverb 'outside' in the D05 text) from Ierousalem as the religious centre (cf. Lk. 24.33), as he himself had been forced to leave it (Lk. 4.29).[25] The message is that following Jesus entails being outside of the domain of the official Jewish institution.

Jesus' attitude towards the religious life of Ierousalem is not, however, shared by his disciples, if even they understand it. No sooner had Jesus

24. See also *General Introduction*, §V.5 on the importance for Luke of the alternative forms of the name for Jerusalem. 'Hierosoluma' and 'the city' are equivalent terms in Luke-Acts (cf. Lk. 19.41; 22.10; 23.19; Acts 4.27; 7.58; 12.10; 21.29, 30; 22.3) just as 'Ierousalem' is equivalent to, for example, 'the holy city' (cf. Matt. 4.5; 27.53).

25. In the case of Jesus, he was 'put outside' the religious centre of Ierousalem because he offended the Jewish people (Lk. 4.29; cf. 20.15; Heb. 13.12–13). Stephen likewise will also be 'taken out' of Ierousalem (Acts 7.58).

left them than they returned to Ierousalem in the religious sense (Lk. 24.52, where the name is coupled with the Temple // Acts 1.12, where it is coupled with the legal restriction of 'a sabbath's day journey' – see on 1.12 below). Luke is too careful a writer to use alternative spellings for no reason; the pattern that emerges in the rest of Acts confirms that here in Acts 1 as elsewhere he employs the alternative forms for the communication of a theological message.

The point of Jesus' order, then, is that the apostles should remain in the city of Jerusalem without undertaking anything (lit. 'remain seated in the city', Lk. 24.49), or setting off on any kind of mission (lit. 'not to leave[26] Hierosoluma', Acts 1.4) as long as they had not received the power of the Holy Spirit, for only then would their activities be successful. For the time being, Luke's hearers do not know from what exactly Jesus has sought to dissuade them, nor which action could compromise the future of the mission. The latter half of the chapter will make clear the dangers the apostles face.

The order not to leave the city is followed by a further command to wait in expectation of the fulfilment of the Father's promise. This promise was the object of great hope in Israel (see *Excursus* 1) and will be referred to in several speeches in Acts (Acts 2.33, 39; 13.23, 32; 26.6; cf. 7.17). It is defined here through the words of Jesus as the gift of the Holy Spirit (cf. Acts 2.33, 39). For the explanation of the promise, Luke moves without any formal transition into a citation of the words of Jesus himself. The AT has Jesus simply saying 'that you heard from me', followed by a justification for the command to wait for the promise. (The reference to the present time at the end of 1.5 AT prevents Jesus' words from being read as a repetition of an earlier saying.) The justification could be viewed as based on an earlier saying that is found in the AT of Lk. 11.13 (*vl* D05, among others), where Jesus specified that the Father would 'give the Holy Spirit to those who ask him'. However, the Bezan reading of Acts 1.4 ('that you heard' – he said – 'from my mouth') is expressed in such a way that the actual words that follow represent the earlier saying of Jesus rather than a justification. The problem, of course, is that the Gospel does not record

26. It should be noted that the present negative infinitive μὴ χωρίζεσθαι used as an imperative can have a preventative force when the action has not yet started, 'do not try to...'; see J. Mateos, *El aspecto verbal en el Nuevo Testamento* (Madrid: Cristiandad, 1977), §§349, 353. Haenchen, p. 141, n. 4 (see Marshall, p. 58) further suggests that Jesus' command was 'intended to preclude the tradition of the disciples' return to Galilee' (as in John 21). In the context of both of Luke's accounts, however, the mention of Hierosoluma/the city has an importance that is theological.

such a saying as coming from Jesus, which may be why the AT avoids giving the impression that the words about John the Baptist and the two kinds of baptism have already been spoken by Jesus.

1.5 Jesus' words echo the declaration of John the Baptist (Lk. 3.16) which contrasted the baptism he administered with water to Jesus' future baptism with the Holy Spirit and fire, except that, unlike John, Jesus makes no reference to the fire (cf. Mk 1.8). Later (Acts 11.16), Peter will tell the Jerusalem church that when he was at Cornelius' house and saw the outpouring of the Holy Spirit on the Gentiles, he remembered these words of the Lord. It is therefore clear that Luke holds this saying to represent the true words of Jesus. It was pointed out with reference to 1.4, that in the AT the comparison of the types of baptism cannot be taken as the actual promise that Jesus gave to his apostles in the past whereas the form of the D05 text allows the saying to be understood as expressing the contents of the promise. Following the citation, Codex Bezae then has Jesus explain, as he predicts the imminent arrival of the Spirit, that this promise made earlier is now about to be fulfilled.

The absence of any mention of fire is significant. The picture painted by John the Baptist in the Gospel is one of a harvester who separates the wheat that he gathers in from the chaff that he burns (Lk. 3.17). Earlier in the episode, John speaks of the trees that do not bear good fruit being thrown into the fire (Lk. 3.9). In this context, fire is thus a symbol of the punishment that was about to fall on those in Israel who did not repent. In the present scene, John's picture of fire could have been inappropriate for it may have prompted the disciples to think in terms of vengeance, especially now when Israel has just put the Messiah to death. Jesus has other concerns at this point when he is about to leave the disciples alone: he wants to reassure them that they will only be deprived of his physical presence for a short time before they receive the divine power that the Holy Spirit will confer on them. They will not have long to wait.

In the Vaticanus text, the brevity of the waiting time is expressed using an understatement characteristic of Luke, 'not many days from now', which qualifies 'you will be baptized'. In the Bezan text, however, the mention of a period of time is connected more specifically to the coming of the Spirit, and the longest they will have to wait is specified as being the Jewish festival of Pentecost which is due to be celebrated shortly.[27]

27. Tradition places Pentecost 10 days after the ascension of Jesus on the basis that the Jews celebrated Pentecost 50 days after Passover and 40 are taken as having

According to this text, Jesus is careful to leave the disciples no excuse for undertaking any action during the waiting period by letting them know the latest end point.

Before going on, it will be useful to summarize the facts that can be gleaned from 1.3–5 in combination with the complementary information supplied by Lk. 24. Jesus makes the last of his appearances to the apostles, at the end of a period that has lasted 40 days since his death. During what turns out to be a farewell meal, Jesus leaves them the last of his instructions:

1. For the time being, they should remain in the city of Jerusalem, but not have anything to do with the religious institution there or undertake any kind of action
2. They are to wait in expectation of the promise of the Father, the sending of the Holy Spirit
3. The period of inactivity and waiting will not be long – up to Pentecost at the most, according to Codex Bezae

[d] 1.6 *The Expectations of the Apostles*

The third part of the opening sequence prepares for the last orders of Jesus, signalling in advance the disparity between the apostles' concerns and those of their master.

In order to understand Luke's message in these verses it is essential to see the apostles in the light of Luke's portrayal of them in the Gospel. Wrong interpretations arise from reading back into this time the knowledge of what the apostles will become later as the account of Acts progresses, instead of picking up the narrative thread from the Gospel. The dangers are two-fold: that of according to them a wisdom and comprehension of Jesus' teaching that they will only acquire with the unfolding of events, and then in differing measures, and also that of projecting onto the apostles the infallibility with which centuries of Church tradition have invested them. Both errors are to be rigorously avoided as the apostles, for the first time in Acts, are now observed directly as they act and speak. What they have understood so far, with the explanations given to them by Jesus during the final meal (Lk. 24.44–46), is how the recent events were in accordance with the Scriptures; specifically they have grasped that they foretold the death and resurrection of the Messiah and that this opened the

already elapsed. Such a calculation a) assumes that the mention of 40 days in Acts 1.3 is to be read literally, and b) begins the count of 40 days from the day of Jesus' death (Passover) rather than his resurrection (three days later). 40 days from the resurrection would leave only eight days before Pentecost.

way for the preaching of repentance and forgiveness to all nations. The Bezan text of Luke's Gospel makes clear how difficult it was for the apostles to reach even this level of understanding.[28] Nonetheless, it will be apparent as the narrative of Acts unfolds that their understanding still remains within the framework of Jewish teaching about the Messianic age in which Israel continues, as ever, to be the privileged people of God, the point of reference for all other peoples and the focus around whom all events revolve. This is precisely what will be seen from the apostles' question in 1.6, their attitude as Jesus is taken away in 1.9–12, and their action in electing a replacement for Judas in 1.15–26; in all of these places the Jewish framework is more clearly and consistently in evidence in the text of D05 than in the text of the other MSS. *Excursus* 1 explores the contents of Jewish Messianic expectations in more detail.

1.6 The passage is introduced by a typical formula μὲν οὖν which Luke uses repeatedly at the start of an episode to signal that an event derives in some way from the previous one (retrospective) and looks forward to a further one (prospective).[29] The two events in this instance are the questioning of Jesus by the apostles and Jesus' response.

The setting here is quite different from that of the preceding verses describing the final meal, for Jesus is taken up during this scene. From Lk. 24.50 ('near Bethany'), it may be presumed that the action takes place on the Mount of Olives. Just as Jesus is about to leave the group for the last time, the apostles start a discussion with him. The initiative comes not from Jesus (in contrast to 1.4) but from the apostles.

This last point is important: the subject of the verb for the first time in Acts is the apostles and what they did was to get themselves together to put a question to Jesus. They had carefully and deliberately worked out

28. The D05 text of the Gospel account shows clearly the struggles experienced by the disciples of Jesus in reconciling the traditional teaching about the Messiah with the actual events that had occurred. See our article 'Emmaous or Oulammaous?'.

29. See Levinsohn, *Textual Connections*, pp. 83–120, on the function of μὲν οὖν in Acts; see also Read-Heimerdinger, *The Bezan Text*, pp. 237–40. οὖν indicates that the event being introduced follows closely in accordance with what has just been reported – here, it is the apostles' question that is presented as arising from what Jesus had said. μέν, on the other hand, anticipates a second, more significant, event, usually introduced with δέ – in this case, the question put to Jesus expects an answer which, according to D05, he does not give but instead cuts short their questioning, as indicated by καί (see *Critical Apparatus*, 1.7).

their question beforehand.[30] The exact wording of the question, which varies according to the MSS (see *Critical Apparatus*), needs to be examined with care; in each case, it is about restoration and the kingdom of Israel. Why did the apostles have a question about these matters and why did they ask it at that time?

The first thing to be taken into account in addressing both these points is the apparent realization of the apostles that they had come to Jesus' last day on earth. This can be deduced from 1.9–11 where there are clear signs that they knew that this was the last opportunity to speak with him (see also *Excursus* 2).

Their realization that Jesus was going away from them was only part of a more general awareness: the apostles had already come to believe throughout the course of Jesus' ministry that his arrival as the longed-for Messiah of Israel heralded the fulfilment of promises in the writings of the Prophets concerning the coming of the kingdom of God and the restoration of Israel. Now what they understood about these matters was largely informed by the traditional teaching they followed as Jews, even though their understanding had been enlightened in some measure by what they had grasped of Jesus' teaching; this topic is more fully explored in *Excursus* 1. Given their expectations, there are elements in Jesus' instructions recorded in Acts 1.4–5 that would sound to them like signals that the time for the restoration of Israel had at last arrived: the announcement of the accomplishment of the promise of the Father, through the coming of the Holy Spirit, which was to take place in Jerusalem; furthermore, it is the resurrected Messiah who speaks with them. All these factors taken together could cause the apostles to understand that the restoration of Israel was about to happen, and happen according to the plan laid out in the Scriptures.

This context accounts for the form that the question takes in all the MSS except D05: 'Is this the time when you will restore the kingdom to Israel?' In other words, since Jesus is the Messiah, and since he has demonstrated the truth of the resurrection and is now about to return to the Father, and since the Holy Spirit is about to be given, are they about to witness the fulfilment of the other prophecies concerning the return of Israel's sovereignty over all the other nations? The question echoes the reference to the kingdom of God in 1.3 but is so much at odds with Jesus'

30. The pre-meditated nature of the apostles' question is indicated in the Greek by the imperfect (ἐπ)ηρώτων (see Zerwick, *Biblical Greek*, §272) followed by the present participle λέγοντες.

teaching about the universal nature of the divine rule that it suggests that the apostles have rather missed the point.[31] The response of Jesus to their question follows in 1.7.

In the text of Codex Bezae, the apostles' question is rather different and focuses on just one aspect of the restoration of Israel. The Greek has an unfinished question, indicated in the translation with ' ... ' , which the apostles put to Jesus insistently: 'Is this the time when you will restore to the kingdom of Israel...?' What is missing from Israel that needs to be restored before Jesus leaves them? On the last occasion recorded by Luke that Jesus spoke to the apostles about the kingdom, at Lk. 22.30, he promised that they would 'sit on thrones judging the twelve tribes of Israel'. Codex Bezae specifies twelve thrones,[32] and thus makes explicit the assimilation of the Twelve apostles with the twelve tribes of Israel (cf. Lk. 6.13–14; 9.1–2). The restoration of the twelve tribes of Israel was a key aspect of the renewal of Israel when the time came for Israel to rule again as a united kingdom under the Davidic Messiah-king. Moreover, according to some writings, it was Elijah who was to reinstate the twelve tribes when it happened. Will Jesus now restore into the kingdom of Israel the representative of the twelfth tribe?

The apostles are faced, however, with a dilemma as Jesus is about to leave them: they have lost one of their members, Judas, who is underlined by Luke as being 'one of the Twelve' (Lk. 22.47) or, more emphatically, 'one of the number of the Twelve' (Lk. 22.3). Since his betrayal of Jesus, they have been left as a group of only 'eleven' (Lk. 24.9, 33; Acts 1.13, 26 B03), which was as incomplete as the number of the sons of Jacob in the absence of Joseph (cf. Gen. 37.9; 42.32). Aware that they had been chosen

31. The nationalistic nature of the apostles' question is recognized by some commentators and acknowledged as contrary to the teaching of Jesus about the universal nature of the kingdom of God, see e.g. Barrett, I, pp. 76–77. Other scholars consider the question to be a proper one because they understand that Israel is indeed restored at some time according to Acts, the inclusion of the Gentiles being part of that restoration, see e.g. J. Jervell, *Luke and the People of God* (Minneapolis: Augsburg, 1972), pp. 41–74; and see D. Ravens, *Luke and the Restoration of Israel* (JSNTSup, 119; Sheffield: Sheffield Academic Press, 1995), pp. 93–94 on the timing of the restoration.

32. Cf. the parallel in Matt. 19.28. Although the D05 text of Lk. 22.30 could be seen as a harmonisation of the Matthew passage, it is equally possible that 'twelve' was felt to be a problem by other MSS of Luke because of the loss of Judas who was part of the group addressed by Jesus (in Matthew's account, the group is wider). The same *vl* occurs in 1 Cor. 15.5 where ℵ A 33 *et al.* change 'twelve' to 'eleven' to make more literal sense. Cf. E.P. Sanders, *Jesus and Judaism* (London: SCM Press, 1985), p. 101.

by God (Luke describes Jesus as spending the night in prayer before he elected them in Lk. 6.12–13, and has specifically mentioned the role of the Holy Spirit in Acts 1.2), the apostles look to Jesus for the replacement of Judas. They find themselves, therefore, in an uncomfortable situation when, not intending Judas to be replaced, Jesus does not respond positively to their request. It is as a consequence of Jesus' lack of action that they go on to organize the replacement themselves, in 1.15–26.

In other words, the apostles have understood something of Jesus' teaching concerning the kingdom of God, namely that they take precedence as the chosen witnesses of the Messiah over the twelve tribes. They have not yet understood how far that aspect of the divine plan has been modified by the death of Judas.

[e] 1.7–8 *The Universal Commission of Jesus*

These two verses constitute the structural climax of the preface to Acts, coming as it does at the end of the first part. They contain the reaction of Jesus to the apostles' questioning and the commission he entrusted to them with regard to their witness to him.

1.7 The absence of any connective in the Vaticanus text to introduce Jesus' reply to the apostles' question indicates that this is not a normal question and answer dialogue and draws attention to the fact that Jesus' response is not what was expected; in the Bezan text, Jesus cuts across the apostles before they have even finished (see *Critical Apparatus*). In either case, he corrects the apostles in a twofold response. Concerning their query 'is this the time?', he gives an answer similar to that recorded by Mark to the question asked by Peter, James, John and Andrew about the time of the destruction of the Temple (Mk 13.4a = Lk. 21.7a): 'Concerning the day or the hour, no-one knows, not even the angels in heaven, nor the Son, but only the Father' (Mk 13.32). Luke had omitted this saying in the parallel passage in his Gospel (Lk. 21.5–28), reserving it for here where he adapts it to the present circumstances.

In fact, Jesus does not answer their question 'is this the time?' but responds instead with a general remark about the inappropriateness of asking the question at all: only the Father knows about every moment in time and the timing of his intervention in the world; if it were otherwise and people also had this knowledge, their freedom would be restricted. But Jesus' rebuke does not allow any certain inference to be drawn at this stage about whether restoration will ever take place at all, for he has quite a different concern, namely, to dissuade the apostles from planning the future, either of Israel or of humanity.[33] It is in the unfolding of the subsequent narrative that the answer to the apostles' question is to be found, by Luke's addressees as well as by later readers. The apostles themselves will also be given the opportunity to see what God has planned for Israel as he acts through their witness to the Messiah.

1.8 The second part of Jesus' response, expressed as a positive affirmation, is introduced with an adversative, 'rather'.[34] He reiterates the promise of the Spirit, reminding them that what they do need to know is that they will receive a power, which the Holy Spirit will give to them and which will enable them to carry out what could, in effect, be understood as an integral part of the restoration ideal. Indeed, the plan that Jesus goes on to lay out before them is not contrary to the Jewish expectation that the arrival of the Messiah will cause the divided kingdom of Israel (the South and the North, Judaea and Samaria) to be reunited; and that the Jewish people will be gathered in from the ends of the earth where also the Jews will bear witness to the Gentiles of the Messiah's arrival (see *Excursus* 1). Christian readers are used to associating the phrase 'the ends of the earth' with the notion of witnessing to the Gentiles,[35] but from a Jewish perspec-

33. There is a great deal of debate over the form of the question in the AT where it relates to the restoration of the kingdom to Israel, with some concluding that Jesus meant to say that the kingdom would not be restored, others that it would be but in God's own time (for discussion on 1.6 and bibliography, see E.P. Sanders, *Jesus and Judaism*, pp. 116–19; see D.L. Tiede, 'The Exaltation of Jesus and the Restoration of Israel in Acts 1', *HTR* 79 (1986), p. 279, n. 2; see also bibliography cited in the notes to *Excursus* 1).

34. ἀλλά signals an opposition, just as in 1.4.

35. The existence of scholarly debate over the exact meaning of ἕως ἐσχάτου τῆς γῆς is a reflection of the possible ambiguity. Whilst it is true that Luke's writings are clear about the universal sense conferred by Jesus on the LXX expression even though it originally had had a Jewish nationalistic sense (see W.C. van Unnik, 'Der Ausdruck ʼΕΩΣ ʼΕΣΧΑΤΟΥ ΤΗΣ ΓΗΣ [Apostelgeschichte 1.8] und sein alttestamentlicher Hintergrund', in *Studia Biblica et Semitica* [Wageningen, 1966], pp. 335–49, who adduces as confirmation of the universal meaning Isa. 8.9; 48.20; 49.6; 62.11; 1 Macc. 3.9; *Ps. Sol.* 1.4), they give no indication that the apostles see it in this way yet. On the contrary, the spread of their witness to the Gentiles does not happen by their own design but by the turn of events and by the direct intervention of God. It is the limited vision of the apostles that causes some to interpret γῆ as meaning the land of Israel (see K.H. Rengstorf, 'Die Zuwahl des Matthias (Apg 1,15ff)', *ST* 15 (1961), pp. 53–56; D.R. Schwartz, 'The End of the γῆ (Acts 1.8): Beginning or End of the Christian Vision?', *JBL* 105 (1986), pp. 669–76; see Barrett, I, pp. 79–80) but the words attributed by Luke to Jesus then become problematic. As for the hypothesis advanced by

tive it is a reminder of the dispersion of the people of Israel among the nations. In Luke's report of Jesus' parting words, the phrase can therefore be thought to be deliberately ambiguous with Jesus knowing how God will act through the apostles' activity to take the good news to the Gentiles, and the apostles hearing a command that fits with their hope of a return of Jews to Israel. It is only once their witnessing activity is well under way, in the order laid down by Jesus, that they will see that the divine plan no longer functions within the religious or nationalistic framework of Israel; the account of this change in the D05 text will be toned down in the AT to produce a more ambiguous, less radical, account of the shift that has taken place.[36]

It may well be that in Jesus' teaching about the kingdom of God (1.3) he included explanations about the shift in the notion of the kingdom of Israel and about the loss of the privileged status of the Jews with respect to the Gentiles. That Luke does not record Jesus as making the change clear as he gives them the commission to be his witnesses to the ends of the earth is an indication that the apostles were unable at that point to understand that the Gentiles were to be included in the people of God on equal terms with the members of Israel. Their lack of a complete grasp of Jesus' message is borne out by their unpreparedness for the conversion of the Gentiles in Acts 10.

It is true that in the Gospel account of the final command of Jesus, Luke includes the mention of 'all nations' which prevents his instructions from being construed as limited to the Jewish people (Lk. 24.47). In the Bezan

H.J. Cadbury in *The Book of Acts in History* (London: A&C Black, 1955), p. 15, and adopted by T.C.G. Thornton ('To the end of the earth: Acts 1[8]', *ExpT* 89 [1977–78], pp. 374–75), according to which the preaching to the ends of the earth would have been accomplished in 8.26–39 with the preaching of the gospel to the Ethiopian, for all that the idea seems attractive (8.1, 4: Judea; 8.5–25: Samaria; 8.26–39: the ends of the earth) it does not correspond to the plan of Luke's work.

36. E.J. Epp (*The Theological Tendency of Codex Bezae Cantabrigiensis in Acts* [Cambridge: Cambridge University Press, 1966]) brought out the more universal outlook of the Bezan text and ascribed it to a later generation of Christians whose concern was to underline the superiority of Christianity over and above Judaism. But this universal outlook belongs to Jesus, and in the Bezan version of Acts it is expressed in terms derived from the Jewish Scriptures and other traditional teachings or literature; it can scarcely, therefore, be the work of Christians who wanted nothing to do with their Jewish roots. On the contrary, there is every sign that Codex Bezae was addressed to Jews whose difficulties in accepting Christianity arose from failing to see how it could be squared with Jewish teaching, and its message of universality is therefore expressed in terms with which they were familiar.

text of this verse, the mention of 'the nations' is made in a carefully worded expression that demonstrates, much more than the AT, that the idea that the apostles are to preach to the Gentiles is new and unexpected information.[37] This is no accident for, at two other places at least in the Bezan text of the Gospel the idea that God's gifts are for anyone other than the Jews is absent where it is present in the AT.[38] At Lk. 2.32 D05, Simeon leaves out the words 'the nations' in his recollection of Isaiah's prophecies (cf. Isa. 42.6; 49.6) and speaks of 'a light for revelation and for glory to your people Israel'. At Lk. 11.13 D05, in Jesus' explanation of the parable of the man who asks his friend for bread at midnight, a parable that he applies to 'everyone' (Lk. 11.10), he simply says that God will give 'a good gift' to those who ask; he does not say, as the AT does, that God will give the Holy Spirit to anyone asking, thus precluding the interpretation that the Gentiles, too, could expect such a request to be granted. These details of the Bezan text correspond to Luke's use of Mark's material concerning Jesus' ministry among the Gentiles for he omits precisely the Markan section in which Jesus goes beyond the frontiers of Israel (Mk 6.45–8.26). The effect of Luke's choice of material is to make the community of apostles the ones who will be the first to carry out the ministry among the Gentile people.

Since, as was noted earlier (on 1.1–3 above), the account in Acts 1 unpacks the condensed account of Luke 24 and thereby pays greater attention to the details of the exchange between Jesus and his disciples, it is striking that no explicit mention is made of witnessing to 'the nations' in Acts. The Acts account, however, seems to be presenting the scene through the eyes of the apostles who, for their part, did not register Jesus' instructions about the Gentiles. That explains why, when they see how God regards them as of equal status with the Jews in giving them the Holy Spirit (Acts 10–11), they are not expecting it.

37. Lk. 24.47–48 D05: γέγραπται ... κηρυχθῆναι ... μετάνοιαν καὶ ἄφεσιν ἁμαρτιῶν ὡς ἐπὶ πάντα τὰ ἔθνη ἀρξαμένων ἀπὸ Ἰερουσαλήμ. καὶ ὑμεῖς δὲ μάρτυρες τούτων, 'it is written that ... there should be preached in his name repentance and forgiveness for sins, indeed to all nations beginning in Ierousalem. And it is you who are the witnesses of these things'.

38. Codex Bezae is usually considered to be *more* open to Gentiles, certainly as far as Acts is concerned (see Epp, *Theological Tendency*, pp. 64–119). This evaluation ignores the highly nuanced nature of the text, and tends to assimilate D05 with the rest of the so-called Western tradition (see Read-Heimerdinger, *The Bezan Text*, pp.151–53).

Yet even within their restricted vision of the witness that they are to bear to the Messiah, Jesus insists that the apostles cannot expect to carry out his instructions while they lack the power of the Holy Spirit. That is why they are meanwhile to remain inactive, without undertaking anything that might jeopardize the future mission (see on 1.4 above). The power that the Holy Spirit will communicate to the disciples will manifest itself as a witness, with the contents of this witness clearly defined: 'you will be witnesses of me'[39] or, as expressed in the Gospel, 'you (will be) witnesses of all this', that is, first, 'that the Messiah had to suffer' (Lk. 24.46a), against all the Messianic expectation of the Jews; secondly, 'that he was to rise (from the dead B03) on the third day' (24.46b), and thirdly, 'that repentance and forgiveness from sins was to be preached to all nations' (24.47a) beginning with, but not restricted to, the Jewish people. It is striking that Jesus allows the apostles to embark on their mission even though they have not clearly grasped the scope of the witness that they are to give. In the initial period, however, their understanding is sufficient to enable them to begin their work, for the departure point is to be the Jewish institution denoted by the religious term 'Ierousalem' (Lk. 24.47b: cf. Acts 1.8b). It is once their mission is under way, and as it progresses, that the success of their testimony will be evaluated against the true scope of the witness intended by Jesus. It will achieve its goal when the apostles see that the idea of Israel as a promised land and the nation as a chosen people has lost all its force, the whole earth having become the object of God's favour.

The book of Acts will be structured around this threefold commission:

1. Witness-denunciation in front of the Jewish council in 'Ierousalem' (cf. Acts 4.5–22: Peter and John; 5.27–41: the apostles; 6.12–15: Stephen)
2. The evangelization of 'Judaea and Samaria' (from 8.1b onwards [cf. 13.47], which was the responsibility of the Hellenists who had to flee as a consequence of Stephen's witness)
3. The preaching of the gospel to 'the ends of the earth' (from 13.1 onwards, where the mission proper to the Gentiles begins when it is entrusted by the Holy Spirit to the Antioch church represented by Barnabas and Saul)

39. The translation 'my witnesses' is incorrect. The position of the genitive pronoun μου, read as it is before the noun, is objective ('of me') and not possessive. When the possessive pronoun is juxtaposed with a noun (here, 'witnesses'), it is typically found after the noun (see Read-Heimerdinger, *The Bezan Text*, p. 108). It is only found before the noun if it is emphatic ('mine rather than someone else's'), which is not the implication here.

Excursus 1

The Restoration of Israel: Two Conflicting Plans

In order to understand how the apostles perceived the last words of Jesus, it is essential to take account of the Jewish conceptual framework and theological perspective of the first century. This is true not only for the first chapter of Acts where the apostles had not yet received the Holy Spirit, but it is equally true afterwards. The Holy Spirit did not suddenly transform Jewish modes of perception into Christian ones, nor was the activity of the Holy Spirit a completely new event, for the operation of the Holy Spirit was known in Judaism long before this manifestation of the divine became associated more especially with Christianity.[40] The apostles were steeped, as faithful Jews would be, in Jewish ways of thinking, and their mentality was unlike those of Christians of even the early second century. Teasing out the purpose of Luke requires, therefore, an awareness of first-century Jewish ways of thinking, in their uniformity (common to all types of Judaism) and in their diversity.[41]

These points may seem obvious for the question of the restoration of Israel but they will be seen later to be just as important for many other matters. An awareness of Jewish issues will often, as here in Acts 1, allow readings of Codex Bezae to be seen for the references and allusions to Judaism that they are. So while a knowledge of the Greco-Roman world of the first century is certainly helpful for an accurate appreciation of the book of Acts (as of the New Testament generally) and is frequently drawn upon by commentators in explaining the text, a knowledge of first-century Judaism (or, more broadly, Second Temple or pre-Rabbinic Judaism) is no less important.

It will be useful to sketch an outline of the expectations of the Jews concerning the restoration of Israel. The hope of Israel becoming one day

40. The term 'Holy Spirit' is rare in the Hebrew text and LXX of the Jewish Scriptures where 'Spirit' is used on its own except for three occasions (Ps. 50.13 [51.11]; Isa. 63.10, 11). However, by the time of the New Testament it appears to have become current in Judaism, as can be seen by comparing the *Isaiah Targum* with the Hebrew or Greek texts. See Read-Heimerdinger, *The Bezan Text*, pp. 153–56.

41. Comprehensive accounts of the diversity of first-century Judaism are to be found in the writings of Jacob Neusner (*The Rabbinic Traditions about the Pharisees before AD 70* [Leiden: E.J. Brill, 1971]; *Judaism in the Beginning of Christianity* [London: SPCK, 1984]); for a summary see J.D.G. Dunn, *The Partings of the Ways Between Christianity and Judaism and their Significance for the Character of Christianity* [London: SCM Press, 1991], pp. 11–15).

a unified and sovereign nation dates from the times of the prophets who gave warnings about, or commented, on the division of the nation and the scattering of the Jewish people among the Gentiles. They interpreted these events, which took place between the eighth and the sixth centuries, as punishment from Yahweh for idolatry and disobedience to his commands, in what can be regarded as either ethical or religious domains although the distinction cannot be rigidly maintained. At the same time, they looked forward to an age when Israel would be purified and reunited as a religious and political nation. These notions are developed and diversified in the post-biblical literature during the period following the building of the Second Temple to such an extent that the Scriptures on their own do not present an adequate picture of the hopes at the time of Jesus or the early Church.[42] While there exists no one formal account, the chief elements of the hopes for the restoration of Israel, initially brought together in the writings of the biblical prophets at such places as Isaiah 11; Jer. 23.1–8; Ezek. 37.24–28, can be summarized as follows:[43]

42. Care needs to be taken with the dating of some of the material of the post-biblical writings and it is important, when attempting to reconstruct the picture of the first century, not to rely on passages that are more likely to stem from Rabbinic, or indeed Christian, thought of the second century CE. Among the most relevant writings to consult is the *Isaiah Targum* (B.D. Chilton [ed.] [Edinburgh: T.&T. Clark, 1987]). See also *2 Baruch*; *4 Ezra*; the *Testaments of the Twelve Patriarchs*; and the *Testament of Abraham*, in J.H. Charlesworth [ed.], *The Old Testament Pseudepigrapha*. I. *Apocalyptic Literature and Testaments* (2 vols.; London: Dartman, Longman and Todd, 1983), and the introductions there to each of these writings. E.P. Sanders (*Jesus and Judaism*) gathers together much useful information on the restoration ideals; but the value of his work for an appreciation of the Jewish hopes in the New Testament is limited in that he only gives consideration to explicit information, which is in itself a denial of Jewish modes of expression. Furthermore, he tends to present the evidence as a set of intellectual propositions and not as a reflection of moral and spiritual life, so missing an intrinsic quality of restoration expectations.

43. More complete lists of references can be found in, e.g., E.P. Sanders *Jesus and Judaism*, pp. 77–119. Biblical references are no more, however, than indications of a rich and living thought system and way of life which, on their own, they are incapable of communicating. Cf. the summary of L.L. Grabbe, *Judaism from Cyrus to Hadrian* (London: SCM Press, 1994), pp. 552–54, on the diversity of Jewish eschatological expectations. Grabbe's scepticism about the possibility of defining an overall 'Jewish view' on the subject of eschatology is a reminder that Luke is concerned in the first chapters of Acts with specific groups of Jews in Palestine, just as he will focus later on the aspirations of the Pharisees through his presentation of Paul.

1. *The reunification of the Jewish people*: Jews from the northern and the southern kingdoms, and from wherever they have been dispersed among the Gentile nations, will be reunited: Isa. 11.11–16; Ezek. 34.11–13
2. *The Messiah*: he will arrive as a Davidic king with the purpose of leading the restored and reunited Israel: Jer. 23.5–8; Ezekiel 34, 37; in places he is seen as an Elijah figure whereas in others, Elijah is represented by the forerunner of the Messiah:[44] 1 Enoch; Mal. 3; Sir. 48.1–12
3. *The land of Israel*: this will be the place for the restored nation to live: Jer. 23.8; 24.6; 2 Macc. 1.27–29; 2.18; *Pss Sol.* 11; 17.28–31, 50
4. *Jerusalem*: the Messiah will arrive in the holy city which will be rebuilt with a new Temple: *Targ. Isa.* 24.23; 31.4;[45] Ezekiel 40–43
5. *The twelve tribes* : they will be restored as leaders of Israel under the rule of the Messiah: Sir. 48.10; Isa. 49.6; Ezek. 47.13–48.29
6. *The Holy Spirit*: he will accompany the Messiah, and God will be revealed once more through prophecy: *Targ. Isa.* 42.1b; 44.3b; Joel 2.28–29
7. *The punishment of the wicked*: in so far as this applies to the Jewish people, some texts (notably from Qumran) speak of only a remnant of Israel being saved: Ezek. 34.17–22; Amos 3.12; Zeph. 3.11–13; Mic. 2.12
8. *The resurrection of the dead*: though denied by the Sadducees, bodily resurrection is a characteristic of the Messianic age in which all the righteous of Israel will participate: Ps. 16.9–11; Ezekiel 37; Dan. 12.2; cf. Acts 26.6–8
9. *Purification*: this would be of an ethical and a religious nature, involving repentance and forgiveness of sins: Isa. 44.22; 55.7; Tob. 13.5–8, 10; *Ps. Sol.* 18.4–7; *Jub.* 1.15, 23
10. *The kingdom of Israel*: self-rule of Israel will be re-established as the rule of the Gentiles is overthrown: Ezek. 34.28–29
11. *The Gentiles*: the hope that the Jews will no longer have to suffer the humiliation of foreign domination derives from the role ascribed to the Messiah as redeemer of Israel.[46] The place of the Gentiles with regard to the restored kingdom of Israel is, however, one concerning which

44. On the merging of the two representations, which is also apparent in the Gospels and Acts, see A. Wiener, *The Prophet Elijah in the Development of Judaism* (London: Routledge and Kegan Paul, 1978), pp. 35–42.

45. On the importance of Jerusalem as the place of revelation of the Messianic kingdom, see B.D. Chilton, *A Galilean Rabbi and his Bible* (London: SPCK, 1984), pp. 53–54, 58–59.

46. In a sociological study of the theme of redemption, B.J. Malina (*Windows on the World of Jesus: Time Travel to Ancient Judea* [Louisville: Westminster/John Knox, 1993], pp. 6–7) has shown how restoration of family or national honour is at the root of the concept. In this sense, the restoration of Israel is inextricably linked to vindication before the Gentiles who have hitherto been enemies of Israel.

there is perhaps the greatest diversity of expectation, even within the biblical prophetic writings:[47]

a. In some writings,[48] the defeat of the Gentiles means that they will be punished by God and, if not completely destroyed, they are seen as being brought under the rule of Israel in total subjection. They will be set apart from the Jews who will remain God's chosen people as a reunited nation occupying the land of Israel. For the preservation of national identity and purity, it is the Torah that is of the utmost importance; indeed, study of the Torah will bring about restoration.[49] This exclusivist view was probably held the more strongly the harsher was the oppression of the Gentiles (notably after 70 CE).

b. There is another view, sometimes concurrent in the same writings as well as in other writings,[50] that is more positive towards the Gentiles. It sees the Gentiles as being drawn by Israel's testimony to worship God in Israel and being granted access to the kingdom. Here, the Torah is of lesser importance than good works. This universalist position may have been the more unusual one in the first century, at least within Palestine, but some would argue otherwise[51].

Although the range of views on the restoration of Israel makes it difficult to assess the prevailing opinion in Palestine in the first century, the scope of the next task is somewhat narrower for it is to determine, given such a diversity, what picture Luke presents of the expectations of the apostles and the teaching of Jesus. The limits of the proposed enquiry should be noted: no attempt is to be made to find a position that harmonizes the views portrayed in Luke's writings with those expressed by the other Gospel writers, nor with those expressed by Paul in his letters. Nonetheless, even if the study is kept within the confines of Luke-Acts, it is evi-

47. For a survey of the variety of positions in the biblical and other Jewish literature, see E.P. Sanders, *Jesus and Judaism*, pp. 213–18.

48. E.g. Isaiah and the *Isaiah Targum* (see Chilton [ed.], p. 59); Micah; *Testament of Moses*; *Joseph and Asenath*.

49. Cf. H.C. Kee, '*Testaments of the Twelve Patriarchs*. Introduction', in Charlesworth (ed.), *The Old Testament Pseudepigrapha*. I, pp. 775–81 (780).

50. E.g. *The Testaments of the Twelve Patriarchs*; *Testament of Abraham*; *2 Enoch*; *3 Baruch*.

51. Chilton (*A Galilean Rabbi*, p. 66) argues that on the basis of the targumic evidence 'the possibility cannot be excluded that this rather more universalistic view of the kingdom ... is characteristic of first century Judaism'. Cf. E.P. Sanders, '*Testament of Abraham*. Introduction', in Charlesworth (ed.), *The Old Testament Pseudepigrapha*. I, pp. 871–81 (876–77).

dent that in the AT there is not a single, consistent message but rather considerable ambiguity.[52] In contrast, the text of Codex Bezae, for both the Gospel and Acts, presents an account that is more sharply drawn and more radical than that of the Alexandrian MSS. According to the Bezan text, the differences between Luke and Paul, and between Jesus and the apostles, are an integral part of the message of the narrator whose purpose is to show at which points the first leaders of the Church did not immediately comprehend or follow the teaching of the Master. In order to disentangle the various points of view, it will be necessary to remember that, throughout his work, Luke uses the speeches he assigns to his characters as a vehicle to express the thinking of the speaker, and not his own beliefs or ideas (see *General Introduction,* §IX). His own views emerge, usually indirectly, through such literary devices as the structure of the narrative, the presentation of the characters or the choice of language.

According to the Bezan text of Luke's writing, there is a progression in the concept of Israel and of its restoration, which involves several shifts in the divine plan. Such shifts are a feature of the history of Israel as recorded in the Jewish Scriptures, arising as they do not out of God's fickleness but out of the freedom people have. Initially, in the prophetic proclamations of the infancy narratives that announce Jesus as the Messiah, the hopes of a restored Israel are given full nationalistic expression, with the mention of the Gentiles omitted by Simeon in his allusion to Isaiah (Lk. 2.32 D05). Moreover, in the same early sections, as likewise in the chapters relating to his ministry, John the Baptist is portrayed as the prophesied forerunner of the Messiah of Israel, as a type of Elijah. The first shift in the concept of Israel comes when neither Jesus nor John is accorded the recognition or the obedience that their status demanded (e.g.

52. It is the attempt to establish Luke's position from the conflicting evidence in the AT of the Gospel and Acts, and/or the search for a single New Testament doctrine that can be distilled from the diversity of positions expressed by different New Testament writers, that has brought about such diverging results in the statements made about the restoration of Israel in Luke's work. Conclusions expressed in recent years alone range from seeing Israel as completely, or temporarily, abandoned in favour of the Church to seeing Israel as restored in the time of the early Church (alternatively in the end times) by virtue of the belief of some Jews in Jesus as the Messiah. It is not possible to enter into debate here with the many viewpoints advocated by contemporary or older works, particularly since our own conclusions depend on the Bezan text. For a summary of the different positions and their own contribution, see R. Bauckham, 'The Restoration of Israel in Luke-Acts', in J.M. Scott (ed.), *Restoration: Old Testament, Jewish, and Christian Perspectives* (Leiden: E.J. Brill, 2001), pp. 435–87; Ravens, *Restoration*, esp. pp. 11–22.

Lk. 7.1–10, 29–30; 10.10–16; 11.29–32; 13.24–30; 14.15–24). The notion of the kingdom of God is thus seen to expand to include the nations who acknowledge the Messiahship of Jesus, entirely in line with scriptural prophecy. A second shift in the plan for Israel is brought about by the decision of the Jewish leaders, including the high priest, to kill Jesus. Their opposition to the Messiah, which is so intense that they hand him over to the Gentiles to be crucified, causes them to lose their authority over God's faithful; they are no longer representatives of God for Israel. This will become clear through their persecution of the disciples of Jesus in Acts 4 and 5. Israel nonetheless retains its identity as the people of God who will finally be redeemed from the oppression of the Gentiles (21.23–28). The important difference is that the Twelve apostles are accorded a higher status than the twelve tribes whom they will judge (Lk. 22.30 D05), their faithfulness to the Messiah being the standard for judgment. According to this changed plan, the apostles and the other disciples of Jesus do not replace Israel, nor are they a 'new' or 'true' Israel, rather they belong to Israel which is being restored under Messianic rule.[53]

This is the position at the end of the Gospel in Codex Bezae, and the one with which the apostles continue to identify in the early part of Acts according to the Bezan text. It is, in most respects, a thoroughly Jewish position, informed and moulded by the scriptural teaching about the Messiah and his reign. As the leaders of the followers of Jesus, the apostles see themselves as representing the twelve tribes of Israel and they associate their leadership with Jerusalem as the religious seat of authority in Judaism. Not only that, but they are depicted by Luke as conscious of being Palestinian Jews; in their expression of a particularly exclusivist type of Judaism,[54] they view Hellenistic Jews, including Jesus-believers,

53. Thus far, we are most in agreement with the analysis of the apostles' role in Israel put forward by Jervell (notably in *People of God*, pp. 75–112, but the position is maintained consistently in his writings) rather than any other explanation that interprets Israel as being superseded by the apostles. Up to the end of the Gospel, Luke presents the changes in the nationalistic perspective as a fulfilment, not a contradiction, of the Scriptures, and Israel continues to exist. We separate from Jervell in his approach to Acts, however, because he does not recognize the radical change that is brought about after the defection of Judas, nor does he distinguish between the understanding of the apostles and that of Luke.

54. In order to describe more exactly this type of Judaism, more precise knowledge is needed concerning the differences between the various kinds of Judaism in the first century. In fact, the book of Acts in the Bezan text serves as primary evidence for this exploration, for it portrays conflicts and tensions between distinct groups (represented by Barnabas, Paul, James, Peter, Apollos, for example) more sharply than the other

as distinct from (and even subordinate to) themselves along with other Jesus-believers from Palestine. They are also extremely cautious about contact with Gentiles and strive to maintain a religious purity among themselves.[55] In the course of the events narrated in Acts, Peter in particular will distance himself from the traditional Palestinian Jewish expectations. James, the brother of the Lord, on the other hand, will come to represent the position that maintains a privileged status for the Jewish race in God's plan for salvation. Paul's stance in all of this is interesting and will be dealt with in a moment.

What the apostles fail to comprehend is that a third shift in the concept of Israel occurs at some time after Jesus' speech recorded in Lk. 22. It follows the defection of Judas from the apostolic group or, more strictly speaking, it follows the death of Judas. When Jesus promised the Twelve apostles that they would sit on twelve thrones (in D05), he already knew that one of them would betray him (Lk. 22.21). The betrayal in itself does not cause a change in the plan concerning Israel. It is made clear in the text of Codex Bezae that the act of Judas is compared with the deceitfulness of Jacob in obtaining the birthright of his twin brother Esau from his father.[56] Despite his cruel trickery, Jacob nevertheless went on to become the one to be called Israel; from this parallel, it can be deduced that it was not the betrayal in itself that deprived Judas of his place as one of the apostles. Peter also betrayed Jesus, but immediately following his promise of the twelve thrones, Jesus tells Peter how he has prayed that he will turn back after his betrayal to strengthen the brethren (Lk. 22.31–34). No such prayer or reassurance is given concerning Judas.

The accounts of the events in Judas' life after he had handed Jesus over to the Jewish authorities are notoriously complex[57] and will be considered

MSS. Claims about the nature of the information that it provides must, however, be made with some degree of tentativeness as long as they cannot be controlled by external evidence.

55. The care taken to avoid foreign contamination, together with the resultant criticism of Hellenistic Jews who were felt to be too open to Gentile influences, was, of course, at the root of the Maccabean revolt which would have still been alive in the collective Jewish memory in first-century Palestine.

56. The sign of the kiss in Lk. 22.47 is described in Codex Bezae with the exact words of Gen. 27.27 LXX, see J. Read-Heimerdinger, 'Where is Emmaus? Clues in the Text of Luke 24 in Codex Bezae', in D.G.K. Taylor (ed.), *Studies in the Early Text of the Gospels and Acts* (Text and Studies, 3/I; Birmingham: University Press, 1999), pp. 229–44 (239).

57. See W. Klassen, *Judas. Betrayer or Friend of Jesus?* (London: SCM Press, 1996), esp. Chapter 9.

more closely in the commentary on Acts 1.16–22 below. Here, it is sufficient to note that the outcome of his death, according to Peter's speech in 1.16–22 and confirmed by Luke in a narrative aside in 1.18–19, is that the Twelve become an incomplete group. The apostles, still holding on to the promise of Jesus of Luke 22, are anxious for Judas to be replaced in order that his function as the twelfth witness to the resurrection of the Messiah can continue to be exercised (Acts 1.6, 25–26); Jesus, in contrast, does not intend to replace him, as shown by his response in 1.7–8 and by the unfolding of events after the election of Matthias (see *Commentary*, 1.15–26, esp. 1.23–24). By means of his comments made throughout the narrative of Acts on the intervention of God in the life of the Christian communities, Luke shows that Israel no longer holds a privileged position in the divine plan and that the notion of the Gentiles being incorporated into Israel, a notion present in the Gospel and derived from the Scriptures, is no longer valid. Nowhere in Acts does the Church represent the restoration of Israel, neither physically nor spiritually, nor is the restoration of Israel mentioned again, implicitly or explicitly, as part of God's will. Whether that silence means that the notion of Israel is permanently abandoned cannot be ascertained from the book of Acts, but what can be affirmed from the Bezan text is that Israel is not part of the programme that God works out through the Church in Acts.

The shifts in the concept of Israel according to the text of Codex Bezae of Luke's Gospel and Acts can be depicted in diagrammatic form in the following way:

Figure 1. *Shifts in the Concept of Israel in the Bezan Text of Luke-Acts*

Beginning of Luke's Gospel	The Messiah arrives to restore Israel as the kingdom of God (no mention of Gentiles, 2.23 D05) Twelve tribes represented by Twelve apostles	
	Shift 1 e.g. 7.29–30; 10.10–16; 11.29–32; 13.34–35	Jesus rejected by many Jewish people
	e.g. 13.29–30; 14.15–24	*Consequence* — The kingdom will be opened to include Gentiles
	Shift 2 20.19–20; 22.2–6	Jewish leaders plot Jesus' death

	22.30 D05	*Consequence* — Twelve apostles (including Judas) will rule over twelve tribes in the kingdom	
	23; 24	Jesus' death and resurrection	
	24.47–48	*Consequence* — The apostles are witnesses of the Messiah, to Jews and Gentiles	
Beginning of Acts	*Shift* 3 1.18–19	Judas buys a field with the betrayal money and dies a godless man	
		Consequences	
		— *The apostles' plan* They want to replace Judas, maintaining the importance of the Twelve apostles. Israel has national and religious identity, with Ierousalem as the seat of authority.	— *Jesus' plan* He does not replace Judas; the Twelve lose their importance as representatives of Israel. Israel is not restored through the Church and is no longer referred to as a national or spiritual identity by Luke as narrator. Ierousalem loses its importance.

It is the Jesus-believers of Hellenistic rather than Palestinian origin, amongst whom Barnabas is portrayed in Codex Bezae as the supreme example, who will be seen to comprehend and embody most closely the plan of Jesus (see *Commentary*, 4.36–37; 11.19–30).

As for Paul, whilst he is more open to the Jews of the Diaspora, and although he understands the new conditions for the Gentiles for their entry into the people of God, his insistence on preaching to the Jews first and on bringing the offering of the Gentiles to Jerusalem is not in accordance with the will of God according to the narrator of the Bezan account[58] (cf. 19.1 D05; 20.3–4, 22–24 D05; 21.11–14 D05). This evaluation of the events involving Paul will become clear as the various stages of his missionary journey are related.

58. We are not concerned here with reconciling Paul's reasoning about Israel in his letters with the portrayal of him in Acts. In fact, there is no difficulty with any possible discrepancies as long as Paul is not regarded as infallible but rather, in a positive sense, as open to growth and development. For an outline of Paul's position in his own writings, see B.D. Chilton and J. Neusner, *Judaism in the New Testament* (London: Routledge, 1995), pp. 58–86.

[a′] 1.9 *The Ascension of Jesus*

The second part of the opening section of Acts begins by expanding on the earlier reference to the ascension of Jesus in the corresponding element [a] of the first part (1.1–2).

The idea of the ascension has already been introduced in the Gospel of Luke (Lk. 24.50–51). There it was said that, once Jesus had given to the disciples the commission to preach repentance and forgiveness of sins in his name to all nations, 'he led them out (outside, D05) in the direction of Bethany' (Lk. 24.50a), that is out of Ierousalem where he had appeared to them (Lk. 24.33, 36). The detail 'outside' in Codex Bezae[59] underlines this last attempt of Jesus while on earth to get the apostles to see that they had to distance themselves once and for all from the Jewish institution. (They will, despite Jesus' instructions, go back to Ierousalem with its religious connotations [Lk. 24.52 // Acts 1.12].) Once outside, Jesus left his disciples, bringing to an end his physical presence with them, and he 'was lifted up into heaven' – a detail omitted by Codex Bezae among other important witnesses (Lk. 24.51).[60]

1.9 From the start of the ascension account, parallels are established with the transfiguration of Jesus (Lk. 9.34–35) as well as the ascension of Elijah (2 Kgs 2.1–18, see *Excursus* 2). The backcloth of the parallel scenes serves to give a depth to the present one but, as variation between the two texts of the Acts narrative continues, the allusions to the earlier events differ. Codex Vaticanus focuses on the similarity between the apostles as they watch Jesus depart from them, and Elisha who similarly had watched his master Elijah being taken from him (2 Kgs 2.9–12a). The Bezan text has stronger echoes of the transfiguration with its focus on the

59. In spite of MSS and versions that omit ἔξω after the verb ἐξήγαγεν (P75 ℵ B C* L 1.33 *pc* a e sys.p), it is possible that Luke has deliberately used this redundant expression (cf. Gen. 15.5 and 19.17 LXX concerning Abraham and Lot) in order to convey the desire of Jesus to bring about the exodus of the disciples 'out of Ierousalem'.

60. ℵ* D it sys omit the reference to ascension in Luke's Gospel. Metzger (*Commentary*, pp. 189–90) explains the reasons that prompted the majority of the committee to refuse the short text and not to accept it as a 'Western non-interpolation' (cf. pp. 191–93). Against their arguments, it should be noted that the short text of Lk. 24.51 shares the same tendency as the text of Acts 1.9–11 (especially D05) to attenuate the drama of Jesus' departure; D05 further uses the verb (ἀπέστη) that Luke typically employs to bring to an end a supernatural presence, cf. Lk. 1.38; 4.13. It is possible that Luke did not wish to introduce the idea of Jesus' ascension until he was able to develop it more fully as he does in Acts 1.9–11.

cloud. The cloud, though, has a slightly different function from that in the transfiguration scene. There, it enveloped the disciples and prevented them from seeing God as he spoke to them about Jesus (Lk. 9.34). At the ascension, it has the function of separating the divine realm, into which Jesus is received, from the human one which he leaves and in which the apostles remain.

[b′] 1.10–11 *The Apparition of Moses and Elijah*
These verses contain echoes of the corresponding element of the first part [b], 1.3 with repetition of a) the verb παρίστημι (referring to Jesus, aorist // referring to the two men, pluperfect), and b) instructions (given by Jesus concerning the Kingdom of God // given by the two men concerning Jesus' return).

1.10 The expectations of the apostles are given more attention than the manner of Jesus' departure. Attention is drawn to their hopes in 1.10–11 by the description of them gazing into the sky, the repetition four (three D05) times of 'into the sky', and in the reproof that Moses and Elijah give.

The 'two men dressed in white' are appropriately brought into the spotlight with the exclamation 'behold!', a literary device typically used to present the arrival on stage of a new character when the scene is being viewed through the eyes of a character already present.[61] Here, it is the apostles who suddenly notice the presence of the two men, whose identity is to be deduced from their previous appearances in the Gospel for, in a typically Lukan threefold pattern, this is the third time that Luke has brought these two figures on the scene: they are first introduced at the transfiguration (Lk. 9.30) where their names are given as Moses and Elijah, and they reappear at the empty tomb (24.4). It is these previous appearances that make it clear that they are not 'angels'.[62] Often associated with one another in Jewish tradition, Moses and Elijah share a pro-

61. Zerwick (*Biblical Greek*, §457) comments that καί, following ὡς, corresponds to a Hebraic construction and serves 'to introduce the main clause after a secondary one'. Whether or not the device is Semitic, the use of καί in D05 to connect a subordinate clause (usually a participle) with a subsequent main clause is frequent and has the function of highlighting the unusual nature of the action expressed in the main clause (Read-Heimerdinger, *The Bezan Text*, pp. 206–10).

62. The two figures are commonly, but erroneously, interpreted as angels, see Barrett, I, p. 83. The clue to their identity lies in the expression (καὶ) ἰδοὺ ἄνδρες δύο which is used first at Lk. 9.30 with the names Moses and Elijah, and again at Lk. 24.4.

phetic intimacy with God that tradition prolongs after their departure from earth and, furthermore, each has a privileged role with regards to the Torah; they are the transmitter and the instructor respectively. In the writings of Luke, they appear at three of the climactic points of Jesus' life. As representatives of the Torah, their function in these three scenes is to confirm that the interpretation that Jesus has given of the meaning of his Messiahship concords with the plan of God such as contained in the Scriptures. Thus, the repeated predictions of Jesus concerning his passion, death and resurrection, just as his insistence on explaining the Scriptures once he had come back to life, are validated by the very characters who personify the divine word. On the three occasions on which they appear, they are always dressed in the characteristic garments of those who already belong to the divine sphere ('in glory', Lk. 9.31; 'in a shining garment', Lk. 24.4; 'in white garments', Acts 1.10).

At the scene of transfiguration, the two men were depicted as talking with Jesus.[63] Their conversation is carefully described by Luke: 'they were talking about the exodus that he was to accomplish in Ierousalem' (Lk. 9.31). The reason for their presence in this singular scene is clear: they confirmed the prediction that Jesus had just made concerning his total rejection by the Jewish institution and that he presented as forming part of the divine plan ('it is necessary', Lk. 9.22). Peter, James and John, being 'asleep', were unable to hear the conversation with Moses and Elijah (a metaphor for their inability to comprehend any talk of apparent Messianic failure), and when they awoke they construed the scene as meaning that Jesus, in keeping with their Messianic expectations, was to acquire a glory similar to that of Moses and Elijah. Peter's idea of the booths was an attempt to retain the three characters in the physical realm and, within it, to give them a place to meet with God, just as Moses put a veil on his face whenever he spoke with Yahweh (Exod. 34.35). The voice of the Father will confirm that the apostles must listen to Jesus, his Son: '*listen* to him' (Lk. 9.35), according to the emphasis of Codex Bezae.[64]

63. The parallels (//) between the ascension scene and that of the transfiguration are striking: καὶ ταῦτα εἰπὼν βλεπόντων αὐτῶν ἐπήρθη καὶ νεφέλη ὑπέλαβεν αὐτόν // ταῦτα δὲ αὐτοῦ λέγοντος ἐγένετο νεφέλη καὶ ἐπεσκίαζεν αὐτούς; καὶ ἰδοὺ ἄνδρες δύο // καὶ ἰδοὺ ἄνδρες δύο; ἐν ἐσθήσεσι λευκαῖς // λευκὸς ... ἐν δόξῃ; οἱ καὶ εἶπαν // οἱ ὀφθέντες ... ἔλεγον; οὗτος ὁ Ἰησοῦς ὁ ἀναλημφθείς // οὗτός ἐστιν ὁ υἱός μου ὁ ἐκλελεγμένος ... Ἰησοῦς; οὕτως... ὃν τρόπον // Ἰησοῦς μόνος.

64. This is the stress of the command in D05 and a few other witnesses (see IGNTP apparatus to Luke's Gospel). By placing the pronoun αὐτοῦ before the verb ἀκούετε,

Later, in the resurrection scene, the two men appeared to the women (the female component of the group of disciples)[65] in order to inform them that Jesus had been raised just as he had predicted while in Galilee (Lk. 24.4). Here again, their function is to remind the women that Jesus' predictions about his death and resurrection were in accordance with the Scriptures (Lk. 24.6–8).

Finally, within the setting of the ascension, the two men are back again, this time to present themselves to the male members of the group (who are slower to understand than the women) in order to dissuade them from their futile hopes. Although Moses and Elijah had been on the scene for some time,[66] standing right beside the apostles, the latter had continued to gaze at the sky. Their action is in imitation of Elisha who was promised a double measure of Elijah's spirit if he saw him being taken away (see *Excursus* 2). The apostles had been so absorbed in watching Jesus that they had failed to notice the presence of the two men.

1.11 They are interrupted in their action of staring into the sky only when the men speak: 'Finally, they spoke...' [67] The form of address 'Men from

the other MSS give marked prominence to the person the disciples are to listen to, rather than to the action of listening (see Read-Heimerdinger, *The Bezan Text*, pp. 68–70), as if Jesus were being contrasted with someone else.

65. A group of women is mentioned by name in positive terms, after the Twelve, at Lk. 8.2–3; two of the names specified are mentioned again at Lk. 24.10 when these women tell the good news to the Eleven and the other disciples who, for their part, do not believe them.

66. The sequence of verb tenses is not without significance: (lit.) 'While (the apostles) were staring (continuous action underlined by the periphrastic construction) into the sky as he (Jesus) was going (present participle, genitive absolute), behold! two men (Moses and Elijah) had presented themselves (pluperfect, denoting that the action of presenting themselves took place before the present moment in time) at their sides in a white garment.' It is common to see this pluperfect interpreted as a simple imperfect, 'were standing', to describe the suddenness of the appearance which breaks into the apostles' gazing (see Barrett, I, p. 83). The pluperfect active of ἵστημι is normally used to render the simple past of the intransitive meaning of the verb, and as such indicates a *state* that had been acquired (see R.A. Young, *Intermediate New Testament Greek* [Nashville, TN: Broadman & Holman, 1994], p. 107 for a summary of research on this denotation of the perfect aspect; cf. the 'Porter/Fanning debate' in S.E. Porter and D.A. Carson [eds.], *Biblical Greek Language and Linguistics* [JSNTSup, 80; Sheffield: Sheffield Academic Press, 1993], pp. 18–82). In this instance, the appearance of the two men does not so much interrupt the gazing of the apostles as go unnoticed, that is until they speak (aorist εἶπαν, 1.11).

67. οἳ καὶ εἶπαν: the adverbial καί introduces a new action after a certain length of

Galilee' is a prompt that reminds the apostles of their origin that they shared with Jesus. Galilee is a place of some significance in the crucifixion and resurrection scenes (cf. Lk. 23.5, 49, 55; 24.6; Acts 13.31).[68] Their message is important, for it puts right the apostles' belief that, as with Elijah, the Spirit would come as Jesus left them. They inform the apostles that it is Jesus himself who will come, and that the manner of his coming will not fulfil any expectations of a Messianic return in victory and glory since he will come as he left, without any signs of triumph or power.

Looking back over this account of Jesus' departure, it is striking that the terms Luke uses to describe the ascension are the same terms he uses in speaking of a messenger – celestial, human or diabolical – whose mission has ended, or of a vision that has come to an end, to indicate a separation as well as a removal.[69] Looking in particular at the final meeting between Jesus and the apostles, it can be seen that Luke has depicted the apostles as not yet clearly understanding the teaching of Jesus, neither on the kingdom of Israel nor on the Spirit nor, indeed, on the nature of his Messiahship. Their expectations have been challenged, first by Jesus who, according to the AT, would not discuss with them the restoration of the kingdom to Israel. According to Codex Bezae, it is a replacement for Judas that he refused to consider with the consequence that when he leaves the apostles they are an incomplete group of Eleven instead of Twelve. Then, as he is taken away from them, they learned that their hopes of receiving the Spirit as they watched him go were false and not to be fulfilled. There is nothing more for them to do but to go back to the city empty-handed; if they obey Jesus' commands, they will stay in Hierosoluma (Acts 1.4) and wait there without doing anything until they receive the promised Spirit. The second part of Acts 1 will show that this is not what happened.

time of inactivity indicated by the pluperfect παρειστήκεισαν; we have translated it with 'finally' in order to signal the time lapse between the arrival on stage of the two characters and the moment at which they began to speak.

68. To say that the address 'came to (Luke) as a simple piece of historical tradition' (Barrett, I, p. 83), is to miss the complex and extremely dense nature of Luke's language in which nothing is superfluous and every word carries significance (see *General Introduction*, §V).

69. See J. Rius-Camps, 'El seguimiento de Jesús, el Señor, y de su Espíritu en los prolegómenos de la misión (Hch 1–12), *Estudios Bíblicos* 51 (1993), pp. 73–116 (81, n. 10), and see 'Las variantes, I', p. 68.

Excursus 2

The Ascension of Jesus and the Parallel with Elijah

The departure of Jesus is described by Luke as a 'taking away' in the presence of chosen witnesses and as such resembles an abundance of other departures of characters who leave the world in a similar way.[70] There are indications that Luke intends a parallel to be seen between Jesus and Elijah, but it is one that exists chiefly in the minds of the apostles for he himself rejects it.

Although there is relatively little information about the figure of Elijah in the Scriptures (1 and 2 Kings; Malachi) or the inter-testamental literature (1 Maccabees; Ben Sira), he emerges in the later Jewish writings of the Mishnah and the Talmud as an established character of considerable significance to the Jewish people.[71] The Gospels themselves witness to the development of traditions and teachings concerning Elijah, which are alluded to in questions relating to Jesus or John but of which there is little prior record in writing. Two chief aspects of Elijah's life that are developed in later Jewish literature are first, his role as the chosen emissary of Yahweh, and secondly, his ascension.

The former is presented in the book of Malachi (3.1–2; 4.5) where Elijah is portrayed as the herald of the Messiah and of the final redemption of Israel. The function of Elijah as envoy of God corresponds to his original function when he appeared in Israel as the prophet who acted on God's behalf to remove idolatry and injustice from Israel (1 Kings 17–2 Kings 1). In Ben Sira 48, Elijah is presented as the redeemer himself who would restore the twelve tribes of Israel (Sir. 48.10).

The ambivalence of the representation of Elijah as the Messiah's forerunner on the one hand, and as the Messiah himself on the other, can be

70. Elijah: 4 Kgdms 2.1–18 LXX; Sir. 48.9, 12; 1 Macc. 2.58; *1 En.* 93.8; *Apoc. Esd.* 7.6; Josephus *Ant.* 9.28; *Acts Pil.* 15.1; Irenaeus *Adv. Haer.* V.5.1; Tertullien *De Anim.* 50. Enoch: Gen. 5.21–24; Sir. 44.16; 49.14; Wis. 4.10–11; *Jub.* 4.23; *1 En.* 70.1–2; 81.6; *2 En.* 67B; *T. Iss.* 4.2; Philo *Mut. Nom.* 34; *Apoc. Abr.* 17; Josephus *Ant.* 1.85; 9.28; 1 Clem. 9.3; Ps.-Clem *Recog.* I.52.4; IV.12.1; IX.3.2; *Acts Pil.* 16.6; 25; Justin *Dial.* 19.3; Irenaeus *Adv. Haer.* IV.16.2; V.5.1; Tertullien *De Anim.* 50; Cyprian *De Mort.* 23. Esdras: *4 Ezra* 12[14].10–50. Baruch: *2 Bar.* 76; cf. 13.3; 25.1. Moses: Josephus *Ant.* 4.315–26; cf. *Ass. Mos.* 10.12.

71. A comprehensive and analytical survey of the role played by Elijah in Judaism up to the present times is found in Wiener, *The Prophet Elijah in the Development of Judaism*.

seen in Luke's work. In the Gospel (Lk. 7.26–28), John the Baptist is identified by Jesus as Elijah whereas here in Acts, the apostles view Jesus as Elijah (see *Commentary,* 1.9–11; cf. Lk. 4.25–27; 9.7–8, 54).[72] The apostles' perception is at odds with Jesus' teaching, for he clearly explained to his disciples that he had come to bring fire on the earth and that he would cause family division (Lk. 12.49–53); his comments echo the prophecy of Malachi who warned of both fire and family strife to accompany the 'day of the Lord' which would be preceded by the arrival of Elijah (Mal. 4.1–5), and they can consequently be interpreted as an attempt to show to his disciples that he was not Elijah.

The tradition that Elijah was taken away to heaven without dying (2 Kings 2) allows him to continue to be active throughout later generations as the messenger of God and, more particularly, as a mediator between men and God. It is essentially his human condition that allows him to know how to help those on earth and it could well be this aspect of his role that caused Jesus, as a man from God, to be identified with Elijah. He lives as a mysterious figure among the Jewish people as helper and guide, appearing unexpectedly in different sites of Palestine because he is not confined to the normal restrictions of time and space. Visions of Elijah (while dreaming or awake) are recounted in Jewish mystical literature in which he appears dressed in white and in which speaking is usually involved, as monologue or dialogue.[73] An important task which he accomplishes is to assist with the study and understanding of the Torah,[74] a task already alluded to in 1 Macc. 2.58. This is undoubtedly one of the reasons, or perhaps an outcome, of his frequent appearances in Rabbinic literature alongside the figure of Moses who was the giver of the Torah (cf. Mal. 4.4–5).[75] Other reasons exist for their association: Elijah like Moses is said by some to be of the tribe of the Levites;[76] they both dialogued directly with God on Mount Horeb (Exod. 3.1–4.17; 1 Kgs 19.9–18) and they both have a role in redemptive history.[77] It has already been seen in the com-

72. At Lk. 9.54, James and John ask Jesus if they should 'bid fire come down and consume [the Samaritans]' in a scene that thus closely mirrors the confrontation between the king of Samaria and Elijah related in 2 Kings 1, a further indication that the disciples understood Jesus to be Elijah.

73. Wiener, *The Prophet Elijah*, pp. 81–86.

74. Wiener, *ibid.*, pp. 54–55.

75. Wiener, *ibid.*, pp. 70–71 and see the Rabbinic references given there.

76. Wiener, *ibid.*, p. 45.

77. 'Moses as the ... first redeemer of Israel and Elijah as the prophet of the final redemption', Wiener, *ibid.*, p. 144.

mentary on 1.10 above that Elijah and Moses are the two men who talk with the apostles after the ascension of Jesus and that they were present on two previous occasions in association with Jesus. The appearance of Elijah on these occasions serves to demonstrate to Luke's addressees that Jesus is not Elijah, though how far the disciples understood that at the time is open to question.

When the narrative of the ascension of Jesus is compared with the account of the ascension of Elijah, a striking number of similarities can be seen.

Elijah in 2 Kings 2

1. Three stages of a preparatory journey, accompanied by his disciple, Elisha: Bethel, Jericho, Jordan (2 Kgs 2.2, 4, 6). The departure finally takes place on the far side of the Jordan, where Elijah had been fed by the ravens during the famine (1 Kgs 17.1–7)
2. The master is being taken (λαμβάνει) by the Lord from Elisha (2 Kgs 2.3, 5)
3. A final request from Elisha (2 Kgs 2.9)
4. The promise of a double measure of Elijah's spirit for Elisha (ἐν πνεύματί σου ἐπ' ἐμέ, 2 Kgs 2.9–10)
5. Elijah leaves as he talks (ἐλάλουν) with Elisha (2 Kgs 2.11)
6. Elijah is taken up (ἀνελήμφθη, 2 Kgs 2.9, 10, 11)
7. To heaven (εἰς τὸν οὐρανόν, 2 Kgs 2.11)
8. Elisha sees (ἐὰν ἴδῃς) Elijah go, following his instructions (2 Kgs 2.10, 12)
9. Elisha is told three times (2 Kgs 2.2, 4, 6) by Elijah to wait ('sit', κάθου) while he continues with the journey prepared for him by Yahweh. Elisha refuses on each occasion to wait. In contrast, after Elijah's departure, he 'sits' (ἐκάθετο) in Jericho while 50 servants of the prophets look for Elijah for three days, knowing that the search is pointless.

Jesus in Luke 24 and Acts 1

1. Three stages of a preparatory journey, accompanied by the apostles: Emmaus (= Bethel,[78] Lk. 24.13 D05), Jerusalem (Lk. 24.33, 36), Mount of Olives (Lk. 24.50, cf. Lk. 19.29; Acts 1.12). The departure finally takes place on the Mount of Olives, at Bethany where Jesus had been accustomed to stay during his last days of ministry in Jerusalem (Lk. 21.37)
2. Jesus, the master, is taken (ὑπέλαβεν) by the cloud from the apostles (1.9)

78. We discuss the identification of Emmaus as Bethel in 'Emmaous or Oulammaous?', pp. 23, 34–36.

3. The apostles' final request (1.6)
4. The Holy Spirit is promised to the apostles (τὴν ἐπαγγελίαν ... ἐφ' ὑμᾶς, Lk. 24.49; ἐπελθόντος τοῦ ἁγίου πνεύματος ἐφ' ὑμᾶς, Acts 1.5, 8)
5. Jesus leaves as he talks (εἰπών B03 / εἰπόντος αὐτοῦ D05) with the apostles (1.9)
6. Jesus is taken up (ἀνελήμφθη, 1.2, 11)
7. To heaven (εἰς τὸν οὐρανόν, 1.10, 11 x 2 D05 / x 3 B03)
8. The apostles watch him as he goes (βλεπόντων αὐτῶν, 1.9 B03, ἀτενίζοντες, 1.10, [ἐμ]βλέποντες, 1.11)
9. Jesus instructs the apostles to 'sit' (καθίσατε) in the city (Lk. 24.49); not to leave but to wait in Hierosoluma (Acts 1.4), while they wait for the Spirit. Instead of obeying Jesus, they set about choosing a twelfth apostle.

The intuitive knowledge of Elijah's disciple, Elisha, that his master was to be taken away before anyone had told him so, is a central element of that narrative in 2 Kings (2 Kgs 2.3, 5). From this it can be deduced that the apostles also realized when the last day of Jesus' life on earth had arrived and that it was this realization that prompted their questioning in Acts 1.6 (see *Commentary*, 1.6–7).

Since Luke has Jesus teach that he was not Elijah, it can be surmised that the reason Luke chose to align Jesus' ascension with that of Elijah was to show that it reflected the mentality of the apostles at that point. The purpose cannot be to convey an accurate theological truth since the events in Acts 1 and beyond contradict any identification of Jesus with Elijah. Indeed, among all the similarities that exist between the two ascension accounts, there is one striking difference: whereas 2 Kings 2 stresses from the outset how the Lord took Elijah away in a whirlwind (2 Kgs 2.1, 11), Acts 1 has Jesus be taken up by a cloud (1.9, more prominent in the D05 text).

The theme of the ascension of Jesus often receives detailed attention in exegetical studies.[79] Certainly the ascension of Jesus has a well-defined function in Luke's theology: to signal the end of Jesus' terrestrial activity and of his physical presence among the disciples. What is not so clear, is

79. The most complete is the monograph by G. Lohfink, *Die Himmelfahrt Jesu. Untersuchungen zu den Himmelfahrts– und Erhhöhungstexten bei Lukas* (München: Kösel-Verlag, 1971), see the review by F. Hahn in *Bib* 55 (1974), pp. 418–26. More recent, is the study by M.C. Parsons, *The Departure of Jesus in Luke-Acts: The Ascension Narratives in Context* (JSNTSup, 21; Sheffield: Sheffield Academic Press, 1987). See also the summary on this topic in E. Grässer, 'Acta-Forschung seit 1960, III', *TR* 42 (1977), pp. 4–6, and the excursus by Schneider, I, pp. 208–11.

the significance that Luke ascribes to it: is it meant to draw attention to a consequence of the resurrection, namely the glorification of Jesus by God as he places him at his right hand, or does it simply signal the end of a certain kind of earthly presence without any notions of glory? This question is intimately connected to a second problem, the nature of the return of Jesus promised to the disciples (1.11): is this to be a second coming heralding the arrival of the kingdom of God, or is it simply a reappearance as and when the circumstances require it?

With regard to the first question, the significance of the ascension, this is traditionally taken to represent the moment when Jesus was received into the glory of his Father. Certainly, Peter associates the resurrection and ascension with the exaltation of Jesus at the right hand of God (2.33; 5.31) and Stephen, too, speaks of him in these terms (7.55–56). But there is no evidence that this is Luke's concern at this point, although if Luke had wanted to confer on the ascension connotations of glory, it would have been very easy for him to do so. The setting lends itself to such a dramatic presentation, and yet he does not take advantage of it. The most spectacular element that he introduces into the scene is a cloud which merely serves to separate the sphere of God from that of men (1.9). Luke's purpose in describing the ascension is rather to signal that the time of Jesus' earthly ministry had come to an end. His departure had been anticipated as early as the scene of the transfiguration when Moses and Elijah spoke of 'his exodus that he was about to complete in Ierousalem' (Lk. 9.31).[80] Another allusion to it follows after the transfiguration scene as a 'taking up' (Lk. 9.51), using the same word as that found for the 'taking up' here at the ascension (Acts 1.11, and also 1.2). From that point onwards in Luke's Gospel, Jesus had set his face towards Ierousalem (Lk. 9.51, 53) and it is now at the ascension, when he is 'taken up' and leaves the apostles for the last time, that his 'exodus' is finally completed.

As for the second question about the return of Jesus, how that is viewed depends on the function attributed to Luke's account of the ascension. If his intention is understood as a wish to describe the moment when Jesus entered into glory, then the promise given by the two men to the apostles, that he will come back, can be taken as a reference to the second coming which Jesus himself described as his return in a cloud, in power and glory (Lk. 21.27; cf. 9.26), and to which Peter also makes less detailed reference

80. D05: εἰς, B03: ἐν. Cf. other instances in Acts D05 where εἰς is used to indicate that an event is to take place in a place following a journey towards it (Read-Heimerdinger, *The Bezan Text*, pp. 193–97).

(Acts 3.20). The qualification, then, that he will come 'thus, in the same way you saw him going to heaven' can be read as a reference to the cloud.[81] Attention has been drawn, however, to the absence of any mention of glory or exaltation in Luke's account of the ascension. The way he went to heaven was precisely without any drama or eschatological signs. True, a cloud obscured Jesus from the sight of the apostles but it was not used as a means to manifest either his glory or his power (unlike at the transfiguration, cf. Lk. 9.34). The return of Jesus as a triumphant Messiah is therefore most likely not what is meant here, even though the apostles cling to this hope in the first stages of their preaching (Acts 3.19–21).

As the story of Acts progresses, it becomes apparent that Jesus allowed himself to be seen by the apostles at critical points and these manifestations could indeed be construed as 'returns' of Jesus (see 10.13–15 and 11.7–9 [Peter]; 9.3–6 and 26.13–18 [Saul]; 18.9–10 and 23.11 [Paul]. At times, rather than appearing himself, he used his angel or an earthquake (see 5.19–20 [the apostles]; 8.26 [Philip]; 12.7–10, 11, 17 [Peter]; 16.26 [Paul and Silas]; 27.23–24 [Paul]). These appearances aside, however, Jesus will be present within the community and in their witnessing activity by means of his Spirit more than anything (see 13.2, 4 [Barnabas and Paul]; 16.6, 7 [Paul and Silas]; 19.1 D05 and 20.3 D05 [Paul]; 21.4 [Paul, in the presence of the 'we'-group]; 21.10–14 [Paul in the presence of the community of Philip and the 'we'-group]).

[c′] 1.12 *The Return of the Apostles to Ierousalem*

The relevance of the report of the apostles' movements in this verse and the next, also included briefly at the end of the Gospel (Lk. 24.52–53), can only be appreciated in the light of the events that follow in the next section of Acts. The setting of the scene corresponds to that of the third element [c] of the episode where Jesus gives his last orders to the apostles: ἀπὸ Ἱεροσολύμων μὴ χωρίζεσθαι, 'not to leave Hierosoluma' (1.4, neutral sense) // ὑπέστρεψαν εἰς Ἰερουσαλήμ, 'they returned to Ierousalem' (1.12, religious sense). The location is in the Temple in Jerusalem.

1.12 Luke stresses in this verse and the next, as he had already in the Gospel, that no sooner had Jesus left them than the apostles returned to the religious centre of Ierousalem and, in fact, to the Temple, as will be seen.

81. Barrett, I, p. 84; Bruce, *Acts*, p. 41; *Text*, p. 72; Conzelmann, p. 27, with an ample bibliography. Note, however, Haenchen's point, p. 150, n. 9, that the passage in Dan. 7.13 alluded to at Lk. 21.27, does *not* refer to the descent to earth of the Son of Man.

The conjunction that introduces their action, 'Then ...', shows that their return took place without any further ado and is also the concluding event of this episode.[82]

The form of the name for the capital used here, in contrast to Jesus' command 1.4, carries theological overtones (see *Commentary*, 1.4). At the end of the Gospel, Luke established that the apostles 'went back to Ierousalem with great (omit B03) joy' (Lk. 24.52), where 'they were continually in the Temple praising God' (Lk. 24.53). They apparently still perceived the Temple as their secure religious base, having not yet realized that the death of Jesus had brought about a total break with the institution of the Temple; this break had been evident in the tearing of the sanctuary curtain (Lk. 23.45), symbolizing an end to the Temple as a place for the presence of God.[83]

The first chapter of Acts presents the same attachment of the apostles to the Temple in spite of Jesus' attempt to distance them from it, this time using the symbol of the Mount of Olives and the sabbath's day journey. The Mount of Olives represents for Luke not only a place of refuge when Jesus became obliged to go into hiding (Lk. 21.37; 22.39, cf. *Excursus* 2), but also a place diametrically opposed to the Temple, 'the village opposite' (Lk. 19.30), that is, opposite Ierousalem (Lk. 19.28 D05; cf. Hierosoluma, B03).[84] At the end of his appearances to the disciples, 'he took them out (of Ierousalem) to Bethany', in other words to the mount called 'of Olives' (24.50, cf. Lk. 24.33). It is the place from which he had to complete his exodus to his Father (see Lk. 9.31, 51 and *Excursus* 2).

82. On this function of τότε, see Read-Heimerdinger, *The Bezan Text*, pp. 212–13.

83. The passive ἐσχίσθη refers to an action of God. The curtain that symbolically was torn in two was that which separated the holy place from the Holy of Holies in the Tabernacle, i.e. the curtain that separated the sacred from the profane was removed. More than a premonition of the destruction of the Temple (I.H. Marshall, *The Gospel of Luke* [New International Greek Testament Commentary; Paternoster: Exeter, 1978], p. 875), what it symbolizes here is the definitive separation from this religious institution and what was to become the Church. Cf. J.B. Green, 'The Demise of the Temple as "Cultural Centre" in Luke-Acts: An Exploration of the Rending of the Temple Veil', *RB* 101–104 (1994), pp. 495–515.

84. τὴν κατέναντι κώμην designates 'Ierousalem' as the 'village opposite', that is, as a place ruled by an ideology opposed to that of Jesus and that hemmed in its inhabitants. Cf. the same contrast at Lk. 21.37: 'in the day' – 'in the Temple' / 'at night' (not D05) – 'on the mount called of Olives'; 22.39–40 (note the term ἐπὶ τοῦ τόπου, which recurs in the Gospel as a technical term, more marked in D05 without the article, for the true place of prayer in contrast with the Temple).

The narrative of Acts is complementary to the Gospel in the way that it underlines the apostles' attitude of total respect with regard to the Jewish law. Not only does it insist on the apostles' return to the Jewish institution (the Hebrew-derived spelling, Ierousalem, is mentioned twice in the same sentence) but also on the distance between the holy city and the Mount of Olives which was that of a sabbath day's journey.[85] The significance of this detail is not to draw attention to a literal measurement (2,000 cubits), even less to underline the apostles' respect for the law of the sabbath, since by any calculation the day of Jesus' ascension was not a sabbath. The point of including the distance would seem to derive from the fact that the measurement of a 'Sabbath day's journey' was based on the distance between the Tabernacle at the centre of the Jewish encampment in the wilderness and the outer limits of the camp. In travelling back to Ierousalem (as opposed to Hierosoluma), the apostles are returning to the centre of Jewish worship, law and authority.[86] This respect for the Jewish authority is in striking contrast to the fact that Jesus had been put to death as a 'transgressor' of the law (Lk. 22.37).

[d′] 1.13 *The List of the Eleven in the Upper Room*

The movements of the apostles continue to be recorded, picking up the theme of waiting from the first part (in [c]: περιμένειν, 'to wait for' [1.4] the Father's promise // καταμένοντες, 'they stayed waiting' [1.13] but at the same time anticipating an action that will go against Jesus' order). The cause of their disobedience is quietly hinted at in the incompleteness of the list of the remaining apostles which will push them to take action rather than continue to wait for the Holy Spirit. The list of only eleven apostles in 1.13 recalls, as far as the Bezan text of the parallel element [d] (1.6) is concerned, their insistent questioning of Jesus about the restoration of the twelfth member of their group. The correspondance between the two elements in the AT is less strong.

1.13 In parallel with the periphrastic construction at the end of the Gospel, 'They *were* continually in the Temple *praising* God' (Lk. 24.53), there is now another periphrastic phrase, 'when they entered (Ierousalem), they

85. For the distance and the regulations involved, see T.S. Kepler, 'Sabbath Day's Journey' (*Interpreter's Dictionary of the Bible*. (G.A. Buttrick [ed.]; Nashville, TN: Abingdon, 1962), IV, p. 141; Strack and Billerbeck, II, pp. 590–94; Barrett, I, pp. 85–86. See also Lohfink, *Die Himmelfahrt*, p. 207.

86. Cf.. Read-Heimerdinger and Rius-Camps, 'Emmaous or Oulammaous?', pp. 35–36.

went up to the upper room where they *stayed waiting*'.[87] The article before 'upper room',[88] not mentioned in Acts until now, designates the meeting place as a known location. In view of the LXX use of the phrase to designate a room in the Temple (1 Chron. 28.11, 20 (some MSS); 2 Chron. 3.9; Jer. 20.2; Ezek. 41.7), the 'upper room' can be understood here as referring to a room in the Temple as a place of meeting for the community. Far from contradicting the information he gave in the Gospel, Luke uses two complementary words to designate the same place: the 'Temple' underlines the sacredness of the place, the 'upper room', its elevation as a high place;[89] both express the apostles' attachment to the place for its religious authority and permanence.

This reference to the upper room, accompanied as it is by the verb 'go up', confirms that the Eleven whose names follow remain firmly fixed in the centre of the Jewish institution, cherishing their belief in their importance (as the next episode will demonstrate) but in disobedience to the command that Jesus had given to them to stay in Hierosoluma, the city without any religious connotations (cf. 1.4). It is highly significant that in his Gospel, at the outset of the section that relates Jesus' final journey, Luke emphasized Jesus' plan to 'confront Ierousalem' (Lk. 9.51, 53) and

87. Periphrastic constructions in Greek are typically used to draw attention to an action, B-D-R, §353, 2a.

88. τὸ ὑπερῷον, with the article, has not been mentioned previously. Zahn, followed by other authors, suggest that it refers to τὸ κατάλυμα described as 'a large room (μέγα, B03; 'a room', οἶκον D05) with couches, on the upper storey (ἀνάγαιον)' at Lk. 22.11–12, where Jesus celebrated Passover with his disciples; others take it to mean an unspecified and unknown location somewhere in the city (Barrett, I, pp. 86–87; Haenchen, p. 152 and n. 2). Others still situate it in the Temple, believing the locality of Acts to correspond to that of Lk. 24.52–53 (Bruce, *Text*, p. 73). The comments of B.B. Thurston are worthy of note ('Τὸ ὑπερῷον in Acts i.13', *ExpT* 80 [1968–9], pp. 21–22): 'If the ὑπερῷον is identified with the place of meeting on the day of Pentecost as it is by Jerome (*Ep.* CIII; cf. Origen, *C. Cel.* VIII.22), then it goes quite naturally that there was no room in a private home (...) But, since they [the apostles] were all Jews the Temple would be open to them and it would correspond to their location on the day of Pentecost. If they agreed upon a ὑπερῷον built into the walls of the outer court, it would present no problem with regard to the women who accompanied them. A chamber east of the court of the women is a possibility.' Cf. 1 Chron. 28.11, 20 LXX. As for the construction of D05, ἀνέβησαν εἰς τὸ ὑπερῷον οὗ ἦσαν καταμένοντες, cf. Acts 2.2; 12.12; 20.8; Lk. 4.16, 17; 23.53. καταμένω is the perfective form of μένω and corresponds to the order of Jesus to περιμένειν τὴν ἐπαγγελίαν (Acts 1.4).

89. ὑπερῷον is a derivative of ὑπέρ + –ώϊος, an ending that indicates 'belonging to', like πατρῷος, μητρῷος.

he placed right at the centre of that section Jesus' severe denunciation of the Jewish institution personified by the holy city (Lk. 13.34–35: 'Ierousalem, Ierousalem...'); but he then passed over in silence Jesus' entry into the city (cf. Mk 11.11), making him enter directly into the Temple in order to bring his denunciation to a head there (Lk. 19.45–46).[90] It is in utter contrast to their Master's example that the apostles not only 'returned to Ierousalem' but no sooner were they in the city than they 'went up' directly to the 'upper room' where they settled themselves to wait.

In the list of the Eleven, there are certain notable differences compared with the details and the order of the list of the Twelve given at the point when they were originally chosen by Jesus (Lk. 6.13). Furthermore, between the two texts of Acts 1.13, there are other slight but important differences. In contrast to the Gospel list, where all the names are given on an equal basis (each linked with the conjunction 'and', as also are the names of the seven Hellenists in the list that is given later in Acts [6.5]), the list here follows something of a hierarchical pattern. In the AT, there is a group of four, headed by Peter who alone carries the article in Greek and is called not by his original name but by the name that Jesus had given him, followed by John, James and Andrew; then two pairs and a group of three. The text of D05 arranges the list in four pairs – the first one singled out by use of the article – and a final group of three. The natural pairs of brothers who were in Jesus' first list – Peter and Andrew, James and John – have been replaced by two pairs whose importance derives from their roles of leadership: Peter and John who repeatedly appear in the early part of Acts as representatives of the group (3.1, 3, 11; 4.13, 19; 8.14); then come James and Andrew. Thomas has moved up the ranks, coming after Philip with whom he makes the third pair; the fourth pair is made up of Bartholomew and Matthew; the list is then brought to a close with three people whose names are qualified in order to distinguish them from the others of the same name in the original list of the Twelve: James (son) of Alphaeus not to be confused with James (son) of Zebedee, Simon the Zealot not to be confused with Simon Peter, and Judas (son) of James not to be confused with Judas Iscariot whose name is obviously missing.

The present list reflects changes – some insignificant, others more important – that have taken place among the apostles since they have first began functioning as a group. Peter (referred to by his new name), John

90. Cf. J. Rius-Camps, 'Lc 10,25–18,30: Una perfecta estructura concèntrica dins la Secció del Viatge (9,51–19,46)', *RCatT* 8 (1983), pp. 283–358 (esp. 337–38; 355).

and James already appear in that order in two important scenes of the Gospel (Lk. 8.51; 9.28). Andrew, it would seem, does not share the same leadership qualities as the other three who head the Gospel list, his place having been taken by John. The group of three names at the end of the list highlights its incompleteness. The original significance that Jesus had conferred on the apostles when he established them as representatives of Israel after the leaders of the nation of Israel had rejected him (Lk. 6.11), has completely disappeared with the death of Judas. It is for this reason that Luke underlines, on the one hand, that Judas was one of the Twelve (Lk. 22.3, 47) and, on the other, that there are only Eleven of them left (Lk. 24.9, 33).

[e′] 1.14 *The Women (and Children, D05) and Members of Jesus' Family*
The record of the presence of not only the families of the apostles but also of Jesus signals the underlying reason why the command of Jesus, given in the corresponding element [e] 1.7–8, has not yet been properly understood. Far from sharing his universal outlook, the group made up of the people described in this verse together with the previous one is closed and restricted to those who consider themselves to be the chosen representatives of Israel and the blood family of the Messiah.

1.14 Another periphrastic construction, 'they were all persevering in unanimity in prayer', echoes the two periphrastic verbs of Lk. 24.53 and Acts 1.13 that draw attention to the action of the apostles (see on 1.13 above). Luke thereby emphasizes the identification of the disciples with the Temple institution, citing their faithfulness in prayer. In view of their Temple association, this prayer, in the singular with the article but with no other qualification (see, in contrast, Lk. 6.12; Acts 12.5), can be no other than formal Jewish prayer (cf. 2.42, 46; 3.1; 6.4; 10.4, 9; 16.13, 16). The mention of prayer in this verse complements the details provided in the other two periphrastic clauses: the first highlights the place, the Temple (ἐν τῷ ἱερῷ); the second, the elevated location (εἰς τὸ ὑπερῷον); the third, the goal which was prayer (τῇ προσευχῇ). All three elements work together to underline an attitude of determination and perseverance. For the time being, the contents of this praying is not specified but the following episode will help to clarify the matter.

On this occasion the Eleven are not alone. They are accompanied by some women, and in addition Mary, the mother of Jesus and his brothers. The reference to these women, mentioned without the article in the Vaticanus text, could be taken to mean the female members of the group of disciples who accompanied Jesus and amongst whom were the first witnesses to his resurrection. Alternatively, the phrase can be seen as a set expression, meaning 'with their wives' (a similar expression is found at 21.5 [D05 *lac.*]).[91] The Bezan text avoids any ambiguity by including the article before 'women' which, since it does not refer to any previously mentioned group, has a possessive function and also includes a mention of children: 'their women and children'. Accordingly, the female disciples mentioned in the Gospel as being among Jesus' followers (Lk. 8.2–3; 23.55; 24.10) are not present in this scene and there is consequently no suggestion that they have any part in what Acts 1.15–26 will show to be a mistaken way of thinking.

In addition to the women (and children, D05), there is another group composed of 'Mary, the mother of Jesus and his brothers'. Luke does not give the names of his brothers but in Mk 6.3 they are given as James, Joses, Judas and Simon. Though it cannot be ruled out that 'brothers' actually means 'cousins', in line with Semitic custom, in the next scene it becomes apparent that there is a significance in the presence of Jesus' brothers (1.15–26). Luke omits any mention of them in the Nazareth episode parallel to Mark's (Lk. 4.22–24; cf. Mk 6.1–4) but they do appear later, standing 'outside' (Lk. 8.19–20) at precisely the moment when Jesus has been revealing the secrets of his kingdom to his disciples (Lk. 8.10) whom he considers to be his real mother and brothers (Lk. 8.21). They may well have been present at the crucifixion (Lk. 23.49), but they are not mentioned in any of the resurrection appearances, although Paul knows of an appearance of Jesus to James, his brother (1 Cor. 15.7). Luke would not have omitted to mention this appearance, supposing that he had known about it, had he wanted to portray Jesus' brothers as integrated into the post-Easter community of disciples.

In the book of Acts, the brothers of Jesus will not reappear as such. When Peter leaves Jerusalem (12.17), it is suddenly made known that James has become the head of the Jerusalem church (or at least a part of it), a position that he will maintain and consolidate as the narrative continues (cf. 12.17b; 15.13; 21.18). James' rise to authority, which will lead in the end to his remaining alone at the helm of the Jerusalem church, can only be explained by reason of his relationship to Jesus.[92]

91. Cf. Zerwick and Grosvenor, *Analysis*, p. 351. See also W. Thiele, 'Eine Bemerkung zu Act 1,14', *ZNW* 53 (1962), pp. 110–11.

92. Cf. P.-A. Bernheim, *James, Brother of Jesus* (London: SCM Press, 1997), esp. pp. 190–222; R. Eisenman, *James, the Brother of Jesus. Recovering the True History of Early Christianity* (London: Faber and Faber, 1997), esp. pp. 93–213; 217–408.

The way that Luke connects Jesus' brothers to the Eleven with the women (or with their wives and children) is to be noted: they join in the united gathering as they pray and persevere in the Temple/upper room, but as newcomers. Their position at the end of the list is highly significant, the more so that this list is intended to prepare the formal meeting in the following episode. On two counts, it says something about the way in which Luke views them:

1. The mention of Mary, the mother of Jesus, together with the wives (and children), at the centre of the list, establishes a clear separation between the eleven proper names and the nameless brethren. The four components of the list are set in a chiastic pattern: eleven apostles (named) / their wives (and children) (unnamed) // Mary, the mother of Jesus (named) / his brothers (unnamed). The mention of the name of Mary confers a certain realism on this second group, whereas the fact of not naming the brothers is typical of the understated way in which Luke generally brings a character (and even a group or a locality) on stage in the second book. As the unnamed participants acquire importance, the mention of their name reflects their changing status; in this case, it will be James who is later named.
2. Since the women and children in the centre of the list would not have had the right to vote in the next episode, the brothers' position in the list can be considered to set them in opposition to the apostles. They occupy, in fact, the place left vacant by Judas (see *Critical Apparatus*).

For the time being, Luke does not explain what prompted the family of Jesus to join the apostolic group but there is an explanation for their presence that can be deduced from the context of this scene and the one to follow. The place left vacant by Judas with his death has not been filled by Jesus before his departure, despite the insistence of the Eleven (Acts 1.6 D05). Neither have they seen their hopes realized of being granted the Spirit of the Prophet as he was going up to heaven. Now they are back once more in Ierousalem, waiting for the promise of the Spirit to be accomplished and still clinging to their belief that the Twelve must in some respect at least be brought back to the full number. It is against that backdrop that Luke depicts them as suddenly surrounded by a larger and new group made up of the closest relatives of Jesus who had always kept their distance from him.

The picture, for all its brevity, is detailed: the two groups remained resolutely in the upper room, waiting together to receive the promise that God had made to the patriarchs and had renewed at intervals to the people of Israel throughout their history, just as Jesus had renewed it to his apostles, equating it with the gift of the Holy Spirit. The promise that all the previous generations had been waiting for is about to be realized in all its fullness. Now, though, the brothers of Jesus are present; if they receive the promise as well, their undeniable family ties with the Messiah will be reinforced and, problematically, could well be a challenge to any rights to represent him to which the Eleven can lay claim. The difficulty for the apostles is that, with the death of Judas, they could be perceived as having lost their privileged status of representatives of the twelve tribes of Israel. The reaction of the Eleven will not be long in becoming apparent.

I. THE REPLACEMENT OF THE TWELFTH APOSTLE
1.15–26

Overview

Following the introductory hinge sequence of Luke's second volume, 1.1–14, whose purpose was to tie together the two volumes by developing themes from the last chapter of the Gospel, the new material of the book of Acts proper is now introduced. The first half of the book (1.15–12.25) divides into two parts: 1.15–5.42 describes the beginnings of the first Jewish Jesus-believing church, the church of Jerusalem; the story then moves on in 6.1–12.25 to relate the creation of the first Christian church, the church of Antioch. The first of these two parts is divided into four sections: I. 1.15–26; II. 2.1–47; III. 3.1–4.35; IV. 4.36–5.42.

Structure and Themes

The first action of the apostles that Luke reports is the replacement of the missing member of their group, Judas. The differences in the telling of the story by the two texts are of the greatest significance for they illustrate the differences in the underlying intentions of the respective narrators. In the familiar version, the AT, the account is a factual one and relates with approval the decision of the apostles to bring their number back to twelve. Not so the Bezan text in which the narrator distances himself from the apostles' action, showing how it was prompted by their own fears and dictated by their inadequate grasp of Jesus' teaching. His lack of endorsement of their behaviour sets the tone for the rest of the book in which he constantly assesses the leaders of the Church against the example of Jesus. It will be of the utmost importance when reading the Bezan text to be open to noticing this critical appreciation of those who are more usually thought of as models of Christian thought and conduct.

The episode consists of four elements arranged in the parallel formation of a b // a′ b′:

[a] 1.15–22 Peter's speech, made up of [α] an Exposition (1.16–17, 20) setting out scriptural justification for the need to replace Judas and [β]

a Parenesis (1.21–22). 1.18–19 constitutes a Narrative aside set into Peter's speech.

[b] 1.23 The presentation of the candidates, by Peter (D05) / the assembly (B03)

[a′] 1.24–25 The prayer of the assembly, asking God to designate the preferred candidate

[b′] 1.26 The result of the election, and the addition of Matthias to (D05) / his incorporation into (B03) the apostolic group

Translation

Codex Bezae D05

[a] **1.15** It was in these days that Peter stood up in the midst of the disciples and said (for the number of people united in purpose was metaphorically 120):

16 'Brethren, it is necessary that this Scripture should be fulfilled which the Holy Spirit spoke beforehand through the mouth of David, concerning Judas who acted as guide for those who arrested Jesus, **17** because he had been numbered among us, the one who was allotted a portion of this ministry and apostleship.'

(**18** Now this Judas, what he did was to buy a field with the reward of his unrighteousness, and he fell headlong and burst in the middle and all his guts were poured out, **19** an incident which became known to all the inhabitants of Jerusalem so that that field was called in their language Akeldamach, which means "Field of Blood".)

20 'For it is written in the book of Psalms:

"Let his estate remain deserted and let there be no-one living in it,

and let another take his office."

21 It is necessary, therefore, that of the men who accompanied us throughout the period of time during which the Lord Jesus Christ went in and out among us, **22** starting from the baptism

Codex Vaticanus B03

1.15 In these days Peter stood up in the midst of the brethren and said (there was a metaphorical number of people united in purpose of 120):

16 'Brethren, it was necessary that the Scripture should be fulfilled which the Holy Spirit spoke beforehand through the mouth of David, concerning Judas who acted as guide for those who arrested Jesus, **17** because he had been numbered among us and he was allotted a portion of this ministry and apostleship.'

(**18** Now this Judas, what he did was to buy a field with the reward of unrighteousness, and he fell headlong and burst in the middle and all his guts were poured out **19** and it became known to all the inhabitants of Jerusalem so that that field was called in their language Akeldamach, which means "Field of Blood".)

20 'For it is written in the book of Psalms:

"Let his estate remain deserted, and let no-one live in it,

and let another take his office."

21 It is necessary, therefore, that of the men who accompanied us during all the time that the Lord Jesus went in and out among us, **22** starting from the baptism of John until the day

	of John until the day when he was taken up from us, one of them should become a witness of his resurrection with us.’	when he was taken up from us, one of them should become a witness of his resurrection with us.’
[b]	**23** He put forward two people, Joseph whom they called Barnabas and who had the name of Righteous, and Matthias.	**23** They put forward two people, Joseph whom they called Barsabbas and who had the name of Righteous, and Matthias.
[a′]	**24** And they prayed and said, ‘Lord who knows all hearts, show us whom you choose out of these two **25** to take up the place of this apostolic ministry from which Judas turned aside to go to his own place.’	**24** And they prayed and said, ‘You Lord, who knows all hearts, show which one you choose out of these two **25** to take the place of this ministry and apostleship from which Judas turned aside to go to his own place’.
[b′]	**26** They gave their votes and the vote fell on Matthias and he was reckoned with the Twelve apostles.	**26** They gave lots for them and the lot fell on Matthias and he was co-opted with the Eleven apostles.

Critical Apparatus

1.15 Καὶ ἐν (ταῖς ἡμέραις ταύταις) B ℵ *rell* || Ἐν δέ D, *In diebus autem* (+ d^{G}) *his* E d a^{2} e p^{2} sy^{hmg} sa mae; Aug.

The opening clause, which establishes a close link between the present scene and the previous one (‘In those very days’), is more neutral in B03 (καί is a simple conjunction of equivalence) than in D05 where δέ indicates a new development and signals, in this instance the beginning proper of Luke’s second volume. For discussion of the reading of καί, see Levinsohn, *Textual Connections*, pp. 104–106; see also Read-Heimerdinger, *The Bezan Text*, pp. 204–206, on the differences between the function of these sentence conjunctions in Acts.

Πέτρος B ℵ *rell* || ὁ Π. D; Chr (ms of Oxford).

The omission of the article causes Peter to be distinguished from the rest of ‘the brethren’. D05 treats the intervention by Peter more as an expected procedure, picking up from the mention of him at 1.12 and recognizing him from the outset as the acknowledged leader of the group of disciples. See Heimerdinger and Levinsohn, ‘The Use of the Definite Article before Names of People’, p. 36.

(ἐν μέσῳ τῶν) ἀδελφῶν B ℵ A C* 33^{vid}. 88. 104. 467. 522. 927^{c}. 945. 1175. 2298 *pc* vg sa bo aeth || μαθητῶν D d (C^{3vid}) E H^{2} Ψ 049. 056. 1. 81. 614. 1739. 2412. 2495 𝔐 e gig p t sy mae geo; Cyp Aug.

According to Metzger, D05 would have substituted ἀδελφῶν with μαθητῶν 'to prevent the reader from confusing these "brethren" with the brothers of Jesus' (*Commentary*, p. 247; cf. Wilcox, 'The Judas-Tradition in Acts 1.15–26', p. 440). Another explanation is also possible: the AT has substituted μαθητῶν for ἀδελφῶν under the influence of the initial greeting of the speech (Ἄνδρες ἀδελφοί). The preference for one term rather than the other is not without significance. According to B03, Peter stood up to speak in the midst of *all the brethren*, described as 120 in the next clause. In D05, on the other hand, he addressed *the disciples* in particular, that is, Jesus' first disciples to whom he is about to propose his plan and who symbolically were of the number 120 (cf. 1.21–22).

ἦν τε B ℵ A E H^2 Ψ 049. 33. 81. 88. 614. 945. 1241. 1739. 2412. 2495 𝔐, *praeterea* d* | ἦν δέ C D^G 056. 876. 1108. 1611. 1765. 2138 d^G e gig p vg sy; Cyp Aug || ἦν γάρ D* vg^{ms}.

This is probably an instance in B03 of confusion between δέ and τε (see B-D-R, §443, n. 4; Read-Heimerdinger, *The Bezan Text*, pp. 210–11). The particle δέ introduces a parenthetical remark about the number of people present in preparation for Peter's speech, for it is the minimum number required for a decision of the kind advocated by Peter to be taken (Wilcox, 'Judas Tradition', p. 440). γάρ also introduces a parenthetical comment but one that looks back rather than forward (on the difference between δέ and γάρ, see Levinsohn, *Textual Connections*, p. 91); the mention of the number of people thus explains that Peter's decision to speak is connected to the number of people present.

ὄχλος B ℵ *rell* || ὁ ὄχλ. D.

The article before ὄχλος in D05 allows it to refer back to the list of 1.13. The articular phrase 'the crowd of names' further recalls the Hebrew expression used repeatedly in the instructions for the first census of Israel as recorded in Numbers 1 (במספר שמות, 'according to the number of names'). This allusion, together with other indications discussed in the *Commentary*, suggests that Luke intends to show that in this scene an actualization of the first census of Israel takes place.

ὡς (ἑκατόν) B D E H^2 049. 056. 33. 614. 1611. 1739^s. 2412. 2495 𝔐; Chr || ὡσεί ℵ A C Ψ 81. 88. 104. 181. 326. 468. 915. 917. 1175. 1642. 1646. 1838. 1875. 1891. 1898. 2492 *pc*, *quasi* d.

The particle ὡς/ὡσεί has the function of signalling a metaphor (rather than an approximate figure) in both texts. The use of ὡς before a number is a practice shared by the other evangelists, but the use of ὡσεί before a number is found only in Luke. In Acts, the two particles constitute an example of the duality of language that Luke deliberately uses to communicate a fine distinction in the purpose of his metaphors (see *General Introduction*, §V.5): whereas ὡσεί insists on the metaphorical *nature* of the comparison, ὡς draws attention to the *origin* of the metaphor and the *point* of comparison. The metaphor in question is the number 120, which represents Israel in its entirety.

1.16 ἔδει B ℵ D^{A} *rell* || δεῖ D* d lat bo; Ir^{lat} Aug Cass.

B03 has the verb in the imperfect, alluding to the Scripture that has been tragically fulfilled with respect to Judas (περὶ Ἰούδα); it can be interpreted as relating either to his death, a death that Luke deals with in an editorial aside (opened with οὗτος μὲν οὖν, 1.18–19), or to his having acted as guide to those who took Jesus despite being part of the group of the Twelve (1.16–17): the passage that best fits the latter is Ps. 41.10, noted by $N\text{-}A^{27}$ in the margin. The verb in D05 is present, relating to a prophecy that has to be fulfilled today, that is, the replacement of Judas.

(τὴν γραφὴν) ταύτην D d C^{3} E Ψ 049. 056. 33. 614. 1611. 1739^{s}. 2412. 2495 𝔐 it vg^{ms} sy^{h} sa mae geo; Ir^{lat} Chr Aug Vig || *om.* B ℵ A C* H^{2} 81. 104. 323. 945. 1175 *al* vg sy^{p}; Eus.

The demonstrative of D05 anticipates the quotation of the Psalms; between the announcement and the quotation proper there is an editorial parenthesis (1.18–19), following the same literary procedure as in 1.15b. Luke introduces it as if it were all one quotation ('Because it is written in the book of the Psalms', 1.20), combining two Psalms without any linking word (Pss 68.26 and 108.8b LXX: cf. below, 1.20). According to D05, δεῖ οὖν of 1.21 serves to pick up the thread of the speech from the first δεῖ here in v. 16.

Ἰησοῦν B ℵ A C*; Eus | τὸν Ἰη. D C^{3} E H^{2} Ψ 049. 056. 33. 81. 614. 1739^{s}. 2147. 2412. 2495 𝔐.

The use of the article in D05 allows attention to centre not on the person of Jesus, a well-known figure who lives on in the memory of the community, but on Judas (without the article).

1.17 καὶ (ἔλαχεν) B ℵ D^{D} *rell*, *et* d || ὅς D*; Aug.

καί in B03 joins two causal clauses introduced – in good Greek style – with a single ὅτι. The relative pronoun in D05 differentiates between a first causal clause (the fact of having been counted among the Twelve *in the past*, conveyed by the periphrastic pluperf. pass.) and a second relative clause (the fact of having been *effectively* entrusted with the apostolic ministry, conveyed by the aor.), thus preparing for the double aspect of the prophecy: his place must remain empty, but his function must be assumed by another.

1.18 (ἀδικίας) αὐτοῦ D d t vg[ms] sy[h**] sa mae aeth; Eus Aug || *om.* B ℵ *rell.*

Unlike the other more general uses of ἀδικία (Lk. 13.27; 16.8, 9; 18.6; Acts 8.23), D05 makes this occurrence specific, 'of *his* unrighteousness', personifying in Judas the evil inherent in money (cf. Lk. 16.9, 11, 13).

1.19 (αὐτοῦ) καί B ℵ[2] *rell*, *et* d || ὃ καί D ℵ* (t) sy[p] bo; Aug.

B03 joins the two clauses of the parenthesis with καί, with the subject ('the deed') understood. The relative pronoun in D05 makes the subject explicit (Delebecque, *Les deux Actes*, p. 214) with καί having adverbial force, '[a deed] which *also* became known', suggesting a progression in time.

τῇ διαλέκτῳ αὐτῶν B* D d ℵ latt || τ. ἰδίᾳ διαλ. αὐτ. A B[2] C H[2] 049. 056. 69. 88. 1175. 1245. 2412. 2495 𝔐 | τ. ἰδ. αὐτ. διαλ. E Ψ 945. 1739.

The omission of ἰδίᾳ in D05 is shared by B03*. In the other two instances in the AT of Acts where the διάλεκτος is qualified by ἴδιος, D05 either changes the expression (2.6) or removes the adjective (2.8). The omission in some witnesses could be due to haplography (Metzger, *Commentary*, p. 248: ΤΗΙΔΙΑΔΙΑΛΕΚΤΩ). It is, of course, the 'Aramaic language' that is meant (cf. 21.40; 22.2; 26.14).

Ἀκελδαμάχ B 1175 *pc*; Eus | Ἀχελ- P[74vid] S A 81 *pc* (gig vg[st.ww]) vg[ms] | Ἀκελδαμά C Ψ 33. 1739[S] 𝔐 vg[cl] | Ἀκελδαιμάχ D (*aceldemach* d).

The closest transliteration of the Aramaic is the form with the second letter of the name as κ (cf. Barrett, I, p. 99 where, however, the form of D05 is wrongly given). On the purpose of the final consonant, see Metzger, *Commentary*, pp. 248–49.

1.20 μὴ ἔστω B ℵ D[C] *rell*; LXX || μὴ ᾖ D* d.

The B03 text harmonizes with Ps. 68.26 LXX. The change of the imperative to subjunctive by D05 could be a way of adapting the Scripture to suit the new situation better.

1.21 ἐν παντὶ χρόνῳ ᾧ B ℵ* *rell*, *in omni tempore quo* d[G] || ἐν π. τῷ χρ. ὡς (ᾧ D[s.m.]) D, *in omni tempore quoniam* d*.

The D05 text makes it clear that the candidate should have been with Jesus not intermittently but throughout 'all *the* period of time *during which*' (for ὡς as a time conjunction, see B-D-R, §455.2) Jesus 'came in' (baptism of John – investiture as Messiah) and 'went out' (ascension–final exodus); cf. 1.22; 10.37.

1.22 (Ἰησοῦς) Χριστός D d 876. 1108. 1611. 1765. 1838 *pc* sy[h] mae aeth; Aug || *om.* B ℵ *rell.*

The addition of Χριστός to the name of Jesus is by no means as characteristic a feature of the 'Western' text, and especially not of D05, as is commonly said (cf. Metzger, *Commentary*, p. 225–26, n. 12). In D05, the full title of Jesus only occurs in liturgical or formal contexts (see Read-Heimerdinger, *The Bezan Text*, pp. 272–74). Its presence here is an indication that Jesus is being referred to primarily in his Messianic function rather than as the human master of the disciples, an interpretation that is fully justified by the mention of his baptism immediately following. Furthermore, the context is a formal one (*Commentary*, 1.15) in which the inheritance of the Messiah is at stake. It is, therefore, inadequate to reject the D05 reading simply as a fondness for the full title of Jesus.

ἄχρι (τῆς ἡμέρας) ℵ A 81. 323. 945. 1175. 1739[s] *al* || ἕως B D *rell.*

Whilst ℵ01 reads ἄχρι, perhaps by assimilation with v. 2 (cf. Lk. 1.20; 17.27; Acts 1.2; 2.29; 23.1; 26.22), B03 and D05 read ἕως (cf. Lk. 11.50 D05; Acts 1.5 D05; 13.11 ἄχρι; 13.20 ὡς; 19.9 D05 614 *pc*).

1.23 ἔστησαν B ℵ D[A] *rell* || –σεν D* d gig; Aug.

The plural of B03 refers to the assembled members of the community. The singular of D05 means that Peter was alone in proposing the candidates. The singling out of the figure of Peter in D05, here as elsewhere, has been interpreted as betraying a later date when 'Peter rules the church with the authority of the monarchical episcopate' (Metzger, *Commentary*, p. 249; but cf. Barrett, I, p. 102). In fact, that Peter acted alone at this point is part of the meaning of the text in D05 (see Read-Heimerdinger, 'Barnabas in Acts', pp. 57, 60–61, and *Commentary*, 1.23).

Βαρσαββᾶν B P[74] ℵ A E Ψ 049. 1. 81. 104. 226*. 330. 945. 1175. 1739[c]. 1828. 1837. 1854 *pm* vg[st.ww] | –σαβᾶν C H[2] 056. 69. 88. 226[c]. 323. 440. 547. 614. 618. 927. 1241. 1243. 1245. 1270. 1505. 1611. 1646. 1739*. 2147. 2412. 2492. 2495 𝔐 vg[cl] || –ναβᾶν D d 6[s] *pc* it vg[mss].

The name cited by B03, meaning 'son of Shabba' (cf. Bruce, *Acts*, p. 50), reappears at 15.22. The alternative reading with one β translates as 'son of the elder'. The meaning of the D05 reading of βαρναβᾶν is explained at 4.36 as 'son of consolation /encouragement'. The confusion between Βαρναβας/Βαρσαββας is repeated at 4.36 in some MSS (181 *pc* [w]). According to D05, it is one and the same person who appears in both episodes; the sequence of tenses τὸν καλούμενον (1.21, pres.) – ὁ ἐπικληθείς (4.36, aor.) looks intentional, and is similar to the pattern used later with John 'Mark' at 12.12, 25.

1.24 σὺ (κύριε) B ℵ *rell* || *om.* D d 440. 1243.

In both texts, the vocative κύριε apparently refers to God (cf. 15.8 where the same title ὁ καρδιογνώστης is applied to God); the D05 text, by omitting σύ, takes away the ambiguity.

ἕνα **1.25** λαβεῖν B ℵ D[D] *rell*, *unum sumere* d || **1.25** ἀναλαβεῖν D* 330.

According to Boismard and Lamouille, II, p. 7: 'L'omission de ενα dans D n'est pas certaine; le scribe a peut-être lié ce mot au verbe suivant pour former αναλαβειν (v. 25)'; Parker, *Codex Bezae*, p. 151, objects: 'According to Boismard-Lamouille, ενα λαβειν stood in the exemplar of D. I see no reason why this should be so'. The reading of D05* does not have much support; not even d05 follows it (*unum sumere locum*). And yet, it cannot be due to a simple error of copying whereby a letter is changed (ΑΝΑΛΑΒΕΙΝ for ΕΝΑΛΑΒΕΙΝ), given that ΑΝΑ is found at the beginning of the line, followed by ΛΑΒΕΙΝ, and not at the end of the previous line which belongs to another clause. The reading of B03, in contrast, links ἕνα with the previous clause. See also the next *vl*.

τὸν τόπον (τῆς διακονίας ταύτης) B P[74] A C* Ψ || τόπον τόν D || τὸν κλῆρον ℵ C[2] E H[2] 049. 056. 33. 69. 81. 88. 104. 614. 945. 1175. 1241. 1739. 2412. 2495 𝔐.

The position of the article in D05 is additional evidence that the previous *vl* in D05 (ανα) is not a straightforward mistake but a variant reading of which account must be taken. In B03, the placing of ἕνα in the previous clause gives to λαβεῖν τὸν τόπον the meaning of 'to occupy *the* place' of the apostolic ministry previously occupied by Judas. ἕνα, however, is pleonastic, since it was enough to say ἀνάδειξον ὃν ἐξελέξω ἐκ τούτων τῶν δύο ('show which you have chosen out of these two') and its presence could be due to the influence of 1.22 (ἕνα τούτων). Furthermore, the reading of ἀναλαβεῖν τόπον in D05*, with the meaning of 'to take up a place' (which is then carefully defined with the article, 'that of this ministry and apostleship deserted by Judas'), is not just an exchange of persons in a specific place or task but the recovery of something that seemed to be irremediably lost. Not only that, but the absence of the article before τόπον shows clearly that Peter was not thinking about a substitution of Judas in every respect (τὸν τόπον of B03) but only with respect to his apostolic ministry (τόπον τὸν τῆς διακονίας ταύτης καὶ ἀποστολῆς D05), thereby leaving vacant the place Judas had held among the Twelve. See *Commentary* for extended discussion on the precise goal of the disciples' vote.

1.25 κλῆρον ℵ C[3] E 33. 1739[s] 𝔐 sy | τόπον B D P[74] A C* Ψ *pc* d lat sy[hmg] co; Did.

The ℵ01 reading is perhaps due to the influence of 1.17. The word play apparent in the reading of τόπον is thereby absent.

1.26 ἔδωκαν κλήρους αὐτοῖς B ℵ A C D[B] 33. 81. 88. 104. 915. 945. 1175. 1704. (1739[s]). 1891. 2298. 2344 *pc* vg co geo aeth; Chr[pt] | ἔδ. κλ. αὐτῆς 1739* || ἔδ. κλ. αὐτῶν D* d E 056. 69. 226. 323. 330. 440. 547. 614. 618. 927. 1241. 1243. 1270. 1505. 1611. 1646. 1828. 1837. 1854. 2412. 2495 𝔐 it vg[ms] sy[h]; Chr[pt] Aug | ἔδωκεν κλ. αὐτῶν H[2] Ψ 2492.

The procedure of 'giving lots' (ἔδωκαν κλήρους), common to both texts, is similar to that referred to in the Pentateuch in connection with the land that God gave to Israel and the distribution of the land among the tribes by Moses. It is quite different from the procedure of 'casting lots' (βάλλειν κλήρους) used in order to make a choice (see Rius-Camps, 'Las variantes, III', p. 63, nn. 34, 35). In the former expression, that found here, it is a matter of personal vote, as something one gives in favour of another. However, by a simple difference in the case of the pronoun, each text manages to convey a different intention: B03 refers to the people for whom the lots were given (αὐτοῖς); D05 confirms that it was a personal (αὐτῶν) vote given by the people present. It is not so much that the pronoun of the D05 is 'easier' (cf. Barrett, I, pp. 104–105) but that it communicates a different meaning.

ὁ κλῆρος B ℵ D^{B} *rell* || κλῆρος D*.

The absence of the article highlights the result of the vote; it also allows for the inconsequential nature of it.

συγκατεψηφίσθη B ℵ^{2} *rell* || συνεψηφίσθη D (–νε– *supra lineam)*, *dinumeratus est* d 1241; Cass | κατεψηφίσθη ℵ* 88.

The preposition συν – gives to the simple verb ψηφίζω, 'to count' (cf. Lk. 14.28), the meaning 'to reckon with'; this is the verb of D05, which reappears at 18.19. The preposition – κατα , also added to the verb, confers on it a perfective sense, 'to co-opt with' (B-A-G); this is the B03 reading, a New Testament hapax.

ἕνδεκα B ℵ *rell* || δώδεκα D d aeth; Eus Tert Aug Cass.

The variation in the choice of verb (see above) matches the different way in which each text numbers the group. Either Matthias was 'co-opted' to the actual group of 'the Eleven apostles' following the defection of Judas (B03); or he was 'counted' alongside the idealized group, symbolized by 'the Twelve apostles' (D05) (see *Commentary*, 1.26, and see on 1.2, n. 11).

Commentary

[a] 1.15–22 *Peter's Speech*

An introductory statement sets the scene for a speech that Peter makes while the assembled disciples and Jesus' family are waiting. The location is the upper room in Jerusalem.

This is the first of several speeches made by Peter in the course of the early chapters of Acts, which serve not only to advance the narrative but also to reveal the stages in the development in his thinking. It is important to distinguish the words Luke attributes to Peter from his own beliefs and ideas concerning the message of Jesus. Because Luke is concerned, in the Bezan text at least, to show that the apostles had to learn to detach themselves from their earlier beliefs and expectations where they did not match the teaching of Jesus, he reconstructs their speeches by means of words that reflect their mentality at the time (see *General Introduction*, §IX).

1.15 The variation in the conjunction used to link this episode to the previous section reveals from the outset that the episode is viewed differently by each of the texts. Whereas the AT, using καί, views the episode as belonging to preliminary information that prefaces the action proper of the book – which begins at 2.5 with the response to the outpouring of the Holy Spirit – Codex Bezae, using δέ, considers it to represent a new development, the preparatory material having been completed by 1.14. It is, therefore, not unexpected that in the Bezan text of this episode the significance and the consequences of choosing the replacement apostle are more forcefully brought out than in the AT.

The time of the action about to be taken is specified and is closely connected with the previous episode: 'In these days', that is, within the brief span of time that Jesus had indicated would elapse between his departure and the coming of the Holy Spirit (cf. 1.5, 'not long after these days'). Luke thereby gives the first signal that the action that follows is in opposition to Jesus' command to the apostles to remain inactive until the coming of the Spirit (see on 1.4, above). It is Peter, acting as spokesman for the Eleven, who ventures to interrupt the inactivity of the waiting period by addressing the assembly precisely during 'these days'. Furthermore, his action is introduced with 'having stood up' (ἀναστάς) in contrast to Jesus' order to 'stay seated' (καθίσατε, Lk. 24.48).

The variant 'brethren/disciples' is indicative of the relative attention to detail paid by the different texts. 'Brethren' (AT) anticipates the expression that will become the habitual one to designate the members of the believing community (cf. Acts 9.30; not to be confused with the expression 'Men, brethren' that opens speeches addressed to fellow Jews); 'disciples' (D05) forms a link with the expression generally used up to the end of the Gospel for the followers of Jesus and, coming as it does after the lists given in 1.13–14, it implicitly distinguishes the disciples from others of the group who have been portrayed until now as not being followers of Jesus, that is his family. Given that the comment is the narrator's, it is not likely that Luke would describe as 'brethren' all the members of a group within which were people who, although literally Jesus' family, were not considered by Jesus himself to be his brethren (cf. Lk. 8.20–21).

In the phrase that speaks of a 'number of people...', only the form of expression in Codex Bezae clearly communicates the purpose of the reference. The literal expression is 'the crowd of names'; it is one not used elsewhere in the New Testament, but it translates the Hebrew phrase used repeatedly in the opening chapter of the book of Numbers describing the first census of Israel taken by Moses and Aaron after their deliverance from Egypt (see *Critical Apparatus*). Each family in each tribe was counted, 'according to the crowd of names'.[1] This allusion to the census of Israel is reinforced by other details of the Acts passage which, together, cause the episode recorded in Acts to be seen as a re-enactment of the first occasion on which the people of Israel were gathered together and numbered by their tribes.

First, by using the article, the Bezan text allows 'the crowd of names' to be related back to something already mentioned in the narrative of Acts, that is, the list of the apostles set out in 1.13 who, as Peter will spell out in his speech, stand for the tribes of Israel. In the first census of Israel, the heads of the tribes of Israel are listed at the outset (Num. 1.4–16) and these leaders are said to have helped Moses and Aaron to call together the entire community (Num. 1.17–18). The problem for the apostles in Acts 1 is that the list is incomplete, there only being eleven names instead of twelve. By evoking Israel's first census in the present scene, Luke demonstrates how firmly the apostles' thinking is rooted within the historical context of Israel and makes clear the reason why the replacement for Judas is such an urgent and important matter: since the apostles represent the tribes of Israel, their twelfth member must be replaced in order to bring back the house of Israel to its full number. As the story of Acts unfolds, Luke will distance himself from the apostles' way of thinking, showing that the incompleteness of their group was no temporary problem, resolved by Peter, but a fundamental and permanent one that could not be rectified by the apostles' action and would never be so.

That the census background is relevant for Peter's plan is meanwhile confirmed by a second detail, the number 120. The figure is not to be understood literally but as a metaphorical number whose non-literal nature

1. Numbers 1 LXX uses ἀριθμός rather than the ὄχλος of Acts 1.15. However, the word used in the Hebrew text means 'crowd' and is usually translated by δῆμος in the LXX. This suggests that Luke was familiar with a non-Greek (i.e. Semitic) tradition on which he draws here.

is signalled by the preceding 'as if' (ὡς D05 and B03, but cf. ὡσεί ℵ01). Usually, when Luke prefaces numbers or analogies with ὡς, he does so in order to establish a link with a reference that is well-known to his addressees and that serves as a point of comparison. In this case, although an original scriptural reference cannot be identified there is evidence that by the time of Acts the number 120 was established in Jewish tradition as a reference to the whole people of Israel. It is recorded in Rabbinic documents as well as others from Qumran, that the presence of 120 adult males was the number necessary to represent Israel at formal gatherings.[2] Accordingly, it may be understood that here the figure 120 stands as another allusion to the house of Israel, and that it is mentioned to show that since Israel was fully represented the situation was right for such a formal event as the election of the twelfth representative of the tribes. Since it is not a literal number, the question of whether it includes the women and children is not relevant. Whether it includes the brothers of Jesus is a more important question which will be answered in a moment when other factors have been examined.

The AT mentions the number of people gathered in a simple parenthetical statement that looks forward to the speech that follows. In contrast, the Bezan text reveals the reason for, or the explanation of, Peter's move; in other words, there is a clear relation between the fact that the number gathered were 120 (Israel was represented) and Peter's decision to speak. This relation is signalled with another literary device, common to both texts, the placing of the redactional parenthetical clause between 'he said' and the beginning of the speech. The unusual position of the parenthesis draws attention to the importance of its contents and relates it to Peter's point of view rather than Luke's as narrator.

2. The requirement of ten men representing each of the twelve tribes in order for formal decisions to be taken is found in Jewish literature, e.g. *m. Sanh.* 1.6; *b. Sanh.* 17a; IQS 6.3f; IQSa 2.22. See Strack and Bilerbeck, II, pp. 594–95 and see M. Wilcox, 'The Judas-Tradition in Acts 1.15–26', *NTS* 19 (1973), pp. 438–52 (440). For discussion about whether this requirement is being referred to here, see Barrett, I, p. 96; Conzelmann, p. 28; Haenchen, p. 159, n. 3. Whether or not some legal regulation is being referred to, the point made by the mention of the number is that Israel is somehow represented. When or how 120 first became a symbol for Israel is not sure; throughout the writings of the Jewish Scriptures, the numbers 10 and 12 can be observed to occur in association with each other, beginning with the construction of the Temple where there were 12 oxen supporting the molten sea in which the priests washed and 10 lavers for the washing of the burnt offerings (2 Chron. 4.4–6; cf. 1 Kgs 7.39, 44).

The phrase 'united in purpose' is found several times in Acts where it acquires the force of a technical term meaning something more than simply 'in fellowship'.[3] (In the Gospel, it occurs only once at Lk. 17.35, with a more straightforward meaning, cf. Matt. 24.41). Of the six (seven D05) occurrences in Acts (1.15; 2.1, 44, 46 D05, 47; 4.26: 16.35 D05), all except the last two are located in the earliest days of the Jerusalem church; the expression always conveys the *purpose*[4] shared by those gathered, whether it be the original group of disciples as here in 1.15, or those who made up the first group of Jesus-believers (2.44, 46 D05) or those who were being added to the church day by day (2.47, especially in the Bezan text). On each occasion, as will be pointed at the appropriate places in the *Commentary*, the common purpose expressed by ἐπὶ τὸ αὐτό distinguishes the Jesus-believers from the wider Jewish community who do not share their outlook; the notion of solidarity is an inherent aspect of the meaning of the phrase when used in Acts.

In the present instance, it will soon become apparent that among the people gathered in the upper room, although they were all united by their attachment in one way or another to Jesus, there was an underlying tension. This is a theme that is developed as the story progresses. It relates to the conflict of the interests of the apostles, on the one hand, and the brothers of Jesus on the other. At this point in the narrative, following the final departure of Jesus, the latter would have had an interest as his blood-family in taking care that Jesus continued to be represented, but their interest is threatened by the existence of the Eleven. These men had been elected initially as a group of Twelve in order to represent the tribes of

3. A good survey of the discussion on meaning of ἐπὶ τὸ αὐτό is provided by P. Serra Zanetti, *ΕΝΩΣΙΣ ΕΠΙ ΤΟ ΑΥΤΟ*, I. *Un 'dossier' preliminare per lo studio dell'unità cristiana al'inizio del 2o secolo* (Bologna: Zanichelli, 1969), pp. 154–63, though we would disagree with the conclusion that in Acts it essentially denotes fellowship (p. 159). On the Semitic origins of the phrase, see M. Wilcox, *The Semitisms of Acts* (Oxford: Clarendon 1965), pp. 93–100.

4. This is the meaning understood by John Chrysostom, *In Act. Ap.* 2,33, Hom. VII: ὅτι δὲ οὐ τόπῳ ἦσαν ἐπὶ τὸ αὐτό, δῆλον ἐξ ὧν ἐπήγαγε λόγων 'καὶ πάντα εἶχον κοινά' (PG LX 65); likewise *In Ac. Ap.* 3,1, Hom. VIII (PG LX 69); and Theophilact, *In Ac. Ap.* 2,44: πάντες δὲ οἱ πιστεύσαντες ἦσαν ἐπὶ τὸ αὐτό· οὐ τόπῳ ἀλλὰ διαθέσει καὶ γνώμῃ καὶ τῇ πρὸς ἀλλήλους ἀδιαστάτῳ ὁμονοίᾳ καὶ στοργῇ. Concerning the pregnant meaning of the phrase ἐπὶ τὸ αὐτό with verbs of state or being, see É. Delebecque, 'Trois simples mots, chargés d'une lumière neuve (Actes des Apôtres, II, 47b)', *RevThom* 80 (1980), pp. 75–85: 'ἐπὶ τὸ αὐτό, après un verbe marquant l'état ou le séjour ... développe spontanément une valeur prégnante de ἐπί, qui implique une intention de réaliser' (p. 78).

Israel, by the express will of Jesus who chose the apostles 'moved by the Holy Spirit' (1.2; cf. Lk. 22.30), and they had been entrusted with a commission to bear witness to Jesus. However, their number had been rendered incomplete by the death of Judas and, according to Codex Bezae, Jesus had not seen fit to re-establish the full number when the apostles pressed him to 'restore (the twelfth tribe) into the kingdom of Israel' (see on 1.6–7 D05 above). The incompleteness of their number put the apostles in a difficult situation for their status as representatives of the tribes of Israel appeared to have been undermined. Furthermore, they had nothing to show for the authority Jesus had conferred on them before his death and his natural brothers could therefore challenge them and set themselves up in their place to continue the work of Jesus. Consequently, when Peter got up to speak, he did so in order to propose a solution to the problem the apostles faced. They were supported by a number of disciples who were of the same mind and who, implicitly, did not sympathize with the claims of the family of Jesus. The presence of their supporters becomes obvious from 1.21 onwards when Peter mentions 'men who accompanied us' and certain names are put forward. It is of this group of apostles and disciples that Luke says that they were 'united in purpose' and that they were symbolically of the number 120; the brothers of Jesus should not be thought as belonging to it.

The flow of the narrative established by the continuous tenses in 1.13–14 ('they stayed waiting' / 'they were continuing steadfastly together') is interrupted by the abruptness of Peter's action, 'he stood up'. At this point in the story a number of questions arise for the attentive reader. How could Peter have decided to move on to undertake some kind of action if he had properly understood Jesus' instruction to 'wait' for the coming of the Holy Spirit? Why, if it was as necessary to replace Judas as Peter thought, had Jesus himself not chosen a new apostle? If the election of the twelfth member was to be the responsibility of the disciples, why did they not at least wait a few more days so that they would have the benefit of the guidance of the Holy Spirit, as Jesus had for the election of the Twelve (1.2)?

The sudden introduction of Jesus' 'brothers' provides the explanation for Peter's hurried intervention. Luke's placing of them in final position in the list of 1.13–14 and at the close of the introductory sequence to the second volume is a highly effective way of drawing attention to their presence as 'a fly in the ointment'. Their appearance, once Jesus had gone away, represented a real threat to the group of the Eleven and justified the steps Peter took as leader of the apostles to prevent the brothers of Jesus from taking advantage of their family relationship with the Messiah in order to assert their superiority over the apostles. It needs to be constantly borne in mind that Peter was still operating within Jewish categories, which is why Luke insists so much on the significance of the '120'. If Peter's plan to restore the number of apostles works, when they receive the inheritance of the Spirit of Jesus they will be able to appeal to their status as representatives of Israel in order to take over his work.

Peter's speech is structured, like the rest of the speeches in Acts, according to the rules of oratory and consists of two parts: [α] the exposition, 1.16–17, 20, and [β] the parenesis, 1.19–21. Both are headed by the impersonal 'it was/is necessary', by which the speaker expresses his conviction that something was or would be fully within the plan of God.[5]

As in the introduction to this speech, Luke also inserts a redactional parenthesis into the exposition (1.18–19). It is introduced by means of a typically Lukan sentence connective (μὲν οὖν) which looks back to what has just been said (the reference to the prophecy in the Psalms relating to Judas in 1.16–17) at the same time as anticipating what is to follow, in this case the actual citation of the Scripture referred to.[6] The presence of two parenthetical comments by the narrator in such a short space of narrative is unusual in Acts but by intruding in this way Luke is able to put a certain distance between himself and Peter. The position of the comments produces a hiatus by interrupting firstly the flow of the narrative (1.15) then the flow of the argument (1.18). In the first case, it allows the narrator to show the thinking that prompted Peter to initiate Judas' replacement, and in the second, to indicate how Peter could justify his appeal to Scripture for what was, as will be seen, a proclamation of profound historical significance.

[α] 1.16–20 *Exposition: The Fulfilment of Scripture.*

1.16 Peter addresses the disciples, as is seen by the several references to 'we/us' in his speech (1.17, 21). That explains why he is able to launch

5. On the divine imperative see C.H. Cosgrove, 'The Divine δεῖ in Luke-Acts', *NovT* 26 (1984), pp. 168–90, and seeD.P. Moessner, 'The "Script" of the Scriptures in Acts: Suffering as God's "Plan" (βουλή) for the World for the "Release of Sins"', in B. Witherington (ed.), *History, Literature and Society in the Book of Acts* (Cambridge: Cambridge University Press, 1996), pp. 218–50.

6. The absence of a δέ clause corresponding to μὲν οὖν can be accounted for by the interruption of the parenthesis. In fact, it is the next step in Peter's argument at 1.20 that is equivalent to it.

straight into the question of Judas' replacement without any preamble. The family of Jesus remain in the background throughout the entire scene.

According to the AT, a scriptural prophecy has already been fulfilled ('it was necessary'); according to Codex Bezae, on the other hand, it is still to be accomplished ('it is necessary'). Although the difference may appear to be minimal, the interpretation of the passage changes quite markedly according to which text is followed.

Following the AT, what has already happened is the betrayal by Judas and/or his gruesome death. Since these are precisely the subject of the parenthesis in 1.17–18, it could look as if this aside is made by Peter, not the narrator.[7] For this reason, it has been suggested that the prophecy of David referred to is Ps. 41.9 (40.10 LXX) , where David laments that his friend has turned against him.[8] More often, it is assumed to be the combined quotation given in Acts 1.20 (Pss 68.26; 108.8 LXX).[9] The difficulty with the latter suggestion is that because the second part of 1.20 refers to the replacement of Judas, the prophecy quoted has so far only partially been fulfilled, in contradiction of 'it *was* necessary'. Needless to say, what Peter meant by saying that Scripture had to be fulfilled depends on which Scripture he was referring to.

Codex Bezae is much less ambiguous for it is clear that the citation from the Psalms is quoted at 1.20; Scripture is alluded to in order to validate an action that is about to be undertaken (the replacement of Judas) – it *is* necessary – and not to speak about his fate that has already been settled.

In referring to the arrest of Jesus, Judas is presented as the 'guide/ leader' of the troops who went to arrest Jesus in accordance with Luke's

7. Some commentators (e.g. Bruce, *Text*, pp. 76–77; *Acts*, pp. 484–89; Marshall, p. 64) correctly recognize that the parenthesis does not belong to Peter's speech.

8. Barrett, I, pp. 97, 100, who thus avoids having to say that part of the quotation of 1.20 is still to be accomplished. Wilcox ('The Judas-Tradition') takes the Scripture to be the allusion to *Targ. Gen.* 44.8 in 1.17, which he sees as confirmed by the ταύτην of D05; this, however, involves taking ὅτι of 1.17 as recitative and assumes the aside of 1.18–19 to be Peter's.

9. Bruce, *Acts*, p. 48; Haenchen, p. 159, n. 9; Marshall, p. 64; Moessner, 'The "script" of the Scriptures', pp. 223–25. The καί joining the two parts of the quotation from the Psalms in 1.20 is taken by UBS^4 and N-A^{27} as separating them rather than conjoining them. It is this interpretation that allows the two parts to be seen as referring to different times, the first past and the second future. See Schneider, I, p. 212, n. c and p. 218, n. 52.

Gospel (Lk. 22.47, 54,[10] but unlike the account of Mark). The Bezan text, in placing the (anaphoric) article before Jesus, treats him as known by the community.[11]

1.17 The precise reason that Peter gives to explain his declaration that Scripture must be fulfilled is of great significance. It is remarkable for what it reveals of the use made of traditional interpretations and teachings associated with the Jewish Scriptures by the followers of Jesus, for it is couched in a phrase used in the Palestinian targums to the book of Genesis (*Targ. Gen.* 44.18) that became a stereotyped definition of the patriarchs of Israel in the haggadic tradition of early Judaism. The Genesis episode in question is that in which the eleven sons of Jacob are on their way back to Israel with the grain they had gone to buy from Joseph in Egypt when the silver cup, hidden in Benjamin's sack by Joseph, is discovered by Joseph's servants. The brothers return to Egypt and Judah pleads on behalf of Benjamin. In the Palestinian targums of the text, his speech is considerably amplified as Judah vows to protect his youngest brother because he was a member of Jacob's family just like the rest of his brothers: 'he was numbered with us and will receive a portion and share with us in the division of the land'.[12]

Peter's use of the label shows how complete was the assimilation between the twelve apostles and the twelve patriarchs of Israel. It is no wonder the apostles thought that Judas had to be replaced for there could no more be only eleven apostles than there could have been eleven patriarchs. In his speech, Peter will show that he recognizes that to some extent

10. Unlike most MSS, which read προήρχετο at Lk. 22.47, D05 (and a few other MSS) have the verb προῆγεν for Judas' action, echoed by ἤγαγον for the action of the authorities in Lk. 22.54.

11. Jesus is typically treated as a known figure by Codex Bezae, see J. Heimerdinger and S.H. Levinsohn, 'The Use of the Definite Article before Names of People in the Greek Text of Acts with Particular Reference to Codex Bezae', *FN* 5 (1992), pp. 15–44 (22–23).

12. This use of targumic material was pointed out by Wilcox in 'The Judas-Tradition'. He is followed by E. Nellessen, 'Tradition und Schrift in der Perikope der Erwählung des Matthias (Apg 1:15–26)', *BZ* 19 (1975), pp. 205–18, and Marshall (p. 64), but otherwise the few commentators who note Wilcox's article tend to be dismissive (e.g., J. Dupont, ' ’ΑΝΕΛΗΜΦΘΗ (Actes 1,2)', *NTS* 8 (1962), pp.154–57. In fact, the use of targumic material here is typical of the use made of Jewish traditional material by Luke generally and by the representatives of the early Church in Acts, especially according to Codex Bezae, as fresh analyses of the text are continuing to demonstrate.

a change has taken place in their status as apostles since the death of Judas but he has yet to grasp the idea that with his desertion the status of the group as leaders of Israel had completely changed within the divine plan. Luke will only cause this fact to become apparent in the course of his story. At this stage, he continues to allow the mentality of the apostles to dominate the narrative, confining the expression of his own thoughts to the structure of the narrative framework, implicit comments and the narrative aside in 1.18–19.

The underlying importance and relevance of the Jewish Scriptures should be noted for, in the space of a brief passage, at least three different ways of drawing on them have been employed: the use of key phrases in 1.15 (the census in Num. 1); direct reference in 1.16, quoted in 1.20 (the prediction made by the Psalms); and the citation of a stereotyped description in 1.17 (the definition from the Genesis targum). It is telling that the comments that Luke makes in his aside (1.18–19), do not explain the targum reference but are limited to further details about Judas' death. This points to addressees who would have recognized the reference but who were not necessarily familiar with the implications of Judas' end.

That Peter was able to apply Scripture to a situation that had just arisen, and that was not foreseen by Jesus (see above on 1.6–8 and *Excursus* 1) is a sign of the authority that he assumed, or with which he was invested, in the company of the disciples. The step that was about to be taken was both profoundly new and radical in so far as it consisted in replacing one of the representatives of the patriarchs of Israel. It shows how thoroughly Peter and, presumably, his hearers (as well as Luke and his hearers) were steeped in Scripture and in traditions of interpretation; and it shows, furthermore, the extent to which Peter had grasped by now that Jesus had come to fulfil the Scriptures. In fact, though, his application of the Psalms to the case of Judas was wrong. Jesus himself never spoke about Judas falling away from the group of apostles, only betraying him, and subsequent events will demonstrate that Peter's appeal to the Psalms as prophetic justification for what he was about to do is not ratified by divine will (see on 1.23, 26 below). Appeal to Scripture was no more then than now a safeguard against misunderstanding God's plan.

1.18–19 *Narrative aside*. There is more to Luke's aim in his parenthesis than to simply inform his addressees about the factual details of the fate of Judas. His purpose is to establish the sin of Judas in terms of Jewish ethical teaching in order for Peter's use of the Psalms to be fully appreciated. He focuses on Judas' purchase of a field with the reward for his betrayal, which is described as 'unrighteousness' (ἀδικία), the opposite of the ethical ideal in the Jewish Scriptures of 'tsedek' (צדק), a perfect harmony of justice and compassion and a quality that will reappear as an epithet of Joseph at 1.23. Judas, who had 'left everything to follow him' (cf. Lk. 5.11, 28; 18.28) just like the other disciples of Jesus, now buys a field. This should not, incidentally, be thought of as the action of a solitary individual; such a purchase would necessarily involve all his family members and it is thus his family honour that is affected by both his deed and his death.

The death of Judas is presented by Luke as a punishment, taking up a term (πρηνής, headlong) from the LXX book of Wisdom (4.19) where the fate of the godless is described: 'They will become a dishonoured corpse..., he will throw them ... headlong (πρηνής)..., they will remain a desert to the end'.[13] When he explains to his audience that the field (χωρίον) where Judas died became known as the 'Field (χωρίον) of Blood' 'in their language' (Aramaic), he is not so much insisting on the Aramaic origin of the name Akeldamach as drawing attention to a play on words that works in Aramaic but not in Greek. According to a typical Jewish exegetical device, the consonants for the Aramaic word for 'portion' (הלק, in Greek κλῆρος, cf. 1.16) can be re-ordered to produce the word for 'field' (הקל).[14] Judas, in other words, exchanged his portion in the land of Israel for a field of blood.

Aramaic is referred to as the language of 'all the inhabitants of Ierousalem'. By employing the Hebrew-derived spelling for the city, an association is created by Luke between the Jewish institution for which Ierousalem stands and the death of Judas. He is not saying, however, that it was the Jews who had themselves made the connection, as the two passive verbs, 'became known' and 'was called', indicate. The point is rather that Judas serves as a warning to them, for Judas is the Greek form of the name Judah, the patriarch who was traditionally the leader and representative of his brethren;[15] Judas' betrayal of the Messiah is of the same nature

13. This parallel is pointed out by W. Klassen, *Judas. Betrayer or Friend of Jesus?* (London: SCM Press, 1996), pp. 168–69.

14. The play on words in Aramaic is presented by Wilcox, 'The Judas-Tradition', pp. 448–49. The significance of the name was presumably lost on anyone not familiar with Aramaic, which could account for the variant spelling in ℵ01, for example. The play on words is repeated at 1.25, though around a different term, τόπος. Again, ℵ01 loses the pun there with its alternative reading κλῆρος.

15. When Peter mentions the Scripture at the beginning of his speech in 1.16 he uses the phrase περὶ Ἰούδα which is the exact translation of the heading for the

as the betrayal of the unbelieving Jews (cf. 3.13–14; 7.52, and 1.16, 17 above).

1.20 *Exposition, continued.* The fusion of the two Psalms (69.25 [68.26 LXX] and 109.8 [108.8 LXX]) is announced at the beginning of the speech (1.16) as a single scriptural reference in the form of a prophecy placed by the Holy Spirit in the mouth of the Psalmist David.[16] The omission of the first hemistich of Ps. 109.8 ('May his days be few') is due precisely to the fact that Peter's purpose is not to use the Psalm to refer to the death of Judas but rather to the need to look for a substitute for the office left vacant with his desertion. The quotation in fact makes a clear distinction between 'his estate'[17] and 'his office': the first is to remain 'deserted'

section of the Hebrew Bible that begins at Gen. 44.18. Cf. R. Brawley, *Text to Text Pours Forth Speech* (Bloomington, Ind.: Indiana University Press, 1995), pp. 72–73; Wilcox 'The Judas-Tradition', p. 446. On Judah as the leader of the tribes, see L. Ginzberg, *The Legends of the Jews* (7 vols.; Philadelphia: The Jewish Publication Society of America, 11th edn, 1982), e.g. II, p. 32; III, p. 170; V, p. 333; VI, p. 245.

16. The καί of the third line or hemistich belongs to the quotation of LXX Ps. 108.8, rather than being a conjunction used by Peter to add a second reference to his first one. Peter was quite free, according to Jewish exegetical practices, to alter the original meaning of a scriptural passage by juxtaposing two or more texts, as well as introducing small changes, omitting a verse, a clause or a word, and so on: see I. Jacobs, *The Midrashic Process* (Cambridge: Cambridge University Press, 1995), pp. 1–20. In fact, the general mention here of the 'book of Psalms' (cf. Lk. 20.42), unlike the specific one by Paul at 13.33, allows the two quotations from the same book to be connected without distinguishing between them. D05, by reading ταύτην with τὴν γραφήν at 1.16, removes any doubt that the quotation is treated by Peter as a single one.

R.H. Fuller ('The Choice of Matthias', *SE* 6 [1973], pp. 140–46) compares the text of 1.20 with the corresponding text of the Psalms in the LXX and the MT, concluding that Luke quotes directly from the LXX and that, in consequence, Peter's entire speech, dependent as it is on the text of the quotation as given, is nothing more than Luke's fabrication; see also Haenchen, p. 161, who says that the interpretation in Acts 1 of Judas' fate is 'early Hellenistic Christian' and not Peter's because Peter would not have used the LXX. Such conclusions are unnecessary. First, while the actual composition of the speech may well be Lukan, Luke as narrator does not share Peter's views or his appeal to Scripture but rather, as explained at the beginning of the *Commentary* on this section, he puts words into his mouth that reflect his mentality at this stage. Secondly, the argument that the text of the Psalms quoted is LXX is ill-founded for there was considerable fluidity in the text of the Scriptures in first-century Judaism and the differences between MT and LXX could well have derived from alternative Aramaic versions of the Psalms (see Nellessen, 'Tradition und Schrift').

17. 'Estate' is perhaps too grand a word. Bruce (*Text*, p. 78) points out that in the papyri the meaning is 'a homestead'.

while the second is to be 'occupied' by another. In what follows, Peter will interpret the office as that of an apostle, as a transferable function; the estate, on the other hand, refers to something fixed that until now had been inhabited by Judas and that, although in theory could now be inhabited by another, has to remain deserted.

In his aside, Luke has explained that the field Judas bought had become a 'field of blood'. In Jewish terms, this meant that it was unfit for habitation (cf. Matthew's account, Matt. 27.7, where the field becomes a burial place). Attention was drawn (on 1.19 above) to the pun in the Aramaic name Akeldamach that expresses the idea that Judas had exchanged his share in the land of Israel for a field of blood. It is this field, his earthly portion in the land and all the family status and honour that go with it, that is to remain deserted (cf. Wis. 4.19, mentioned with reference to 1.18 above). According to Peter's explanation, Judas' apostolic office must, in contrast, be carried on, a necessity governed by his former position among the apostles who have to take over the leadership function of the twelve patriarchs of Israel (cf. 1.17).

The distinction drawn by Peter has several complex implications. In order to understand how far reaching these are, it is important to keep in mind the constant interplay between past and present in the role assigned to the apostles by Jesus. By insisting that Judas' estate is to be left vacant, Peter is demonstrating that the replacement of Judas will not be so complete a representative of the patriarch Judah as Judas himself had been – the assimilation between the apostles and the tribes of Israel will not continue to be as total as was originally intended with the election of the apostles by Jesus.[18] The dislocation of the apostolic group brought about by the circumstances surrounding Judas' death has caused the patriarchal group to be effectively reduced to the number eleven. The number of the apostles is to remain incomplete in so far as they stand for the twelve tribes of Israel as distinct family groups – the tribe of Judah is not to be replaced. In this way, Peter respects Jesus' refusal to restore the twelfth tribe back into the kingdom of Israel (see on 1.6 D05 above and *Excursus* 1) and shows an awareness that the historic identity of Israel is changing.

At the same time, it is important for Peter at this stage in his thinking that there should be twelve apostles to carry on the *function* or the work assigned to them as representatives of the patriarchs of Israel: they will continue to serve Israel as leaders and as witnesses to the Messiah even

18. The pluperfect form of the verb used by Peter in 1.17, ὅτι κατηριθμημένος ἦν ἐν ὑμῖν, indicates a state of affairs that already belongs to the past.

though the idea of individual tribal representativity has been abandoned. For this purpose, Judas has to be replaced but the new member will never be on a par with the Eleven. The difference between the status of the original Twelve appointed by Jesus and that of the new member who is about to be elected, will be signalled in the final verse of the episode by the wording of Codex Bezae. In this same text at 1.23, Peter will reveal his own preference for a candidate from the tribe of Levi, which was originally excluded from the leadership functions of the twelve other tribes (Num. 1.49; 2.33); this is in itself a sign of his openness to accept change within the deeply-rooted concepts of Israel's national identity as defined by the traditions of the Torah (see on 1.22, 26 below).

Peter's decision not to re-attribute Judas' estate to his replacement means that the ancient notion of the twelve tribes of Israel and of a division of the land among them has been superseded. Such an understanding tallies with the absence in Acts of any reference by any of the apostles to Jesus' words that in his kingdom they would rule over, or judge, the twelve tribes of Israel (cf. Lk. 22.30). It tallies similarly with the change in the contents of the promise of the Father, originally relating to a share of the land (Gen. 12.7) but now bestowed as the gift of the Holy Spirit.

(β) 1.21–22 *Parenesis: The conditions to be met by the candidates.*

1.21–22 In the parenetic part of his speech, Peter takes up from 1.16 (especially in the Bezan text where he referred to a present need) his idea that a replacement for Judas is necessary, as he goes on to set out his plan. The impersonal 'it is necessary' indicates that it enters into the plan of God – that is, in Peter's understanding – for the group he is addressing. In accordance with the (supposed) plan of God, he sets out the condition for Judas' successor and the basis on which the election will take place. He is insistent about the condition to be met by the candidates: they have to have been fellow-disciples from the beginning (baptism) to the end (ascension)[19] of the ministry not just of Jesus the man but of the Lord Jesus (Christ D05, where the full title underlines his Messianic status).[20] The condition is a reminder that the election of the Twelve had taken place right at the beginning of Jesus' ministry (Lk. 6.12–16). It carefully ex-

19. The verbs εἰσῆλθεν, ἐξῆλθεν are aorist because they do not represent linear time (cf. Barrett, I, p. 101) but specific moments when Jesus entered and left the earthly sphere.

20. On the variations in the use of christological titles in the text of Acts, see Read-Heimerdinger, *The Bezan Text*, pp. 254–74.

cludes the brothers of Jesus who were not his disciples during his lifetime, and prevents them from appealing to their family links with the Messiah in order to qualify as candidates.

Peter restricts the scope of the apostolic testimony to the fact of the resurrection of Jesus or, more specifically in Codex Bezae, of Jesus as Messiah. As far as the apostles were concerned, it was the resurrection that had convinced them that Jesus was the Messiah (cf. Lk. 24.31–45) and Peter focuses here on this fact instead of the broader contents of the witness that Jesus commanded them to bear (Lk. 24.46–48; cf. Acts 1.8, 'of me').[21] He has, in other words, given a narrower interpretation to the contents of the apostolic witness than that which Jesus intended. The witness of which he speaks is an active 'bearing of testimony', rather than a passive 'eye-witness' which many of the disciples could already claim to be, including even James the Lord's brother (see 1 Cor. 15.7).

[b] 1.23 *The Presentation of the Candidates*

1.23 The AT has the assembly intervene at this point as it proposes two suitable candidates. In Codex Bezae, it is Peter personally who takes this initiative. Of the successful candidate, it is only known that his name is Matthias and that he presumably fulfils the stipulated condition. No-one ever speaks of him again in Acts. In contrast, rather more is said of the candidate who is named first, Joseph. It is odd that the rejected candidate should be the one named first and described more fully than the other. The implication in the Bezan text of the fuller, positive information concerning Joseph is that he was Peter's preferred choice, and perhaps the same deduction should be made with reference to the assembly in the AT.

Joseph is cited along with two other names, the latter of which is the Latin form (Ἰοῦστος, *Justus*, cf. 18.7; Col. 4.11) of the Hebrew word 'tsadik' (צדיק, 'righteous'), the highest ethical quality that a Jew was exhorted to achieve.[22] According to Codex Bezae (by no means alone, see *Critical Apparatus*), Joseph is none other than Barnabas who next appears selling his field (note the contrast with Judas!) at 4.36. There, Luke provides the translation of this name, given by the apostles, as 'the Son of Encouragement'. The present participle here in 1.23 (lit. 'being called')

21. This detail is made much of by J. Jervell, *Luke and the People of God* (Minneapolis: Augsburg, 1972), pp. 82, 86, although he does not see the restriction as a negation of Jesus' command.

22. For some fine discussion of the meaning of this concept, see the writings of the French Jewish psychiatrist Henri Baruk, *Tsedek, droit hébraïque, et science de la paix* (Paris: Zikaron, 1970).

shows that he was currently acquiring this name, suggesting that he was then exercising the function of encourager. In contrast, the Latin name had been acquired in the past (aorist) and, apparently, in a Latin-speaking context since one could think he would otherwise have been given a Greek name (Δίκαιος, cf. 3.14; 7.52; 22.14). It is possible that this Joseph belonged to the circle of the Hellenistic disciples who appear in Luke's Gospel for he will be seen on several counts to have been from a group of Hellenistic origin. Luke is the only evangelist to speak of the call by Jesus of these 'seventy(-two) others' (Lk. 10.1), after the failure of the Twelve in Samaria (cf. Lk. 9.52–55).

The combination of the names, Joseph/Son of Encouragement/the Righteous is a clue that the first candidate is being assimilated with the patriarch Joseph because of what the latter had come to stand for (see *Excursus* 5). In the intertestamental literature, the character of Joseph is considerably developed compared with the biblical account: he is the heroic figure without fault or failing, the supreme example of a wise, pious and generous man, who displayed impeccable conduct even when living in exile in Egypt. He serves as an example of purity for Jews among foreigners, at the same time as being their representative.[23] Two titles are especially associated with him: Joseph the Righteous (cf. *4 Macc*. 2.2) and Joseph the Son of Encouragement (cf. Gen. 50.15–21 and the Rabbinic Midrash *Gen.R.C.* IX 2). The clue could hardly be more explicit for anyone who was familiar with the Joseph stories still developing in the first century:[24] the first of the candidates put forward to replace Judas is to be viewed as 'Joseph'.

The coincidence of epithets for Joseph the son of Jacob and Joseph Barnabas the Just is strong evidence that the name given in the Bezan text

23. For an excellent presentation of the Joseph traditions, see J. Kugel, 'The Case Against Joseph', in T. Abusch, J. Huehnergard and P. Steinkeller (eds.), *Lingering over Words* (Atlanta: Scholars Press, 1990), pp. 71–87; *In Potiphar's House* (Cambridge, MA.: Harvard University Press, 1994). J. Read-Heimerdinger in 'Barnabas in Acts. A Study of his Role in the Text of Codex Bezae' (*JSNT* 72 [1998], pp. 23–66), pp. 12–14, discusses the significance of the Joseph traditions for the narrative of Acts. See also Brawley, *Text to Text*, pp. 61–74.

24. The targums to the Pentateuch, the writings that are now referred to as apocryphal (especially the *Testaments of the Twelve Patriarchs*), together with the Jewish legends and traditions that emerged in the first century in such works as the romance *Joseph and Aseneth*, all bear ample witness to the importance that Joseph acquired in the history of Israel over the course of the centuries and that was continued by the Rabbinic teachings.

is correct.[25] It does, however, raise tricky questions concerning the reasons for which Barnabas was rejected (another similarity with Joseph), especially given his later leading role in the Christian community (again resembling the popularity and success of Joseph in the latter part of the Genesis story). It could well be this theological difficulty that prompted a change of name to Barsabbas, altogether less contentious. The text of Codex Bezae will maintain a stronger interest in Barnabas than the other manuscripts do, as will be seen more particularly in Acts 4, 11 and 15.

The reasons for Joseph's rejection will be considered at 1.26. Meanwhile, it can be noted that Joseph, otherwise known as Barnabas, was a native of Cyprus and a Levite (see 4.36). That information means that he was a Hellenistic Jew, not a Palestinian Jew as were all the other apostles. The fact that it is Peter, according to the Codex Bezae, who has a preference for the first candidate is a sign that he acknowledges a wider scope to the integrity of Israel beyond the confines of Palestine. The other apostles, and notably James the brother of Jesus, have greater difficulty in recognizing this, being more narrowly and rigidly nationalistic in their thinking and so reflecting conflicts within Judaism in the first century that will reappear in the narrative of Acts (see *General Introduction*, §X). In wanting to open up the apostleship to include a Jew from outside the land of Israel, Peter is at least showing some kind of understanding of the wider acceptance of the people in countries outside Israel displayed by Jesus during his ministry and in his final command. The greater readiness of Peter to change his old way of thinking is seen again on several occasions in the story of Acts (see *Commentary*, Acts 10–12). But the result of the election does not go in favour of his plan.

[a′] 1.24–25 *The Prayer of the Assembly*

The penultimate movement of the episode corresponds to the first [a] (Peter's speech) and contains three parallel elements in the prayer addressed to God by the disciples: 1. they ask him to choose 'one of these', ἕνα τούτων [a] // 'which one ... out of these two', ὃν ... ἐκ τούτων τῶν δύο (ἕνα B03) [a′]; 2. he will assume 'the portion of this ministry', τὸν κλῆρον τῆς διακονίας ταύτης [a] // 'the place of this ministry and

25. Not only does Luke attach significance to names for either their etymological sense (e.g. 'Jesus' = 'Saviour') or for what they say about the background of a person (Aramaic, Greek or Latin), but more than that, he attaches great importance to the meaning of second names or pseudonyms. He makes use of such names to stress a person's suitability for a certain function, for example.

apostleship', τὸν τόπον τῆς διακονίας ταύτης καὶ ἀποστολῆς [a′]; 3. this was a role fulfilled by 'Judas who acted as guide for those who arrested Jesus' [a], and thus it had been // 'abandoned by Judas' [a′].

1.24–25 According to Codex Bezae, prayer is made by the group of disciples, those addressed by Peter in 1.15; there is still no suggestion that the family of Jesus is involved. In contrast, according to the reading of 1.15 in the AT, the implication could be the whole gathering in the upper room who join in prayer. This prayer of election is parallel to the prayer Jesus made prior to the election of the Twelve (Lk. 6.12), to be distinguished from the type of investiture prayer accompanied by the laying on of hands that will occur later (cf. Acts 6.6 and 13.3). It was addressed to God[26] as 'Lord who knows the hearts of all' (cf. 15.8), in other words as he who judges not according to external appearances but according to the hidden intentions. The community were dependent on divine knowledge, being as they were without the discernment that Jesus had when he 'chose the apostles inspired by the Holy Spirit' (1.2) in the knowledge that apostleship was a divine appointment. Their prayer was that God should show them his preference for which of the two candidates best displayed the required qualities to take up the place left vacant by the death of Judas.

It is important to recognize the limited scope of the 'place' meant here. It was noted in the discussion on 1.20 that Peter appears to acknowledge something of the change in the status of Judas' replacement, compared with that of Judas, in so far as he equates one aspect of the place occupied by Judas among the apostles with the 'estate' that had to remain 'deserted'/'no-one living there' (1.20). He perseveres, nonetheless, with the idea that there must be twelve apostles to carry out the function assigned to them. It is the place 'of this apostolic ministry' (B03 'of this ministry and apostleship') deserted by Judas[27] that has to be filled. The position of the article after 'place' in the text of D05 makes it clear that Peter has in mind *only* the place of the ministry (1.17) associated with the function of

26. The use of the same verb as in 1.2 (ἐξελέξω/ἐξελέξατο) leads some to conclude that Jesus is meant by κύριε (Bruce, *Acts*, p. 50; cf. Barrett, I, p. 103; Marshall, p. 66). In omitting Σύ, D05 removes the note of familiarity and thus reduces the ambiguity of κύριε. The community obviously are aware that Jesus did not choose Judas' replacement while he was with the apostles and are unlikely therefore to ask him to do so now.

27. The phrase λαβεῖν τὸν τόπον τῆς διακονίας ταύτης καὶ ἀποστολῆς ἀφ' ἧς παρέβη Ἰούδας does not link the desertion of Judas with the τόπος, but with the διακονία and ἀποστολή: ἀφ' ἧς is feminine.

apostle or, using the terms of his quotation from the Psalms, the 'office' that had to be 'taken by another' (1.20). Judas has left vacant 'this place' to go 'to his own place', a euphemism to indicate 'the place of death'.[28] Just as in 1.18–19 where Luke introduced the pun in Aramaic that showed how Judas exchanged his share in the land of Israel for a field of death unfit for human habitation, so here there is a play on the word for 'place': Judas left his 'place' of apostolic ministry to go to his own 'place', that is of death.

[b′] 1.26 *The Result of the Election*

The last movement [b′] corresponds to the second [b] (1.23), the presentation of the candidates: 'He (Peter D05) / They (B03) put forward two people, Joseph..., and Matthias' // 'the vote fell on Matthias'.

1.26 It is important to see that the procedure of 'casting lots' here is different from the practice recorded in the Jewish Scriptures. The usual expression there, 'to cast lots',[29] signifies the operation of chance or divine intervention without any notion of a personal choice on the part of those who, for example, throw the pebbles. It does not have the same connotations as the expression used here by Luke, 'they gave lots',[30] which has the sense of giving something that necessitates a counting of the votes. In the AT, a formal vote is not excluded: 'they gave lots/votes *for them*'; in Codex Bezae, it is even made explicit: 'they gave *their* lots/votes'.[31] That is, the process is not an election, such as allows God to

28. Ignatius seems to refer to this euphemism in his *Letter to the Trallians* (5.1). See Bruce, *Acts*, p. 51, n. 75.

29. LXX: βάλλειν κλήρους (see 1 Chron. 25.8; 26.13, 14; Neh. 10.34 [35]; 11.1*vl*; Est. 3.7; Joel 3 [4].3; Hab. 1.11; Jon. 1.7; Nah. 3.10; Isa. 34.17). The use of 'give' lots is only found in the singular, διδόναι κλῆρον; the references are countless and chiefly refer to the distribution of land to the twelve tribes.

30. See E. Stauffer, 'Jüdisches Erbe im urchristlichen Kirchenrecht', *TLZ* 77 (1952), pp. 201–206 (204), who cites Est. 9.24 and DSM (=IQS) 6.16, 18, 22 as instances where the expression has the meaning of a ballot, not chance.

31. K.H. Rengstorf, 'Die Zuwahl des Matthias (Apg 1,15ff)', *ST* 15 (1961), pp. 53–56 (56, n. 36). Contra Haenchen, p. 162: '...in this election the human factor is excluded: it is God who is choosing'. The burden of proof is his. A. Jaubert ('L'élection de Matthias et le tirage au sort', *SE* 6 [1973], pp. 274–80) admits of a preliminary deliberation of the kind indicated at Qumran followed by an election by means of lots. Likewise, W.A. Beardslee, 'The Casting of Lots at Qumran', *NovT* 4 (1960), pp. 245–52: 'it appears possible that the tradition available to Luke used the term "Lot" in the sense of "decision by the community, reflecting God's decision", as at Qumran and

work through 'chance', but rather it is one carried out by the disciples themselves. It is significant that in the whole of the New Testament, after the giving of the Holy Spirit this procedure is not repeated (see the selection of Barnabas and Saul, 13.2).

The result of the election is difficult to reconcile with the Alexandrian reading of 1.23, for it is inexplicable that an assembly should be aware of the qualities of the first candidate ('the Righteous') and then without further comment go on to elect the second who was presented without any kind of qualifying description. If, on the other hand, it were Peter (as in the reading of Codex Bezae) who acknowledged the qualities of Joseph, ('Barnabas', a name that the apostles themselves gave him because of his gift of encouragement, as well as 'the Righteous') when he proposed him, then the decision of the disciples could be understood as a vote against Peter's preferred choice.

Why would some disciples refuse Barnabas? His Hellenistic origin in Cyprus was most probably a factor, as noted earlier with reference to 1.23, for a Diaspora Jew could be thought not to qualify for the role of a representative of Israel. That Peter could accept a Diaspora Jew on equal terms suggests that he had comprehended something of the scope of Jesus' mission outside the land, if not the people, of Israel. The conflict that would later erupt within the Jerusalem community between Hebrews and Hellenists (cf. 6.1) was, from the Bezan point of view, nothing new or strange but was latent from the beginning within the Jerusalem church. Joseph Barnabas' quality as a Levite may also have counted against him[32] in view of the underlying scene of the first census of Israel in Numbers (see on 1.15 above), where the detailed instructions specify that the Levites should have no portion of the land given to them as a tribe (Num. 1.49; 2.33).[33] Some at least among the disciples in Acts 1 continue to

that Luke has recast the story to make explicit the mechanism by which the divine will was revealed' (p. 250). The Qumran parallel is debatable, however: cf. Barrett, I, p. 104. Concerning the Western reading, see E. Grässer, 'Acta-Forschung seit 1960', *TR* 41 (1976), pp. 141–94 (173). R. Eckart (*Pseudo-Philo und Lukas*, Tübingen: J.C.B. Mohr [Paul Siebeck], 1994) discusses interesting similarities between the account of Acts and the book of Judges in Pseudo-Philo.

32. For fuller discussion of this point and the variant readings of 4.36, see Read-Heimerdinger, 'Barnabas in Acts', pp. 34–37, 61. In the *Testaments of the Twelve Patriarchs* there is a focus on the eschatological roles played by Judah and Levi that would be worth exploring for its possible bearing on Acts 1.15–26 where Judas and Barnabas could be construed as acting out the roles of Judah and Levi respectively.

33. The parallels between the LXX text of Num. 1.49 and 2.33 and the D05 text of Acts are worthy of note: τὴν φυλὴν τὴν Λευὶ (λευίτης τῷ γένει, 4.36).οὐ συνε–

reason in terms of the legal conditions of the Torah: a Levite cannot have a portion in Israel in the same way as the other tribes. Peter, on the other hand, has apparently grasped how the patriarchal system has been superseded, enabling him to claim that the portion of Judas/Judah in Israel was to remain vacant (see on 1.20 above).

According to the MSS that read Barnabas, choosing Matthias in preference to him will prove to have been the wrong choice and a negative reflection on the spiritual judgment of the disciples, for later in the narrative of Acts (13.2) the Holy Spirit will single out Barnabas for service – certainly, together with Saul but as the first-named of the pair. By his own personal qualities, he will effectively rise up as an example and a leader among the early followers of Jesus, without having to submit to any process of election other than the appointing by the Holy Spirit. He will only disappear from the narrative of Acts when Paul disagrees with him, a disagreement that is, given Barnabas' qualities, a telling comment on Paul's spiritual judgement, too (see *Commentary*, 15.36–40).

In place of the reading of all the Greek MSS 'and he was co-opted with the Eleven apostles', the Bezan text reads the last line as 'he was reckoned with the Twelve apostles',[34] thus making it is clear that, in line with Peter's plan (1.20), Matthias was not enlisted as a full member of the original apostolic group but only as a replacement to fill the 'office', leaving the patriarchal seat vacant. In the Bezan text, therefore, the replacement of Judas did not involve the full integration of Matthias into the group of the Twelve; the new member stood alongside that original group whose membership had been fixed by the choice of Jesus. No-one could fully replace any of those chosen members. To recapitulate the thinking of the apostles in Codex Bezae: only the original Twelve represented the twelve patriarchs of Israel; their representativity ceased after the death of Judas,

πισκέψῃ (συνεψηφίσθη, 1.26) καὶ τὸν ἀριθμὸν αὐτῶν οὐ λήμψῃ (ἀναλαβεῖν τόπον, 1.25) ἐν μέσῳ τῶν υἱῶν ᾿Ισραὴλ (ἐν μέσῳ τῶν μαθητῶν, 1.15).

34. The basic meaning of the verb ψηφίζω, 'to count with pebbles or fingers', comes to mean 'to count, calculate'. The B03 verb συγκαταψηφίζω is found elsewhere only in Plutarch, *Temistocles* 21, with the meaning of 'join in a vote to condemn' (B-A-G). The Vulgate translates it as 'adnumeratus est'; similarly the Syriac, Armenian, Coptic and Ethiopic versions. The preposition συγ – underlines the idea of a community decision and the preposition –κατα– confers on the verb a perfective nuance, 'completely, totally', two aspects which the English translation seeks to convey with 'co-opted with'. In contrast, the simpler reading συμψηφίζω of the Bezan text contains only the first nuance: in other words, the community of disciples took a joint decision that it should be Matthias who should take the position left vacant by Judas, he was 'reckoned with' the apostles.

but the apostles must still continue as a group of twelve members in order to imitate the established pattern of leadership of Israel. What has been done with the election of Matthias is sufficient to re-establish this pattern. Furthermore, with the vacant place filled, the family of Jesus has been prevented from laying claim to their family ties.

The more familiar text shows a different perspective, for the implication there is that Matthias was co-opted on an identical footing to the eleven other apostles. This leaves unexplained the contents of the first part of the curse that Peter applied to Judas (namely that his land was to remain unoccupied).

It is worth observing that in both forms of the text, it is not the number alone that is stressed (as in the Gospel, 'the Eleven' [cf. Lk. 24.9, 33] / 'the Twelve' [cf. Lk. 22.3, 47]), but rather the apostolic office: 'together with the Eleven/Twelve apostles (cf. 1.25: 'the place of this apostolic ministry'). This subtle detail reinforces the picture provided by the Bezan text by showing how the assembly reconstructs the apostolic group while leaving unoccupied Judas' role among the Twelve (1.17). By their scheme, the apostles have managed to respect the unwillingness of Jesus to reconstitute the group when they asked him to (1.6 D05) at the same time as avoiding the possibility of Jesus' brothers taking advantage of their blood relationship with him in order to insist on joining the leadership of Israel.

Excursus 3

The Replacement of Judas and its Consequences

The interweaving of the narrative text of 1.15–26 and the portion of direct speech contained within it has the function of depicting and commenting on the mentality of the apostles during the brief period of time that elapsed between Jesus leaving them and the Holy Spirit arriving. Luke skilfully uses his literary craft not only to relate an event that took place during these few days but also to express his evaluation of the motives and the reasoning that prompted the action. It is imperative to put aside from the very start of the book of Acts the traditional expectation that Luke's evaluation of the apostles will be always positive for, just as in the Gospel so too in Acts, Luke's treatment of Jesus' disciples is much more subtle and realistic than blanket approbation. In point of fact, the present episode constitutes the first link in a long chain of both positive and negative actions on the part of the apostolic group that will later lead to their final acceptance of the mission entrusted to them by Jesus. Failure to discern Luke's overall intention to portray the growth and development of the apostles, or confusing Luke's understanding of Jesus with the ideas and concepts expressed in the apostolic speeches, leads to Luke being attributed with theological notions of a Judaizing nature that do not fit with the universalizing message of Acts. The consequences of an incorrect understanding of Luke's procedures are especially serious when tackling the complex matter of the relationship between the Church and Israel in Acts. It is essentially this relationship that is at issue in 1.15–26.

It can be noticed that the election of Matthias (1.15–26) has been organized by Luke on the basis of the pattern established by the election of the Twelve (Lk. 6.12–16), but with some notable differences:

1. Both elections are preceded by a *prayer* addressed to God.
2. Election was made from an already *existing group.*
3. In both cases, the *apostolic function* is made explicit.
4. In both elections, *the betrayal of Judas* is alluded to.

But this parallelism is not uniform. There are contrasting elements, too, that stand in antithesis:

1. The *duration* of the prayer: Jesus' was lengthy (periphrastic construction) // the disciples' was brief (aorist)
2. The *means* of election: Jesus by the Holy Spirit // the 120 by prayer and the casting of votes
3. The *manner* of election: Jesus 'chose Twelve from among them' // Matthias 'was co-opted/reckoned with the eleven/twelve apostles'

The main consequence that follows from this election is that with the restoration of the number twelve the apostles have restricted the universal scope of the witness that Jesus had ordered them to bear.[35] They have held on to their understanding that the apostolic group was to mirror the patriarchal pattern of the leadership of Israel. Their understanding will conflict with the breadth of vision that was a distinguishing feature of Jesus' commission, for the disciples will find that they have erected a barrier to their witness with their failure to realize that Jesus did not intend the ancient pattern of leadership to be maintained after the death of Judas.

35. Cf. Rengstorf, 'Die Zuwahl des Matthias', p. 52, who shows a clear realization of this. In contrast, J.A. Jáuregui (*Testimonio – apostolado – misión. Justificación teológica del concepto lucano Apóstol – Testigo de la Resurrección. Análisis exegético de Act 1,15–26* [Bilbao: Universidad de Deusto, 1973]) summarizes very well the opinion of the majority of commentators: 'El aspecto de los Doce, como testigos ante el pueblo, con carácter jurídico va a ser el que más le interesa recalcar a Lucas en la reconstrucción de los Doce de los orígenes. Ellos representan el verdadero Israel desde los comienzos en su calidad de testigos con carácter jurídico' (p. 150).

Luke does not question Peter's good faith in setting out the plan to replace Judas, nor his desire to avoid a worse evil. He simply observes that he had not fully understood the universal scope of the Messiahship of Jesus after his ascension, as he had not understood it either during his lifetime. The third evangelist is precisely the one who underlines the most the total incomprehension of the Twelve faced with the project of the universal kingdom which Jesus wanted to establish with their collaboration (cf. Lk. 9.21–22, 32, 44–45, 46–48, 49–50, 54–55; 18.31–34; 22.21–23, 24–27, 31–34, 47–48, 54–62; 24.21–27, 46; Acts 1.6–8).

All in all, the number 'twelve', symbolizing Israel, will be scarcely of relevance in the book of Acts. Of the four (five D05) occurrences, only one (two D05) relate to the apostles. It will be helpful to briefly look at those occurrences alongside the occurrences of the number 'eleven'.

The first occurrence appears – as we have seen – in the Bezan text of 1.26. There, in place of the reading: 'and (Matthias) was co-opted with the *Eleven* apostles', D05 reads: 'he was reckoned with the *Twelve* apostles'. Codex Bezae thereby indicates that those gathered together never really envisaged a true inclusion of Matthias into the apostolic group – a move that would have contradicted Jesus' thinking – but rather they saw him as a simple addition to the original group which they still saw as having a validity despite the desertion of Judas.

In accordance with this view of Judas' replacement, the Bezan text specifies that at Pentecost, 'Peter, standing up with the *ten*, raised his voice...' (2.14); the usual text, on the other hand, persists in the idea that the group of the Twelve has been fully reconstituted with the inclusion of Matthias: 'Peter, standing with the *Eleven*, raised his voice...'.

Following these references, 'twelve' does not reappear until the beginning of Acts 6 (6.2). This passage is of prime importance for understanding the scope of the restoration of the apostolic group. For the first time, the audience of Acts is told explicitly that the Jerusalem community is not a united one (the Bezan text has already hinted at some tension by indicating that the 120 had preferred Matthias to Joseph 'Barnabas', a Hellenist), and not only that, but that it is composed of Hebrews and Hellenists with the former disregarding the weaker and less advantaged members (6.1: the Hellenistic widows). The nature of the distinction will be examined in detail in the *Commentary*, 6.1–6. Meanwhile, it is sufficient to note that the Twelve call together all the Hellenistic community, inviting them to organize themselves on the basis of the number seven, a number with universal connotations (6.2–6). The reason why this passage is so significant that it marks the end of the domination of the Twelve and the beginning of their downfall. They will no longer appear as the successors of the patriarchs of Israel. It is not by chance that from the time of this conflict (although the exact time is not specified) James the brother of the Lord takes up the reins of the Jerusalem church.

The other three occurrences of the number 'twelve' (7.8; 19.7; 24.11) do not relate to the apostles but are references to the twelve tribes of Israel. They are either direct or are based on analogy. In the case of Stephen's speech, the reference is to 'the twelve patriarchs' who are the origin of the analogy drawn upon in the other two occurrences. Thus, in 19.7 Luke specifies that the first disciples who were the founding members of the church of Ephesus were 'altogether as twelve men'; the particle before the number, ὡσεὶ δώδεκα, signals the metaphorical nature of the comparison (cf. the discussion in the *Critical Apparatus* on its occurrence at 1.14 in א01). At 19.7, Luke's intention is to express the fact that the church has been founded on a judaizing basis (baptism of John, 12 members). At 24.11, Paul defends himself in front of the Roman governor inviting him to check personally that 'I spent no more than twelve days in Jerusalem from the time I went up there to participate in the worship (of the Temple)', where the number of days[36] just like the religious name Ἰερουσαλήμ and the participle προσκυνήσων establish a connection with the twelve tribes of Israel, whereby Luke underlines the attitude of the total, and even aggressive, respect of Paul towards the institutions of Israel.

36. See J. Rius-Camps, *El camino de Pablo a la misión de los paganos* (Madrid: Cristiandad, 1984), p. 271, n. 610.

II. THE OUTPOURING OF THE HOLY SPIRIT
2.1–47

General Overview

Now that the apostolic leadership has been brought back to its full number with the replacement of the twelfth member, the narrative moves on from its close focus on the group of the apostles and their associates to consider them in a wider setting. With the arrival of the Holy Spirit, it is this group that will form the core of the first community of Jewish Jesus-believers, the church of Jerusalem.

There are four sequences in this section, the latter serving as a summary to the narrative so far:

[A] 2.1–4 The first outpouring of the Holy Spirit
[B] 2.5–13 The reaction of the people in Jerusalem to the manifestation of the Spirit
[B′] 2.14–40 Peter's two-part response and its outcome
[A′] 2.41–47 The first summary: the way of life of the Jerusalem church

[A] 2.1–4 *The First Outpouring of the Holy Spirit*

Overwiew

The moment has come for the fulfilment of the promise of the Holy Spirit, announced by Jesus before his ascension (1.4–5). The action takes place in Jerusalem.

Structure and Themes
The first sequence is made up of four elements:

[a] 2.1 The gathering of the apostle-led group
[b] 2.2 The sound of the wind, precursor of the Holy Spirit
[b′] 2.3 The appearance of tongues of fire, representing the Spirit
[a′] 2.4 The filling of the group with the Spirit

Translation

	Codex Bezae D05	*Codex Vaticanus B03*
[a]	**2.1** And it happened in those days that the day of Pentecost was drawing to a close, they being all united in purpose,	**2.1** When the day of Pentecost was drawing to a close, they were all together united in purpose,
[b]	**2** and suddenly there it came, a sound from heaven like that of a wind, a violent one, being driven in and it filled all the house where they were sitting.	**2** and suddenly there was a sound from heaven like that of a violent wind being driven in and it filled the whole house where they were seated.
[b′]	**3** And there appeared to them tongues as if of fire, which were being divided and then they sat on each person individually,	**3** And there appeared to them tongues as if of fire, which were being divided, and it sat on each person individually,
[a′]	**4** and they were all filled with the Holy Spirit and each began to talk in other tongues as the Spirit gave them the means to utter proclamations.	**4** and they were all filled with the Holy Spirit and they began to talk in other tongues as the Spirit gave them the means to utter proclamations.

Critical Apparatus

2.1 Καὶ ἐν τῷ συμπληροῦσθαι B ℵ *rell* || Καὶ ἐγένετο ἐν ταῖς ἡμέραις ἐκείναις τοῦ συμπληροῦσθαι D d.

B03 links the outpouring of the Holy Spirit to the previous episode with a simple καί. Indeed, in this text, all the incidents from the beginning of the book up to 2.5 are conjoined in a similar way, as if they were being grouped together as preparatory material for the action of the book that begins with the reaction of the people to the Spirit-filled disciples in 2.5 (introduced with δέ; see *Critical Apparatus*, 1.15; Levinsohn, *Textual Connections*, p. 106). D05, on the other hand, presented the appointment of the replacement apostle as the start of the action of the book (1.15 D05, δέ), and links this section to the previous one by setting it within the same time framework (the time of the early episodes in Acts is a preoccupation of the Bezan text, cf. 2.41 D05; 3.1 D05; 6.1 D05, Read-Heimerdinger, *The Bezan Text*, pp. 103–107). The timing of this scene is of greater importance for D05 than B03 given that according to D05 Jesus had already specified that the Spirit would be received within the period between his ascension and Pentecost (1.5 D05).

The dative expression of B03 could mean either a) that the counting of the days up to Pentecost had come to an end, or b) that the first day of Pentecost, the most important of the seven-day festival, was coming to an end having begun at sunset the previous evening. The latter is more likely in view of the present infinitive with its durative aspect (cf. Lk. 9.51 B03). Various interpretations of the genitival infinitive construction of D05 could be considered: a) the genitive is dependent on ἐν ταῖς ἡμέραις ἐκείναις, so 'it happened in those days of the arrival of the day of Pentecost' (Delebecque, *Ascension*, pp. 84–86; Ropes, *The Text of Acts*, p. 10), anticipating the main clause beginning καὶ ἰδοὺ ἐγένετο ἄφνω; this formula has a partial parallel in the Jewish Scriptures (Ruth 1.1) but it involves taking συνπληροῦσθαι as meaning 'arrive'; b) the genitival infinitive expresses purpose, so 'in order to fulfil the day of Pentecost', i.e. fulfil the promise that had been made by Jesus concerning it (1.5 D05) but, in fact, Jesus' promise was not attached strictly to the day of Pentecost; c) the genitive is to be taken as a nominative, with the infinitive the subject of ἐγένετο (Robertson, *Grammar,* p. 1067), so 'there came about in those days the completion of the day of Pentecost', i.e the day was drawing to a close. This option best concords with the narrator's intention in D05 of showing how the disciples had caused the promise to be delayed to the last minute by their action of appointing a replacement for Judas.

ἦσαν πάντες (–ℵ*) ὁμοῦ B ℵ^2 A C* 81. 323. 945. 1704 *pc*, *erant simul omnes* d latt sy co || ὄντων αὐτῶν πάντων D sy^p sa mae.

In B03, 'they were all together' is the main clause of this introductory sentence, with the time of the event a secondary consideration. In D05, both the timing (see above) and the gathering of the group are circumstances that prepares for the arrival of the Spirit in the next clause.

2.2 (καὶ) ἰδού D mae; Cyr^{pt} || *om.* B ℵ *rell* d.

More than a dramatic declaration, echoing the Semitic phrase found in scriptural narratives, καὶ ἰδού has the function of presenting the scene through the eyes of the participants, from their psychological stance.

πνοῆς βιαίας B ℵ *rell* || βιαίας πνοῆς D d 383. 917. 945. 1874. 2495 *pc.*

In Luke's writing, placing the adjective in front of an anarthrous noun has the effect of highlighting it because it is not the usual order (Read-Heimerdinger, *The Bezan Text,* p. 90). Attention is thus drawn in D05 to the force necessary to prepare the arrival of the Spirit; at the same time, the emphatic word order may serve as a device intended to recall the manifestation of divine power to Elijah on Mount Horeb (1 Kgs 19.11).

ὅλον (τὸν οἶκον) B ℵ *rell* | *totam* d || πάντα D.

Both ὅλος (entirety) and πᾶς (totality) are found in Acts qualifying οἶκος (ὅλος 7.10; 18.8; πᾶς 2.36; 10.2 [D05 *lac.*]; 11.14; 16.15 D05) where the noun is used in each case in the figurative sense of household/family. If the meaning of οἶκος here is understood as literal, ὅλος conveys better the idea that the wind filled the entire building ('through and through'). If, on the other hand, οἶκος represents something more than the material building, πᾶς would express the totality of that entity.

(ἦσαν) καθήμενοι B ℵ *rell* || καθεζόμενοι D C.

κάθημαι suggests a fixed position of inactivity (cf. 2 Kgs 1.9; 2.2, 4, 6; Jon. 4.5). καθέζομαι, in contrast, is durative and expresses the disciples' attitude of ongoing waiting.

2.3 ὡσεὶ πυρός B D d ℵ^2 *rell* || πυρός ℵ*.

Without ὡσεί, ℵ01 omits the metaphorical aspect of the fire.

καὶ ἐκάθισεν B ℵ^2 81. 88. 453. 1175 *pc*, *et sedit* d; (PsDion) CyrJ | ἐκάθισέν τε P^{74vid} A C^2 E H^2 Ψ 049. 056. 1. 33. 614. 945. 1245. 1611. 1739^s. 2412. 2495 𝔐 | ἐκάθισεν δέ C* || καί (– D$^{s.m.}$) ἐκάθισάν τε D* | καὶ ἐκάθισαν ℵ* sy; Eus.

The singular verb of B03 could refer to each of the tongues (Zerwick and Grosvenor, *Analysis*, p. 353) or could anticipate the mention of the Holy Spirit; it is less likely that it refers to the fire. On the face of it, the plural looks like a simple *lectio facilior* but the complexity of the *vll* suggests that the issue is more complicated than that. The double connective of D05 underlines the intimate connection between the tongues appearing to the disciples (ὤφθησαν αὐτοῖς) and sitting on them (καὶ ἐκάθισάν τε), a link that is more forceful when one bears in mind that in D05 this scene is being described from the point of view of the participants (see on 1.2 above).

2.4 ἤρξαντο B D^A *rell* || ἤρξατο D.

This *vl* is similar to the previous one, but with D05 reading the singular in this instance. The insistence on the individual speakers is unexpected in view of the plural verb with πάντες in the previous line and αὐτοῖς in the following one.

Commentary

[a] 2.1 *The Gathering of the Apostle-led Group*

2.1 The characters on stage as this new scene opens are the same as those of the previous episode, in other words the group of '120' (approximate [B03] or metaphorical [D05]) made up of the apostles and other disciples, who see themselves as representing Israel. They will be later characterized in this section as 'Galileans' (2.7). The exact location is more difficult to determine and is examined more closely below (2.2).

Codex Bezae ties this episode closely to the previous one by setting it within the same time frame, 'in those days', recalling from the outset the short period of time ('not many days') that Jesus had told the apostles would elapse before their baptism in the Holy Spirit (1.5). Codex Vaticanus begins more abruptly by referring straightaway to the day of Pentecost, a first mention in this text but not in the Bezan text where Pentecost had already been mentioned by Jesus (1.5 D05) as the latest time for the realization of his promise. The time of the Jewish feast of Pentecost, according to Biblical tradition at least, was the 50th day after the sabbath of Passover week, that is on the day after the sabbath seven weeks later; since Jesus had been raised on the day after the sabbath of Passover and had ascended 40 days after his resurrection, the present scene takes place some 10 days after his ascension.[1]

The Greek expression situating the event in relation to Pentecost can be taken in two ways because the verb used can mean either 'be completed' or 'be fulfilled'. So this could be a reference to the counting of the days from Passover to Pentecost and a way of saying that the period had come to an end; the use of a term in Hebrew to describe a day as being 'fulfilled' in reference to the counting down of a regulation number of days, suggests that could be the meaning in mind here, giving the translation: 'When the day of Pentecost had arrived'. However, the tense of the verb indicates that the time was not yet finished but rather was still being completed.[2] This leads to the interpretation that the day itself of Pentecost was coming to an end having started, according to the Jewish method of reckoning days, at sunset the previous evening. Against this interpretation it may be pointed out that at 2.15 Peter will use the Roman way of reckoning when he speaks of the time of day as being 'the third hour', a reference to 9 a.m. but it is quite conceivable that the religious days were viewed from the Jewish point of view and time on a daily basis from the secular one.

1. According to J. Potin (*La fête juive de la Pentecôte*, 1. *Études des textes liturgiques* [Lectio Divina, 65; Paris: Cerf, 1971], pp. 121–22), the Pharisees altered the calculation of the day of Pentecost so that it fell 50 days after the day of Passover itself (because that day was viewed as a sabbath whatever day of the week it fell). For more details on the date of Pentecost, see *Shavuot* in *Enc. Jud.*, XIV, cols.1319–22. It is not clear if the change had already been made by the time of Jesus. If so, then the day of Pentecost would have occurred less than 10 days after the ascension.

2. The present infinitive of συμπληρόω here should be compared with its occurrence at Lk. 9.51 where the 'days of his [Jesus'] lifting up' are said to be drawing near, and the use of an analogous expression using the aorist of πίμπλημι at Lk. 1.23; 2.6, 21, 22 to express that a period of time 'had been completed'.

The significance of the feast of Pentecost is worth exploring.[3] In the Jewish Bible, it was an important harvest celebration timed to coincide with the ripening of the wheat (Exod. 23.16a; Lev. 23.15–20). It was designed to be celebrated by all people, not just of Israel but foreigners, too (Deut. 16.10). Because its date was reckoned by counting seven weeks from Passover, the time when the fruit of the first crop of the year (that is, barley) was offered (Lev. 23.15), it was commonly known as the Feast of Weeks (Exod. 34.22a; Num. 28.26). Pentecost was thus closely linked to Passover, not only because its date depended on the date of Passover but because there was an offering of crops on each occasion. The appropriateness of Pentecost for the sending of the Holy Spirit may derive from the fact that it is then that the first fruits of the new creation following the death of Jesus are formed as the disciples are filled with the Spirit and emerge as the core of the new people of God (Jer. 31[38 LXX].33–34; Ezek. 36.22–32). The parallel further fits with the fact that the outpouring of the Spirit at Pentecost does not represent a unique happening that cannot be repeated but is simply the first among other occasions.

By the time of the 1st century CE, however, there was rather more to Pentecost than a celebration of the first-fruits, just as there was rather more to the arrival of the Spirit than the birth of a new community. Exactly what was the meaning of the Jewish festival in the mid-thirties is difficult to determine but the echoes in Luke's account of traditions known from later writings to be associated with Pentecost indicate that certain developments had taken place by that time and were sufficiently well established for Luke to draw on their theological implications. The most clearly attested development was the association of Pentecost with the renewal of the covenant.[4] In the *Book of Jubilees* (*Jub.* 6.17–20), the origin of this celebration on the day of Pentecost is traced back to Noah with whom the first covenant was made (Gen. 9.16–17) and, indeed, the major promises made by God to Israel are presented as occurring on this day, including the covenant given to Moses at Sinai (Exod. 19.5; cf. 24.7,8). This aspect of the Pentecost festival adds another strand to the rooting of the sending of the Spirit in Jewish religious tradition, for Jesus specifically foresees the event as 'the promise of the Father' (1.4). The universal nature of the covenant made with Noah ('between God and

3. Potin (*La fête juive*) presents a comprehensive exploration of the meaning of the festival from its earliest celebration to the Rabbinic period. See also R. Le Déaut, *La nuit pascale* (Rome: Biblical Institute Press, 1963), p. 126.

4. Potin, *La fête juive*, pp. 124–31, 301.

every living creature of all flesh that is upon the earth', Gen. 1.16) comes forcefully to the fore in the subsequent narrative of Acts 2 and will be the primary theme of the first part of Peter's speech in 2.14.21. It also underlies the allusions to the Tower of Babel (Gen. 11.1–9; see on 2.5 below), an event that destroyed the unity of humanity and that Luke now presents as reversed by the unifying power of the Spirit who makes God once more accessible to 'all flesh'.

By the Rabbinic period, the feast of Pentecost had become the anniversary of the giving of the Torah at Sinai, a specific aspect of covenant renewal that reinforces the connection of Pentecost with the Exodus. In the Acts account, the importance of the Torah as such is not in evidence (on the contrary, the freedom of the Holy Spirit could be said to be in contradiction to the regulations of the law), and there is no explicit attestation of the association of the giving of the Torah with Pentecost until the 2nd century CE. At this time, too, there is also the first evidence of traditions (Rabbinic and targumic, for example) that had developed from the Biblical account of God's revelation at Sinai. All of this would be of no consequence except that there are traces in the Acts narrative of the later traditions surrounding the Exodus story, aswell as elements of the Biblical account itself, that suggest, at the very least, that the revelation of God at Sinai was one of the strands of the Pentecost celebration and that Luke sought to activate it in his account of the outpouring of the Spirit.[5] In sum,

5. The following are the chief elements of the Acts account that may be intended as echoes of the Sinai story, either Biblical or traditional (summarised from Potin, *La fête juive*, pp. 303–314; see A. Del Agua, *El método midrásico y la exégesis del Nuevo Testamento* (Valencia: Institución San Jerónimo, 1985), pp. 217–22):

2.1. The day of Pentecost (*Targ. Ps.-J. Exod.* 19.1: the revelation of God at Sinai takes place on the day of Pentecost). The unity of the assembled disciples (*Targ. Ps.-J. Exod.* 19.2; Exod. 19.8a; 24.3).

2.2. Noise precedes revelation (Exod. 19.16 [LXX = ἦχος]). All the house (of Israel, represented by the 120) was shaken (*Targ. Ps.-J. Exod.* 19.3; Exod. 19.18 [LXX = ὁ λαός]).

2.3. Tongues as if of fire (Exod. 19.18). Division of tongues (*Targ. Deut.* 33.2: God's voice divided into four).

2.5. People from every nation (*Targ. Deut.* 33.2: the law was offered to all nations).

2.6. People in Jerusalem heard the noise and gathered near it (Exod. 19.16: all the people heard the thunder on Sinai and Moses brought them to the mountain).

2.6, 8. They each heard their own language (*Targ. Deut.* 33.2; *Exod. R.* 5.9).

the revelation of God at Sinai where he spoke his word to Moses, is replaced by the revelation of God through his Spirit to the 120 waiting in Jerusalem. This is a revelation that properly belongs to the Messianic age (Joel 3.1–2) in which the people themselves, rather than God, are the ones who declare the divine word (Acts 2.4,11).

The references made by Jesus before his departure to the imminent fulfilment of the Father's promise and the sending of the Spirit must have aroused a considerable feeling of expectation among the group of disciples as they waited in Jerusalem. The sense of urgency is enhanced in the Bezan text by a number of factors, not least among which is the echo of Jesus' promise that the baptism in the Spirit would happen 'until Pentecost' (1.5 D05). Time has almost run out and the suggestion may be that a delay was occasioned by the decision of the apostolic group to select a replacement for Judas. For this was contrary not only to Jesus' commandment to them to 'wait' in the city (Lk. 24.49) / Hierosoluma (Acts 1.4) but also to the fact that he had not chosen to replace Judas before he left them (see *Commentary*, Acts 1). Now, as the day is coming to an end, they are all sharing the same thoughts and feelings, no doubt of hope and maybe even fear of disappointment. That explains why the unity of the disciples is presented in the Bezan text as closely linked to the time element for both of them are circumstances that prepare for the arrival of the Holy Spirit. The phrase used to express their unity is the same as was used of the 120 disciples (D05; brethren B03) at 1.15 where, as pointed out in the Commentary, the unity Luke has in mind is not a localised gathering in one place but a sharing of thought and purpose among the 120 and especially their solidarity within the larger group to which they belong. It is important to be clear that at this stage, the disciples still remain attached to the Temple even though they are under the leadership of the Twelve apostles (see *Commentary*, 1.26).

[b] 2.2 *The Sound of the Wind, Precursor of the Holy Spirit*

2.2 Codex Bezae continues to view the scene through the eyes of the expectant disciples as the dramatic action suddenly begins. The Greek literally means 'and behold!' but it is an expression that Luke frequently uses to present a scene from the point of view of his characters rather than his own point of view as narrator. Here, at last, is what they have been waiting for. The first sign of anything happening is the sound of a violent wind which was being 'driven in', implying that there is some kind of resistance to be overcome before the arrival of the Spirit.[6] The forcefulness of the scene, repeated in the earthquake at the second manifestation of the Spirit in Acts (4.31), contrasts with the gentleness of Jesus' experience at his baptism when the Holy Spirit came down on him 'like a dove' (Lk. 3.22). The strong wind is reminiscent of the manifestation of divine power to Elijah (1 Kgs 19.11–12) and is typical of the cosmic disturbance that precedes God's revelation to his people (for example, on Mount Sinai, Exod. 19.16–19, and cf. the citation of Joel in Peter's speech, Acts 2.16–21).

It should be noted that the sound is made by the wind and not the Spirit. The noun πνεῦμα designating the Spirit does, in fact, also mean 'wind' but by using another term, πνοή, Luke indicates that he intended no confusion between the two here.[7] The meaning of 'the house' that was filled by the sound needs to be clarified. There are two words used by Luke in his writings to refer to a house (οἶκος/οἰκία); they can both denote a material building but also have a metaphorical sense, with the former being used (in general, not just by Luke) to refer to a tribal or ethnic group (as in 'the house of Jacob', 7.46) and the other being adopted by Luke as a term to designate a community of disciples (so 'the house of Mary', 12.12). Here, it is a question of the former term and on one level, the reference is simply to the building, the place where the group were seated (B03) / were sitting expectantly (D05).[8] Where exactly that was is not made clear though it would be reasonable to take it as the last location mentioned, the upper room (1.13),[9] since that is where the disciples went to wait after Jesus' ascension. It has already been noted (see *Commentary* on 1,13–14) that the upper room corresponds to the Temple of Lk. 24.53, and οἶκος is precisely a term by which the Temple was known.[10] So the meaning is apparently not just that some house was filled with the sound

6. Delebecque expresses the driving force of the wind by translating φερομένης as 'pratiquement irrésistible' (*Les deux Actes*, pp. 32–33).

7. In LXX the term πνοή often has a negative force; cf. *Jub.* 10.26 which describes the tower of Babel being destroyed by a violent wind. For further discussion of the Babel paradigm, see 2.5 below.

8. 'Sitting' in the Jewish Scriptures is used to express waiting expectantly: e.g. LXX 4 Kgdms 1.9 (Elijah); 2.2,4,6, (Elisha); Jon. 4.5 (Jonah). Jesus had told his disciples to 'sit' (καθίσατε) in the city until they received power from above (Lk. 24.49).

9. The use of οἶκος by D05 to refer to the upper room at Lk. 22.12 tends to reinforce the connection between the location of Acts 2.2 and the upper room.

10. οἶκος occurs frequently in the LXX as a synonym for the Temple and as a more oblique reference in Luke's writing at Lk. 6.4; 19.46; Acts 7.47, 49.

of the wind but the Temple itself – and it will be to the Temple that the people flocked when they heard the noise and where they listened to Peter (2.6). In Codex Bezae, 'the house' acquires a further symbolic meaning from the theological intent that has been noted as part of the message of Acts so far. The Bezan text of 1.15 presented the group of disciples, those who, according to this text, were sitting expectantly in the house, as representing Israel (see 1.15 D05), and since οἶκος is a term used to refer to Israel, especially with the particular adjective for 'all' selected by Codex Bezae (πᾶς, cf. 2.36) but not by the AT which uses a synonym (ὅλος), then the comment here at 2.2 can be taken to mean that the sound of the wind 'filled all of Israel'.[11] This is a revelation, in other words, not just for a select few but for the benefit of all the people.

[b′] 2.3 *The Appearance of Tongues of Fire*

2.3 The manifestation of the Holy Spirit is firstly a visual one, seen by the assembled disciples. This visual disclosure of God's presence has been common enough in previous cases of his self-revelation but here it is not as a personal representation of God (as it was, e.g., to Abraham [Acts 7.2, cf. Gen. 15.1–6]) or some other spiritual being (e.g. the angel of the Lord [Lk. 1.11] or Jesus [Lk. 22.43 D05/א01*]) or a symbolic creature (e.g. a dove at Jesus' baptism [Lk. 3.22]) but as 'tongues, as if of fire'.[12] The initial manifestation of the Spirit is thus in one sense a metaphorical one which will be actualized in the following verse as Luke plays on the double meaning of the word 'tongues'.

As the tongues separate and settle on each person, the people receive the 'Father's promise' which Jesus had referred to as the gift of the Holy Spirit (Lk. 24.49; Acts 1.4). Originally, the promise made by God to his people had consisted in the possession of the land of Israel which was divided up among the twelve tribes (διεμερίσθη, Gen. 10.25 = 1 Chron. 1.19; Josh. 21.43a). Luke uses the same technical term διαμεριζόμεναι (lit. 'being divided') to refer to the new promise, the sharing out of the Spirit. This time it is not an earthly possession that is involved but a prophetic power for proclaiming the wonders of God to all who want to hear.

Although John the Baptist had proclaimed that the one coming after

11. Note that the reading of Exod. 19.18 LXX concerning the revelation at Sinai, says that 'all the people' ('all the mountain' in Hebrew) were shaken when the Lord descended in fire.

12. There are further parallels between the fire in the midst of which God spoke to Moses (Exod. 3.1–6, cf. Deut. 4.36) and the coming of the Holy Spirit as fire which enables the disciples to make divine utterance.

him would baptise them 'with the Holy Spirit and fire' (Lk. 3.16), Jesus himself omitted any reference to the aspect of punishment and purification contained in the notion of eschatological fire (cf. Lk. 3.9, 17). Even so, Luke cannot be unaware of a connection between the fire of John's prophecy and the fire by which the Spirit is now symbolically represented although the fire at Pentecost is not a symbol of destruction but of power.

[a′] 2.4 *The Filling of the Group with the Spirit*

2.4 The meaning of the symbol of the fire is now made clear: 'they were all filled with the Holy Spirit', that is, the whole gathering which includes the apostles but others besides (cf. 2.1). A certain parallel can be seen in this scene with the coming of the Holy Spirit on Jesus at his baptism, so making a connection between the beginning of the ministry of Jesus and the start of the mission of the Jerusalem church. However, a much stronger parallel with Jesus' baptism is drawn by Luke in his presentation of the mission of the Antioch church.[13] The parallel here is rather with the promise made by John the Baptist to Israel, as noted above (2.3). Any echo of Jesus' baptism is a negative rather than a positive one, for in the case of Jesus it was said that he was 'full of the Holy Spirit' (Lk. 4.1), a fulness that will be a requirement for the future representatives of the Hellenistic disciples (Acts 6.3) and that will be used especially of Stephen (6.5, 8; 7.55) and Barnabas (11.24). In contrast, in the case of the gathering in the upper room, it is simply said that they were 'filled with the Holy Spirit'. The adjective 'full' (πλήρης) implies a permanent state while the aorist of the verb 'to fill' (ἐπλήσθησαν) denotes the result of an action,[14] which may or may not be lasting. Thus, it will be later said of those present that they were again 'filled' (Peter, 4.8; all those gathered at Pentecost together with others who had joined them, 4.31), implying that the effects of the coming of the Holy Spirit described here are only valid for this scene. Luke deliberately distinguishes between the punctual moment at which an individual or a group begins or starts again to act under the impulse of the Holy Spirit and the ongoing state of acting under his influence.[15] As long as it is not said that an individual or a group is 'full' of the Holy Spirit, there is no guarantee that all the subsequent actions that are

13. See J. Rius-Camps, *El camino de Pablo a la misión de los paganos* (Madrid: Cristiandad, 1984), §§10-16, 17–25, and 27–28.

14. J. Mateos, *El aspecto verbal en el Nuevo Testamento* (Madrid: Cristiandad, 1977), §367.

15. Rius-Camps, *El camino de Pablo*, p. 47, n. 61.

narrated are undertaken under his inspiration. Only when it is expressly stated is there any certainty (e.g. 4.8, Peter; 13.9, Saul/Paul). The consequence of this distinction is that 'being filled' with the Holy Spirit does not make the believer infallible and this will apply as much to the apostles as to anyone else.

When Peter later refers back to this scene following the events at the house of Cornelius (11.16), he will describe the present happening in terms of the fulfilment of the prophecy of Jesus concerning baptism in the Holy Spirit (1.5). It is a baptism that belongs distinctly to Jesus, in contrast to the water baptism that was John's (Lk. 3.16). It will be mentioned again in subsequent episodes as a sign of the acceptance by God of believers in Jesus, functioning alongside water baptism in the name of Jesus as the outward demonstration of a person's turning to him.

The effect of the people being filled with the Spirit was that they began to make proclamations in languages hitherto unknown to them. Whether these are intelligible, known languages or incomprehensible, 'spiritual' languages (the phenomenon known as 'glossolalia') is an important question but one that cannot be answered until a later point in the narrative. What is worthy of note, meanwhile, is just how much prophetic utterance is the chief characteristic of baptism in the Holy Spirit. Its significance is brought out in Luke's description of the event, by the chiastic arrangement of the metaphorical elements and their actual realization.

Metaphor:
- [a] There appeared to them, ὤφθησαν αὐτοῖς, aorist passive, marking the onset of the vision,
- [b] as they were being divided out, διαμεριζόμεναι, present participle progressive,
- [c] tongues, as if of fire, γλῶσσαι
- [d] which sat on each of them, ἐκάθισεν / -αν, punctual aorist

Resulting action:
- [d′] All were filled with the Holy Spirit, ἐπλήσθησαν, punctual aorist,
- [c′] they began to talk in other tongues, γλώσσαις
- [b′] as the Spirit went on giving them, ἐδίδου, progressive imperfect,
- [a′] the means to make proclamation, ἀποφθέγγεσθαι, habitual infinitive, marking the continuing outcome

In this arrangement, there is a close correspondance between all the components except the outer ones where a marked change occurs between the onset of the vision [a], perceived only by those present, and the final outcome [a′] which is an ongoing public proclamation. Baptism in the Holy Spirit is thus seen to be precisely for the purpose indicated by Jesus, that is witness to himself (cf. 1.8).

[B] 2.5–13 *The Reaction of the People in Jerusalem to the Manifestation of the Spirit*

Overview

In order to follow the development of the narrative, it is imperative to recognize that throughout the second chapter of Acts Luke uses a dual register, writing on one level that is historical and on another that is spiritual, the two constantly overlapping and impinging on one another. The opening scene is presented as a literal reality but thereafter a fictional element is introduced into the story which must be disentangled from the literal strand. The historical scene is played out by Jewish characters, that is the apostolic group and subsequently the Jews present in Jerusalem. Another group, who represent the whole of humanity, take part in the episode but their presence is a device of literary fiction: they are not literally present though they have a purpose with respect to the historical scene which is to serve as a foil to show up the negative reaction of the Jews by their more positive response. Introducing a fictional, universal aspect to explain events in the history of Israel is characteristic of a certain type of Jewish exegesis, notably with reference to the revelation of God on Sinai which, as has already been indicated (see on 2.1 above), belongs to the template used for the Pentecost narrative.[16] The way Luke uses the fictional characters to act as foils who bring out the weaknesses of certain dominant characters in both the Gospel and Acts is typical of his narrative art and will be seen again, notably in the presence of the anonymous 'we'-group in the second half of the book.

Structure and Themes

The theme of this sequence is the reaction to the manifestation of the Holy Spirit, both on the part of those who were literally present and those who were figuratively present The structure is arranged as follows:

[a] 2.5 Introduction of the people living in Jerusalem
[b] 2.6 The gathering of the crowd who hear their own languages
[c] 2.7–11 The crowd express amazement; the list of their countries.
[b′] 2.12 The positive reaction of the crowd
[a′] 2.13 The negative reaction of the crowd

17. See the discussion of *Exod. R.* 5.9, in Potin, *La fête juive*, pp. 248–50.

Translation

	Codex Bezae D05	*Codex Vaticanus B03*
[a]	**2.5** In Jerusalem, there were living [Jews,] devout men from every nation under heaven.	**2.5** There were Jews living in Jerusalem, devout men from every nation under heaven.
[b]	**6** At the sound of this noise, the crowd gathered and they were confused; and each one of them heard that they were speaking in their language.	**6** At the sound of this noise, the crowd gathered and they were confused because each one of them heard them speaking in their own language.
[c]	**7** They were utterly amazed and they marvelled as they said to one another, 'Look! is not every one of these people who are speaking Galileans? **8** Then how is it that we each hear our language in which we were born **9** – Parthians and Medes and Elamites; and people living in Mesopotamia, Judaea and Cappadocia, **10** Pontus and Asia, Phrygia and Pamphilia, Egypt as also the regions of Libya belonging to Cyrene; and those temporarily residing here from Rome (Jews as well as proselytes), **11** Cretans and Arabians – how is it that we hear the great deeds of God as they speak in our languages?'	**7** They were utterly amazed and they marvelled, saying, 'Look, surely all these people who are speaking are Galileans? **8** Then how is it that we each hear in our own native language? **9** – Parthians and Medes and Elamites, people living in Mesopotamia, Judaea and also Cappadocia, **10** Pontus and Asia, Phrygia as well as Pamphilia, Egypt and the regions of Libya belonging to Cyrene, and those temporarily residing here from Rome (Jews as well as proselytes), **11** Cretans and Arabians – we hear them telling in our languages the great deeds of God.'
[b′]	**12** All of them were utterly amazed and puzzled to one another over what had come about, saying, 'What does this mean?'	**12** All of them were utterly amazed and were puzzled as they said to one another, 'What does this mean?'
[a′]	**13** Others, in contrast, mocked as they said, 'These people are full of sweet wine!'	**13** Others, in contrast, mocking said, 'They are full of sweet wine!'

Critical Apparatus

2.5 ˀἮσαν δὲ εἰς (ἐν ℵ^{2}) Ἰερουσαλὴμ κατοικοῦντες ἄνδρες εὐλαβεῖς ℵ* *l* 844 ph vg^{ms} | ˀἮσ. δὲ εἰς Ἰερ. κατ. Ἰουδαῖοι, ἄνδ. εὐλ. A 88. 1175 ‖ ˀἮσ. δὲ ἐν Ἰερ. κατ. Ἰουδαῖοι, ἄνδ. εὐλ. B H^{2} Ψ 049. 056. 33. 69. 81. 323. 330. 614. 945. 1175. 1241. 1245. 1270. 1505. 1739. 2412. 2492. 2495 𝔐 it vg sy co arm geo; Chr Hil Hier | ˀἮσ. δὲ ἐν Ἰερ. Ἰουδ. κατ., ἄνδ. εὐλ. E | ˀἮσ. δὲ κατ. ἐν Ἰερ. ἄνδ. Ἰουδ. εὐλ. C*

| Ἠσ. δὲ κατ. ἐν Ἰερ. Ἰουδ., ἄνδ. εὐλ. C[3] || Ἐν Ἰερ. ἦσ. κατ. Ἰουδ., εὐλ. ἄνδ. D, *In Hierusalem erant habitantes Iudaei, timorati viri* d; Aug | Ἐν Ἰερ. ἦσ. κατ. εὐλ. ἄνδ. *coni.*

A fuller list of readings has been given than simply those of ℵ01/B03/D05 to show the complexity of this variant. Several issues are involved:

1. All MSS except D05 treat this verse as the opening of a new development in the narrative, introduced as it is with δέ. As such, it constitutes a parenthetical explanation that anticipates the next stage of the action at 2.6 (also introduced with δέ to mark the onset of a new action). The asyndeton of D05 indicates that the information of this verse is of special interest and is not to be viewed as a straightforward development of the story so far (Read-Heimerdinger, *The Bezan Text*, p. 247): it signals, in fact, a change in register from historical to fictional, combining with word order variants to underline the extreme importance of the information contained within the clause.
2. The word order of all MSS except D05, which open the clause with the verb, is unmarked although it is unusual to find that the change of participant or topic is not signalled by being fronted. In D05, it is the location that is fronted and the importance of the comment concerning Jerusalem is thereby heightened (Levinsohn, *Textual Connections*, pp. 61–65), especially in combination with the absence of connective (see above).
3. ἐν is the word Luke generally uses to express fixed location. Nonetheless, the choice of εἰς in ℵ01 and others can be accounted for by the fact that the people had come from other countries into Jerusalem to stay there, this pregnant use of the preposition being found elsewhere in Acts (*The Bezan Text*, pp. 192–97, esp. p. 195. εἰς is never used in a purely locative [i.e. non-pregnant] sense in the Bezan text, though this does happen occasionally in the Alexandrian MSS).
4. The placing of the adjective εὐλαβεῖς before the noun ἄνδρες in D05 draws attention to the devoutness of the men (*The Bezan Text*, p. 91).
5. The variety of positions in the sentence of Ἰουδαῖοι strongly suggests that it was not present in the autograph. The difficulty posed by its omission is sufficiently great for its addition to have occurred as a means to avoid implying that there was a large number of Gentiles living in Jerusalem and involved in witnessing the gift of the Holy Spirit. On the other hand, its presence could seem superfluous and even in contradiction with the statement that the Jews were from every nation (see Metzger, *Commentary*, p. 251, for an analysis of the arguments and the conclusion that it should be retained as being the *lectio difficilior*). The solution to the apparent impasse lies in recognizing that Luke uses in these verses a narrative procedure that allows him to speak on two levels at once: he does mean to say that there was a large number of Gentiles living in Jerusalem at the time of the arrival of the Spirit but this is a literary fiction whereby a universal dimension is introduced into the story, distinct from the literal reality to which the Jews belong. Although D05 contains Ἰουδαῖοι, the conjectured reading otherwise adopts the Bezan text

because in every other respect it has been seen to be cohesively emphatic in drawing attention to the contents of the parenthetical statement. The underlining of Jerusalem and the devoutness of the men (see above) is consistent with the fact they were Gentiles.

2.6 ὅτι ἤκουσεν B ℵ 36. 181. 241. 307. 327. 614. 917. 1646. 1874 (*quia audiebant* d); Eus || καὶ ἤκουον D.

According to B03, the cause of the crowd's bewilderment was that each person heard (sing.) their own language being spoken. In D05, it was the sound of the wind that occasioned the bewilderment and a new clause adds that everyone heard (pl.), or understood (cf. Gen. 11.7 LXX), people speaking in their languages (see below).

εἷς ἕκαστος B D d *rell* || ἕκ. ℵ E Ψ 049. 945. 1270. 1739. 1854.

ℵ01 insists less on each and every one in the crowd.

τῇ ἰδίᾳ διαλέκτῳ λαλούντων αὐτῶν B ℵ *rell* || λαλοῦντας ταῖς γλώσσαις αὐτῶν D d sy^p.(hmg)^; Aug^pt^.

A subtle yet important difference exists between the two forms attested. The B03 text explains that the everyone in the crowd *heard* in their language people talking, with διάλεκτος in the singular to accord with the singular verb (see above) and the genitive participle expressing the personal object of the verb ἀκούω. The explanation is curiously close to the Jewish tradition that when God gave the Torah on Mount Sinai his voice divided into several languages (*Targ. Deut.* 33.2, where it is initially a question of three languages but the number increases to 70 in later tradition; see Potin *La fête juive*, pp. 248–59) and each nation heard God speaking in their own language; the Rabbinic commentary is insistent that God spoke one language but was heard in different languages (*Exod. R.* 5.9).

The D05 text retains the same word for language as for the tongues of fire (2.3) and spoken tongues (2.4), in the plural in accordance with the plural verb (see above); furthermore, it is the speaking that occurs in their languages, not the hearing (Ropes, *The Text of Acts*, p. 13). The accusative after ἀκούω expresses the idea that the people hear not so much 'them speaking in their languages' as 'the fact they were speaking in their languages' (see Delebecque, *Les deux Actes*, p. 32).

2.7 ἐξίσταντο δέ B D H^2 056. 096. 69. 226. 330. 340. 614. 618. 1828. 1241. 1243. 1245. 1646. 1854. 2147. 2412. 2492 *pm*, *et admirabantur* d gig r mae; Eus Aug || ἐξίσταντο δὲ πάντες (ἅπ– ℵ*) $ℵ^2$ A C E Ψ 049. 096^vid^. 1. 33. 81. 88. 104. 181. 323. 547. 927. 945. 1175. 1270. 1505. 1611. 1739. 1837. 2495 *pm* lat sy sa bo.

The mention of 'all' could have been under the influence of 2.12a; there, however, it is necessary to draw together the diverse peoples listed whereas here no distinction among the crowd has yet been made.

(ἐθαύμαζον) λέγοντες B P^{74} ℵ A C* 81. 1175 *pc* r w vg sa bo; Eus || λέγ. πρὸς ἀλλήλους D d C^3 E H^2 049. 056. 096. 323. 330. 614. 945. 1241. 1611. 1739. 2412. 2492 𝔐 a gig p t sy.

It is a frequent characteristic of D05 to specify the addressee of verbs of speaking where B03 does not do so (Read-Heimerdinger, *The Bezan Text*, pp. 180–82). The formula is different from that used at 2.12a. The detail that the people spoke among themselves echoes the Babel account (Gen. 11.3), in both cases presenting them as bonded together in their puzzlement against the power of the supernatural.

οὐχί B || οὐχ D ℵ E 81. 88. 98. 794. 915. 1175. 1827. 1891 | οὐκ P^{74} A C H^2 Ψ 049. 056. 33. 614. 1739. 2412. 2495 𝔐; Eus.

Both negatives expect an affirmative answer (B-A-G, οὐ 4.c; οὐχί 3), the B03 reading being the more emphatic. It could have been possible that the iota of οὐχί fell out before ἰδού, and οὐχ subsequently corrected to οὐκ, but the explanation is unlikely because it would mean that the error was universally reproduced.

πάντες B* E H^2 Ψ 049. 056. 33. 81. 88. 614. 1175. 1245. 1611. 2412. 2492 𝔐 || ἅπ– D P^{74} ℵ A B^2 C 096. 323. 945. 1739 *al.*

There is frequent variation between these two forms in Acts, with ἅπας being more emphatic, 'absolutely all, every single one' (ἅπας in the common text: 4.31; 11.10; 16.28; in ℵ01: 2.7a; 4.32; in ℵ01/B03: 2.44; 5.16; 16.3; 16.33; in ℵ01/D05: 2.7; 5.12).

2.8–11

The *vll* that concern the connectives in these verses causes the text to be punctuated differently. The omission by D05 of καί before οἱ κατοικοῦντες causes the three subordinate verbs ἐν ᾗ ἐγεννήθημεν ... οἱ κατοικοῦντες ... καὶ οἱ ἐπιδημοῦντες to form three parallel statements enclosed between the two occurrences of ἀκούω (2.8a, 11b) the second picking up the first by repeating the question of 2.8a (see *Translation* 2.8–11). This is the punctuation proposed by Bover (5th edition) and Merk (9th edition), as also by N-A^{25} but not by subsequent editions (see *apparatus* GNT^4, 2.8–11).

The genitival phrase λαλούντων αὐτῶν in 2.11 constitutes the object of ἀκούομεν in B03, in line with the same construction in 2.6. According to D05, the accusative τὰ μεγαλεῖα τοῦ θεοῦ could be construed as the object of ἀκούω just like the accusative τὴν ἰδίαν διάλεκτον in 2.6, with the genitival phrase in 2.11 standing as a genitive absolute.

2.8 τῇ ἰδίᾳ διαλέκτῳ ἡμῶν B ℵ A C D^B (E) *rell*, *propria lingua nostra* d || τὴν διάλεκτον ἡμ. D* p^c w vg^{cl}.

B03 uses once more the dative (cf. 2.6 above) to express that it is the *hearing* that takes place in the different languages, whereas D05 maintains the notion that the people hear the different languages (being spoken).

2.9 καὶ Ἐλαμῖται B D d ℵ^2 *rell* || *om.* ℵ*.
καὶ (οἱ κατοικοῦντες) B ℵ D^B *rell*, *et* d || *om.* D*.

See on 2.8–11 above.

2.9–10 (Ἰουδαίαν) τε B P^{74} ℵ D^E *rell* || *om.* D* d.
(Φρυγίαν) τε B P^{74} ℵ *rell* || *om.* D d.
(Αἴγυπτόν) τε D || *om.* B P^{74} ℵ *rell* d.

The presence of Judaea causes a problem because of the mention of Ἰουδαῖοι in 2.5 (some witnesses replace it with another country, see N-A^{27}). B03 links it closely with Cappadocia by the use of τε. A similar difference in the linking of countries is seen with respect to Phrygia, which B03 links closely to Pamphilia, and Egypt which D05 links closely to the regions of Libya. The connections between the countries give rise to different patterns in the way they are arranged.

2.11 Κρῆτες καὶ Ἄραβες B ℵ D^D *rell*, *cretenses et arabi* d || Κρήτης κ. Ἄραβοι D*.

In B03 the qualification 'Jews and proselytes' applies to the name preceding it, the Romans. In D05 the spelling of Κρήτης makes it a genitive of Κρήτη, the name of the country, so causing the description to apply to the people of Crete. There are reasons for thinking that this is a phonetic confusion and that the genitive is not intended:

1. The purpose of restricting the population of Crete to Jews and proselytes is not clear; although Paul records (Tit. 1.12) that Cretans had a reputation for being 'liars, evil beasts, lazy gluttons', there is no evidence that they were the worst in the world or that the Jewish population were any better (cf. Tit. 1.10–11).
2. The reading 'Crete' interrupts the pattern of what would otherwise be three peoples corresponding to the three peoples at the head of the list in 2.9.
3. The confusion between ε and η is not uncommon in the MS of D05.

2.12 διηποροῦντο B ℵ A 076 *pc* || διηπόρουν D, *obstupescebant* d C E H^2 Ψ 049. 056. 096. 33. 614. 1175. 1611. 1739. 2412. 2492 𝔐.

B03 uses the middle voice (deemed to be 'an Alexandrian refinement', Metzger, *Commentary*, p. 254) meaning 'were completely perplexed' and thus causes the phrase ἄλλος πρὸς ἄλλον to depend on the following participle λέγοντες (see below). D05 reads the active which allows ἄλλος πρὸς ἄλλον to be taken with this verb and conveys the meaning that they expressed their bewilderment to each other.

λέγοντες B ℵ *rell* || ἐπὶ τῷ γεγονότι καὶ λέγ. D d (sy^{hmg}); Aug.

The active voice, διηπόρουν, of D05 (see above) is more appropriate since the indirect object is specified in this text. καί between a participle and a main verb is a characteristic device of D05 used to draw attention to the main verb (Read-Heimerdinger, *The Bezan Text*, pp. 208–10).

2.13 διαχλευάζοντες ἔλεγον B ℵ A C D^{D+F} 33. 81. 88. 226^{c}. 945. 1175. 1245. 1739. 1611 | χλευάζοντες ἔλ. E H^{3} Ψ 049. 056. 69. 226*. 614. 1270. 2412. 2495 𝔐 || διεχλεύαζον λέγοντες D* d a b sy^{p} co; Aug.

The D05 text creates a grammatical parallel between the two clauses, διηπόρουν καὶ λέγοντες and διεχλεύαζον λέγοντες, repeating the imperfect active + present participle each time. The existence of two separate groups among the crowd as a whole (πάντες, 2.12a) is thus established: ἄλλος πρὸς ἄλλον and ἕτεροι, each with different reactions to the outpouring of the Spirit. The difference in the construction of the clauses in the B03 text makes it much less clear that two distinct groups of people among the crowd are intended.

(γλεύκους) οὗτοι D d (t w vg) sy^{p} bo; Aug || *om.* B ℵ *rell.*

The inclusion of the demonstrative pronoun in D05 confers a distinct tone of disrespect on the comment of the second group.

Commentary

[a] 2.5 *Introduction of the People Living in Jerusalem*

2.5 The narrative switches now from its focus on those speaking in other tongues to look at events from the point of view of those witnessing them. These people are brought into the story in an aside (the storyline continues in 2.6) which the Bezan text expresses in emphatic terms (see *Critical Apparatus*), letting the audience know that what is said about the people living in Jerusalem is particularly important. The question of their identity must be resolved at this point in order to understand the rest of the episode.

One possibility is to consider that they were all Jews, some of whom would have been local residents (note the presence of Judaea in the list of countries, 2.9) but others from all over the Diaspora (the countries listed 2.9–11) would have made a pilgrimage to Jerusalem for the Feast of Pentecost. This is to take the narration as a purely factual, historical account and is based on the reading of 'Jews' in this verse. The word is indeed present in both manuscript traditions but is omitted by certain important witnesses (see *Critical Apparatus*). Its presence poses a serious problem: not only is it illogical to say that the Jews came from 'every nation under heaven' since they viewed themselves as one nation[17] but, more than that, the idea that only the Jews heard the prophetic proclamations jars with the various indications throughout the rest of the chapter that the outpouring of the Holy Spirit was universally valid and effective for the whole of mankind. Essentially, to treat all the inhabitants of Jerusalem as Jews is to misunderstand Luke's theological intention. We therefore suggest that the word 'Jews' was not originally present in this verse, but that the primitive text is otherwise that of Codex Bezae because of the way all the readings work together to draw attention to its contents.

What happens then at this point is that Luke changes register and introduces a symbolic dimension into the narrative. He presents the outpouring of the Spirit as valid for the whole of mankind whom he imagines as present at the Pentecost scene; this dimension will become more apparent in the list of nations (2.9–11) and in the reaction of part of the crowd. Not that the historical reality disappears, however, for the Jews who were really present in Jerusalem, many of them from the Diaspora who had come up for the Feast of Pentecost, remain included among the crowd who gather in 2.6. Luke thus fuses the historical dimension of his narrative with a spiritual reality, thereby anticipating the universal character of the gift of the Holy Spirit and the unification of all humanity under the one God.

The scriptural paradigm for the Pentecost scene is a complex one for there are elements drawn both from the revelation at Sinai (Exodus 19–24) as well as from the story of Babel (Gen. 11.1–9). The Jewish traditions that became associated with the former explained that all of humanity was present when God revealed the Torah and that, although his voice divided into different languages so that all the nations could understand his words, Israel was the only people prepared to accept the divine gift.[18] Now when the Spirit is given in God's new revelation, Israel will be the people to reject him in an ironic reversal of the ancient Jewish position of superiority. So Luke, in bringing into his narrative the whole of humanity, is picking up details of the Sinai traditions and actualizing the Exodus story.

Parallels with the Babel story have already been suggested with reference to the theme of universality in 2.2. There is, in fact, an extensive

17. Metzger, *Commentary*, p. 290: 'Most amazing of all is the statement that these Jews were persons from every nation under heaven. Out of all *lands* under heaven could be understood – but since Jews were already an ἔθνος, to say that these were from another ἔθνος, is tantamount to a contradiction of terms.'

18. *Targ. Deut.* 33.2; *Exod. R.* 5.9; see Potin, *La fête juive*, pp. 248–59.

series of verbal similarities between the text of Acts and the LXX of Genesis 11 by which the Babel story is established as a paradigm for Luke's account.[19] Here, the reference to the people 'from every nation under heaven' living in Jerusalem echoes the theme of people from the whole earth settling in Shinar where the tower reaching to heaven was to be built (Gen. 11.1–2). It is probable that the Babel story was already connected to the Sinai story in Jewish tradition before Luke used the two in association with one another;[20] the effect of using them as a combined template for

19. The allusions to the Babel model are numerous: πᾶσα ἡ γῆ ... ἕως τοῦ οὐρανοῦ, Gen. 11.1 // ἀπὸ παντὸς ἔθνους τῶν ὑπὸ τὸν οὐρανόν, Acts 2.5; φωνὴ μία, Gen. 11.1 // τῆς φωνῆς ταύτης, Acts 2.6; κατῴκησαν, Gen. 11.2 // ἦσαν ... κατοικοῦντες, Acts 2.5; πυρί, Gen. 11.3 // ὡσεὶ πυρός, Acts 2.3; ἤρξαντο ποιῆσαι, Gen. 11.6 // ἤρξαντο λαλεῖν, Acts 2.4; συγχέωμεν, Σύγχυσις, συνέχεεν, Gen. 11.7, 9a,b // συνεχύθη, Acts 2.6; συγχέωμεν ἐκεῖ αὐτῶν τὴν γλῶσσαν, Gen. 11.7 // συνεχύθη καὶ ἤκουον εἷς ἕκαστος λαλοῦντας ταῖς γλώσσαις αὐτῶν, Acts 2.6; ἵνα μὴ ἀκούσωσιν ἕκαστος τὴν φωνὴν τοῦ πλησίον, Gen. 11.7 // ἀκούομεν ἕκαστος τὴν διάλεκτον ἡμῶν, Acts 2.8 D05; χεῖλος ἕν, τὰ χείλη, Gen. 11.1, 6, 9 // διάλεκτος, γλῶσσαι, Acts 2.3, 4, 6, 8, 11; the whole of humanity came from the east: ἀπὸ ἀνατολῶν, Gen. 11.1 // the whole of humanity was gathered in Jerusalem and the list of their countries starts in the east, Acts 2.9. The parallels operate in such a way as to set up a contrast between God's act of punishment and his act of salvation: the confusion created at Babel as a result of arrogance is transformed into a language comprehensible to all humanity as the Holy Spirit acts as a kind of simultaneous translator.

20. Although there is no direct evidence that Babel and Sinai were explicitly linked in Jewish tradition, they have several elements in common which suggests that a connection may well have been made:

1. The theme of the many languages created by God at Babel emerges in the Sinai traditions concerning the hearing of the word of God in different languages, the number 70 (or 72) appearing in stories associated with both events (J.L. Kugel, *Traditions of the Bible. A Guide to the Bible as it was at the Start of the Common Era* [Cambridge, MA.; Harward University Press, 1998], pp. 236–37).
2. The making of bricks for the tower of Babel (Gen. 11.3) is echoed in the reference to the 'pavement like sapphire stone' under the feet of God when he appeared to the leaders of Israel (Exod. 24.10) which is explained as being a brick from the time of Israel's slavery in Egypt: the story is that when a woman gave birth, she dropped the baby into a brick mould and that brick was carried up to heaven to become God's footstool (*Targ. Ps.-J. Exod.* 24.10; Potin, *La fête juive*, pp. 155–59).
3. A similar story exists about a pregnant woman giving birth to a child while making the bricks for Babel, except that in that instance she hid the child under her clothes (*3 Baruch* [Greek] 3.5; Kugel, *Traditions*, pp. 240–41).

the Pentecost revelation is to insist powerfully on the universal nature of the divine gift of the Holy Spirit. Even so, though such is Luke's message, he is careful to distinguish the divine intention and spiritual ideal from the present reality. Hence, although Peter will demonstrate an inspired, universal interpretation of the outpouring of the Holy Spirit in the first part of his speech (2.14–21), he will fall back to a more restricted view once the historical reality takes over as he addresses the 'Men of Israel' (2.15).

[b] 2.6 *The Gathering of the Crowd who Hear their Own Languages*
2.6 The allusions to Babel come to the fore in this verse with the use of the verb 'confused' (συνέχυθη) to describe the residents of Jerusalem who are drawn by the noise (lit. 'this voice'), echoing the Greek name given to Babel (Σύγχυσις) when the Lord 'confused their language' (Gen. 11.7, 9) because they were of 'one voice'. This time, the confusion is positive for God's punishment is reversed as the Holy Spirit speaks through those whom he has filled and the noise is heard by the representatives of all the nations of the earth as an intelligible language. In the AT, the confusion arises because everyone hears in their diverse languages, an exact replica of the traditional interpretation of the situation when God revealed himself on Mt Sinai (see *Critical Apparatus*); this is a little different from the Bezan text where the people are confused by the fact that those who have received the Spirit are *speaking* in the different tongues of the listeners, picking up the comment made in 2.4 and mirroring more closely the Babel scene. In either case, instead of the confusion of languages leading to dispersion and disunity, here the multiplicity of languages enables comprehension and draws people together. Humanity has recovered the capacity to understand in diverse languages the single language of the Spirit, and God has thus re-established the unity of creation.[21]

[c] 2.7–11 *The Crowd Express Amazement; the List of their Countries*
2.7–8 The literary fiction advances by means of an imaginary dialogue among the representatives of the nations. They are 'amazed', an adjective that will be repeated after their speech (2.12), and express their wonder (to each other, according to the Bezan text which frequently seeks to confer this type of human realism on the narrative) at the scene they are witnessing. The miracle lies in the fact that the diverse peoples clearly hear and understand their languages all being spoken by Galileans whose usual language would have been Aramaic. From a Jewish standpoint, the very

21. J.G. Davies, 'Pentecost and Glossolalia', *JTS*, NS, 3 (1952), pp. 228–31 (229).

name 'Galileans' carries with it a certain note of disrespect, for the people from Galilee were looked down upon by other Jews and regarded as inferior;[22] that Galileans should be the first to receive the gift of the Holy Spirit and proclaim the great deeds of God (2.11) is therefore especially surprising.

The question asked by the onlookers, 'how is it that we hear...' will be picked up again after the list of peoples in 2.9–10.

2.9–11a The list of peoples that follows forms a parenthesis between the reiterated question of 2.8b and 2.11b. Because the register at this point in the narrative is not one of literal reality, the list is not to be understood as a historical record of the people present at the Feast of Pentecost in Jerusalem. Nor should it be thought of as referring exclusively to Jews given the secondary nature of the reading of 'Jews' at 2.5. The 15 names specified in the list correspond rather to the whole of humanity: not just geographically, in the way that they are distributed around the four points of the compass, but also historically in their associations with the past, the present and the future. Luke may have drawn on existing lists to create his own but in so doing he has turned them to his own special purpose.

Following the structure created by the conjunctions of the Bezan text (that of the AT is less clear), the 15 countries or peoples fall into three groups which are marked by the presence of three verbs: 'born' (Parthians, Medes and Elamites), 'living' (nine countries from Mesopotamia to Libya) and 'temporarily residing' (Romans, Cretans and Arabs). The use of the number three, which forms the basis of each of the divisions in the list, expresses the symbolic completeness of each group by virtue of the representative names, so an exhaustive list of all the known countries does not need to be given.[23] Geographically, the peoples and nations are

22. The disregard with which the Galilean Jews were viewed by other Jews seems to have been due in part to their largely peasant status and also the extent to which the region of Galilee had accepted Hellenising influences. S. Freyne, *Galilee from Alexander the Great to Hadrian, 323 BCE to 135 CE* (Wilmington: Michael Glazier, Inc/Notre Dame: University of Notre Dame Press, 1980), pp. 22–50; 245–46; and *idem*, 'The Geography of Restoration: Galilee–Jerusalem Relations in Early Christian and Jewish Experience', in J.M. Scott (ed.), *Restoration: Old Testament, Jewish, and Christian Perspectives* (Leiden: E.J. Brill, 2001), pp. 405–33.

23. One aspect of the symbolic force of the number three is that Israel is taken as the reference point; see L. Ginzberg (*The Legends of the Jews* [7 vols.; Philadelphia: The Jewish Publication Society of America,11th edn, 1982], III, p. 79) who comments: 'Everything that is closely connected with the Torah and with Israel is triple in number.'

organized in the list according to an imaginary itinerary around the four points of the compass, starting in the east with the first group of three peoples together with Mesopotamia; it goes on through Palestine viewed as the centre of the world (Judaea), then turns towards the north (Asia) and back down towards the south (Egypt) then towards the extreme west (Libya as far as Cyrene), turning back to the centre by means of the last group of three peoples. In the list of the nine nations, the first, Mesopotamia, has the article (situated in the extreme east), then the central one (Asia, in the north) and finally, Libya at the other extreme. The list can be plotted geographically as follows:

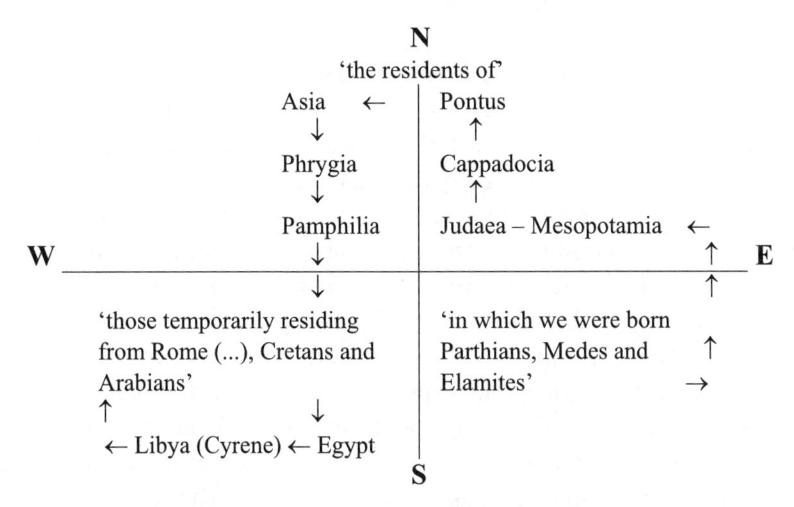

The starting point in the east is reminiscent of the origin of the people who gathered at Shinar for the building of the tower of Babel, in the early days of humanity. The first three names belong to peoples of the past, a fact borne out in the Bezan text where the conjunctions allow each of them to be linked to the past tense verb of the statement 'languages in which we were born'.

In the centre of this structure are those living in the nine countries that stand for the whole of the present era (three groups of three). Among them is Judaea, standing, as the diagram demonstrates, at the centre of the axis of geographical coordinates created by the diverse peoples and nations in the list.

The final group of three peoples are introduced as 'temporarily residing'.[24] Like the first three, these are ethnic groups rather than geographical

24. Concerning the meaning of ἐπιδημέω, cf. 17.21; 18.27 D05: they are 'outsiders', as opposed to κατοικοῦντες who reside in a place.

areas,[25] but rather than recalling the past they anticipate the future. The Romans were in the process of expanding their empire, just as the Cretans were expanding at sea and the Arabs in the desert. The qualification of the Romans as 'Jews and proselytes' would seem to aim to exclude the Roman army of occupation from among those taking part in the scene. This aside confirms by implication that all the other people were not limited to Jews or proselytes.

2.11b The topic of the inspired speech is now specified as 'the great deeds of God', an expression of praise found again at 10.46 in a similar context. This clarifies the meaning of 'utter proclamations' at 2.4.

[b′] 2.12 *The Positive Response of the Crowd*
2.12 The amazement of the crowd, already stated at 2.7, is reiterated. The initial adjective 'all' underlines the way that the outpouring of the Holy Spirit has drawn all of humanity together and that they can talk together. At this point, however, the idea that there is some division among the crowd is subtly introduced by means of the phrase 'one to another'. Luke uses this expression to distinguish between two responses to the miracle they have witnessed, with the Bezan text keeping the focus precisely on this event, 'what had happened'. First, there is the positive enquiry as to the significance of the event which can be viewed as emanating from those who were genuinely open to being enlightened, the 'devout men' of 2.5, including both Gentiles and Jews. This group belongs to the register of literary fiction, although must include some Jews who were historically present (cf. 2.36b).

[a′] 2.13 *The Negative Response of the Crowd*
2.13 In recording a second response of the crowd, Luke now reactivates the literal dimension of his narrative as he reports the scornful ridicule of 'the others', who were among those who were historically present in Jerusalem on this occasion. Instead of wanting to know more, they dismiss the speaking in tongues as drunken nonsense. The use of the demonstrative pronoun in Codex Bezae emphasizes the disrespectful tone of their remarks. As he speaks to the crowd, Peter will address the two groups separately.

25. The distinction is well made by W. Stenger in 'Beobachtungen zur sogenannten Völkerliste des Pfingstwunders (Apg 2,7–11)', *Kairos* 21 (1979), pp. 211–12.

[B′] 2.14–40 *Peter's Two-Part Response and its Outcome*

Overview

This sequence contains the second of Peter's speeches in Acts and is important for revealing his thinking at this stage in his understanding of Jesus' message. As with all the speeches, it must be borne in mind that the words Luke attributes to the speakers are by no means necessarily to be equated with his own ideas and beliefs. His concern is not to communicate official Christian doctrine but to illustrate how difficult it was for the disciples of Jesus to change their traditional ways of thinking (see *General Introduction*, §IX). Such an interpretation of the purpose of the speeches is particularly true of the Bezan text.

Structure and Themes

[a]	2.14–21, 22–36	The speech of Peter with its dual aspect: universal and Israelite
[b]	2.37a	The response of the crowd to Peter's speech
[c]	2.37b	The positive response of some of the crowd
[b′]	2.38–39	Peter's exhortation to Israel to repent and be baptized
[a′]	2.40	Summary of Peter's message

Translation

Codex Bezae D05

[a] **2.14** So then Peter stood up with the ten apostles and was the first to lift up his voice and say, 'Men of Judaea and all of the people living in Jerusalem. Let this be known to you; give ear to my words. **15** For these men are not drunk, as you imagine, since the hour of the day is the third. **16** Rather this is what was spoken through the prophet: **17** "It shall be in the last days, says the Lord, I will pour out from my spirit onto all flesh and their sons and their daughters shall prophesy and the young men shall see visions and the old men shall dream; **18** both on my male servants and on my female servants I myself will pour out from my spirit; **19** and I will give wonders in heaven

Codex Vaticanus B03

2.14 Peter stood up with the Eleven and lifted up his voice and proclaimed, 'Men of Judaea and all the people living in Jerusalem. Let this be known to you and give ear to my words. **15** For these men are not drunk, as you imagine, for it is the third hour of the day. **16** Rather this is what was spoken through the prophet Joel: **17** "And it shall be after that, says God, I will pour out from my spirit onto all flesh and your sons and your daughters shall prophesy and your young men shall see visions and your old men shall dream dreams; **18** indeed, onto both my male servants and my female servants in those days I will pour out from my spirit and above and signs on earth below; **20** the sun turns into darkness and the moon into blood before the great day of the Lord comes **21** and it shall be that anyone who calls on the name of the Lord shall be rescued." **22** Men of Israel, hear these words: Jesus the Nazorene, a man from God, proved among us by powerful deeds and wonders and signs, all of which God did through him in the midst of you, just as you know, **23** this man who was given up by the deliberate plan and foreknowledge of God, you held in your power through the hands of men outside the Law, and you nailed him and killed him. **24** God resurrected him after he had loosened the labour pains of Hades, since it was not possible for him to be held in its grasp. **25** For David says about him, "I saw my Lord before me at all times because he is at my right hand I will not be shaken. **26** Because of this, my heart was glad and my tongue rejoiced, and more than that, my flesh will also dwell in hope **27** that you will not abandon my soul in Hades nor will you allow your Holy One to see corruption. **28** When you have made known to me the ways of life you will fill me with gladness in your presence". **29** Brethren, concerning the patriarch David it can authoritatively be said to you with confidence that he both died and was buried and that his tomb is still with us to this day. **30** So what it means is that, because he was a prophet and knew that God had sworn to him with an oath that out of the fruit of his innermost thoughts he would physically raise up the Messiah and sit him on his throne, **31** he foresaw and spoke about the resurrection of the Messiah, to the effect that he was neither abandoned in Hades nor

they shall prophesy. **19** And I will give wonders in heaven above and signs on earth below, blood and fire and clouds of smoke; **20** the sun shall be turned into darkness and the moon into blood before the great and glorious day of the Lord comes **21** and it will be that everyone that calls on the name of the Lord will be rescued." **22** Men of Israel, listen to these words: Jesus the Nazorene, a man attested among you by God with powerful deeds and wonders and signs that God did through him in the midst of you, just as you know, **23** this man who was given up in line with the deliberate plan and foreknowledge of God, through the hands of men outside the Law you nailed and killed him. **24** God resurrected him after he had loosened the labour pains of death, since it was not possible for him to be held in its grasp. **25** For David says about him, "I saw the Lord before me at all times because he is at my right hand I will not be shaken. **26** Because of this, my heart was glad and my tongue rejoiced, and more than that, my flesh will also dwell in hope **27** that you will not abandon my soul in Hades nor will you allow your Holy One to see corruption. **28** You made known to me the ways of life, You will fill me with gladness in your presence". **29** Brethren, concerning the patriarch David it can authoritatively be said to you with confidence that he both died and was buried and that his tomb is still among us to this day. **30** So what it means is that, because he was a prophet and knew that God had sworn to him with an oath to sit one of his descendants on his throne, **31** he foresaw and spoke about the resurrection of the Messiah,

	did his flesh see corruption. **32** Accordingly, God resurrected this man, Jesus, of which we are all witnesses. **33** Consequently, having been exalted to the right hand of God and having received the promise of the Holy Spirit from his Father, he poured out for you what you both see and hear. **34** For it was not David who ascended into the heavens since he said himself, "The Lord says to my Lord Be seated at my right hand **35** until I place your enemies as a stool for your feet." **36** Accordingly, let all of the house of Israel know with certainty that God appointed as both Lord and Messiah this Jesus whom you crucified.'	to the effect that he was neither abandoned in Hades nor did his flesh see corruption. **32** God resurrected this man Jesus, of which we are all witnesses. **33** Consequently, having been exalted to the right hand of God and, what is more, having received the promise of the Holy Spirit from his Father, he poured out for you what you both see and hear. **34** For it was not David who ascended into the heavens since he said himself, "The Lord says to my Lord Be seated at my right hand **35** until I place your enemies as a stool for your feet." **36** Accordingly, let all the house of Israel know with certainty that God appointed him both Lord and Messiah, this Jesus whom you crucified.'
[b]	**37a** Then all of those who had come together and had listened were cut to the heart,	**37a** When they heard they were cut to the heart,
[c]	**37b** and some of them said to Peter and the apostles, 'So what shall we do, brethren; show us.'	**37b** and said to Peter and the rest of the apostles, 'What are we to do, brethren?'
[b′]	**38** Peter says to them, 'Repent and be baptized, each one of you, in the name of the Lord Jesus, the Messiah, for the forgiveness of sins and you will receive the gift of the Holy Spirit; **39** for the promise belongs to us and to our children and to any of those who are far off whom the Lord our God will call.'	**38** Peter said to them, 'Repent and be baptized, each one of you, upon the name of Jesus, the Messiah, for the forgiveness of your sins and you will receive the gift of the Holy Spirit; **39** for the promise belongs to you and to your children and to any of those who are far off whom the Lord our God will call.'
[a′]	**40** With many and varied arguments he continued testifying and repeatedly exhorted them saying, 'Be saved from this perverse generation.'	**40** With many and varied arguments he continued testifying and repeatedly exhorted them saying, 'Be saved from this perverse generation.'

Critical Apparatus

2.14 σταθεὶς δέ B P^{74} ℵ *rell*, *cum stetisset autem* d || τότε στ. δέ D sy^{p} mae.

τότε in D05 indicates that Peter took up his position to respond to the crowd without any delay (Read-Heimerdinger, *The Bezan Text*, pp. 221–22). The place of δέ after the participle prevents τότε from being separated from the verb it qualifies and also avoids the juxtaposition of τότε and δέ which may have seemed odd. That δέ should thus be the third word of the sentence is not a difficulty for similar examples are found elsewhere in the New Testament (see Winer, *Grammar*, pp. 698–99).

(σὺν τοῖς) ἕνδεκα B P^{74} ℵ (D^{E}) *rell* || δέκα ἀποστόλοις D* d.

The mention of 'ten' apostles in D05 is entirely in accordance with the Bezan text of 1.26 (see *Commentary*).

(ἐπῆρεν) πρῶτος D* d (πρότερον E) p^{c} w vg^{ms} mae || *om.* B ℵ $D^{s.m.}$ *rell.*

Not only is Peter viewed by D05 as the spokesman for the apostles but his speech as the first among other apostolic discourses not cited in the Acts account (cf. 2.42).

καὶ ἀπεφθέγξατο αὐτοῖς B P^{74} ℵ *rell* || κ. εἶπεν D d it (sy).

B03 picks up the verb ἀποφθέγγεσθαι used in 2.4 to describe the proclamations made in diverse languages, even though Peter's speech that follows is not made in a foreign tongue.

καὶ οἱ κατοικοῦντες 'Ιερουσαλὴμ πάντες B P^{74vid} ℵ A C 81. 88. 1828* || κ. πάντες οἱ κατ. 'Ιερ. D d.

The position of πάντες at the end of the phrase in D05 allows Peter's address to be interpreted as distinguishing between the two groups already distinguished in 2.5 and again 2.12–13 (see *Commentary*), that is, the Jewish people literally present in Jerusalem and the universal audience present only as a literary fiction.

καὶ ἐνωτίσασθε B ℵ rell || ἐνωτίσατε D, *ausilate* (pro: *aures date [uerbis meis]*?) d (*auscultate* d^{G}).

All MSS except Codex Bezae agree in using the deponent verb ἐνωτίζομαι, 'pay attention', found on several occasions in the LXX though a hapax of the New Testament. D05 reads the active voice not used elsewhere by biblical authors. The absence of καί between the two commands is a typical rhetorical device used by speakers in Acts to give force to a parallel idea (Read-Heimerdinger, *The Bezan Text*, pp. 250–53). Possibly it serves to distinguish here between the two separate groups to whom the distinct commands are addressed.

2.15 ἔστιν γὰρ ὥρα τρίτη τῆς ἡμέρας B P^{74} ℵ D^{Avid} *rell*, *est enim hora tertia diei* d || οὔσης ὥρας τ. ἡμ. τρίτης D* lat; Ir^{lat} GrElv Aug Hes Cass.

D05, with a range of Latin support, reads a circumstantial clause in place of the explicative γάρ and underlines the time of day by the emphatic position of the adjective.

2.16 (προφήτου) Ἰωήλ B ℵ *rell* || *om.* D d r; Ju Ir^{lat} Rebapt Hil GrElv Aug.

Apart from this mention of Joel in the AT, Luke never specifies the name of the prophets except Isaiah.

2.17 Καὶ ἔσται μετὰ ταῦτα B 076 sa^{mss}; LXX (Theoph) | Κ. ἔσται ἐν τ. ἐσχ. ἡμ. ℵ A E H^{2} I P Ψ 028. 049. 056. 33. 614. 945. 1241. 1245. 1739. 2412. 2492. 2495 𝔐 vg sy; Ir Hil Mac Chr Aug *al* || Ἔσται ἐν τ. ἐσχ. ἡμ. D d gig p sy^{p} co; Ir^{lat} Rebapt Hil Ephr Aug.

B03 follows Joel 3.1 LXX; both the Sinaiticus and the Bezan texts change a phrase describing an eschatological event to the equivalent of 'day of the Lord' referred to earlier in Joel's prophecy (Joel 2.1).

(λέγει) ὁ θεός B ℵ *rell* || κύριος D d E 242. 467. 1845 d latt sa bo^{mss}; Ir^{lat} Rebapt Hil Chr Aug GrNys PassPerp JacEd.

Peter's parenthetical aside, not included in the book of Joel, specifies the speaker of the prophetic words. Whereas ὁ θεός is a reference to God, κύριος is potentially ambiguous since it can mean Yahweh, as in LXX, or Jesus. 2.33 will make clear that Jesus is intended; it is typical of B03 to avoid identification of Jesus with the Lord who spoke to Israel in the past (Read-Heimerdinger, *The Bezan Text*, p. 293).

ἐπὶ πᾶσαν σάρκα B ℵ D^{A} *rell*, *super omnem carnem* d; LXX || ἐπὶ πάσας σάρκας D*.

The plural, read by D05 alone as a modification of the Joel LXX text, is one contribution among others in the Bezan form of this speech to the universal application of Joel's prophecy.

οἱ υἱοὶ ὑμῶν καὶ αἱ θυγατέρες ὑμῶν B ℵ *rell*; LXX || οἱ υἱοὶ αὐτῶν καὶ αἱ θυγ. αὐτῶν D d gig r; Rebapt Hil GrElv PassPerp.
(οἱ νεανίσκοι) ὑμῶν B P^{74} ℵ *rell*; LXX || *om.* D d (p*) r; Rebapt GrElv PassPerp.

The further modification by D05 of the second person pronoun to the third, followed by the omission of the second person pronoun both here and after οἱ πρεσβύτεροι (see below), removes the restriction of Joel's prophecy to the Jewish people.

ὁράσεις B P^{74} ℵ D^{A} *rell*, *visiones* d; LXX || ὁράσει D*.

D05 alone departs from the LXX of Joel by reading the singular dative ('in vision', lit.).

(οἱ πρεσβύτεροι) ὑμῶν B P^{74} ℵ A C^{3} D^{B} *rell*; LXX || *om.* D* d C* (p*) r; Rebapt GrElv PassPerp.

See on (οἱ νεανίσκοι) ὑμῶν above.

ἐνυπνίοις ἐνυπνιασθήσονται B P74 ℵ A C D[B] 049. 1. 33. 81. 945. 1175. 1739 *al* | ἐνύπνια ἐνυπ. E H2 P 056. 69. 88. 614. 1241. 1245. 1611. 2412. 2495 *pm, somnia somniabunt* d; LXX || ἐνυπνιασθήσονται D*.

D05 is once more alone in omitting the cognate noun 'dreams' while B03 follows more closely Joel LXX.

2.18 καί γε B P74 ℵ D[D] *rell* || κ. ἐγώ D* *(!)* d.

γε, not present in Joel LXX, confers a note of insistence on the declaration concerning the servants whom Peter qualifies with the possessive 'my' (of God/Jesus, cf. 2.17). The combination of the possessive adjective with ἐγώ in D05 has the effect of reinforcing the relationship between Jesus (ἐγώ), his people (μου) and, in the following sentence, his Spirit (μου), thereby establishing a clearer distinction between the Jews on the one hand and, on the other, humanity as a whole to whom the previous affirmations have been applied by Peter according to the Bezan text.

ἐν ταῖς ἡμέραις ἐκείναις (ἐκχεῶ) B P74 ℵ *rell*; LXX || *om.* D d gig r ro* vg[mss]; Ju Did Rebapt Asterius Prisc Did Hier.

The omission of the time specification in D05 is in accordance with the inclusion of this phrase in 2.17 where it is given an eschatological meaning.

(πνεύματός μου) καὶ προφητεύσουσιν B P74 ℵ *rell* || *om.* D d p*; Tert Rebapt Prisc PassPerp.

The omission of the time phrase (see above) and the absence of the repeated reference to prophesying means that in the D05 text a pattern is created in which the two applications of Joel's prophecy in 2.17b–18 (universal and Jewish) are mirrored:

[a] I will pour out my Spirit
  [b] on all flesh
    [c] they will prophesy ... see in visions ... have dreams
  [b′] on my male servants and female servants
[a′] I will pour out my Spirit

2.19 (κάτω) αἷμα καὶ πῦρ καὶ ἀτμίδα καπνοῦ B P74vid ℵ *rell*; LXX || *om.* D d it; Prisc.

B03 again retains an element from LXX Joel that D05 discards.

2.20 μεταστραφήσεται B ℵ D[K.B] *rell, convertetur* d; LXX || μεταστρέφεται D*.

In place of the future of Joel LXX, reproduced by B03, D05 actualizes the prophecy by the use of a present. A reference to the darkening of the sun at the time of the crucifixion (Lk. 23.44) may be intended.

πρὶν ἤ B C H^2 P Ψ 056. 614. 1739. 1891. 2147*. 2412. 2492 𝔐 || πρίν D ℵ A C E Ψ 33. 81. 1175. 1505. 1611. 1891. 2495 *al.*

A few MSS of Joel LXX read an unusual ἤ after πρίν, suggesting that the editors or scribes of the MSS of Acts have followed the text of LXX with which they were familiar.

(τὴν μεγάλην) καὶ ἐπιφανῆ B P^{74} A C E H^2 P 049. 056. 33. 614. 945. 1175. 1611. 2412. 2495 𝔐 vg; LXX || *om.* D d ℵ gig r; Prisc.

In line with the omission of the details in 2.19 (see above), D05 also omits from the quotation of Joel LXX the description of the day of the Lord as 'glorious'. These modifications allow the prophecy concerning the day of the Lord to be more easily applied to the present manifestation of the Holy Spirit rather than to a future apocalyptic moment.

2.21 καὶ ἔσται πᾶς ὃς ἂν ἐπικαλήσεται τὸ ὄνομα τοῦ (– D*) κυρίου σωθήσεται B D P^{74} *rell*; LXX || *om.* ℵ

While ℵ01 omits the verse altogether, D05 differs from the rest of the MSS that read it in placing the article before κύριος, thereby undoing, so to speak, the fixed nature of the expression used to refer to the name of the Lord in the LXX. In consequence, the reference to 'Lord' in this instance can mean Jesus, in line with the introduction of the reference to him in 2.17 D05 (see above; Read-Heimerdinger, *The Bezan Text*, p. 279).

2.22 (ἄνδρα) ἀποδεδειγμένον ἀπὸ τοῦ θεοῦ εἰς ὑμᾶς B ℵ C 69. 81. 88. 104. 323. 945. 1175. 1245. 1646. 1739 | ἀπὸ τ. θε. ἀποδεδειγμένον εἰς ὑμᾶς A D^B E P H^2 Ψ 049. 056 33. 614. 1241. 1611. 2344. 2412. 2492. 2495 𝔐 || ἀπὸ τ. θε. δεδοκι–μασμένον εἰς ἡμᾶς D^{*vid}, *a deo probatum* d lat.

The variant ὑμᾶς/ἡμᾶς could be due to itacism but the D05 reading may equally be intended (see *Commentary*). The particular verb used in D05, δοκιμάζω, 'test, prove' (following the reconstruction of the MS proposed by Scrivener, but see Boismard and Lamouille, II, p. 13), means that ἀπὸ τοῦ θεοῦ is unlikely to be the agent, for analysis of Luke's practice indicates that he does not use ἀπό to introduce the agent of a passive verb unless the verb is one of sending (as here in B03; see Read-Heimerdinger, *The Bezan Text*, p. 183). ἀπὸ τοῦ θεοῦ in D05 should therefore be taken instead as referring to the origin of Jesus ('a man from God').

οἷς (ἐποίησεν) B ℵ D^B *rell* || ὅσα D*, *quae* d; Ephr.

The dative of the relative pronoun in B03 arises through attraction and creates something of a meaningless repetition: 'Jesus was attested to you by God by means of miracles… which God did among you (as you know).' No wonder that Boismard and

Lamouille see this as evidence of two similar texts that have been ineptly joined together (Boismard and Lamouille, II, p. 14)! With the accusative relative pronoun and the 1st person pronoun in the first part of the sentence in D05 (see above), there is no redundancy; rather, Peter moves from speaking about the activity of Jesus for the benefit of the apostolic group to remind his audience that these deeds were performed publicly.

2.23 (ἔκδοτον) λαβόντες D d $ℵ^2$ C^3 E H^2 P Ψ 049. 056. 33. 88. 614. 945. 1611. 1175. 2412. 2495 𝔐 sy^h; Eus || *om.* B P^{74} ℵ A C* 81. 323. 1739. 1891 *pc* lat; Ir^{lat} Ath.

Although Metzger describes the additional participle in D05 as 'a typical scribal expansion' (*Commentary*, p. 258), the juxtaposition of ἔκδοτον and λαβόντες is attested in similar contexts by both Polybius and Josephus with the meaning 'held in one's power/at one's mercy' (see Epp, *The Theological Tendency*, pp. 59–61).

2.24 (ὠδῖνας) τοῦ θανάτου B ℵ *rell* || τ. ᾅδου D, *inferiorum* d latt sy^p mae bo; Polyc Ir^{lat} Ephr Aug.

D05 anticipates the mention of Hades at 2.27, 31. ὠδῖνες θανάτου is an expression found in Pss 17.5; 114.3 LXX while ὠδῖνες ᾅδου is found at Ps. 17.6 LXX.

2.25 (τὸν κύριόν) μου D d ℵ 614. 2495 *pc* sy^p || *om.* B *rell*; LXX.

B03 follows Ps. 15.8 LXX.

2.26 μου ἡ καρδία B ℵ*; Cl || ἡ καρδία μου D d P^{74vid} $ℵ^2$ A C E H^2 P Ψ 049. 056. 095. 33. 323. 614. 945. 1175. 1739. 2412. 2495 𝔐; LXX Ir^{lat}.

The situation here is unusual in so far as it is the B03 text with little support that does not follow Ps. 15.9 LXX in the continuation of the quotation. The placing of the possessive pronoun before the noun generally tends to make the expression of feeling more intimate (Read-Heimerdinger, *The Bezan Text*, pp. 108–109) though there is no apparent reason for that in this instance.

2.28 ἐγνώρισας B P^{74vid} ℵ D^B *rell*, *notas fecisti* d; LXX || γνωρίσας D.

The aorist participle in D05 in place of the aorist indicative could have arisen through a copyist's error. If it is intentional, it causes the verb to refer to a future time, 'When you have made known to me...', rather than the past, which matches the future tense of the verbs in v. 27.

2.29 τὸ μνῆμα B ℵ *rell* || τ. μνημεῖον D, *monumentum* d P^{74vid} gig.

Unlike τὸ μνῆμα which refers to the tomb or grave (as in 7.16, speaking of Joseph's bones), τὸ μνημεῖον can mean the memorial erected on the grave (as understood by d05), although not necessarily, as illustrated by the reference to the placing of Jesus' body in a grave, μνημεῖον, at 13.29.

ἐν ἡμῖν B P^{74} ℵ *rell* || παρ' ἡμῖν D d Ψ e gig p r t vg sy^{p}; Ir^{lat}.

B03 has Peter refer to the grave of David as a physical reality within the city. The combination in D05 of παρ' ἡμῖν with the previous variant reading could mean instead that Peter is referring to the memorial to David as an ongoing record.

2.30 ὀσφύος B ℵ $D^{H.G}$ *rell* || καρδίας D*, *praecordia* d.

This variant functions in conjunction with the following one. The reading ὀσφύος ('loins') in conjunction with 'the fruit', is a reference to the physical descendance of David, in line with Ps. 131.11 LXX where κοιλία ('belly, organ of reproduction, innermost recesses of the human body'; see B-A-G) is read. The 'fruit of his heart (καρδίας)', on the other hand, is a metaphorical expression rather than a physical one since the heart was seen as the seat of the intellect, and can therefore be construed as a reference to the fruit of David's thoughts, that is, his prophesying.

κατὰ σάρκα ἀναστῆσαι τὸν Χριστὸν καί D* d* (33. 36. 88 *pc*) mae || *om.* B P^{74vid} ℵ A C D^{A} 81. 1175 d^{A}.

The absence of these words, combined with the variant reading of the noun ὀσφύος noted above, results in a meaning that is different from that of D05. According to B03, God had promised David he would place one of his physical descendants on his throne. The reading of D05, further supported with slight variation by E Ψ 𝔐 sy^{h} and Or, means that God promised David that out of his prophecies he would raise up (i.e. 'create', one of the meanings of ἀναστῆσαι) the Messiah in the flesh and place him on his throne (cf. 2 Sam. [2 Kgdms LXX] 7.12–13). The subsequent references to ἀναστῆσαι in the next two verses play on the alternative meaning of the verb, 'to resurrect'.

2.31 προϊδὼν ἐλάλησεν περὶ τῆς ἀναστάσεως τοῦ Χριστοῦ B P^{74} ℵ *rell* || ἀναστ. τ. Χρ. D*, *resurrectione Christi* d* | προειδὼς ἐλ. π. τ. ἀν. τ. Χρ. D^{F} d^{mg} 33. 88. 104. (945. 1739. 1891) *al* sa; Cyr^{pt}.

As the sentence does not make sense as it stands in D05 and d05, the omission of these words would seem due to a copyist's error which must have arisen at an early stage in the composition of the text since the Greek and Latin pages do not derive from the same exemplar.

οὔτε ... οὐδέ B E H^{2} P Ψ 049. 056. 69. 88. 614. 1241. 1611 𝔐; LXX || οὔτε ... οὔτε D, *neque ... neque* d ℵ A C 81. 945. 1175. 1270. 1739. 1891. 2147. 2495 *al*; Or Eus.

The use of οὐδέ by B03 confers a stronger emphasis on the second of the two affirmations.

εἰς ᾅδην B ℵ 81. 88. 323. 440. 547. 927. 945. 1175. 1270. 1505. 1739. 1891. 2344 *al*; LXX Eus || εἰς ᾅδου D A C^{vid} E H^{2} P Ψ 049. 056. 69. 614. 1611. 2412. 2495 𝔐.

The accusative is found in Ps. 15.10 LXX to which this verse appears to refer. The genitive stands, in a construction usual in Classical Greek, for εἰς ᾅδου οἶκον and can assumed to be intentional since it varies not only from the LXX reference but also from the previous reference in Peter's speech at 2.27.

εἶδεν (διαφθοράν) B ℵ D[s.m.] *rell*, *vidit* d || ἰδεῖν D* 1175; LXX.

2.32 τοῦτον τὸν Ἰησοῦν B ℵ D[H] *rell* || τ. οὖν, Ἰη. D* d gig p r mae; MVict Amb.

Without any linking word, B03 relates the mention of the resurrection of the Messiah to 'this Jesus', with the demonstrative adjective and the anaphoric article picking up the earlier reference to him in 2.22. In D05, the demonstrative is a pronoun referring to the Messiah to whom the name 'Jesus' stands in apposition, revealing the Messiah's identity (cf. 2.36 D05); οὖν links this next stage in Peter's reasoning to the previous argument, and belongs to the series of steps in Peter's speech connected in a similar way (2.30, 32, 33 D05, 36) (see Read-Heimerdinger, *The Bezan Text*, p. 227).

(οὗ) πάντες ἡμεῖς ἐσμεν μάρτυρες B P[74vid] *rell* | π. ἐσ. ἡμ. μαρτ. ℵ || π. ἡμ. μάρτυρές ἐσμεν D, *nos omnes testes sumus* d 1518 c gig p t vg; MVict Amb.

By its place before the verb, the Bezan text emphasises the word 'witnesses'.

2.33 τήν τε ἐπαγγελίαν τοῦ πνεύματος τοῦ ἁγίου B ℵ A C E Ψ 33. 81. 88. 945. 1175. 1611. 1739. 1891. 2147 || καὶ τὴν ἐπ. τ. ἁγίου πν. D | τήν τε ἐπ. τ. ἁγ. πν. P H[2] 049. 056. 69. 614. 2412. 2492. 2495 𝔐, *et pollicitationem spiritus sancti* d.

With the connective τε, B03 presents the receiving of the Holy Spirit by Jesus as closely connected to his exaltation to God's right hand, or even as of greater significance for what follows (Read-Heimerdinger, *The Bezan Text*, p. 205); the order of words in the phrase referring to the Holy Spirit is that typically used in Acts in the context of an explanation such as Peter is giving here (*The Bezan Text*, pp. 163–64, 168). The Bezan text does not highlight the receiving of the promise in the same way but it refers to the Holy Spirit with the expression reserved in Acts for the intimate relationship between the Spirit and either Christians or Jesus himself.

(ἐξέχεεν) τοῦτο ὃ ὑμεῖς καί B D[F] | τ. ὃ ὑμ. P[74vid] ℵ A C* 81. 323. 1175. 1739. 1891 *al* vg[cl.st.ww]; Cyr || ὑμῖν ὃ καί D*, *vobis quod et* d.

B03 focuses on the action of the glorified Jesus pouring out the Spirit, the effects of which Peter's audience (nominative, ὑμεῖς) can (both, B03) see and hear. In contrast, with the dative pronoun ὑμῖν, D05 focuses on the people as the intended benefactors of the Spirit who was poured out 'for you'.

2.34 λέγει δὲ αὐτός· Εἶπεν B ℵ *rell* || εἴρηκεν γὰρ αὐτός· Λέγει D (*dixit enim ipse: Dixit* d p sy[p] mae).

B03 introduces David's words with a historic present and thereafter follows the LXX of Ps. 109.1. In D05, as elsewhere in the Bezan text, the logical structure of Peter's speech is more apparent by virtue of the connective γάρ which, following on immediately from a previous clause introduced by γάρ, serves to confirm the contents of the first affirmation (Read-Heimerdinger, *The Bezan Text*, p. 241); the perfect tense to introduce the quotation tends to present David's speech more as a scriptural record than his personal words. The use of the present tense in the opening verb of the speech has the effect of making David's words relevant to the present situation; the same change from the LXX text occurs in Jesus' quotation of these words in Lk. 20.41.

2.35 ἕως ἂν θῶ B P^{74} ℵ D^{B} *rell* || ἕως θῶ D*, *donec ponam* d.

B03 again follows the LXX where D05 differs (Lk. 20.41 D05 reads ἕως τιθῶ rather than the more usual ἕως ἂν θῶ).

2.36 πᾶς οἶκος B P^{74} ℵ *rell* || π. ὁ οἶκος D C 1518 sa mae.

The phrase without the article underlines the collectivity of Israel; with the article, the totality.

(κύριον) αὐτόν B P^{74} ℵ A C D^{B} Ψ 88. 323. 945. 1175. 1611. 1739. 1891 || *om.* D d E H^{2} P 049. 056. 81. 614. 2412. 2495 𝔐.

The variant readings function in conjunction with the variant in the same verse concerning the article before Jesus (see below).

ἐποίησεν ὁ θεός B ℵ Ψ 81 *pc* || ὁ θ. ἐπ. D d P^{74} A C E H^{2} P 049. 056. 614. 1739. 2412. 2495 𝔐 p r t vg; Ir^{lat} $Ath^{pt.}$

The order of words in D05 not only underlines God as the subject by placing it before the verb but also causes 'God' to follow directly the two titles 'Lord and Messiah' so highlighting the divine activity in relation to the bestowing of these roles on Jesus.

τοῦτον τὸν Ἰησοῦν B ℵ D^{B} *rell* || τοῦτον, Ἰη. D* d.

It is conceivable that τόν has been omitted from D05 by haplography. However, since the same reading as that of 2.32 D05 is reproduced, this time without an intervening οὖν, it is more likely to be intentional. The demonstrative is again a pronoun and the name of Jesus stands in apposition. In the alternative reading, the demonstrative is an adjective qualifying Jesus, the whole phrase standing in apposition to αὐτόν, absent in D05.

2.37a ἀκούσαντες δέ B ℵ *rell* || τότε πάντες οἱ συνελθόντες καὶ ἀκ. D, *tunc omnes qui convenerant exaudientes* d sy^{hmg}.

B03 simply moves on to the next development of the story, introduced with δέ, as the narrative switches back to focus on the people who had heard Peter's speech. With τότε, D05 presents the immediate response of the people who are referred to as a whole before the separate response of one element among them is recorded in the question that follows.

τὴν καρδίαν B P^{74vid} ℵ A C 81. 1175 || τῇ καρδίᾳ D d E H^2 P Ψ 049. 056. 69. 88. 614. 945. 1245. 1611. 1739. 2412. 2495 𝔐.

Both the accusative and the dative may be used to express the relationship of the noun to the verb κατανύσσομαι (B-A-G).

2.37b εἶπόν τε B A C H^2 P 056. 69. 88. 945. 1175. 1245. 1739. 2412. 2495 𝔐 | εἰπόντες ℵ D^B 049. 614. 1245. 1611. 2412 *pc* sy^h || καί τινες ἐξ αὐτῶν εἶπαν D* d mae; Ephr.

D05 identifies those who seek to pursue the discussion with Peter as only a part of his Jewish audience (see v. 37a above).

τοὺς λοιποὺς ἀποστόλους B ℵ *rell* || τοὺς ἀπ. D d 241 gig r bo^{mss}; Aug Qu.

B03 makes it quite clear that Peter operates as one of the apostles, numbered as 'the Eleven' in 2.14. The apostles have already been named as such in D05 at 2.14 and the term here therefore is anaphoric.

Τί B ℵ *rell* || Τί οὖν D d gig mae; Ir^{lat} Aug.

The next three variants, in the report of the people's response, function together. The connective in D05 makes clear that the question of the people arises as a consequence of Peter's words.

ποιήσωμεν B ℵ *rell* || ποιήσομεν D 1739 *al*; Chr.

The future instead of the deliberative subjunctive in the AT confers a certain note of urgency on the people's question. In the parallel scene relating the baptism by John in Luke's Gospel, the people ask Τί οὖν (omit D05) ποιήσωμεν (Lk. 3.10).

(ἀδελφοί,) ὑποδείξατε ἡμῖν D d E it vg^{mss} sy^{hmg} mae | *om.* B P^{74} ℵ *rell.*

The urgency is continued in the second question recorded by D05, using a word that echoes the cry of John the Baptist (Lk. 3.7).

2.38 πρὸς αὐτούς· Μετανοήσατε B P^{74vid} 218. 606. 630. 1835. 1838 *al*; Aug^{pt} | ἔφη πρ. αὐτούς· Μετ. E H^2 P Ψ 049. 056. 69. 323. 614. 1241. 1611. 2147. 2344. 2412. 2492. 2495 𝔐 gig t vg^{mss} | πρ. αὐτούς· Μετ., φησίν ℵ A C 36. 81. 86. 630. 945.

1175. 1642*. 1704. 1739. 1891. 2298 vg || πρ. αὐτοὺς φησίν· Μετ. D d (1505) p r vg^{ms}; Ir$^{lat\ vid}$.

The varying places of φησίν reflect stylistic variation rather than any difference in meaning. Its occurrence in ℵ01 after the first word of the direct speech can be observed in the speeches reported in the later chapters of Acts (D05 *lac.*), though there, too, variant readings arise (23.35; 25.5; 26.25). In the only comparable occurrence in Luke's Gospel, D05 reads ἔφη before the two words spoken rather than after (Lk. 7.40).

ἐν (τῷ ὀνόματι) B D d C 429. 522. 945. 1739. 1891. 2298; Ir^{lat} Did || ἐπί ℵ A E H^{2} P Ψ 049. 056 33. 614. 1270. 1611. 2412. 2492. 2495 𝔐.

ℵ01 seems to encourage the people to be baptized *on the basis of* the name of Jesus; both B03 and D05, *in* his name.

τοῦ κυρίου (Ἰησοῦ Χριστοῦ) D d E 614. 945. 1270. 1739. 1891. 2412 *al* r (p) vg^{ms} sy$^{(h)}$ (sa mae); Cyp Bas || *om.* B ℵ *rell.*

It is typical of the Bezan text to use the full title with the name of Jesus in the formal context of a baptism (Read-Heimerdinger, *The Bezan Text*, p. 267).

(εἰς ἄφεσιν) τῶν ἁμαρτιῶν ὑμῶν B ℵ A (C) 81 *pc* t w vg || ἁμαρτιῶν D d E H^{2} P Ψ 049. 056. 33. 614. 1245. 1270. 1611. 1739. 2344. 2412. 2495 𝔐 it sy; Ir^{lat} Cyp.

The expression of B03 is not found elsewhere. The shorter D05 reading is the one that recurs in similar solemn circumstances: Mk 1.4; Matt. 26.28; Lk. 1.77; 3.3 (another echo of John's baptism); 24.47; Acts 5.31; 10.43; 13.38; 19.5 D05; 26.18 (D05 *lac.*).

2.39 ὑμῖν ... τοῖς τέκνοις ὑμῶν B P^{74} ℵ *rell* || ἡμῖν ... τ. τέκ. ἡμῶν D d (p) mae; Aug.

The variant could have arisen through itacism (cf. 13.26 where ὑμῖν is read by P^{45} C E 1739 𝔐 lat sy bo aeth geo). On the other hand, Luke alone among the evangelists respects the classical rule which dictates that εἶναι + dative underlines the possession (rather than the possessor for which εἶναι + genitive is required; see B-D-R, §189.1). Since Peter's audience do not yet possess 'the promise', that is, the Holy Spirit, the second person pronoun is not appropriate here, and the reading of D05 makes better sense.

2.40 (ἑτέροις) τε B P^{74} ℵ *rell*, *quoque* d || δέ D 489 vg^{mss} co.

The connective views δέ Peter's other words as a separate development which continued (imperfect verb and present participle) after his first discourse whereas τε sees them as of parallel significance (Read-Heimerdinger, *The Bezan Text*, p. 205).

(ἀπὸ τῆς γενεᾶς) τῆς σκολιᾶς ταύτης B P^{74} ℵ *rell* || ταύτης τ. σκ. D, *(ex progenie) ha[n]c prava* d 614. 1646. 1837. 1838. (1891*). 2412. 2495 gig p r t vg; Aug Lcf.

The place of the adjective at the end of the phrase has the effect of accentuating it (Delebecque, *Les deux Actes*, p. 36).

Commentary

[a] 2.14–36 *The Speech of Peter with its Dual Aspect: Universal and Israelite*

Peter makes his speech in response to the twofold reaction of the crowd. It consists of a long *Exposition* (2.14b–35) and a brief *Parenesis* (2.36). The Exposition itself is divided into two distinct parts, the first (2.14b–21) addressed to a universal audience and the second (2.22–35) restricted to Peter's Jewish listeners. Each part is accompanied by appropriate scriptural references which form the backbone of the speech. The following schema can be observed:

[α] *Exposition* (2.14b–35):
- *First part* (2.14b–21):
  - Theme: New humanity, the first fruits of the Spirit
  - Addressees: The Jews (historically) together with the representatives of the nations living (figuratively) in Jerusalem (v. 14b)
  - Event: The outpouring of the Holy Spirit (v. 14c [cf. vv. 2–4])
  - Thesis: The Holy Spirit is the heritage of all humanity (vv. 15–16)
  - Scripture: Joel 3.1–5a (vv. 17–21)
- *Second part*: (2.22–35)
  - Theme: The Messiah-Lord, resurrected and exalted at the right hand of God
  - Addressees: The Jews (v. 22a)
  - Event: The death of Jesus (vv. 22b–23)
  - Thesis 1: The Messiah has been resurrected (vv. 24, 29–32)
  - Scripture: Ps. 15.8–11 (vv. 25–28)
  - Thesis 2: ...as Lord, he has been exalted at the right hand of God (vv. 33–34a)
  - Scripture: Ps. 109.1 (vv. 34b–35)

[β] *Parenesis* (2.36)
- The resurrected Jesus is Messiah and Lord (v. 36)

The parenesis is interrupted by the reaction of the audience (2.37) but is resumed immediately (2.38–40) in response to the question they ask.

It is important to notice that only the first part of Peter's speech has a universal application and, as such, demands a radically new interpretation of the Scriptures under the inspiration of the Holy Spirit. Once Peter limits his audience to the people of Israel, however, it must be supposed that he is no longer speaking as inspired but from his own understanding. To see how this can be so, it should be noted that the apostles have been (and will only ever be) described as 'filled with the Holy Spirit' (2.4) rather than 'full of the Holy Spirit' (cf. Jesus, Lk. 4.1). Consequently, not everything that they do and say will be inspired. That Peter speaks from his own thoughts in the second part of his speech in this chapter is borne out by the fact that his attitude towards his fellow-Jews will change as he understands more precisely the message of Jesus. For the time being, his concern is to convince the Jews of the status of Jesus as the Messiah and of his resurrection, and of the means for them to be saved from the consequences of having killed him. In due course, he will come to realize that salvation lies outside a Jewish way of thinking and that the Messiahship of Jesus goes beyond the prophecies of the Scriptures.

2.14a The tone of the introduction to Peter's speech is solemn, with the Bezan text making explicit the close connection between the crowd's reaction and the apostolic response, 'So then...'. Peter does not speak on his own but on behalf of the other apostles and the different ways the two texts count them is entirely in line with what has been said earlier about the replacement of Judas: since the election of Matthias was seen by the AT to cause the group of Twelve to be reconstituted (see *Commentary*, 1.26), there were eleven apostles apart from Peter; in the Bezan text, however, the narrator had indicated that Matthias was not considered to fully replace Judas and therefore only ten apostles remained in addition to Peter. Later (Acts 6), the apostolic group will rely on their claim to represent Israel as a body of Twelve, even in the Bezan text, but for the time being, certainly in the first part of Peter's speech with its universal application, that is not an issue.

[α] 2.14b–35 *Exposition*

2.14b According to Codex Bezae, Peter's speech is the first among others (cf. 2.42). His role as spokesman is thereby underlined while according at the same time some teaching responsibility to the other apostles.

Two distinct elements of Peter's audience are apparent in the wording of the Bezan text which distinguishes between the (literal) people of Judaea and all the other people (figuratively) present in Jerusalem (see *Commentary*, 2.5–8). The position of the adjective 'all' in the AT groups the listeners together indifferently. It will be helpful, as an aid to understanding how the two registers can operate at once in the Bezan text, to bear in mind the parallel from the traditional Jewish account of the giving of the law on Mount Sinai, which has not only the Israelites as historical witnesses of the event but, alongside them, all the people of the world as present on another level of reality. In Acts, the universal element is present as the intended, and potential, recipients of the gift of the Holy Spirit, alongside the Jews of the time who had come to Jerusalem for the Passover. The two groups have already been seen to have responded to the arrival of the Holy Spirit in different ways (2.12–13). It is possible that the distinction made in Codex Bezae is maintained in Peter's opening commands: to the Jews, it should 'be known' (γνωστὸν ἔστω, the same expression being found with reference to Jews at 4.10; 13.38; 28.22, 28), implying that they are to understand correctly things already heard; and the others, the nations, are to listen carefully (ἐνωτίσασθε [ἐνωτίσατε D05], New Testament hapax), suggesting that what they are about to hear is new knowledge. A similar duality of address is seen in the opening words of Joel's prophecy (Joel 1.2; cf. 2.1) which will be extensively cited by Peter in the following verses. The absence of connective in the Bezan text may serve to express the distinction.

2.15 The dual register is maintained as Peter responds to the two reactions of the crowd. In answer to the charge of those actually present (2.13) that the disciples are drunk, he points out that it is too early. The 'third hour' is counted from the rising of the sun and corresponds to nine o'clock in the morning; this information tallies with the statement in 2.1 that the day of Pentecost was coming to an end, having begun the previous evening. The significance of the time is underlined by the expression of Codex Bezae, reflecting the attention Luke pays more generally to times (Lk. 23.44; Acts 3.1; 10.3, 9, 30). Since the third hour was that at which the crucifixion began (Mk 15.25), a correlation is thus established between the death of Jesus and the arrival of the Spirit as the first fruit of his death.

2.16 Peter then goes on, in opposition to the accusation of drunkenness, to answer the more positive questioning of the universal audience, 'What does this mean?' (2.12). 'This' is what had been foretold through prophecy as recorded in the Jewish Scriptures. There is in the passage Peter expounds an element of universalism which makes sense of the account Luke gives of the whole world having gathered in Jerusalem, the centre of the Jewish religion, to witness the event that would put an end to their dispersion and their spiritual alienation. Peter will present the coming of the Spirit on the disciples of Jesus as the first manifestation of the realization of Joel's prophecy.

Allusions to the book of Joel in fact begin before Peter's citation of it. As noted above (see 2.14), Joel addresses two sets of people in his opening words: the 'elders', and 'all the inhabitants of the earth' (a distinction repeated in 2.1 with 'Sion', and 'all the habitants of the earth' once again), paralleled by the 'men of Judaea' and 'all the inhabitants of Jerusalem' in the Bezan text of Acts 2.14. Joel exhorts the people to 'hear this ... give ear (ἐνωτίσασθε)...' (Joel 1.2), just as Peter says 'let it be known ... give ear (ἐνωτίσασθε/ἐνωτίσατε)...' (Acts 2.14).

2.17 More than simply citing the passage of Joel 2.28–32a LXX word for word, Peter will interpret and adapt it to so as apply it to the current situation. This is more apparent in the Bezan text which departs at numerous places from the LXX text.[26]

The opening words of Joel 2.28 LXX read as in Codex Vaticanus. The modification of the time phrase in Codex Bezae (and, indeed, Codex Sinaiticus) draws on the earlier references in Joel's prophecy to 'the day of the Lord' (1.15; 2.1, 11) as a time of final blessing and revelation. Peter's application of this prophecy to the present time when the Holy Spirit has been given, especially in its more universal form in Codex Bezae, requires a radical reworking of the original promise which was made to the people of Israel (Joel 3.16) following their lamentation (Joel 2.12–17) for the pitiful state of their land (Joel 1.4–20). It is in the creation of such new interpretations that the inspiration of the Spirit is clearly apparent, and evidence that he is indeed present.

The coming of the Spirit is presented by Peter as marking the start of a final, and definitive, era for humankind. Following the original thrust of Joel's prophecy it could look as if Peter is distinguishing between the outpouring of the Spirit as marking the beginning of the age of the Church and the judgment of unbelievers, which will take place, following signs of cosmic turbulence, on 'the day of the Lord' (2.20) at the end of this age.[27] Contrary to this interpretation, however, the reworking of Joel's text, especially in its Bezan form, results in its being applied in its totality to the present event and to the ongoing presence of the Lord Jesus through his Spirit in the community.

In the Bezan text, Joel's prophecy is attributed to 'the Lord', a term which is potentially ambiguous but which 2.33 makes clear means Jesus. The words 'all flesh' in Greek are then changed from the singular to the

26. See J. Rius-Camps, 'La utilización del libro de Joel (Jl 2,28-32A LXX) en el discurso de Pedro (Hch 2,14–21): Estudio comparativo de dos tradiciones manuscritas', in D.G.K. Taylor (ed.), *Studies in the Early Text of the Gospels and Acts* (Text and Studies, 3/I; Birmingham: University Press, 1999), pp. 245–70.

27. See, e.g., Barrett, I, pp. 138–39. Passages such as Lk. 17.26–36; 21.25–27 may be appealed to in support of this interpretation.

plural (as if to emphasise 'all mortals'), the first of a series of modifications that extend the application of Joel's prophecy beyond the limits of Israel and truly signal the onset of a new epoch. Further changes follow as the original recipients of the divine Spirit, already envisaged by Joel as a wider group than the usual limited group of prophets, are no longer 'yours' (i.e. belonging to Israel) but 'theirs' (belonging to 'all flesh'). Both texts portray a community of a family type, composed of parents and children, old and young, but whereas in the AT it is to the group of disciples (which include women, cf. 1.13) actually present in this scene that the words can be immediately applied, in the Bezan text the local application is merely a small element of a universal one.

2.18 Modifications to the text of Joel are made in both the AT and D05 which are significant, for Peter qualifies the servants as 'my' and thereby restricts the repetition of 'I will pour out my Spirit' to the Jews. The relationship between Jesus as the divine giver (cf. 2.17, 33) and his people is further reinforced by the Bezan text with the additional emphatic pronoun ἐγώ, 'I myself'. The AT, in introducing the Jewish people, simply repeats the earlier affirmation, restating that they will prophesy and that the Spirit will be poured out in these days. By omitting those two details, the Bezan text creates a concentric pattern according to which the move from the universal and to the Jewish application of the prophecy is apparent:

[a] I will pour out my Spirit
  [b] on all flesh
    [c] they will prophesy ... see in visions ... have dreams
  [b′] on my male servants and female servants
[a′] I will pour out my Spirit

The first mention of the outpouring of the Spirit is a general one, relating to all humanity [a, b], and the second is specific to the Jewish people [b′, a′]. In the centre of the structure is a list of the recipients of the Spirit (sons and daughters, young men, old men) and their activities, who are members of both groups.

2.19–20 In several writings of the New Testament, notably Paul's so-called 'Pastoral Epistles', the signs of cosmic upheaval are cited as portents of the end of the world and precursors of the splendour of the second coming of Jesus (2 Thess. 2.8; 1 Tim. 6.14; 2 Tim. 4.1; Tit. 2.13). It is therefore easy to assume that Peter has in mind such events here as he refers to dramatic events on earth and in heaven. If attention is paid, however, to the way Peter adapts the text of Joel to the present situation, it becomes clear that he interprets these signs not as an indication of the end of the world but as anticipating the onset of the final age of humanity, for 'the day of the Lord', when people may be saved by calling on his name, will be seen to be the present time (cf. 2.39–40).

Peter's adaptation of Joel's prophecy to the present age is all the more consistent in the Bezan text which omits, first, the reference to 'blood, fire and clouds of smoke'. Although these aspects of Joel's vision of the day of the Lord (Joel 2.30) fit with John the Baptist's warning of an eschatological, Messianic baptism with 'the Spirit and with fire' (Mk 1.8), Jesus himself removed the punitive aspect of this prophetic statement (see *Commentary,* 1.5; 11.16). Likewise, the second omission in Codex Bezae of the description of the day of the Lord as 'glorious', an adjective with connotations of the splendour associated with the theophany of the second coming, is in keeping with the way Jesus presented himself to the world and would continue to maintain his presence through his Spirit.

That said, other modifications to Joel's text occur in both texts of Peter's speech: the addition of the adjectives 'above/below' to qualify heaven and earth; the introduction of the term 'signs' on a par with 'wonders', which thus stands as the first mention of 'signs and wonders', a motif that will be repeated throughout the missionary speeches as a way of tracking the progressively positive interaction of the disciples of Jesus with both Jewish and Gentile society (2.22, 43; 4.30; 5.12; 6.8; 7.36; 14.3; 15.12). In the context of the day of Pentecost on which Peter makes his speech, 'the wonders in heaven above' could refer to the noise of the wind (2.2) and the 'signs on earth below' to the tongues of fire that settled on the disciples (2.3).

The cosmic upheaval is presented in the Bezan text as a present, not a future, reality, yet another means to remove the future dimension from the prophecy and signal its realization in current events. There is an echo of the comment that the sun was darkened at the moment of the crucifixion (Lk. 23.44) but more than anything, the cosmic signs reflect the profound change in the order of things as a new era for the whole of humankind is born.

2.21 Peter stops short of the words concluding the section he cites from the book of Joel, for there the deliverance of those who call on the name of the Lord is limited to those on Mount Zion and Jerusalem (Joel 3.5 LXX). In his reworking of the ancient prophecy, Peter avoids according any privilege to a faithful remnant of the people of Israel by giving it once more a universal application.

The almost literal quotation of Joel from the LXX text in the AT of Peter's speech gives the impression that the point he wants to make is simply that what his audience see and hear, the outpouring of the Spirit which precedes a final judgment day, has been foreseen in the Jewish Scriptures. In the Bezan text, where Joel's text is considerably modified, Peter has quite a different purpose: on the basis of a prophecy addressed to the people of Israel, he constructs a new prophecy which proclaims that the gift of the Spirit is for all of humankind and marks the beginning of a new era; it is as much for the Jews attending the Feast of Passover in Jerusalem as it is for all the representatives of the nations who were figuratively present. The creative use of Scripture, bringing it up to date so as to make it relevant to new circumstances, is a typically Jewish approach to exegesis (see *Introduction,* §V).

There is no need to see in the universalism that characterizes the Bezan form of Peter's speech a trait of later Gentile Christianity. On the contrary, in Luke's Gospel Jesus has already shown how the gospel is for all nations and it is entirely right that under the inspiration of the Spirit Peter's teaching should be in keeping with the message of his master. The extensive alteration to the text of Joel could, on the other hand, have been felt to be a difficulty among Christian communities that accorded a high status to the fixed nature of the written text, and it could have been this attitude that prompted an editor to replace the Bezan form of Joel's prophecy with one more in line with the LXX.

2.22 With the change of addressee to 'Men of Israel', Peter also changes his theme from the outpouring of the Spirit to the person of 'Jesus the Nazorene'[28] who was known to his audience. His concern will be to demonstrate that this man whom the Jews killed was none other than the Messiah and that he has been raised from the dead. The designation 'Nazorene' identifies Jesus as the Messiah of the line of David (cf. Isa. 11.1, which describes the Messiah as a sprout (נצר) blossoming from the root of Jesse, the father of David; cf. Isa. 11.10).[29]

28. Peter uses the term Ναζωραῖος, a Messianic designation lacking the political, nationalistic connotations of the alternative Ναζαρηνός. The same term will be used exclusively in Acts (cf. 3.6; 4.10; 6.14; 22.8; 24.5; 26.9) where the context is always Messianic; the more nationalistic form is found in Luke's Gospel, usually with variant readings (Lk. 4.34; 18.37 D05; 24.19 ℵ01/B03), where Luke plays on the dual terminology to underline the political hopes of certain of his characters.

29. See Zerwick, *Biblical Greek*, §417.

The main verb of Peter's long introductory sentence (typical of Peter's speeches in Acts, almost as if Luke represents him thinking aloud as he works out what he wants to say) comes at the end of 2.23, 'you killed'. By the time Peter gets to it, he will have summarized all the work of God through Jesus, starting with the miracles, signs and wonders, echoing the first mention of the latter two terms in 2.19 and setting up a point of reference with which the future miraculous activity of the apostles can be compared (see on 2.19 above). By these, Jesus has been 'attested' (AT) or 'tested' (D05), the perfect tense conveying the notion of a state that has been achieved (as opposed to a past event now over and done with, as would have been suggested by the use of the aorist). The difference between the two texts is, in fact, not just the verb but the overall structure of the sentence and variation, too, affecting one of the pronouns. The result is that in the AT Peter speaks of Jesus with reference only to his audience, apparently affirming twice the same idea that God did wonderful things through him among the people.

The Bezan text first of all considers Jesus from the point of view of the disciples. He was a man from God, and it is among the circle of his followers ('we') that he has been tested, or indeed 'proved by testing', by the manifestations of supernatural power; Jesus' credentials, in other words, have been given for the benefit of the disciples for whom they are necessary since they are to witness to him. Yet they were performed not in secret but publicly among the people Peter is addressing, as well the other inhabitants of Palestine (cf. Lk. 24.19) including Gentiles (cf. Acts 10.37–38). Peter goes on to set the Jews' rejection of Jesus against this open demonstration of God's power.

2.23 Peter moves constantly throughout this part of his speech between the action of God and the action of the people, showing at each turn how everything that happened to Jesus during his life as a man was foreseen. Here he stresses how the failure of Jesus to be accepted by his people was decreed by God, knowing their weakness. Jesus himself did not weary of teaching this notion to the disciples, using the impersonal 'it is necessary' to indicate the divine plan (Lk. 9.22; 17.25; 22.37; 24.7, 26, 44), or using the Scriptures (Lk. 9.30–31; 18.31–33; 22.37; 24.25, 27, 44–46) or even the term 'a decree' of God (Lk. 22.22). The Jews used the Romans, called here 'lawless' which can be taken in its literal sense of 'without the (Jewish) law'. Their part was essential in order for the crucifixion to be carried out but Peter in no way puts this forward as an excuse to diminish the responsibility of the Jews for the death of Jesus. The Bezan text, if anything, emphasizes it for Jesus is described as being in their power, when they could do with him what they chose (cf. Saul who was said to be in the power of David, 1 Sam. 26.6–25).

2.24 The contrast between the killing of Jesus by the Jews and his resurrection by God is underlined by the use of a relative pronoun to link the two sentences. The same construction is frequently repeated to similar effect in later speeches (2.36b, c; 3.13a, b; 15a, b; 4.10c, d; 5.30b, 31; 10.39b, 40; 13.29, 30 D05), sometimes with the same juxtaposition of the theme of the resurrection with a prior denunciation of the death of Jesus, the two elements of the earliest nucleus of apostolic preaching.

Four expressions are used in Luke's writings to speak of the resurrection and often are found with variant readings:

1. The passive voice of the verb ἐγείρω, 'be raised (from the dead)': about John the Baptist, Lk. 9.7 (not D05); about Jesus, 9.22 (not D05), by himself; 24.6 (omit D05), by the two men in the garden
2. The active voice of the verb ἐγείρω, 'raise', always with God as the subject: Acts 3.15; 4.10; 5.30; 10.40; 13.30, 37
3. An intransitive tense of the verb ἀνίστημι, 'rise': Lk. 9.7 D05, 22 D05; 18.33; 24.7, 46; Acts 10.41; 17.3
4. A transitive tense of ἀνίστημι, 'resurrect', with God as subject: Acts 2.24, 32; 3.26; 13.32, 34; 17.31

From the above list, it can be noticed that in Acts (and in Luke's Gospel, too, in Codex Bezae) the two recurring expressions specify God as subject and include either ἐγείρω in the active voice, or ἀνίστημι used transitively. It is the latter that Peter uses here.

The metaphor Peter employs to describe the resurrection is both unique and striking. The phrase 'the labour pains of death' arises in the translation of Ps. 114.3 LXX and 'the labour pains of Sheol (= Hades)' in Ps. 17.5 LXX, where the Hebrew reads the ambiguous word חבל that can mean either 'bonds' or 'labour pains'. Although the comparison of death to a woman giving birth is not known in the Hebrew Scriptures, the LXX adopts the latter meaning, translating the noun as ὠδῖνες, which Peter uses here – in fact, in a conflation of ideas since he combines 'labour pains' with the verb 'loosen' which fits better with the idea of 'bonds'. Though the idea of death giving birth is unusual, there nevertheless occurs in the Hebrew Scriptures the association of the pains of childbirth with the redemption of Israel (see, e.g., Isa. 66.7; Hos. 13.13; Jer. 13.21; 22.23; 49.24) and it may be that notion that informs Peter's imagery at this point. He personifies death (especially with the name Hades in D05, anticipating the reference in Ps. 15 LXX that Peter is about to cite, Acts 2.27) as a woman in labour holding back her child (cf. Hos. 13.13) whom God releases, creating the powerful picture of death giving birth to life.[30]

2.25–28 Peter backs up the claim that God has resurrected Jesus by referring to Scripture, quoting Ps. 15.8–11 LXX. The passage underlines the security promised to David because of his faithfulness to his Lord, including deliverance from death and decay and the assurance of joy as he is shown the paths to life. The Greek text, in going further than the Hebrew which implies simply that the psalmist is protected from premature death, lends itself to being interpreted as meaning resurrection after death. Although Peter cites the passage in full (unlike Paul who will take just the half verse that speaks of 'not seeing corruption', Ps. 15.10b, cf. Acts 13.35) only two elements from the quotation are directly relevant to the point he wishes to make: first, that the 'Messiah will not be abandoned in Hades' (cf. 2.27a with 2.31b), adduced as evidence that God caused him to be released from death (cf. 2.24a); and second, that 'his flesh will not see corruption' (cf. 2.26, 27b with 2.31c), proof that death could not hold him (cf. 2.24b).

2.29 With a new term of address, Peter creates a fresh sense of intimacy with his audience of fellow-Jews, as he prepares to reinterpret the text of the Psalm he has quoted. He takes them step by step through his reasoning, seeking to demonstrate that the Scripture refers in reality to the Messiah. The qualification of David as 'the patriarch' is unusual but tallies with the idea that the Messiah is his descendance. The first point to establish is that David did die, the proof being the known existence of his tomb in Jerusalem.

2.30–31 The next step is to explain why, since he was not referring to himself, David speaks in the first person. The answer lies in the fact that David was speaking as a prophet which enabled him to speak about the future Messiah.[31] His exact relationship with the Messiah may depend on

30. Wilcox (*The Semitisms of Acts* [Oxford: Clarendon Press, 1965], pp. 46–48) identifies the phrase 'the pangs of death will compass (people) about' in a document from Qumran, 1QH 3.28, where it occurs in an eschatological context and as an allusion to Ps. 18 (17 LXX).4. This shows, at the very least, that the association of death – labour pains – bonds was known outside Acts and may indicate a tradition familiar to Peter as also his audience.

31. The idea that David was a prophet does not date from David's own lifetime (he

which text is followed. According to the AT, he contained within his 'loins', a euphemism for his genital organs, all of his descendance including the Messiah who would sit on his throne as King of Israel. The 'oath' Peter relates this to is first found in 2 Sam. 7.12–13, where God promised David he would 'raise up' (ἀναστήσω LXX) his son who would come from his 'loins' (ἐκ τῆς κοιλίας LXX) to take over his throne after his death, and is repeated in Ps. 132 (131 LXX).11 where the Psalmist says that God swore to David to set 'from the fruit of your loins' (ἐκ καρποῦ τῆς κοιλίας σου LXX) 'on your throne' (ἐπὶ τὸν θρόνον σου). It is the words of Ps. 131.11 LXX that Peter uses in the AT of Acts 2.30, presenting Jesus as the Davidic Messiah who will assume a worldly reign over Israel. There is a difficulty, however, for while such a concept is certainly in line with Jewish expectation of the time, it is in contradiction with the teaching of Jesus who explicitly refused the title 'Son of David' (Lk. 20.41–44; cf. 18.38–39); he had not come as a nationalistic Messiah whose claim to the title is dependent on his blood ancestry, but as a Messiah for all, not attached to any privileged ethnic group.

The text of Codex Bezae avoids any reference to David's physical descendants by using the expression 'fruit of his heart' instead of 'fruit of his loins'. Now the heart in Greek represents the seat of intellectual faculties, that is 'thinking', and the same figurative meaning is expressed by the two synonymous Hebrew terms used in 2 Sam. 7.12, מעים, 'loins' (cf. Prov. 22.18; Job 15.2, 35) and Ps. 132.11, בטן, 'belly' (cf. Ps. 40.9) although both words are more frequently euphemistic references to the reproductive organs. The result in the Bezan text of Acts 2.30 is that the Messiah is envisaged as issuing from David's innermost thoughts, as coming out of his prophesying. Thus any concept of a Messiah who is the physical son of David is avoided.

At the same time, it is the Bezan text that makes specific reference to the physical 'raising up' of the Messiah in a play on the word ἀνίστημι which means both 'raise up' (i.e. 'cause to be born') or 'resurrect', qualifying it with 'according to the flesh'. In the original context of 2 Sam. 7.12 LXX, it has the first meaning but the ambiguity leads perfectly to the next step in Peter's argument as he moves on to apply David's prophecy

was the king and Nathan the prophet) but seems to have arisen gradually at a relatively late date though it was established by the time of the NT writings; see J. Kugel (*Poetry and Prophecy* [Ithaca and London: Cornell University Press, 1990]), pp. 45.55: 'David the prophet, that is, the prophetic author of the Psalms, was a notion already in the air at the turn of the era, if not before', p. 54.

not to Jesus' life on earth but precisely to his resurrection after his death. What David foresaw was that Jesus would be physically resurrected after his death, that though he would die he would not remain dead. It is imperative that Peter deals with this issue for in terms of Jewish hopes, the death of the Messiah, before he had taken up the throne of Israel, would be a total contradiction of traditional expectation.

The implication, though it is not spelt out by Peter, is that following his resurrection he would subsequently rule over Israel as king. It may be precisely to avoid the nationalistic connotations of such a claim that Peter avoids developing this aspect of David's prophecy but instead focuses on the exaltation of Jesus to the right hand of God (2.33).

2.32 Having developed his argument about the resurrection, Peter picks up his first reference to it (2.24) bringing in a new element, the witness of the apostles. Once again, he restricts the apostolic testimony to the resurrection, as was already observed at 1.22, despite Jesus' command to them to witness to his *person* (1.8). The overriding concern at this stage is not to speak of Jesus' life or his work or teaching but to prove, on the grounds of the resurrection, that despite being put to death Jesus was the Messiah.

2.33 The exaltation of the resurrected Jesus to the right hand of God is equivalent to his enthronement. It proves that the death of Jesus did not mean the failure of the Messiah, as it must have seemed, but the opportunity for God to resurrect him and set him beside him, effectively sharing his throne with him. Peter then shows how this provided the occasion for God to fulfil his promise, the promise spoken of by Jesus after his resurrection (Lk. 24.49; Acts 1.4). In saying that Jesus received the Holy Spirit from the Father, he echoes Jesus' words at the cross, 'Father, I hand over my spirit into your hands' (Lk. 23.46). He has taken back his spirit and has poured it out – the verb harks back to the Joel passage – and it is the results of this that Peter's audience have observed first hand. Codex Bezae clarifies that the Spirit has been poured out for them, for Israel, a detail that is consistent with the orientation of this part of Peter's speech towards his fellow-Jews. The manifestation of the Spirit as a tangible phenomena is not something that they can ignore.

2.34–35 The final step in Peter's reasoning concerning Jesus consists in demonstrating that his exaltation at the right hand of God was the enthronement foreseen by David, seeking to ratify thereby his claim that Jesus is the Messiah. For this purpose, he refers to another of David's psalms, Ps. 110 (109 LXX).1, again wishing to show that it applies to the Messiah and not David himself. Now Jesus himself cited this psalm when he was teaching in the Temple (Lk. 20.1–4), but precisely for the purpose of proving to the scribes the error of their belief that the Messiah was to be 'the son of David'. As has been noted above, Jesus repudiated the notion held by the Jews that the Messiah was a political figure, a warrior-king for Israel (cf. Lk. 24.21). For Jesus, the prototype of the Messiah is not David but God himself; the privileged position of Israel has been lost and is no longer part of the divine plan, and consequently the expectation that the Messiah would be a successor to David is a false hope. Peter, however, takes the psalm in order to show that the exaltation of the Messiah after his death was foreseen and that, with its language of enthronement (the Messiah is 'at the right hand' of God with his enemies 'as a footstool' for his feet) it is a heavenly counterpart to David's reign over Israel on earth. So although Peter has understood the idea that Jesus was not an earthly Messiah with political goals and military resources, he continues for the time being to see Jesus the Messiah as closely associated with David as king of Israel. It is no problem that Luke has Peter say something opposed to what, as narrator of the Gospel, he presents Jesus as saying as long as it is remembered that Luke, as any good narrator, puts in the mouth of his participants their own thoughts and manner of expression rather than using them as vehicles for his own theology.

[β] 2.36 *Parenesis*

2.36 Peter sums up his reasoning by drawing together the contrasting actions of the 'house of Israel' who crucified Jesus and the action of God who appointed him both Lord and Messiah, returning in effect to the same point with which he started his speech. The question arises as to when exactly does Peter mean God appointed Jesus to these positions. Was it after the crucifixion? Such an understanding would go against Luke's portrayal of Jesus' investiture as Messiah beginning with his baptism (Lk. 3.22), but this would merely confirm that Peter had not yet understood accurately the things concerning Jesus. More critically, though, it also contradicts Peter's own realization early on in his life as a disciple of Jesus that he whom he was following was the Messiah (Lk. 9.20, cf. 24.21). Rather than implying anything about the time of the divine appointment of Jesus to his role as Lord and Messiah, Peter is simply contrasting the two actions (both expressed with an aorist main verb) of God on the one hand and the people of Israel on the other, highlighting the awfulness of the crime of killing the one who was the longed-for Messiah.

[b] 2.37a *The Response of the Crowd to Peter's Speech*
2.37a Peter is interrupted by the reaction of his audience at this point who are greatly affected by what he is saying. A division among the Jewish listeners is apparent only in Codex Bezae where reference is first of all made to the whole crowd, only some of whom will want to know what they can do about the crime Peter has exposed.

[c] 2.37b *The Positive Response of Some of the Crowd*
2.37b The question put to the apostles reveals that the people felt remorse, expressed only by part of the listeners in the Bezan text, and that they depend on them to advise them as to what they can do about the dreadful situation that they have created. The real need for a solution and the urgency of it emerges more clearly from the Bezan text, echoing as it does the cry of John the Baptist to repentance (Lk. 3.7), and corresponds to the horror of the plight of the Jews that has been exposed by Peter's speech.

[b′] 2.38–39 *Peter's Exhortation to Israel to Repent and be Baptized*
2.38 As Peter responds to their plea, he urges the people to repent and to be baptized. His words are similar to those of John the Baptist, more so in the Bezan text with the general 'forgiveness of sins' in place of 'your sins' (cf. Lk. 3.3). Peter, though, now links this water baptism, to be undertaken by each person individually, specifically to the person of Jesus whom he refers to with the title Messiah, and also Lord according to Codex Bezae, so restating the declaration he has just made and making quite clear that Jesus is to be acknowledged in both his functions. The gift of the Holy Spirit is promised to the people as a whole, and not individually, as following water baptism but without indicating when this will happen. In the event, the coming of the Holy Spirit will not be mentioned until 4.31 when the community of the disciples of Jesus were gathered in prayer.

2.39 With the mention of the Holy Spirit, Peter returns to the point he made earlier about the promise of the Father (2.33). The AT considers him to be distancing himself from his audience by relating the promise to 'you' 'your children', whereas the Bezan text has him include himself and all the rest of the apostolic group in the use of 'us', 'our', more consistent with the use of 'our God' at the end of the verse. Their common identity as Jews is marked out by the contrast with 'those who are far off', a typical expression to refer to Gentiles. Here, Peter takes up the last part of the verse from the Joel passage (Joel 3.5c) which he had omitted earlier in his speech (see *Commentary,* 2.21), though changing the tense of the verb from 'God has called' to a future 'will call'.

[a′] 2.40 *Summary of Peter's Message*

2.40 Luke indicates that Peter did not stop discussing with the people but continued at some length. The focus of his exhortation is the need for them to be saved from 'this perverse generation', once more taking up the verb 'save' that is found in the quotation from Joel (σωθήσεται, Joel 3.5 // σώθητε, Acts 2.40). The attention drawn to the adjective 'perverse' in the Bezan text underscores the importance of the phrase, one that is applied paradigmatically to the generation that abandoned God in the desert (Deut. 32.5; Ps. 78 [77 LXX].8). Thus, a comparison is implied between the faithless people of Israel in the desert and those who have rejected the Messiah in the present. The comparison tallies with the denunciation of 'the tree ... that does not bear good fruit' by John the Baptist (Lk. 3.7–9; cf. 3.17).

Furthermore, the terms of this statement that brings Peter's speech, and indeed this section, to a close strongly resemble those in which the preaching of John the Baptist are described: 'With many and varied exhortations he preached good news to the people' (Lk. 3.18). These echoes of John the Baptist function in combination with other similarities mentioned earlier: the question put by those who wish to take action in response to the preaching (Acts 2.37b // Lk. 3.10, 12, 14); the use of the verb 'show' (Lk. 3.7 // Acts 2.37c D05); a baptism for the forgiveness of sin (Lk. 3.3 // Acts 2.38b, especially D05); the promise of the Holy Spirit (Lk. 3.16 // Acts 2.38c). The effect of the similarities is to establish a comparison between Peter and John the Baptist. In so far as both advocate baptism for the forgiveness of sins the comparison is to some extent inevitable, but Luke seems to be deliberately reinforcing it by the inclusion in both scenes of other similar themes and vocabulary. The overall result is create a sense at the end of Peter's speech that the community of Jesus-believers, led by Peter and the apostles, are still waiting for the Messiah, that they are preparing for his return as a powerful ruler who will be acclaimed on earth. This is yet another mark of the imperfect and incomplete understanding that the disciples have of the person of Jesus, one that will be gradually corrected and refined in the course of ensuing events.

[A′] 2.41–47 *The First Summary: The Way of Life of the Jerusalem Church*

Overview

The first summary of the book of Acts brings to a close the second section. Several of the themes will be taken up in the second summary, which forms a bridge between the third and the fourth sections (4.32–35). The two summaries are compared in *Excursus* 4.

Structure and Themes

The structure of the first summary follows a carefully crafted pattern in the Bezan text, constructed by means of the sentence connectives. The variants of the AT result in a structure that is not only looser and less adapted to the message to be communicated, but also ambiguous in several places.

The structure according to Codex Bezae:

[a] 2.41–42 The growth of the believing community
[b] 2.43–47a The tension in the life of the community created by fear
[a′] 2.47b The action of God

It will be helpful to set out the Greek text of Codex Bezae in order to see how the various elements fit together:

[a] **41** οἱ μὲν οὖν πιστεύσαντες τὸν λόγον αὐτοῦ ἐβαπτίσθησαν
καὶ προσετέθησαν ἐν ἐκείνῃ τῇ ἡμέρᾳ ψυχαὶ ὡσεὶ τρισχίλιαι
42 καὶ ἦσαν προσκαρτεροῦντες τῇ διδαχῇ τῶν ἀποστόλων ἐν Ἰερουσαλὴμ
καὶ τῇ κοινωνίᾳ,
τῇ κλάσει τοῦ ἄρτου
καὶ ταῖς προσευχαῖς·
[b] **43** ἐγίνετο δὲ πάσῃ ψυχῇ φόβος,
πολλά τε τέρατα καὶ σημεῖα διὰ τῶν ἀποστόλων ἐγίνετο,
44 πάντες τε οἱ πιστεύοντες ἦσαν ἐπὶ τὸ αὐτὸ
καὶ εἶχον πάντα κοινὰ
45 καὶ ὅσοι κτήματα εἶχον ἢ ὑπάρξεις ἐπίπρασκον
καὶ διεμέριζον αὐτὰ καθ’ ἡμέραν τοῖς ἄν τις χρείαν εἶχεν,
46 πάντες τε προσεκαρτέρουν ἐν τῷ ἱερῷ
καὶ κατ’ οἴκους <ἦσ>αν ἐπὶ τὸ αὐτό,
κλῶντές τε ἄρτον μετελάμβανον τροφῆς ἐν ἀγαλλιάσει
καὶ ἀφελότητι καρδίας
47a αἰνοῦντες τὸν θεὸν
καὶ ἔχοντες χάριν πρὸς ὅλον τὸν κόσμον·
[a′] **47b** ὁ δὲ κύριος προσετίθει τοὺς σῳζομένους καθ’ ἡμέραν ἐπὶ τὸ αὐτὸ
ἐν τῇ ἐκκλησίᾳ.

The opening sentence is connected to the preceding narrative with μὲν οὖν in v. 41 [a] which anticipates δέ to follow in v. 43 [b]. Typically in Acts, μὲν οὖν ... δέ introduces two consequences of the preceding events, the second of which is the most significant.[32] The dependance of the one upon the other demands that the two clauses belong to the same paragraph. The subject of [a] is those who had believed Peter's message, whereas [b] introduces a new subject, 'every soul', more inclusive than those who had believed, before switching back once more to focus on the believing community 'all the believers', v. 44.

The two main clauses linked with καί in [a], and the four linked with τε in [b], constitute a series of elements associated with the principal statement in each case. There are further elements connected with καί το the second and third τε clauses. Whereas [a] deals with the positive outcome of the believers' baptism, concentrating on the life of the community among themselves, [b] presents the outcome of the fear that affects the population in general and is initially associated with the apostles' working of signs and wonders (v. 43). But it will also cause tension among the believing community between their public and private lives. The latter is indicated by the phrase ἐπὶ τὸ αὐτό (of which the exact meaning will be discussed in the commentary below), arising first in v. 44 as 'all the believers' are distinguished from 'every soul'. It occurs for a second time in v. 46 in direct contrast with the intervening statement that these 'all' also continued attendance in the Temple, a second manifestation of their public life.

The concluding part of the summary in v. 47b [a′], reflects the opening part by describing the saving action of God.

In the AT, the opening sentence of the summary also begins with μὲν οὖν, but with the corresponding δέ clause located at v. 42 so that the two consequences following Peter's exhortations are presented as the baptisms and the increase in numbers of the believing community. Even here, though, because of the structural connection between the two clauses, it is incorrect to detach v. 42 from v. 41 with a paragraph break (as in the current Greek editions). Thereafter, three new developments are signalled with separate δέ clauses (vv. 43a, 43b, 44). V. 46a has τε in a participial phrase relating the attendance of the believers at the Temple, which is probably to be seen as connected to vv. 44–45 as an additional element in the description of the community life. It is unlikely to be connected to the final statement of v. 46b, also introduced with τε, as such a reading would

32. Read-Heimerdinger, *The Bezan Text*, pp. 237–38.

cause two participles (προσκαρτεροῦντες, κλῶντες) to be linked with τε, an occurrence not found elsewhere in Acts.

Translation

	Codex Bezae D05	*Codex Vaticanus B03*
[a]	**2.41** So those who believed his message were baptized and there were added that same day about 3,000 souls. **42** They continued steadfastly in the teaching of the apostles in Jerusalem and in fellowship, in the breaking of bread and the prayers.	**2.41** So those who accepted his message were baptized and there were added that day about 3,000 souls. **42** They continued steadfastly in the teaching of the apostles and in fellowship, in the breaking of bread and the prayers.
[b]	**43** On every soul came fear: many signs and wonders were happening through the apostles; **44** all the believers were united and had everything in common, **45** and whoever had properties or possessions sold them and distributed them to those who might be in need; **46** they all continued steadfastly in the Temple and in their houses constituted a united group; as they broke bread, they partook of food with gladness and simplicity of heart, **47a** praising God and having favour with all of the world.	**43** On every soul came fear. Many signs and wonders were happening through the apostles. **44** All those who had believed in unity had all things in common, **45** and they sold their properties and possessions and distributed them according to whoever was in need, **46** continuing each day steadfastly in the Temple together; furthermore, breaking bread in their houses, they partook of food with gladness and simplicity of heart, **47a** praising God and having favour with all of the people.
[a′]	**47b** The Lord added daily those being saved to the group united in the Church.	**47b** The Lord added daily to the united group those being saved.

Critical Apparatus

2.41 ἀποδεξάμενοι (τὸν λόγον) B P^{74} ℵ A C 81. 1175. 1505. 2147 *pc* lat; Cl Or Eus | ἀσμένως ἀποδ. E H^{2} P Ψ 049. 056. 33. 614. (1243). 1739. 2492 𝔐 sy mae geo arm; Aug || πιστεύσαντες D, *credentes* d | ἀποδ. ... ἐπίστευσαν καί p r vg^{ms} $sy^{p.hmg}$ mae; Aug.

The verb ἀποδέχομαι, 'welcome, approve', of B03 is exclusive to Luke in the NT, but when he uses it elsewhere the object is always a person (Lk. x 2; Acts x 5). When 'the word' is the object as here, Luke only ever uses the simple verb δέχομαι, so on both counts the expression of B03 in this verse constitutes an exceptional usage. Many MSS qualify the verb with the adverb 'with joy' (cf. 21.17 for the only other occurrence of the same adverb). Codex Bezae, in its Greek and Latin pages, is alone in reading πιστεύω with 'the word' as direct object, a rare construction. Support is found for the verb, in a conflation of readings, in a number of versions.

ἐν τῇ ἡμέρᾳ ἐκείνῃ B ℵ A C 81. 1175. 1245 || ἐν ἐκ. τ. ἡμ. D d gig p r t vg; Aug

The particular day, which was the day of Pentecost, is underlined in D05 by the placing of the demonstrative before the noun (Read-Heimerdinger, *The Bezan Text*, pp. 103–106).

ὡσεὶ (τρισχίλιαι) B D, *quasi* d *rell* || ὡς ℵ.

ὡσεί and ὡς operate as a pair of alternative words to introduce a comparison with quite specific contrasting meanings in D05 (ὡσεί indicates a metaphorical comparison, ὡς an allusion to a scriptural paradigm), but no such pattern has been observed in ℵ01. Here, both texts would appear to have the same meaning of 'as if'.

2.42 ἦσαν δέ B ℵ *rell* || καὶ ἦσαν D d arm.

This is the clause viewed by B03 as corresponding to the μὲν οὖν clause that opens the section whereas D05 groups them together as one, the corresponding δέ clause beginning at 2.43. The difference affects the overall structure of the section.

(τῶν ἀποστόλων) ἐν Ἰερουσαλήμ D d (t y vg^{ms}) || *om.* B ℵ *rell.*

The mention of the city of Jerusalem is superfluous information since the text can be readily understood without it. It has a theological purpose, however, in the D05 text for it underlines the continuing association of the apostles with the Jewish institution. The detail is included in some MSS in 2.43 (see below).

2.43 (πολλὰ) δέ B ℵ 81 *pc* | τε A C D^{C} E H^{2} P Ψ 049. 056. 33. 614. 945. 1175. 1611. 1739. 2412. 2495 𝔐, *etiam* d lat || *om.* D* 69 *pc.*

The omission of τε in the original hand of D05 is due to haplography (ΤΕΤΕΡ–ΑΤΑ). Phonetic confusion between τε and δέ arises frequently among the MSS of Acts (Read-Heimerdinger, *The Bezan Text*, pp. 205–206). With the reading τε, there emerges a clear pattern of parallel elements all introduced with the same particle.

(... ἐγίνετο) ἐν Ἰερουσαλήμ (E) 33. 104. (181*). 1409. (2344) sy^{p} | ἐν Ἰερ., φόβος τε ἦν μέγας ἐπὶ πάντας (+ αὐτούς Ψ *pc*) P^{74vid} ℵ A C Ψ (36. 326). 1175. (2495) *pc* lat (mae) bo || *om.* B D d H^{2} P 049. 69. 81. 614. 945. 1739. 1891. 2412 𝔐 gig p* r sy^{h} sa; Chr.

The mention of Jerusalem is included in some MSS in 2.42 (see above) and is widely attested here, though by neither B03 or D05. The repetition of the theme of fear may have arisen through a conflation of readings because some MSS (in particular mae, see Boismard and Lamouille, *ad loc.*) only include this mention of fear at the end of the verse.

2.44 πάντες δέ B E H² P 049. 056. 33. 614. 1739. 1891. 2412. 2495 𝔐 | καὶ πάν. δέ P⁷⁴ ℵ A C Ψ 81. 88. 1175 || πάν. τε D d c gig r t vg.

τε introduces the second of four parallel elements, viewed as a separate development with δέ.

οἱ πιστεύσαντες B ℵ H² 056. 0142. 28. 36. 42. 88. 104. 255. 257. 383. 431. 453. 522. 915. 1311. 1838. 2401. 2495 co || οἱ πιστεύοντες D, *credentes* d P⁷⁴ᵛⁱᵈ A C E P Ψ 049. 33. 81. 1175. 1739. 2412. 2495 𝔐; Bas.

With the aorist participle, the act of believing is seen as accomplished and corresponds to its occurrence in 2.41 D05. The use of the present participle focuses on the ongoing act of belief and, in contrast to the aorist of v. 41 D05, allows it to refer to a wider group of believers than those who have recently accepted Peter's teaching.

ἐπὶ τὸ αὐτὸ (εἶχον) B 254 (2495 gig) m p r; Orig Spec Salvian || ἦσαν ἐπὶ τὸ αὐτὸ καί D d P⁷⁴ ℵ A C E H² P Ψ 049. 056. 33. 81. 610. 614. 945. 1175. 1739. 1891. 2344. 2412 𝔐 ar c dem e ph ro t w vg syᵖ arm aeth geo; Bas Chr.

The B03 text links the unity (ἐπὶ τὸ αὐτό) of the believers with the sharing of their property. D05, along with most other MSS, presents the unity of the group as a general condition, followed by a series of three practices (each linked with καί) associated with that unity. The importance accorded to the phrase ἐπὶ τὸ αὐτό in D05 is reflected in its occurring three times in the space of this summary (cf. 2.46, 47).

ἅπαντα (κοινά) B ℵ *rell* || πάντα D d.

ἅπας is more emphatic that πᾶς underlining the entirety of the believers (see *Critical Apparatus,* 2.7, for a list of references in Acts).

2.45 καὶ τὰ κτήματα καὶ τὰς ὑπάρξεις ἐπίπρασκον B P⁷⁴ ℵ *rell* || καὶ ὅσοι κτ. εἶχον ἢ ὑπ. ἐπ. D d syᵖ.

The clause in the B03 text stands in parallel to the previous statement, explaining how the believers had everything in common. D05, on the other hand, introduces a new idea by describing the action of a certain group among the believers, those who had possessions.

(αὐτὰ) καθ' ἡμέραν D d || *om.* B ℵ *rell*; cf. 2.46.

The description in D05 continues to be more detailed than in B03: it is those who had sold their goods who distributed the money on a daily basis.

(πᾶσι) καθότι ἄν B P⁷⁴ ℵ Dᶠ *rell, secundum quod* d || τοῖς ἄν D*.

Continuing the general description in B03, it is said that money was given according to the need. D05 is again more precise in defining some members of the community as being in need.

2.46 καθ' ἡμέραν τε προσκαρτεροῦντες ὁμοθυμαδὸν ἐν τῷ ἱερῷ B P^{74} ℵ *rell* || πάντες τε προσεκαρτέρουν ἐν τ. ἱερῷ D d.

The final elements of the summary are subordinated in B03 by means of participles to one main verb in the last clause, the sharing of food. D05 has a main verb here and will introduce another one to follow (see below). B03 places the adverb καθ' ἡμέραν at this point and underlines the unity of the believers with ὁμοθυμαδόν (cf. 1.14; 5.12 D05).

κλῶντές τε κατ' οἶκον B P^{74} ℵ *rell* || καὶ κατ' οἴκους <ἦσ>αν (κατοικουσαν D*) ἐπὶ τὸ αὐτὸ κλῶντές τε D$^{C.coni}$, *et per domos in* (+ d^{G}) *idipsum capiebant* d (mae).

The use of τε in B03 to link two participles (προσκαρτεροῦντες / κλῶντες) is rare in Luke's writing. This text associates the breaking of bread with the meeting of the believers in private houses. D05 reads an additional main verb which places their meeting in the houses on an equal footing (καί) with their continued fidelity to the Temple in the previous clause (the omission of the first two letters of ἦσαν by the original hand of D05, corrected by Corrector C, is probably due to haplography); a new sentence begins with κλῶντές τε. A second occurrence in this summary of the phrase ἐπὶ τὸ αὐτό would be clumsy and repetitive were it not so important to the narrator of the D05 text to stress the solidarity of the believers as a group within the adherents of the Temple. The breaking of bread is presented, with the fourth connective τε, as a final identifying mark of this community.

2.47 (πρὸς ὅλον) τὸν λαόν B ℵ *rell* | τ. κόσμον D d.

The use of ὅλον replaces the more usual πᾶς to qualify ὁ λαός, a technical term that always signifies Israel in Luke's writing. The reading of ὁ κόσμος in D05 widens the scope of the favour enjoyed by the believers to include the whole world – a reading which is entirely in keeping with the presence, on a figurative level, of people from every nation at the outpouring of the Spirit (see *Commentary*, 2.5). The use of λαός instead keeps the narrative on a purely historical level.

ἐπὶ τὸ αὐτό B P$^{74vid.91vid}$ ℵ A C 095. 81. 1175 *pc* lat sa bo arm aeth || ἐπὶ τ. αὐ. ἐν τῇ ἐκκλησίᾳ D d | τ. ἐκκλ. ἐπὶ τ. αὐ. 69. 307. 945. 1739. 1891. (1243). 1245 *pc* | τ. ἐκκλησία E H^{2} P Ψ 049. 056. 33. 610. 614. 2344 𝔐 sy mae; Chr (see below).

At the third mention of ἐπὶ τὸ αὐτό, D05 makes clearer the sense of it in the narrative of this text by qualifying it with the phrase 'in the church'. This is the first occurrence of the word ἐκκλησία in Acts.

Commentary

[a] 2.41–42 *The Growth of the Believing Community*

2.41 The similarities between the account of the preparatory mission of John the Baptist and that of the apostles in this chapter were noted above (see 2.40). The outcome of John's ministry was summarized in a two-part statement about first, his ongoing evangelistic activity and then his imprisonment by Herod: 'So (μὲν οὖν), with many different exhortations he announced the good news to the people. Then (δέ), Herod the tetrarch ... to all the evils he had committed, added (προσέθηκεν) this, that he shut up John in prison' (Lk. 3.18–20). Despite the similarity with the structure that has been noted as present in this first summary of the book of Acts, Peter's preaching leads not to imprisonment but to 3,000 souls being added through baptism (προσετέθησαν) to the apostolic community. The use of the same verb in the two similarly constructed summaries serves to highlight the essential difference in the outcome of the apostles' preaching.

The number is not to be taken literally nor even approximately but as a metaphorical figure. The number three and its multiples was already an important figure in the Jewish Scriptures where it represented completeness (see *Commentary*, 2.9–11a). The term 'souls' may be contrasted with the use of 'men' (ἄνδρες) when the narrative next summarizes the effect of the apostles' teaching by giving the number of people believing as 5,000 (4.4). The second term, in comparison with the first, designates the believers as mature and it is only at that point that the Holy Spirit is given (4.31). Here, the 3,000 had accepted Peter's message or, according to Codex Bezae, had believed it. 'Belief' will come to be a characteristic mark of those who follow Jesus (cf. 2.44).

2.42 Those who are baptized, in the name of (the Lord, D05) Jesus Christ (cf. 2.38) signal publicly thereby their separation from 'this perverse generation' (cf. 2.40). The correlative to that is their adherence to the teaching of the apostles and fellowship. The radical nature of the transfer is qualified, nevertheless, by a reminder in the Bezan text that the apostles remain attached to Jerusalem as the religious centre (Hebrew-derived spelling, see *Commentary*, 1.4, 8). The comment is unecessary except to highlight the fact that the apostles continued to function within the framework of the traditions of Judaism. Fellowship is identified as consisting of the breaking of bread and prayers. While the first activity would seem to be a reference to what will in time become a distinctively Christian celebration, the second with the article could well mean the official Jewish prayers. The tension inherent between the two practices will become more marked in the next section of the summary.

[b] 2.43–47a *The Tension in the Life of the Community Created by Fear*
2.43 Attention now switches to the more general effect of Peter's preaching, on 'every soul' among the 3,000 just mentioned. In the Bezan text,

this is the second, and more significant, consequence, namely the fear that it engendered (see the notes on structure at the beginning of this sequence). Fear among believers and non-believers alike will again be noted in the second summary of Acts (5.5, 11). The cause of the fear is not explained directly but may be deduced in part from the context and in part from the subsequent text. Certainly, it is difficult to overestimate how terrifying the charges made by Peter, that the Jews had killed the Messiah, must have been. Furthermore, the account of the large-scale response to Peter's teaching, including the baptism of thousands of people, suggests an upheaval in the local life of the city that must have been nothing short of dramatic and, in many of its practical consequences, overwhelming.

In Codex Bezae, a series of four sentences follows, all introduced with the connective τε which sets them on an equal footing and relates them all to the principal statement concerning the fear that was experienced. The first, viewed by the AT as a separate development, links the fear to the miraculous deeds that were being performed by the apostles, a public manifestation of spiritual power (cf. 5.16–17). An element of the fear may well have been to do with the fact that these apostles were not recognized as religious leaders or people with authority, causing confusion and uncertainty as to where their power came from.

2.44–45 In the second τε clause (another new development in the AT), the narrative moves back again to consider all of the believers, not just, according to the Bezan text, those who had newly believed (cf. 2.41 D05). Their common bond is indicated by means of the expression ἐπὶ τὸ αὐτό. This is the third occurrence of the phrase in Acts (cf. 1.15; 2.1) where it is used as a leitmotif to signal the solidarity of the Jesus-believers and their existence as an identifiable group among the Jewish people as a whole. The Bezan text spells this out in an independent clause, whereas in the AT the force of the phrase is attenuated as it simply has the force of an adverb qualifying 'those who had believed'.

The unity of the believers is expressed through a sharing of goods, in accordance with Jesus' teaching (cf. Lk. 12.33; 18.22). The Bezan picture is more nuanced, suggesting that only some members of the community had things to sell and that they saw to the distribution to those in need, which took place day by day rather than as the occasion arose.

2.46–47a The AT adds that while enjoying the unity of sharing their goods, the believers continued to attend the Temple together on a daily basis. It then adds a final further comment describing the joy of their shared meals held in private as they praised God and enjoyed the approbation of the people, that is, the Jews. This information is expressed in the Bezan text by means of two more parallel τε clauses. The first sets side by side the public attendance in the Temple and then, in an explicit statement, the private meeting in houses where the believers are once more said to have been united, ἐπὶ τὸ αὐτό. The juxtaposition of these two places of meeting throws into relief the problems facing those who accepted Peter's teaching that Jesus was the Messiah and publicly acknowledged their belief by baptism. As Jews, they continued to adhere to the Temple and to be under the religious authority of its leaders; it could hardly have been otherwise but, given that their belief in Jesus was an open denial of the verdict of the Jewish authorities on him, there would be the continual threat of reprisal. The solidarity of the Jesus-believing community within the confines of Judaism, and the conflict thus created for its members, will be always to the fore in the first half of the book of Acts according to the Bezan text.

The final τε clause develops the picture of the meetings in the houses with the decscription of the joyful meals already noted in the AT. But here, in the Bezan text, it is with 'all the world' that they find favour, an echo of the universal theme of the earlier part of the book and, further back than that, of the universal nature of the revelation of God at Sinai according to Jewish tradition (see *Commentary*, 2.5).

[a′] 2.47b *The Action of God*

2.47b The concluding statement of this section draws together elements from the previous verses: the verb προστίθημι, 'add', is taken up from the first part of the summary, with the subject now specified as God; the verb σῴζω, 'save', is taken up from the precis of Peter's message (v. 40); the adverb καθ' ἡμέραν, 'daily', has already occurred in v. 45 D05 where it was associated with the distribution of goods, and thus links the growth in numbers to this example of practical fellowship – a less happy connection is made in the AT with the 'daily' attendance in the Temple (v. 46); finally, the motif ἐπὶ τὸ αὐτό is repeated (cf. vv. 44, 46 D05) – as the group grows beyond the 3,000, it is united in its solidarity within the Jewish institution. The Bezan text introduces at this point the term that will come to denote this new group of Jesus-believers, ἡ ἐκκλησία, 'the church'. The Greek word was well-known as the LXX translation of the word found throughout the Hebrew Bible denoting 'the assembly' of Israel. Thus the narrator leaves one of the earliest hints that the people of God is no longer Israel but the Jesus-believers.

III. The Sign of the Lame Man's Healing
3.1–4.35

General Overview

The third section of the book of Acts presents an account of how the Jesus-believing Jewish community emerged from the midst of Israel. It follows the description of the Jesus-believing community that concludes Section II (2.41–47). There, the disciples were still attached to the Temple and under the authority of the Jewish religious leaders, though identifiable as a separate group. This section marks a break with the official Jewish institution as the community of believers begin to organize themselves independently.

Structure and Themes

The principal theme of this third section of the book of Acts is the release of the apostles and the community of Jesus-believers from the old religious order. This is initially prompted by the healing of the lame man in the name of Jesus, which serves as a sign of the power of Jesus to overthrow purity regulations concerning the worship of God. The subsequent hostile opposition shown by the religious leaders to the liberating power of Jesus leads to the apostles' realization that their authority is no longer valid.

Five sequences can be identified, arranged concentrically around the opposition of the Jewish authorities to the apostles. A summary, that stands outside the main structure serves as a bridge to the fourth section of the book of Acts:

[A] 3.1–10 The healing of the lame man
[B] 3.11–26 Peter's speech in Solomon's Porch
[C] 4.1–4 The imprisonment of Peter and John
[B′] 4.5–22 The meeting of the Sanhedrin
[A′] 4.23–31 The release of the Jesus-believing community
4.32–35 Bridging (Second) Summary: The community ideal

The first sequence introduces a man lame from even before his birth begging for alms at one of the Temple gates. His healing by Peter, together with John, is followed by his entry into the Temple, to the great amazement of the people who observed what happened. Peter responds to their astonishment with a speech that occupies the second sequence, using the healing as a starting point to teach the people about Jesus.

The third and fourth sequences present the reaction of the Temple authorities to the teaching of the people by the two apostles. The focus throughout is on the perplexity of the Jewish leaders and the inefficacity of their attempts to control the new movement. Their response to the apostles will cause Peter to change from expressing his own thoughts to speaking through the Holy Spirit as he takes a firm stand against the religious authorities to whom, as a Jew, he has so far been in submission. Although the Sanhedrin will decide to release them, their opposition to the power of Jesus will bring about a fundamental shift in the Jesus-believing community as they place themselves under the authority of the apostles instead of the Temple authorities.

[A] 3.1–10 *The Healing of the Lame Man*

Overview

Much more than a simple physical miracle, the healing of the lame man constitutes nothing less than his release from the regulations of the Temple that excluded him from the presence of God. This healing represents the first in a progression of steps set out by the narrator in Acts 1 to 10 as a demonstration of how freedom from the restrictive regulations controlling access to God was gradually seen to be achieved. The culmination of the process will be the outpouring of the Holy Spirit on the Gentiles as a manifestation of their acceptance by God (Acts 10). The steps begin with a man who, although Jewish, was prevented by his physical condition of lameness from entering God's presence on the grounds of impurity. The healing carried out in the name of Jesus will remove this obstacle and the angry response of the Jewish leaders will make quite evident their unrelenting rejection of Jesus as the Messiah.

The model for this healing is found in Luke's Gospel in the healing of the paralytic by Jesus (Lk. 5.18–26). It will be later paralleled in the book of Acts by the healing by Paul of the cripple in Lystra (Acts 14.8–10). The differences between the parallel accounts highlight the distinctive features of each one, as will be pointed out at the relevant places.

Structure and Themes

A clear structural pattern is apparent in Codex Bezae, though it is less evident in the AT. At the centre is Peter's declaration of healing which is mirrored by his act of helping the lame man to stand:

[a]	1	Peter and John's attendance at the Temple
[b]	2a	The lame man at the Beautiful Gate
[c]	2b–3	His plea for alms from Peter and John
[d]	4	Peter's command to the lame man
[e]	5	The lame man's acquiescence
[f]	6	Peter's declaration of healing
[f′]	7a	Peter's act of raising the lame man
[e′]	7b	The man's healing
[d′]	8a	The consequences of his healing
[c′]	8b	The entry of the healed man into the Temple with Peter and John
[b′]	9–10a	Attention turns to the onlookers
[a′]	10b	The people's amazement

The scene takes place at the Temple and focuses on the lame man. The scene culminates with the reaction of the onlookers who, despite being present throughout, are not mentioned until the end. They will provide the link leading to the next sequence [B].

Translation

	Codex Bezae D05	*Codex Vaticanus B03*
[a]	**3.1** It was in those days that Peter and John were going up to the Temple in the afternoon at the ninth hour of prayer,	**3.1** Peter and John were going up to the Temple at the ninth hour of prayer
[b]	**2a** and behold! a certain man, lame from his mother's womb, was also being carried up; they used to place him daily at the gate of the Temple, the one called Beautiful, so that he could ask them for alms.	**2** and a certain man, who was lame from his mother's womb, was also being carried up; they used to place him daily at the gate of the Temple, the one called Beautiful, so that he could ask for alms from the people entering the Temple.
[c]	**2b** As they were entering the Temple, **3** this man searched intently with his eyes and when he saw Peter and John about to be in the Temple, he started asking them for alms.	**3** When he saw Peter and John about to go into the Temple, he started asking to receive alms.
[d]	**4** Peter, together with John, considered him and said, 'Look intently at us.'	**4** Peter, together with John, looked intently at him and said, 'Look at us.'
[e]	**5** He looked intently at them, expecting to receive something from them.	**5** He focused his attention on them, expecting to receive something from them.

[f]	**6** Peter said to him, 'Silver and gold I do not possess; but what I do have, I give to you. In the name of Jesus Christ the Nazorene, walk',	**6** Peter said to him, 'Silver and gold I do not possess; but what I do have, I give to you. In the name of Jesus Christ the Nazorene, walk',
[f′]	**7a** and having seized him by the right hand, he raised him up.	**7a** and having seized him by the right hand, he raised him up.
[e′]	**7b** And at once he was made to stand and his feet and his ankles were made firm;	**7b** At once, his feet and his ankles were made firm;
[d′]	**8a** and, jumping up, he stood and walked around rejoicing;	**8a** and, jumping up, he stood and walked around
[c′]	**8b** and he went with them into the Temple, praising God.	**8b** and he went with them into the Temple, walking and leaping and praising God.
[b′]	**9** And all the people saw him walking and praising God **10a** and they gradually recognized that this was the man who used to sit asking for alms at the Beautiful Gate of the Temple;	**9** And all the people saw him walking and praising God. **10a** They gradually recognized that he was the man who sat asking for alms at the Beautiful Gate of the Temple,
[a′]	**10b** and they were filled with amazement and utter stupefaction by the change in him.	**10b** and they were filled with amazement and utter stupefaction at what had happened to him.

Critical Apparatus

3.1 Πέτρος δὲ καὶ ᾿Ιωάνν(–ν– B)ης B P^{74} ℵ A C 095. 81. 945. 1175. 1505. 1739. 1891 *pc* lat sa bo | ᾿Επὶ τὸ αὐτὸ δὲ Π. κ. ᾿Ιωάννης E H^{2} P Ψ 049. 056. 33. 181. 614. 2344 𝔐 sy mae; Chr. | Π. κ. ᾿Ιωάννης 69. 1243. 1245. 2495 || ᾿Εν δὲ ταῖς ἡμέραις ταύταις Π. κ. ᾿Ιωάνης D d (p r) mae.

In B03, the narrator continues the story by simply picking up the reference to the apostles going to the Temple in 2.46. In D05, with the introduction of a time phrase at the head of the sentence, a new section of the narrative is indicated, corresponding to the first section (cf. 1.15) and the second (cf. 2.1 D05). The same procedure can be noted at the opening of later sections throughout Acts (cf. 6.1; 8.1b; 12.1 etc.), as well as in Luke's Gospel.

(ἱερὸν) τὸ δειλινόν D d mae || *om.* B P^{74} ℵ *rell.*

D05 spells out that the incident took place in the afternoon, that is, the time of the afternoon sacrifice at 3 pm.

(ἐπὶ τὴν ὥραν) τῆς προσευχῆς τὴν ἐνάτην B P^{74} ℵ *rell* || (+ τὴν D^{C}) ἐν. τ. προσ. D* d sa.

The order of words in the time phrase of B03 is that used in an explanation, as if the audience were not familiar with the hours of prayer in the Temple. In comparison, D05 treats the information as self-explanatory, as if the audience knew the prayer customs of the Temple (Read-Heimerdinger, *The Bezan Text*, p. 97).

3.2 (καὶ) ἰδού D* d p^2 t vg^{mss} sy^p mae; Chr || *om.* B ℵ $D^{s.m.}$ *rell.*

ἰδού has the function of introducing a new element into the story that is seen from the perspective of the participant already present. This, then, keeps the focus on Peter and John throughout the initial verses of the episode. It cannot be translated with one word in English, but has the force of 'And this is what happened to them'.

ὑπάρχων (ἐβαστάζετο) B P^{74} ℵ *rell* || *om.* D d lat sy^p sa (mae) arm; Chr Lcf.

The construction ὑπάρχων + attributive is common in Luke's writings (Lk. x 15; Acts x 25 [+ 3 D05]; Matt. x 3 [+ 1 D05]; none in Mk or Jn). It is not clear why the participle should be omitted in D05 here, though it is not necessary for the meaning.

παρὰ τῶν εἰσπορευομένων εἰς τὸ ἱερόν B P^{74} ℵ A C $D^{s.m.}$, *ab his qui ingrediebantur in templum* d || παρ' αὐτῶν· Εἰσπορ. αὐτῶν εἰς τ. ἱερ. D*.

The variant readings make a significant difference to the meaning. B03 has the lame man seeking for alms from the people entering the Temple; D05 has him specifically waiting for Peter and John and then begins a new sentence with a genitive absolute clause, saying that it was as they were entering the Temple that the lame man saw them.

3.3 ὃς ἰδών B P^{74} ℵ *rell* gig p r t vg; Lcf || οὗτος ἀτενίσας τοῖς ὀφθαλμοῖς αὐτοῦ καὶ ἰδών D, *hic respiciens oculis suis et* (– d^G) *vidit* d* h mae.

The use of the demonstrative οὗτος is appropriate in D05 in order to shift attention temporarily from Peter and John, through whose eyes the scene has been seen so far (cf. on 3.2, above), to the lame man. There occurs the first of a series of four *vll* involving the verb ἀτενίζω. In D05, it is always used of the lame man (cf. 3.4, 5) with the sense that it has elsewhere in Luke-Acts of a gaze directed towards divine power (cf. Acts 1.10; 7.55; 11.6); it is otherwise restricted to a gaze of someone exercising divine power (13.9; 14.9). B03 omits the reference here and also in 3.5, and in 3.4 uses it of Peter and John looking at the lame man (see below).

(μέλλοντας) εἰσιέναι B ℵ D^C *rell*, *introire* d || εἶναι D*.

D05 reads the simple infinitive instead of the compound. This may be a case of the middle letters of the word being accidentally dropped (ΕΙ<ΣΙΕ>ΝΑΙ). Alternatively, the use of the stative verb in D05 may intentionally refer to the apostles' presence in the Temple as opposed simply to their movement into it, thus complementing the reference in 3.2b D05 to their entering of the Temple.

(ἠρώτα) αὐτούς D d h p* || *om.* B P^{74} ℵ *rell.*

Peter and John are once more brought into focus in D05 by the inclusion of the pronoun. The B03 text does not portray the begging as directed to the apostles in particular (cf. on 3.2 above).

(ἐλεημοσύνην) λαβεῖν B P^{74} ℵ A C (+ παρ' αὐτῶν E) Ψ 095. 33. 81. 88. 614. 1175. 1739. 2412 *al* vg || *om.* D d H^2 P 049. 056. 69. 323. 945. 1241. 1245. 1611. 2492. 2495 𝔐 it sy^h; Lcf.

The infinitive is not necessary in the expression αἰτεῖν ἐλεημοσύνην. The pronoun in the D05 text (see above) renders it especially superfluous.

3.4 ἀτενίσας B P^{74} ℵ *rell, intuitus* d || ἐμβλέψας D h p^2 vg.

In the D05 text, the verb ἀτενίζω is reserved for the man (cf. on 3.3 above). ἐμβλέπω can have the sense of 'consider' which may be its meaning here.

Πέτρος εἰς (πρὸς ℵ 2147*) αὐτὸν σὺν τῷ 'Ιωάννῃ εἶπεν B P^{74} ℵ $D^{s.m.}$ *rell*, $d^{s.m.}$ || ὁ Π. εἰς αὐ. σὺν 'Ιωάνην καὶ εἶπεν D* d*.

D05 treat Peter and John as already established on the scene (anaphoric article) and acting as a united pair (one article for them both – see Read-Heimerdinger, *The Bezan Text*, pp. 135–37). In omitting the article before Peter, B03 highlights Peter as speaker, in accordance with its usual pattern (see *The Bezan Text*, p. 132).

βλέψον B P^{74} ℵ *rell* || ἀτένισον D d gig h p r t vg^{mss} sy^p mae.

This is the third *vl* involving the verb ἀτενίζω, with D05 using it, as usual, of the lame man.

3.5 ἐπεῖχεν B P^{74} ℵ *rell, adtendebat* d || ἀτενίσας D h.

The final occurrence in D05 of the verb ἀτενίζω, used once again of the lame man, confirms that he responds obediently to Peter's command (cf. above).

τι παρ' αὐτῶν λαβεῖν B P^{74} ℵ *rell* || τι λαβ. παρ' αὐ. D d (E) 104. 1838 gig (h) p r vg sa; Chr Lcf.

The position of the pronominal phrase before the verb in B03 highlights the apostles. This concords with the fact that it is only now that they become the object of the lame man's attention, since his begging has so far been described in general terms in B03. In contrast, in the D05 text the lame man has been portrayed as deliberately seeking out the apostles from the outset of the scene and so there is no need to highlight them now.

3.6 εἶπεν δὲ Πέτρος B ℵ E H^2 P Ψ 049. 056. 33. 69. 81. 323. 614. 945. 1611. 2412. 2492 𝔐 || εἶπ. δὲ ὁ Π. D 242.

B03 again omits the article before Peter as he speaks (cf. comments on 3.4 above).

3.7 (ἤγειρεν) αὐτόν B ℵ A C 81. 88. 1175. 1611 || *om.* D d E H^2 P Ψ 049. 056. 33. 69. 614. 945. 1739. 2412. 2495 𝔐 vg^{ms}.

The omission by D05 of the second occurrence of the pronoun is correct Greek (Delebecque, *Les deux Actes*, p. 38.); if it has any effect on the telling of the story, it is that it directs attention to Peter's first action, that of touching the lame man.

παραχρῆμα δέ B ℵ *rell* || καὶ παρ. D d (gig) e h p vg sy^p mae; Ir^{lat} Chr.

While B03 views the effects of Peter's healing commands and gestures as a new development marked by δέ, D05 conjoins with καί each of the successive stages of healing, including the people's reaction, to Peter's performative act, so presenting the whole as part of the same unit of development.

ἐστάθη καί D d h mae; Cyp || *om.* B ℵ *rell.*

The verb read by D05 is in the passive, showing the positive result of Peter's gesture.

αἱ βάσεις αὐτοῦ B ℵ A C 81. 88. 945. 1175. 1739. 1891 || αὐ. αἱ β. D d E H^2 P Ψ 049. 056. 33. 69. 323. 614. 1245. 1611. 2412. 2495 𝔐; Ir^{lat}.

The position of the possessive pronoun in B03 is the unmarked (neutral) one. The fronting of it in D05 functions in combination with the supplementary verb (see above) to maintain the spotlight on the man.

3.8 (περιεπάτει) χαιρόμενος D d (χαίρων E) h mae || *om.* B ℵ *rell.*

The mention of 'rejoicing' in D05 echoes the text of Isaiah 35 that describes the joy of the sick, the lame man among them, on being healed by God. The middle voice of χαίρω is unusual, and incorrect in Classical Greek (Delebecque, *Les deux Actes*, p. 38); the active voice of E08 could be due to a retroversion from the Latin *gaudens*.

περιπατῶν καὶ ἁλλόμενος καὶ (αἰνῶν) B (P^{74} ℵ) *rell* || *om.* D d h mae.

The details included in B03 intensify the description of the miracle (see Lake, *English Translation and Commentary*, IV, p. 34: 'The Neutral Text with its "walking and jumping" seems intended to magnify the miracle'). Their absence in D05 allows the physical effects of the healing to be kept separate from the spiritual consequences, that is, the entering into the Temple and the praising of God.

3.10 (ἐπεγίνωσκον) δέ B P[74] ℵ A C Ψ 81 || τε D, *(cognoscebant)que* d E H[2] P 049. 056. 33. 69. 323. 614. 1175. 1505. 1611. 1739. 2344. 2412. 2495 𝔐.

δέ in B03 causes the switch to the people's thoughts to be presented as a new development, which is logical in so far as the scene has not been viewed through their eyes before. D05, with τε, introduces the reaction of the people as an additional and final element in the sequence of consequences following Peter's command in 2.6 (Read-Heimerdinger, *The Bezan Text*, pp. 204–206). This is the information that will lead onto the next stage of the narrative.

οὗτος (ἦν) B D, *hic* d E H[2] P Ψ 049. 056. 33. 69. 323. 614. 945. 1175. 1241. 1611. 1739. 2412. 2495 𝔐 sy || αὐτός P[74] ℵ A C 36. 81. 181. 453. 1505. 1646 *pc* gig h p r vg; Lcf.

With the demonstrative pronoun, both B03 and D05 imply a contrast between the condition of the man now, walking and entering the Temple, and his earlier condition as he sat begging at the entrance. D05 frequently reads the demonstrative pronoun οὗτος in place of αὐτός: Lk. 2.8; 4.6; 6.33; 13.14, 31; 24.20; Acts 3.10; 16.16; 17.25; 20.35.

καθήμενος B P[74] ℵ *rell* || καθεζόμενος D.

The form of the verb in B03 is derived from κάθημαι (cf. 2.2 B03, 34; 6.15 D05; 8.28; 14.8; 23.3); the D05 form is from καθέζομαι (cf. 2.2 D05; 6.15 B03; 20.9). In so far as a distinction can be made, the former expresses a fixed state, the latter an ongoing activity (see *Critical Apparatus*, 2.2).

συμβεβηκότι B P[74] ℵ *rell, contegerat* d || γεγενημένῳ D (1828) sy[p].

συμβαίνω used in B03 refers to an event that happened, as it were, by chance; the verb γίνομαι in D05 implies that a much more deliberate change of state has come about.

Commentary

[a] 3.1 *Peter and John's Attendance at the Temple*

3.1 Whereas the AT opens this new section rather abruptly with a change of scene and characters, Codex Bezae has an introductory time clause that characterizes the opening of all the major divisions of the book of Acts (cf. previous sections 1.15; 2.1 and later sections 6.1; 8.1b; 12.1). A connection with the previous section, Section II, is thus established, clearly indicating a time frame for the incidents about to be related.[1] The close linking of the sections causes attention to be drawn to the fact that

1. Read-Heimerdinger, *The Bezan Text*, pp. 103–107.

the apostles continued going to the Temple, already alluded to at the end of the previous section (2.46), even when the Jesus-believing community was growing in strength and numbers (2.47).

Codex Bezae further underlines the specific time at which Peter and John went to the Temple with the mention of ‘in the afternoon/evening’ which indicates the time of the second daily sacrifice, being also ‘the ninth hour of prayer’ (3 pm). This is, of course, the time recorded by Luke for the death of Jesus on the cross and when the veil of the Temple was torn down the middle (Lk. 23.44–46). At this stage, the apostles have not yet grasped the significance of the veil being torn, for their continued attendance at the Temple is evidence that they have not understood that access to God has been made open through the death of Jesus and is no longer dependent on Temple ritual.

Note should be taken at this point of the first mention of the word for ‘evening’ in the Jewish Scriptures, where God is said to have ‘walked in the (garden of) paradise in the evening’ (περιπατοῦντος ἐν τῷ παραδείσῳ τὸ δειλινόν, Gen. 3.8 LXX). Already in the Gospel, Luke has associated the reference to the evening sacrifice with a mention of paradise (Lk. 23.43). It is no coincidence that the repeated use of the verb ‘walk’ in the Temple episode (Acts 3.8b; cf. vv. 6d, 8c B03, 9a, 12d) combines with ‘in the evening’ to echo the Genesis text. The purpose of the echo will be seen in 3.3.

The imperfect of the Greek verb in v. 1 could express the idea that they went to the Temple daily (‘they used to go’) which may well have been the case (cf. 2.46 ℵ01/B03), but it could also mean that on a particular day they were on their way (‘were going’) when they were stopped by a crippled beggar.

[b] 3.2a *The Lame Man at the Beautiful Gate*

3.2a Attention in the Bezan text is focused on the lame man by the use of ‘behold!’, but he is seen through the eyes of the apostles (see *Critical Apparatus*). The man, introduced by the indefinite τις, is to be taken as a representative of a certain group of people.[2] He is, in fact, one of a number

2. The use of τις to introduce a representative of a type is very common in Luke’s writings, even more so in D05. It is found with anonymous characters: Lk. 7.2; 8.27 B03; 10.25, 30; 11.37 D05; 12.16; 14.2; 16.1, 19; 18.35; 19.12; Acts 3.2; 14.8; 16.9, 16; 19.9 D05; and with proper names: Lk. 1.5; 2.25; 10.38; 16.20; 23.26; Acts 5.1, 34; 7.58 D05; 8.9, 27 D05; 9.10, 33, 36, 43; 10.1, 5, 6, 22 D05; 13.6; 16.1, 14; 17.34 D05; 18.2, 7, 24; 19.14, 24; 20.9; 21.10, 16; 22.12; 24.1 (D05 *lac.*). It is also used with objects (Acts 10.11; 11.5) or places (Acts 27.8, D05 *lac.*).

of people excluded from full participation in the Temple because he was considered to be impure (see 2 Sam. 5.6–8).[3] His lameness, what is more, was innate since he had been lame since his mother's womb (cf. Acts 14.8); it was an intrinsic part of his being.

Everyday, unspecified people used to carry him to one of the entrances to the Temple, the Beautiful Gate. As there is no record of a gate known by this name, it is difficult to determine its exact location with certainty. Two things are sure, however: 1) it must have been one of the outer gates since a lame man would not have been permitted to enter the Temple proper;[4] 2) it is unlikely to have been the external eastern gate that was hardly used, if at all, for entering the Temple and consequently not useful for the purpose of begging. The gate where there would have been many people around (cf. 'all the people' who witnessed the healing, 3.9) was the main entrance on the south side of the Temple, the Hulda Gate that led from the city through an underground passageway into the outer court of the Herodian extension, built around the Temple proper. Although there is no evidence for the name 'Beautiful' being attributed to this gate, the rich decoration of the internal surfaces may have given rise to the name.

There is, however, a deeper level of significance in the naming of the gate as 'Beautiful' (Ὡραῖα) that must not be overlooked. The echo in this episode of the Genesis account of God walking in the garden of paradise in the evening (Gen. 3.8) was pointed out above with reference to 3.2. In the garden, God had set (ἔθετο, Gen. 2.8; cf. Acts 3.2, ἐτίθουν) a man and made all kinds of trees to grow that were 'beautiful' (ὡραῖος, Gen. 2.9; 3.6) to look at. The implication of the verbal links between the Genesis passage and the present one is that the episode recorded in Acts marks the beginning of a new act of divine creation, as fundamental in its nature as the first creation of the world.

3. The interpretation of 2 Samuel 5, the Scripture in which the reference to the 'blind and the lame not entering the house' is first found, is far from straightforward, nor is it clear how the regulation developed over the centuries. It is worth noting, nonetheless, that in the targum to 2 Samuel, the text reads 'the sinners and the guilty' in place of 'the blind and the lame'.

4. For this reason, the Beautiful Gate cannot be the Nicanor or Corinthian Gate (cf. Barrett, I, pp. 179–80) which separated the Court of Prayer (or Women) from the Court of Israel. An excellent scale model of the Second Temple, based on research of source material in the Bible, the Mishnah and Josephus, has been constructed by Alec Garrard and reproduced in colour photographs (*The Splendour of the Temple* [Eye, Suffolk: Moat Farm Publications, 1997]). The model recreates a precise picture of the Temple, its gates and its courts, which is helpful in order to understand this episode.

In the AT, the end of 3.2 belongs to the previous sentence: the man asked alms of people who were going into the Temple. The different sentence structure of Codex Bezae causes the intention of the lame man and his friends to be more specific: he sat by the entrance of the Temple to ask alms of Peter and John. In this case, 'kind deeds' is possibly more appropriate as the meaning of 'alms' than 'money'.[5] The Bezan detail suggests that these people have recognized the power of the apostles to free the lame man from the burden and restrictions of his impurity, just as the friends who lowered the paralytic through the roof in Luke's Gospel (Lk. 5.18) had recognized the power of Jesus to heal. In the Gospel parallel, however, Jesus was already active in healing the sick when the paralytic was brought to him. In the Acts account, it is the sick man and his anonymous helpers who take the initiative in seeking an encounter with the apostles at precisely the time that coincides with the second daily Temple sacrifice, and also the death of Jesus. Within the context of Luke's writings, the man, the gesture and the timing all have symbolic value: together, they constitute an attempt to draw the attention of the apostles to the effect of Jesus' sacrifice and the abolition of the distinction between pure and impure. But the apostles, for their part, are preoccupied with maintaining Temple worship rather than imitating the example given by Jesus in the Gospel account.

[c] 3.2b–3 *His Plea for Alms from Peter and John*

3.2b–3 As he asks for alms, the Bezan text once more specifies that his begging is directed at Peter and John rather than people in general; this is no chance meeting but a fully intentional one. That it is the lame man who takes the initiative and not the apostles is reinforced in this sentence that spells out in more detail how the cripple stopped Peter and John to ask for alms. The words 'when he saw Peter and John' echo the Lukan parallel passage 'when he [Jesus] saw their faith' (Lk. 5.20), underlining the initial passivity of the apostles in the Acts scene. Codex Bezae insists further on the activity of the man: he has been searching for Peter and John and when he finally spots them, they are about to go into the Temple, apparently paying him no attention.

The verb that is used in Codex Bezae to describe the lame man 'searching intently' will be used twice more in this episode ('look intently', 3.4, 5), always with reference to the cripple looking at the apostles. The Alexandrian text omits the reference here and also in 3.5; in 3.4, it is used of

5. The word in Greek has both meanings (B-A-G, ἐλεημοσύνη).

Peter and John looking at the lame man. The Bezan insistence on this verb, a Lukan favourite,[6] is typical of its use elsewhere in Acts where it generally denotes a gaze directed towards heaven (1.10; 7.55; 11.6) or a heavenly representative (6.15). On two other occasions, it is used of Paul (13.9, Paul looks at Simon Magus prior to declaring his deceit; 14.9, Paul looks at the paralytic prior to healing him), where Paul acts with divine empowerment. The choice of the verb in this passage is another indication that the apostles' God-given power was recognized, first by the man in need of healing (3.3), and only subsequently by the apostles themselves (3.4).

Inherent in the verb in the imperfect, 'asking' (ἠρώτα), is the sense that it was a tentative request rather than a confident demand.

[d] 3.4 *Peter's Command to the Lame Man*

3.4 Peter and John at last react to the presence of the crippled beggar. In the Bezan text, Peter and John are treated as already established participants in the incident, working together (one article for the pair), whereas the AT highlights Peter as speaker.[7] The choice in the AT of the verb 'look intently' (ἀτενίζω) to describe Peter and John's reaction anticipates the awareness of divine help that will empower Paul's response to certain people he meets (see 3.3 above); the more neutral verb βλέπω is then used by Peter in commanding the lame man to look at them. In the Bezan text, the verb used of Peter and John seeing the beggar (ἐμβλέπω) can have the sense of 'to consider', suggesting that they were caught unawares and did not immediately exercise their power by the use of their gaze; on the contrary, they require the lame man to direct *his* gaze towards *them* ('look at us intently', ἀτένισον). He is the one who must be active.

[e] 3.5 *The Lame Man's Acquiescence*

3.5 The response of the lame man concords with the respective command of each text. In the AT, he pays special attention to the apostles, in effect for the first time, whereas in the Bezan text he does exactly as he is told, 'look intently' being used of him now for the third time.

His expectation of receiving something is to be defined differently according to what has preceded in each of the two texts. In the AT, there

6. ἀτενίζω only occurs 14 times in the New Testament, of which two are in Lk., 10 in Acts (+ 2 D05).

7. Read-Heimerdinger, *The Bezan Text*, pp. 132; 136–37. Peter has already been established as leader of the apostles from the first mention of his name at the head of the list at 1.13 (cf. 1.15 D05).

has been no indication that the lame man was looking for anything but money from Peter and John. In contrast, several indications have been given in Codex Bezae that it was Peter and John whom he was waiting for at the Temple gate, and consequently that it was something other than money that he was hoping for. Indeed, the verb 'expect' (προσδοκῶν) and the associated word 'expectation' (προσδοκία) often have a technical sense in Luke, alluding to the Messianic expectation of the people of Israel (Lk. 1.21; 3.15; 7.19, 20; 8.40; 12.46; 21.26; Acts 12.11).

[f] 3.6 *Peter's Declaration of Healing*

3.6 As Peter responds to the lame man, he disappoints or fulfills his hopes according to which text is followed. His declaration that he has no money is consistent with the earlier account of the Jesus-believing community having no personal possessions (2.44–45; 4.32, 34–35).[8] The promise of healing for his lameness will have come as no surprise to the man according to the Bezan account (see on 3.5 above). Peter's words will nonetheless have been utterly surprising to the onlookers, in the Alexandrian as in the Bezan text, who are already present though not yet introduced (see 3.9).

Peter's invocation contains a series of references to a) the 'name' which is the equivalent of the person (cf. in the present section 4.7, 10, 12, 17, 18, as also the baptismal declaration at 2.38); b) 'Jesus' with its meaning of Saviour / Deliverer; c) his function as 'Messiah' (cf. 1.21 D05; 2.30 D05, 31, 36, 38); d) the qualification 'the Nazorene' (as distinct from 'Nazarean') which is always the term used in the book of Acts;[9] e) the order discussed by Jesus with reference to the paralytic in the Gospel, though given in a different form when addressed directly to the man (ἔγειρε καὶ περιπάτει, Lk. 5.23, cf. 5.24).

In both the texts under consideration, Peter's command is limited to telling the man to 'walk'. The absence of the command to 'get up' contrasts with the parallel scenes involving Jesus (ἔγειρε, Lk. 5.24) and Paul (ἀνάστηθι, Acts 14.10) where only the command to 'get up' is given.

[f′] 3.7a *Peter's Act of Raising the Lame Man*

3.7a It would seem to be a lack of confidence in his power to heal that caused Peter to limit his command, for he takes the man by the right

8. The verb ὑπάρχω functions in association with a) the noun ὑπάρξεις (2.45), b) the participle τὰ ὑπάρχοντα (4.32) and c) the same verb (4.34).

9. See *Commentary*, 2.22.

hand and helps him to stand up. Neither Jesus nor Paul assist the paralytics they heal, but in both cases the person is recorded as standing up 'immediately' (Lk. 5.25; Acts 14.10 D05), the same adverb that is used here with reference to the lame man.[10] Jesus and Paul, however, were conscious of their ability to heal and took the initiative in doing so, whereas Peter and John had not set out to exercise their power, hence the hesitancy of the command.

[e′] 3.7b *The Man's Healing*

3.7b The healing of the lame man in this instance is described accordingly as a progressive one, rather more so in Codex Bezae. In the AT, the man's feet and ankles are straightaway made firm, before he jumps up and walks around. In the Bezan text, the man is made to stand first before the other signs of healing occur.

[d′] 3.8a *The Consequences of his Healing*

3.8a The act of 'jumping up' is an expression of the freedom that the lame man experiences for the first time in his life. It is likewise mentioned with reference to the paralytic Paul heals who had also been crippled from birth (οὐδέποτε περιεπάτησεν [aorist B03] / περιεπεπατήκει [pluperfect D05], 14.8), but not the paralytic in Luke's Gospel who was responsible for his own paralysis (Lk. 5.20, 21, 23, 24). The word 'jumping up' echoes Isa. 35.6 where the lame man 'leaping like a deer' appears in the prophetic description of the return of Israel to Zion after God's destruction of her enemies. The overall scene of Isaiah 35 is characterized by great jubilation, and it is therefore appropriate that when the man by the Temple in Jerusalem finally walks, Codex Bezae should describe him as 'rejoicing'.

[c′] 3.8b *The Entry of the Healed Man into the Temple with Peter and John*

3.8b The series of actions performed by the man as a manifestation of his healing concludes with his going into the Temple with Peter and John. Not only is this the consequence of his new-found ability to walk but much more it is a demonstration that he has been released from the prohibition that had prevented him from entering the Temple. At this stage, Peter and John do not see that following Jesus has far-reaching implications for the whole question of Temple worship; this will come later. For

10. παραχρῆμα is found 10 times in Luke's Gospel and six times in Acts (+ 2 D05) but only twice elsewhere in the New Testament (Matt. 21.19, 20).

the time being, they continue with their intention of praying in the Temple, accompanied now by the healed man.

[b′] 3.9–10a *Attention Turns to the Onlookers*
3.9 A new character is mentioned, 'all the people', who collectively represent Israel in Luke's writings.[11] The way that the narrator refers to them, with the connective καί and the aorist verb in first position, points to the fact that they are viewed as having been present all along rather than arriving freshly on the scene (which would have been shown by the connective δέ and the noun phrase in first position). Their presence, in other words, is taken for granted; it is their viewpoint that is now considered as they see the healed man walking and praising God.

3.10a There has been a series of steps over the last few verses (conjoined with καί), starting from the command of Peter to the lame man (3.6) which led to a progressive manifestation of healing (3.7–8) and finally to his being seen by the people (3.9). The gradual realization (ἐπεγίνωσκον, imperfect) that the man was the one who used to sit begging at the Beautiful Gate, is presented in the Alexandrian text as a new development (δέ). In the Bezan text, the realization is linked closely to the previous series of steps, and as the culminating point (τε). The contrast between the present state of the man and his previous condition is emphasized in this text with the demonstrative pronoun 'this (man)'.

[a′] 3.10b *The People's Amazement*
3.10b The recognition leads to extreme feelings of amazement and bewilderment. The strength of the people's surprise cannot be explained simply by the fact that the man has been healed, for it was not unknown for Jewish healers to perform similar acts. Nor can it be attributed to their ignorance of the powers of the apostles since what causes their amazement is said to be 'what had happened to him' (B03) or 'the change in him' (D05). Now the difference between the lame man begging at the Temple gate and the one walking and praising God in the Temple is, certainly, that he has been physically healed but more astonishing still, is that he has gone from being an impure person, excluded from the Temple,

11. πᾶς ὁ λαός is not found in Mark, only once in Matthew (Matt. 27.25), but 15 times in Luke (Lk. x 9 [+ 1 in pl.]; Acts x 6); the equivalent ἅπας ὁ λαός, exclusive to Luke (Lk. x 3), reinforces the idea of totality; ὅλος ὁ λαός is only found in Acts 2.47 (not D05 which reads ὅλον τὸν κόσμον, see *Commentary*, 2.47).

to a pure person, a participant in Temple worship. The lame do not go into the Temple but this man has gone in, walking.

No mention is made of the ritual cleansing that, according to Jewish law, the healed man should have gone through before entering the Temple. This suggests that Peter and John took upon themselves the authority to permit him to enter without performing the legal requirements. Such a step may well have contributed to the utter bewilderment of the people (lit.: they were 'out of themselves'). It will also account for the strength of the opposition of the Temple authorities in Acts 4.

[B] 3.11–26 *Peter's Speech in Solomon's Porch*

Overview

The narrative moves on to the moment when the group come out again from the Temple (D05) and Peter addresses the onlookers who witnessed the healing of the lame man.

Structure and Themes

This is the second of Peter's speeches about Jesus recorded in Acts. Spoken to a Jewish audience, its main topic is the power of the resurrected Jesus to heal and to obtain forgiveness for those who had brought about the crucifixion of the Messiah. It expresses hope for the restoration of Israel based on Scripture, reserving the universal aspect of the Messiah for a distant, indefinite future. The structural divisions that have been identified follow Codex Bezae:

[a] 3.11a The healed man's exit from the Temple with Peter and John
[b] 3.11b The people in Solomon's porch
[a′] 3.12–26 Peter's speech

Translation

	Codex Bezae D05	*Codex Vaticanus B03*
[a]	**3.11a** As Peter and John were coming out together, he came out with them, clinging on to them.	**3.11a** While he was clinging to Peter and John,
[b]	**11b** Those people who had been left amazed were standing in the portico called Solomon's.	**3,11b** all the people ran towards them in the portico called Solomon's, stunned.
[a′]	[α] **12** Peter responded and said to them, 'Men of Israel, why do you	**12** When Peter saw it, he responded to the people, 'Men of Israel, why do

marvel at this man? or why do you look intently at us as if it were we who by our own power or piety had done this, that is made him walk? **13** The God of Abraham and the God of Isaac and the God of Jacob, the God of our fathers, glorified his servant Jesus the Messiah whom you delivered up for judgment; and you denied him before Pilate who had judged him and was wanting to release him. **14** For the Holy and Righteous One you made the situation worse and asked for a murderer to be granted to you. **15** And instead, you killed the author of life whom God raised from the dead, to which we are witnesses. **16** It is by virtue of faith in his name that you see this man and know that his name made him strong and it is precisely the faith that came to him through Jesus that has given him this wholeness in the presence of you all.

you marvel at this man? or why do you look intently at us as if by our own power or piety we had made him walk? **13** The God of Abraham and of Isaac and of Jacob, the God of our fathers, glorified his servant Jesus whom you betrayed and denied before Pilate when he had decided to release him. **14** You denied the Holy and Righteous One and asked for a murderer to be granted to you. **15** And instead, you killed the author of life whom God raised from the dead, to which we are witnesses. **16** By faith in his name, this man whom you see and know, his name has made him strong; and it is precisely the faith that came to him through Jesus that has given him this wholeness in the presence of you all.

[β] **17** Now, men and brethren, we know that you for your part through ignorance committed a wicked deed, behaving like your rulers. **18** God, however, fulfilled thereby that which he had announced in advance through the mouths of all the prophets, the suffering of his Messiah. **19** So repent and turn around for your sins to be wiped away, **20** and in order that there may come times of refreshing from the presence of the Lord, and that he may send the one who has been apppointed Messiah for you, Jesus, **21** whom heaven must, in fact, retain until the time for the restoration of everything that God spoke about through the mouths of his holy ones, the prophets. **22** Moses said to our fathers "The Lord your God shall raise up again for you a prophet from among your brethren; listen to him as you have listened to

17 Now, brethren, I know that you acted in ignorance just like your rulers. **18** But God fulfilled thereby the things he had announced in advance through the mouths of all the prophets, the suffering of his Messiah. **19** So repent and turn around with a view to your sins being wiped away, **20** and in order that there may come times of refreshing from the presence of the Lord, and that he may send the one who has been apppointed Messiah for you, Jesus, **21** whom heaven must, in fact, retain until the time for the restoration of everything that God spoke about through the mouths of his holy prophets from of old. **22** There was Moses, on the one hand, who said "The Lord your God shall raise up again for you a prophet like me from among your brethren; listen to him in everything me, in everything he says to you. **23** Any soul who does not listen to the prophet, that person will be removed from the people." **24** All the prophets from Samuel on, from among the things to follow, wath he spoke they also announced, namely these days. **25** You are the sons of the prophets and of the covenant that God made with our fathers, when he said to Abraham, "All the families of the earth shall be blessed in your seed." **26** For you first God raised up his servant and sent him out to bless you as you each turn away from your sins.'

he says to you. **23** Any soul who does not listen to the prophet, that person will be removed from the people." **24** On the other hand, there were all the prophets, from Samuel and those after him, all those who spoke, and they also announced these days. **25** It is you who are the sons of the prophets and of the covenant that God made with your fathers, when he said to Abraham, "All the families of the earth shall be blessed in your seed." **26** For you first God raised up his servant and sent him to bless you as you each turn away from sin.'

Critical Apparatus

3.11 κρατοῦντος δὲ αὐτοῦ τὸν Πέτρον καὶ τὸν ᾿Ιωάνν(–ν– B)ην B P[74] ℵ *rell* || ἐκπορευομένου δὲ τοῦ Π. κ. ᾿Ιωάνου D d h mae.

The *vll* in this verse entail a significant difference in the narrative, corresponding to that of 3.2–3. The B03 text has the healed man clinging to Peter and John (viewed separately since both have the anaphoric article), and the people running towards them and meeting up with them in Solomon's Porch (see below); it is not clear whether they have been into the Temple proper or not. The D05 text is explicit: as the apostles (with a single article, i.e. still a united pair, cf. 3.4) come out of the Temple, he comes out with them, clinging to them.

συνέδραμεν πᾶς ὁ λαὸς πρὸς αὐτούς B P[74] ℵ A C Ψ 057. 81. 88. 323. 1175 | συνέδραμεν πρὸς αὐτοὺς πᾶς ὁ λαός E (H[2]) P 049. 056. 33. 614. (945). 1245. 1611. 1739. 2412. 2495 𝔐 || συνεξεπορεύετο κρατῶν αὐτούς D d.

See above on this *vl*. The B03 phrase 'all the people' is repeated from 3.9 where the verb is in the singular, as here, although in 3.10 it switched to the plural. ὁ λαός is a technical term in Luke's writing to refer to the people of Israel.

ἐπὶ τῇ στοᾷ τῇ καλουμένῃ Σολομῶντος ἔκθαμβοι B ℵ *rell* || οἱ δὲ θαμβηθέντες ἔστησαν ἐν τ. στ. —ἡ καλουμένη (τῇ –νῃ D[C]) Σολομῶνος— ἔκθ. D, *stupentes autem stabant in porticum qui vocatur Solomonis [stupebant]* d (mae).

The use of ἐπί with the dative in B03 is not usually associated with movement, suggesting that it is the apostles and the healed man (αὐτούς) who are already in Solomon's Porch when the people meet up with them (Read-Heimerdinger, *The Bezan Text*, p. 199); the plural adjective ἔκθαμβοι, used with the singular 'all the people', matches the plural verb ἐπλήσθησαν θάμβους used in 3.10. D05 refers back to the people by picking up this verb from v. 10 with the aorist passive participle θαμ-βηθέντες in the plural, and the adjective ἔκθαμβοι reiterates their amazement. It is they who are standing in Solomon's Porch as Peter and John leave the Temple with the healed man. The use of the nominative singular in D05 for the name of the porch indicates that it is considered to be in apposition (Delebecque, *Les deux Actes*, p. 39). The spelling Σολομῶντος in B03 is found only here and in the AT of Acts 5.12; D05 uses the spelling found elsewhere in the New Testament: Matt. 1.6; 12.42 (x 2); Lk. 11.31 (x 2); Jn 10.23; Acts 5.12 D05.

3.12 ἰδὼν δὲ ὁ Πέτρος B ℵ A C 057^vid. 33. 81. 88. 323. 440. 927. 1175. 2147^c. 2344 | ἰδ. δὲ Π. E H² P Ψ 049. 056. 614. 1241. 1270. 1611. 1739. 1891. 2147*. 2412. 2495 𝔐 || ἀποκριθεὶς δὲ ὁ Π. D d (gig mae).

The *vll* are consistent with the diverse readings of the previous verse. According to B03, Peter first of all sees the people running up then responds to them (see below). In D05, Peter would necessarily pass by the people standing in the porch as he left the Temple and there is no need to specify that he saw them.

ἀπεκρίνατο πρὸς τὸν λαόν B P⁷⁴ ℵ *rell* || εἶπεν πρὸς αὐτούς D d.

B03 repeats the technical term ὁ λαός here, as also in 3.11 (cf. 2.47 AT), so insisting that the onlookers were the Jews and that Peter's speech is addressed to them. The corresponding lack of insistence in D05 suggests that the Jewish context of the episode was more readily apparent to the audience of that text.

ὡς ἰδίᾳ δυνάμει B ℵ *rell* || ὡς ἡμῶν τῇ ἰδ. δυν. D d p* r.

This *vl* functions in combination with the following one.

πεποιηκόσιν B ℵ *rell* || τοῦτο πεποιηκότων D d (0236^vid) gig (p) r.

The construction of B03 is typically Lukan (cf. Lk. 16.1; 23.14; Acts 23.15, 20; 27.30), with the dative perfect participle agreeing with the object pronoun of the previous verb. D05 uses a genitive absolute construction in which the 1st person pronoun stands in contrast to the neuter demonstrative τοῦτο.

3.13 (ὁ θεὸς 'Αβραὰμ) καὶ 'Ισαὰκ καὶ 'Ιακώβ B E H² P Ψ (049). 056. 69. 81. 323. 614. 945. 1739. 2147^c. 2412. 2495 𝔐 || κ. θεὸς 'Ισὰκ κ. θεὸς 'Ιακ. D (A) | ὁ θε. 'Ισαὰκ κ. ὁ θε. 'Ιακ. P⁷⁴ ℵ C 88. 104. 1175. 2147*.

The repetition of θεός before each of the patriarchs in D05, each time without the article, creates an echo of Exod. 3.6 when God first declared himself to Moses: cf. Exod. 3.6, ὁ θεὸς τοῦ πατρός σου, θεὸς 'Αβραὰμ καὶ θεὸς 'Ισαὰκ καὶ θεὸς 'Ιακώβ // Acts 3.13 D05, ὁ θεὸς 'Αβραὰμ καὶ θεὸς 'Ισαὰκ καὶ θεὸς 'Ιακὼβ ὁ θεὸς τῶν πατέρων ἡμῶν. Cf. Lk. 20.37.

(᾽Ιησοῦν) Χριστόν D d h^{vid} mae || *om.* B P^{74} ℵ *rell.*

The mention of Χριστόν is not merely a reverential use of a title but, given that Peter is addressing Jews, a meaningful reference to Jesus as the Messiah. The concurrence of the term 'the Messiah' with God's servant is found in the *Targum of Isaiah* 52, a passage to which there are several allusions throughout Peter's speech (see Heimerdinger, 'Unintentional Sins in Peter's Speech', pp. 269–76).

(ὑμεῖς) μέν B P^{74} ℵ *rell* || *om.* D d 049. 6. 69. 383. 1854. 2147 *pc* sy^{p}; Chr Theoph Oecum.

The use of μέν in B03 anticipates a contrast with the Jews' action of delivering up Jesus. Though not signalled with a corresponding δέ as it would normally be, the contrasting action consists in Pilate's decision to release Jesus (Read-Heimerdinger, *The Bezan Text*, p. 235). D05 establishes a contrast instead between the action of God, just stated, and that of the Jews (repeated in reverse order in 3.15).

(παρεδώκατε) εἰς κρίσιν D d (E) h p* sy^{hmg} mae; Ir^{lat} || *om.* B P^{74} ℵ *rell.*

The detail of D05 concords with Lk. 24.20.

ἠρνήσασθε B P^{74} ℵ *rell*, *negastis* d || ἀπηρ– D e gig p* t vg^{mss}.

The intensive form of the verb used by D05 is the same as that Jesus used of Peter's denial in the Gospel (Lk. 22.34, 61).

([ἀπ]ηρνήσασθε) αὐτόν D d E H^{2} P Ψ 049. 056. 33. 69. 88. 614. 1241. 1611. 2147^{c}. 2412. 2495 𝔐 || *om.* B P^{74} ℵ A C 81. 323. 945. 1175. 1739. 2147*.

The additional pronoun in D05, together with the additional phrase εἰς κρίσιν, has the effect of distinguishing between the two actions of handing Jesus over and denying him. It will be specifically the second action that is seen to be in opposition to Pilate's judgment of Jesus (Read-Heimerdinger, *The Bezan Text*, p. 235).

κρίναντος ἐκείνου ἀπολύειν B P^{74} ℵ (+ αὐτόν D$^{s.m.}$) *rell* || τοῦ κρίναντος, ἐκείνου ἀπολ. αὐτὸν θέλοντος D* d h; Ir^{lat}.

B03 uses the verb κρίνω with the sense of 'decide'; D05 uses the same verb but with the sense of 'judge', adding that when Pilate had judged 'he wanted to release him (Jesus)'; the same words are used of Pilate in the Gospel: θέλων ἀπολῦσαι τὸν ᾽Ιησοῦν (Lk. 23.20). The account of the conflict between the Jewish people and Pilate is more explicit in D05, with an insistence on the people's determination to go against the governor's wishes.

3.14 ἠρνήσασθε B P^{74} ℵ *rell* || ἐβαρύνατε D d mae; Ir^{lat} (Aug).

While in B03 Peter repeats the accusation already made in 3.13, in D05 he adds a further charge, literally ‘you aggravated’. This consisted in demanding his crucifixion, stated three times in Luke’s Gospel (Lk. 23.18, 21, 23).

ᾐτήσασθε B P^{74} ℵ *rell* || –σατε D d.

The middle (B03) and the active (D05) of the verb αἰτέω, though practically interchangeable, tend to be used in distinct ways in Luke-Acts. The middle is generally used of asking for an action to happen (Lk. 23.23 [but not 23.25]; Acts 7.46; 12.20; 13.38 [*vl* D05]), whereas the active is used of asking for something concrete to be given (Lk. 1.63; 6.30; 11.11, 13; 23.52; Acts 16.29). Both voices can be justified here, since the B03 text focuses on the action of ‘being granted to you’ and the D05 text on ‘a murderer’.

3.16 τῇ πίστει B P^{74} ℵ* 0236^{vid}. 81. 1175 *pc* || ἐπὶ τ. πίσ. D, *in fide* d ℵ^{c} A C E H^{2} P Ψ 049. 056. 33. 323. 614. 945. 1739. 2344. 2412. 2495 𝔐 latt; Ir^{lat}.

D05 clarifies that it is on the basis of faith in the name of Jesus that the name has made him strong.

τοῦτον ὃν θεωρεῖτε καὶ οἴδατε ἐστερέωσεν B ℵ D^{C} *rell*, *hunc quem vidistis et scitis consolidavit* d || τοῦτον θεωρ. κ. οἴδ. ὅτι ἐστ. D* aeth^{mss}.

This long sentence in 3.16 is difficult to unravel, as often happens in Peter’s speeches. In B03, τοῦτον (the healed man) is the object of the main verb ἐστερέωσεν, with two verbs in an intervening relative clause referring to him (‘this man whom you see and you know’). The D05 sentence is more disjointed without the relative pronoun though it nevertheless makes sense because of ὅτι after οἴδατε: ‘you see this man and you know that...’.

3.17 ἄνδρες (ἀδελφοί) D d E 33. 88. 1311 *pc* h p q w t vg^{ms} mae || *om.* B ℵ *rell.*

The term of address in D05 is similar to that with which Peter begins his speech, ἄνδρες Ἰσραηλῖται (also found in the previous speech, 2.22).

οἶδα B ℵ *rell* || ἐπιστάμεθα D, *scimus* d^{G} h mae arm^{mss}; Ephr.

With the plural in D05, Peter speaks on behalf of himself and John, or even of the rest of the apostles, rather than for himself as in B03. The appeal to a wider circle fits better with the charge that Peter will bring against the people of Israel, made all the stronger in D05 (see below).

(ὅτι) ὑμεῖς μέν D d (h) || *om.* B ℵ *rell.*

D05 introduces a contrast (μέν) between the action of his audience (ὑμεῖς) and that of God (δέ, 3.18). The opposition between the two is attenuated in B03 where the charge reads more as a straightforward matter of fact.

(ἐπράξατε + τὸ D^{C}) πονηρόν D* d gig h p q w t vg^{mss} sy^{hmg} mae; Ir^{lat} Aug^{pt} Ambst || *om.* B ℵ *rell.*

The description of the action of the people as 'wicked' intensifies the severity of Peter's charge.

3.18 ἃ (προκατήγγειλεν) B P^{74} ℵ *rell, quae* d || ὃ D h | ὅς 467 a b c dem gig vg^{mss}; Vig.

The plural pronoun in B03 refers to that which God has foreseen in general; the singular in D05 refers more specifically to the suffering of the Messiah.

3.19 πρὸς (τὸ ἐξαλειφθῆναι) B ℵ || εἰς D P^{74} A C E H^{2} P Ψ 049. 056. 33. 69. 81. 614. 1611. 1739. 2412. 2495 𝔐.

Both prepositions introduce a purpose clause in this instance. πρός + infinitive is found elsewhere only at Lk. 18.1.

ὑμῶν τὰς ἁμαρτίας B ℵ *rell* || τ. ἁμ. ὑμῶν D d b dem gig h m p s t vg^{mss}; Ir^{lat} Tert.

B03 emphasizes 'your' sins by placing the possessive pronoun before the noun (Read-Heimerdinger, *The Bezan Text*, pp. 108–109). This *vl*, together with the previous one, may have arisen because the different editors of Acts were familiar with different texts of the Jewish Scriptures to which Peter's exhortation alludes.

3.20 ἔλθωσιν B ℵ *rell, veniant* d || ἐπέλθ– D h; Tert.

The compound verb underlines the eschatological character of the times of refreshing 'coming upon' the world (cf. Lk. 1.35; 21.26; Acts 1.8; Eph. 2.7; Jas 5.1).

3.21(τῶν ἁγίων) ἀπ' αἰῶνος αὐτοῦ προφητῶν B* P^{74vid} ℵ* A C 81. 1175. 1739 *pc* e (vg); (Or) | τῶν ἀπ' αἰ. αὐ. πρ. $ℵ^{2}$ B^{2} E (33^{vid}). 945 *pc* | αὐ. πρ. ἀπ' αἰ. (614) 𝔐 vg^{mss} | αὐ. πρ. τῶν ἀπ' αἰ. Ψ 1505 *pc* sy^{h} || αὐτοῦ, τῶν (– $D^{p.m.}$) πρ. D* d *pc* it; (Tert).

τῶν προφητῶν in D05 are to be read as in apposition to τῶν ἁγίων αὐτοῦ. The expression of B03 reproduces the words of Zacharias in Lk. 1.70 (P^{74} B L Δ 0130): καθὼς ἐλάλησεν διὰ στόματος τῶν ἁγίων ἀπ' αἰῶνος προφητῶν αὐτοῦ. It should be noted, however, that Lk. 1.70 D05 (it Ir^{lat}) reads διὰ στόματος ἁγίων προφητῶν αὐτοῦ, τῶν ἀπ' αἰ., with the same appositional construction as here in Acts 3.21 D05.

3.22 εἶπεν B P^{74} ℵ A C 81. 1175. 1739 *pc* (vg); Or || εἶπ. πρὸς τοὺς πατέρας ἡμῶν D d E 33^{vid}. 88. 1837. 2344^{vid}. (2495) *pc* it sa mae arm; Ir^{lat} (Mss $gr^{sec.\ Beda}$) | εἶπ. πρ. τ. πατ. Ψ 383. 467. 876. 945. 1108. 1611. 1739. 1891. 2138. 2147 sy^{h}; Chr | πρ. τ. πατ. εἶπ. H^{2} P 049. 056. 69. 323. 614. 1241. 1245. 1270. 1505. 2412. 2492 𝔐.

The phrase 'our fathers' occurs three times in Peter's speech according to D05 (cf. 3.13, 35), thereby strengthening his identification with his addressees and anchoring his teaching in the history of Israel.

(ὁ θεὸς) ὑμῶν D d ℵ[2] A H[2] 049. 056. 69. 81. 323. 610. 945. 1175. 1505. 1739. 1891. 2147 𝔐 [pt] lat; Ir[lat] Or[pt] Chr Cyr || ἡμῶν ℵ* C E P Ψ 33. 614. 1241. 1245. 1270. 1611. 2344[vid]. 2412. 2495 𝔐 [pt] sy[h] sa[mss]; Or[pt] Cl[hom] Ambr | *om.* B h p sa[ms] bo; Eus Dyd Qu.

In Peter's citation of Deut. 18.15–16, D05 introduces two changes compared with the LXX text. The first is the plural of the second person pronoun, in place of σου, to accord with the plural ὑμῖν earlier in the sentence. While B03 omits the pronoun altogether, ℵ01* reads the first person which, if intentional, tends to distance Moses/Peter from the audience.

ὡς ἐμέ· αὐτοῦ ἀκούσεσθε B ℵ *rell* || ὡς ἐμοῦ αὐτοῦ ἀκ. D d.

B03 follows the LXX whereas D05 makes an interesting alteration, so that it is no longer a question of comparing the new prophet with Moses but the manner of listening to the new prophet with that of listening to Moses.

3.24 (καὶ πάντες) δέ B P[74] ℵ *rell* || *om.* D d gig h p vg bo; Ir[lat].

The connective δέ in B03, corresponding to μέν in 3.22, distinguishes Moses from the later prophets, with καί at the beginning of the sentence having adverbial force. In D05, if καὶ (πάντες) is taken as the correlative to μέν (as happens also in Classical Greek, see Winer, *Grammar*, p. 721), the same distinction is implicit. Alternatively, the correlative clause in D05 may be understood as not occurring until 3.25: Ὑμεῖς ἐστε υἱοὶ τῶν προφητῶν.

ὅσοι ἐλάλησαν B P[74] A C* E H[3] P Ψ 049. 056. 69. 81. 614. 945. 1175. 1739. 2412. 2495 𝔐, *quodquod locuti sunt* d | οἳ ἐλ. ℵ C* D[B] | οἳ ἐπροφήτευσαν C[2] || ὃ ἐλάλησεν D*.

The plural verb in B03 groups together Samuel and all the later prophets. The singular verb in D05 could be interpreted as applying to Samuel and all the prophets after him (as in B03), the singular reflecting the fact that they all spoke in agreement; the difficulty with this suggestion is the neuter pronoun ὅ where a masculine would have been required. An alternative suggestion, that makes better grammatical sense and fits with Peter's argument, is to take the verb as applying to Moses (or even God, cf. v. 21), with the neuter pronoun referring to the content of his speech ('what he spoke'). On this understanding of D05, the genitive phrase καὶ τῶν καθεξῆς refers not to the prophets who came after Samuel but to the succession of events foreseen by Moses – 'from among them (genitive of the neuter article), what Moses spoke all the later prophets also announced, namely these days', where τὰς ἡμέρας ταύτας is in apposition to τῶν καθεξῆς; καί both before the genitive phrase and after ὃ ἐλάλησεν are adverbial, meaning 'even', or 'also'.

3.25 οἱ (υἱοί) B P[74] ℵ A C E 056. 0165. 81. 88. 226. 547. 927. 945. 1175. 1739. 1854. 1891. 2147 || *om.* D H[3] P Ψ 049. 323. 614. 1241. 1245. 1270. 1505. 1611. 2412. 2495 𝔐; Chr.

The omission of the article before the complement (D05) is in accordance with the usual Greek practice. The presence of the article in B03 therefore implies that Peter is carefully restricting his present definition of 'the sons of the prophets' to his Jewish audience. It cannot be necessarily concluded that D05 is being less restrictive than B03, but the limiting in B03 is clearly underlined.

ἧς ὁ θεὸς διέθετο B D[B] 0165[vid] *pc* h p; Ir[lat] | ἧς δι. ὁ θε. P[74] ℵ A C E H[3] P Ψ 049. 056. 33[vid]. 69. 81. 323. 945. 1175. 1241. 1505. 1611. 1739. 2147. 2344. 2412. 2495 𝔐 lat || ἣν ὁ θε. δι. D d.

The attraction of the relative pronoun in B03 is a common occurrence. The position of the subject before the verb in both B03 and D05 is emphatic.

(πατέρας) ὑμῶν B P[74] ℵ[2] A E 81. 88. 104. 453. 547. 927. 945. 1175. 1505. 1739. 2147. 2344. 2492 vg[st.ww] sa[ms] bo[mss]; Ir[lat vid] Chr || ἡμῶν D d ℵ* C[vid] H[3] P Ψ 049. 056. 0165. 69. 181. 323. 614. 1891. 2344. 2412. 2495 𝔐 it vg[cl] sy co; Ir[lat v.l.] Fulg.

It is usual, more so in D05 than in B03, for the apostles and other Christian leaders to identify with their Jewish audience in speaking of the patriarchs by using the first person pronoun: Peter (3.13, 22 D05, 25 D05; 5.30; 15.10), Stephen (7.4 D05, 11, 12, 15, 38, 39, 44, 45a, 45b), Paul (13.17, 32 D05; 26.6 [D05 *lac.*]) and Ananias (22.14). The second person pronoun expresses criticism and a distancing of the speaker from the Jewish audience: Stephen (7.51, 52 [ἐκεῖνοι D05]) and Paul (28.25 [D05 *lac.*; ἡμῶν 𝔐 gig vg]).

εὐλογηθήσονται B A* Ψ 323. 383. 945. 1739. 1243. 1854 *pc;* Ir[lat] || ἐνευλ– D P[74] ℵ A[2] E H[3] P 049. 056. 0165. 33. 69. 614. 1175. 1245. 1611. 2412. 2495 𝔐.

D05 retains the compound verb from Gen. 22.18; 26.4 LXX, the source of Peter's quotation at this point, although at the same time it introduces changes to the passage in common with B03.

3.26 ἀναστήσας ὁ θεός B ℵ C 0165. 36. 88. 104. 323. 1175 *pc* | ἀν. 049. 547*. 1270. 1854 || ὁ θε. ἀν. D d P[74] A E H[3] Ψ 056. 33. 69. 81. 614. 945. 1241. 1611. 1739. 2412. 2495 𝔐 lat; Ir[lat].

D05 highlights God as the subject while B03 adopts a more neutral word order of subject–verb. The latter word order, however, also creates potential ambiguity, allowing πρῶτον to be taken as qualifying either the pronoun ὑμῖν, 'for you first', or the participle ἀναστήσας, 'having first raised up...'.

ἀπέστειλεν αὐτόν B P[74] ℵ *rell*, *misit* d | ἀπ. 945. 1611. 2344 || ἐξαπ– D.

The verb ἀποστέλλω is shared by all the Gospel writers (Matt. x 22; Mk x 20; Jn x 27; Lk. x 25 [+ 1 D05]; Acts x 26 [– 2 D05]) whereas ἐξαποστέλλω is used only by Luke (Lk. 1.53; 20.10, 11, 12 D05; 24.49 B03 [ἀπο – D05]; Acts 3.26 D05; 7.12; 9.30 [D05 *lac.*]; 11.22; 12.11; 13.26; 17.14; 22.21 D05 [ἀπο – B03]).

The absence of the second object pronoun αὐτόν in D05 tends to accord more importance to the first action of raising up (ἀναστήσας) Jesus.

ἕκαστον ἀπὸ τῶν πονηριῶν B ℵ *rell* || ἕκαστος (–ον D[B]) ἐκ τ. πονηρῶν D* (104 (– ιῶν D[C]), *unusquisque a nequitiis* d.

B03 uses the noun αἱ πονηρίαι whereas D05 reads the neuter adjective τὰ πον–ηρά. It is possible that the variation in preposition does not affect the meaning. However, ἐκ together with the personal pronoun qualifying τῶν πονηρῶν could mean that Peter's audience need to extract themselves 'out of' their sins rather than more generally turn away 'from' sin (Read-Heimerdinger, *The Bezan Text*, p. 189).

(πονηρῶν) ὑμῶν D ℵ *rell* || πονηριῶν αὐτῶν C* 33, *suis* d gig h p vg; Lcf | αὐτοῦ 323. 945. 1739. 1891 | *om.* B Chr.

The pronoun may have been omitted by haplography. The third person pronouns, referring to ἕκαστον, can be seen as attempts to supply a suitable pronoun rather than as modifications of the second person pronoun of D05.

Commentary

[a] 3.11a *The Healed Man's Exit from the Temple with Peter and John*

3.11a In the AT, it is not clear whether Peter, John and the healed man clinging to them had already been into the Temple proper (into the Court of Israel, beyond the Court of the Gentiles) or whether they were on their way there; the Bezan text makes it clear that they had indeed been inside the Temple and that as they were going out the healed man was clinging to them.

The attitude of the healed man is, on the face of it, surprising for he clearly does not require Peter and John's assistance to walk. However, if he has been into the Temple without following the ritual acts of purification prescribed by the Jewish law he will be dependent on their support once he is confronted by the Temple authorities. His need for protection is apparent in the Bezan picture of him clinging to the apostles as he went out of the Temple with them.

[b] 3.11b *The People in Solomon's Porch*

3.11b In the AT, whether the apostles and the healed man had been into the Temple proper or not, the people ran up to meet them in Solomon's Porch. This was a covered portico that ran along the eastern wall of the Temple, with sections of it in the Courts of Israel and the Gentiles as well as in the Herodian extensions, and was where Jewish teachers used to meet to discuss with the people.[12] According to the Bezan text, the people were waiting there for the group to come out of the Temple.

[a′] 3.12–26 *Peter's Speech*

This speech, like all the speeches in Acts, is made up of [α] an Exposition (3.12–16) and [α′] a corresponding Parenesis (3.17–26). However, despite the formality of its construction, it is very digressive with a piling up of relative clauses and half-finished sentences that characterize other apologetic speeches of Peter's (cf. second half of the Pentecost speech, 2.22–36).

[α] 3.12–16 *Exposition*. In the exposition, four points are made in a chiastic pattern: [*a*] (3.12) a twofold question ('why do you marvel... why do you look intently?') is answered with [*a′*] (3.16) a twofold response ('by virtue of faith in his name... the faith that came to him through Jesus'). Between these, stands an account of the action of God, [*b*] (3.13–14), in glorifying his servant when he had been betrayed by the people and [*b′*] (3.15) in resurrecting him when he had been killed.

3.12 Once again, the apostles do not take the initiative in explaining the miracle to the people, but rather it is in response to the stunned crowd, as they gaze at Peter and John, that the former speaks. His speech is specifically addressed to the people of Israel, they are fellow-Jews (cf. 2.22). He opens with two questions, the first relating to their stupefaction at the healed cripple, and the second to the attention they are concentrating on himself and John ('look intently' picks up the verb used earlier, exclusively of the lame man in Codex Bezae [3.4a B03; 3.3a, 4b, 5 D05]). He deduces that the people attribute the man's healing to their abilities or qualities, a supposition that acts as a springboard for speaking about Jesus as he contradicts it.

12. The location of Solomon's porch is described differently according to the various reconstructions of the Temple that have been proposed. In Garrard's model, Solomon's porch is partly within the Temple walls and partly in the Herodian extensions, outside the sacred area (*The Splendour of the Temple*), pp. 29, 46–47.

3.13 Peter's reference to the God of Israel is a solemn declaration and in the Bezan text echoes the wording of Exod. 3.15–16 LXX when God reveals his name to Moses; they are words also repeated by Jesus according to Lk. 20.37. Peter thus makes clear his position of Jewish orthodoxy as the basis on which he will go on to identify Jesus as the Messiah. Jesus has already been referred to as a man (2.22). The description of him now as God's servant is an allusion to the term used in Isaiah (52.13; 53.7–8, 11; cf. Acts 8.32–35). The Bezan text, furthermore, makes an explicit mention of his role as 'Messiah', a term not found in the Massoretic text of Isaiah but one that does occur, also in association with the 'servant of God', in the *Targ. Isa.* 52.13.[13] The use of the term in the Bezan text is therefore by no means evidence of a later, Christian modification but could reflect a Jewish tradition known to Peter and his audience.

The problem facing Peter is how to convince the Jewish people that Jesus is the Messiah for he is known to them as a man who died a criminal's death, utterly contradicting all expectations of the splendour that should accompany the arrival of the Messiah. The argument of his speech will therefore concentrate on demonstrating that the apparent failure of Jesus was due to his rejection by the people of Israel, and that God has overruled their killing of him by glorifying him after his death. He begins his explanation here in 3.13 with a relative pronoun ('whom you...') and will pick it up again in 3.16 after a digression.

The responsibility of the Jews for the death of Jesus is attributed to two actions: handing Jesus over and standing against him even though Pilate wanted to release him. The Alexandrian text groups the two actions together, setting the Jews in contrast (using μέν) with Pilate. In the Bezan text, the Jews are rather seen in contrast with God (3.13a; no μέν), and the actions are viewed as separate: firstly, they handed him over to judgment and secondly, when Pilate had judged him, they stood against him even though Pilate wanted to release him (cf. Lk. 23.17 ℵ01 [= v. 19 D05]). The two actions of handing Jesus over and denying him correspond exactly to the deeds attributed by Luke in the Gospel to Peter and Judas, the first and the last named of the apostles (Lk. 6.14–16). It is Judas who hands Jesus over (the same verb, παραδίδωμι, which also translates as 'betray' in English) to the Jewish authorities when he leads them to him on the Mount of Olives (Lk. 22.47–48, 52–53). In the Gospel, the action

13. On the *Isaiah Targum* reading of 'Messiah' and other ideas expressed in Peter's speech, see J. Heimerdinger, 'Unintentional Sins in Peter's Speech: Acts 3:12–26', *RCatT* 20 (1995), pp. 269–76.

of handing over or betrayal is not principally attributed to the Jewish people, but to Judas and the religious leaders.[14] Similarly, it was Peter who denied knowing Jesus (Lk. 22.34, 57, 58, 60, 61),[15] not the Jewish people. The Jewish people are implicated to some extent in the Gospel by the words addressed by Pilate to 'the chief priests, the rulers and the people' when he sees Jesus for the second time, 'You brought me this man... ' (Lk. 22.13–14; cf. 'the chief priests and the multitudes', 23.4), but it was not they who initiated the process of trial and judgment. Indeed, until the last moment the people had ben eager to hear his teaching and stood out against the authorities (Lk. 19.48; 20.1, 9, 19, 45; 21.38). Luke is thus portraying Peter here in Solomon's porch as doctoring the facts by omitting any mention of the responsibility of the apostolic group and by laying the blame for Jesus' death on the Jewish people.

3.14 The AT repeats the accusation of denial, expanding on the description of Jesus as 'holy' and 'righteous', both Messianic terms used by Isaiah (Isa. 54.5 and 53.11 respectively). Codex Bezae continues with the progression of unjust actions started in 3.13 by adding further accusations against the Jews (in which the apostles had no part): they made things worse for the Messiah by bringing about his crucifixion (cf. Lk. 23.18, 21,

14. Jesus predicted on several occasions to his disciples that he would be handed over, or betrayed, but without specifying the agent (note the passives: μέλλει παραδίδοσθαι, Lk. 9.44; παραδοθήσεται, 18.32; δεῖ παραδοθῆναι, 24.7). However, once Judas has taken the decision to betray him (πῶς ... παραδῷ αὐτόν, 22.4; τοῦ παραδοῦναι αὐτόν, 22.6), Jesus will show who he is (πλὴν οὐαί ... δι᾽ οὗ παραδίδοται, 22.21) and will unmask his betrayal (φιλήματι ... παραδίδως, 22.48). Luke also uses the verb in its active form with reference to the Jewish leaders when they are looking for arguments to hand Jesus over to the Roman governor (ὥστε παραδοῦναι αὐτόν, 20.20) and when the disciples on the road to Emmaus refer back to this event (παρέδωκεν αὐτόν, 24.20); also with reference to Pilate who, in turn, handed Jesus over to the will of the Jewish leaders (παρέδωκεν τῷ θελήματι αὐτῶν, 23.25). Stephen will refer to all the Jews, without distinction, as 'traitors' (προδόται, Acts 7.52) using the same technical term as that used to qualify Judas in the list of the Twelve (cf. Lk. 6.16).

15. The ordinary verb 'deny' (ἀρνέομαι) is used once in Luke's Gospel of Peter (22.57) and the intensive form (ἀπ–αρνέομαι) twice (22.34, 61). In Acts 3, the AT uses the ordinary form in vv. 13 and 14, whereas the Bezan text uses the intensive form in v. 13 and a different verb in v. 14 (see *Commentary*, 3.14). The intensive form makes a more obvious link with Peter's denial and makes his present distortion of the facts more apparent. He has still some way to go before making a full conversion: the process was begun in Lk. 22.61–62 but will only become complete in Acts 12.

23). The overall effect of the Bezan text is that Peter's accusations against the Jews are considerably stronger than in the AT.

Both texts refer to the people asking for Barabbas to be released rather than Jesus (Lk. 23.18–19, 25) despite Pilate's repeated intention to the contrary (Lk. 23.16, 20, 22). The intercalation of Pilate's judgment between the two sets of accusations, both introduced as they are with the emphatic pronoun 'you...' (ὑμεῖς, 3.13b, 14), underlines the responsibility of the Jews rather than the Roman authorities for Jesus' death.

3.15 Peter expresses this fact in the strongest terms, referring to Jesus as the author of life who has been killled. This then leads him by means of a second relative pronoun (cf. 3.13) back to considering the action of God in favour of the Messiah, raising him from the dead in direct opposition to the rejection of the people. A third relative pronoun introduces the testimony of the apostles to the fact of the resurrection.

3.16 The speech now returns to its original topic, the healing of the crippled man. It is because Jesus has been raised from the dead that the man has been healed, and his healing glorifies Jesus (cf. 3.13) because it has been carried out by his name.

The explanation for the healing which rests on the effectiveness of the name of Jesus is tangled, as Peter's explanations sometimes are (cf. Acts 10.36–37). Seeing the structure of the sentence, however, makes the meaning clearer. Essentially, the same thing is said twice, with a pattern of parallel elements that is more obvious in the Bezan text:

A	It is by virtue of faith in his name	A′	and it is precisely the faith that came through Jesus
a	that you see this man and you know	b′	that has given him this wholeness
b	that his name made (him) strong,	a′	in the presence of you all.

In the case of the last two elements, the order is reversed in the second half of the sentence so as to produce a chiastic form.

While the pattern may well help to clarify the meaning, however, the exact sense remains imprecise. Whose is the faith that stands as the topic of the two parts of the sentence? In the parallel Gospel scene where Jesus heals the paralytic lowered down through the roof (Lk. 5.18–26), Luke says that Jesus 'saw their faith' (5.20), referring to the men who carried the paralytic on his bed. In the present scene, those who carried the lame man to the Temple have only been mentioned briefly and indirectly (Acts 3.2). According to the Bezan text, it may nevertheless be partly their faith that was active in obtaining healing for the lame man for they deliberately used to set him by the Temple so that he could encounter Peter and John, presumably because they saw them as representatives of Jesus (3.2 D05). Peter specifies, though, in v. 16 that it was faith in and through the name of Jesus that was effective in bringing about healing, and the name was only invoked in the words of healing (3.6b). The faith, then, that has been principally operative is that of the lame man as he responded to Peter's command. That faith is twofold for it came through Jesus (v. 16b) and had Jesus' name as its object (v. 16a).

The name represents the person of Jesus himself which is why it is the name that is said first to have made the man strong. The result was 'wholeness' (τὴν ὁλοκληρίαν), a word used only here in the New Testament but otherwise found in some manuscripts of Isa. 1.6 LXX where the prophet reports on the pitiful condition of rebellious Judah and Jerusalem, saying that there is no 'wholeness' in them.[16] In this context, and within the logic of Peter's argument, the release of the lame man from his impurity, which had prevented him from freely worshipping God in the Temple, is an example for the people of Israel to follow so that they, too, can be restored following their killing of the Messiah. The bringing in of the notion of faith prepares for Peter's exhortation of the Jewish people to believe in Jesus.

[β] 3.17–26 *Parenesis*. The parenetic section of the speech also consists of four points arranged in a chiastic pattern: the first *[a]* (vv. 17–18) and the last *[a′]* (vv. 25–26) both make an emphatic contrast between the people ('you', vv. 17 // 25) and 'God' (vv. 17 // 26). The central elements contain an invitation to conversion *[b]* (vv. 19–21), and a warning of the consequences if it is not accepted *[b′]* (vv. 22–24).

3.17 Having drawn attention to the responsibility of his Jewish audience for the death of the Messiah, Peter goes on to address the question of how things can be put right. In the AT, Peter speaks for himself whereas the Bezan text has him speak on behalf of himself and John or even the apostolic circle. He speaks now very much as one of them ([men and] brethren), in other words from a Jewish perspective.

He goes on to point out that the dreadful deeds that he has been describing were committed in ignorance. In the AT, the meaning seems to be that

16. ἡ ὁλοκληρία is found in certain recensions of Isa. 1.6 LXX (L C O sub *; see Rahlfs' edition).

the Jewish people and their leaders acted independently ('you acted in ignorance just like your rulers'), and it is generally understood that Peter is offering 'ignorance' as a means to excuse their actions. Under Jewish law, the deeds summarised by Peter (3.13–15) would incur the death penalty: on its own, killing another person (3.15) was a capital offence (cf. Exod. 21.12–14; Num. 35), and in this case it is compounded by the fact that Jesus was the Messiah; false witness was borne (3.13); and the release of a known murderer was asked for (3.14).

The Bezan text spells out that it is a wicked act that has been committed and so appears to undermine the excuse by insisting on the evil nature of their actions. The word πονηρόν is found throughout the LXX to describe wickedness as an absolute concept and also as transgression against the law or the will or the judgment of God.[17] Such a perspective concords with Jewish legal regulations under which all evil deeds incur blame; if they were comitted in ignorance that is not an excuse for sin but rather it is the cause of it (cf. Lev. 5.17).[18] The sin becomes something more awful when committed in ignorance ('we have done wrong and did not realise it'), not something lesser. At this point, then, in the Bezan text, Peter is not seeking to exculpate the Jews by pointing to their ignorance as a circumstance that will let them off the penalty. On the contrary, he is establishing the cause of their guilt for which he will offer in a moment (3.19) the means whereby the consequences can be escaped.

The detail 'a wicked deed' allows better sense to be made of the comparison of the people with their rulers. According to the Bezan text, the ignorance can be read as describing only the condition of the people, which caused them to commit the same wicked deed as their rulers. Their ignorance was of the Scriptures concerning the Messiah, and because they were ignorant they followed their rulers. Again, this does not let them 'off the hook', for the evil deed has been committed whatever the cause, but it does account for how it came about. An awareness of the Jewish view of wrong-doing is important for an understanding of Peter's progression of

17. In the AT, πονηρόν is only found as an abstract noun in Acts 28.21. In the Bezan text, it is used again by Peter of Ananias in Acts 5.4 D05 and in the plural at 3.26 D05 in place of πονηρία (see *Critical Apparatus*). Additional Bezan references in Luke's Gospel are found in the mouth of Jesus, referring to the thoughts of the religious leaders who were accusing him of blasphemy (pl. πονηρά, 5.22 D05; cf. // Matt. 9.4); and of one of the two crucified criminals who declared that Jesus had done no wrong (οὗτος ... οὐδὲν πονηρόν ἔπραξεν, 23.41 D05).

18. The problem of sins committed in ignorance is dealt with in the tractate of the Mishnah *Horayoth*.

thought, at least in the Bezan text. He is not seeking to tone down in any way the dreadfulness of the killing of the Messiah by introducing the notion of ignorance. He is identifying with his audience in sharing their awareness that death must be the consequence for them and that is why he offers them a way to be saved from that punishment.[19]

3.18 The ignorance of the people (and their rulers, AT) contrasts (more pointedly in Codex Bezae) with the planned action of God who brought about the fulfilment of the prophetic writings concerning the suffering of the Messiah by means of their lack of understanding.[20] At last Peter has seen that the suffering of the Messiah was foreseen. Not so long ago, Peter and the other apostles had been in exactly the same position as the Jewish people he is now addressing, for Jesus had been attempting throughout his ministry to convince them of the need for him to suffer but they had persistently resisted the idea (Lk. 9.22, 44–45; 17.25; 18.31–34; 22.15), even after his resurrection according to Codex Bezae (Lk. 24.32).[21] They, too, had been 'ignorant' (Lk. 18.34).

3.19 In accordance with (οὖν) Peter's presentation of the situation of his audience, he puts forward the solution, namely that the people should acknowledge that they have done wrong ('repent') and return to God ('turn around').[22] The action of turning is expressed by a verb often used

19. J.L. Epp (*The Theological Tendency of Codex Bezae Cantabrigiensis in Acts* [Cambridge: Cambridge University Press, 1966], pp. 42–44) concludes that the Bezan text reveals 'calculated anti-Judaic sentiment'. The contention here is that, on the contrary, Peter in the Bezan text shows a clearer awareness of the situation of the Jews according to a Jewish perspective. His appreciation of the awfulness of their wrongdoing is expressed not from an accusatory standpoint but one of compassion.

20. Present-day readers may well be concerned at this point in Peter's speech with issues of freewill and predestination: if God had previously announced the suffering of the Messiah and used the rejection by his people to fulfill the prophecies, to what extent can the Jews be held responsible for their actions? But in Jewish thought such matters do not present themselves as a problem. The central point Peter is making is that nothing happens outside the plan of God and therefore there is a solution for the awfulness of their actions.

21. In the Bezan text of Luke's Gospel, the apostles do not fully understand the necessity for the Messiah to suffer until his final meeting with them in Jerusalem (24.44–47). See J. Read-Heimerdinger and J. Rius-Camps, 'Emmaous or Oulammaous? Luke's Use of the Jewish Scriptures in the Text of Luke 24 in Codex Bezae' (*RCatT* 27 [2002], pp. 23–42).

22. Of the 34 occurrences of μετανοέω in the New Testament, 14 are in Luke (Lk.

in the Greek Scriptures of re-establishing a broken contact. The relationship may be one between the Jews and God (see Lk. 1.16–17; Mk 4.12 [// Matt. 13.15] and Acts 28.27, all citing Isa. 6.10), or Jesus (specifically of Peter, Lk. 22.32; Acts 9.35; 11.21), or a neighbour (Lk. 17.4). It is also used by extension of Gentiles turning to God (Acts 14.15; 15.19; 26.18). Here in Acts 3, it is a matter of the Jews turning back to God rather than to Jesus who, according to Peter at this stage in his understanding, is still retained in heaven (3.21).

No mention is made of baptism, although it is likely that those who accepted Peter's exhortation were in fact baptized. The omission of any mention of this outward manifestation of a change of heart may be due to the fact that the speech was interrupted (4.1).

The effect of repentance and returning to God is the 'wiping away of sins', an action referred to in the Jewish Scriptures as the removal from a written record. The verb is used specifically of the erasure by God of sins in Isa. 43.25.[23]

3.20–21 Peter goes on to bring in ideas from Jewish eschatological expectation and it is critical at this point not to confuse Peter's thought with that of the narrator. Peter is not speaking here under the inspiration of the Holy Spirit, as he will do subsequently, and his speech reveals clear traces of Jewish traditional thinking that are presented elsewhere in Luke's work as superceded through the events of Jesus' life, death and resurrection. It is important to recognize that Luke has left these elements in Peter's speech as evidence of his deficient understanding in the early days of the Church. Seeing his explanations in this light will account for some of the contradictions between various speeches in Acts and also with the thought expressed by Luke as the narrator in Acts or in his Gospel (see *General Introduction*, §IX).

x 9; Acts x 5). If the references to the noun (μετάνοια) are also included (x 22 in the NT, of which 11 in Luke: Lk. x 5; Acts x 6 [+ 1 D05]), the frequency of the word in Luke is striking. As for ἐπιστρέφω, of the 36 occurrences in the New Testament, half are in Luke (Lk. x 7; Acts x 11 [+ 1 D05]); ἐπιστροφή is only found in Acts 15.3. The two verbs are found together three times in Luke (Lk. 17.4; Acts 3.19; 26.20).

23. The equivalent term 'forgiveness for sins' (ἄφεσις ἁμαρτιῶν) is found associated with 'repentance' (μετάνοια) in the preaching of John the Baptist (Lk. 3.3), in the command of Jesus to his apostles (24.47), the apostolic preaching to Israel (Acts 2.38; 5.31) and Peter's invitation to Simon Magus (8.22). ἐπιστρέφω and ἄφ. ἁμ. is used in the command given to Saul on the Damascus road as he is sent to the Gentiles (26.18).

Peter has already alluded to Jesus as Messiah in his Pentecost speech (2.36) where he distinguished between the action of the Jews in crucifying Jesus and that of God in making him Lord and Messiah (see *Commentary*, 2.36). In this speech, Peter has moved on to recognize that the suffering and rejection of the Messiah was foreordained and that the coming of Jesus is the fulfilment of this Messianic failure. He continues, nevertheless, to hold on to the idea that there is a glorious arrival of the Messiah still to take place and that the privileged status of Israel as God's chosen people is still intact.

The times of refreshing with which he begins the description of the future form part of the overall picture in the Jewish Scriptures of the expected final and glorious restoration of Israel (though they may not have been specifically identified there as a characteristic of the end times).[24] Since Peter cannot accept that the ignominious rejection of Jesus already represents the anticipated coming of the Messiah and since he sees that Israel has in no way been restored, he interprets events to construct another coming in the future which will be more in line with the ancient promises. In other terms, the promises that could not be fulfilled in the first coming are to be realised in the second coming.

The disappointment that Israel had not been restored by Jesus was already noted in the apostles' questioning of Jesus in 1.6. When he had not responded to their concerns, it was the apostles, led by Peter, who had taken their own steps to prepare for restoration by ensuring that there were twelve apostles in place to represent the twelve tribes (see *Commentary* on Acts 1).

Peter presents the arrival of the times of refreshing as dependent on the repentance of Israel.[25] Despite their rejection, denial and killing of him, the Messiah is still viewed by Peter as appointed as Christ for the Jews and reserved for them. In the meantime, he is portrayed as retained in heaven until God sends him once Israel is restored (cf. Ps. 110.1).[26] Only here in all of Luke's writings is the Messiah presented as to be 'sent'

24. D.L. Bock, *Proclamation from Prophecy and Pattern: Lucan Old Testament Christology* (JSNTSup, 12; Sheffield: JSOT Press, 1987, p. 190), but cf. possible scriptural evidence for the phrase 'the times of refreshing' in R. Bauckham, 'The Restoration of Israel in Luke-Acts', in J.M. Scott (ed.), *Restoration: Old Testament, Jewish, and Christian Perspectives* (Leiden: E.J. Brill, 2001), pp. 435–87 (478–79).

25. ὅπως ἄν, cf. Lk. 2.35; Acts 15.17 (introducing a quotation), is a literary archaism expressing purpose; see B-D-R, §369,5.

26. It is not 'all things' that are to be restored but 'all things of which the prophets spoke', that is, Israel to its status of glory and blessing.

again in the way Peter proclaims, accompanied by 'times of refreshing' and 'restoration'. In fact, both Moses and Elijah (two of the prophets whom Peter will refer to, 3.22–24) told the apostles that they should not expect the return of Jesus to be spectacular in this kind of way: it would be as discreet as his manner of departing (1.11, see *Commentary*).

In Peter's anticipation of future restoration there are echoes of Zachariah's joyful confidence that the prophecies of Israel's messianic salvation were about to be realised, and would be announced through his son, John (the Baptist) (Lk. 1.67–79). In particular, the use of the introductory phrase 'as he spoke by the mouth of his holy prophets from of old' in Lk. 1.70 is taken up at the end of Acts 3.21, though less exactly by the Bezan text (see *Critical Apparatus*). Zachariah, for his part, spoke under the inspiration of the Holy Spirit and recognized that the coming of Jesus would be the fulfilment of the scriptural prophecies. Peter, in contrast, sees in Jesus a failure to bring about the promised restoration to Israel and therefore continues to see it as reserved for the future as a spectacular and glorious event.

The parallel, observed in the previous chapter (see *Commentary*, 2.40), between the ministry of John the Baptist who prepared the people to receive the Messiah, and that of Peter and the entire apostolic community by association, is continued in this speech as Peter prepares the people for the return of the Messiah. What he has failed to grasp is the reinterpretation Jesus gave of the scriptural promise to Israel, in identifying the Father's promise as the gift of the Holy Spirit (Lk. 24.49; Acts 1.4–5). Peter and the other disciples have already received that promise as Peter himself has announced (2.33, 38–39).

Luke pursues in the book of Acts the portrayal of the apostles he first created in the Gospel, showing them to be severely handicapped in their understanding of Jesus' message by their nationalistic view of Israel and their religious traditions. For the moment, the Holy Spirit has not yet changed their way of thinking in this respect. But Jesus will continue to act through circumstances and more direct intervention until a more accurate understanding of his teaching is finally achieved. Luke's aim in portraying the early difficulties faced by the apostles is a pedagogical one in that he will show how progress was made and the obstacles overcome and thereby encourage his audience to persevere in their pursuit of the gospel message.

3.22–24 The references that Peter makes to the prophets do not directly provide evidence for the restoration of all things (3.21) but rather back up the exhortation to repent (3.19) and acknowledge Jesus as the Messiah, incorporating at the same time justification for the idea that the Jews have a privileged place in God's plan (3.20). Specifically, Peter seeks to prove that

1. Jesus is the prophet like Moses foreseen by himself
2. His coming was foreseen by all the prophets
3. God's covenant with Abraham and the patriarchs continues

He makes a series of scriptural allusions that are cited in a form that departs to some extent from the LXX.[27] The first is to Deut. 18.15 (18) where Moses repeats to Israel God's promise to raise up a prophet like him when they come into the holy land, whom they are to obey. In Codex Bezae, Peter specifies that Moses spoke 'to our fathers', so underlining his identification with the people of Israel (the Bezan text has three references to 'our fathers' in Peter's speech, cf. 3.13, 25). Another difference in the Bezan text compared with the LXX makes the pronoun 'me' depend on the verb 'listen to' ('listen to him as to me', D05) rather than on the comparison of the new prophet with Moses ('a prophet like me', B03). The effect is to place greater emphasis on the command to listen to the new prophet. As is often the case, the AT follows the Greek of the LXX text more closely.

The verb 'raise up' takes on a double meaning in Peter's speech in view of its use in Luke's writings not only in a literal sense but also as a reference to the resurrection. Peter makes use of the two meanings here. In the former sense, Jesus has already spoken to Israel as the new Moses raised up by God. But the people did not listen to him and so Peter plays on the second meaning of resurrection, giving them another chance to listen to him 'in everything he says to you'. These last words are in fact not read in the Deuteronomy text but may well have been present in some other text used in Palestine. Whatever their origin, they allow Peter to extend the possibility for the people to pay attention to Jesus, now as the Messiah in heaven.

Not, however, that they will hear him directly but through the apostles who are his witnesses (cf. 3.15) and who see themselves are representatives of the nation of Israel as it is about to be restored. It is the message

27. Wilcox (*Semitisms*, pp. 32–33) concludes that Luke may have used a Greek text that differed from the LXX. His judgment is supported by that of J. de Waard, *A Comparative Study of the Old Testament Text in the Dead Sea Scrolls and in the New Testament* (Studies on the Texts of the Desert of Judah, 4; Leiden: E.J. Brill, 1966), pp. 21–24.

of Jesus, which they transmit, that must therefore be heeded. The warning of their removal from the people if they fail to do so echoes Deut. 18.19 but also appears to draw on Lev. 23.29 where, using the same verb ἐξολεθρεύω, 'cut out', reference is made to those who do not repent on the day of atonement being 'cut out' of Israel. This is a threat of the utmost seriousness, since to be excluded from the people of Israel was the ultimate punishment.[28] By issuing the warning, Peter takes the bold step of redefining the people of Israel as those who accept Jesus as the Messiah.

The AT anticipates two prophetic expressions of God's words (μὲν ... δέ): Moses who communicated the promise of a future prophet and then the prophets, 'all those who spoke', later confirming that announcement. In Codex Bezae, there is a contrast implied between Moses and all the prophets on the one hand, and Peter's audience as 'sons of the prophets', on the other. The way the prophets who came after Samuel are presented in the AT is odd: literally, 'all the prophets from Samuel and from those who followed, all those who spoke'. In the Bezan text, a different point is made: 'all the prophets from Samuel on' repeated the same message that God had spoken through Moses (cf. v. 21), and from among the events predicted by him (that a prophet like him would be raised up whom everyone should listen to lest they be destroyed) they too have announced 'these days'. In other words, the events foreseen by Moses were the essence of the later prophets' message, too, 'these days' referring to the time of the coming of the 'prophet like Moses'.[29]

3.25–26 The Israelite audience are not only the beneficiaries of the prophecies but are the descendants of the prophets and of the covenant made with Abraham, as distinct from the Gentiles. The AT carefully restricts the definition of 'the sons of the prophets' to Peter's Jewish audience. There is little room at this point in Peter's thinking for the inclusion of the Gentiles. Although the notion is anticipated in v. 26, in the affirmation that God's servant has been raised up for the Jews 'first', it will still be

28.On the exclusion of a Jew from Israel, see L.H. Schiffman, *Who was a Jew?* (Huboken, N.J.: KTAV, 1985).

29. It would be tempting to interpret the phrase 'these days' as meaning the present time, but analysis of the position of the demonstrative adjective in time expressions indicates that the adjective (ταύτας) would be placed before the noun (τὰς ἡμέρας) it qualifies when reference to the present is intended (Read-Heimerdinger, *The Bezan Text*, pp, 101–107). In this instance, the demonstrative is placed after the noun, making it a simple reference to 'these days already mentioned'.

some time before Peter is ready to understand that the prophecies apply to Jews and Gentiles equally.

[C] 4.1–4 *The Imprisonment of Peter and John*

Overview

This is a brief sequence consisting only of four verses, but its central position within the third section of Acts focuses attention on the first manifestation in the narrative of the conflict between the Jewish authorities and the apostles of Jesus, a conflict that will again move on the story at various points in the future.

These opening verses, and continuing up to 4.7, have a remarkably close parallel in the scene in Luke's Gospel when the religious authorities suddenly arrive to question Jesus (Lk. 20.1–20):

1. The construction Ἐγένετο δέ + finite verb: Lk. 20.1 D05 // Acts 4.5 D05
2. Both Jesus and the apostles are interrupted as they teach: διδάσκοντες αὐτοῦ τὸν λαόν, Lk. 20.1 // λαλούντων αὐτῶν πρὸς τὸν λαόν, Acts 4.1
3. They are in the Temple: ἐν τῷ ἱερῷ, Lk. 20.1 // Solomon's Porch, Acts 3.12
4. The authorities suddenly turn up: ἐπέστησαν, Lk. 20.1 // ἐπέστησαν, Acts 4.1
5. The same groups of authorities are listed: οἱ ἀρχιερεῖς καὶ οἱ γραμματεῖς σὺν τοῖς πρεσβυτέροις, Lk. 20.1 // οἱ πρεσβύτεροι καὶ γραμματεῖς ... καὶ Ἄννας ὁ ἀρχιερεύς ... καὶ ὅσοι ἦσαν ἐκ γένους ἀρχιερατικοῦ, Acts 4.5–6 D05
6. Similar questions are asked: ἐν ποίᾳ ἐξουσίᾳ ταῦτα ποιεῖς ἢ (καὶ D05) τίς ἐστιν ὁ δούς σοι τὴν ἐξουσίαν ταύτην; Lk. 20.2 // ἐν ποίᾳ δυνάμει ἢ ἐν ποίῳ ὀνόματι ἐποιήσατε τοῦτο ὑμεῖς; Acts 4.7 D05
7. Reference is made to Ps. 118 (117 LXX).22: Jesus, Lk. 20.17 // Peter, Acts 4.11

Structure and Themes

These few verses set the scene, in a remarkably concise way, for the trial by the Sanhedrin that is to follow. For the first time in Acts, Luke brings on stage the priests (high priests, B03) and the Sadducees who are presented from the outset as hostile to the Jesus-believers. There are three elements, with the imprisonment of the apostles at the centre and the reaction of the religious leaders at the beginning standing in contrast to the willingness of the people to believe the apostolic message at the end:

[a] 4.1–2 The arrival of the Jewish authorities
[b] 4.3 The arrest of Peter and John
[a′] 4.4 The growing number of Jesus-believers

Translation

	Codex Bezae D05	*Codex Vaticanus B03*
[a]	**4.1** As they were speaking these words to the people, the priests and the Sadducees suddenly appeared, **2** extremely upset because they were teaching the people and announcing Jesus in the resurrection of the dead,	**4.1** As they were speaking to the people, the high priests and the captain of the guard and the Sadducees came upon them, **2** greatly annoyed because they were teaching the people and proclaiming in Jesus the resurrection, from the dead,
[b]	**3** and having laid hands on them, they went so far as to put them into custody until the next day, for it was evening now.	**3** and they laid hands on them and put them into custody until the next day, for it was evening now.
[a′]	**4** Many of those who heard the speech believed and, what is more, the number of men became symbolically 5,000.	**4** Many of those who heard the speech believed and the number of men became about 5,000.

Critical Apparatus

4.1 (λαὸν) τὰ ῥήματα ταῦτα D d (E) 876. 913. 1518. 1611. 2138 h (gig p q) w sy$^{(p).hmg}$; (Lcf) Theoph Cass || *om.* B ℵ *rell.*

By means of the anaphoric reference, the D05 text focuses on the teaching of the apostles, which was interrupted by the religious authorities. In B03, it is the speakers who were interrupted.

(ἐπέστησαν) αὐτοῖς B ℵ *rell* || *om.* D d gig h p vg; Lcf.

The pronoun in B03 directs attention on the characters whereas, as noted above, the interest in D05 is on the teaching.

οἱ ἀρχιερεῖς B C 467 (gig) arm^{mss} || οἱ ἱερεῖς D d ℵ A E H^{3} P Ψ 049. 056. 0165. 33. 36. 69. 81. 88. 181. 307. 453. 610. 614. 945. 1175. 1243. 1409. 1678. 1739. 1891. 2344. 2412. 2492. 2495 𝔐 lat sy co; Tert Chr.

The presence of the high priests makes the persecution all the more serious (Metzger, *Commentary*, p. 275). Their absence at this stage in D05 allows for a harsher degree of persecution to be introduced at 5.21, when persecution arises again.

καὶ ὁ στρατηγὸς τοῦ ἱεροῦ B ℵ *rell* || *om.* D d gig.

The presence of the guard of the Temple in B03 again increases the seriousness of the opposition to the apostles (cf. previous variant).

4.2 διαπονούμενοι B ℵ *rell* || και(τ D[G])απον – D*, *dolore percussi* d.

διαπονέομαι (middle voice), meaning to be 'greatly annoyed' (B-A-G), is used to describe the feelings of the authorities as they arrive on the scene. The D05 verb has been corrected from ΚΑΙΑΠΟΝΟΥΜΕΝΟΙ to ΚΑΤΑΠΟΝ –, the middle-passive voice of καταπονέω which has the stronger sense of 'oppressed, tormented' (B-A-G).

καταγγέλλειν B ℵ *rell* || ἀναγγ – D, *adnuntiarent* d Ψ.

The difference in the verbs is accounted for by their different objects (see below). d05 translates both by *adnuntiare* (καταγγέλλω: Acts 3.24; 13.5, 38; 15.36; 17.3, 13, 23; ἀναγγέλλω: Acts 20.20, 27) (*pace* Boismard and Lamouille, II, p. 25).

ἐν τῷ 'Ιησοῦ τὴν ἀνάστασιν B ℵ *rell* || τὸν 'Ιησοῦν ἐν τῇ ἀναστάσει D d (mae).

See below.

τὴν ἐκ νεκρῶν B P[74] ℵ A C E 33. 81. 88. 104. 323. 927. 1175. 1646. 1739 || τῶν νεκ. D d H[3] P Ψ 049. 056. 614. 945. 1611. 2412. 2495 𝔐 e gig h p sa mae; Ir[gr] Lcf.

The three last variants in this verse function as one unit to express a subtle difference between the two texts. According to B03, the apostles proclaimed the resurrection, specifically that from the dead, by taking Jesus as a particular example in order to defend it; D05, in contrast, has the apostles announcing Jesus within the framework of the resurrection of the dead, where the lack of explanatory insistence on the nature of the resurrection could be a cue to the focus on the person of Jesus instead.

4.3 καὶ ἐπέβαλον ... καὶ ἔθεντο B ℵ *rell*, *et inmiserunt ... et posuerunt* d || κ. ἐπιβαλόντες ... καὶ (– D[s.m.]) ἔθεντο D* (h).

B03 marks out three main actions on the part of the protagonists, each expressed by a finite verb (ἐπέστησαν ... ἐπέβαλον ... ἔθεντο) and linked with καί. D05 has only two main verbs instead of the three, expressing the second by means of a participle (ἐπιβαλόντες) that is connected to the following main verb by means of an adverbial καί; this is a device used typically in D05 to highlight an action (Read-Heimerdinger, *The Bezan Text*, pp. 208–10).

(εἰς τὴν) αὔριον B ℵ *rell* || ἐπαύριον D d 0165 *pc* h.

The two adverbs are equivalent.

4.4 καὶ ἐγενήθη ἀριθμὸς τῶν ἀνδρῶν B ℵ 0165*, *et factus est numerus virorum* d | κ. ἐγ. ὁ ἀρ. τ. ἀνδ. P[74] A E H[3] P Ψ 049. 33. 69. 81. 614. 1175. 1611. 1739. 2412. 2495 𝔐 || κ. ἀρ. τε (– D[s.m.]) ἐγ. ἀνδ. D* (h) sa mae bo[mss].

Since it makes little sense to take the absence of the article before ἀριθμός in B03 as an indication of indefiniteness ('a number') when the genitive noun following is articular (τῶν ἀνδρῶν), it should be interpreted as a device to underline the word. For a discussion of the reason for its importance, see *Commentary*. The position of ἀριθμός between καί and τε in D05, as well as the use of adverbial καί in conjunction with the connective τε, underlines the word even more forcibly. The article with ἀνδρῶν in B03 appears to apply the comment literally to men only. With the inarticulate noun, ἀνδρῶν can have a more theological sense of 'adult believers'.

ὡς (χιλιάδες) B D 0165*. 876. 1108. 1611. 2138. 2344 || ὡσεί E H³ P Ψ 049. 056. 33. 69. 88. 614. 1739. 2412. 2495 𝔐, *ad* d h | *om.* P⁷⁴ ℵ A 0165ᶜ. 81. 1175. 2147 *pc* vg.

The distinction made by D05 between ὡς and ὡσεί has been noted with reference to 1.15 and 2.41 (see *Critical Apparatus* and *Commentary, ad loc.*). Both can have metaphorical force in Luke's writings but with the use of ὡς the comparison is being made specifically with an earlier, paradigmatic event. The absence of either word in ℵ01 suggests that the number was regarded as literal rather than metaphorical, and as absolute rather than approximate.

Commentary

[a] 4.1–2 *The Arrival of the Jewish Authorities*

4.1–2 The speech addressed to the people of Israel by Peter (and indirectly by John, too: note the plural 'they were speaking') is interrupted by the sudden arrival of the Temple authorities in Solomon's Porch. The AT has three groups, including the chief (high) priests according to Codex Vaticanus, as well as the Captain of the Temple. Although there was only one high priest, previous holders of the office together with other members of his family appear to have been identified with him (cf. 4.6). The Captain of the Temple was a priest, next in rank to the high priest, who had oversight of the Temple Guard, in charge of law enforcement within the Temple and with powers of arrest.[30] The hostility of the attack is less intense at this point in the Bezan text where it is a question only of the priests and the Sadducees who appear on the scene,[31] though their disquiet is described in stronger terms: they were 'tormented'. Many of the priests (and all the high priests at this time) were associated with the party of the

30 E. Schürer, *The History of the Jewish People in the Age of Jesus Christ* (3 vols.; rev. and ed. G. Vermes, F. Millar and M. Black; Edinburgh: T&T Clark, 1973), II, pp. 275–79.

31. The verb ἐφίστημι is practically exclusive to Luke (Lk. x 7; Acts x 11) and has connotations of a sudden, and sometimes violent, appearance.

Sadducees, wealthy aristocrats whose influence in the Temple was particularly powerful.

The two reasons given for the reaction to the apostles correspond to the two groups mentioned: they were teaching the people, taking on one of the priests' duties, and they mentioned the resurrection of, or from, the dead, a doctrine denied by the Sadducees. The difference in the way reference is made to the resurrection in the two texts is one of focus – either on the resurrection as such, using Jesus as a particular example (Vaticanus), or on Jesus, taking for granted the truth of the resurrection as a general fact (Bezae). Indeed, Peter's speech is interrupted precisely at the point when he begins to speak about the resurrection of Jesus (cf. 3.26).

[b] 4.3 *The Arrest of Peter and John*

4.3 The apostles are detained by the Jewish authorities so that they can be examined the next day. The presence of the Captain of the Guard at some point would be necessary in order for the arrest to be made. The note that it was evening fits with the time given in 3.1 D05 for the healing of the lame man by Peter and John that has led to their arrest. The late hour suggests a parallel with the arrest of Jesus at Lk. 22.53 when Jesus himself referred to the darkness of the hour; the holding of the apostles until the meeting of the Sanhedrin the next day further echoes the trial of Jesus (cf. Lk. 22.66; Acts 22.30).

[a′] 4.4 *The Growing Number of Jesus-Believers*

4.4 The negative response of the Temple authorities stands in contrast to the positive response of the people, whose acceptance of the word is emphasized by being sandwiched in the middle of the description of the attack of the leaders. The large number of believers now reaches the figure of 5,000, representing considerable growth from the last figure of 3,000 cited just before the healing of the lame man (2.41, cf. 2.47). The number can be understood literally in the AT, but the qualifying word ὡς used by Codex Bezae regularly signifies an allusion to a previous use of a figure (or one of its multiples) and ultimately to its original occurrence in some scriptural story that is being taken as a paradigm (cf. 1.15). Within Luke's writings, there is an immediate echo of the feeding of the 5,000 where Codex Bezae records that the crowd was ὡς πεντακισχίλιοι (Lk. 9.14), with the same word introducing the figure of 5,000 (the other MSS read ὡσεί which, although sometimes used by Luke to indicate a metaphor, could mean 'approximately' here). There, the crowd was welcomed by Jesus and he taught them and healed them; the time of day was also evening. The Twelve had wanted to send them away on that occasion whereas now the apostles are responsible for attracting the people to belief in Jesus. The number five recurs throughout the whole of that episode (9.13, 16, five loaves; 9.14, groups of 50, 5,000 men), and is also associated with the day of Pentecost (50 days after Passover) when the Holy Spirit was given for the first time. It therefore prepares for the second outpouring of the Holy Spirit on the present assembly (4.31).

In both Acts 4 and Luke 9, the people numbered at 5,000 are said specifically to be ἄνδρες, 'men', that is mature adults.[32] In the Jewish Scriptures, it is the number 50 that is typically associated with adult prophetic communities,[33] with the first mention of a multiple of five occurring in the course of Yahweh's instructions to Moses concerning the Tabernacle: 500 shekels was to be the base measure of the ingredients for the anointing oil in the Tabernacle, to be used to make both objects and people holy for the service of Yahweh (Exod. 30.22–33). More would need to be known about the use made in Jewish tradition of the measures in these instructions in order to ascertain what exactly might be evoked by an allusion to them by Luke, but the notion of holiness in the service of the Lord could potentially add substance to the brief summary description of the people who believed in Jesus as the Messiah.

Emphasis is given to the word itself ἀριθμός, 'number', in both texts, though more forcefully in Codex Bezae. The reason for it is not immediately clear, though once more, it may arise from the existence of a motif in Jewish exegesis to which allusion is being made. One possibility lies in the consideration that the adjective 'numerous' was a technical term to designate 'the faithful to the Torah'.[34] The word 'number' will again be used at 5.36.

[B′] 4.5–22 *The Meeting of the Sanhedrin*

Overview

It is the formality of the opening sentence, introducing the convocation of the council meeting, ἐγένετο δὲ ἐπὶ τὴν αὔριον [ἡμέραν D05]

32. The wording of Lk. 9.14 D05 confers particular emphasis on the 'men': ἦσαν γὰρ ἄνδρες ὡς πεντακισχίλιοι; cf. B03: ἦσαν γὰρ ὡσεὶ ἄνδρες πεντακισχίλιοι.

33. 3 Kgdms 18.4, 13 LXX; 4 Kgdms 2.7 LXX: πεντήκοντα ἄνδρες υἱοὶ τῶν προφητῶν.

34. See B. Barc, *Les arpenteurs du temps: Essai sur l'histoire religieuse de la Judée à la période héllenistique* (Lausanne: Éditions du Zèbre, 2000), p. 174.

συνήχθησαν, that marks this fourth sequence out as separate from the previous one in which the trial scene was prepared. There are a number of elements in Peter's speech made here to the Sanhedrin under the inspiration of the Holy Spirit, and his speech to the people in the second sequence, [B] when he was speaking his own thoughts.

The Sanhedrin is now encountered for the first time in the narrative of Acts, although its power and opposition to Jesus have already been made evident in Luke's first volume (Lk. 22.66–23.5) in events that took place only a matter of weeks earlier. Its composition is difficult to determine with precision, and it will be seen that there is some difference between Codex Bezae and the AT in this respect. This first meeting of the Sanhedrin will anticipate a second one that occurs in the fourth section of Acts, 5.21b–40.

Structure and Themes

The trial consists of a series of steps and is prolonged by the fact that the council members find themselves at a loss when they hear Peter's account and are confronted with the evidence of the man who has been healed. Their inability to deal with the situation is the fulcrum of the sequence. Leading up to it, is the interrogation, with Peter's response, inspired by the Holy Spirit, repeating the same teaching they have already heard from Jesus (Lk. 20.17–18). They arrive at a solution which, however, Peter refuses to accept. Notwithstanding his refusal, the Sanhedrin are forced to release the apostles in view of the positive feeling towards them on the part of the people. The sequence concludes with a narrative aside that gives a clue as to the true meaning of the sign of the lame man's healing.

[a]	4.5–6	The authorities gather together
[b]	4.7	The interrogation of the apostles
[c]	4.8–12	Peter's testimony before the Sanhedrin
[d]	4.13a	The Sanhedrin's reaction
[e]	4.13b	Their recognition of Jesus' influence
[f]	4.14	Their perplexity
[e′]	4.15–17	A solution is sought
[d′]	4.18	The Sanhedrin's decision
[c′]	4.19–20	Peter's response
[b′]	4.21	The release of the apostles
[a′]	4.22	The meaning of the sign

A number of thematic parallels, positive and negative, may be noted between the corresponding elements on either side of the centre, [f]. Of particular interest, is the contrast between [a] the opening list of the participants in the Sanhedrin meeting, including a series of high priests representing the highest religious authority, and [a′] the aside (from the narrator in Codex Bezae) which, as the lame man is mentioned for the last time, finally informs the audience about the significance of his healing, a significance that had gone unnoticed by the great religious powers despite their responsibility for teaching the people of Israel.

Translation

	Codex Bezae D05	*Codex Vaticanus B03*
[a]	**4.5** It was on the next day that the rulers and the elders and scribes gathered in Jerusalem, **6** and there was Annas the high priest and Caiphas and Jonathan and Alexander and all who were of the high-priestly family,	**4.5** It was on the next day that their rulers and elders and scribes gathered in Jerusalem, **6** there was Annas the high priest and Caiaphas and John and Alexander and all who were of the high-priestly family,
[b]	**7** and they placed them in the centre and started to enquire, 'By what kind of power or name did *you* do *this*?'	**7** and they placed them in the centre and started to enquire, 'By what kind of power or name did *you* do *this*?'
[c]	**8** Then Peter, filled with the Holy Spirit, said to them, 'Rulers of the people and elders of Israel, **9** if *we* are being examined by *you* today about a good deed done to a sick man, to ascertain by what this man has been restored, **10** let it be known to you and to all the people of Israel that by the name of Jesus Christ the Nazorene, whom you crucified and whom God raised from the dead, by this name this man is standing before you whole **11** (it is he the stone that was treated with contempt by you, the builders, but that has become the cornerstone), **12** and it is by none other for there is no other kind of name under heaven that has been given to men by which we must be saved.'	**8.** Then Peter, filled with the Holy Spirit, said to them, 'Rulers of the people and elders, **9** since we are being examined today about a good deed done to a sick man, to ascertain by what this man has been restored, **10** let it be known to you and to all the people of Israel that by the name of Jesus Christ the Nazorene, whom you crucified and whom God raised from the dead, by this name this man is standing before you whole. **11** (It is he the stone that was treated with contempt by you, the builders, but that has become the cornerstone.) **12** And salvation is in no-one else, since neither is there any other name under heaven given among men by which you must be saved.'
[d]	**13a** Seeing the boldness of Peter, and John, too, and when they understood that they were without training in the law, they were astonished.	**13a** Seeing the boldness of Peter and John, and when they understood that they were unlettered and laymen, they were astonished.
[e]	**13b** They recognized that they had been with Jesus.	**13b** They recognized that they had been with Jesus;

[f]	**14** And seeing the man who was healed standing there with them, they could do or say nothing to oppose them.	**14** moreover, seeing the man who was healed standing there with them, they had nothing to say in opposition.
[e′]	**15** They ordered them to be led out of the council and conferred amongst themselves, **16** saying, 'What shall we do with these men? For that an intelligible sign has taken place through them is perfectly obvious to everyone living in Jerusalem, and we cannot deny it **17** for fear that something greater spread among the people. Accordingly, we will warn the men to speak no more about this name to any one among men whatsoever.'	**15** They ordered them out of the council and conferred amongst themselves, **16** saying, 'What can we do with these men? For that an intelligible sign has taken place through them is obvious to everyone living in Jerusalem, and we cannot deny it; **17** but, lest the news spread further among the people, let us warn them to speak no more about this name to any one among men whatsoever.'
[d′]	**18** Since they were in agreement over this decision, they called them and charged them not to mention or to teach about the name of Jesus under any circumstance.	**18** And they called them and charged them not to mention or to teach about the name of Jesus under any circumstance.
[c′]	**19** But Peter and John answered, and said to them, 'Whether it is right in the sight of God to obey you rather than God, you judge. **20** For can we not speak of the things that we have seen and heard?'	**19** Peter and John answered and said to them, 'Whether it is right in the sight of God to obey you rather than God, you judge. **20** For we cannot but speak of the things that we have seen and heard.'
[b′]	**21** When they had further threatened them, finding no cause for which to have them punished, they let them go, on account of the people because everyone was praising God for what had taken place	**21** When they had further threatened them, finding nothing for which to have them punished, they let them go, on account of the people because everyone was praising God for what had taken place
[a′]	**22** (for the man to whom the sign of healing had happened was more than forty years old).	**22** (for the man to whom this sign of healing had happened was more than forty years old).

Critical Apparatus

4.5 (Ἐγένετο δὲ) ἐπὶ τὴν αὔριον συναχθῆναι αὐτῶν τοὺς ἄρχοντας καὶ τοὺς πρεσβυτέρους καὶ τοὺς γραμματεῖς B P[74] ℵ *rell* ‖ ἐπὶ τ. αὔρ. ἡμέραν (– D[s.m.]) συνήχθησαν οἱ ἄρχοντες κ. οἱ πρεσβύτεροι κ. γραμμ. D* d h sy[p] aeth.

The accusative-infinitive construction following ἐγένετο, as it does in B03, is found frequently in Luke's work. However, the alternative ἐγένετο + finite verb is by no means uncommon in the Gospel (with the verb in the aorist: Lk. 1.8, 23, 41, 59; 2.1, 6 (*vl* D05), 15 D05, 46; 5.1 D05; 7.11 (*vl* D05); 8.22 (*vl* D05), 40 S01 (*vl* B03/D05); 9.18 (*vl* D05), 33, 51; 11.1, 27; 17.14; 19.15 (*vl* D05), 29; 20.1; 24.4, 30, 51; with the verb in the imperfect: Lk. 2.15 (*vl* D05); 3,21–23 (*vl* D05); 5.1 (*vl* D05), 17 (*vl* D05); 8.1; 9.18 [aorist B03]; 14.1; 17.11; 18.35; 24.15). See B-D-R, §442,4a and n. 11.

With the subjects in the accusative in B03, the relationship between them and the high priestly family in 4.6 (in the nom.) is unclear; v. 6 could be construed as a parenthesis detailing the prominent people among the rulers or elders of the council. With all the subjects in the nominative in D05, the various groups and individuals are more easily understood as different people.

The possessive pronoun in B03 closely associates the authorities with the believers, whereas D05 avoids making such a close connection at this point.

With the triple repetition of the article before each of the groups of leaders, B03 treats each as distinct. D05 groups the latter two, so creating a twofold distinction between the rulers and the religious authorities (see on 4.8 below and *Commentary*, 4.5–6 for further discussion of the distinction).

ἐν Ἰερουσαλήμ B D d P[74] A E Ψ 33. 81. 226[c]. 323. 440. 927. 1175. 1245. 1739. 1891 *pm* || εἰς Ἰερ. ℵ H[3] P 049. 056. 0165. 69. 88. 226*. 330. 614. 945. 1241. 1505. 1611. 1646. 1828. 1854. 2412. 2495 *pm*.

The choice of εἰς in place of ἐν suggests that some of the people who gathered in the city came from outside, although this may simply be a case of εἰς taking over the function of ἐν in the development of the Greek language (Read-Heimerdinger, *The Bezan Text*, p. 195).

4.6 Καϊάφας B ℵ A 1175 d[G] | –φαν E H[3] P Ψ 049. 056. 33. 69. 323. 614. 945. 1241. 1611. 1739. 2412. 2495 𝔐 || Καίφας D d* 0165 gig h p vg sa mae.

The form of the name in D05 is also read by this MS in the Gospels of Matthew, John and Luke. The alternative form corresponds to the Aramaic .

Ἰωάννης B ℵ A 0165. 1175 | –ην E H[3] P Ψ 049. 33. 69. 88. 614. 945. 1241. 1243. 1611. 1739. 2147. 2412. 2492. 2495 || Ἰωναθᾶς D, *Io(on* d[G]*)athas* d gig p* vg[ms*]; Hier.

Jonathan was the name of the son of Annas, according to Josephus (*Ant.* 18.4.3).

4.7 ἐν τῷ μέσῳ B ℵ A 81. 323. 330. 945. 2147 || ἐν μ. D E H[3] P Ψ 049. 056. 0165. 33. 69. 88. 614. 1245. 2412. 2495 𝔐.

The use of ἐν (τῷ) μέσῳ in an absolute sense (i.e. without a dependent gen.) occurs with the article in Matt. 14.6 and without in Jn 8.3, 9 (which properly belongs to Luke's Gospel, see Rius-Camps, 'Origen lucano de la perícopa de la mujer adúltera', pp. 149–76).

ἐποιήσατε τοῦτο ὑμεῖς B D *rell* || τοῦτο ἐποιήσατε ὑμεῖς ℵ E.

ℵ01 highlights the miracle (τοῦτο) performed by the apostles; the word order of B03 and D05 places the miracle in contrast with the apostles (ὑμεῖς) as agents, thereby the perceived incongruity.

4.8 (πρεσβύτεροι) τοῦ Ἰσραήλ D d E H^{3} P Ψ 049. 056. 33. 69. 323. 614. 945. 1739. 1891. 2344. 2412. 2495 𝔐 e gig h p$^{*(2)}$ (q w vg^{mss}) sy$^{(p).h}$ mae arm; Ir^{lat} Cyp Chr Amb Mss gr$^{sec.\ Beda}$ || *om.* B P^{74} ℵ A 0165. 1175. 1409* *pc* ar c pt vg sa bo; Cyr.

By qualifying the elders as 'of Israel' in D05, Peter distinguishes them from the ἄρχοντες, the 'rulers of the people' (cf. 4.5 above).

4.9 (ἀνακρινόμεθα) ἀφ' ὑμῶν D d E 88. 876. 915. 1108. 1611. 2138 it sy mae; Ir^{lat} Cyp Chr || *om.* B P^{74} ℵ A H^{3} P Ψ 049. 056. 0165. 33. 69. 614. 1175. 1245. 1270. 1739. 1891. 2344. 2412. 2495 𝔐 vg sa.

Although ἀπό eventually took over from ὑπό as the preposition to introduce the agent of a passive verb, and is found with this sense in the Alexandrian MSS, it is highly unusual to find it replacing ὑπό in D05 (Read-Heimerdinger, *The Bezan Text*, pp. 184–87). In fact, it is more likely that in this instance, rather than referring to the agent of ἀνακρινόμεθα, ἀφ' ὑμῶν means 'on your own, by yourselves' (cf. Lk. 21.30; Jn 15.4, for this meaning of the phrase). On this understanding, Peter is referring not to the present interrogation, as in B03, but to the fact that the authorities have already carried out deliberations before the present meeting. Bruce (*Text*, p. 120) comments that the verb ἀνακρίνω is used in Attic Greek of a preliminary enquiry and only in later Greek did it come to refer to legal interrogation more generally. Cf. Paul, Acts 24.21, who had proclaimed to his Jewish accusers that it was on account of the resurrection that he was being tried, ἐγὼ κρίνομαι σήμερον ἐφ' ὑμῶν, complaining that they had *not* worked out the charges against him beforehand.

4.11 ὑμῶν B ℵ *rell* d || ἡμῶν D 614. 2412.

It is possible that the pronouns have been confused through itacism in D05 unless it should be thought that Peter is including all Jews, not just the authorities he is addressing, in this adaptation of Ps. 118 (117 LXX).22 (see Wilcox, *Semitisms*, p. 173). Cf. the same variant in 4.12 below.

4.12 (οὐδενὶ) ἡ σωτηρία B ℵ *rell* || *om.* D d p*.

In D05, every instance of ἐν + dative in this episode has causal or instrumental force and the phrases in which it occurs echo each other: cf. 4.7b ἐν ποίᾳ δυνάμει ἢ ἐν ποίῳ ὀνόματι, 9 ἐν τίνι, 10 ἐν τῷ ὀνόματι ... ἐν τούτῳ, 12 ἐν ἄλλῳ οὐδενί ... (ὄνομα) ἐν ᾧ... The presence of ἡ σωτηρία in B03 disrupts the pattern.

οὐδὲ (γάρ) B ℵ A 0165. 33. 88. 226^{c}. 323. 440. 927. 945. 1175. 1739. 1837. 1891. 2147. 2495, *nequ[a]e* d^{G} | οὔτε E H^{3} P Ψ 049. 056. 69. 104. 226*. 330. 547. 614. 1243. 1245. 1611. 2412. 2492 || οὐ D h; Ir^{lat} Cyp Did Aug.

In accordance with the previous variant, B03 introduces a fresh affirmation whereas D05 develops the earlier one.

ὄνομά ἐστιν ἕτερον B H^{3} P 049. 056. 1. 226. 323. 330. 440. 547. 614. 618. 927. 1241. 1245. 2147. 2412. 2492 || ἐστὶν ἕτ. ὄν. D (*aliud est nomen* d) p; Ir^{lat} Aug | ἕτ. ὄν. ἐστ. ℵ gig | ὄν. ἕτ. ἐστιν A E Ψ 0165. 33. 69. 88. 104. 945. 1175. 1611. 1739. 1837. 1891. 2495.

The emphatic position of ὄνομα in B03 is justified because it is the subject of a new statement (see above).

τὸ δεδομένον ἐν ἀνθρώποις B ℵ *rell* || ὃ (τὸ D^{C}) δεδ. ἀνθρ. D* d lat; Ir^{lat} Cyp.

Again in keeping with the B03 readings in the earlier part of the sentence (see above), the article with the participle confers emphasis on the one name that has been given and that has also been known among men (Bruce, *Text*, p. 121). D05 reads the relative pronoun, referring not to the name of Jesus but to 'any other name' given 'to men' (*pace* Delebecque, *Les deux Actes*, p. 42).

ὑμᾶς B 547. 1270. 1704 *pc* || ἡμᾶς D d ℵ *rell.*

B03 has Peter direct his message of salvation exclusively to the authorities whereas D05 rather more realistically makes Peter's message apply to Jews generally, including John and himself, or possibly to a wider audience still. Cf. 4.11 above.

4.13 καὶ ἰδιῶται B P^{74} ℵ *rell* || *om.* D d.

The reference to Peter and John as 'laymen' (Zerwick and Grosvenor, *Analysis*; 'untrained', B-A-G; cf. Barrett, I, pp. 233–34) gives greater justification to the surprise felt by the authorities. The technical sense of the first adjective ἀγράμματοι is 'without training in the law' in contrast to the scribes, οἱ γραμματεῖς, in which case the second adjective does not add anything. If, however, the adjective were taken with its broader meaning of 'unlettered', then some further description may have been felt necessary.

(ἐπεγίνωσκόν) τε B ℵ A E H^{3} P 049. 056. 0165^{c}. 33. 69. 614. 945. 1175. 1241. 1611. 1739. 2412. 2495 𝔐 || δέ D d P^{74} Ψ 0165*. 1. 36 *pc* e.

Since τε generally introduces the final point in a series (Levinsohn, *Textual Connections*, pp. 121–36) the two successive occurrences of the particle in B03 (see 4.14 below) are unusual, and it looks as if one of them may have arisen through phonetic confusion with δέ (Read-Heimerdinger, *The Bezan Text*, pp. 210–11). It makes more sense of the narrative development to assume that the B03 reading in this verse should be δέ, as in D05, and in 4.14 τε. With δέ, a concise, isolated comment is made, accounting for the bewilderment of the authorities as the scene develops.

4.14 (τόν) τε (ἄνθρωπον) B P^{74} ℵ A E Ψ D^{C} 049. 33. 69. 88. 440. 945. 1175. 1245. 1611. 1646. 1739. 1837. 1891. 2495, *quoque* d | δέ H^{3} P 056. 1. 226. 330. 547. 614. 618. 927. 1243. 1828. 2147. 2412. 2492 || *om.* D*.

On the basis of the argument above, it is likely that τε was the intended particle in this verse of B03, making the confusion of the authorities an additional factor to their recognition of the apostles as disciples of Jesus. In D05, the absence of connective linking the new clause with the previous one typifies the use of asyndeton to create tension (Read-Heimerdinger, *The Bezan Text*, pp. 252–53), in this instance increasing the drama of the situation as the authorities find themselves not knowing what to do or say. If a second instance of asyndeton follows immediately in 4.15 D05 (see below), it further intensifies the overall disjointed nature of 4.13–15 which reflects the authorities' perplexity.

σὺν αὐτοῖς B P^{74} ℵ D^{B} *rell*, *cum ipsis* d || σὺν αὐτῶν D.

The use of the genitive following σύν, as after μετά, is exceptional (Robertson, *Grammar*, p. 628).

ποιῆσαι ἢ (ἀντειπεῖν) D h x || *om.* B ℵ *rell* d.

The powerlessness of the authorities is augmented in D05. Their intention of doing something against the apostles is apparent from their question in 4.16: Τί ποιήσωμεν (ποιήσομεν D05) ...;

4.15 (κελεύσαντες) δέ B ℵ *rell*, *autem* d || *om.* D (ΚΑΙΛΕΥΣΑΝΤΕΣ) 1518. 2147 sa^{mss}.

δέ introduces a new development in B03. The opening letters of the sentence in D05 could be interpreted either as κε– which has been written as και because of the phonetic resemblance, or as an instance of haplography whereby κε– has dropped out because of the phonetic similarity. In the first case, this produces a second example of asyndeton following on directly from the previous one (see above on 4.14); in the second, the connective καί presents the deliberations of the council on an equal footing with their bewilderment.

ἀπελθεῖν B ℵ *rell*, *[h]abire* d^{G} || ἀπαχθῆναι D h sy.

The verb ἀπέρχομαι used by B03 is common in Luke as in the other Gospel writers to signify simply 'go' to a place. In contrast, ἀπάγω of D05, 'go out' of a place, has connotations of violence and is used by each of the Synoptic writers with reference to the trial of Jesus: cf. Lk. 22.66; 23.26.

συνέβαλλον B ℵ A E H[3] P 049. 33. 69. 614. 945. 1175. 1245. 1739. 2147. 2412. 2492 𝔐, *conferebant* d e || –βαλον D Ψ 618. 1611. 2495 sy[h] sa arm.

The aorist is used in D05 in place of the imperfect of B03.

4.16 (Τί) ποιήσωμεν B ℵ d || ποιήσομεν D 242. 257. 323. 614. 876. 945. 1108. 1518. 1611. 1739. 2298. 2318. 2412. 2495. e g h p Vg Lcf Chr.

With the future indicative in D05, rather than the aorist subjunctive, the question is more direct and more urgent in keeping with the tone of the speech overall in D05 (cf. the same variant in 2.37; Read-Heimerdinger, *The Bezan Text*, pp. 227–28). Alternatively, ο in place of ω in D05 may be due to phonetic confusion (cf. φανερότερον below) but the use of the subjunctive by D05 in similar phrases at Lk. 3.10, 12, 14 rather tells against that explanation.

ὅτι ... γέγονεν ... φανερόν B ℵ *rell*, *quoniam ... factum est ... manifestum est* d || ὅτι ... γεγονέναι (–νεν D[s.m.]) ... φανερότερόν ἐστιν D*.

ὅτι introduces the noun clause as subject (the causal sense is excluded by the presence of γάρ, *pace* Zerwick and Grosvenor, *Analysis*) for which the infinitive, though unusual, is nevertheless correct (B-D-R, § 397.5; *pace* Delebecque, *Les deux Actes*, p. 42). The verb ἐστιν, elided in B03, is made explicit in D05 where the adjective is further strengthened by use of the comparative form (which correctly should be φανερώτερον) to convey intensity.

4.17 ἀλλ' (ἵνα) B ℵ *rell*, *sed* d || *om.* D.

There is considerable difference in the structure of this sentence, resulting in somewhat different meanings. B03 presents, at this point, the solution to the problem summarized by the authorities, beginning a new sentence with ἀλλά and the purpose clause (ἀλλ' ἵνα) depending on the main verb following, ἀπειλησώμεθα. In D05, the ἵνα clause depends on the previous main verb, οὐ δυνάμεθα ἀρνεῖσθαι, and the solution will follow in the next clause with οὖν (see 4.17 below).

πλεῖον B ℵ *rell* || πλέον τι D d h p.

The subject of the verb διανεμηθῇ is not expressed in B03 but is to be understood as 'the news' (Zerwick and Grosvenor, *Analysis*); πλεῖον qualifies the verb, 'any further' (B-A-G, πολύς, II.c). The indefinite τι in D05 supplies the subject which, combined with πλέον as an adjective, means 'something greater'. The neuter comparative adjective πλέον is found in Luke's writings at Lk. 3.13; Acts 15.28 (πλεῖον

D05), and as a *vl* for πλεῖον in D05 at Lk. 7.42; 9.13; 11.31. πλέον is only used elsewhere in the New Testament at Jn 21.15, without *vl.*

ἀπειλησώμεθα B P[74] ℵ A 323. 945. 1175. 1739. 1891 | ἀπειλῇ ἀπειλ. E H[3] P Ψ 049. 056. 33. 69. 614. 1245. 1611. 2412. 2495 𝔐 sy[h] || ἀπειλησόμεθα οὖν D d.

The solution to the problem is offered now in D05 (see 4.17 above), introduced by οὖν and with the future of the verb expressing a firm intention. B03 continues the sentence already started, with the subjunctive used to express a suggested course of action.

αὐτοῖς B d || ουτοις D.

The impossible reading of D05 is an error either for the B03 reading (cf. τουτοι 21.20 D05 for οὗτοι) or τούτοις with the same disrespectful tone it has at 4.16a.

4.18 συγκατατιθεμένων δὲ αὐτῶν τῇ γνώμῃ D d gig h (vg[ms]) sy[hmg] mae; (Lcf) || *om.* B P[74] ℵ *rell.*

D05 spells out the agreement of the Sanhedrin with the decision, beginning a new development with the connective δέ.

καὶ καλέσαντες B P[74] ℵ *rell* || φωνήσαντες D d gig sy[hmg] mae; Lcf.

B03 continues from the report of the deliberations with καί, not having mentioned the agreement of the Sanhedrin. Luke generally uses the verbs καλέω and φωνέω with distinct meanings: καλέω has the particular meaning of 'invite, invoke, call by name' (Lk. x 36 [+ 7 B03; + 4 D05]; Acts x 16 [+ 3 B03; + 1 D05]); φωνέω is less specific and simply means 'call' (Lk. x 9 [+ 1 B03; + 2 D05]; Acts x 4 [+ 3 D05]). The use of καλέω in B03 therefore is not in line with Luke's usual practice (cf. φωνέω in Lk. 6.13 D05; 14.12; 16.2; 19.15; Acts 9.41 [D05 *lac.*]; 10.7 [D05 *lac.*]).

παρήγγειλαν καθόλου B ℵ* || παρ. τὸ καθ. P[74] ℵ[1] A (παρήγγειλαν τὸ κατὰ τό D) E 0165. 33. 88. 927. 945. 1175. 1611. 1646. 1739. 1837. 1891. 2412. 2495 *pm* | παρ. αὐτοῖς τὸ καθ. H[3] P Ψ 049. 056. 69. 614. 1243. 2412. 2492 *pm*, *praeceperunt illis ne omnino* d.

D05 appears to have confused ΠΑΡΗΓΓΕΙΛΑΝ ΤΟ ΚΑΘΟΛΟΥ with ΠΑΡΗΓΓΕΙΛΑΝΤΟ ΚΑΤΑ ΤΟ. The omission of the article in B03 is unusual (B-D-R, §§160, n. 3; 399, n. 5).

τοῦ (᾿Ιησοῦ) D P[74] ℵ B[2] *rell* || *om.* B* 36. 431. 614. 618. 1243. 2147. 2412 *pc.*

As the reference to Jesus is anaphoric, it is in accordance with Luke's usual practice to retain the article. Its omission in B03 suggests that the phrase ἐπὶ τὸ ὀνόματι ᾿Ιησοῦ has been taken as a fixed expression which is out of place in this context.

4.19 ὁ δὲ Πέτρος καὶ (+ ὁ A Ψ) Ἰωάννης ἀποκριθέντες εἶπον B P[74] ℵ *rell* || ἀποκριθεὶς (–θέντες gig *cet*) δὲ Π. κ. Ἰωάνης εἶπον D d (gig sy[p]; Lcf).

The B03 text, retaining the article and placing the names before the verb, treats the fact that Peter and John answered the Sanhedrin as expected; the single article presents them as a united pair, despite the plural participle. In D05, it is the singular participle that expresses their unity but here the fact that they responded to the Sanhedrin is treated as not entirely expected: the absence of the article, together with the participle in first position, draws attention to their speech and switches the focus from the Sanhedrin back to Peter and John (Read-Heimerdinger, *The Bezan Text*, pp. 132–33).

4.20 μὴ λαλεῖν B P[74] ℵ D[E] *rell, non loqui* d[E] || λαλεῖν; *(interrog.)* D*, *loqui?* d*.

The absence of μή in D05 is explicable if the sentence is understood as a question and not as a statement; the negative οὐ at the beginning of the question would signify that a positive answer is implied (B-D-R, §§427.2; 440).

4.21 μηδὲν εὑρίσκοντες B ℵ A P E 049. 056. 33. 69. 323. 614. 1175. 1245. 2412. 2495 𝔐 | μὴ εὑρ. Ψ 927. 945. 1739. 1891 || μὴ εὑρ. αἰτίαν D (*nihil invenientes causam* d) p[*.2] sy[p] mae bo.

With the mention of αἰτία in D05, there is an echo of the statement that 'no cause of death was found' in Jesus: Lk. 23.22 D05; Acts 13.28 D05. See Epp, *Theological Tendency*, p. 126. B03 remains more vague with 'nothing'.

κολάσωσιν B* || –σωνται D ℵ B[2] *rell.*

The active voice of κολάζω, 'punish' is not found elsewhere in the New Testament. The middle voice signifies 'have someone punished' (Zerwick and Grosvenor, *Analysis*).

4.22 γεγόνει B D *pc* || ἐγεγ– ℵ A E H[3] P Ψ 049. 056. 33. 69. 614. 945. 1175. 1270. 1611. 1739. 2412. 2495 𝔐, *factum erat* d.

Both B03 and D05 omit the augment in the pluperfect, as happens frequently in the New Testament.

(τὸ σημεῖον) τοῦτο B ℵ *rell* d (?) || *om.* D gig p mae bo[mss]; Ir[lat] Lcf.

The use of the anaphoric demonstrative pronoun in B03 makes it clearer that the reason for the people's praising God is a narrative aside. The reading of *hoc* in d05 does not necessarily mean that τοῦτο was read in the exemplar since, in the previous clause of this verse, *his* (*sic.* = *hic*) is read before *homo* even though the demonstrative adjective is not read in any Greek MS. The two demonstratives in d05, as well as the translation of γάρ by *autem* at the beginning of the sentence, also make it clear that the sentence is understood as the narrator's comment.

Commentary

[a] 4.5–6 *The Authorities Gather Together*

4.5–6 It was seen at the beginning of this episode that the people disturbed by the apostles' teaching were the priests and the Sadducees. In order to confront Peter and John, they bring them before the Sanhedrin, the supreme council responsible for dealing with all matters concerning Jewish life. The Sanhedrin will not be mentioned by name until 4.15 but its coming together is described in detail here. The exact composition of the Sanhedrin while Jerusalem was under the rule of the Roman governors is uncertain and may have changed over time.[35] It is probably safe to say that among its members there were always the high priests, the Sadducees, the Pharisees and the scribes (including Pharisee scribes) but, for all that it was a Jewish court, it was, indirectly at least, dependent on and controlled by the Roman authorities, especially as permission had to be sought for it to convene.[36]

The various mentions of the Sanhedrin in the New Testament do not clarify the composition of the court. Here, the AT names three groups on an equal footing (the rulers, the elders, the scribes, see *Critical Apparatus*), followed by the names of the high priests together with the high priestly family. The list of high priestly members could be seen as an explanation of who is meant by the rulers, with the name of Annas dominating the list. Although Annas had ceased to occupy the office of high priest in 15 CE, his five sons (including Theophilus, see *Commentary*, 1.1) were high priests at one time or another up to 62 CE and his son-in law, Caiaphas, was the current holder of the title. Codex Bezae, on the other hand, distinguishes between the first group, the rulers, and a second one composed of the elders and scribes, followed by the high priestly group. It is not impossible that in this text, too, the description of the high priests is meant to expand on the mention of the 'rulers' but this suggestion does not match Luke's presentation of the Jewish leaders elsewhere.

There is, indeed, a difficulty in identifying the rulers on this, and on other occasions, in Luke's work. The same combination as that found in

35. The problem arises because the Rabbinic evidence does not fit the facts given by Josephus, leading some to conclude that there were two different Sanhedrins, see E.M. Smallwood, *The Jews under Roman Rule* (Leiden: E.J. Brill, 1976), p. 32, n. 36; cf. M. Grant, *The Jews in the Roman World* (London: Weidenfeld and Nicolson, 1973), pp. 92–93.

36. Smallwood, *The Jews under Roman Rule,* pp. 147–50.

the Bezan text of 4.5–6, of the high priests and the scribes with the elders, appears in the parallel scene in the Gospel to interrogate Jesus (Lk. 20.1) in the Temple, but with no mention of the rulers in that instance. Elsewhere in the Gospel they are twice mentioned alongside the high priests (Lk. 23.13: Pilate 'called together the high priests and the rulers and [all, D05] the people'; 24.20: 'our high priests and rulers handed [Jesus] over to be condemned to death'). When the same term ἄρχοντες was used by Peter at 3.17, it was apparently as a general term referring to the leaders of the Jews. At 4.8, Peter will address the meeting as 'rulers of the people and elders (of Israel D05)'; and when the apostles are tried by the Sanhedrin for a second time, Gamaliel will speak to 'the rulers and the Sanhedrin members' (5.35 D05) as he makes a plea on their behalf. Taking all these references to ἄρχοντες together, it looks as if, when it is a question of a Sanhedrin setting, they do not include any of the other groups mentioned, and are distinguishable from the Sanhedrin members (or, at the very, least, from the other members). On this understanding, they could represent the presence of Roman authorities who, as noted above, exercised some measure of control over the Jewish court and by their military presence constituted a visible power. Later, in the interpretation of Psalm 2 given by the apostles (4.25–27), ἄρχοντες will mean precisely the secular powers under Pilate (see *Commentary*, 4.27). Too little is known, however, about the actual Roman involvement in the Sanhedrin to be sure that the rulers in that context is a reference to the attendance of Roman officials, although the possibility cannot be excluded.

The detail that the council met in Jerusalem is superfluous from a factual point of view since it is clear that the events have been taking place there. It has the theological purpose, however, of carefully setting the scene for the imminent rejection of Jesus as Messiah in the holy city; it also anticipates the declaration of the disciples at 4.27 that powers of all kinds had come against the Messiah 'in this city', taking up the reference to 'Zion, my holy hill' from Ps. 2.6 (see *Commentary*, 4.27). The precise meeting place of the Sanhedrin is debatable but Rabbinic writings suggest that sometime around 30 CE it moved to the abside at the end of the Royal Portico,[37] which was within the Herodian extension to the Temple.

The high priest in power at the time of the incident was Caiaphas (18–36 AD). However, Annas who is named as high priest was his father-in-

37. *Sab.* 15a; *Ros Has.* 31a; *Sanh.* 41a; *'Abod. Zar.* 8b. For an idea of what the abside of the Royal Portico looked like, see the photographic illustrations of the scale model of the Temple in Garrard, *The Splendour of the Temple*, pp. 38, 44

law who held office from 6–15 CE and who appears to have continued to dominate the high priesthood with his influence even after he was deposed by the Romans (cf. Lk. 3.2). Caiaphas was succeeded by five sons of Annas, including Jonathan (the D05 reading) who followed Caiaphas in 36 CE. Another of his sons, Theophilus (see *Commentary*, 1.1), had a son called John who is perhaps the person meant by the AT reading.[38] The identity of Alexander is unknown.

The mention of Annas and Caiaphas echoes the reference to their high priesthood at the time of the beginning of the ministry of John the Baptist (Lk. 3.2, [where D05 again reads Καίφας]), and contributes a further element to the parallel between John the Baptist and the Jerusalem church (cf. Acts 3.20–21).

[b] 4.7 *The Interrogation of the Apostles*

4.7 The interrogation by the Sanhedrin is reported in direct speech and focuses on knowing what power the apostles have called upon to bring about the healing of the lame man. The same word, δύναμις, is used as the one Peter used in explaining the healing to the people in 3.12 but, unlike the people, the religious authorities do not imagine for a moment that the apostles might have drawn upon their own power – having interrogated Jesus himself in much the same terms when they first tried to find cause to denounce him ('Tell us by what authority you do these things, or who it is who gave you this authority', Lk. 20.2), they are only too aware that some 'name' other than the apostles' own has been involved. The matter of the resurrection is not brought up, possibly because it was not a problem that affected the Sanhedrin as a whole, some of the members being Pharisees who themselves believed in the resurrection.

[c] 4.8–12 *Peter's Testimony before the Sanhedrin*

Peter's response to the council is inspired by the Holy Spirit, and stands in contrast to his earlier speech to the people where he was not said to have been filled with the Spirit as he spoke. A series of parallels between the two speeches can be noted:

1. ἄνδρες Ἰσραηλῖται, 3.12 // πρεσβύτεροι τοῦ Ἰσραήλ, 4.8 D05
2. ἀπεκτείνατε, ὃν ὁ θεὸς ἤγειρεν ἐκ νεκρῶν, 3.14 // ἐσταυρώσατε, ὃν ὁ θεὸς ἤγειρεν ἐκ νεκρῶν, 4.10

38. R. Anderson, 'A la recherche de Théophile', in *Saint Luc, évangéliste et historien* (*Dossiers d'Archéologie* 279 [2002–3]), p. 66.

3. ἐπὶ τῇ πίστει τοῦ ὀνόματος αὐτοῦ ... τὸ ὄνομα αὐτοῦ, 3.16a // ἐν τῷ ὀνόματι Ἰησοῦ ... ἐν τούτῳ, 4.10
4. τὴν ὁλοκληρίαν ταύτην ἀπέναντι πάντων ὑμῶν, 3.16b // ἐνώπιον ὑμῶν ὑγιής, 4.10

4.8 When Peter, together with the other disciples, was filled with the Spirit at Pentecost (2.4), the term used by Luke was πλησθείς, the aorist participle of the verb πίμπλημι. The aorist of the same verb was used in the Gospel, to speak of Elizabeth (Lk. 1.41) and Zachariah (Lk. 1.67) having been filled with the Holy Spirit. It is the adjective πλήρης, however, that is used to refer to Jesus being full of the Spirit after his baptism (Lk. 4.1); it will be used again of the seven Hellenists (6.3), especially Stephen (6.5; 7.55), and of Barnabas (11.24). The difference is that the adjective refers to a permanent state whereas the aorist of the verb refers to an action that is repeated as the occasion requires.[39] Consequently, as Peter is filled now for a second time, the implication is that he was not full of the Spirit in the intervening period, as could be deduced from the nature of his earlier speech. The fact that he now speaks under the guidance of the Holy Spirit is a way of indicating that Peter is in harmony with the thinking of Jesus as he replies to the Sanhedrin.

He addresses his audience as both rulers of the people and elders – with Codex Bezae qualifying the latter as 'of Israel'. As discussed above (see *Commentary*, 4.5–6), these are probably to be thought of as two separate groups, with 'the rulers of the people' and 'the elders of Israel' representing different types of leaders, as listed in 4.5–6. Peter, it is to be noted, is still very much part of Israel at this stage, these are *his* leaders whom he addresses.

4.9 Peter's response makes it clear that he views the hearing as a formal interrogation.[40] In the Bezan text, he draws a contrast between the authorities who are conducting the hearing, and John and himself who stand accused, with the suggestion that the real discussion about their case is not being carried out in front of them but rather has already taken place amongst the authorities before the meeting (see *Critical Apparatus*). The

39. See Bruce, *Acts*, p. 99, n. 16.

40. ἀνακρίνω as a judicial term is part of Luke's technical terminology: cf. Lk. 23.14 (Pilate); Acts 12.19 (Herod); 24.8 (Felix); 28.18 (the Romans). The cognate noun ἀνάκρισις, a New Testament hapax, is found at 25.26 (Festus and Agrippa II).

use of the word σήμερον, 'today', is a typically Lukan signal indicating that the present represents a critical moment.[41]

Peter does not immediately answer the Sanhedrin's question about the power or name but first spells out the contents of their unmentionable 'this' (4.7): by what has a sick man been restored to health? The verb used, σῴζω, has a fuller meaning that simply physical healing and will be used by Peter at the end of his speech to mean spiritual salvation. Although it will not become clear until later, the healed man is, in fact, standing with Peter and John in the middle of the Sanhedrin.

4.10 The answer to the question 'by what?' is now proclaimed, with a solemn introductory formula exclusive to Luke: γωστὸν ἔστω, 'let it be known'.[42] The declaration that follows, addressed not just to the Sanhedrin but to the whole of Israel, shows that Peter is aware that the healing of the lame man has a significance far beyond the immediate situation, and that his answer has a validity for the belief system of Judaism in general. The content is similar to the explanation Peter had already given to the people in Solomon's porch (cf. 3.16), namely that it is by the name of Jesus that the healing has taken place, the qualification 'the Nazorene' being a reference to his Messianic status.[43] Once again, too, Peter attaches to the mention of Jesus a reference to the crucifixion and resurrection, opposing the action of the Jews with that of God. He makes no distinction here between the rulers and the people nor does he bring in the motive of ignorance (cf. 3.17).

4.11 A scriptural quotation, referring to the rejection of the stone by the builders, forms a parenthetical comment which, in the AT, is an independent statement with a new sentence beginning at 4.12, whereas in the Bezan text it is an explanatory insertion in the middle of a sentence that continues in v. 12. In both cases, it is sandwiched between a positive and a negative declaration about the name of Jesus, and takes up the brief accusation of 4.10 by expanding on it:

41. All 'todays' in the Gospel are significant: see, e.g., Lk. 2.11; 3.22 D05; 4.21; 5.26; 19.5, 9; 23.45; 24.21 D05. Coming from Peter, it echoes the 'today' of Jesus' warning to him of his denial (Lk. 22.34, 61 [not D05]).

42. γνωστὸν ἔστω is found in speeches, at the beginning (Acts 2.14; 4.10) and in the parenesis (13.38; 28.28); γνωστὸν ἐγένετο is found in narrative (1.19; 9.42; 19.17).

43. See *Commentary*, 2.22 and 3.6 on the significance of Ναζωραῖος and how it differs from Ναζαρηνός.

v. 10 'whom you crucified' // v. 11 'the stone that was treated with contempt by you, the builders'
v. 10 'whom God raised from the dead' // v. 11 'that has become the cornerstone'

The quotation, from Ps. 118.22, was already cited by Jesus, but in its LXX form (= Ps. 117 LXX), in the parallel scene of Luke 20 where he applied it to his interrogators – the chief priests and the scribes with the elders, Lk. 20.1 (cf. 20.19). The differences in Peter's wording are due to the fact that he now identifies the stone as Jesus, explicitly applying the prophecy to his rejection by the Jewish leaders. In particular, the verb used by Peter, ἐξουθενηθείς, 'treated with contempt', was that chosen by Luke to describe the treatment of Jesus by Herod and his soldiers (ἐξουθενήσας, Lk. 23.11). It is no surprise that the wording of the LXX should have been modified by Peter if one considers the amount of re-wording of the LXX apparent elsewhere in the Bezan text of Acts, for example, Peter's use of Joel in Acts 2. There is certainly no need to think that Luke has used some source that differed from the LXX.[44]

4.12 The AT introduces a new subject at this point, namely salvation. The second part of the sentence beginning οὐδὲ γάρ, 'since neither...' is ambiguous, partly because of the somewhat odd word order. The usual interpretation, given in the translation, is that no other name under heaven (i.e. on earth) than that of Jesus has been given among men for them to be saved by. Another possible meaning is that the name given among men (i.e. of Jesus) by which people must be saved, is not different in nature[45] under heaven (from its nature *in* heaven, where Jesus is to be found since he has been resurrected, cf. v. 10).

The Bezan text has a different word order and the sentence picks up from the end of v. 10 with the same subject: by the name of Jesus this man has been healed (v. 10) and it is by no other (v. 11). There is thus a consistent focus on the matter of the name throughout 4.10 and 4.12, with the references creating a chiastic pattern:

44. The debate about Luke's sources for this reference to Psalm 117/118 ignores the fact that Luke, like his speakers, is quite at ease in modifying scriptural passages in order to show how they apply to new situations.

45. The word for 'different' in 4.12b is ἕτερος, which can mean 'of a different kind or nature', especially in contrast to the word used in the previous clause of 4.12a, ἄλλος, which means 'another, a different one'.

10b by the name of Jesus Christ the Nazorene
    10e by this name
    12a it is by none other (name)
12b no other kind of name ... has been given ... by which we must be saved

4.12 reflects the first set of positive affirmations of 4.10 with their negative counterparts, mirroring the pattern of noun-pronoun in reverse order. The two-fold question of the council is thus answered: the power is the name, and the name is that of Jesus. By use of the impersonal imperative δεῖ, 'it is necessary' (lit.), Peter implies that what he is claiming is sanctioned by God; it is not his own opinion.

The speech opens with 'a sick man ... has been restored' and closes with 'a name given to men by which you (B03) / we (D05) must be saved', with the same verb σῴζω used in the passive in each instance and the same noun ἄνθρωπος. Codex Vaticanus has Peter instruct the leaders whom he is addressing on the means of salvation. In Codex Bezae (as Codex Sinaiticus and most MSS), 'we' could be taken to apply only to the Jewish people, but Peter's declaration that the name of Jesus had been given to 'men' in general means that his vision of the salvation offered by Jesus has already started to widen and to extend beyond the confines of the Jewish people. Certainly, it extends fully to a 'man' considered unclean under Jewish law.

[d] 4.13a *The Sanhedrin's Reaction*

4.13a The astonishment of the leaders is occasioned by several factors, which Luke expresses through their own eyes. First, they 'see' the boldness (παρρησία) of Peter, principally, but also of John. This is no doubt a comment not just on the apostles' open and fearless attitude in response to the interrogation but on their radically new interpretation and application of Scripture, which could properly be called 'daring' – both in the sense that they dared to rethink traditional teaching in so revolutionary way and in the sense that they had the courage to declare it. The word παρρησία does, indeed, have this dual meaning in Acts, where it signifies the inner freedom given by the Holy Spirit for properly understanding the message of Jesus which is reflected in the outward liberty to proclaim it.[46] Thus, in

46. S.C. Winter ('ΠΑΡΡΗΣΙΑ in Acts', in J.T. Fitzgerald [ed.], *Friendship, Flattery, and Frankness of Speech: Studies on Friendship in the New Testament World* [Leiden: E.J. Brill, 1996], pp. 185–202) distinguishes between the meaning of παρρησία in classical usage – characterized by speaking the truth in public, with authority and in the face of opposition (e.g. pp. 191–92) – and that expressed in

the apostles' prayer following the return of Peter and John to the community at the end of the present scene, they will request the ability to speak 'with complete boldness' (μετὰ πάσης παρρησίας, 4.29). Their request is only partially answered, as they are subsequently described as enabled by the Spirit to speak 'with boldness' (μετὰ παρρησίας, 4.31), just as at 2.29 (cf. 2.4) and in the present scene, 4.13 (cf. 4.8).

Their reworking of Scripture is especially surprising because the leaders realize that they were not trained in the law. Such is the technical meaning of the word ἀγράμματοι, which contrasts the apostles with the scribes, οἱ γραμματεῖς, who were the ones with the formal expertise to examine and understand the Scriptures. The AT appears to have taken ἀγράμματοι with its ordinary meaning of 'unlettered' and therefore adds that they were 'laymen' (ἰδιῶται), in other words, not formally trained. Not only does the content of Peter's speech indicate a sophisticated degree of understanding of the Scriptures, but its form is highly crafted and displays considerable evidence of rhetorical style, as the analysis above has sought to demonstrate. How could an untrained person come out with such things?

[e] 4.13b *Their Recognition of Jesus' Influence*

4.13b The leaders, of course, do not recognize that Peter is speaking through the Holy Spirit, the spirit of prophecy who enables him to understand God's thoughts. What they do recognize is that the apostles had been with Jesus. What does this recognition mean? It is unlikely that until that moment they had not known that Peter and John were disciples of Jesus. But the particular line of Peter's argument must have sounded remarkably similar to what they had heard from Jesus not so long before (cf. Lk. 20.1–19), down to his use of Psalm 118 to attack the religious authorities. The statement further anticipates their increasing perplexity as they consider the healed man: the sign conveyed by the healing – the release of a lame man from purity regulations – is indeed similar to the works performed by Jesus, in whose name these disciples of his claim to have acted.

Hellenistic usage – the moral virtue of frank speech in a philosophical setting (e.g. pp. 196–97). He wishes to demonstrate a shift from the former to the latter in the successive occurrences of the word in Acts. His thorough study has much that is of interest, but it fails to take account of the Jewish context from which the formulation and declaration of the message of Jesus stemmed. It is especially because of this context that the radical nature of Jesus' message requires παρρησία, given by the Holy Spirit, for its proper understanding and transmission. The cognate verb παρρησιάζομαι is not used by Luke as a technical term in the same way as the noun (see 9.27, 28 [Paul]; 13.46 and 14.3 [Paul and Barnabas]; 18.26 [Apollo]; 19.8 and 26.26 [Paul]).

[f] 4.14 *Their Perplexity*

4.14 The confusion and the bewilderment of the leaders marks the height of the drama: the most powerful people among the Jews, responsible for all matters pertaining to the Temple, are at a loss as to how to deal with the situation. Their perplexity is conveyed not just by the words of Luke's account but by the disjointed construction, especially in Codex Bezae where the short, sharp sentence at the end of v. 13 is followed by a sentence without, unusually for Luke, any introductory connecting word. Their powerlessness is further underlined in the Bezan text with the comment that they did not know what to *do* or say in opposition. This would seem to be a clear reference to Jesus' warning to his disciples not to meditate beforehand what they would say to their persecutors, since Jesus himself would give them words that could be neither resisted nor contradicted (Lk. 21.15).[47] In this instance, Peter and John had allowed the Holy Spirit to speak through them (cf. 4.8) and Jesus' prophecy was fulfilled.

[e′] 4.15–17 *A Solution is Sought*

4.15 Since the leaders do not know how to react to Peter and John or to the man who stands as evidence of their healing, they discuss what to do amongst themselves after sending their prisoners out of the meeting. The verb used by Codex Bezae to describe their removal from the meeting (ἀπαχθῆναι) is the same as that used by Luke to describe how Jesus was led away to be tried by the Sanhedrin (Lk. 22.66).

While the AT moves the narrative here on to a new development, Codex Bezae continues to express the confusion of the council by a second absence of connective (see *Critical Apparatus*).

4.16–17 The discussion is reported in direct speech, with a statement of the problem followed by a proposed solution. Although the problem and solution are stated in much the same terms in the two texts (though expressed more forcibly in Codex Bezae, see *Critical Apparatus*), the attitude of the council members is presented differently. The council need to decide what to do with Peter and John, but their course of action will have to take account of the fact that everyone in Jerusalem is aware of the 'sign' (σημεῖον) that has happened through them, a sign that can be

47. In most MSS, Lk. 21.15 reads ἀντιστῆναι ἢ ἀντειπεῖν, the second verb being that found in Acts 4.14 (AT and Bezan text). However, Lk. 21.15 D05 (supported by numerous early versions) omits the second verb. The verbal parallel between Acts and Luke is thereby absent, although the parallel of sense remains.

recognized or known (γνωστόν) for what it is.[48] The involvement of the people has been underlined since the beginning of this incident (by the narrator, 3.9, 11 B03, 12a B03; 4.1; by Peter, 3.12b; 4.10; by the Jewish authorities, 4.2).

According to the AT, the council have no wish to deny what has happened; their concern is rather that even more people might hear of it if they do nothing about it and so they propose to forbid the apostles to continue speaking about Jesus. In the Bezan text, in contrast, the council are inclined to deny the sign but are afraid that if they do, something even more dramatic will happen. They therefore take a definite decision to stop any further talk about Jesus. The point is this: the significance of the healing of the lame man is not so much that a miracle, a display of divine power, has occurred, as that a particular sign (cf. 4.22 below) that all have understood (γνωστόν) has been effected – he has been made pure and free to enter the Temple, and all in the name of Jesus, without the intervention of the Temple rulers or even their authority. The use of the perfect tense (γέγονεν [B03] / γεγονέναι [D05], and cf. a perfect form of γίνομαι in 4.21, 22) is important, for it expresses a change of state with lasting effect rather than the occurrence of an event which would have been expressed with the aorist.[49] It would be in the interests of the Temple leaders to publicly repudiate the sign (even though they cannot contest that a healing had taken place), in order to protect their prestige and prevent the power of Jesus from challenging their own; but in so doing, they could encourage the apostles to perform some greater challenge to the Temple institution. They know about Jesus and what he taught concerning them (cf. Lk. 20.9–19), and they recognize that his disciples are carrying out his teaching (cf. 4.13). The best they can do, therefore, is to use their authority to intimidate them and to forbid Jesus' name to be mentioned at all so that his unacceptable, revolutionary message cannot be heard nor his power be exercised.

Literally, the prohibition applies to 'anyone among men', using the word ἄνθρωπος that first appeared at the end of Peter's speech, 4.8, and that has recurred since ('a sick man', 4.9; a 'name given to men', 4.12; 'the man who was healed', 4.14; 'the man to whom the sign ... had happened', 4.22). By means of the repeated use of the term, Luke shows how the

48. γνωστός recurs throughout Acts (1.19; 2.14; 4.10, 16; 9.42; 13.38; 15.18; 19.17; 28.22, 28) not so much with the sense of factual knowledge but more of intelligible facts.

49. For discussion on the perfect aspect to convey an alteration of state see S.E. Porter, *Verbal Aspect in the Greek of the New Testament, with Reference to Tense and Mood* (Studies in Biblical Greek, I; New York: Peter Lang, 1989), p. 259.

scope of the message of Jesus has changed from being restricted to the people of Israel (cf. 3.2, 10, 12; 4.1–2) to being extended to all of humanity (see *Commentary*, 4.8). In the same way, he presents the Sanhedrin as seeking to exclude all of humanity from hearing the apostles' teaching about Jesus, as if they were aware of the universal significance of 'the sign'.

[d′] 4.18 *The Sanhedrin's Decision*

4.18 Codex Bezae specifies that the decision met with general agreement, it was not imposed by any individual or group within the council. Bearing in mind the presentation in Codex Bezae of the participants in the meeting as including Roman representatives (see *Commentary*, 4.5–6), this agreement has a special significance that will become more apparent later on (see *Commentary*, 4.27–28). At that point, the apostles were recalled, as in the AT, and the ban on the continued use of the name of Jesus communicated to them. Since no threat was made as to what might happen if they were to disobey the order, it can be assumed that the council took for granted that their command would be obeyed.

[c′] 4.19–20 *Peter's Response*

4.19–20 The Bezan wording of the clause introducing Peter and John's response reflects the fact that they were not expected to challenge the command. (The wording of the AT does not treat it as unusual.) In different ways, both texts indicate that the apostles act as a united pair (see *Critical Apparatus*), though the word order of Codex Bezae indicates that it is Peter who takes the initiative as he has done throughout this episode (cf. 3.4, 12; 4.8, 13).

The challenge takes the form of an indirect rhetorical question in which appeal is made to a widely accepted principle,[50] namely that it is better to obey God than people. The implication that the council did not itself represent divine law would be highly offensive to the Jewish leaders. Since they are told to judge whether it was 'right *in the sight of God*' to listen to God, the answer is inescapable.

Although in the AT the apostles state that they are bound to speak of what they have witnessed, in Codex Bezae they ask another rhetorical question – are they not allowed to speak of what they have witnessed? In neither case, do they accept the council's order but the refusal in the Bezan text is attenuated. It will only be at their second appearance before

50. Barrett, I, p. 237.

the council, at 5.32, that they will make their position clear as they declare their obedience to God.

[b′] 4.21–22 *The Release of the Apostles*

4.21 At this point, threats are added to the ban on mentioning the name of Jesus. Just what punishment may have been possible or appropriate is not indicated, but on their second appearance before the council the apostles will be beaten for refusing to obey their orders. The motive adduced for letting them go on this occasion is that they find nothing to punish them for (or no cause, as the Bezan text expresses it); there is therefore no basis on which to determine a punishment. The wording of the Bezan text echoes parallel passages in the Gospel concerning the trial of Jesus: Lk. 19.47–48; 24.19; but especially 23.22 D05: οὐδεμίαν αἰτίαν θανάτου εὑρίσκω ἐν αὐτῷ, cf. Acts 13.28 D05: μηδεμίαν αἰτίαν θανάτου εὑρόντες ἐν αὐτῷ.

Again, the presence of the people and their positive response to what has been effected through the healing of the lame man (note the second use of the perfect γεγονότι, cf. 4.16) are evoked, contrasting with the hostile reaction of the Sanhedrin. The people's approval of the apostles is, as already hinted in v. 16, what prevents the council from taking stronger action against them.

[a′] 4.22 *The Meaning of the Sign*

4.22 Reference is made to the age of the man in an aside that is a comment made by the narrator and not just an expression of the people's own awareness. It is typical of Luke to use a brief parenthetical comment to express information that, as will be seen, is of critical importance (cf. 1.15, for example).

The man's healing is described once again as a 'sign', a reminder that more is involved than a healing miracle (see *Commentary*, 4.16). And again a perfect tense is used, to express the permanent change of state that has been effected (see *Commentary*, 4.16, 21) appropriately enough since, as was seen in the discussion of 3.1–10, the healing of the lame man in the name of Jesus stands for something much greater than his own personal well-being: it represents nothing less than the power of Jesus to release the Jewish people from the regulations preventing those with an impurity from worshipping God.

The underlying significance of the healing is important in order to understand the mention of the fact that he was more than 40 years old. This reference to his age functions in combination with the comment at the beginning of this long third sequence of Acts that he had been lame 'from his mother's womb' (3.2), since his conception.[51] He had suffered from his lameness, and consequently his impurity, from the very beginning and had continued to do so after the age of 40; he was more than 40 when he was healed. In view of the symbolic meaning that Luke attaches to the healing, it is legitimate to take the 40 years in a non-literal sense, as an allusion to the 40 years the people of Israel spent in the desert before entering the Promised Land. On this understanding, the laws of impurity controlling access to God are said to have existed since the very beginning of the people of Israel and to have continued even after their arrival in the Promised Land. The marginalization of the impure is indissoluble from the existence of the people of Israel. Even though they had escaped from their condition of slavery in Egypt, yet they had continued to oppress certain categories of people and cause them to be excluded from the most central of concerns of Jewish life, access to worship in the Temple. It is this fundamental feature of religious regulations, the distinction between the pure and the impure, that Jesus finally has succeeded in abolishing. Little wonder, then, that the people praised God on account of what had happened!

[A'] 4.23–31. *The Release of the Jesus-Believing Community*

Overview

The final sequence of the third section of Acts stands in stark contrast to the first sequence at the beginning of Acts 3. There, Peter and John are seen attending Temple prayer but, once confronted by the lame man and his situation with regard to participation in Temple worship, they find themselves performing a miracle of healing in the name of Jesus that allows him to gain the status of purity necessary for access to the Temple. When the two apostles publicly proclaim the healing as evidence of the power and authority of the resurrected Jesus, the Temple authorities are disturbed by the challenge to their authority represented by the sign of the healing and, with the agreement of the Roman authorities, they impose a ban on the continued mention of the name of Jesus. In consequence, Peter

51. Luke makes similar comments on the remarkable age of characters at Lk. 1.7, 18 (Zechariah and Elizabeth), 36 (Elizabeth); 2.36, 37 (Anna), where their old age signifies not only the unexpected nature of God's intervention but also the great length of time that Israel had had to wait for it. Age is specified likewise at Lk. 3.23 (Jesus); 8.42 (Jairus' daughter), 43 (the woman with a flow of blood).

and John go back to their own community where their separation from the religious authority of the Temple leadership becomes evident.

The precise identity of the group present in this final sequence is ambiguous. It is tempting to think that it is composed solely of the apostles, given that no place would be large enough for the 5,000 believers last mentioned (4.4), and that the elements of the petition in their prayer (speaking the word; with boldness; healing, signs and wonders) are only used elsewhere of the apostles.[52] Furthermore, the concepts expressed in the prayer reflect a level of sophistication in the understanding of the Scriptures and in the interpretation of recent events that should probably be attributed to the apostles rather than the community in general.

The use, however, of ἅπαντες to describe those who were filled with the Holy Spirit following the prayer (see *Commentary*, 4.31) confirms that a wider group than the apostles was present, for Luke uses this term to signify 'absolutely all' the people as opposed to simply 'the totality'.[53] As for the material problem of what place might be large enough and suitable for all the believers to gather, the question becomes, in fact, irrelevant once the symbolic nature of the scene is understood for what it is. For Luke presents this gathering very much as a metaphorical expression of the reality of the changes taking place among the Jesus-believers and the divine response to their situation, rather than as a literal event. That is not to say that nothing of the kind ever occurred but simply that Luke has chosen to portray it in its fullest dimension, as affecting all the Jesus-believers as a unified community and in terms that go beyond physical reality, as will be seen.

Whilst it is no doubt true that the prayer itself reflects thinking and concerns more appropriate to the apostles than the believers in general, this does not exclude the involvement of the whole of the believing community in the prayer since all are united under the leadership of the apostles. On the contrary, it conveys the extent to which it is the apostles who have replaced the Temple authorities as the leaders of the Jesus-believing Jews.

Structure and Themes

The sequence relates the return of the apostles, once they have been released from the Sanhedrin, to the community of Jesus-believers. The

52. See J. Dupont, 'La prière des apôtres persécutés', in *idem*, *Études sur les Actes des Apôtres* (Lectio Divina, 45; Paris: Cerf, 1967), pp. 521–22.

53. ἅπαντες is used by Luke as a term distinct from πάντες and carries the sense of 'absolutely all, entirely everything', as opposed to the total number, see *Critical Apparatus*, 2.7, 44.

community's response, under the guidance of the apostles, is expressed as a prayer in which the Sanhedrin's prohibition on any mention of the name of Jesus is interpreted as an accomplishment of scriptural prophecy and, as such, is not acceded to. Confirmation of the weakening of the power of the official Jewish leadership and of God's presence with the Jesus-believers is given as the Temple building is shaken and the Holy Spirit is received for a second time.

Following the initial report of the apostles to the rest of the Jesus-believers, the bulk of the sequence is taken up by their prayer and the divine ratification of it:

[a]	4.23	The community are informed of the Sanhedrin's decision
[b]	4.24–30	The prayer of the community
[a′]	4.31	Divine ratification of the prayer

Translation

Codex Bezae D05

[a] **4.23** Once released, they went to their own community and reported what the high priests and elders had said to them.

[b] **24** They, when they heard and realized how God had acted, lifted their voices together towards God and said, 'Master, you are the God who made the heavens and the earth and the sea and all that is in them, **25** who spoke through the Holy Spirit through the mouth of your servant David, "Why did the nations rage and the peoples devise vain projects? **26** The kings of the earth took position, and the rulers gathered, all with a common purpose against the Lord and his anointed." **27** For in truth there gathered in this city against your holy servant Jesus whom you anointed, both Herod and Pontius Pilate with the nations and the peoples of Israel **28** to do what your hand and your plan had foreordained to happen. **29** And now, Lord, look on their threats and grant to your servants to speak your word with complete

Codex Vaticanus B03

4.23 Once released, they went to their own community and reported the things the high priests and elders had said to them.

24 When they heard, they lifted their voices together towards God and said, 'Master, you who made the heavens and the earth and the sea and all that is in them, **25** who said through the Holy Spirit through the mouth of our father David, your servant, "Why did the nations rage and the peoples devise vain projects? **26** The kings of the earth took position and the rulers gathered, all with a common purpose against the Lord and his anointed." **27** For in truth there gathered in this city against your holy servant Jesus whom you anointed, both Herod and Pontius Pilate with the nations and the peoples of Israel **28** to do what your hand and plan had foreordained to happen. **29** And now, Lord, look on their threats and grant to your servants to speak your word with all boldness, **30** as you stretch out your hand to heal boldness, **30** as you stretch out your hand to heal and signs and wonders are performed through the name of your holy servant Jesus.'

[a′] **31** And when they had finished praying, the place in which they were gathered was shaken and all of them were filled with the Holy Spirit and they started to speak the word of God with boldness to all those who wished to believe.

and signs and wonders are performed through the name of your holy servant Jesus.'

31 And when they had finished praying, the place in which they were gathered was shaken and all of them were filled with the Holy Spirit and they started to speak the word of God with boldness.

Critical Apparatus

4.23 ἀπήγγειλαν B D, *renuntiaverunt* d A E Ψ *rell* || ἀνήγ– ℵ 226.

A *vl* involving ἀναγγέλλω was noted at 4.2 above where B03 reads καταγγέλλω. The meaning of both verbs used here would seem to be equivalent (B-A-G, ἀναγγέλλω, 2).

4.24 (ἀκούσαντες) καὶ ἐπιγνόντες τὴν τοῦ θεοῦ ἐνέργειαν D d mae; (Chr) || *om.* B P^{74} ℵ *rell.*

The reading of D05 has echoes of 2 Macc. 3.29; *3 Macc.* 4.21; 5.12, 28 where the word ἐνέργεια is found with the same meaning as here (see Epp, *The Theological Tendency*, p. 127). It contrasts with the use of the same word referring to the Jewish authorities in 4.13. Far from being a pious addition, the comment has a profound theological meaning, for the recognition that what has happened with the Temple authorities is the work of God implies a radical shift in attitudes towards the Temple and its regulations.

(Σὺ) ὁ θεός D d E H^{3} P Ψ 049. 056. (33). 69. 323. 610. 614. 945. 1175. 1505. 1611. 1739. 1891. 2412. 2492 𝔐 gig p (vg^{mss}) sy sa mae; (Ir^{lat}) Lcf || *om.* B P^{74} ℵ A 2495 *pc* dem ph ro w $vg^{(cl)}$ bo; Ath^{pt} (Hil Aug).

A similar use of ὁ θεός before a participle of ποιέω in apposition is found at Acts 14.15 D05; 17.24 (cf. Ps. 145.5–6 LXX).

4.25 ὁ τοῦ πατρὸς ἡμῶν διὰ πνεύματος ἁγίου στόματος Δαυὶδ παιδός σου εἰπών B P^{74} ℵ A E Ψ 33. 36. 88. 307. 323. 453. 610. (927. 945). 1175. 1739. 1891. 2344 *al* | ὁ διὰ στ. Δ. παι. σου εἰπών H^{3} P 049. 056. 69. 614. 1241. 1245. 1611. 2412. 2492 𝔐 (τοῦ παιδός 326. 1505 *al*) || ὃς διὰ πν. ἁγ. διὰ τοῦ στ. λαλήσας Δ. παιδός σου D, *qui per spiritum sanctum per os locutus est David puero[-i] tuo[-i]* d (sy^{p}).

There is a number of difficulties with the reading as it stands in B03: between ὁ and εἰπών, which is in parallel to ὁ ποιήσας of the previous clause, there is a series of phrases that qualifies David as both ancestor (τοῦ πατρὸς ἡμῶν) and servant of God (παιδός σου), they are all in the genitive, apparently because God is represented as speaking through the Holy Spirit and through (supplied by some witnesses) the mouth of David. D05 has a somewhat different structure: the relative pronoun ὅς refers back to God, identified as the one to whom the prayer is addressed in v. 24 (see above), and begins a fresh clause with a participle, λαλήσας, standing for a finite verb (B-D-R §468,2 and n. 3); it is thus clearly stated that God spoke through the Holy Spirit and through the mouth of David (Read-Heimerdinger, *The Bezan Text*, p. 162).

4.27 παῖδά σου B P^{74} ℵ *rell, puerum tuum* d || σου παῖδα D 614. 2412; Hil.

The position of the pronoun before the noun not only places the name of Jesus adjacent to the word παῖς, but further establishes a connection between Jesus and David by creating a chiastic pattern: 4.25: Δανὶδ παῖδός σου // 4.27: σου παῖδα Ἰησοῦν. A further chiasmus is created between this mention of Jesus and the closing words of the prayer, 4.30: παῖδός σου Ἰησοῦ.

4.28 (ἡ βουλή) σου D d ℵ A^{2} E^{2} H^{3} P Ψ 049. 056. 33. 69. 614. 1270. 1611. 1891. 2344. 2412. 2495 𝔐 sy; Ir^{lat} || *om.* B A* E* 242. 323. 467. 945. 1175. 1739 *pc* a c e gig vg^{cl}; Lcf Hil Aug.

By the repetition of the pronoun, not necessary for the basic sense, D05 differentiates between what happened (γενέσθαι) through the hand of God and what was foreseen (προώρισεν) by his counsel, a distinction that is further brought out by the chiastic pattern of the nouns and the associated verbs.

4.29 ἔπιδε B ℵ H^{3} P Ψ 049. 056. 33. 69. 614. 945. 1245. 1270. 1505. 1611. 1739. 2344. 2412. 2495 𝔐 || ἔφιδε D A E 88. 1175.

Although Delebecque describes the D05 reading as an error (*Les deux Actes*, p. 45), the aspiration before the verb ἰδεῖν occurs elsewhere in the Bezan text of Luke's work (Lk. 1.25, ἐφεῖδεν; 6.35, ἀφελπίζοντες; Acts 2.7, οὐχ᾽ ἰδού). Rendel Harris identifies it as an early pronunciation (Rendel Harris, *Codex Bezae*, p. 138).

τὰς ἀπειλάς B P^{74} ℵ D^{A} *rell, minacias* d || τὰς ἅγιας D*.

The nonsensical reading of D05 can be explained by the confusion of letters: of ΑΠΕΙΛΑΣ, Π was read for Γ, ΕΙ was read for Ι because of itacism, Λ was suppressed because of its juxtaposition with the similar-looking Α.

παρρησίας πάσης B P^{74} ℵ *rell, fiducia omni* d || πάσης παρρ. D E gig p vg; Lcf Hil.

The position of πᾶς pre-noun is the one most frequently found in Acts (Read-

Heimerdinger, *The Bezan Text*, pp. 97–99), expressing the emphasis inherent in the meaning of the adjective. The reason for the emphasis becomes clear with the contrast that appears in 4.31 where the boldness with which the word was spoken was not complete (μετὰ παρρησίας), as indeed it had not been when Peter and John spoke to the Sanhedrin (cf. 4.13). Total boldness will remain an elusive goal until the end of the book of Acts, except for the case of Stephen (6.10 D05, cf. 28.31).

4.30 (τὴν χεῖρά) σου D P^{45} ℵ E H^{3} Ψ 049. 056. 33. 614. 1505. 1739. 2412. 2495 𝔐 || *om.* B* d gig; Lcf.

D05 repeats the phrase with the possessive pronoun used earlier in the prayer (4.28); B03 makes the reference to God clear through the accusative pronoun as the subject of the infinitive (see below).

ἐκτείνειν σε B ℵ* H^{3} P 049. 056. 36. 69. 104. 330. 614. 1243. 1505. 1611. 2147. 2412. 2495 *al* | σε ἐκτ. P^{74} A 1175 *pc* || ἐκτ. D d (P^{45}) $ℵ^{2}$ E Ψ 33. 323. 945. 1241. 1270. 1739 𝔐.

This variant is connected to the one above.

γίνεσθαι B P^{74} ℵ D^{C} *rell* || γενέσθαι D* d 1. 330. 629. 1241. 1838. 2492 *pc;* $Theoph^{lat}$ Oec^{lat}.

B03 reads the present infinitive, like ἐκτείνειν, both of them dependent on ἐν τῷ. By the use of the aorist, D05 may be considering not so much the repeated occurrences of signs and wonders as the accomplishment *per se* of this manifestation of divine power, already identified as a particular marker of the Messianic age (2.19, 22; cf. 5.12).

4.31 (παρρησίας) παντὶ τῷ θέλοντι πιστεύειν D d E r w vg^{mss} mae; Ir Ephr Mss $gr^{sec.\ Beda}$ Aug || *om.* B P^{8} ℵ *rell.*

The detail in D05 may well conform ‘to the spirit of the recital’ but it is far from ‘naive’ (cf. Metzger, *Commentary*, p. 282). On the contrary, it corresponds to the theological implications of the ‘shaking of the place’ by which Luke symbolically expresses the disintegration of the Temple authority and rule in the lives of the Jesus-believers (see *Commentary*). The consequence of this profound change is that the community began freely speaking the message about Jesus, no longer within the confines of the Temple but to everyone who wished to believe.

Commentary

[a] 4.23 *The Community are Informed of the Sanhedrin's Decision*

4.23 The scene now changes as Peter and John leave the Sanhedrin and go back to join the other disciples, πρὸς τοὺς ἰδίους. This expression is used for the first time (cf. 5.18 D05, εἰς τὰ ἴδια; 21.6, εἰς τὰ ἴδια; 24.23, τῶν ἰδίων αὐτοῦ). The community that they go back to is a distinct group. Their existence has been apparent before (e.g. 2.47, ἐν τῇ ἐκκλησίᾳ; 4.4, the 5,000 believers), but the gap that has been gradually widening between the Jesus-believers and the rest of the Jews is finally made quite clear with this expression to 'their own'. The result is that they will become a group no longer under the authority of the Jewish leaders but under the authority of the apostles.

As they relate the decision of the Sanhedrin, mention is made only of the high priest and the elders, an indication of their dominance in the Council; and also telling of the fact that it is the threat to the Temple institution that lies at the heart of the Sanhedrin's anxiety about the apostles, a concern that would be of lesser importance to the scribes and the Roman authorities (see *Commentary*, 4.5).

[b] 4.24–30 *The Prayer of the Community*

A series of features distinguish this prayer from the speech of Peter (and John) in Solomon's Porch, demonstrating how the Jesus-believers are becoming more precise in their understanding of Jesus:

1. Peter invokes 'the God of Abraham, the God of Isaac and the God of Jacob', 3.13; the Jesus-believers invoke 'God who made the heavens and the earth and the sea and all that is in them', 4.24. A move has been made away from Jewish exclusivism to a more universal way of thinking.
2. Peter allows for the part played by ignorance in the role played by the Jews for the death of Jesus, 3.17; the disciples perceive the opposition to Jesus as intentional and acknowledge an informed collaboration between the Jews and the Romans, 4.27.
3. Peter exhorts his fellow Jews to repent as a means to escape the punishment due, even for acts committed in ignorance, 3.19; no pardon for the Jewish leaders is sought in the prayer of the community, but rather they ask God to pay attention to their threats, 4.29.
4. Peter speaks of the Messiah being retained in heaven until the time of his second coming, 3.20–21; the Jesus-believers focus on the power of the name of Jesus to act already, 4.30.

4.24 The prayer made in response to the news brought by Peter and John demonstrates a growing awareness of how God is working. The Bezan text spells out this realization. The prohibition placed on them by the Sanhedrin was not, therefore, perceived as a hindrance to Jesus' message but, on the contrary, as a positive development.

God is addressed as δέσποτα (cf. Simeon's prayer, Lk. 2.29), a term found occasionally in the LXX in referring to God. The further inclusion of ὁ θεός in the Bezan text removes any ambiguity, or possibility that prayer was made to Jesus, and echoes the two mentions of God in the introduction to the prayer in such a way as to ensure a distinction, with a sharpness that is unusual in Acts, between God and Jesus.[54] He is addressed above all as creator, in terms that resemble the description of creation in the Jewish Scriptures (Exod. 20.11; Ps. 146 [145 LXX].6). Paul has recourse to the same description in his address of the Greek community of Lystra (14.15) and in a slightly modified form in Athens (17.14). Thus, a universal tone is established which concords with the very gradual realization, already noted in Peter's speeches (see *Commentary*, 4.12, 22) and now communicated among the Jesus-believers, that God is not limited to the God of Israel.

4.25–26 There follows a citation from Psalm 2 which, despite its nationalistic tone in its original context, will be used to explain the current situation in a thorough re-working of its application. This same Psalm has already been cited by Luke according to the Bezan account of the baptism of Jesus (Lk. 3.22 D05 = Ps. 2.6 LXX), where its function was to identify Jesus as God's anointed, ὁ Χριστός, the Messiah.

The Psalm is attributed to David who is presented both as God's servant and as the mouthpiece of the Holy Spirit.[55] By virtue of each of these two characteristics, David is assimilated with Jesus, whom Peter referred to as the servant of God in his speech in Solomon's Porch (3.13, 26) and as receiving the Holy Spirit. In this way, what originally was said of David's situation could be interpreted as a prophetic communication about Jesus (see *Commentary*, 2.30, on David as prophet). Whilst the application of Davidic language to a contemporary ruler was not new,[56] the use that is about to be made of Psalm 2 in this instance will introduce a radical reversal of the original meaning.

54. For discussion of possible ambiguity when prayer is addressed to κύριος, see Read-Heimerdinger, *The Bezan Text*, pp. 278–93.

55. The notion that God spoke through the Holy Spirit is apparent in the *Targum of Isaiah* (*Targ. Isa.* 40.13a; 59.21); see Read-Heimerdinger, *The Bezan Text*, pp. 154–55.

56. The application to contemporary rulers of concepts originally referring to Davidic rule was not new; cf., e.g., Isa. 45.1–3 (Cyrus) and Ps. 2.1–9 (David), and see J. Tromp, 'The Davidic Messiah in Jewish Eschatology of the First Century BCE', in J.M. Scott (ed.), *Restoration: Old Testament, Jewish, and Christian Perspectives* (Leiden: E.J. Brill, 2001), pp. 179–201 [191–94].

The citation of Ps. 2.1–2 corresponds exactly to the LXX text that, in turn, renders the Hebrew faithfully. There are two pairs of doublets, the nouns and verbs of each arranged in chiastic form as the following literal translation shows:

> Why raged nations
> and peoples devised vain projects?
> Took position the kings of the earth,
> and the rulers gathered, with a common purpose
> against the Lord and his anointed.

In the Jewish Scriptures, it is the Gentiles who are being referred to in the two parallel expressions: neither the nations (ἔθνη) nor the peoples (λαοί) are of Israel. They are represented by their kings (οἱ βασιλεῖς) and their rulers (οἱ ἄρχοντες). In other words, in the original context, the Psalm represents a warning uttered against the Gentiles and their various leaders who are attacking the Israelites and their king, David; in so doing, they are rebelling against God. David has been appointed and anointed by God and made his son (Ps. 2.7); he has been established in Jerusalem, 'on Zion, my holy hill' (2.6).

The expression 'with a common purpose', ἐπὶ τὸ αὐτό, should be noted as this is the fourth (fifth, D05) time that it has been used in the early chapters of Acts (1.15; 2.1, 44, 46, 47 D05). On previous occasions it has served to mark out the disciples of Jesus from the rest of the Jews, as a group united in their solidarity against the opponents of Jesus (see *Commentary*, 1.15). For the first time, it refers here to a group united in their attack against the people of God (cf. 16.35 D05).

4.27–28 The Psalm is now used to interpret present events, but in the process the Scripture itself has to be properly interpreted, ἐπ' ἀληθείας, if its true meaning is to be understood.[57] Thus, on the one hand, Jesus is identified as the servant of God and anointed by him, taking the Psalm as a prophecy that, like other Psalms (cf., e.g., 3.25–30), foresaw his coming. Then, on the other hand, the opponents have to be identified. First, the 'kings' and 'rulers' are named as Herod and Pontius Pilate, two names that are expected enough. There follows the identification of their subjects

57. Luke uses ἐπ' ἀληθείας elsewhere to express the concordance between two things: a present event and a situation in the past (Lk. 4.25–28); an individual and the group he belongs to (Lk. 22.59); a present understanding of a previous declaration (Acts 10.34).

with an almost exact reproduction of the terms used in the Psalm but with a shocking twist: 'nations and peoples *of Israel*'.

What this means is that the enemies of 'the Lord and his anointed', although originally Gentiles who had operated a united campaign, have become a mixed alliance of Gentiles (Pontius Pilate and the nations) and *Jews* (Herod and the people of Israel). One element of each doublet in Ps. 2.1–2 has been assigned to Gentiles and the other to Jews. The Jews have joined forces with the Gentiles to oppose their own God and their Messiah. As far as can be determined, this is a radically new interpretation of the Psalm; a group of Jews, the Jesus-believers, have identified their own people as the enemies of God, working in collaboration with the Gentiles.

Again the chiastic pattern reinforces the message:

Herod
    Pontius Pilate
    the nations
the people of Israel

The Herod in question was Antipas who was tetrarch of Galilee and Peraea from 4 BCE–40 CE, appointed by and serving on behalf of the Romans. While not strictly speaking a king, he was part of the great Jewish Herodian dynasty, and the title 'king' was used of him (cf. ὁ βασιλεύς, Matt. 14.9; Mk 6.14, 22, 25, 26, 27). Although his mother was a Samaritan, he was brought up as a Jew and was recognized as Jewish (as opposed to a Gentile) ruler.[58] Pontius Pilate, for his part, was a Roman, serving as governor of Judaea from 26–36/37 CE (Lk. 3.1).

The place of this hostility is further identified as 'this city', Jerusalem, the equivalent of 'Zion, my holy hill' (Ps. 2.6), although this is not said to be the location of the enemy attack in the Psalm itself. It is though, of course, where Jesus was tried and put to death. Already in the Gospel, Luke underlined the connivance of Herod and Pilate when they collaborated over the trial of Jesus despite, he said, being enemies before that time (Lk. 23.12).[59] In the absence of any evidence for an actual quarrel

58. Despite questions raised over the Jewish identity of the Herods, it seems clear that they were regarded positively by the Jews themselves; see W. Horbury, 'Herod's Temple and "Herod's Days"', in *idem* (ed.), *Templum Amicitiae*, (JSNTSup, 48; Sheffield: JSOT Press, 1991), pp. 103–49; P. Richardson, *Herod: King of the Jews and Friend of the Romans* (Colombia, S. Carolina: University of South Carolina, 1996), pp. 305–13.

59. The word order of the Bezan text of Lk. 23.12 draws attention to the unexpected nature of the friendship between Herod and Pilate: ὄντες δὲ ἐν ἀηδίᾳ ὁ Πιλᾶτος καὶ

between the two, it may be surmised that the enmity he had in mind was more of a racial than personal nature, that between Gentile and Jew, and that the mention of it was to underline the theological significance of their newly found friendship which is not fully evident until now in his second volume.

The mention of Jerusalem has another function, for it serves as a key to point out the parallel between the trial of Jesus and the trial that has just taken place of his disciples. It was in Jerusalem that the leaders, headed by the 'rulers', had gathered to try the apostles (cf. this apparently superfluous detail in 4.5). This event was itself described by Luke in the words of Ps. 2.2: συνήχθησαν οἱ ἄρχοντες, that are repeated in the application of the Psalm here (cf. 4.26). As was pointed out earlier (*Commentary*, 4.5–6), the rulers present at the Sanhedrin meeting could perhaps be thought of as representatives of the Roman authorities, not as Jews. On this understanding, the reason why the Bezan text made a point of spelling out the agreement of those present at the meeting with the plan proposed (4.18) becomes apparent now as the disciples make much of the concordance of both Gentiles and Jews in their opposition to Jesus: at the trial that has just taken place, there has been agreement between the Jewish leaders and the Roman authorities about the need to silence the disciples.

Step by step, the prayer of the Jesus-believers reveals their developing awareness of the significance of Jesus' death. Seeing the hostile attitude of the Sanhedrin to the apostles' teaching and acting in his name, they display a greater consciousness of the awfulness of the role played by their own people in the death of Jesus, of their working together with the Gentiles to become opponents of God. The consequences of this realization will be that they become increasingly independent of the Temple authorities and organize themselves under their own leaders, the apostles.

That the tragic alliance between Gentiles and Jews against the Messiah can be identified in Scripture means that it has long been part of God's foreknowledge. The importance of ensuring all things that are contained within the will and control of God has already been seen in Peter's speeches (2.23; 3.18) and has been prepared for in this prayer by the opening address to God as the creator of everything. Even though the significance of the Scripture has only just been realized, since only now has it become clear that Jews themselves were included among the opponents of God, the authority of the Psalms is such that the event can confidently be attributed to God's plan and indeed, to his intervention, his 'hand'. The refer-

ὁ Ἡρῴδης ἐγένοντο φίλοι ἐν αὐτῇ τῇ ἡμέρᾳ.

ence to God's hand will be repeated at the end of the prayer (4.30) in a request for God to act now, another pointer in this series of parallels between Jesus and his disciples.

4.29 The similarity between the opposition to Jesus and the attacks on the apostles is made explicit by those praying as they go on from describing the situation to ask for God's assistance in the present circumstances to resist the threats made against them (cf. 4.21).[60] Far from intending to obey the Sanhedrin's orders they intend to announce God's word, for which they require divine empowering. Their request shows the conviction of the community that they are in line with God's will and that, in contrast, the Sanhedrin are not. Luke has so far portrayed the apostles as speaking with 'boldness' (μετὰ παρρησίας, 2.29; 4.13), a term that was seen to designate the openness given by the Holy Spirit to comprehend accurately the message of Jesus and to communicate it freely. Here, the community seek 'all boldness', to have full courage and confidence as they speak about Jesus.

4.30 The proclamation of the God's word is to be accompanied by his action, expressed by 'stretch out your hand',[61] with the reference to God's hand echoing the mention of his hand in the events concerning Jesus (4.28). This divine hand is mentioned by Luke in the context of creation (7.50), and protection (Lk. 1.66; Acts 11.21). Here, it is a question of healing, signs and wonders, characteristics of Jesus' own ministry (cf. 2.22) and it is in his name that they will continue to be performed. Signs and wonders, in particular, will be said to be manifested as a demonstration of God's power at various stages of the spread of the gospel message (5.12; 6.8; 14.3; 15.12).

[b′] 4.31 *Divine Ratification of the Prayer*

4.31 The new way of thinking expressed by the prayer is confirmed, even as the disciples are speaking, by manifestations of God's power. Events occur in precisely the reverse order in which they are requested in the petition made at the end of the prayer:

60. The link between the expository part of the prayer and the petition is marked by a connecting phrase typically used by Luke in such instances: (καὶ) τὰ νῦν, cf. 5.28; 17.30; 20.32; 27.22; καὶ νῦν, cf. 3.17; 10.5; 13.11; 22.16; 23.21; 26.6.

61. ἐκτείνω τὴν χεῖρα in Luke's work can signify either the onset of action (Lk. 5.13; Acts 4.30) or speech (Acts 26.1).

Petition:
  with all boldness
    speak your word
      signs and wonders
Response:
      the place is shaken
    they begin to speak the word of God
  with boldness

Each of the elements of the response has a particular significance. A tremor shakes 'the place', ὁ τόπος, in which they were praying. In Biblical language, which Luke adopts, 'the place' is none other than the Temple. If one retraces the steps of Jesus' disciples, it can be observed that so far they had been faithful to the Temple and its practices. After Jesus had left them, they had gone back to Jerusalem (in the religious sense, 1.12, cf. Lk. 24.52) and stayed there in the 'upper room', another phrase used by Luke to denote the Temple (cf. Acts 1.13 and Lk. 24.53), waiting for the Holy Spirit. They had continued to participate in Temple worship (1.14; cf. 2.2, 46; 3.1, 3, 8). At the first outpouring of the Holy Spirit, the Temple (this time referred to as 'the house', ὁ οἶκος, 2.2) had been filled with a tremendous noise.

Now, in a more dramatic way still, the place is shaken. On the one hand, this demonstration of God's power can be understood as a positive sign of his acceptance of the community's prayer: he has allowed them to perceive his presence. And yet the verb used, σαλεύω, is commonly found in the LXX to refer to a sign of God's action, but when referring to the earth or its foundations, always implies God's judgment or punishment (cf. Pss 17.8; 45.7; 76.19; 81.5; Sir. 16.18; Amos 9.5; Mic. 1.4; Nah. 1.5; Hab. 3.6) or the subsequent submission to his lordship on the part of these natural elements (cf. Pss 95.9; 96.4; 98.1; 113.7). In reality, the shaking of the Temple corresponds to the new consciousness of the disciples that all is not well with it. It symbolizes the fact that the Temple institution, which no-one would have ever dared to question, is in the process of being demolished because the Jesus-believers have recognized the role played by its authorities in the death of Jesus and have refused to accept their continued opposition to his power. The security of the ancient Temple system is crumbling, in a picture that recalls the tearing of the veil at the moment of Jesus' death (Lk. 23.45), a symbol of the removal of obstacles preventing access to God. Gradually, the attitude of the disciples towards the Temple has been brought into line with the significance of this earlier sign.

Whether or not the disciples have distanced themselves from the Temple in a complete or permanent fashion remains to be seen, but for the time being it has been sufficient for all to be filled with the Holy Spirit in a fresh outpouring. The expression used, with the aorist passive of the verb πίμπλημι, describes an event that is renewable rather than a lasting state of affairs (see *Commentary*, 4.8). The arrival of the Spirit is followed straightaway[62] by the proclamation of the word of God, with boldness. Note that it is not said that the disciples spoke with 'all boldness' as they had requested (see *Commentary*, 4.30) but only with some measure of boldness. It is no accident that Luke reserves the perfect fulfilment of the prayer to the end of the book when the message of Jesus has finally been understood and accepted in its entirety and without any obstacle (28.31).

On the first occasion, the arrival of the Spirit was followed by speaking in other languages about 'the great deeds of God' (2.11); this time it is followed by a proclamation of the word of God with no mention of other tongues. In Luke's writings, the expression the 'word of God' is used alongside the alternative expression the 'word of the Lord', each with a quite distinct meaning and application.[63] This is the first occurrence of either in the book of Acts, the 'word of the Lord' not appearing until 6.7 and then only in the Bezan text. When the 'word of God' is used with reference to Jews, as is the case at this stage in the narrative of Acts, it carries the same force as it has when it is used in Luke's Gospel of Jesus speaking with the people (Lk. 5.1; cf. 8.11, 15 D05; 8.21; 11.28). It is a general term meaning the precepts and commandments that God has already communicated to his people, although a fresh interpretation or focus may be given to them. It is not specifically the message about, or of, Jesus, which will be expressed by the 'word of the Lord'. For the time being, the Jesus-believers are concerned with expounding to the people in Jerusalem the word revealed by God through the Scriptures, no doubt explaining them in the light of the arrival of Jesus as Messiah in the way that has been seen in the apostolic speeches and the recent prayer, but not yet teaching Jesus' radically new message that goes beyond earlier expectations and beliefs. His disciples have yet to understand this properly for themselves.

Codex Bezae specifies that they spoke 'to all those who wished to believe'. This detail signifies a marked change from earlier attempts to

62. The immediate succession of being filled and speaking is indicated by the sequence of the aorist (ἐπλήσθησαν) and imperfect (ἐλάλουν) tenses.

63. The references in Luke-Acts to 'the word of God' and 'the word of the Lord', and their respective connotations, are examined in detail in Read-Heimerdinger, *The Bezan Text*, pp. 297–310.

convince anyone who was listening, on the day of Pentecost (everyone in Jerusalem, 2.14; cf. all Israel, 2.36), or in Solomon's Porch (3.11–12; 4.1–2), inviting them all to repent (2.38, 40; 3.19, 26) but with only some accepting what was preached (2.41; 4.4). Now, given the recognition that some were voluntarily hostile to hearing the truth and not prepared to accept it, the proclamation of the word is limited to those who have a desire to believe. It excludes no-one but neither is it indiscriminate.

With the shaking of the Temple and the second outpouring of the Holy Spirit, a new stage has been reached in the development of the Jerusalem church: all its members (the 120, 1.15; the 3,000, 2.41; the 5,000, 4.4) have been empowered by the Spirit in a sign of divine acceptance. There are clear resonances here of Jesus' promises of the help of the Spirit in times of persecution (Lk. 12.11–12; 21.12–19) and warnings of the highest powers being brought down (Lk. 21.26).

4.32–35. *Bridging (Second) Summary: The Community Ideal*

Overview

The concluding sequence of the third section of Acts forms a summary, just like the concluding sequence of the second section. Unlike the first summary, however, which clearly belonged within the structure of Section II, this second summary stands outside the structure because it acts as a bridge between the third and fourth sections of Acts. It draws together features of the third and anticipates the two sequences of the fourth.[64]

Structure and Themes

Three specific characteristics of the ideal community are briefly described, leading to a fourth general feature. It will be seen as the narrative develops that the description given here (and expressed in a series of verbs in the imperfect) represents an ideal, and in this sense is not to be taken as an account of a literal reality.

The first two points describe the unity of the believers, both spiritually and materially. The third point relates to the apostles and their witness. The last one is an overall comment describing all the members as highly

64. Different commentators of Acts consider different passages of the book to be summaries. Most identify three summaries: 2.41(2)–47; 4.32–37; 5.12–16, but there are variations (see, e.g., Barrett, I, 251, 159, 272–73). For reasons that will be explained at the appropriate places, we identify the second summary as finishing at 4.35 and the so-called third summary to be an integral part of the fourth and final section of this first stage of the book of Acts.

esteemed. This comment is then explained,[65] by picking up the second point about the sharing of possessions and giving more detail about how this worked in practice, including the leading role played by the apostles. The four steps can be represented thus:

[a] 4.32a The unity of the believers
[b] 4.32b The sharing of possessions
[c] 4.33a The witness of the apostles
[d] 4.33b–35 The respect for the community, for
[α] no-one was in need, because
[β] the proceeds of possessions sold were brought to the apostles, and
[α′] distributed to the needy

There are similarities and differences between this summary and the first one at 2.41–47. They are analysed in *Excursus* 4.

Two themes of the summary, the sharing of possessions and the leadership of the apostles, will be developed in the fourth section of Acts.

Translation

	Codex Bezae D05	*Codex Vaticanus B03*
[a]	**4.32a** The entire group of those who came to believe had one heart and one soul and there was no distinction among them.	**4.32a** The entire group of those who came to believe had one heart and one soul.
[b]	**32b** No-one said that anything of their possessions was their own, but they had everything in common,	**32b** No-one at all said that anything of their possessions was their own, but they had everything in common,
[c]	**33a** and with great power the apostles gave witness to the resurrection of the Lord Jesus Christ,	**33a** and with great power the apostles of the Lord Jesus gave witness to his resurrection,
[d]	**33b** and they were all held in high esteem. [α] **34a** There was, indeed, no needy person among them, [β] **34b** for all those who were owners of fields or houses took the initiative in selling them and bringing the money of those who were selling, **35a** and they placed it at the feet of the apostles. [α′] **35b** It was distributed to each one according to anyone who was in need.	**33b** and they were all held in high esteem. **34** There was, indeed, no needy person among them, for all the owners of fields or houses sold them and brought the proceeds of what had been sold, **35** and they placed it at the feet of the apostles. It was distributed to each as had need.

65. It is possible to interpret otherwise the explicative sentences of 4.34, both beginning with γάρ, as expanded comments on all four points made in the summary so far, rather than the last one alone.

Critical Apparatus

4.32 καὶ οὐκ ἦν διάκρισις ἐν αὐτοῖς οὐδεμία D de r mae; Cyp (Zen) Ambr | κ. οὐκ ἦν χωρισμὸς ἐν αὐ. τις E || *om.* B P^{74} ℵ *rell.*

If διάκρισις is taken with its meaning of 'discrimination', the absence of distinction among the believers noted by D05 signals a difference between the community of disciples and the hierarchical organization of the Temple. Alternatively, the meaning of 'quarrel' could be intended here (B-A-G).

οὐδὲ εἷς B P^{45} ℵ *rell* || οὐδείς D d 056. 88. 330. 618. 915. 1270. 1522. 2492; Chr $Theoph^{lem}$.

The separation of the words οὐδὲ εἷς without elision insists on 'not even one' (Bailly, 1420, C).

τι B (P^{45}) ℵ *rell*, *quicquam* d || *om.* D 2344. 2495* *pc.*

The omission of τι in D05 is probably due to haplography (ΤΙΤΩΝ).

(τῶν ὑπαρχόντων) αὐτῷ B ℵ A E 049. 056. 33. 88. 614. 1175. 1739. 1611. 2344. 2412. 2495 *al* || –τοῦ D P^{8} 2147 *pc* | –τῶν P 69. 104. 330. 462. 618. 1241. 1243. 1270. 1646. 1891. 2492 *pm* r; Cyp Zen | –τοῖς $Theoph^{lem}$ | *om.* 36. 945 *pc;* Chr.

The dative of the possessor (B03) focuses on the act of possessing, whereas the genitive (D05) focuses on the person to whom the things belong (B-D-R, §189.1).

ἔλεγον B* P^{74} 049. 945. 1241 *pc*, *dicebant* d || –γεν D P^{8} ℵ A B^{2} E H^{3} P Ψ 056. 33. 69. 462. 614. 945. 1175. 1241. 1270. 1505. 1611. 1739. 1891. 2412. 2495 𝔐.

The plural verb in B03 does not concord grammatically with the singular pronouns in this sentence for all that it corresponds to the many people of the community.

πάντα B D d $P^{8.45vid}$ *pc;* Chr $Theoph^{lem}$ || ἅπ– ℵ A E H^{3} P Ψ 049. 056. 33. 69. 88. 614. 945. 1175. 1270. 1611. 1739. 2344. 2412. 2495 𝔐.

The form ἅπαντα is intensive, signifying 'all manner of things'. The same variant is found in the equivalent context of the first summary at 2.44 where D05 also reads πάντα.

4.33 (οἱ ἀπόστολοι) τοῦ κυρίου Ἰησοῦ τῆς ἀναστάσεως B || τῆς ἀν. τ. κυ. Ἰη. Χριστοῦ D d E 323. 945. 1739. 1854. 1891. 2495 *al* e (ph) r arm^{mss} | τῆς ἀν. τ. κυ. Ἰη. P^{8} H^{3} P Ψ 049. 056. 33. 69. 88. 181. 462. 614. 927. 1611. 1646. 1243. 2147. 2344. 2412. 2492 𝔐 gig p t sy^{h} sa arm^{mss} aeth; Ir^{lat} $Orsiesius^{lat}$ Aug | τῆς ἀν. Ἰη. Χριστοῦ τ. κυ. (+ ἡμῶν 36. 307. 453. 610. 1678 vg^{cl}) ℵ A 36. 1175. 1409 *pc* vg.

The genitive phrase τοῦ κυρίου Ἰησοῦ in B03 should probably be taken with οἱ ἀπόστολοι, as its position is unjustifiably emphatic if it is understood as dependent on τῆς ἀναστάσεως (Ropes, *The Text*, p. 44). In D05 (as in א01, in a different order again), the phrase is dependent on τῆς ἀναστάσεως, and it includes the description of Jesus as the Messiah, characteristic of D05 when the setting is Jewish (cf. 2.30; 3.13; Read-Heimerdinger, *The Bezan Text*, 265–66).

4.34 (ἐνδεής) ἦν τις B | τις ἦν P^{74} א A 226^{c}. 323. 945. 1175. 1505. 1739. 1891 *al* || τις ὑπῆρχεν D P^{8} E H^{3} P Ψ 049. 056. 33. 69. 614. 1241. 1245. 1611. 2412. 2495 𝔐.

ὑπάρχω is frequently found as a synonym of εἶναι (B-A-G, ὑπάρχω, 2) and as an occasional *vl* between B03 and D05 (16.21; 17.27; 19.31, 40); the use of it here in D05 may be due to the use of εἶναι in the next line (see below).

(κτήτορες) ἦσαν D d || *om.* B P^{74} א *rell.*

This *vl* operates in conjunction with the two following ones.

(ἢ οἰκιῶν) ὑπῆρχον B D* $P^{8.45.74}$ $א^{2}$ *rell* || *om.* א* $D^{s.m.}$ d.

This *vl* is examined below.

πωλοῦντες ἔφερον τὰς τιμάς B $P^{8.74}$ א D^{B} *rell* || πωλ. καὶ φέροντες τιμάς D* (*vendentes et adferebant praetia* d).

The sentence is constructed differently in B03 and D05. B03 has as the subject ὅσοι ... ὑπῆρχον, qualified by the participle πωλοῦντες, with the main clause ἔφερον τὰς τιμάς... D05 has the same subject but with the verb ἦσαν; ὑπῆρχον is then the main verb followed by two parallel participles, πωλοῦντες and φέροντες, with the meaning of 'taking the initiative in doing something' (L-S-J, ὑπάρχω, A 3). The omission of the article before τιμάς in D05 may signify money in general rather than certain specified sums of money.

τῶν πιπρασκομένων B $P^{8.45.74}$ א D^{B} *rell* || τ. πιπρασκόντων D*, *quae ven<d>ebant* d.

B03 confirms that specific sums are meant with the passive participle: it was the sums of money corresponding to the things being sold that were brought. D05 has the active voice: the money of those who were selling.

4.35 ἑνὶ (ἑκάστῳ) D || *om.* B P^{45} א *rell, singulis* d.

The individual recipients are singled out with ἑνί in D05, in a phrase that occurs frequently in Luke's writings (Lk. 4.40; 16.5; Acts 2.3, 6; 4.35 D05; 5.18 D05; 17.27; 20.31; 21.19 B03, 26).

Commentary

[a] 4.32a *The Unity of the Believers*

4.32a The description that follows applies to all those who have become believers in Jesus since the beginning. Although there is every reason to think that the figures given previously (120, 1.15; 3,000, 2.41; 5,000, 4.4) have a symbolic rather than a literal value, it would seem that there is a large number of such believers.

Unity is experienced in two areas – the heart, as the faculty of thinking, and the soul, as the seat of the emotions – though they are unlikely to have been specified at the expense of others. Codex Bezae balances the positive comment with a negative one, equivalent in meaning but important to underline the absence of division in the community. This feature is seen, in the course of the present scene to be especially true of the total harmony between the apostles as leaders of the community and the members of themselves. It also prepares, by way of anticipated contrast, for the dissension among the believers that will be portrayed later in Acts 6.

[b] 4.32b *The Sharing of Possessions*

4.32b The pattern of positive and negative statements observed in the Bezan text of 4.32a is repeated, this time without variant, in the reverse order (negative/positive) as the second feature of the community ideal is described: no-one (emphasized in the AT) laid claim to their possessions, rather everything was shared. This particular feature will be expanded at the end of the summary.

[c] 4.33a *The Witness of the Apostles*

4.33a The third characteristic relates only to the apostles and to their witness of Jesus. The different position of the phrase 'of the Lord Jesus' in Codex Vaticanus and Codex Bezae does not affect the sense since in both texts it is said that the apostles' witness was powerful and that it concentrated on the resurrection or, as the Bezan text specifies, to the resurrection of Jesus the Messiah. It is typical of the Bezan text to associate the resurrection with the Messiah when a Jewish audience is involved (see *Critical Apparatus*). In respect of the content of the testimony, the wording is important and should be carefully noted: the apostles testified to the resurrection.[66] They continue to restrict the scope of their witness exclu-

66. The resurrection is emphasized as the object of the witness by its position at the end of the sentence, separated from 'the witness' by the subject of the verb: τὸ μαρτύριον οἱ ἀπόστολοι τῆς ἀναστάσεως.

sively to the resurrection (cf. 1.22; 2.24–32, 36; 3.15; 4.2, 10) which, whilst good as far as it goes, falls short of the commandment given by Jesus before he left them that they should witness to himself (1.8, see *Commentary*).

[d] 4.33b–35 *The Respect for the Community*

4.33b–35 A culminating point (expressed by the connecting word τε) is reached in the list of characteristics with the general comment that all were held in esteem. The word χάρις probably has this sense here,[67] rather than the alternative 'divine favour', in view of its use with this meaning in the first summary (see *Commentary*, 2.47). Justification is then given for this comment by explaining that everyone had what they needed ([α], 4.34a), adopting wording that echoes the promise recorded in the Torah: ὅτι οὐκ ἔσται ἐν σοὶ ἐνδεής (Deut. 15.4 LXX). The system adopted to this end is then described in detail, corresponding to the commandment contained in the same passage of Deuteronomy (15.11: 'You shall open your hand wide to you brother (τῷ ἀδελφῷ σου τῷ πένητι) ... to the needy'): property was sold and the proceeds put at the disposition of the apostles ([β], 4.34b–35a); the funds were then shared out to the needy ([α'], 4.35b). It is implicitly under the supervision of the apostles that this distribution was carried out, for the expression 'place at the feet' of someone (παρὰ τοὺς πόδας) is a sign of recognition of their authority or power.[68] It is questionable, in fact, whether they should ever have taken on the administration of the distribution for later, when a conflict becomes apparent over the fairness of the way it is carried out, the apostles will recognize that the task gets in the way of their preaching of the word of God (6.2, cf. 6.4).

The system of the rich sharing their goods with the poor was not, of itself, a new idea among the Jews for there already existed charity funds that were held at the Temple under the responsibility of the religious leaders.[69] It is therefore all the more significant that the Jesus-believers set up their own funds independently and that the apostles took responsibility

67. Zerwick and Grosvenor, *Analysis*, p. 363.

68. 'Fuß als Symbol der Macht oder Autorität einer Person: "zu *Füßen* legen" Mt 15,30; Apg 4,35.37; 5,2' (R. Bergmeier), in H. Balz and G. Schneider (eds), *Exegetisches Wörterbuch zum Neuen Testament* (3 vols.; Stuttgart-Berlin-Köln-Mainz: W. Kohlhammer, 1980, 1981, 1983), III, p. 344.

69. S. Safrai and M. Stern (eds), *The Jewish People in the First Century* (2 vols.; I. Philadelphia: Fortress Press, 1974; II. Assen-Amsterdam: Van Gorcum, 1976), I, p. 417.

for them in place of the central administration. The transfer of authority from official Jewish leaders to the apostles will be a principal theme of the next section of the book of Acts.

Excursus 4

Similarities and Differences between the First and Second Summaries

There are a number of elements in parallel between the two summaries, which must be carefully compared in order to note some slight, but significant, changes that have taken place in the period that has elapsed since the assembly (2.47 D05) of Jesus-believers was first described:

1. *The unity of the believers*: at 2.44a, it was described with the expression ἦσαν ἐπὶ τὸ αὐτό which, especially in Codex Bezae, conveys the sense of the solidarity of the believers in the midst of a larger group, that is, the Jews in general. Following the reaction of the Jewish authorities to the power of Jesus, however, the Jesus-believers are seen to withdraw from the official Jewish leadership to create their own distinct community under the leadership of the apostles. In this sense, they no longer form a minority group within, but opposed to, a larger one; rather they constitute a separate (because separated) community. (That is not to say that they no longer considered themselves to be Jewish; such a step is still a long way off.) Thus, their unity is described in different terms at 4.32a, with reference only to the inner cohesion of the group obtained through the unity of thought and feeling: ἦν καρδία καὶ ψυχὴ μία.
2. *The sharing of possessions*: in both summaries, it is said that everything was held in common ownership, the terms being reproduced exactly in Codex Bezae (πάντα κοινά, 2.44 // 4.32). The community ideal thus continues to be the same at both stages.
3. *The selling of goods*: mention is likewise made on each occasion of the selling of properties by those who possessed them, with Codex Bezae further clarifying at both places that only some people were in such a fortunate position (ὅσοι κτήματα εἶχον ἢ ὑπάρξεις ἐπίπρασκον, 2.45 D05 // ὅσοι γὰρ κτήτορες ἦσαν χωρίων ἢ οἰκιῶν ὑπῆρχον πωλοῦντες, 4.34 D05).
4. *The distribution of the proceeds of things sold*: initially, the distribution was undertaken by those who had sold their goods (διεμέριζον αὐτὰ πᾶσιν, 2.45). This later became the responsibility of the apostles (διεδίδετο δὲ [ἑνὶ D05] ἑκάστῳ, 4.35).
5. *The apostles*: in the first summary, they were portrayed as teaching the believers (2.42) whereas in the second they have turned their attention outwards and are engaged in witnessing, an activity that can be presumed to reach outside the community. Note that Codex

> Bezae made a point of specifying that the teaching of the apostles took place 'in Jerusalem' (2.42 D05), underscoring the continued attachment to the religious traditions and the central authority of the Temple. This attachment has been broken at the time of the second summary, by the force of events that followed.

Overall, it may be observed that progress has been made with respect to the relationship between the Jesus-believing community and the rest of the Jews. The gap between them is widening and, at the same time, the new community is beginning to turn outwards. The principal element of continuity resides in the sharing of goods, and in the chapters that follow the importance of this theme will continue to be developed.

IV. The Jerusalem Church
4.36–5.42

General Overview

The division between the sections at this point in the narrative is not as clear as it is elsewhere. The difficulty in identifying section boundaries can be explained by the fact that the passage of 4.36–5.42 does not so much introduce new material as develop the topics dealt with in the summary at the end of Section III. Commentators generally detect a third summary at 5.12–16 but there is a problem with this division for it causes a new section to start at 5.17, with an aorist participle in first position in the sentence. The initial position of the participle is, on the contrary, an indication that the following passage continues the situation of the previous one (from 5.12), with the same participants, in the same time frame and in the same place, the presence of the high priest and his circle being taken for granted all along.[1] If 5.17 started a new section, one would expect the new subject (the high priest) or some indication of time or place to be placed before the verb in order to introduce it (cf. 4.36, Ἰωσὴφ δέ...). Consequently, 5.12–16 is not to be regarded as a new summary but as the beginning of a narrative unit that extends to the end of Acts 5.

Structure and Themes

Following the summary describing the life of the Jerusalem church at the end of Section III, Luke selects the two features mentioned there, namely the sharing of goods (4.32, 34–35) and the witness of the apostles (4.33), and develops them in more detail. When the activity of the apostles provokes the hostility of the Temple authorities, this leads to their imprisonment, with consequences that dominate the narrative of the latter part of this section.

1. Levinsohn (*Textual Connections*, pp. 65–69) sets out the conditions for identifying a change of situation in the narrative of Acts. He goes so far as to argue that when a circumstantial participle is placed at the beginning of a sentence as in 5.17, it 'indicates continuity of situation and even unity of topic between the independent clauses that are contiguous to it' (p. 67).

The two aspects of the community life are dealt with separately, allowing two sequences to be distinguished, [A] (4.36–5.11) developing the theme of the sharing of goods, and [B] (5.12–42) expanding on the theme of the apostolic witness. Each of them moves rapidly through a series of dramas that are built around their own inner structure, indicated by [AA] and [AB], and from [BA] through to [BA′]:

[A]	4.36–5.11	The selling of a field
[AA]	4.36–37	A perfect example
[AB]	5.1–11	Two flawed examples
[B]	5.12–42	The testimony of the apostles
[BA]	5.12–16	Signs and wonders
[BB]	5.17–21a	The jealousy of the high priest
[BC]	5.21b–26	The calling of the Sanhedrin
[BC′]	5.27–33	The Sanhedrin meeting
[BB′]	5.34–40	Gamaliel's intervention
[BA′]	5.41–42	The liberation of the apostles

This section brings to a close the first stage of the narrative of Acts, ending on a positive note of triumph over the opposition of the hostile Jewish authorities. In the next stage, the topic of the administration of relief to the needy in the church will be taken up, introducing notes of discord between the two groups of the Jesus-believers, the Hebrews and the Hellenists. For the time being, in this section the Hellenists will be seen to be represented by Barnabas. Though this aspect of his identity is alluded to only obliquely, it is significant that he is an entirely positive figure.

[A] 4.36–5.11 *The Selling of a Field*

Overview

The first aspect of the bridging summary that is developed in this section is the selling of property and the sharing of the proceeds among the community (cf. 4.32, 34–35). The change in the tense of the verbs from the imperfect to the aorist signals the shift from a description of a general situation to an account of specific incidents.[2] The repetition of terms, or

2. It should not be thought that the relationship of the general summary to the specific incidents is one of an idealized description to the less than perfect reality. Rather, the summary presents the actual situation in the church, perfectly exemplified by Barnabas, and sets against that the account of people whose failure to live up to the new way of it resulted in their death.

their synonyms, taken up from the summary demonstrates the close relationship between the two passages. The following aspects of the bridging summary are found in the first sequence of this section:

Summary	Barnabas	Ananias	Sapphira
κτήτορες ... ὑπῆρχον	ὑπάρχοντος αὐτῷ	κτῆμα, ὑπῆρχεν	
χωρίων	ἀγροῦ/χωρίου	τοῦ χ–ου	τὸ χ–ον
πωλοῦντες, τῶν πιπρασκο μένων	πωλήσας	ἐπώλησεν, πραθέν	ἀπέδοσθε
ἔφερον/φέροντες	ἤνεγκεν	ἐνέγκας	
τὰς τιμάς	τὸ χρῆμα	τῆς τιμῆς x 2	τοσούτου x 2
ἐτίθουν	ἔθηκεν	ἔθηκεν/ἔθετο	
παρὰ τοὺς πόδας τῶν ἀποστόλων	πρὸς/παρὰ τ. π. τ. ἀπ.	παρὰ τ. π. τ. ἀπ.	πρὸς τ.π. αὐτοῦ

Structure and Themes

On one level, this sequence describes first a positive example of generosity and sharing in the community before relating in more detail the story of a man and his wife who pretended to follow the example but were not sincere about it. On another level, the account stands as a real-life parable, expressing the conflict between the old order of Israel and the new order of the church. The characters of the parable are members of the Jerusalem community – Barnabas who represents the perfect acceptance of the new order, and the married couple, Ananias and Sapphira, who represent the destructive attempt to cling to the old while embracing the new at the same time (see *Excursus* 6 on the symbol of the field).

The positive example is presented with very little circumstantial detail in one sentence. The two negative examples are presented in two parallel accounts that follow the identical patterns except for the inversion of the last two elements:

[AA]	4.36–37	A perfect example: Barnabas
[AB]	5.1–11	Two flawed examples
[a]	5.1–2	Ananias
[b]	5.3–4	Peter's rebuke
[c]	5.5a	Ananias' death
[d]	5.5b	Great fear on everyone
[e]	5.6	The young men bury Ananias
[a′]	5.7	Sapphira
[b′]	5.8–9	Peter's rebuke
[c′]	5.10a	Sapphira's death
[d′]	5.10b	The young men bury Sapphira
[e′]	5.11	Great fear on the church and everyone

Translation

	Codex Bezae D05	*Codex Vaticanus B03*
[AA]	**4.36** Joseph, who had been named Barnabas by the apostles (which means in translation 'Son of Encouragement'), and who was from Cyprus, a Levite by birth, **37** since he had a field he sold it and brought the proceeds and placed them at the feet of the apostles.	**4.36** Joseph, who had been named of Barnabas by the apostles (meaning 'Son of Encouragement'), and who was a Levite, a Cypriot by birth, **37** since he had some land he sold it and brought the proceeds and placed them at the feet of the apostles.
[AB]		
[a]	**5.1** A certain man by the name of Ananias, together with his wife, sold a property **2** and took something for himself out of the money (his wife knew about it, too), and he brought a certain part of it and placed it at the feet of the apostles.	**5.1** A certain man, Ananias by name, together with his wife, sold a property **2** and kept something back from the money (his wife knew about it, too), and he brought a certain part of it and placed it at the feet of the apostles.
[b]	**3** Peter said to Ananias, 'For what reason did Satan dare you to test the Holy Spirit, and to keep something back for yourself from the price of the field? **4** Was it not still yours in the meantime, and even when it was sold was it not in your authority? How did it happen that you put it in your heart to do this deed of wickedness? You lied not to men but to God.'	**3** Peter said 'Ananias, for what reason did Satan dare you to test the Holy Spirit, and to keep something back from the price of the field? **4** Was it not yours while it remained in your possession, and even when it was sold was it not in your authority? How did it happen that you put this deed in your heart? You lied not to men but to God.'
[c]	**5a** As soon as he heard this, he at once fell down and died.	**5a** Hearing this, he fell down and died.
[d]	**5b** And great fear came on everyone when they heard.	**5b** And great fear came on everyone when they heard.
[e]	**6** The response of the young men was to wrap him up, carry him out and bury him.	**6** The response of the young men was to wrap him up, carry him out and bury him.
[a′]	**7** There was a three hour interval; then his wife, not knowing what had happened, came in.	**7** There was a three hour interval; then his wife, not knowing what had happened, came in.
[b′]	**8** Peter said to her, 'I will ask you, did you really sell the field for such and such?' She stated, 'Yes, for that much.' **9** Peter said to her, 'Why did it agree with you to put to the test the Spirit of the Lord? Listen, the feet of those who	**8** Peter responded to her, 'Tell me, if you sold the field for such and such?' She said, 'Yes, for that much.' **9** Peter said to her, 'Why was it agreed between you to put to the test the Spirit of the Lord? Listen, the feet of

	have just buried your husband are at the door and they will carry you out.’	those who have just buried your husband are at the door and they will carry you out.’
[c′]	**10a** And she immediately fell at his feet and died.	**10a** She immediately fell at his feet and died.
[d′]	**10b** The young men came in and found her dead; they wrapped her up, carried her out and buried her next to her husband.	**10b** The young men came in and found her dead; they carried her out and buried her next to her husband.
[e′]	**11** And great fear came on the whole church and on everyone when they heard these things.	**11** And great fear came on the whole church and on everyone when they heard these things.

Critical Apparatus

4.36 ἀπὸ (τῶν ἀποστόλων) B P[8] ℵ A E H[3] P Ψ 049. 33. 69. 88. 104. 614. 945. 1175. 1241. 1243. 1270. 1505. 1646. 1739. 1891. 2412. 2492 *pm* || ὑπό D 056. 323. 440. 547. 618. 927. 1245. 1611. 1854. 2147. 2344. 2495 *al.*

ἀπό gradually supplanted ὑπό to introduce the agent of a passive verb. D05 is consistent in using the older preposition unless the verb is one of separation (Read-Heimerdinger, *The Bezan Text*, pp. 183–87).

ἑρμηνευόμενον B* P[8] || μεθ– D P[74vid] ℵ A B[2] E P Ψ *rell.*

Whereas the verb on its own (B03) simply means 'interpret', the prefix μετα– signifies the change from one language to another (Zerwick and Grosvenor, *Analysis*), and so 'translate'.

Λευίτης, Κύπριος τῷ γένει B P[8] ℵ *rell* || Κύπρ., Λευ. τ. γέν. D d.

The varying order of words alters somewhat the account given of Barnabas' origins. According to B03, he is a Levite, of Cypriot race or origin; according to D05, a Cypriot, of Levite descent. The first supposes that he was a proselyte while the second considers him to be of a Jewish family (Read-Heimerdinger, *The Bezan Text*, pp. 83–84).

4.37 ἀγροῦ B ℵ *rell*, *ager* d || χωρίον (–ου D[B]) D* e p.

The term χωρίον is used by D05 to establish parallels between Barnabas and Judas (1.18, 19) on the one hand, and Ananias and Sapphira (5.3, 8) on the other. The connections between these characters are weakened in B03 and the theological implications of the parallels obscured.

παρὰ (τοὺς πόδας) B D d P[57.74] A H[3] P Ψ 049. 056. 33. 69. 614. 945. 1175. 1611. 1739. 2412. 2495 𝔐 || πρός ℵ E 36. 94. 180. 307. 327. 453. 1844 *pc* e p; Theoph[lem].

παρὰ τοὺς πόδας is the expression also read at 4.35 and 5.2, all three occurrences referring to the same action of placing proceeds at the disposition of the apostles. At 5.10, in contrast, πρὸς τοὺς πόδας will be used because it is a different situation of Sapphira falling down at Peter's feet. πρός in ℵ01, like ἀγρός noted above, removes a key that links Barnabas to the incident involving Ananias and Sapphira that follows.

5.1 Ἁνανίας ὀνόματι B P74 ℵ E H3 P Ψ 049. 056. 88. 614. 945. 1175. 2412. 2495 𝔐 || ὀν. Ἁν. D d A 36. 69. 453. 522. 876. 1108. 1518. 1611. 1765. 1838. 2138 *pc* gig r t vg; Chr.

In Luke's work, the usual position of ὀνόματι is before the name of the person (Read-Heimerdinger, *The Bezan Text*, pp. 85–88). By disrupting the usual pattern, B03 draws attention to the name. In the subsequent development of the episode, however, the events will be viewed as more important than the participants in B03 (*The Bezan Text*, pp. 132–33).

5.2 ἀπὸ (τῆς τιμῆς) B ℵ *rell* || ἐκ D.

The use of ἀπό in B03 following νοσφίζομαι, meaning that Ananias and Sapphira 'held back for themselves something from the money paid', is repeated without variant in the next verse. ἐκ in D05 is used as a partitive genitive with the sense that they 'took something for themselves out of the money paid' (cf. d05: *subtraxit*, 5.2; *intercipere te* 5.3).

ἔθηκεν B P8.74 ℵ *rell* || ἔθετο D.

B03 uses the active voice of τίθημι, 'placed', as at 4.37; D05 uses the middle voice, 'placed for himself', as at 5.4.

5.3 ὁ (Πέτρος) B P8.74 ℵ A Ψ 33. 69. 323. 945. 1175. 1270. 1739. 1891. 2344 || *om.* D P 049. 056. 614. 1241. 1611. 2412. 2495 𝔐.

The omission of the article by D05 is in line with Luke's usual practice (deduced from the non-variant readings) of using this device to bring back a participant into the narrative (Read-Heimerdinger, *The Bezan Text*, pp. 123–25).

Ἁνανία B P8.74 ℵ *rell* || πρὸς Ἁνανίαν D Ψ *pc* d w vgmss | πρ. αὐτόν· Ἁνανία E *pc* (p) r syh**.

In sentences introducing speech in Acts, the addressee is introduced either with the name in the dative case or in the accusative preceded by πρός, as here in D05. The choice between them is not simply a matter of stylistic preference but is a means to identify the relationship between speaker and addressee (Read-Heimerdinger, *The Bezan Text*, 176–82). The latter expresses a personal, direct relationship, whereas the former idiom is more impersonal and distant. The D05 reading is in keeping with the consistent interest the Bezan text displays in the relationships between the participants of the narrative.

In B03, the addressee is not specified but the name of Ananias occurs in the vocative at the beginning of Peter's address to him.

ἐπλήρωσεν B D d P[8] ℵ[2] A E H[3] Ψ 049. 056. 0189. 33[vid]. 69. 614. 945. 1175. 1611. 1739. 1891. 2344. 2412. 2495 𝔐 e gig p* r t sy co arm; Or Marc CyrJ GrNy Did Epiph[pt] Chr Cyp Lcf Ambst Ambr Qu Fulg Mss gr[*sec. Beda*] || ἐπήρωσεν ℵ* 330. 808 *pc* | ἐπείρασεν P[74] ar c dem p[2] (ph) ro w vg; Ath Epiph[pt] SevGab | ἐπώρωσεν 2492; Chr[pt].

The expression shared by B03 and D05, 'filled your heart' with the verb πληρόω, has been much debated because of its harshness but it is appropriate in the context, especially since it translates an expression from the Hebrew Bible meaning 'to dare' (see Metzger, *Commentary*, pp. 285–86). The ℵ01reading, meaning 'disabled, maimed' (πηρόω), could have arisen by the accidental omission of the λ, or in error for ἐπώρωσεν, 'harden', as at Jn 12.40 (cf. Boismard and Lamouille, II, 33–34).

τὸ πνεῦμα τὸ ἅγιον B P[8.74] ℵ *rell, spiritui sancto* d || τὸ ἅγ. πν. D; Epiph.

The form of the reference to the Holy Spirit in Luke's work varies according to the context in which the Spirit is mentioned (Read-Heimerdinger, *The Bezan Text*, pp. 145–72, esp. 165–67, 168–69). The form adopted by B03 is that generally used in teaching and explanatory contexts; the form of D05 is used in the Bezan text only with reference to believers in Jesus, who have a personal relationship with the Spirit.

(νοσφίσασθαί) σε D d A H[3] P Ψ 049. 69. 2495 𝔐 || *om.* B P[8.74] ℵ A E 056. 88. 104. 323. 440. 547. 614. 927. 945. 1175. 1270. 1611. 1739. 1891. 2344. 2412 *al.*

The repetition of the pronoun by D05 is not necessary for the sense but it underlines Ananias's guilt.

5.4 μένον B P[74] ℵ[2] D[B] *rell, manens* d | ἔμενον ℵ* || μέσον D*.

The D05 reading could be an error for μένον, but it could quite easily be a valid reading meaning 'in the meantime' (B-A-G, μέσος 3), that is, between the sale of the land and the handing over of the money to the apostles.

ἐν τῇ σῇ ἐξουσίᾳ B P[8.74] ℵ *rell, in tua potestate* d || ἐν τ. ἐξ. D.

The similarity of vowels in consecutive words could have caused σῇ to have been overlooked by the copyist of D05 (Delebecque, *Les deux Actes*, p. 46).

τὸ πρᾶγμα τοῦτο B P[8] ℵ *rell* || ποιῆσαι (+ τὸ D[B]) πονηρὸν τοῦτο D*, *facere dolose rem istam* d sy[p] (sa mae) | ποι. τὸ πρᾶγμα τοῦτο P[74].

In B03, the noun phrase is the direct object of the verb ἔθου. In D05, the object is the infinitive ποιῆσαι, which is followed by its own object. If πονηρόν is read as a noun, qualified by the demonstrative adjective τοῦτο, the article inserted by Corrector B is indispensable. However, if πονηρόν is understood as an adverb instead, as it is by d05, then τοῦτο is a demonstrative pronoun and no article is necessary.

ἐψεύσω B $P^{8.74}$ ℵ D^{B} *rell* || –σου D*.

The variation reflects the alternative endings of the 2nd person singular of the aorist middle-passive.

5.5 ἀκούων B $P^{8.74}$ ℵ *rell*, *audiens* d || ἀκούσας D 547.

B03 (pres. part.) presents Ananias as falling down dead while Peter was still speaking, whereas D05 (aor. part.) views Peter as having finished.

ὁ (Ἀνανίας) B P^{8} ℵ A E H^{3} P 049. 33. 69. 88. 1175. 1243. 1245. 1270. 1891. 2147. 2344 *al* || *om.* D Ψ 056. 383. 522. 547. 614. 618. 876. 913. 915. 945. 1108. 1241. 1518. 1611. 1739. 1765. 1838. 2138. 2298. 2412. 2492. 2495; $Oecum^{lem}$.

For the second time (cf. 5.3 above), B03 retains the article before the name of a person where D05 omits it. The omission of the article here is not expected since Ananias is an established character in the episode, and it thus causes special attention to be drawn to him.

παραχρῆμα (πεσών) D d (E) p || *om.* B $P^{8.74}$ ℵ *rell.*

The adverb is unnecessary in B03 since the present participle was used at the beginning of the sentence (see above) to refer to Ananias' dying while Peter was speaking, unlike D05 which reads the participle in the aorist.

5.8 ἀπεκρίθη δὲ πρὸς αὐτὴν Πέτρος B P^{74vid} ℵ A 0189^{vid}. (36). 1175. 2344 *pc* $vg^{st.ww}$ | ἀπ. δὲ πρ. αὐ. ὁ Π. P^{8} 69. 88. 945. 1646. 1739. 1891 || εἶπεν δὲ πρ. αὐ. ὁ Π. D d it vg^{cl} sy co; Lcf | πρ. ἣν ὁ Π. ἔφη E | ἀπ. δὲ αὐτῇ ὁ (– Ψ 2147 *pc*) Π. H^{3} P Ψ 049. 056. (614). 1505. 2412. 2495 𝔐.

There is a tendency for B03 to use the verb ἀποκρίνομαι where D05 has a verb of speaking (5.8, 29; 10.46; 15.13; 21.13) or the equivalent (11.9). As an introduction to a dialogue, it may reflect Semitic practice (Boismard and Lamouille, II, 34), but it spoils the parallelism between Peter's speech to Sapphira and that to Ananias if the present one is treated as an independent dialogue. In the D05 text, the speeches are introduced in identical fashion (cf. 5.3), except for the anaphoric article in D05.

B03 typically omits the article before Peter as he is about to speak (Read-Heimerdinger, *The Bezan Text*, pp. 133–34). D05 does not usually draw attention to the speakers in this way when the reference is anaphoric, unless the speech is a presentation of the gospel.

Εἰπέ μοι, εἰ B $P^{8.74}$ ℵ *rell, Dic mihi, si* d || Ἐπερωτήσω σε, εἰ ἄρα D (mae).

The verb ἐπερωτάω is found frequently in Luke's work, especially in the text of D05 (Lk: x 17 [x 20 D05]; Acts x 2 [x 6 D05]). The expression Ἐπερωτήσω σε, εἰ... is found twice in the D05 text of Luke's Gospel (6.9 D05; 20.3 D05) (cf. C.A. Phillips, *The Bulletin of the Bezan Club* 8 [1930], pp. 23–24, as cited by Metzger, *Commentary*, p. 286). The construction εἰ ἄρα is found at Acts 5.8 D05; 7.1 D05; 8.22; 17.27.

τοσούτου τὸ χωρίον B $P^{8.74}$ ℵ *rell, tanti praedium* d || τὸ χωρίον τοσούτου D.

The theme of the field (τὸ χωρίον) is central to this story and is the motif that establishes parallels with other narratives (cf. 4.37 above). Attention is drawn to the term by displacing it nearer the beginning of the sentence (Read-Heimerdinger, *The Bezan Text*, pp. 68–70), suggesting that D05 recognized its significance and wished to highlight it in this way.

ἡ δέ B $P^{8.74}$ ℵ D^{A} *rell* || ἡ δή D* d.

The emphatic particle δή is rare in the New Testament outside Luke's writings (Matt. 13.23 [but τότε D05]) where it is found several times: Lk. 2.15; Acts 5.8 D05 (δέ ℵ01 B03); 6.3 A02 (δέ ℵ01 B03; om. D05); 13.2; 15.36. Here in D05 it presents Sapphira's affirmative reply with greater force (B-A-G, δή 1).

5.9 Τί ὅτι B D, *quid utique* d P^{74} *rell* || Τί οὖν ὅτι ℵ.

The conjunction in ℵ01 softens the abruptness and unexpected nature of Peter's second question. Without it, the expression τί ὅτι repeats the wording of Peter's question to Ananias in v. 4.

συνεφωνήθη B P^{74} ℵ *rell* || –φώνησεν D d.

The passive voice of συμφωνέω in B03 is used impersonally to mean 'Why was it agreed between you' (Zerwick and Grosvenor, *Analysis*). The active voice may also be used impersonally in D05: 'Why did it agree with you', or else the implied subject is Satan: 'Why did he agree with you.'

(τὸ πνεῦμα) κυρίου B ℵ A E H^{3} P Ψ 049. 33. 614. 945. 1739. 2412. 2495 𝔐 || τοῦ κυρ. D 056. 927 || τὸ ἅγιον P^{74} 1522. 1838 *pc* geo.

The anarthrous reference τὸ πνεῦμα κυρίου is found as a set phrase in the LXX (cf. Lk. 4.18 quoting Isa. 61.1), where the Lord means Yahweh. The articular expression allows τοῦ κυρίου to refer to Jesus, and the expression is thus equivalent to Peter's reference to the Holy Spirit in his question to Ananias, especially in its more intimate, Bezan form (see above, 5.3).

5.10 ἔπεσεν δέ B $P^{57.74}$ ℵ *rell* || καὶ ἔπ. D, *et cecidit[que]* (– $d^{s.m.}$) d* gig (*ceciditque* h) p r t vg^{mss}; Chr Lcf.

The immediacy of the consequence of Peter's words is expressed by the conjunction καί for, unlike δέ, it presents Sapphira's death as expected and as part of the same narrative unit as the speech (Levinsohn, *Textual Connections*, pp. 83–84).

ἐξενέγκαντες B P^{45vid} ℵ *rell, cum extulissent* d || συστείλαντες ἐξήνεγκαν καί D (sy^{p}).

The parallelism between husband and wife is reinforced in the D05 text by the inclusion of the detail that her body, like Ananias's (cf. 5.6), was wrapped before being carried away for burial.

Commentary

[AA] 4.36–37 *A Perfect Example: Barnabas*

4.36 In the AT, Barnabas is introduced into the story for the first time at this point. The presentation is unusually abrupt with no ἀνήρ τις or any other such phrase that normally accompanies the inital introduction of a character into the narrative of Acts. The absence of an introductory phrase is not a problem in the Bezan text, however, for this is the second mention of Barnabas who has already been presented at 1.23 D05, as the first of the candidates put forward by Peter to replace Judas (see *Commentary*, 1.23). Barnabas will play an important role in the events of Acts, notably as the companion of Paul. The Bezan text generally has a greater interest in him than the AT, setting him up as a model disciple and a foil to show up the weaknesses of Paul.[3]

The information that the narrator provides concerning Barnabas is extremely succinct but of the greatest importance. At 1.23 D05, as here, his real name is Joseph and Barnabas is the name given to him by the apostles. The translation, or meaning, of the Aramaic name in Greek, rendered here in English as 'Son of Encouragement', can be explained in various ways, for the Greek word παράκλησις has a wide semantic field encompassing the senses of 'comfort', 'consolation', 'exhortation' or 'encouragement', so determining the underlying Aramaic word is not straightforward. For reasons that are discussed in *Excursus* 5, the explanation that fits best with Luke's Greek translation is that it is a Hellenization of the Jewish name 'Bar-Nahama', a name not uncommon among first-century Palestinian Jews of which the root נחם signifies 'to comfort, to

3. The portrait of Barnabas presented by the Bezan text is examined in Read-Heimerdinger, 'Barnabas in Acts: A Study of his Role in the Text of Codex Bezae', *JSNT* 72 (1998), pp. 23–66.

console'.[4] Apart from the close correspondance in meaning between the Greek παράκλησις and the Aramaic verb, the notion of 'comfort' or 'consolation' calls to mind Joseph, the son of Jacob, who was known in Jewish tradition as the 'Son of Consolation'. It is precisely with this ancient heroic figure that the character of Barnabas is assimilated according to the Bezan text of Acts 1, the translation Luke gives of his name being one of the keys to recognizing that Barnabas is modelled on the ancestral figure of Israel's past (see *Commentary*, 1.23 and *Excursus* 5).

At 1.23 in Codex Bezae, Joseph was 'being called' (τὸν καλούμενον, present participle) Barnabas, indicating that he was acquiring his function at a point when Jesus had left them for the last time and when the role of comforter was certainly appropriate. Now, the function is established ('had been called', ἐπικληθείς, aorist participle), and it is made clear that it was the apostles who were responsible for acknowledging his role. The esteem in which they held him will be apparent in later episodes of Acts as he introduces Paul to them and acts on their behalf in the Antioch church (cf. 9.27–28; 11.22–24). The rendering in English of the Greek translation of Barnabas, υἱὸς παρακλήσεως, as 'Son of Encouragement' brings together the aspects of both consolation and exhortation expressed by the verb and united in the ministry of Barnabas among the Jesus-believers (cf. 11.23, 26 D05).

The matter of Barnabas's origin is treated differently in the AT and Codex Bezae. According to the former, he is a Levite but Cypriot 'by race', τῷ γένει, but in the Bezan text the order is inverted so that he is a Cypriot but Levite by race. Since γένος refers to the biological descent of a person, the blood relationship,[5] in the first case the family of Barnabas would be from Cyprus and he would therefore apparently be a proselyte Jew. In the Bezan text, his family would be Jewish and living in the Diaspora; the fact that he was from Cyprus is a secondary factor as far as his identity as a Levite is concerned. On the question of a Levite owning fields, see on 4.37 below.

The connection of Barnabas with Cyprus establishes him as a Hellenistic Jew, not from the land of Israel as the apostles were. The mention of Barnabas's origin anticipates the quarrel between the Hebrews and the

4. The most commonly advanced alternative suggestion for the origin of 'Barnabas' is that it was derived from the Aramaic word for prophet (נביא), reflecting the aspect of 'exhortation' expressed by παράκλησις (Barrett, I, pp. 258–59; S. Brock, 'ΒΑΡΝΑΒΑΣ ΥΙΟΣ ΠΑΡΑΚΛΗΣΕΩΣ', *JTS* 25 [1974], pp. 93–98).

5. Louw and Nida, 10.1, γένος.

Hellenists related in Acts 6. The name of Cyprus will be picked up in Acts as a place of openness to the Gentiles (11.20–22 [indirectly]; 13.4; 15.39), in the mission to whom Barnabas will be chosen by the Holy Spirit to play a leading role (13.1–2).

4.37 Barnabas had a field which seems, at first sight, to be contradictory with his being a Levite since under the rules given at the time of the distribution of the land a Levite did not have a share in the land but was given cities and fields, in addition to tithes, by the other tribes (Num. 35.1–8). Though the cities could be redeemed by individual Levites, the fields could not (Lev. 25.34). It may be that in the person of Barnabas, it is being demonstrated that these ancient laws are being revoked here and that the new community of believers are free from the restrictions of the Torah.

Quite apart from the connection between Barnabas's status as a Levite and the selling of his field, there is another significance in the mention of his tribal origin. It was the Levites who substituted for the first-born of each of the other tribes, being dedicated to the Lord in their place (Num. 3.40–45). They thus had an important role to play in representing the people of Israel before God. In the same way, Barnabas shows himself to be wholly dedicated to the service of Jesus in putting his money at the disposal of the Jesus-believers and submitting to the authority of the leaders chosen by him. He is a model of perfect surrender to God and dependence on him. Further significance still in the detail that Barnabas was a Levite is derived from his assimilation with Joseph the patriarch (see *Excursus* 5).

The word used in the Bezan text to refer to Barnabas's field, χωρίον, not only prepares for the contrasting example of Ananias and Sapphira (cf. χωρίον 5.4, 8) but also is an echo of the story of Judas, parallels that are obscured by the AT synonym in 4.37 of ἀγρός. It was seen in the case of Judas (see *Commentary*, 1.18–19) that the field Judas bought with the payment for his betrayal of Jesus and in which he died has a symbolic value that goes beyond the literal reality. It represents his portion in Israel according to the ancient division of land among the twelve tribes (see *Excursus* 6). This symbolic meaning of the field enhances the significance of the selling of the field by Barnabas. First, a comparison between Judas and Barnabas is established by the repeated use of the word χωρίον in the Bezan text. The comparison between the two is already made at 1.23 D05 when Barnabas is proposed as a worthy replacement for Judas as the Twelfth apostle; on both counts, it has the effect of showing Barnabas as a positive model. Concerning the field, whereas Judas used his betrayal payment to buy back land (after giving up everything to follow Jesus), Barnabas renounces his possessions for the good of the followers of Jesus.

Secondly, the paradigm of Joseph on whom Barnabas is modelled serves to bring out his generosity even further. Joseph had one field of his own, given to him by Jacob just before his death (Gen. 48.22; Jos. 24.32; cf. Jn 4.5). This one field was the only portion of the land of Israel that belonged to Joseph personally. Joseph Barnabas sells his sole possession and gives up his share in the heritage of Israel. In placing the proceeds at the disposition of the apostles, he accepts their leadership for the new community (for the significance of the feet as symbol of authority, cf. Lk. 7.38 [x 3]; 8.35, 41; 17.16; 20.43; Acts 4.35; 22.3)

Finally, comparison is made between Barnabas and Ananias/Sapphira, the one giving up all that he has and the latter holding back a part of their 'field'. The underlying message of their insincere action will be examined below.

Barnabas should be seen not just as a character in his own right but as a representative of those among the Jesus-believers who accepted their growing separation from the traditional Temple authority and entrusted the apostles with the care and organization of their community. The fact that he stands alone as a perfect example against two negative counterparts may be an indication that those whom he represents are in the minority.

[AB] 5.1–11 *Two Flawed Examples*
[a] 5.1–2 *Ananias*

5.1 Ananias is introduced also as a representative, with the indefinite pronoun τις which typically marks out a person as a type in Luke's writings. He is not alone but is the husband of Sapphira, so part of a married couple. Their Hebrew names identify them as belonging to the Hebrew section of the community, unlike Barnabas who was a Hellenist (see above; cf. 6.1). Their unity, and at the same time their independence from each other, is expressed by the reports concerning each one which repeat the same facts yet remain distinct accounts.

The property that they sold (κτῆμα) belongs to them jointly and picks up the word κτήτορες ('owners', 4.34) used in the bridging summary that is being expanded in the present passage. So far, everything is in order.

5.2 The pair continue to act in unison as Ananias, with his wife's knowledge, keeps back (ἐνοσφίσατο) some of the proceeds and delivers only a part to the apostles. The Greek word evokes the story told in Joshua 7 of the Israelites who, when the city of Jericho was taken at the point of entry into the Promised Land, kept for themselves (ἐνοσφίσαντο, Jos. 7.1 LXX) some of the objects in the city that God had ordered to be set apart either for destruction (6.17–18) or for the treasury (6.19). Achan from the tribe of Judah is the one singled out in the story, and when his deed was discovered and he confessed to it (7.19–21), he and all his family were stoned to death and burned, along with his possessions including the forbidden objects (7.25).

The evocation of this event in the Scriptures is, nevertheless, limited; it is a means with which to underline the seriousness (for the individual and for the community) of keeping back a part of the money and to remind the hearers of Acts that the divine judgment executed on Ananias and his wife has a precedence. There are too many differences between the two incidents, both in their form and in their underlying intent to claim that the story of Achan acts as a paradigm with which to interpret the present story, or that the ancient event is now being re-enacted.[6]

In placing the proceeds of the sale at the feet of the apostles, Ananias is demonstrating his apparent acceptance of their leadership and authority. The drama arises out of the fact that his acceptance is not complete since he has retained a part of the money. The middle voice of the verb 'placed' in the Bezan text expresses well the interest he had in carrying out this act of pseudo-submission.

[b] 5.3–4 *Peter's Rebuke*

5.3 Peter challenges Ananias as he brings the money to the apostles, acting as usual as their spokesman. He asks him a series of three questions, though apparently without expecting a reply. The first uses the expression 'fill your heart' which has a Hebrew equivalent, meaning 'dare' (cf. Eccl. 8.11 LXX; Jn 16.6). The seriousness of his deception, aswell as its spiritual nature, is indicated by the mention of both Satan, as the one who 'dared' Ananias, and the Holy Spirit as the one who was lied to. Peter's charge recalls the description at 4.31 of all the community of Jesus-believers

6. D. Marguerat (*The First Christian Historian. Writing the 'Acts of the Apostles'* [trans. K. McKinney, G.L Laughery and R. Bauckham; SNTS, 121; Cambridge: Cambridge University Press 2002]) enumerates the reasons why the story of Achan cannot be viewed as a model for the Ananias/Sapphira episode (pp. 172–76). He proposes that the real scriptural parallel is that of Adam and Eve, a suggestive idea that would need to be explored by examining more thoroughly the forms of the Genesis story in 1st century Judaism. His narrative analysis of the story of Ananias and Sapphira in general, exploring as it does the purpose of the account within the wider narrative context, has several points of interest.

being filled with the Holy Spirit (the identical expression τὸ ἅγιον πνεῦμα, reserved by the Bezan text of Acts for reference to the Spirit in relation to believers, is used at both places in Codex Bezae). It is because the believers have had this experience that the deception is an act against the Spirit. As in the case of Achan whose deception affected the whole of the people of Israel (Jos. 6.18; 7.1, 25), so in the case of Ananias, his deed will affect all the community (cf. Acts 5.5).

5.4 Two more questions follow: the first insists on Ananias's rights over his own field – his freedom to sell it and, if he did, to do what he wanted with the money. In other words, he was under no compulsion to follow the example of people such as Barnabas. Not doing so, however, would mean that he could not be part of the group of Jesus-believers, since it was a mark of the community that they did have all things in common (cf. the description 4.32–35). So the point of Peter's rhetorical question is not just that Ananias could have done what he wanted with his field or the proceeds from it, but more that he was under no obligation to remain with the Jesus-believers. If he did not want to join in the pooling of resources or hand over his money to the responsibility of the apostles and recognize their authority, he could have left the new community and remained among the rest of the Jews under the authority of the Temple.

It is clear that the wrongdoing is the secret retaining for himself of part of the proceeds of the sale, but the problem is not an ethical one concerning generosity and love. It goes deeper than that, for what Ananias has done is to appear to have been joining in with the Jesus-believers but not wholeheartedly. The next question is similar to the one Peter began with, asking again how Ananias could have let this happen. The Bezan text insists on the wickedness of the deed.

Peter's questions show to what extent he is taken aback by the deception and also thoroughly perplexed as to what has made Ananias act in the way he has. Why would he want to look as if he were a believer in Jesus without fully participating in the community life and without fully accepting the authority of the apostles? The obvious explanation would seem to be that he had not fully made up his mind to become a disciple of Jesus but wanted to hold on to the life he was used to, clinging on to something of the old order of Israel, without the Messiah and without the Holy Spirit. His belonging to the old system is symbolized by his field which he only relinquishes in part (see *Excursus* 6). There is, in other words, a conflict of interests between the new life and the old, the authority of the Temple and that of the apostles. Now that the Jesus-believers are organized separately from the Temple, they are more clearly distinguished from the rest of the Jews than they had been hitherto, and thus Ananias's hesitating between the two shows up in a way that it would not have done earlier.

Peter's charge that Ananias has lied to God, not to men, corresponds to his apparent acknowledgment of Jesus as Messiah (seeming to join with the other believers) whilst not fully giving himself to the implications of that belief. Lying to the Holy Spirit has the gravest of consequences with no remission possible (cf. Lk. 12.10) and Peter's accusation means that his death is inevitable.

[c] 5.5a *Ananias' Death*

5.5a Ananias does not die at the hand of the people but simply falls dead (cf. Sapphira, 5.10; and Herod, 12.23). The AT has him die even as Peter is speaking whereas in the Bezan text he dies as soon as Peter has finished. In neither case, however, is it Peter's words that produce the death – this is not the reverse of a miracle in which the words spoken cause a healing to occur. Rather, Peter recognizes the nature and the extent of Ananias's deception, prompted by Satan and in opposition to God, and it is God himself who intervenes to protect his people from such evil.

Bearing in mind that Ananias represents a section of the Jesus-believers (cf. 5.1), his death means the death of a whole group, those who were unwilling to fully separate themselves from the old system and accept the leadership of the apostles. In a way death is not so much a punishment as an inevitable consequence of such a double life.

[d] 5.5b *Great Fear on Everyone*

5.5b The news of the incident creates fear in everyone who heard about it – the unqualified noun πάντες suggests that people outside the group of believers as well as those inside were affected but for the moment they are not distinguished. The only qualification is that fear affected people when they heard about what had happened, the implication being that Sapphira was not among them since she is not aware of the situation when she arrives (5.7).

[e] 5.6 *The Young Men Bury Ananias*

5.6 The scene should probably not be viewed as some kind of church meeting in which the young men stood up to deal with the body of Ananias. Although the participle ἀναστάντες is used literally elsewhere by Luke, the metaphorical sense of a 'reaction' on the part of the young men is more appropriate here (cf. 5.36, 37; 7.18; 20.30):

1. No mention of a meeting of the community has been made, only of the apostles (5.2).
2. No mention is made of anyone else seeing the incident, only of people who heard of it (5.5).
3. Sapphira, for one, was not present but comes in later (5.7).
4. The church as a whole is not mentioned until the end (5.11).

What Luke seems to have in mind is rather a gathering of the apostles as the administrators of the funds to be distributed to those in need (cf. 4.35).

The word used for those who took out the body to bury it is, in fact, the comparative, 'the younger men' (οἱ νεώτεροι), implying that Ananias was one of the older members (οἱ πρεσβύτεροι) probably in the literal sense (cf. Lk. 15.12–13, 25; 1 Pet. 5.5), though not necessarily so. The fact that it is the younger members of the community who take the initiative in removing the dead body is not without significance: it is they who are the life of the recently formed community, they who 'bury', quite literally, the past with its attachment to the old values and systems.

[a′] 5.7 *Sapphira*

5.7 Sapphira is mentioned for the third time as the wife of Ananias (cf. 5.1, 2). The three hour interval between Ananias's death and his wife's arrival may be a literal duration but it is also a metaphorical one, introduced as it is by ὡς (see *Commentary*, 1.15). There are several possibilities as to the nature of the comparison:

1. Three is a number of completeness throughout the Scriptures, an indication that Sapphira had all the time necessary to consider her action, without being taken unawares by what follows.
2. Three hours was the duration between the times of Jewish cultic prayer.[7]
3. An analogous situation arises in the scene describing Peter's denial of Jesus when, between his second and third denial, a single hour is said to have elapsed (διαστάσης ὡσεὶ ὥρας μιᾶς, Lk. 22.59). Several similarities exist between the two passages, including the figure three in the number of times Peter denied Jesus.[8]

Sapphira, it should be noted, came in of her own accord, having not even heard of her husband's death.

7. Marguerat (*The First Christian Historian*), p.166.

8. Other features in common are: παραχρῆμα, συνειδυίης – μὴ εἰδυῖα (οὐκ οἶδα x 2), συνεφωνήθη (ἐφώνησεν).

[b′] 5.8–9 *Peter's Rebuke*

5.8 The role played by Peter is more deliberately active in the Bezan text than in the AT, contrasting with the comparatively passive role he played in the earlier healing of the lame man, when he responded to events rather than taking the intiative (cf. 3.3, 12). It is a measure of his progress that he is very much in charge in the present scene and directs events. Again in the Bezan text, the question he asks Sapphira is emphatically expressed, 'Did you really...' with the mention of the field in focus (see *Critical Apparatus*). The verb 'sell' is in the plural, viewing the action as a joint one rather than considering the responsibility of Sapphira alone. The verb itself is noteworthy: in place of the more usual πωλέω (4.34, 37; 5.2) or πιπράσκω (2.45; 4.34; 5.4), ἀποδίδωμι is used. It is found elsewhere in the New Testament only at Acts 7.9, with reference to the selling of Joseph into Egypt. In the LXX, it is found in the same context (Gen. 37.27, 28, 36; 45.4, 5) and, among other places, for the selling of the fields by the Egyptians in the time of famine under Joseph's supervision (Gen. 47.20, 22). The idea in all of these instances is not just that things were sold as a commercial enterprise but that the person 'rid themselves of something', whether in a positive or a negative sense. This is relevant to the significance of the selling of the fields – beyond providing funds for the relief of the poor, the people who sold their fields were doing away with their properties.

Sapphira's reply is qualified in the Bezan text as being particularly affirmative (see *Critical Apparatus*).

5.9 It is possible that with both the passive form of the AT and the active of the Bezan text Satan is the implied agent/subject of the verb 'agree', as he was the explicit subject of the verb in Peter's rebuke to Ananias (cf. 5.3). This interpretation is perhaps suggested by the expression 'put to the test the Spirit of the Lord', especially in Codex Bezae where it means the Spirit of Jesus (see *Critical Apparatus*). The idea that simply concealing the true value of the property could in itself put God to the test seems exaggerated, but it makes sense if the underlying nature of the wrongdoing is borne in mind. Pretending to follow the practice of the Jesus-believers whilst secretly retaining part of the value of their field is equivalent to dividing their loyalties, appearing to accept the consequences of following Jesus but continuing to maintain their adherence to the traditional ways of Israel (see on 5.3–4 above and *Excursus* 6). The outcome is bound to be disaster for the two are incompatible, being the extremes of the Jewish law, on the one hand, and of the Spirit on the other. In other circumstances, Peter will again speak of imposing the law (on Gentiles) as putting God to the test (cf. 15.10).

Peter's warning of the imminence of her death is not what causes Sapphira to die – that is, it does not have a performative force, no more than his words to Ananias (cf. on 5.5 above) – but rather it demonstrates Peter's prophetic gift and his accurate understanding of God's view of the situation.

[c′] 5.10a *Sapphira's Death*

5.10a The death of Sapphira is as immediate as that of Ananias, with the word 'immediately' repeated in the case of the Bezan text (cf. 5.5 D05). She falls 'at his feet', where her husband had placed the money from the sale of the field, so that the punishment occurs at the place of the crime (cf. Judas, 1.18–19); in both cases, the feet represent the apostolic power and authority.

[d′] 5.10b *The Young Men Bury Sapphira*

5.10b Those who buried Ananias, having initially been introduced as the 'younger men', are now referred to as 'the young men' (οἱ νεανίσκοι), a sign that the use of the comparative in the first instance was deliberate. They carry out the same procedure for Sapphira as for her husband, burying her beside him.

Throughout this incident, attention has been drawn to the fact that it concerns a married couple. Three times the word 'man' is used (ἀνήρ, 5.1, 9, 10) as also the word 'wife' (γυνή, 5.1, 2, 7); three times their joint action is underlined by means of the preposition 'together' (σύν), either alone or in a compound verb (5.1, σὺν Σαπφίρῃ; 5.2, συνειδυίης; 5.9, συνεφωνήθη). Since they appear not as individuals but as representatives of a certain type among the Jesus-believers, the implications of their unity and, at the same time, completeness is that it is an entire section of the community that is destroyed. A stage is thus marked in the development of the community of believers, a time when, as the Temple authorities had been rejected because of their opposition to Jesus and the apostles took upon themselves the leadership of the community, a considerable number were united in their unwillingness to give up the old in order to wholeheartedly embrace the new, and so brought death upon themselves. In this way, the community was purified from those who did not devote themselves entirely to adherence to the Messiah and at the same time was protected from the danger of accommodating their faith in him to the traditional views and attitudes dictated by the Jewish authorities.

[e′] 5.11 *Great Fear on the Church and Everyone*

5.11 The fear caused by the sudden death of Ananias is aroused again by the death of his wife, as people hear the news. It is mentioned this time at the end of the account so that it is the closing note on which the story overall ends.

This time, all the members of the church are included, too, among those who are moved by fear. This means all the believers who were in Jerusalem, no-one having yet entered the community from outside the city. In the AT, the church is mentioned for the first time here in the book of Acts, at precisely the point when the Jesus-believing community has separated itself from the Temple, replacing the ἐκκλησία of Israel as the assembly of the people of God which is referred to throughout the LXX. In Codex Bezae, the word ἐκκλησία was already used at 2.47 when it was said that 'the Lord added to the church daily those who were being saved' (see *Commentary*, 2.47). Since it is not certain that the believers themselves were aware at that point that they constituted a community alongside, or outside, the 'assembly of Israel', the comment would seem to be being made with hindsight or, as it were, from the Lord's point of view.

All the Jews generally, then, inside and outside the church were afraid when they heard the news of what had happened to Ananias and Sapphira. These were no ordinary events and the authority and power of the apostles must have seemed, indeed, strange and frightening.

Excursus 5

Joseph Barnabas and Joseph the Son of Jacob

From the first mention of Barnabas in Acts at 1.23 in the text of Codex Bezae, Luke leaves clues to show that this character is modelled on the son of Jacob of the same name. The nature of the comparison between them is not typological in the sense that Joseph the patriarch prefigured Barnabas the disciple of Jesus. That understanding of scriptural models is essentially a later, Christian one. The assimilation of Barnabas and Joseph in the Bezan text of Acts is rather of a Jewish type, whereby Barnabas re-enacts events that occurred in the life of Joseph whose place in the Torah establishes him as a paradigmatic figure (see *General Introduction*, V.10).

In order to appreciate the significance of the assimilation, account must be taken not just of the Genesis narrative but of the stories of Joseph in later tradition. For the Targums to the Pentateuch, in addition to the writings that are now referred to as apocryphal (especially the *Testaments of the Twelve Patriarchs*, together with the Jewish legends and traditions that emerged in the first century CE in such works as the romance *Joseph and Aseneth*), all bear ample witness to the importance that Joseph acquired in the history of Israel over the course of the centuries and that was continued by the Rabbinic teachings.[9] In the intertestamental period, Joseph who had been sold into slavery in Egypt by his jealous brothers, is praised and honoured above all the other sons of Jacob. He is the heroic figure without fault or failing, the supreme example of a wise, pious and generous man who, despite having being badly treated himself, served in an exceptional capacity to comfort and encourage his father and brothers when they joined him in Egypt.

Two outstanding qualities are attributed to the person of Joseph in Jewish tradition. On the one hand, he is Joseph the Righteous, the Virtuous, the 'tsadik' (יוסף הצדיק), which is found as a standard epithet in Jewish tradition (see *4 Macc.* 2.2; cf. Acts 1.23, Ἰοῦστος). On the other hand, he is a source of comfort and encouragement, his reputation in this respect being due in large measure to the fact that even after his father's death, he never turned against his brothers for having sold him to the Egyptian merchants. The consolation he offered them in their bereavement, at the time when they feared that he would treat them harshly, is perceived as remarkable. Mention is made of the fact in Gen.50.15–21 where it is said that 'he reassured them and comforted them' (v. 21). The verb in the LXX text is παρακαλέω, in Hebrew נחם, the verb that could be Hellenized as (Bar)-nabas.[10]

If Barnabas is Joseph but also a Levite, he has a dual identity in terms

9. For a thorough and highly skilful treatment of the Joseph traditions, see J.L. Kugel, 'The Case Against Joseph', in T. Abusch, J. Huehnergard and P. Steinkeller (eds.), *Lingering Over Words* (Atlanta: Scholars Press, 1990), pp. 271–87. The subject is developed in more detail in his *In Potiphar's House. The Interpretative Life of Biblical Texts* (Cambridge, MA.: Harvard University Press, 2nd edn, 1994).

10. A later Rabbinic Midrash develops the theme of Joseph's consoling presence in Gen. 50.21: 'Now if Joseph who spoke mild words to the hearts of the tribal fathers and thereby comforted them, when the Holy One, blessed be he, comes to comfort Jerusalem, how much more so: "Comfort, comfort, my people" (Isa. 40.1)' (*Gen. R.* 100.9). Cf. comments made from a Jewish perspective by J. Neusner in his edition, *Genesis Rabbah: The Judaic Commentary to the Book of Genesis* (Atlanta: Scholars Press, 1985), III, p. 391: '[This Rabbinic Midrash] provides an important link to the eschatological salvation of Israel, so that the present scene prefigures Israel's future history.' Joseph, in other words, is viewed as the forerunner of divine consolation on a messianic scale. Cf. *Targ. Ps.-J. Gen.* 50.21 where the theme of Joseph's consolation is also more extensively developed than in the Hebrew text.

of assimilation with the patriarchs of Israel.[11] Far from being self-contradictory, this combination of historical templates strengthens and enriches the patriarchal typology, for an important aspect of the life of Joseph was his marriage into the Egyptian family of Potiphera, priest of On, through his wife Aseneth (Gen. 41.45).[12] The identification of Joseph with the priests of Egypt through his marriage to Aseneth leads to seeing another significance in Barnabas's selling of his field. It is especially in the sharing out of the land in Egypt, once Joseph is joined there by his father and his brothers, that his wisdom and fairness become most apparent (Genesis 47, see notably the expanded comments and the exegesis of the passage in the Targums and *Midrash Rabbah*). He makes careful arrangements for the Egyptians to sell their land in order to buy food with the profits so that no-one goes hungry; even when the famine is at its worst, everyone is provided for thanks to the skilful management of Joseph as Pharoah's overseer. Only the priests (Egyptian, that is) do not have to sell their land in order to buy food for, not being farmers, they receive a fixed income from Pharaoh – the point is made three times in the space of a few sentences (Gen. 47.22–26). In contrast, Barnabas, despite his Levitical (i.e. priestly status), does sell his land in order to contribute to the well-being of the community.

The Hellenistic origin of Barnabas (from Cyprus, 4.36) is another element in his identity that connects him with Joseph, the hero of Jews living in a foreign land, who kept himself pure even though he was in exile.[13]

11. If Peter's proposal that he should replace Judas (representing Judah, see *Commentary,* 1.16–26) is taken into account, Barnabas is assimilated, in fact, with three patriarchs: Judah, Joseph and Levi. This trio has a place in the history of Israel as the sons to whom Jacob gives the inheritance of the first-born, Reuben: the double portion of land (Joseph), the kingship (Judah) and the high priesthood (Levi) (*Targ. Neof. Gen.* 49.3). See J.L. Kugel, *Traditions of the Bible. A Guide to the Bible as it was at the Start of the Common Era* [Cambridge, MA.: Harvard University Press, 1998], pp. 463–66).

12. The effect of Joseph's marriage into the priestly family of Egypt on the history of the Jews, in particular the connection with the Jewish high priestly family of the Oniads, would be a profitable line of investigation for understanding the importance of Joseph for first-century Judaism, including the Jesus-believers (cf. the importance of Joseph in Stephen's speech in Acts 7).

13. As the 'land of the Kittim', Cyprus is a place that arises in legends surrounding Joseph. Another possible significance may derive from the consonants of the name in Hebrew, כפר, which are the same as those in the word 'atonement'.

Excursus 6

The Symbol of the Field

The first sequence [A] of the fourth section of Acts (IV) presents a drama that is in many ways repugnant to those accustomed to the notion of a merciful and benign God. The idea of people being struck dead for 'lying to the Holy Spirit' looks on the face of it like the response of a cruel and vengeful God, reminiscent of Old Testament scenes that one hoped were over for good with the revelation by Jesus of God as a father showing grace and love to his children instead of harsh punishment. The worst of it is that the crime, if we are honest, seems hardly serious enough to warrant death. Surely other Christians have cheated and lied in church matters and yet have continued to live despite their wrongdoing. What, then, is to be made of this scene?

The answer lies in the essential theme of the episode which is the selling of land and the handing over of the proceeds to the apostles. Certainly, there is every reason to suppose that the selling of property actually took place among the early Jesus-believers, and that its purpose was to enable all the members of the community of Jesus-believers to benefit from the wealth of the few landowners among them. The story that contrasts the positive example of Barnabas with the failure of Ananias and his wife to live up to it is a striking illustration of the themes of generosity versus self-interest. That there is, however, another, theological, significance to the action is indicated by the recurrence of a key term in this and other episodes of the Acts narrative, the word for a 'field', χωρίον. The word is found in 5.3 with reference to Ananias, and 5.8 with reference to Sapphira (in a position of salience in the wording of the Bezan text); in Codex Bezae, it is also found with reference to Joseph Barnabas at 4.37 D05 (ἀγρός AT), thus making clearer the parallel between the two examples. But there have been earlier mentions of a 'field', firstly at 1.18–19 with reference to Judas and again in the second summary at 4.34; and there will be one more in Acts referring to the lands belonging to Publius, the chief man of the island of Malta, at 28.7. An examination of the context of these other references will be helpful to clarify the connection between them.

The mention of a field in Acts 1, the first occurrence of the term in Luke's work, is repeated three times in Greek and once in Aramaic. In a narrative aside, Luke speaks of the χωρίον that Judas bought with the money that he gained for betraying Jesus to the Jewish leaders (ἐκτήσατο χωρίον, 1.18, cf. Lk. 22.5) but, because he died in it, that field (τὸ χωρίον ἐκεῖνο) became known as a 'field of blood' (χωρίον αἵματος, 1.19), for which Luke then gives the Aramaic equivalent, 'Akeldemach'. The underlying theological significance of Judas' field, representing his heritage in Israel and expressed in part through the play on words in Aramaic, has been discussed in the *Commentary* (1.18–19). The force that the word χωρίον acquires at this first occurrence will inform subsequent occurrences which will, in turn, reflect further nuances back onto the Judas episode.

The second mention of a field arises in the second summary, where it is said that anyone who owned fields (κτήτορες χωρίων, 4.35) sold them in order for the proceeds to be distributed among all the believers. Two further closely related notions are common to the Judas passage, the second summary, and the particular examples of Barnabas and Anania/Sapphira: the action of 'buying' (κτάομαι, cf. ἐκτήσατο, 1.18; κτήτορες, 4.34; κτῆμα, 5.1, and its correlate 'selling': πωλέω, 4.34, 37; 5.1; πιπράσκω, 4.34; 5.4; ἀποδίδομαι, 5.8), and the noun 'payment' (μισθός, 1.18, cf. ἡ τιμή, 4.34; 5.2, 3; τὸ χρῆμα, 4.37). These parallels are by no means coincidental but serve, on the contrary, to compare and contrast the actions of the various characters. On the one hand, Judas attempted to buy back his heritage in Israel by betraying the Messiah. On the other, the believers in Jesus gave up their fields at the point when they relinquished the traditional authority of the Jewish leaders and began to organize themselves under the leadership of the apostles. The old patterns and systems that had provided for so long the defining structure of the identity of Israel as the people of God are disintegrating.

Barnabas perfectly exemplified the reununciation of the traditional system of Israel's leadership and the acceptance of the apostolic leadership in its place. In Codex Bezae, he was already introduced as a possible replacement for Judas (1.23), the upright counterpart to his wickedness: he was Joseph, the son of Jacob who, when sold into slavery by his brothers, kept himself pure in Egypt and became the model of holiness and righteousness (see *Excursus* 5). Now in 4.36–37, it becomes clearer how much Barnabas stood for everything that was opposite to Judas' treachery. For Joseph had been given just one field by his father on his deathbed (Gen. 48.22; Jos. 24.32; cf. Jn 4.5) since his own share in Israel was divided between his two sons. But Joseph Barnabas sells his one field and places all of the proceeds at the disposition of the apostles for the sharing out among the community. In contrast, Ananias and Sapphira do not bring all the proceeds but hold onto part of them. The symbolic meaning of the field allows this holding back to be interpreted theologically, as a failure to renounce totally the old religious system and to trust the apostles as the chosen leaders of the Jesus-believers. The comparison with Judas is thus made more apparent: Judas sought to return to the ancient, pre-Messianic understanding of Israel by denouncing the Messiah, and Ananias and Sapphira sought to cling on to something of this notion.

The symbolic interpretation of the field is seen in the final example in Acts, though this time the context is one of paganism and not Judaism. The scene relating the encounter between Paul, with his companions, and Publius, the leading citizen of Malta (28.7–10), is closely linked to the bridging summary of 4.32–35 as well as the opening sequence of Section IV by a series of repeated words and phrases: he is described as possessing fields with the same expression used of Joseph Barnabas (ὑπῆρχεν χωρία τῷ πρώτῳ τῆς νήσου, 28.7); Paul's company are presented with many gifts, using the plural of the term referring in the earlier passages to the 'price' or 'proceeds' (πολλαῖς τιμαῖς ἐτίμησαν ἡμᾶς, 28.10a; cf. 4.34; 5.2, 3); and they were given all that was necessary (τὰ πρὸς τὰς χρείας, 28.10b; cf. 4.35). Many further echoes are heard of the earlier passages,[14] a deliberate attempt on the part of the narrator to draw them together. The effect of this technique is to show how Publius, when Paul first met him, had a rich heritage in his pagan traditions and values. However, with the miracles of healing performed on his father and then on the rest of the inhabitants of the island (28.8–9), even though Publius' fields were not expressly sold, Paul and his companions were nevertheless the beneficiaries of 'many gifts' (πολλαῖς τιμαῖς) in exactly the same way as the first communities of Jesus-believers benefitted from the sale of the fields owned by their members.

In short, the word χωρίον serves as a peg on which these diverse episodes hang, forming a connection between the passages and causing them to mutually inform and interpret each other.

Two points may be noted with reference to Barnabas and Ananias/ Sapphira. On the one hand, Barnabas is a Jew from the Diaspora and thus a 'Hellenist' rather than a 'Hebrew'. The favourable way in which he is presented prepares for the approval shown by the narrator of the Hellenists generally after Acts 6, for it is they who are the first to move out from Jerusalem (8.1 D05) and to speak to those who were on the fringes of Jewish society (8.5, 26; 11.20 D05). On the other hand, Ananias and his wife represent those believers who were more firmly attached to the

14. There are numerous other links between the passages in addition to the ones listed: 28.7a // 4.31; 28.7a // 5.1; 28.7b // 5.7; 28.8 // 5.12; 28.9 // 5.16; 28.10a // 4.34; 5.3; 28.10b // 4.35.

traditional order, who wanted to be part of the new community but without giving up all of the past. Significantly, it is the 'younger people' who remove each of them in turn when they die and it is they who bury, as it were, the past.

It should not be thought that the selling of the fields by the Jewish Jesus-believers represents a complete break with Israel at this stage in the development of the church, for they will continue to be enlightened as God intervenes in their evangelizing activity to show them further aspects of the traditional beliefs – notably the separation of the pure and the impure, preventing the admission of Gentiles – that have been changed by the coming of the Messiah. For the time being, it is the status of the twelve tribes of Israel that has been recognized as changed, replaced by the leadership of the apostles which produces a new sense of belonging and freedom.

[B] 5.12–42 *The Testimony of the Apostles*

General Overview

The new sequence relating the apostles' activities in Jerusalem is juxtaposed with the last observation of the previous sequence, namely that fear was experienced among both the Jesus-believers of the church and the people. Exactly the same juxtaposition is found in the first summary as the narrator describes the effect of Peter's preaching at Pentecost and associates the 'signs and wonders' worked by the apostles with the fear 'on every soul' (see *Commentary*, 2.43).

What is new here, compared with the earlier description, is that the apostles are seen performing signs and wonders in the Temple. This leads to the culmination of the conflict between the high priest, together with the aristocratic Sadducee party from which his family came, and the apostles as leaders of those Jews who believed in Jesus as the Messiah.

This sequence brings the first stage of the apostles' mission to a close as their witness in Jerusalem is completed.

Structure and Themes

The theme of the apostles' witness is picked up from its mention in the second summary (4.33), just as the matter of the selling of fields was taken up in the previous sequence of this section. The placing of the 'hands of the apostles' in first position before the verb in the opening sentence in Greek shows that there is a change of subject at 5.12 from what has gone before. A new sequence or section should not be seen as starting at 5.17 for reasons explained in the *General Overview* to Section IV. In addition to the structural indications that show continuity between 5.16 and 5.17, there is also an important continuity of theme since allusions to the Exodus start at 5.12 and are maintained (more clearly in the Bezan text) throughout the rest of the section (discussed in detail in *Excursus* 8).

Initially, the focus is on the apostles' testimony by signs and wonders, in the Temple. At the end of the sequence, the apostles are back in the Temple, but their activity by now is teaching and preaching about Jesus the Messiah. What has happened in the meantime is their imprisonment by the high priest and his circle and their release by the angel of the Lord, leading to their re-arrest and appearance before the Sanhedrin. It is in response to the instructions that they moved on from performing miracles in the Temple to teaching 'all the words of this life'.

This sequence divides naturally into a series of sub-sequences stet will each be treated separately. At the centre of the section stand two passages relating the calling of the Sanhedrin and their meeting:

[BA] 5.12–16 Signs and wonders through the hands of the apostles
[BB] 5.17–21a The jealousy of the high priest
[BC] 5.21b–26 Preparations for the Sanhedrin meeting
[BC′] 5.27–33 The Sanhedrin meeting
[BB′] 5.34–40 Gamaliel's intervention
[BA′] 5.41–42 The liberation of the apostles

[BA] 5.12–16 *Signs and Wonders through the Hands of the Apostles*

Overview

In the opening verses of this sequence, ideas are taken up from both the first summary (the apostles' signs and wonders, 5.12a: 2.43b; the unity of the believers, 5.12b: 2.44, 46a; favour with those outside, 5.13b: 2.47a; growth in the number of believers, 5.14: 2.41, 47b) and the second (the apostles' testimony, 5.12a: 4.33a; meeting in the Temple, 5.12b: 4.32a; favour with those outside, 5.13b: 4.33b). In addition, in the latter two verses, 5.15–16, Luke adapts the summary of the life of Jesus found in Mark's Gospel (Mk 6.53–56), to apply it to Peter as the leader of the apostles (see *Excursus* 7).

Structure and Themes

The main theme that is singled out and developed, however, is the witness of the apostles through the performance of signs and wonders in the Temple. It is precisely this activity that will arouse the jealousy of the high priest and the Sadducees. It is also in connection with the theme of healing miracles that allusions to the Exodus are made in these verses, so establishing this critical event in Israel's history as the paradigm for the narrative that follows.

Elements of this description of the activity of the apostles in the life of the Jesus-believing community will be echoed in the description of Paul's activity in Ephesus (19.11–19).[15]

The narrative focuses on the activity of the apostles among the people outside the circle of believers, relating what drew the people to them and the effect of their contact with them. Four steps can be identified in the development of the narrative, following the structure of the Bezan text which differs in this passage from the AT in 5.13 (see *Critical Apparatus*):

[a]	5.12a	The apostles among the people
[b]	5.12b–13	The church in Solomon's Porch
[b′]	5.14–15	An increase in believers who sought healing
[a′]	5.16	People gathered from outside Jerusalem

For the first time, the apostles witness to people from outside Jerusalem – albeit still within the city and within the Temple as Codex Bezae is careful to point out – marking a significant move forward in the mission entrusted to them by Jesus.

Translation

	Codex Bezae D05	*Codex Vaticanus B03*
[BA]		
[a]	**5.12a** Through the hands of the apostles many signs and wonders happened among the people;	**5.12a** And through the hands of the apostles many signs and wonders happened among the people;
[b]	**12b** and all of them were united in the Temple, in the porch of Solomon, **13** and none of the rest dared to be joined to them, but the people praised them greatly.	**12b** and they were all united in Solomon's porch. **13** Of the rest, none dared to be joined to them, but the people praised them greatly.

15. The parallels between 5.12–16 and 19.11–19 will be studied in more detail in the *Commentary* on Acts 19. In summary, the similarities are: working of miracles: 5.12a // 19.11; distinction between believers and non-believers: 5.13a // 19.18–19; praise: 5.13b // 19.17c; addition of new believers: 5.14 // 19.18 (especially D05); the healing power emitted by Peter // Paul: 5.15 // 19.12a; release from all sicknesses: 5.15d D05, 16b // 19.12b; expulsion of unclean spirits: 5.16b // 19.12b. Further echoes of earlier verses are heard: everyone was afraid: 5.5b, 11: 19.17b; the prices of the land sold // books burned: 4.34: 19.19.

[b′]	**14** More than ever, believers were added to the Lord, multitudes of men and of women, too, **15** with the result that they carried out their sick in the streets and laid them on beds and mattresses so that when Peter came at least his shadow might fall on some of them, for they were set free from all the sicknesses according to whatever each one of them had.	**14** More than ever, believers were added to the Lord, multitudes of men and of women, too, **15** with the result that they even carried out the sick into the streets and laid them on beds and mattresses so that when Peter came at least his shadow would fall on some of them.
[a′]	**16** A crowd of people from the cities round about gathered in Jerusalem, carrying sick people and those tormented by unclean spirits, and they were all healed.	**16** Even the multitude from the cities around Jerusalem gathered, carrying sick people and those tormented by unclean spirits, all of whom were cured.

Critical Apparatus

5.12 (Διά) τε B || δέ D d ℵ *rell.*

The change of subject in 5.12, indicated by the fronting of Διὰ δὲ τῶν χειρῶν τῶν ἀποστόλων, calls for the connective δέ in order to signal a new unit of development in the narrative (Levinsohn, *Textual Connections*, pp. 83–85).

πάντες B A E 0189. 1646 *pc* || ἅπ– D, *universi* d P^{74vid} ℵ H^{3} P Ψ 049. 056. 33. 69. 945. 1739. 1891. 2412. 2495 𝔐.

Within Luke's writing, the adjective ἅπαντες is emphatic, with the sense of 'absolutely all'.

ἐν τῷ ἱερῷ D, *in tem<plo>* d sa^{mss} mae aeth | ἐν τ. ναῷ συνηγμένοι E e || *om.* B $P^{45.74}$ ℵ *rell.*

Without the mention of the Temple in B03, the believers are described as being together in the porch of Solomon while the apostles performed signs and wonders. The D05 account has a different focus: they are together in the Temple but not in the inner courts, only in the porch of Solomon; cf. 3.11 D05 where Solomon's porch is likewise presented as outside the inner, restricted areas.

τῇ (Σολομῶνος) D | τοῦ H^{3} 440. 927. 2412 || *om.* B P^{45} ℵ *rell.*

For the second time, D05 carefully specifies the name of the porch; cf. 3.11: ἐν τῇ στοᾷ – ἡ καλουμένη Σολομῶνος – D05, ἐπὶ τῇ στοᾷ τῇ καλουμένῃ Σολομῶντος B03.

5.13 τῶν δὲ λοιπῶν οὐδείς (–θείς P^{45} B 0189) B P^{45} ℵ *rell* || καὶ οὐδεὶς τ. λοι. D d (t sy).

By means of the conjunction δέ as well as the unusual initial position of the partitive genitive, B03 treats the introduction of ‘the rest’ as contrasting with those who were of one mind in the porch of Solomon. In contrast, D05 has the two sentences in parallel, the first as a positive statement describing ‘all’ (the believers) and the second as a negative statement describing ‘the rest’.

5.15 (ὥστε) καὶ εἰς τὰς πλατείας B P^{74} ℵ A D^{E} Ψ 33. 88. 927. 945. 1175. (1611). 1739. 1891. 2147 || κατὰ πλ. D^{*} d 1646 | κατὰ τὰς πλ. H^{3} P 049. 056 69. 323. 614. 1245. 1505. 2412. 2495 𝔐; Chr.

Where D05 simply states the location where the sick were brought (‘into the streets’), B03 expresses it more forcefully (‘even into the streets’).

(τοὺς ἀσθενεῖς) αὐτῶν D d 453 p sy^{p}; Cass || *om.* B P^{45} ℵ *rell.*

The inclusion of the personal pronoun is characteristic of the interest shown by D05 in the participants in the narrative.

ἐπισκιάσει B 33. 69. 104. 226. 614. 1241. 1505. 1646. 2344. 2412. 2495 *al* || –σῃ D d P^{74} ℵ A E H^{3} P Ψ 049. 056. 88. 945. 1175. 1245. 1611. 1739. 1891. 2147. 2492 𝔐.

Purpose clauses with ἵνα may have the verb in the indicative (B03, future) though more usually the subjunctive (D05) (B-D-R, §369.2).

(τινὶ αὐτῶν·) ἀπηλλάσσοντο γὰρ ἀπὸ πάσης ἀσθενείας ὡς εἶχεν ἕκαστος αὐτῶν D, *et li<b>erabantur ab omne[m] valetudine[m] qu<a>m habebant unusquisque eorum* d (gig p vg^{cl} mae; Lcf) | καὶ ῥυσθῶσιν ἀπὸ π. ἀσθ. ἧς εἶχον. διό E || *om.* B P^{74} ℵ *rell.*

D05 clarifies that the consequence of Peter’s shadow falling on some of the sick who had been brought out into the streets was that everyone was healed of all their sicknesses.

Clark (*Acts*) suggests that the reading ὡς should be substituted with ἧς, but Delebecque argues that there is no difficulty if ὡς is taken as meaning ‘according to the seriousness of each case’ (*Les deux Actes*, pp. 46–47).

5.16 καὶ τὸ (πλῆθος) B P^{74} ℵ D^{B} *rell* || *om.* D^{*} d 547 a b gig t y vg^{mss}; Lcf.

For a second time in this passage, B03 is emphatic (cf. 5.15), this time stressing that people also came for healing from outside Jerusalem (see the next two *vll.*).

τῶν περὶξ πόλεων *codd.* ($D^{E?}$) || τ. περιπόλεων D^{*} (*finium undique* d?).

This *vl.* functions in combination with the following one.

῾Ιερουσαλήμ B P[74] ℵ A 0189. 927 *pc* lat sy; Lcf || εἰς᾽ Ιερ. D d E H[3] P Ψ 049. 056. 69. 323. 614. 945. 1175. 1241. 1270. 1505. 1739. 1891. 2412. 2495 𝔐 c dem vg[mss] bo.

B03 envisages a crowd gathering that is made up of the people from the cities around Jerusalem. D03 speaks of a crowd coming into Jerusalem from the cities round about (see above). An alternative interpretation of τῶν περιπόλεων could be that they are 'vagrants' (L-S-J, περίπολις, εως, ὁ, ἡ).

ὑπὸ (πνευμάτων) B P[74] ℵ *rell* || ἀπό D.

Although ἀπό gradually supplanted ὑπό to introduce the agent of a passive verb, D05 (unlike B03) is generally consistent in restricting the use of ἀπό to verbs that include the idea of sending or movement away from the agent (Read-Heimerdinger, *The Bezan Text*, pp. 183–86). In view of the high degree of regularity in D05, the choice of ἀπό in this instance could have been prompted by the notion of movement implicit in the meaning of the verb (L-S-J, ὀχλέω I. 'move, disturb', II. 'trouble, importune'). An identical reading at Lk. 6.18 D05, ὀχλούμενοι ἀπὸ πνευμάτων ἀκαθάρτων ἐθεραπεύοντο, indicates that the preposition is not simply a matter of scribal error or preference.

οἵτινες ἐθεραπεύοντο ἅπαντες B P[74] ℵ *rell*, *qui curabantur universi* d || καὶ ἰῶντο πάντες D (gig) p sy[p]; Lcf.

The difference in meaning between θεραπεύω (mid. or pass., B03) and ἰάομαι (mid. dep. or pass., D05) is slight. The semantic field of the former is wider in scope, being used of physical healing as well as deliverance from evil spirits (Lk. 6.18; 7.21; 8.2), which is appropriate here if the relative οἵτινες is taken to refer to both the sick and those tormented by evil spirits as the pronoun ἅπαντες would indicate. ἰάομαι is a more limited, technical term for healing but its significance may derive from its use in the Exodus paradigm which is activated (more clearly by D05) throughout this episode: while in the wilderness, the Israelites were healed of every disease by the Lord 'your healer' (Exod. 15.27, ἰώμενος LXX). πάντες in D05 presents those healed as every individual person rather than as an overall group (cf. ἕκαστος αὐτῶν 5.16 D05). Delebecque interprets ἐθεραπεύοντο as a middle and ἰῶντο as a passive (*Les deux Actes*, pp. 48–49).

Commentary

[a] 5.12a *The Apostles among the People*

5.12a In the bridging summary, among the features of the Jesus-believing community was noted the activity of the apostles: 'with great power the apostles gave witness to the resurrection of the Lord Jesus Christ' (4.33 D05; 'with great power the apostles of the Lord Jesus gave witness to his resurrection' B03). Their witness to the resurrection had already been presented in Peter's teaching of the people in Solomon's porch following the healing of the lame man (3.11–26, especially vv. 15, 26) and again in his speech to the Sanhedrin (4.10; cf. 4.2). Indeed, Peter claimed that the healing had taken place because Jesus had been raised to life by God, and that they, the apostles, were witnesses of the resurrection (3.15). As a continuation of that first miracle, interpreted as a sign of the liberating power of Jesus (4.16, 22), Luke shows the apostles to have pursued their witness to Jesus by performing more 'signs and wonders'. This was in accordance with the prayer made by the Jesus-believers following the first persecution of the apostles by the Jewish authorities ('grant to your servants to speak your word with complete boldness, as you stretch out your hand to heal and signs and wonders are performed through the name of your holy servant Jesus', 4.29–30). It is also in imitation of their master (cf. 2.22), as Luke's adaptation of the summary relating to Jesus in Mark's Gospel (Mk 6.53–56) to the apostles implies. Despite these indications of positive evaluation of the apostles, and despite the evidence of the success of their witnessing that is about to be supplied, a note of criticism will be sounded: according to Luke's presentation, the apostles' primary witness to Jesus was to his resurrection, and that through the practical demonstration of miracles of healing of one kind or another. Jesus, in contrast, had instructed them to be witnesses of himself, with a much wider remit than simply his resurrection (1.8; cf. Lk. 24.48). Accordingly, the angel of the Lord will instruct them to 'speak in the Temple to the people all the words of this life' (see *Commentary*, 5.20) and at the end of this section, they will be seen teaching and preaching about Jesus (5.42).

The mention of 'signs and wonders', without distinguishing between the two terms, refers back not only to previous occurrences of the term in Acts but is the first in the passage 5.12–42 of a series of discreet allusions to the Exodus, the deliverance of Israel under the leadership of Moses from their slavery in Egypt. Moses performed signs and wonders in Egypt (Exod. 7.3), especially at the Red Sea as the people of Israel were about to leave their place of enslavement (Wisd. 19.8b; cf. Acts 7.36; see *Excursus* 8).

[b] 5.12b–13 *The Church in Solomon's Porch*

5.12b The unity of the Jesus-believers is a recurring idea, already emphasized in the bridging summary by Codex Bezae (4.32a D05). As noted above, Solomon's porch was the place where Peter had spoken to the people to explain to them about the healing of the lame man. Prior to the opposition of the high priest and other Temple authorities to their preaching about Jesus, the Jesus-believers had continued to attend the Temple for prayer (1.14; 2.46; 3.1, 3, 11), but they would appear to have ceased once the authorities had demonstrated their refusal to accept the apostles' testimony to Jesus and the believers had organized themselves in some kind of separate community under the leadership of the apostles, for no further mention will be made of their joining in the Temple activities.

The detail 'in the Temple' in Codex Bezae is not strictly necessary, as if anyone did not know where Solomon's porch was, but it serves the purpose of highlighting the Temple as the focus of the apostles' activity which is a key theme in this part of the narrative of Acts.

Solomon's porch was outside the area of the Temple reserved for Jews, running as it did along the eastern wall of the Herodian extensions; it was used as a place for teaching by lesser rabbis so the apostles would not have been the only ones speaking there (see *Commentary,* 3.10).

5.13 There are various possibilities for understanding who is meant by 'the rest' in this verse, the problems arising because of an apparent contradiction in the following verse:

1. It refers to anyone outside the group of Jesus-believers ('all of them', v. 12b), that is, 'the people', who dared not join them but who nevertheless recognized their greatness and praised them, from a distance so to speak. Problem: the information is contradicted by the observation that more and more men and women did become believers (v. 14)
2. It refers only to those among the people of Israel who were not added by the Lord to the number of believers (v. 14; cf. Lk. 8.10: 'to you it has been given to know the secrets of the kingdom of God but for the rest [τοῖς λοιποῖς] they are in parables...'). Problem: the term 'the rest' is odd, since the comment that the Lord added many does not come until the next verse
3. It refers to other rabbis, as distinct from the ordinary people. Problem: is the context sufficiently clear for 'the rest' to be understood as meaning other Jewish teachers?
4. It refers to believers other than the apostles. Problem: the last named participants with whom 'the rest' are compared are not the apostles but 'all of them' (emphatic in the Bezan text) whose unity is highlighted (v. 12b); since there is no need to underline the unity of the apostles, these 'all' must mean the whole community of Jesus-believers

The difficulties are made more acute in the AT by the contrastive particle introducing 'the rest' (τῶν δὲ λοιπῶν). In order to resolve the difficulty of reconciling v. 13 with v. 14, it is necessary to see that each is speaking of a different situation. Thus, v. 13 portrays the situation of the community of believers in the Temple, with all the other Jews, the 'people', keeping at a safe distance from them even though they recognized the greatness of what they were doing; the conjunction καί in the Bezan text expresses this kind of parallel (rather than contrastive) presentation of the believers and the other people in the Temple. For this reason, v. 12b has been grouped with v. 13 in the structural analysis. Then, in v. 14, where the scene is no longer confined to the Temple, Luke turns the attention of his hearers to the spectacular growth of the community in general.

The observation that those who dared not join the Jesus-believers praised them (presumably the apostles in particular but, since the community act in perfect unity, they are not singled out) is another implicit criticism of the situation the apostles have created. For unease is suggested by the application to people of a verb (μεγαλύνω) usually reserved by Luke for praise of God.

[b′] 5.14–15 *An Increase in Believers who Sought Healing*

5.14 As attention now moves away from the activity of the established community in the Temple to a consideration of the more general situation, it is the great numbers of those who are drawn to belief in Jesus who become the focus of the narrative.[16] This is the third reference to the numerical growth of the Jesus-believers: 3,000 souls (ψυχαί) were added on the day of Pentecost, repesenting an identificable group (the figure 'three' expressing completeness) but as yet taking tentative steps for they had only been baptized in water (2.41); then, the number reached 5,000 after the sign of the healing of the lame man, the believers now reaching a more mature status ('the number of men', ἀριθμὸς τῶν ἀνδρῶν, 4.4) and anticipating the second outpouring of the Holy Spirit on them (see *Commentary*, 4.31; the figure 'five' expresses the idea of holiness); and

16. In theory, τῷ κυρίῳ could mean either people believed in the Lord (πιστεύοντες) or that they were added to the Lord (προσετίθεντο). Account needs to be taken, however, of the fact, first, that earlier it was said that it was the Lord who took the initiative in the building up of the community (2.47); secondly, that it will later be said that 'a considerable crowd was added to the Lord (προσετέθη ὄχλος ἱκανὸς τῷ κυρίῳ, 11.24); thirdly, that Luke always expresses belief in Jesus with the formula πιστεύω + εἰς/ἐπὶ τὸν κύριον (9.42; 11.17; 16.31 / 14.23; 18.8 D05) – the only exception is the dative construction at 18.8 in MSS other than D05. All these considerations taken together point to τῷ κυρίῳ belonging to 'were added' in 5.14.

now, the increase is indicated by the general term 'multitudes', and the balance in the group by the mention of 'women' (πλήθη ... γυναικῶν) as well as men.

The community is defined by its belonging to the Lord, that is, to Jesus. It can hardly be God who is intended here since the Jews already belonged to him and it would make no sense to say that they were 'added to him' (even less that they 'believed' in him).

5.15 The new believers have been drawn to Jesus by the miracles performed by the apostles in his name. The consequence of their belief is that they seek to obtain healing from sickness and the oppression of unclean spirits by the power of Peter's shadow.[17] The mention of divine power contained within a shadow and communicated by it echoes the shadow of God's presence that guided the people of Israel in the wilderness (e.g. Exod. 40.35) – another allusion to the Exodus story (see *Excursus* 8). The fact that people would not actually touch Peter is an indication of their view of his holiness (comparison being implied with Jesus whose garment people touched, cf. Mk 6.56, see *Excursus* 7). This is the point of saying 'at least his shadow': those seeking healing neither expect or need anything more.

The new location is specified as 'in the streets' which the AT underlines. The Bezan text portrays their quest as being for their families rather than for themselves ('their sick') and gives the reason as the fact that they themselves have experienced, every one of them, liberation from disease. Without these details, the AT seems to view the ones bringing their sick as the general public, not the believers at all; the connection with the previous sentence is thus weak and causes some to view vv. 12b-14 as parenthetical.[18]

[a′] 5.16 *People Gathered from Outside Jerusalem*

5.16 When the sphere of the apostles' activity moved from the limited area of the Temple to the larger area of the streets, it was not at their initiative but because of the new believers' response to their own healing (so Codex Bezae; the picture is not necessarily progressive at all, nor

17. The idea that a shadow had any power is found in the warnings that even the shadow of a dead body could make a person impure (see *Eliyahu Rabbah* [4b, 6], a commentary on Mishnah *Tohoroth* by Elijah Ben Solomon, Gaon of Vilna [Brünn, 1802]).

18. E.g. Barrett, I, p. 276.

outside the control of the apostles, in the AT). A further step away from the centrality of the Temple occurs when people from outside Jerusalem bring their sick to be healed, again not at the initiative of the apostles. It is noticeable that at each new step, the apostles are moved along by events rather than setting out to develop their mission according to some plan worked out in advance.

The widening of the circle of those healed corresponds to the parable of the banquet of the kingdom told by Luke in his Gospel (Lk. 14.16–24): first, those invited make excuses, of which three examples are cited; then, the servants are ordered to bring in those from 'the streets and the lanes of the city' who, having accepted, still leave room for more; so finally, people are brought in from the 'highways and hedges'. The reminiscence of Jesus' parable may allow the Greek word τῶν περιπόλεων to be understood as 'the vagrants' instead of 'the cities round about' (see *Critical Apparatus*).

The wording of the Bezan text emphasizes that the apostles nevertheless remain in Jerusalem, for that is where the sick were brought. In any case, they were all healed. In view of the Exodus paradigm that is being established in these verses (see *Excursus* 8), there is an echo in this comment (reinforced by the choice of verb in the Bezan text) of God's healing of his people in the wilderness before they could be allowed to enter the Promised Land (see *Excursus* 8).

Excursus 7

Luke's Adaptation of Mk 6.53–56

In his Gospel, Luke does not make use of the summary Mark gives of Jesus' healing ministry at Mk 6.53–56 (cf. Matt. 14.34–36), for he omits the entire Markan section which, following the feeding of the five thousand, relates among other things Jesus' journey to Tyre and Sidon and the Decapolis, leading to the feeding of the four thousand in Gentile territory (Mk 6.45–8.26). The reason for his omission is that he holds over the mission to the Gentiles to his second volume where it is the responsibility of the apostles, in line with Jesus' command (Lk. 24.47; Acts 1.8). Consequently, Luke adapts the Markan summary of Jesus' healings to apply it to Peter in 5.15–16, as he will later apply it to Paul (19.11–12).

There are numerous parallels (//) between Mark's summary and Acts 5.15–16. They are listed below, with the Acts text followed by the Markan parallel:

Acts 5.15a // Mk 6.55b

- ὥστε καί (– D05), Acts 5.15a // καὶ ἤρξαντο, Mk 6.55b
- εἰς τὰς (κατὰ D05) πλατείας, 15b // ἐν ταῖς ἀγοραῖς, 56c
- ἐκφέρειν, 15c // περιφέρειν, 55e
- τοὺς ἀσθενεῖς (+ αὐτῶν D05), 15d // τοὺς κακῶς ἔχοντας, 55d
- καὶ τιθέναι, 15e // ἐτίθεσαν, 56d
- ἐπὶ κλιναρίων καὶ κραβάττων, 15f // ἐπὶ τοῖς κραβάττοις, 55c
- ἵνα, 15g // καὶ παρεκάλουν αὐτὸν ἵνα, 56f
- ἐρχομένου Πέτρου, 15h // καὶ ὅπου ἂν εἰσπορεύετο (᾿Ιησοῦς), 56a
- κἂν ἡ σκιὰ ἐπισκιάσῃ τινὶ αὐτῶν, 15i // κἂν τοῦ κρασπέδου τοῦ ἱματίου αὐτοῦ ἅψωνται, 56g
- + (ἀπηλλάσσοντο γὰρ ἀπὸ πάσης ἀσθενείας ὡς εἶχεν ἕκαστος αὐτῶν), 15j D05 // –
- συνήρχετο δὲ καὶ (– D05) τὸ πλῆθος, 16a // ὅπου ἤκουον ὅτι ἐστίν, 55f
- τῶν πέριξ πόλεων (περιπόλεων εἰς D05) ᾿Ιερουσαλήμ, 16b // εἰς κώμας ἢ εἰς πόλεις ἢ εἰς ἀγρούς, 56b
- φέροντες ἀσθενεῖς καὶ ὀχλουμένους ὑπὸ (ἀπὸ D05) πνευμάτων ἀκαθάρτων, 16c // ἐτίθεσαν τοὺς ἀσθενοῦντας, 56e
- οἵτινες ἐθεραπεύοντο ἅπαντες (καὶ ἰῶντο πάντες D05), 16d // καὶ ὅσοι ἂν ἥψαντο αὐτοῦ ἐσῴζοντο, 56h

The most striking difference between Peter and Jesus is that Jesus allowed people to touch the hem of his clothes and they were healed by doing so, whereas Peter did not come into contact at all with those seeking healing but people were cured simply by his shadow. The verb 'touch' (ἅπτω) is a term to do with purity with reference to the Jewish law (cf. Mk 1.40–42; 5.25–34, etc.). When Jesus 'touches with his hand' or lets himself 'be touched', he demonstrates his complete freedom with regard to the law separating the pure and the impure. Peter has still some way to go before achieving this same freedom (cf. Acts 10.14–15, 28; 11.8–9).

[BB] 5.17–21a *The Jealousy of the High Priest*

Overview

The allusions to the Exodus, which the previous verses have been establishing as the model for the current events, are intensified in this passage (see *Excursus* 8). As the Exodus is re-enacted, but in a tragic reversal of roles, the episode will be seen to work on a figurative level as well as a literal one. This is as much a story about inner attitudes as historical events.

Structure and Themes

The imprisonment of the apostles is dealt with very briefly, in a similar way to their first arrest by the Jewish leaders (4.1–3). The intervention of the angel of the Lord to release them follows without further ado, and is described equally briefly. In accordance with his instructions to them to return to the Temple, they do so. Three steps can be identified:

[a]	5.17–18	The imprisonment of the apostles
[b]	5.19–20	The deliverance of the apostles
[a′]	5.21a	The obedience of the apostles to the angel's command

Translation

	Codex Bezae D05	Codex Vaticanus B03
[BB]		
[a]	**5.17** In reaction, the high priest and all those of his circle, the sect of the Sadducees as it was, were filled with jealousy **18** and they laid hands on the apostles and publicly put them in custody, and everyone went to their own home.	**5.17** In reaction, the high priest and all those of his circle, the sect of the Sadducees as it was, were filled with jealousy **18** and they laid hands on the apostles and publicly put them in custody.
[b]	**19** So in the night an angel of the Lord opened the doors of the prison **20** and led them out and said, 'Go and take up your stand in the Temple and speak to the people all the words of this life.'	**19** But an angel of the Lord in the night opened the doors of the prison; **20** having led them out he said, 'Go and take up your stand in the Temple and speak to the people all the words of this life.'
[a′]	**21a** On hearing this, they entered the Temple about dawn and began teaching.	**21a** On hearing this, they entered the Temple about dawn and began teaching.

Critical Apparatus

5.18 καὶ ἐπορεύθη εἶς ἕκαστος εἰς τὰ ἴδια D d mae || *om.* B P[45.74] א *rell.*

The comment in D05 is far from being a 'circumstantial detail' (Metzger, *Commentary*, p. 288); rather it contributes to the activation of the Exodus paradigm underlying this episode (cf. Exod. 12.22), in combination with other details (cf. 5.21 D05 below; see *Excursus* 8). It is one among several comments that serve to show how the high priest and the Sadducees thought of themselves as protected by God. Epp (*Theological Tendency*, p. 129) thinks the subject of the verb is ambiguous and could mean the apostles but the obvious existence of a collective prison as opposed to individual cells (5.21, 22 D05) excludes this interpretation. There is a striking similarity between the

D05 comment, coupled with the D05 reading of 5.21b, and Jn 7.53–8.2 (see Rius-Camps, 'Origen lucano de la perícopa de la mujer adúltera', pp. 149–76).

5.19 ἄγγελος δὲ κυρίου διὰ νυκτός B P^{74} ℵ* A 88. 104. 1175. 1646. 1739. 2344 | ἀγγ. δὲ κυρ. διὰ τῆς νυκ. ℵ^{2} H^{3} P Ψ 056. 33. 69. 323. 614. 945. 1241. 1505. 1611. 2412 || τότε διὰ νυκ. ἀγγ. κυρ. D (*per nocte<m> vero angelus domini* d) sy^{p}.

With τότε, D05 presents the arrival of the angel of the Lord as a direct response to the action of the Jewish leaders (Read-Heimerdinger, *The Bezan Text*, pp. 213–14). The promptness of the divine intervention is further signalled by the position of the adverbial expression of time, διὰ νυκτός. In comparison, the B03 text underlines the presence of the angel of the Lord.

ἤνοιξε B E H^{3} P Ψ 056. 0189. 69. 614. 945. 1241. 1270. 1739. 1891. 2412. 2495 𝔐 | ἀνοίξας P^{74} ℵ A 36. 453. 1175 *pc* || ἀνέῳξεν (–αν D*) D^{H} d.

The two forms of the aorist indicative of ἀνοίγω are equivalent, although the form with ἠν– is the later of the two (Bailly, *ad loc.*).

ἐξαγαγὼν δέ B Ψ 0189. 2344 || ἐξ. τε D d P^{74} ℵ A P 049. 056. 33. 945. 1175. 1241. 1270. 1505. 1739. 1891 𝔐 | καὶ ἐξ. E H^{3} 69. 614. 2412. 2495.

By using the connective δέ, B03 treats the opening of the prison by the angel as an action distinct from that of leading the prisoners out and speaking to them. D05 links them closely with τε and anticipates the next development (Levinsohn, *Textual Connections*, pp. 121–30). Most of the witnesses that read the participle ἀνοίξας (see above) support the D05 reading here.

Commentary

[a] 5.17–18 *The Imprisonment of the Apostles*

5.17 The sudden mention of the high priest and his associates implies that they had been in the background throughout the previous scene. That this is indeed the case is shown by the reference to their jealousy without any explanation that they had seen anything to provoke them to envy. The high priest in question can be assumed to be Annas and his family (cf. 4.6), including Caiaphas who was technically holding office at the time, and Theophilus, one of Annas's sons who would become high priest within a few years of these events (see *Commentary*, 1.1 and *General Introduction* §X).

The use of the participle ἀναστάς has already been noted with reference to the young men who reacted to the death of Ananias in the church community (see *Commentary*, 5.6). More than a mere 'graphic' participle,[19] in Luke's work it introduces a fresh initiative on the part of a participant who had hitherto not been active.[20] The repeated occurrence of the participle to present the action of Gamaliel, the representative of the Pharisees, (5.34) will serve to strengthen the comparison between the two rival parties and their influence in the Sanhedrin.

The tense of the verbs passes from the imperfect to the aorist: the action of the apostles had been going on over a period of time before the Jewish leaders had had enough and took action.

This is not the first time, of course, that the high priest and the Sadducees have been seen to have problems with the apostles (cf. 4.1, 5–6, 23). On the contrary, underlying the whole of this sequence is their earlier imprisonment of Peter and John for having performed a 'sign' of healing and spoken to the people about Jesus and his resurrection (4.2). In the meantime, the apostles had separated themselves from the Temple authorities and organized the community of Jesus-believers under their own leadership (4.32–35). They have lost any hopes they might have once had about the Jewish leaders repenting or acknowledging Jesus as Messiah and their realization that the Sanhedrin does not represent the mind of God will be apparent in the brief speech Peter makes in answer to their charge on this occasion.

The fact that the Sadducean faction continue to actively oppose the Jesus-believers is symptomatic of the threat they felt was posed to their authority and role among the people as representatives of the Temple. It is the detachment of the apostles from the Temple institution rather than the miracles or the teaching as such – which could have disturbed the Pharisees as much as any other group – that was presumably the cause of the Sadducees' hostility. A dominant motif throughout this scene is established by the five (six D05) references to 'the Temple' (5.12 D05, 20, 21, 24, 25, 42), not as a place of prayer but as a place of witness to Jesus either through miracles done in his name or through teaching about him. In this, the apostles imitated Jesus' own use of the Temple, though it will be seen in due course (notably Acts 12) that they have not yet completely detached themselves from it.

The Sadducees, however, were by no means the only voice within the Sanhedrin and a more tolerant attitude will later be demonstrated by a representative of the Pharisees which, in the end, prevents the council

19. *Pace* Zerwick, *Biblical Greek*, §363.

20. The use of ἀναστάς to express a reaction on the part of a participant in an episode is seen at, e.g., Lk. 10.25; Acts 1.15; 5.17, 34; 6.9; 15.7; 23.9.

from annihilating the apostles as they would have wished (5.33 AT; or had even decided, D05).

The motive of jealousy is cited at other places in Acts as the cause of opposition to the Jesus-believers (13.45; 17.5). It has a biblical precedence in the envy felt by the sons of Jacob towards their brother Joseph (7.9), but more importantly for the present scene in the feelings of Pharaoh towards Moses when he worked miracles, as recorded by tradition.[21] The analysis of the reason for the attack of the high priest and the Sadducees thus evokes once more the Exodus event, as confirmed by other details in the verses that follow (see *Excursus* 8).

5.18 Unlike the first arrest that involved only Peter and John (cf. 4.3), this time all the apostles are concerned. The detail that they are put into prison publicly[22] draws attention to the desire of the Sadducees to manifest their authority before the people. On releasing Peter and John after the earlier occasion, they had carefully warned them not to mention again the name of Jesus (4.21). Now that they have not only continued to teach about this detested name but have set themselves up in opposition to the priestly authorities, their situation is much more serious.[23]

A detail is included in the Bezan text that at first sight is an unnecessary clarification but in reality is rich in resonances. The information that those who had publicly put the apostles into prison then went to their own homes reveals an attitude of arrogance and individual concern for their own comfort which contrasts with the sharing and sense of community expressed among the Jesus-believers. More telling still, is the echo in this detail of Moses' instructions to the Israelites on the night of Passover: they were to shut themselves up safely in their houses while the angel of the Lord 'passed over' the land (Exod. 12.22). Several allusions to the Exodus paradigm have already been noted in earlier verses in this passage

21. Eusebius, *Praep. Ev.*, 9.27.7,17; and Josephus, *Ant.*, 2.254–55

22. When the adjective δημοσίᾳ is used elsewhere in Acts, it is always in an adverbial sense (16.37; 18.28; 20.20); see Delebecque, *Les deux Actes*, p. 48. It is not used by any other New Testament author nor in the LXX but, in contrast, is found three times in the books of the Maccabees: 2 Macc. 6.10; *3 Macc.* 2.27; 4.7, each time as an adverb.

23. Under Jewish law, an offence could not be punished if a person was not aware of the consequences of their act. A warning had, therefore, to be given first, in front of witnesses, and action could only be taken if the offence was repeated. Cf. 4.13 (the apostles were untrained), 4.17 (a legal warning: ἀπειλή, –έω; 4.21: προσαπειλέω; cf. 4.29) and 5.28.

(see *Excursus* 8 for a full list and discussion of the theme), and because the parallel has already been established the Sadducees are seen to be aligning themselves with those who are approved and protected by God, in contrast to their prisoners. In an ironic development, however, while they are safely shut up in their houses, the angel of the Lord will open the doors of the prison and release their captives. It is no longer the official authorities who are protected but those chosen by Jesus to witness to him.

[b] 5.19–20 *The Deliverance of the Apostles*

5.19 The angel of the Lord intervenes in the apostles' favour to bring them out of the prison and to send them back to the Temple. In the Bezan text, the action of the angel is presented as a direct response to the action of the Jewish leaders, underlining at the same time that the release took place at night. On both counts, the Exodus parallels are strengthened (*Excursus* 8) and anticipate a further allusion in the use of the verb ἐξάγω typically associated with the deliverance of the people of Israel from Egypt. The angel thus undoes the attempts of the authorities to put an end to the apostles' activities, to the point of ordering them to return to the Temple.

5.20 It is not simply a question, however, of returning to their previous activity for they are to speak to the people 'the words of this life'. The relationship between the apostles and the people becomes aligned with that of Moses to the people of Israel after he had been appointed to lead them out of Egypt and into the Promised Land (cf. Deut. 5.31, 33, with verbal parallels between the LXX and the text of Acts, on which see *Excursus* 8). They are to take up position in the Temple as orators (σταθέντες), addressing the people with authority.

The 'life' to which they are to testify is not confined to the way of life experienced by the Jesus-believing community but embraces the entire message of salvation. For Moses, this meant the laws and ordinances of God by following which the people would live; for the apostles, it means the acceptance of Jesus as the means chosen by God for salvation (cf. 4.12) even though he has been rejected by the Jewish leaders (cf. 4.11, 27–28). In view of the apostles' limited testimony at the outset of the episode (see *Commentary*, 5.12), the angel's insistence on 'all' the words anticipates the fuller testimony given by the apostles to Jesus at the end of the episode compared with the beginning (cf. 5.42).

On one level, the apostles need an angel to deliver them from prison because they have not yet acquired a full understanding of Jesus which would allow them to break free from the oppression of the old order of

Israel. Jesus himself was never imprisoned despite the many attempts to silence him on the part of various authorities (the high priest, Lk. 22.54; the Sanhedrin, 22.66; Pilate, 23.1; Herod, 23.7; and again Pilate, 23.11 from where he was taken to the place of crucifixion, 23.26, 33). The difference with the apostles is that they still cling to the identity of Israel as a people distinct from the rest of humanity (cf. 5.31). Complete deliverance from the traditional expectations and hopes of Israel will not come until the prison (Exodus) scene is repeated once more with Peter, this time on his own (Acts 12).[24]

[a′] 5.21a *The Obedience of the Apostles to the Angel's Command*
5.21a The apostles obedience to the angel's command was immediate and complete. They went at dawn, at the hour of the morning sacrifice, when the doors of the Temple were unlocked and people would be congregating. In this, they again imitated Jesus' example (Lk. 21.38; cf. Jn 8.2).

[BC] 5.21b–26 *Preparations for the Sanhedrin Meeting*

Overview

This passage is full of dramatic irony for the audience know about the release of the apostles and that God has delivered them from the hostility of the high priest and the Sadducees, yet the religious authorities themselves have still to learn of the escape and they will behave as if they are in control. The Sanhedrin will be called for the second time in Acts to deal with the apostles (cf. 4.5–21)

Structure and Themes
The Temple remains at the centre of the story, a sign that it is this institution that is at the heart of the conflict. The re-arrest of the apostles was inevitable once they were discovered teaching there, and yet this does not make their miraculous deliverance a pointless intervention. For themselves, they are prompted to progress from performing signs and wonders to teaching about Jesus, and they are reassured that God supports them against the hostility of the greatest authority in Israel. As for the leaders,

24. The symbolism of Peter's miraculous deliverance from prison in Acts 12 will be dealt with in detail in the *Commentary*; meanwhile, see Heimerdinger, 'The Seven Steps of Codex Bezae: A Prophetic Interpretation of Acts 12' in D.C. Parker and C.-B. Amphoux (eds.), *Codex Bezae: Studies from the Lunel Colloquium June 1994* (Leiden: E.J. Brill, 1996), pp. 303–10.

they discover that there are powers stronger than theirs working against them although it is debatable whether they ever recognize that this is from God since, in the Bezan text at least, they continue to present themselves as representing God among the people of Israel (5.29 D05). Finally, from the point of view of the narrative, the deliverance of the apostles is critical to bring out the assimilation of the high priest and his circle with Pharaoh and their oppression of the apostles with Pharaoh's oppression of the people of God in Egpyt.

The amount of verbal repetition in this passage is striking, reinforcing the impression of intense activity:

1. Three occurrences of the aorist participle παραγενόμενος (vv. 21b, 22, 25)
2. Three occurrences of the verb ἄγω (vv. 21b, 26, 27)
3. Three occurrences of the verb εὑρίσκω (vv. 22, 23a, 23b)
4. Two occurrences of the verb ἀπαγγέλλω (vv. 22, 25)
5. Four mentions of the prison, twice δεσμωτήριον (vv. 21, 23) alternating twice with φυλακή (vv. 22, 25)
6. Two mentions of the Temple, ἱερόν (vv. 24, 25)
7. Two mentions each of the following characters: the high priest, ἀρχιερεύς (vv. 21b, 24); the commander of the Temple, στρατηγός (vv. 24, 26); the officers, ὑπηρέτης (vv. 22, 26); the people, λαός (vv. 25, 26)

The anxiety of the high priests and the Temple guard about the escape and how things will end is at the centre of the episode, just as their perplexity was the focus of the parallel arrest in the previous chapter (cf. 4.13–17):

[a]	5.21b	The calling of the Sanhedrin
[b]	5.22–23	The discovery of the empty prison
[c]	5.24	The authorities are worried
[b′]	5.25	An anonymous informer
[a′]	5.26	The re-arrest of the apostles

Translation

	Codex Bezae D05	*Codex Vaticanus B03*
[BC]		
[a]	**5.21b** When the high priest and his supporters arrived (having been roused early), and they had called together the Sanhedrin, that is the full senate of the sons of Israel, they sent to the jail to have them brought.	**5.21b** When the high priest and his supporters arrived, they called together the Sanhedrin, that is the full senate of the sons of Israel, and sent to the jail to have them brought.

[b] **22** When the officers arrived and opened the prison, they did not find them inside. **23** They went back again and reported the fact, saying, 'We found the prison securely locked and the guards standing at the doors, but when we opened them we found no-one inside.'

22 When the officers arrived, they did not find them in the prison. **23** They went back again and reported the fact, saying, 'We found the prison securely locked and the guards standing at the doors, but when we opened them we found no-one inside.'

[c] **24** On hearing these words both the commander of the Temple guard and the high priests were perplexed about them, not knowing what would happen next.

24 On hearing these words both the commander of the Temple guard and the high priests were perplexed about them, not knowing what might happen next.

[b′] **25** But then someone arrived and announced to them, 'The men whom you put in prison are standing in the Temple and teaching the people.'

25 But then someone arrived and announced to them, 'The men whom you put in prison are standing in the Temple and teaching the people.'

[a′] **26** Then the commander went with the officers and brought them with force, afraid that the people might stone them.

26 Then the commander went with the officers and brought them, but without force because they were afraid that the people might stone them.

Critical Apparatus

5.21b Παραγενόμενοι B* p || –μενος D d P74 א B2 *rell.*

The singular participle of D05 highlights the role of the high priest in leading the opposition to the apostles (cf. ἀναστάς, 5.17).

συνεκάλεσαν B P74 א *rell* || ἐγερθέντες τὸ πρωῒ καὶ συγκαλεσάμενοι D d mae; (Ephr).

In place of the one finite verb in B03, D05 has two aorist participles. The first stands in a phrase that, on the one hand, operates in conjunction with the D05 reading at 5.18 (see above) to evoke the commandment to the Israelites to stay in their houses until the morning during the night of the Passover (cf. Exod. 12.22, τὸ πρωΐ). On the other hand, the phrase corresponds to the time of the morning sacrifice offered in the Temple at dawn, the time when the apostles had started teaching there (cf. ὑπὸ τὸν ὄρθρον, 5.21a [*ante lucem* d05 at both places]). The second participle subordinates the action of calling together the council to that of sending (καὶ ἀπέστειλαν) for the prisoners. The latter is forcefully underlined in D05 by means of the construction of participle + καί + finite verb, a device typical of Codex Bezae to highlight tension in a narrative (Read-Heimerdinger, *The Bezan Text*, 208–10; Rius-Camps, 'Le substrat grec de la version latine des Actes dans le codex de Bèze', pp. 271–95 [283–84]).

The voice of the second participle συγκαλεσάμενοι is the middle in D05, expressing the dominating interest of the high priest and his circle in the affair; B03 has the active voice in the aorist indicative.

5.22 οἱ δὲ παραγενόμενοι ὑπηρέται B P^{74} ℵ A 36. 88. 945. 1175. 1739. 1891. 2495 *al* gig vg sy^{p} sa; Lcf || οἱ δὲ ὑπ. παρ. D d E H^{3} P Ψ 049. 056. 33. 69. 323. 614. 1241. 1505. 1611. 2412. 2495 𝔐 p sy^{h} mae sa.

The position of the noun after the participle in B03 plays down the role of the officers. In D05, more attention is paid to the officers who are further described in the next D05 reading (see below).

καὶ ἀνοίξαντες τὴν φυλακήν D d 876. 1611. 2138 p t.7 vg sy^{h**} mae || *om.* B P^{74} ℵ *rell.*

The officers continue to be in focus in D05 as they are seen opening the prison once they arrive there: the action is related in detail to highlight the drama of the scene. The sentence ironically echoes the description of the angel opening the doors of the prison during the night (cf. 5.19).

(αὐτοὺς) ἐν τῇ φυλακῇ B P^{74} ℵ *rell* || ἔσω D d mae.

The *vl.* arises from the previous one. With the prior mention of the prison in D05, it is sufficient to say 'inside' at this point, but in B03 the prison is mentioned for the first time.

(ἀναστρέψαντες) δέ B P^{74} ℵ D^{A} *rell* || καί D^{*} d.

B03 continues to develop the narrative in a series of steps with the conjunction δέ. In D05, the new sentence is introduced without any connective, another device to highlight the drama of the scene (see Read-Heimerdinger, *The Bezan Text*, pp. 247–50, where this example should be added to the list on p. 247). Furthermore, with καί separating the participle from the following finite verb for a second time in these verses (cf. 5.21 D05), the report of the officers is also highlighted.

5.23 κεκλεισμένον B ℵ $D^{s.m.}$ *rell* || ἐγκ[λ]εκλ– D^{*}.

B03 reads the perfect participle of κλείω, D05 the perfect participle of ἐγλείω (cf. Lk. 3.20 but one instance of dittography has corrupted the text which reads: ΕΥ–ΡΟΜΕΝΕΝΚΛΕΚΛΕΙΣΜΕΝΟΝ.

5.24 τί ἂν γένοιτο B P^{74} $ℵ^{2}$ D^{D} *rell* | τὸ τί ἂν γέν. $ℵ^{*}$ || τί ἂν γένηται D^{*}.

In place of the optative aorist, $D05^{*}$ reads the subjunctive. Both express uncertainty about how things might end.

5.25 οἱ (ἄνδρες) B D P^{74} ℵ^{2} *rell* || *om.* ℵ* H^{3} 1245*.

ℵ01* does not identify the escaped prisoners as a particular group, possibly meaning 'there are some men whom you put in prison...'. See also below.

ἑστῶτες καὶ διδάσκοντες B D P^{74} ℵ^{2} *rell* || *om.* ℵ*.

In keeping with omission of the article (see above), according to ℵ01* it is simply reported that there are some escaped prisoners in the Temple, without describing what they are doing there. Both readings are a way of avoiding identifying the men in the Temple.

5.26 ἦγεν B P^{74vid} ℵ D^{D} 88. 915 (*deducebant* d) || ἤγαγον D* 1243. 1245. 2495 *pc* vg^{OW} sy^{p} mae | ἤγαγεν A E H^{3} P Ψ 049. 056. 33^{vid}. 69. 323. 462. 614. 945. 1175. 1270. 1505. 1611. 1739. 2412. 2492 𝔐 gig h p t vg; Lcf.

The imperfect of B03 expresses the tentative nature of the guards attempts to take the apostles away, whereas the aorist of D05 is more definite. See also below.

οὐ (μετὰ βίας) B P^{74} ℵ D$^{C/E}$ *rell* || *om.* D* d*.

What looks at first sight like a copyist's error in D05 may, in fact, be a deliberate reading. In line with the verb in the aorist tense (see above), D05 portrays the re-arrest of the apostles as forceful and determined because the guards feared they would be stoned by the people.

ἐφοβοῦντο B P^{74} ℵ *rell*, *timebant* d | ἐφοβεῖτο Ψ || φοβούμενοι D.

The participle in D05 views the guard's fear from their perspective, unlike the finite verb that stands as a narrator's comment.

Commentary

[a] 5.21b *The Calling of the Sanhedrin*

5.21b Having spent the night safely in their houses, the high priest and the Sadducees arrive at the Temple to bring the apostles before the Jewish supreme court, in a move reminiscent of the earlier occasion on which Peter and John appeared before the Sanhedrin (4.5). Codex Bezae specifies that they had been roused early, a reference probably to the priests' role in the morning sacrifice (see *Commentary*, 5.21) but also a detail recalling Moses' order to the Israelites to stay in their houses until the morning (Exod. 12.22, ἕως πρωΐ LXX), corresponding to the comment in the Bezan text of 5.18 that they had each gone to spend the night in their own house.

Yet another contribution to the activation of the Exodus paradigm is the description of the Sanhedrin as 'the full senate of the sons of Israel'. The expression recalls Moses' action of calling together 'the full senate of the sons of Israel' (Exod. 12.21, πᾶσαν γερουσίαν υἱῶν Ἰσραήλ LXX) in order to convey to them instructions concerning the Passover. Once again, the high priest and his circle are carrying out their role as leaders of Israel, unaware that they have been replaced by the apostles chosen by Jesus. Their ignorance creates narrative tension for the audience have been following the progress of the apostles as, after recognizing the part played by the Jewish leaders in the killing of the Messiah (4.27–29), they have assumed their role of leaders among the Jesus-believers.

The dramatic irony of the episode continues as the council have the prisoners sent for, not knowing anything about their release with the help of the angel. The word used to refer to the prison in this instance (and repeated in the report of the officers, 5.23) is not the usual word, φυλακή (cf. 5.19, 22, 25), but δεσμωτήριον (cf. 5.23 below). This term is rare in the New Testament (only Matt. 11.2; Acts 16.26, outside this passage); in the LXX, four of the seven occurrences arise in connection with Joseph in prison in Egypt.

[b] 5.22–23 *The Discovery of the Empty Prison*

5.22 The officers, like the commander of the Temple in 5.24 whose authority they were under, are not Roman soldiers but the Temple guard who were Jews, frequently connected with the family of the high priest.[25] The insistence of the Bezan text that they first opened the prison links their action back to the opening of the prison by the angel during the previous night (5.19); the fact that they found no-one inside, to the angel's leading the apostles out (5.20).

5.23 The officers' report stresses how everything in the prison seemed in order, as securely closed up and guarded as the authorities had left it. The contrast is striking between the Sadducees who had called upon all means humanly possible to put a stop to the apostles, and God who had destroyed their manifestations of power and, against all hope, had freed the apostles so that they could proclaim to the people of Israel Jesus' message of liberation. Luke uses the prison, in other words, as a symbol to express as strongly as possible the force of the oppression of the apostles by the ruling parties of Israel. The activation of the Exodus theme in the previous verses (see *Excursus* 8) causes the prison to represent the slavery of Israel in Egypt, a comparison that assimilates the

25. See Barrett, I, p. 286, quoting the Mishnah.

Jewish religious authorities with Pharaoh and the apostles with the people of God.

[c] 5.24 *The Authorities are Worried*

5.24 The commander of the Temple is mentioned for the first time, confirming that the apostles had been in prison in the Temple and therefore his responsibility. His position as 'second-in-command' to the high priest justifies the mention of him here along with the high priests generally (cf. 4.6) who shared a common anxiety about what was going on and where it was leading.

[b′] 5.25 *An Anonymous Informer*

5.25 The report of the anonymous person who has seen the apostles follows exactly the instructions of the angel: in the Temple, standing, teaching, the people. For the second time, the verb ἵστημι is used with reference to the apostles (cf. 5.20), here underlined with the periphrastic form εἰσὶν ... ἑστῶτες; with its force of 'take up a position', it contrasts with the guards who had taken up their posts in the prison, ἑστῶτες, 5.23.

For the third time (cf. 5.20, 21), the apostles are presented as teaching in the Temple: they have gone beyond working miracles to focus on explaining about Jesus, in clear contravention of the orders imposed on them by the Sanhedrin (cf. 4.18; 5.28).

[a′] 5.26 *The Re-arrest of the Apostles*

5.26 The commander goes with his officers to re-arrest the apostles. Their fear of being stoned by the people, who obviously have taken the apostles' side, leads them, according to the AT, to exercise caution and to take hold of them without using violence; according to the Bezan text, on the other hand, their fear of the people causes them to act violently, no doubt to get out of the people's way and back to the Sanhedrin as quickly as possible.

The siding of the people (a term reserved by Luke to refer to the people of Israel) is a reminder of how they also supported Jesus (cf. Lk. 19.48; 20.19). The authority of Israel's religious leaders is continuing to weaken.

[BC′] 5.27–33 *The Sanhedrin Meeting*

Overview

As the Sanhedrin meeting finally gets underway, the tension between the traditional Jewish authorities and the apostles reaches a peak.

Structure and Themes

The centre of the sequence is a divided one, with this passage, in which the Sanhedrin meeting finally gets underway, acting as the counterpart to the previous one in which the meeting was held up in the absence of the prisoners. It is taken up by the account of the charges brought against the apostles by the council and Peter's response on behalf of the apostles, concluding with the decision (D05; 'wish', AT) to kill them:

[a]	5.27a	The appearance of the apostles in the Sanhedrin
[b]	5.27b–29a	The questioning by the priest
[b′]	5.29b–32	Peter's response
[a′]	5.33	The Sanhedrin's decision

Translation

	Codex Bezae D05	Codex Vaticanus B03
[BC′]		
[a]	**5.27a** They brought them and stood them in the council;	**5.27a** They brought them and stood them in the council;
[b]	**27b** and the priest questioned them saying, **28** 'Did we not give you an absolute order not to preach about this name? Look, you have filled Jerusalem with your teaching and you wish to bring on us the blood of that man. **29a** It is necessary to obey God not men.'	**27b** and the high priest questioned them saying, **28** 'We gave you an absolute order not to preach about this name, and look, you have filled Jerusalem with your teaching and you wish to bring on us the blood of this man.'
[b′]	**29b** Peter said to them, **30** 'The God of our Fathers raised Jesus whom you had killed by hanging him on a tree. **31** This man God exalted as a ruler and saviour for his glory to give repentance to Israel and forgiveness of sins in him. **32** And we are witnesses of all these things, and the Holy Spirit whom God gave to those obeying him.	**29** Peter and the apostles said in reply, 'It is necessary to obey God rather than men. **30** The God of our Fathers raised Jesus whom you had killed by hanging him on a tree. **31** This man God exalted as a ruler and saviour at his right hand to give repentance to Israel and forgiveness of sins. **32** And we are witnesses in him of these things, and God gave the Holy Spirit to those obeying him.'
[a′]	**33** Having heard this, they were infuriated and were intending to kill them.	**33** Having heard this, they were infuriated and were wanting to kill them.

Critical Apparatus

5.27 ὁ ἀρχιερεύς B P^{74} ℵ *rell* || ὁ ἱερεύς D*, *pontefix (pontifex!)* d gig; Lcf | *praetor* h.

A similar *vl.* is found at 4.1 where D05 reads οἱ ἱερεῖς instead of οἱ ἀρχιερεῖς in

B03. It is clear that the high priest is involved in the present scene (cf. 5.17) but it may be that the person speaking here on behalf of the Sanhedrin is not actually the high priest but a lower priest.

5.28 Παραγγελίᾳ παρηγγείλαμεν B P^{74} $ℵ^{*}$ A 1175 *pc*, *Denuntiatione praecipimus* d lat sa^{ms} bo mae; Ath $Cyr^{2/3}$ Lcf || Οὐ παρ. παρηγγείλαμεν...; *(interrog.)* D $ℵ^{2}$ E P S (Ψ) 36. 181. 307. 453. 462. 610. 614. 945. 1409. 1678. 1739. 1891. 2344 𝔐 e h p w sy sa^{mss} mae aeth; Bas Chr $Cyr^{1/3}$ Ambst.

The interrogative of D05 may be less direct than the categorical statement of B03 but, on the other hand, it corresponds to the verb ἐπηρώτησεν of the previous verse. Metzger (*Commentary*, p. 289) suggests that it could have been the wish to have the high priest utter a rebuke that prompted a copyist to change the question into a statement.

καὶ (ἰδού) B ℵ D^{B} *rell* || *om.* D^{*} d.

Because the opening sentence of the speech is a statement in B03 (see below), a conjunction is necessary to introduce the accusation. Following a question, however, no such connective is required; on the contrary, the asyndeton confers greater force on the accusation (cf. a similar construction of an interrogative followed by asyndeton in Lk. 2.48; 7.25; Acts 5.9).

πεπληρώκατε B D E H^{3} P Ψ *rell* || ἐπληρώσατε P^{74} ℵ A 1175. 2147.

The perfect of B03 and D05 is appropriate since the apostles have created a state of affairs in Jerusalem, conveyed by the perfective aspect.

(τοῦ ἀνθρώπου) τούτου B P^{74} ℵ D^{H} *rell*, *huius* d || ἐκείνου D^{*} gig h p sa; Lcf.

Both readings avoid pronouncing the name of Jesus with the demonstrative of D05 causing the council spokesman to place himself at a greater distance from a man he despises.

5.29 πειθαρχεῖν δε<ῖ> (D^{H}) θεῷ μᾶλλον ἢ ἀνθρώποις D^{*} d^{*} (h) sy^{p}; (Aug Lcf) || *om.* B P^{74} ℵ $D^{s.m.}$ *rell* $d^{s.m.}$: cf. below.

These words are attributed by B03 to Peter, being read as the opening declaration of his speech in the second part of the verse (see below). They thus serve as a corrective to the council's accusation, justifying the apostles' action because they are in obedience to the commands of God rather than to the human orders of the council. D05 attributes them to the priest where they take on a rather different meaning, for in this case, the priest is expressing the accepted belief that the council speak for God, and should be obeyed in preference to the man Jesus.

ἀποκριθεὶς δὲ (+ ὁ 056. 33. 88. 547) Πέτρος καὶ οἱ ἀπόστολοι εἶπαν· Πειθαρχεῖν δεῖ θεῷ μᾶλλον ἢ ἀνθρώποις B P^{74} ℵ D$^{s.m.}$ *rell* d$^{s.m.}$ || ὁ δὲ Π. εἶπεν πρὸς αὐτούς D* d gig (h) sy^{p}; (Aug Lcf).

The difference in the introduction to Peter's speech is accounted for by the placing of the sentence about obeying God in his mouth in B03, rather than the priest's (see above), a sign that the displacement of the sentence was not simply a copyist's error. Peter uses this argument to respond to the accusation of the council, and attention is drawn to his bold declaration by the typical omission of the article before his name (see Read-Heimerdinger, *The Bezan Text*, pp. 133–35); furthermore, it is explicitly shared by the other apostles. Where it is the priest, however, who appeals to the need to obey God rather than men, Peter alone addresses the council in a less detached fashion (expressed by πρὸς αὐτούς, see *The Bezan Text*, pp. 176–82). The anaphoric reference to Peter in D05 is justified by the mention of him at 5.15 where he is singled out from among the other apostles.

5. ʽΟ θεός B D E H P Ψ *rell* || ʽΟ δὲ θε. P^{74} ℵ A.

Where the proclamation of the resurrection of Jesus is the opening sentence of Peter's speech, as in D05, no connective is required. In B03, where this is the second sentence, it is not formally connected to the first.

5.31 τῇ δεξιᾷ B P$^{45.74}$ ℵ D^{B} || τ. δόξῃ D*, *c<l>aritate* d^{coni} gig p sa; Ir^{lat} Aug.

The confusion between the two words could be a copyist's error since it is also found in the LXX (see Metzger, *Commentary*, p. 290). On the other hand, both readings make sense, that of D05 being equivalent to ἐδόξασεν; cf. 3.13; Pss 3.4; 111.9 LXX.

τοῦ (δοῦναι) B ℵ* 915 || *om.* D, (*dare*) d ℵ^{2} A H P Ψ *rell.*

The presence of the article before the infinitive in B03 makes explicit the notion of purpose expressed by the infinitive (B-D-R, §§390.2; 400.2). Luke uses infinitives of purpose both with and without the article, sometimes in the same sentence (cf. Lk. 2.22, 24). A systematic analysis of all occurrences, and the variant readings, would be necessary to determine any fine distinction between the two constructions.

(ἁμαρτιῶν) ἐν αὐτῷ D* d h p sa mae aeth; Aug || *om.* B P^{74} ℵ D$^{s.m.}$ *rell.*

D05 makes clear the role of Jesus in being the source, or instrument, of forgiveness. B03 reads the words ἐν αὐτῷ in the next sentence (see below).

5.32 (καὶ ἡμεῖς) ἐν αὐτῷ μάρτυρες B *pc*; Ir^{lat} | ἐν αὐ. ἐσμεν μάρτ. 945. 1739. (1891) *pc* bo^{ms} || ἐσμεν μάρτ. D* P^{74vid} ℵ 104. 181. 614. 915. 1175 *pc* lat sy^{p} co arm^{mss} aeth; Did? | μάρτ. ἐσμεν A (Ψ) 1409, *testes sumus* d gig h p^{2} vg^{AO}; Var | ἐσμεν αὐτοῦ μάρτ. D^{E} E H P S 049. 056. 36. (69). 323. 1241. 1505. 2344. 2495 𝔐 e (p*) sy^{h} arm^{mss}; Chr.

B03 reads the words ἐν αὐτῷ here instead of in the previous sentence as in D05 (see above). Since ἐσμὲν μάρτυρες is already followed by an object in the genitive, the prepositional phrase is clumsy here.

πάντων (τῶν ῥημάτων) D* d h p mae || *om.* B ℵ D$^{s.m.}$ *rell.*

D05 underlines the completeness of the apostolic testimony.

τὸ πνεῦμα τὸ ἅγιον B 876. 2401 *pc* sa bo; CyrJ || τ. πν. τ. ἅγ. ὅν D* | τ. πν. τ. ἅγ. ὅ P^{45} ℵ A 69. 88. 945. 1175. 1646*. 1739. 1891 | τ. πν. δὲ τ. ἅγ. ὅ D^{C} E H P S Ψ 049. 056. 614. 1245. 1595. 1611. 2412. 2495 𝔐.

The omission of the relative pronoun in B03 may be due to homoeoteleuton (ΑΓΙΟΝΟΝ). If not, the sense is altered so that instead of being mentioned as a witness supporting the apostolic testimony, the Spirit is referred to only as a gift of God to those obeying him. D05 regularly refers to the Holy Spirit, as indeed an unclean spirit, with a masculine pronoun (cf., e.g., D05 Mk 1.10, 26; 3.11; 5.10, 13; 9.26 etc.). ℵ01 reads the neuter pronoun here.

5.33 ἐβούλοντο B A E Ψ 049. 36. 104. 431. 614. 876. 1611. 1838. 2138. 2412 *pc* co aeth; Chr || –εύοντο D, *cogitabant* d ℵ H P S 056. 181. 307. 323. 453. 610. 945. (–εύσαντο 1175. 1241). 1678. 1739. 1891. 2344 𝔐 lat sy^{p} arm; Lcf.

The same variant involving the two verbs βούλομαι and βουλεύομαι arises at 15.37. The latter expresses a stronger sense of intention rather than simply a wish as expressed by the former.

Commentary

[a] 5.27a *The Appearance of the Apostles in the Sanhedrin*

When the apostles are brought by the guard they are positioned (ἔστησαν) in the Sanhedrin. The third use of the verb ἵστημι with regard to the apostles contrasts with the two previous occurrences that described the apostles taking up position in the Temple (cf. on 5.25 above): whereas the apostles had obeyed the angel's command to stand in the Temple (cf. 5.20), the Jewish authorities stand them in the council to be accused of not obeying God.

[b] 5.27b–29a *The Questioning by the Priest*

5.27b–28 Although the high priest presided over the Sanhedrin and therefore may have been the one to address the apostles ('We gave you an absolute order...' [AT]), the Bezan text has an ordinary priest do this, asking a rhetorical question rather than making a statement ('Did we not...?'). The reminder in either case is of the vehement warning given by the Sanhedrin to Peter and John (4.18, 21), and is expressed forcefully.[26] Not only have the apostles continued their teaching about 'this' name (as if the name of Jesus could not be mentioned) but they have 'filled Jerusalem' with it. The form of the name of the city is the Hebrew-derived spelling, Ἰηρουσαλήμ, designating the religious centre of Judaism and not the town.[27] Exceptionally, the article is used before Jerusalem, as if expressing the close association, even the identification, of the Sanhedrin with Jerusalem as the seat of Jewish authority and the centre of worship in the Temple. They thus unwittingly demonstrate that the apostles have fulfilled the first part of the mission entrusted to them by Jesus, for they were to start announcing his message in Jerusalem: ἀρξαμένων ἀπὸ Ἰηρουσαλήμ (Lk. 24.47 D05; cf. Acts 1.8).

Worse still, the apostles have been attributing responsibility for the death of Jesus to the Jewish leaders (see 4.10). The audience of Acts, being privy to the development in the understanding of the apostles, know that their awareness of the Jewish leaders' role in Jesus' death had become more acute following the appearance of Peter and John before the Sanhedrin (cf. 4.27–28) and will not be surprised by the displeasure of the Sanhedrin. The Jewish authorities are threatened not only by the spread of teaching about Jesus as the resurrected Messiah, which they reject (4.1–2), and by the power the apostles claim they exercise in his name, which they cannot deny (4.16–17), but on top of all that they are being held responsible for putting an innocent man to death. More precisely, the apostles are accusing them of murdering the Messiah of Israel (cf. 3.15) which for any man would be bad enough, but for the rulers of Israel the consequences are unthinkable. The apostles must be stopped at all costs.

5.29a In the AT, Peter and the apostles answer the Sanhedrin at this point, beginning with a rephrasing of Peter and John's challenge to them at the

26. The use of a verb with its associated noun, παραγγελίᾳ παρηγγείλαμεν, is a typical Hebraic construction, appropriately attributed to the (high) priest; see B-D-R, §198.6; Zerwick and Grosvenor, *Analysis*, p. 366. For other occurrences of the same construction, cf. 2.17 x 2; 7.34; 28.26.

27 In the text of Codex Bezae, Luke adopts the dual spelling of the name of Jerusalem to distinguish between the geographical place and the centre of the Jewish religion; the pattern is less clear in the AT. See Read-Heimerdinger, *The Bezan Text*, pp. 311–44; and for an eclectic view of the variation among the MSS on this point, J.K. Elliott, 'An Eclectic Textual Study of the Book of Acts', in T. Nicklas and M. Tilly (eds.), *Apostelgeschichte als Kirchengeschichte. Text, Traditionen und antike Auslegungen* (BZNW, 122; Berlin: Walter de Gruyter, 2003), pp. 9–30.

previous hearing: 'Whether it is right in the sight of God to obey you rather than God, you judge' (4.19). The current wording is stronger and in the affirmative, taking the form of a typical apologetic formula,[28] but essentially it repeats what had been said to the Sanhedrin earlier. In Codex Bezae, however, the force of the saying changes for it is spoken as the priest's concluding sentence. As such, it answers the question put to the Sanhedrin on the earlier occasion, indicating that God is indeed to be obeyed and implying that, since the Sanhedrin represent God's authority among the Jews, the apostles must comply with their orders.

[b′] 5.29b–32 *Peter's Response*

5.29b In the Bezan text, Peter speaks on behalf of the apostles, as he has done on most occasions so far.

5.30–31 The speech of Peter (D05) / the apostles (AT) does not seek to answer the charges put to them by the Sanhedrin. If anything, it confirms their accuracy! The principal beliefs concerning Jesus are summarized in three points. First, the resurrection of Jesus (cf. 2.24, 32; 3.15; 4.2, 10), now named for the first time in this scene, is affirmed. 'The God of our Fathers' is designated as the agent of the resurrection (cf. 3.13 but not 4.10), making an appeal to their common heritage and, more especially, showing that Jesus was no common criminal but must have been approved by God. The language firmly sets Jesus within the context of Israel. The Jewish authorities are accused of having crucified him (cf. 2.23, 36; 3.15; 4.10), using an expression 'hanging on a tree' that will return in Peter's speech to Cornelius (10.39).

Secondly, Jesus is proclaimed as having been exalted by God, at his right hand (AT) or for his glory (D05), as a ruler and saviour. The proclamation takes up elements of the speech made by Peter to the people of Israel at Pentecost ('exalted at his right hand', 2.33, cf. 2.34; 'made Lord and Messiah', 2.36). The focus of these beliefs is important for it reveals an interpretation and application of the gospel message that is narrower and more exclusive than Jesus intended, as Peter himself will later understand. So, although it is not excluded in the understanding of the apostles at this stage that even before his death Jesus was Messiah, Lord, ruler and saviour, Peter presents these qualities each time in relation to his resurrection by God and to his exalted status. That is, his vision of the resurrection

28. The sentence is spoken by, e.g., Socrates; see Plato, *Apologia* 29D: πείσομαι δὲ μᾶλλον τῷ θεῷ ἢ ὑμῖν.

as a kind of heavenly enthronement tends to obscure the mission and rule of Jesus during his lifetime.

Moreover, he also restricts at this point Jesus' role as ruler and saviour solely for the benefit of Israel. This limiting of Jesus to the Jews has been seen in Peter's earlier speeches, with only infrequent glimpses of a more universal application when he was noted by Luke to be 'filled with the Spirit' (2.16–21; 4.8–12). Specifically, Peter announces here that the aim of Jesus' exaltation was for the repentance of Israel and the forgiveness of their sins. This was, indeed, where it was to begin but the apostles had been told by Jesus that his message of repentance and forgiveness was for all nations (Lk. 24.47).

The weaknesses in the arguments put forward by Peter (or by all the apostles, AT) correspond to the absence of any mention of his being filled with the Spirit as he speaks, or of the boldness that was a mark of the Spirit (cf. 4.13, 31) and apparent at the earlier hearing. In consequence, it is Gamaliel who will come onto the stage as an instrument to assist in the defence of the apostles.

5.32 Insisting on the testimony of the apostles (cf. 2.32, 36; 3.15; 4.33) which is confirmed by the witness of the Holy Spirit, Peter responds to the matter of obeying God, raised by the priest according to Codex Bezae: the fact that they have been given the Holy Spirit by God is evidence that they obey him. The unsaid corollorary is, of course, that those who have not been given the Holy Spirit, the Sanhedrin, have not obeyed him, calling into question their authority and claim to speak for God.

In the text of Codex Vaticanus, the Spirit is not mentioned as a corroborative witness but only as the gift of God to those obeying him.

By his reference to the gift of the Spirit, Peter may be alluding to Pentecost but is also likely to have in mind the second, more recent, occasion when the Spirit was given following their release from the Sanhedrin (4.31). Then, the whole community had been given boldness to speak the word of God, that same boldness that had struck the Sanhedrin when Peter, filled with the Spirit, had spoken to them on the first occasion (4.8, cf. 4.13). No more now than then, however, are they likely to recognize God's presence with the apostles. The Sadducees in particular, with their doctrine excluding God's intervention in the world, will not be moved by the claims that God has acted either through Jesus or the Holy Spirit.

[a'] 5.33 *The Sanhedrin's Decision*

5.33 Having heard him to the end, the Sanhedrin are totally exasperated. The Bezan text goes further than the AT in saying not only that they 'wished' to kill the apostles but that they 'intended' to do so. Similarly, the high priests and the scribes had sought to kill Jesus (Lk. 22.2) because he had systematically undermined their authority when he was teaching in the Temple (cf. 19.27–22.2). In order to proceed with their wish or intention, the Sanhedrin may have needed to bring in the Roman authorities if, as some evidence suggests, they did not have the power to impose the death sentence without them.[29] The evidence, however, for killing the apostles is lacking, as Gamaliel will point out to them.

The same combination of verbs (ἀκούσαντες ... διεπρίοντο) will be used later to describe the reaction of the members of the Sanhedrin when they hear Stephen (ἀκούοντες ... διεπρίοντο, 7.54). He, in contrast to the apostles, will be more outspoken in his opposition to the Temple institution and will distance himself from Israel and the Fathers of Israel (7.51–53), causing the Sanhedrin to act upon their fury and stone him to death. Stephen's death will serve retrospectively to show up the weaknesses of Peter's speech to the Sanhedrin on this occasion.

[BB′] 5.34–40 *Gamaliel's Intervention*

Overview

For the first time in Acts, the party of the Pharisees are mentioned. There would have been a number of Pharisees among the Sanhedrin and Gamaliel, a well-known and influential rabbi, intervenes as their representative (see *Excursus* 9).

Structure and Themes

The introduction to the new character, Gamaliel, leads directly into his speech, to which the council respond by releasing their prisoners:

[a] 5.34–39 Gamaliel's speech
[a′] 5.40 The Sanhedrin's response

The speech itself is divided, following Luke's normal pattern of speeches, into two parts, an Exposition (5.35–37) and a Parenesis (5.38–39).

29. Cf. E.M. Smallwood, *The Jews under Roman Rule: From Pompey to Diocletian* (Leiden: E.J. Brill, 1996), pp. 149–50; J.-P. Lemonon, *Pilate et le gouvernement de la Judée* (EBib.; Paris: J. Gabalda, 1981), pp. 74–75; 79–96.

Translation

	Codex Bezae D05	*Codex Vaticanus B03*
[BB′]		
[a]	**5.34** However, a certain member of the Sanhedrin intervened, a Pharisee called Gamaliel who was a teacher of the law revered by all the people, and he ordered the apostles to be put outside for a little while before saying to the rulers and the Sanhedrin members, **35** 'Men of Israel, take careful thought over what you are about to do to these men. **36** For not so long ago there rose up Theudas, saying that he was someone great, and indeed, a number of men adhered to him, about 400 of them, and he killed himself, and all those who followed him likewise were reduced to nothing. **37** After him rose up Judas the Galilean in the days of the census and attracted many people as his followers. He, too, perished and those who followed him were scattered. **38** As for the present case, they are brethren; I tell you, keep away from these men and leave them alone, not defiling your hands; because if this plan or this enterprise should be of men, it will be destroyed; **39** but if it is of God, you will not be able to destroy them, neither you nor kings nor tyrants. Accordingly, keep away from these men lest you be found fighters against God.'	**5.34** However, someone in the Sanhedrin intervened, a Pharisee called Gamaliel who was a teacher of the law revered by all the people, and he ordered the men to be put outside for a little while before saying to them, **35** 'Men of Israel, take careful thought over what you are about to do to these men. **36** For not so long ago there rose up Theudas, saying that he was somebody, and a number of men adhered to him, about 400 of them, and he was killed, and all those who followed him were scattered and they came to nothing. **37** After him rose up Judas the Galilean in the days of the census and attracted people as his followers. He, too, perished and all those who followed him were scattered. **38** And now I say to you, keep away from these men and release them; because if this plan or this enterprise should be of men, it will be destroyed; **39** but if it is of God, you will not be able to destroy them. You could perhaps be found fighters against God.'
[a′]	**5.40** They believed him, and having called in the apostles, they beat them and charged them not to speak about the name of Jesus, and they released them.	**5.40** They were persuaded by him, and having called in the apostles, they beat them and charged them not to speak about the name of Jesus, and they released them.

Critical Apparatus

5.34 ἐν τῷ συνεδρίῳ Φαρισαῖος B P45.74 ℵ *rell, in concilio pharisaeus* d || ἐκ τοῦ συνεδρίου (+ αὐτῶν E) Φαρ. D E h p bo aeth.

The D05 reading has to be taken as a partitive genitive, meaning either 'a certain Pharisee from (belonging to) the Sanhedrin', or 'a certain member of the Sanhedrin, a Pharisee...'. The B03 reading could have either of these two meanings, too, but the preposition ἐν creates a further ambiguity for it could have a locative sense, meaning that 'someone stood up *in* the Sanhedrin, a Pharisee...'.

(ἐκέλευσεν) ἔξω (– P^{74}) βραχὺ τοὺς ἀνθρώπους B ($P^{45.74}$) ℵ A 614 *pc* p vg bo || τοὺς ἀποστόλους ἔξω βραχύ D d gig h sy^{h} | ἔξω τ. ἀποστ. βρ. τι H S 049. 056. 330. 440. 1241. 1505. 1854. 2492 | ἔξω βρ. τι τ. ἀποστ. P 33^{vid}. 2147 | ἔξω βρ. τ. ἀποστ. E Ψ 0140. 69. 88. 614. 945. 1175. 1245. 1270. 1611. 1739. 2412. 2495 𝔐 sy^{p} sa mae.

The designation of the prisoners as 'men' by B03 anticipates Gamaliel's two references to them in 5.35, 38. D05 draws attention to the identity of the prisoners by placing the noun before the adverb and using the term 'apostles'.

5.35 πρὸς αὐτούς B P^{74} ℵ *rell* || πρ. τοὺς ἄρχοντας καὶ τοὺς συνεδρίους D d sa (mae).

The 'rulers' are distinguished from the council members by D05, possibly referring to the high priestly circle who were, to some extent, a distinct group and whose power was controlled by the council (see Grant, *The Jews in the Roman World*, p. 92). Alternatively, 'rulers' may refer to the presence of Roman authorities. See *Commentary*, 4.5–6.

Although the pronoun in B03 is potentially confusing, for it could be taken as signifying the apostles (Delebecque, *Les deux Actes*, p. 249), the context makes it clear enough who is meant, so it is unlikely to have prompted the clarification provided by the D05 reading. It is more probable that D05 saw a need to underline the different groups of authorities whom Gamaliel was addressing.

(προσέχετε) ἑαυτοῖς B ℵ $D^{s.m.}$ (*vobis* d) | αὐτοῖς $P^{45.74}$ C 69 || ἑαυτούς D^{*}.

The dative of B03 is correct, as noted by a later copyist of D05.

5.36 (τινα) ἑαυτόν B $P^{45.74}$ ℵ A^{*} C H P Ψ 049. 056. 945. 1175. 1739. 1891. 2492 𝔐 || μέγαν ἑαυ. D (*magnum ipsorum* d) sy^{p} mae | ἑαυ. μέγ. A^{2} E 36. 255. 257. 431. 522. 614. 927. 1270. 1837. 2147. 2298. 2412 *pc* a gig h vg^{mss} aeth; Or Cyr Hier.

Theudas' self-designation as 'someone great' in D05 is a way of identifying himself as the Messiah. Particular emphasis is conferred on the adjective by the word order of D05.

ᾧ προσεκλίθη B $P^{45.74}$ ℵ A C^{2} E H P Ψ 049. 056. 945. 1175. 1245. 1270^{c}. 1739. 1891. 2147 *pm*, *cui adsensum est* d | ᾧ προσεκλίθησαν C^{*} 1270^{*} | ᾧ προσεκολλήθη 104.

226. 323. 440. 614. 927. 1241. 1505. 1611. 2344. 2412. 2495 || ᾧ καὶ προσεκλίθη D* (–θησαν D^A^).

Adverbial καί in D05 draws attention to the comment about the men who were attached to Theudas.

ἀνδρῶν ἀριθμός B P74 ℵ A C E 69. 88. 945. 1175. 1739. 1891. 2147 || ἀριθ. ἀνδρ. D d H P S Ψ 049. 056. 232. 383. 614. 1245. 1270. 1505. 1611. 1837. 2412. 2495 𝔐 a b g h p s vg^AD^.

It is B03 that modifies the usual order of noun + dependent genitive to place the noun ἀριθμός closer to the figure cited (Read-Heimerdinger, *The Bezan Text*, pp. 110–13).

This reading of D05 operates in combination with the previous two readings to accentuate the size and importance of the uprising under Theudas.

ὃς ἀνηρέθη B P74 ℵ D^D^ *rell*, *qui interfectus est* d || ὃς διελύθη αὐτὸς δι᾽ αὐτοῦ D* p mae.

Whereas B03 describes Theudas as simply being killed (cf. 5.33), D05 specifies that he committed suicide, using the verb διαλύω. This is the same verb that B03 will use to describe the fate of Theudas' supporters (see below).

(αὐτῷ) διελύθησαν B P74 ℵ D^F^ *rell* | διεσκορπίσθησαν 614. 1611. 2412 || *om.* D* d (p).

In the D05 reading above, διαλύω means 'destroyed' whereas here in B03 it could mean either that Theudas' many supporters were dispersed or destroyed. As for D05, instead of a second verb to describe their fate, this text applies the same verb to both the leader and his followers (see above).

5.37 (ἀπέστησεν) λαόν B P74 ℵ A* 88. 915. 1175. 1241 *pc*, *populum* d ar c dem ph ro vg sa^mss^ bo; Eus Cyr || λαὸν πολύν D C (e) gig (h) p (w) mae aeth; (Or) | λα. ἱκανόν A² H P S 049. 056. 0140. 36. 37. 69. 453. 610. 945. 1245. 1409. 1678. 1739. 1891 𝔐 sy^P^ | ἱκαν. λα. E Ψ 33. 181. 431. 614. 1108. 1611. 1270. 1611. 1898. 2138. 2344. 2412. 2412. (2495) *pc*; Chr.

As in the case of Theudas, so in the account of Judas the Galilean D05 insists on the size of the uprising.

πάντες (ὅσοι) B P74 ℵ *rell* || *om.* D P45 209 it; Ephr.

Having emphasized the number of Judas' followers, it is now sufficient for D05 to say that all perished without exception by using the relative pronoun ὅσοι. B03 stresses the fact with the adjective πάντες.

5.38 καὶ νῦν B* E || κ. τὰ νῦν D P74 ℵ *rell.*

B03 omits the neuter plural article referring to the matters of the present (Zerwick and Grosvenor, *Analysis*) and introduces the parenesis of his speech with a simple adverb. The formula καὶ *τὰ* νῦν is used elsewhere to move from the expository section of a speech to the present application (references including τά are in italics): 3.17; *4.29*; *5.38*; 10.5, 33 (νῦν οὖν); 13.11; 15.10 (νῦν οὖν); *17.30*; 20.22, 25, 32.

εἰσὶν (– Ds.m.) ἀδελφοί D* (*fratres* d) h mae || *om.* B P45.74 ℵ *rell.*

The D05 reading is an important part of Gamaliel's defence of the apostles according to that text, for he draws the attention of the council to the fact that they are Jews, which affects how they should be treated.

ἄφετε (αὐτούς) B P74vid ℵ A C Ψ 88. 1175 *pc* || ἐάσατε D E H P S 049. 056. 0140. 33vid. 383. 614. 945. 1611. 1739. 1891. 2412 𝔐; Chr.

The verb of B03, ἀφίημι, is potentially ambiguous since it can mean 'let go' or 'forgive'. ἐάω in D05 conveys an exhortation to 'leave them alone', reinforcing Gamaliel's first command to 'stand away from them'.

μὴ μιαίναντες τὰς χεῖρας D d 61 mae | μὴ μολύνοντες τ. χεῖ. ὑμῶν E h Beda || *om.* B P74vid ℵ *rell.*

Gamaliel is unlikely to be saying in D05 that the Sanhedrin should let the apostles go because defilement would ensue from unlawfully killing them (cf., e.g., Num. 35.33–34), for the consequences of the Temple authorities' committing such a sin would be enormous, and disastrous for the whole of the land of Israel. Possibly he is referring to the ritual impurity that could arise from the Temple authorities' being in the presence of a dead body, even without physical contact according to one school of rabbinic thought (see *Eliyahu Rabbah*, a commentary on Mishnah *Tohoroth* by Elijah Ben Solomon, Gaon of Vilna [Brünn, 1802]), in which case his concern with the 'defiling of hands' could be connected with the requirement for the priests to be pure in order to handle sacrifices.

5.39 (αὐτοὺς) οὔτε ὑμεῖς οὔτε βασιλεῖς οὔτε τύραννοι D *(nec vos nec imperatores nec reges* d) 876. 913. 1108. 1611. 2138 (h) syh** mae | οὔτε ὑμεῖς οὔτε οἱ ἄρχοντες ὑμῶν E gig dem w vgD (sa); Beda || *om.* B P74 ℵ *rell.*

The phrase of D05, listing those powers who will not be able to destroy the apostles, resembles that of Wisd. 12.14, but the context there is the opposite: none will be able to *defend* those whom God has punished. It may be that Gamaliel is making an allusion to a Jewish tradition in which these words figure, but none has been identified so far.

ἀπέχεσθε οὖν ἀπὸ τῶν ἀνθρώπων τούτων D d 913 h (w dem) mae | ἀπόσχεσθε οὖν ἀπὸ τῶν ἀνδρῶν τού. 431. 614. 876. 1108. 1611. 2138. 2401^{c}. 2412 h sy^{h**} mae || *om.* B P^{74} ℵ *rell.*

Gamaliel's initial exhortation of 5.38a is repeated at the end of his speech in D05, with a change only of the verb.

The result of the variants in D05 is that Gamaliel's sympathy and support for the apostles is stronger than in the B03 text.

(μήποτε) καί B P^{74} ℵ D^{B} *rell* || *om.* D* d 630. 1311. 2138. 2495 *pc* p vg^{O} sy co.

The adverbial καί in B03 arises from the fact that this final clause of Gamaliel's speech follows on directly from the second conditional clause, εἰ ... ἐστίν, without the intervening material of D05. If the clause is to be linked in sense to the conditional, μήποτε must mean 'maybe'; but it is also possible to link it to the imperative of 5.38a (Barrett, I, p. 297).

ἐπείσθησαν (δὲ αὐτῷ) B P^{74} ℵ D^{B} *rell* || <π>επιστ<ευκότ>ες D$^{p.m.?}$.

The reconstruction of the D05 reading, illegible in the MS, is based on Scrivener's comments that one letter is missing from the beginning of the word and four from the middle (Scrivener, *Bezae Codex*, pp. 441–42). Luke frequently employs πιστεύω + dative (cf. Lk. 20.5; Acts 8.12; 16.34; 17.34; 18.8a, 8c D05; 26.27; 27.25). At Lk. 16.31 D05, there is the similar reading of πιστεύσουσιν instead of πεισθήσονται.

5.40 (ἀπέλυσαν) αὐτούς D E H P S Ψ 049. 056. 33. 88. 614. 1270. 1505. 1611. 1739. 2412. 2495 𝔐 lat sy; Lcf || *om.* B P^{74} ℵ A C 1175 *pc.*

The pronoun is not strictly necessary but it establishes a clear parallel with 4.21 (οἱ δὲ προσαπειλησάμενοι ἀπέλυσαν αὐτούς).

Commentary

[a] 5.34–39 *Gamaliel's Speech*

5.34 Until now, the action has been directed by the high priests and the Sadducees, although the Pharisees have obviously been involved as members of the Sanhedrin. They were an influential voice in the council because they enjoyed greater popular support than the aristocratic Sadducees, though they were in the minority and, it seems, played a more passive than active role.[30] On this occasion, as later in the case of Paul (23.9), they are portrayed by Luke as defending the Jesus-believers in

30. M. Grant, *The Jews in the Roman World* (London: Weidenfeld and Nicolson, 1973), pp. 92–93.

the Sanhedrin. Gamaliel is introduced as their representative (τις), and Luke's information that he was a well-known and respected teacher of the law is backed up by Rabbinic evidence.[31] Paul's own teacher (22.3), he belonged to the moderate school of rabbis who advocated peaceful obedience to the law rather than aggressive action to enforce it. He died in 62 CE but he continued to be remembered and honoured, as Luke's audience would no doubt be aware.

As a representative of the Pharisees, he speaks on their behalf. The participle ἀναστάς used to introduce his intervention is the same as that used to introduce the reaction of the high priest and the Sadducees at 5.17 (see *Commentary*, 5.17), thus creating a correspondance between them.

At the same time, there are echoes of the earlier Sanhedrin meeting, in which Gamaliel would presumably have also participated. There, the Sanhedrin in general gave the order (κελεύσαντες) for Peter and John to be taken out of the council chamber to allow a discussion to be held out of their hearing (4.15); here, it is Gamaliel alone (ἐκέλευσεν) who asks for them to be put outside.

5.35 In the Bezan text, Gamaliel's addressees are noted as being the 'rulers and Sanhedrin members', possibly distinguishing the high priestly circle from the other Sanhedrin members, or alluding to the presence of Roman authorities (see *Commentary*, 4.5–6). The form of address that he adopts, 'Men of Israel', is the same that Peter uses when he addresses his fellow-Jews (cf. 2.22; 3.12) and situates the issue under discussion quite clearly in its Jewish context.

The thrust of Gamaliel's argument is a warning to the Sanhedrin not to rush into action and kill the apostles. There may have been several reasons why he wanted to prevent their deaths: on the one hand, he would have sympathized with certain aspects of the apostolic teaching, the resurrection in particular, and supported them against the Sadducees' doctrines; on the other hand, it would be in keeping with his own philosophy to allow events to work themselves out in accordance with the will of God rather than taking violent action.

5.36 In order to prepare the way for his advice to the Sanhedrin to leave the apostles alone, Gamaliel reminds them of two previous instigators of

31. See *Mishnah Sot.* 9.15 which describes him as a 'rabban' (great master): 'When Rabban Gamaliel the Elder died, the glory of the law ceased and purity and abstinence died.'

uprisings who came to nothing. Both date from some years earlier since Judas the Galilean, whom he cites as coming after Theudas, was active in the days of the census, that is 6–7 CE. There were, by all accounts, numerous individuals who attempted to lead rebellions against the Romans in the first century, some of them claiming to be the Messiah.[32] Although Josephus speaks of a certain Theudas who claimed to be a prophet and attracted a large following, this happened later in 44–46 CE; his following was larger than the 400 mentioned by Gamaliel and he was killed by having his head being cut off which does not concord with the detail in the Bezan text that Theudas committed suicide. All things considered it looks as if it is not the Theudas of Josephus who is being referred to.

According to Gamaliel, Theudas claimed to be 'somebody' – the Bezan reading 'someone great' is a euphemism for the Messiah which has been obscured by the AT by the omission of the adjective. The number of his followers is no approximation but, as usual, the particle ὡς introduces a number that has a symbolic significance. Multiples of 4 – 40, 400, 4,000[33] – establish a connection with the early history of Israel and, although in the case of Theudas not enough is known about him to determine precisely the significance of the number 400, it tallies with his pretension to be the redeemer of Israel and confirms his nationalist aims.[34]

5.37 Judas the Galilean is considerably easier to identify.[35] He led a movement among the people of Israel to oppose the census decreed by Quirinius that caused Judaea to be annexed to Syria, protesting that God was the king of Israel and the Jews should be subject only to him. He was unsuccessful in his attempt to gain political independence for the Jews and his movement was disbanded but his associate, a Pharisee by the name of Sadduk, went on to lead a militant wing of the Pharisees known in some quarters as the 'Zealots'.[36] Once again, the size of the revolt is emphasized in the Bezan text.

32. E.g. Origen (*C.Cels.*, I.57) who mentions not only a Theudas from before the time of Jesus' birth but also Judas the Galilean, in addition to two Samaritans who claimed to be messiahs.

33. See 21.38, '4,000 men of the Assassins'. Cf. the 4,000 people who were fed by Jesus in Gentile territory (Mk 8.9, 20; Matt. 15.38; 16.10), a pericope omitted by Luke.

34. 400 is the number of soldiers in a military formation in the shape of a square that faced the enemy on four sides.

35. See E. Schürer, *The History of the Jewish People in the Age of Jesus Christ* (3 vols.; rev. and ed. G. Vermes, F. Millar, M. Black; Edinburgh: T&T Clark, 1973), I, pp. 332, 381–82.

36. Josephus, *Ant.* 18.1.1.6.

Luke, however, does not report Gamaliel's reference to these revolutionary leaders in order to simply confer historical realism on his account but to draw lessons from the historical examples.[37] Gamaliel will make his point in the second part of his speech. Indirectly, meanwhile, he has revealed how the apostles were seen by the Jewish leaders. For if Gamaliel compares the apostolic movement with those of Theudas and Judas, it is not only that they all were Jews from recent times or that each had a large group of followers but also that they were all, in one way or another, claiming to represent the interests of Israel. The people he selects for comparison confirm that the apostles were perceived by the Jews as leading a nationalist movement.

5.38a Gamaliel's advice is clear: the leaders should keep well clear of the apostles and should let them go. In the Bezan text, Gamaliel makes clear his own position: 'they are brethren (εἰσὶν ἀδελφοί), I tell you', insisting on the fact that they are Jews, not enemies from another nation. Having urged the Sanhedrin to let them go, he then goes on in the Bezan text to qualify his advice by adding 'not defiling hands' (μὴ μιάναντες τὰς χεῖρας). The point of the comment is not entirely clear for whilst Gamaliel's preoccupation with defilement certainly corresponds to his position as a Pharisee, just what he means will cause the defilement of hands is difficult to determine.[38] On the one hand, the words can be read as indicating the consequence that will arise if the prisoners are not released. However, the difficulties of interpreting Gamaliel's words as meaning that the Sanhedrin should release the apostles because they would defile their hands by killing them have been pointed out in the *Critical Apparatus*: by committing an unlawful killing, they would be morally impure and defile not only their hands but the land of Israel (the implication of their fury that the apostles have been 'bringing the blood' of Jesus on them, 5.28). An alternative suggestion is that the impurity Gamaliel has in mind is ritual, as if he is thinking of the hands of the priests becoming impure through contact with the dead bodies and therefore unfit to perform sacrificial duties.

37. Cf. Lk. 13.1–5, where Jesus compares his present audience of Jews with two examples of groups of people who had recently been killed, for the purpose of teaching a lesson about sin and repentance.

38. The categories of defilement in ancient Judaism and the regulations concerning them are notoriously complex. A useful survey has been made by J. Klawans, *Impurity and Sin in Ancient Judaism* (Oxford: Oxford University Press, 2000), see esp. pp. 3–60.

Another rather different line of investigation is suggested by taking the words 'not defiling hands' as an adverbial clause describing the manner in which the Sanhedrin should let the apostles go, qualifying the command. In other words, they should release them in an honourable fashion, taking account of the fact that 'they are brethren'. On this understanding, Gamaliel's concern is with justice and the suggestion is that the priests' hands would be made impure for sacrifice if they mistreated their prisoners. In the event, they apparently did not heed the advice, since they beat them (5.40, δείραντες, active) before releasing them.

5.38b–39 Gamaliel continues by applying the lesson drawn from the two examples he cited. He puts forward two possibilities, that the apostles' activities are from men or from God. The debate among the Jewish authorities over whether a religious activity was of men or God has already arisen over Jesus, precisely concerning his teaching in the Temple (Lk. 20.1–7), and on that occasion they did not obtain an answer to their question. Gamaliel, for his part, makes his opinion clear by his choice of expressions. For the first hypothesis, he uses a particular Greek construction that shows he does not support it: supposing that their activity is a merely human enterprise, then they will be destroyed, in the same way as the uprisings of Theudas and Judas came to nothing.[39] In the second case, he proposes not a remote hypothesis but a real possibility: 'if it is of God, you will not be able to destroy them'. He makes the point emphatically in the Bezan text, saying that no matter what their human, earthly power might be, no-one could not destroy the apostles (see *Critical Apparatus*). This, of course, is precisely what has been seen to have happened in the attempt to get rid of Jesus, though it is not clear how far Gamaliel, let alone the high priests or the other members of the Sanhedrin, have realized that.

A final, emphatic command is repeated in the Bezan text, reiterating Gamaliel's advice to the Sanhedrin to stay clear of the apostles, 'these men' as he calls them for the third time (cf. 5.35, 38). His sympathy for the Jesus believers is quite obvious in this text, though there is no indication that it derives from an inclination to accept their teaching; it is more likely to reflect his Pharisaic principles of moderation and tolerance and, as shown by his last words of caution, a fear of opposing God.

39. The conditional in this first case is expressed by the construction ἐάν + subjunctive verb (cf. Lk. 23.35). The second conditional clause of v. 39 is, in contrast, expressed by εἰ + indicative verb, presenting a real possibility.

[a′] 5.40 *The Sanhedrin's Response*

5.40 The reaction of the Sanhedrin to Gamaliel is noted, not without a hint of irony, with the same verb (aorist, ἐπείθησαν δὲ αὐτῷ) as that used to express the support given to Theudas and Judas the Galilean (imperfect, ἐπείθοντο αὐτῷ, 5.36, 37), meaning that they were persuaded by him, or they accepted what he said. The text of Codex Bezae appears to say that they 'believed' him (see *Critical Apparatus*).

In consequence, the apostles were called back into the council chamber and were released. They were first punished, nonetheless, with a beating (which seems to have taken place there and then) followed by a repeat warning (cf. 4.18) not to mention the name of Jesus.

This is the last time that the apostles come into direct conflict with the Jewish authorities in Jerusalem. It seems that following this attempt to suppress the Jesus-believers, future attempts are made indirectly, notably through Herod (Agrippa I) when the apostle James is killed and Peter imprisoned (12.1–13).

[BA′] 5.41–42 *The Liberation of the Apostles*

Overview

The final two verses of the chapter stand as a kind of epilogue to Section IV and bring to a close the first part of the book of Acts.

Structure and Themes

The two verses describe the release of the apostles and, echoing earlier summaries, conclude with a positive statement about their ongoing activity:

[a] 5.41 The apostles' joy
[a′] 5.42 Their continued teaching

Translation

Codex Bezae D05

[BA′]

[a] **5.41** So the apostles went rejoicing from their appearance before the Sanhedrin, because on behalf of the name they were deemed worthy to be dishonoured.

[a′] **42** Every day, in the Temple and in the houses, they did not cease teaching and announcing that the Lord was Jesus, the Messiah.

Codex Vaticanus B03

5.41 So they went rejoicing from their appearance before the Sanhedrin, because they were deemed worthy to be dishonoured on behalf of the name.

42 And every day, in the Temple and in the houses, they did not cease teaching and announcing that the Messiah was Jesus.

Critical Apparatus

5.41 (Οἱ μὲν οὖν) ἀπόστολοι D d 614. 1611. 2412 *pc* p sy^{h} mae; Ambst || *om.* B P^{74} ℵ *rell.*

This is the second time in this passage that D05 has specified that the people concerned are the apostles (cf. 5.34 above). On both occasions, a clearer contrast is made between the apostles and the Jewish council.

κατηξιώθησαν ὑπὲρ τοῦ ὀνόματος B P^{74} ℵ A C (056). 69. (88). 323. (945. 1175). 1505. 1739. 1891. 2147 || ὑπ. τ. ὀν. κατηξ. D d H P 049*. 1. 1646. 2495 | ὑπ. τ. ὀν. Ἰησοῦ κατηξ. Ψ 33. (330). 440. 927. 1270. 1837 𝔐 gig h p vg | ὑπ. τ. ὀν. τοῦ κυρίου Ἰη. κατεξ. E 547. 614. 1241. 1611. 2412.

The order of words in D05 underlines the cause for which the apostles had suffered, that is, the name of Jesus.

5.42 πᾶσάν τε ἡμέραν B ℵ *rell* || πᾶσαν δὲ ἡμ. D d 242 e gig h vg sa bo; Lcf.

With the particle τε, B03 views the apostles' presence in the Temple and in the houses as an additional event leading on from their departure from the council (5.41). D05, on the other hand, presents it as a new development, which brings out the fact that the apostles' teaching and evangelizing activities represent a change from their miracle working in the Temple before their arrest.

(εὐαγγελιζόμενοι) τὸν Χριστὸν Ἰησοῦν B P^{74} ℵ A 88. 323. 440. 547. 614. 945. 1175. 1270. 1739. 1837. 1891. 2147. 2412. 2495 | Ἰη. Χρ. E Ψ 1245. 1646 | Ἰη. τὸν Χρ. H P 049. 056. 1. 226. 330. 618. 1241. 1243. 1505. 1828. 1854. 2492 || τ. κύριον Ἰη. Χρ. D d 1898 gig h p vg^{CT} sy^{p} sa aeth; Ephr Lcf | τ. κύρ. Ἰη. C 33. 927. 2344.

This is one of several variant readings that cause the order of the name and title/function of Jesus to be interchanged and/or an additional element to be specified (see Read-Heimerdinger, *The Bezan Text*, pp. 261–74). An examination of such variant readings demonstrates that, contrary to popular opinion, D05 does not simply add elements to make the name of Jesus complete; on the contrary, where there are more elements in D05, there is always an underlying reason. In view of these findings, it can be said that according to B03, the apostles were engaged in announcing that the Messiah was Jesus. Not so D05 which has the apostles announce that the Lord of the Jewish Scriptures was Jesus, the Messiah. It is a much more bold step to identify the Lord as Jesus, and one that B03 will systematically avoid making (*The Bezan Text*, p. 293).

Commentary

[a] 5.41 *The Apostles' Joy*

5.41 In the concluding verses to this section, Luke describes two effects of the apostles' release from the Sanhedrin, from which they had escaped with a beating although there had been talk of putting them to death (5.33). The first effect is immediate and consists in the apostles' rejoicing that they had done something to merit their punishment, that they had been mistreated for having proclaimed the name of Jesus, exactly as he himself had forewarned (cf. Lk. 21.12). Although they have not been 'hated by all' (cf. 21.17), the apostolic community has had a foretaste of the persecution Jesus promised his disciples (cf. 6.22–23).

[a′] 5.42 *Their Continued Teaching*

5.42 The second effect of the apostles' release is a lasting one and builds on the order given to the apostles during the previous night. Their teaching and proclamation about Jesus was carried on without ceasing both in the Temple and in private houses. In the Temple, it would be addressed to the people of Israel, in a public place of meeting, while in the houses, the setting would be more personal and private. The same combination of public and private meetings was seen in the first summary (cf. 2.46) but there, all the believers were involved and the activity was limited to worship and the breaking of bread. Here, it is a question of the apostles and in comparison with the first summary, it is striking how their activity is now described as directed outward, taking the message of the gospel beyond the community although without excluding by any means ministry among the Jesus-believers.

This is the first time that the verb εὐαγγελίζομαι has been encountered in Acts. The verb used so far for speaking about Jesus has been 'speaking' (4.1, 17, 20, 31; 5.20, 40) or 'teaching' (4.2, 18; 5.21, 25, 28). Evangelizing in Acts is a more public proclamation than teaching (cf. e.g., 8.4, 12, 25, 35, 40; 10.36; 11.20; 14.7; 17.18); and the fact that it is chosen here for the first time is a sign that the apostles are beginning to enjoy a greater inner freedom and boldness to speak about Jesus as the Messiah. Its equivalent was used by Luke in describing Jesus' instructions to his apostles: he ordered them 'to preach the gospel', κηρύσσειν τὸ εὐαγγέλιον (1.2 D05: cf. Lk. 9.2 and Mk 3.14 D05).

So something of a landmark is reached as the apostles fulfil their mission to testify to Jesus in Jerusalem. It has been noted in this section that Luke has been drawing attention throughout the last episodes to the fact that witness has been borne to Jesus among the Jewish people, among the Jewish leaders and in the centre of Jewish worship, all of them in Jerusalem. He has also been pointing out where the witness has been incomplete, because it has focused on his resurrection and has tended to restrict his role as being for the benefit of Israel; and because the apostles have continued to cling to the idea of Israel as the privileged people of God. Nonetheless, they have progressed in their understanding and have modified some of their core beliefs, notably as they recognized the part played by the Jewish authorities in Jesus' death and realized that they themselves were to replace the traditional leadership among the Jesus-believers.

The next stage of the narrative will continue to look at how the apostles exercised their leadership function and will develop the hints that have been made in the course of the first chapters concerning the importance of the Hellenist members of the church. For the time being, persecution from the high priest and his circle has been stopped but further, more indirect, persecution will be reported as the Jesus-believing community move away from Jerusalem to preach the good news of Jesus to people who have so far been excluded by Jewish law from the people of God.

Excursus 8

The Re-enactment of the Exodus[40]

At several places in the commentary on 5.12–42 parallels were noted with the story of the Exodus, the event recorded in the book of Exodus that undergirds so much of Jewish theology and that is foundational for Jewish self-awareness as the chosen people of God. In his Gospel, Luke already made use of the Exodus paradigm to show how Jesus carried out his own exodus, but in a new way that turned upside down the ancient model (ἔλεγον τὴν ἔξοδον αὐτοῦ ἣν ἤμελλεν πληροῦν ἐν Ἰερουσαλήμ, Lk. 9.31, cf. 9.51). For Jesus made his exodus out of Jerusalem, in contradiction of the idea that Jerusalem was the holy city, the centre of Jewish existence where the Messiah would appear.

After his resurrection, he likewise attempted to take his disciples out of Jerusalem: he 'led them outside (ἐξήγαγεν αὐτοὺς ἔξω, Lk. 24.50 D05;

40. The treatment of the Exodus theme in Acts has been examined in more detail in Read-Heimerdinger, 'The Re-enactment of the History of Israel: Exodus Traditions in the Bezan Text of Acts', in R. Pope (ed.), *Remembering the Past and Shaping the Future: Religious and Biblical Studies in Wales* (Leominster: Gracewing, 2003), pp. 81–96.

AT: ἕως) near Bethany', using the verb that characterized the Exodus (ἐξάγω LXX, e.g. Exod. 12.17, 42, 51; see Stephen speaking of the Exodus, Acts 7.36, 40). On each of these occasions, the spelling adopted for Jerusalem is the Hebrew-derived spelling, Ἰερουσαλήμ (on the significance of the spelling of Jerusalem, see *General Introduction*, §V.5). It is therefore significant that before leaving them for the last time, Jesus instructed the apostles to go back to the city (Lk. 24.49) or Ἱεροσόλυμα (Acts 1.4, see *Commentary*). Instead, however, not yet understanding that Jerusalem no longer had any religious significance or that their function as leaders was not attached to the place, they returned to Ἰερουσαλήμ (Acts 1.12, see *Commentary*), even to the Temple (cf. Lk. 24.52).

Once the apostles have realized the part played by the Jewish religious authorities in the death of Jesus and have experienced first hand their continued opposition to his role as Messiah (and their own as his witnesses) they are also able to understand that the Temple, the seat of authority for the Jewish leaders, can no longer be the place of worship for the Jesus-believers. It is at that point that the Lord intervenes to free them from the control of the high priest and the other religious leaders. It will be the first step towards their total release from their attachment to Jerusalem, a deliverance that will first be accomplished by the leader of the apostles, Peter, in Acts 12.

The theological importance Luke accords to the liberation of the apostles is shown by the way he builds into his narrative in Acts 5 the Exodus paradigm. The way he causes his characters to re-enact the Exodus is more apparent in the text of Codex Bezae than in the AT, not only because it displays more complete and more complex allusions to the Exodus event but because it uses the ancient event in a typically Jewish way as a paradigm to interpret the recent developments in the history of Israel (see *General Introduction*, §§V, XI). The result is that, as often, where the AT relates a historical, factual incident, the Bezan text makes use of the incident to draw out profound theological truths, in this case that the Jewish religious leaders, chief of whom is the high priest, have taken on the role of Pharaoh as they oppress the witnesses to Jesus as the Messiah.

Within the imprisonment scene, the series of markers that recall the deliverance of the Israelites from Egypt can be identified as follows:

1. The motive of the high priest and the Sadducees for attacking the apostles was jealousy (5.17), concording with a tradition that Pharaoh sought to get rid of Moses because he was jealous of his success.[41]

41. The evidence for this tradition is found in the work of Artapanus, a Hellenistic

2. After the Jewish authorities had put the apostles in custody, Codex Bezae records that 'each one went to his own house' (5.18 D05). There they remained until they were 'roused early in the morning (τὸ πρωΐ)' (5.21 D05). These details echo the command Moses gave to the people of Israel as they prepared for the night when the Lord would pass through Egypt to kill the firstborn: 'none of you shall go out of the door of his house until the morning' (Exod. 12.22, ἕως πρωΐ LXX). They show how the authorities believed themselves to be on the side of God, favoured and protected by him.
3. The angel of the Lord intervenes to release the prisoners (ἄγγελος κυρίου, 5.19). Initially in the Exodus account, it is the Lord himself who effected the deliverance of the people of Israel (Exod. 12.23, 29, 50) but in subsequent accounts the angel of the Lord is mentioned (Num. 20.16, cf. Exod. 14.19).[42]
4. The escape happens at night (διὰ νυκτός, 5.19), the time when the drama of the Exodus from Egypt took place (Exod. 12.12, 29–31, 42). The Greek text of Codex Bezae gives special prominence to the timing of the escape of the apostles by positioning the temporal adverb in first place in the sentence after the initial conjunction:
   5.19 B03: ἄγγελος δὲ κυρίου διὰ νυκτὸς ἤνοιξε τὰς θύρας...
   D05: Τότε διὰ νυκτὸς ἄγγελος κυρίου ἀνέωξεν τὰς θύρας...
5. The angel brings the apostles out of the prison (ἐξαγαγών τε αὐτούς, 5.20), just as so often the Lord is said to have brought the people out of Egypt (e.g. Exod. 12.17, 42, 51, ἐξάγω LXX).[43]
6. The angel commands the apostles to 'go and stand in the Temple (σταθέντες ἐν τῷ ἱερῷ) and speak (λαλεῖτε) to the people (τῷ λαῷ) all the words of this life (τῆς ζωῆς ταύτης)' (5.20). The connection between words and life is an intimate one, seen in the traditional idea that the Torah was the tree of life.[44] The association

Jew from 3th/2nd century BCE, cited by Eusebius, *Praep. Ev.*, 9.27.7,17; and Josephus, *Ant.*, 2.254–55.

42. For further examples of the tradition concerning the Exodus angel see Kugel, *Traditions of the Bible*, pp. 584–85. D. Daube (*The Exodus Pattern in the Bible* [London: Faber and Faber, 1963]) draws attention to the tradition, evident in Exod. 33.2–6, that the presence of an angel in place of God himself was viewed as a consequence of the people's sinfulness (pp. 40–41).

43. Though the notion of God 'bringing out' his people recurs in diverse contexts in the Hebrew Bible, its importance has been shown to be derived from its first occurrence in the Exodus narrative (Daube, *The Exodus Pattern*, pp. 32–33).

44. The idea that the Torah was the tree of life is extensively represented in the Rabbinic writings, apparently developed at a much earlier date: 'As I shall breathe the breath of life into the nostrils of man, so will I do for Israel – I will give the Torah unto him, the tree of life' (cited by L. Ginzberg, *The Legends of the Jews* [7 vols.; Philadelphia: The Jewish Publication Society of America, 11th edn., 1982], I, p. 51; see also Kugel, *Traditions of the Bible*, pp. 614–15; 627.

is found in the order given by God on Mount Sinai to Moses after he had left Egypt: 'But you, stand here by me (στῆθι μετ᾽ ἐμοῦ), and I will tell (λαλήσω) you all the commandments and the statutes and the ordinances that you shall teach them [= the people, ὁ λαός, Deut. 5.28 LXX)] ... you shall walk in the way that the Lord your God has commanded you ... that you may live long (μακροημερεύσητε, cf. Deut. 4.1 LXX: ἵνα ζῆτε) in the land that you shall possess' (Deut. 5.31, 33 LXX).

7. The view that the high priestly circle had of themselves is reinforced in the statement 'they called together the Sanhedrin, that is all the senate of the sons of Israel (πᾶσαν τὴν γερουσίαν τῶν υἱῶν 'Ισραήλ)' (5.21), for this echoes the action Moses took when he transmitted the instructions concerning the passover to the people of Israel: 'Moses called all the senate of the sons of Israel' (Exod. 12.21, πᾶσαν γερουσίαν υἱῶν 'Ισραήλ LXX). As leaders of Israel, they see themselves as having the role of Moses but the narrative has established in the preceding scene (5.12–17) that it is the apostles, those who believe in and follow Jesus as Messiah, who have been given the divine power to teach, heal and lead the people of God. There is, in other words, an implicit conflict over who exactly is leading Israel.

Four further allusions to the Exodus event in Acts 5 may be detected in the account of the apostles' activity just prior to the imprisonment scene (vv. 12–16), deriving as much from later Jewish tradition as the biblical account. They establish a comparison between the happy state of the Israelites just after their deliverance from Egypt and the success and harmony enjoyed by the apostolic community:

8. The apostles are portrayed as engaged in performing many signs and wonders among the people (σημεῖα καὶ τέρατα πολλὰ ἐν τῷ λαῷ, 5.12a), reminiscent of the wonders accomplished by God through Moses in Egypt (Exod. 7.3, τέρατα LXX). The parallel with Moses is bolstered by the traditional teaching concerning the many miracles he is said to have carried out among the Israelites throughout the Exodus, especially at the Red Sea: Wis. 19.8b; cf. Acts 7.36, 'he brought them out doing wonders and signs (τέρατα καὶ σημεῖα) in the land of Egypt, at the Red Sea and in the desert'.[45]

45. *Targ. Ps.-J. Exod.* 15.11 amplifies the Hebrew text when it speaks of the Lord 'performing signs and wonders for your people, the house of Israel' at the Red Sea. The tradition concerning the performance of miracles by Moses at the Red Sea is investigated by P. Enns, *Exodus Retold: Ancient Exegesis of the Departure from Egypt in Wis 10:15–21 and 19:1–9* (Harvard Semitic Museum Monographs, 57; Atlanta, Georgia: Scholars Press, 1997), pp. 128–30.

9. The whole of the apostolic community is described as being united (ὁμοθυμαδόν, 5.12). The unity of the Israelites as they left Egypt is likewise a theme that was stressed in later Jewish tradition, partly based on Exod. 12.31–32 (cf. Wis. 10.20, ὁμοθυμαδόν; 18.9; 19.8).[46] A consequence of this unity is that whilst it is true that only the apostles were physically imprisoned, the whole of the Jesus-believing community cannot but have been affected by the hostility of the Jewish authorities.
10. Peter is presented as especially active in miracles of healing and is invested with such divine power that people were brought out to lie on the streets of Jerusalem so that 'his shadow (σκιά) might rest upon (ἐπισκιάσῃ, lit. "overshadow") some of them' (5.15). In the Exodus story, it was the cloud that went before the Israelites as they journeyed out of Egypt and through the wilderness that 'overshadowed' (ἐπεσκίαζεν LXX, e.g. Exod. 40.35) the tent of meeting and contained within it, as it were, the divine presence (cf. Isa. 4.6, where God is depicted as creating a cloud [by day, and a fire by night] to be like a 'shadow' [σκιά LXX] for the protection of the people in Jerusalem).
11. The Bezan text goes on to specify that everyone was thus liberated from whatever sickness they might have had (5.15 D05). Both texts then conclude, before introducing the high priest and the Sadducees onto the scene, with the statement that all the sick and those with unclean spirits from around Jerusalem were healed (5.16, ἐθεραπεύοντο B03; ἰῶντο D05). Similarly, the Israelites were healed of every disease by the Lord 'your healer' in the wilderness (ἰώμενος LXX, Exod. 15.27).[47]

It may be noted that in the Exodus account, the Israelites are particularly blessed by God after their deliverance from Egypt, whereas in the case of the apostles they are portrayed as having already attained this state before they are arrested. Within the traditions of Jewish exegesis, however, it is not necessary for the exact chronology of an event to be respected in order for it to serve as a paradigm for interpreting subsequent events in the history of Israel. The re-enacting of the key elements of the event are of more significance than the order in which they occur. Yet one more allusion to the Exodus may lie behind the plea Gamaliel makes to the Sanhedrin:

46. For further discussion of the reasons behind the tradition concerning the unity of the Israelites, see Enns, *Exodus Retold*, pp. 75–82; 123–24.

47. There was a Jewish legend that the giving of the Torah had to be delayed when the Israelites left Egypt because the Lord wanted first of all to heal all their sicknesses (Ginzberg, *Legends of the Jews,* III, p. 78).

12. Although neither text of 5.38 (ἄφετε αὐτούς AT / ἐάσατε αὐτούς D05) uses the verb ἀποστέλλω found in the repeated references to 'let my people go' in the LXX text of Exodus, there is possibly an intended echo of the plea in Gamaliel's exhortation. If so, the Sanhedrin letting the apostles go is being equated with Pharaoh letting the Israelites go from slavery. Associated with the release of slaves throughout the Torah are orders for their good treatment on the part of the masters when they 'let them go'[48]. Seen in such a light, the Sanhedrin's mistreatment of the apostles (5.40) is all the more significant.

The implication of the comparison made between the detention and miraculous release of the apostles, on the one hand, and the Exodus on the other, is that the Jewish leaders, the very ones who should have guided the people in an acceptance of the Messiah, have become the enemies of God's people. The Acts narrative is thus expressing strong criticism of the religious leaders in their failure to fulfil their appointed roles. They have become the new oppressors of the people of God.

Excursus 9

The Parallel Roles of Gamaliel and Judas Iscariot

It is thanks to the intervention of Gamaliel, the Pharisee, that the apostles are released by the Sanhedrin and that they are able to continue their witnessing activity to Jesus as the Messiah. That they were able to do this unhindered by the Temple authorities, and apparently without opposition in Jerusalem (until, that is, the time of Herod Agrippa I [Acts 12]), is an indication that the Jesus-believers were tolerated by the Jewish religious leaders. This situation is in stark contrast to the situation of Jesus following his appearance before the Sanhedrin (Lk. 22.66–71) for he, for his part, met with outright rejection. Parallels between the opposition to Jesus' teaching in the Temple by the Jewish authorities and the apostles' first confrontation with them have been noted with reference to 4.1–7 (see *Commentary*, 4.1–4, *Overview*). Further parallels exist between Jesus' trial by the Sanhedrin and the apostles' second appearance before the council in Acts 5. First of all may be noted the similarities of circumstance (readings of D05 are in square brackets):

48. On the conditions for the proper release of a slave, see Daube, *The Exodus Pattern*, pp. 55–61.

1. Both Jesus and the apostles are involved in teaching the people in the Temple (Lk. 21.38 // Acts 5.20, 21, 25, 28).
2. The high priests are involved in both instances, together with the scribes in the Gospel (Lk. 22.2; cf. 23.23 D05 // Acts 5.17, 21), and they seek to put their prisoners to death (Lk. 22.2: ἐζήτουν πῶς ἀνέλωσιν [ἀπολέσωσιν] αὐτόν // Acts 5.33: ἐβούλοντο [-εύοντο] ἀνελεῖν αὐτούς).
3. On both occasions, the authorities are afraid of the people (Lk. 22.2: ἐφοβοῦντο γὰρ τὸν λαόν // Acts 5.26: ἐφοβοῦντο γὰρ τὸν λαόν, μὴ λιθασθῶσιν).
4. The arrest takes place at night with the meeting of the council held the following morning (Lk. 22.52–52, 66 // Acts 5.17–18, 21).
5. Jesus' trial is explicitly said to occur at the time of Passover (Lk. 22.1), while the theme of the Passover runs throughout that of the apostles by the allusions to the first Passover in Egypt (see *Excursus* 8).

The most surprising similarities are those that relate to the contrasting effects achieved by one individual on the outcome of the trial:

6. The plan to kill the prisoners is interrupted on each occasion (imperfect ἐζήτουν // ἐβούλοντο followed by a verb in the aorist) by the intervention of an individual who represents a certain group (Lk. 22.3, Judas: εἰσῆλθεν δὲ Σατανᾶς εἰς [τὸν] Ἰούδαν τὸν καλούμενον Ἰσκαριώτην [Ἰσκαριώδ] ὄντα ἐκ τοῦ ἀριθμοῦ [ἐκ] τῶν δώδεκα; cf. 22.47 // Acts 5.34, Gamaliel: ἀναστὰς δέ τις ἐν τῷ συνεδρίῳ [ἐκ τοῦ σ–ίου] Φαρισαῖος ὀνόματι Γαμαλιήλ)
7. Judas speaks (συνελάλησεν) with the high priests and the officers [omit D05] about how to deliver Jesus to them (Lk. 22.4; cf. 22.23: ὁ τοῦτο μέλλων πράσσειν) // Gamaliel says to (εἶπεν πρός) the rulers and members of the Sanhedrin, 'Men of Israel, take careful thought over what you are about to do (τί μέλλετε πράσσειν) to these men' (Acts 5.34)
8. Jesus was beaten (Lk. 22.63: δέροντες [omit D05]); Pilate wanted to let him go (ἀπολύσω) after chastising him (23.16, 20, 22) // The apostles were beaten (δείραντες) after which they released them (ἀπέλυσαν) (Acts 5.40)
9. The Jewish leaders rejoiced (ἐχάρησεν) at the arrival of Judas and the agreement reached with him (Lk. 22.5) // The apostles, following the intervention of Gamaliel, they left the Sanhedrin rejoicing (χαίροντες) at what they had suffered (Acts 5.41).

Judas and Gamaliel are both responsible in their own way for the particular conclusion reached by the Sanhedrin in the trials of Jesus and the apostles respectively: Judas, representing the Jewish people and also one of the Twelve, sets in motion the process that culminates in the death of Jesus; Gamaliel, as a leading Pharisee and member of the Sanhedrin, successfully dismantles the case set up by the high priestly circle against the apostles and, by obtaining their release, is indirectly responsible for their continuing ministry.

BIBLIOGRAPHY

I. *Works of Reference and Frequently Cited Works*

The following works are referred to by a short title (indicated in brackets after the entry) or, in the case of commentaries on Acts, by the name of the author.

Aland, B. and K., *et al.* (eds.), *Novum Testamentum Graece* (Stuttgart: Deutsche Bibelgesellschaft, 27th edn, 1993). (N-A^{27})

— *The Greek New Testament* (Stuttgart: Deutsche Bibelgesellschaft/United Bible Societies, 4th edn, 1993). (UBS^{4})

The American and British Committees of the International Greek New Testament Project (eds.), *The Gospel According to St. Luke*. Part I. Chapters 1–12; Part II, Chapters 13–28 (Oxford: Clarendon Press, 1984, 1987). (IGNTP)

Bailly, A., *Dictionnaire grec-français* (Paris: Hachette, 16th edn, 1950). (Bailly)

Barrett, C.K., *A Critical and Exegetical Commentary on the Acts of the Apostles* (2 vols.; Edinburgh: T.&T. Clark, 1994, 1998).

Bauer, W., *A Greek English Lexicon of the New Testament and Other Early Christian Literature* (ed. and trans. W.F. Arndt and F.W. Gingrich; Chicago: Chicago University Press, 1957). (B-A-G)

Blass, F., and A. Debrunner, *Grammatik des neutestamentlichen Griechisch* (Göttingen: Vandenhoeck & Ruprecht, 15th edn, 1979). (B-D-R)

Boismard, M.-É., and A. Lamouille, *Le texte occidental des Actes des Apôtres: Reconstitution et réhabilitation*. I. *Introduction et textes*; II. *Apparat Critique* (Paris: Éditions Recherche sur les Civilisations, 1984). (Boismard and Lamouille)

Bruce, F.F., *The Acts of the Apostles. The Greek Text with Introduction and Commentary* (London: The Tyndale Press, 1951). (*Text*)

— *Commentary on the Book of Acts. The English Text with Introduction, Exposition and Notes* (London: Marshall, Morgan and Scott, 1954). (*Acts*)

Clark, A.C., *The Acts of the Apostles* (Oxford: Clarendon Press, 1933; repr. 1970). (*Acts*)

Conzelmann, H., *Acts of the Apostles* (trans. J. Limburg, A.T. Kraabel and D.H. Juel; ed. E.J. Epp; Philadelphia: Fortress Press, 1987).

Delebecque, É., *Les Actes des Apôtres* (Paris: Belles Lettres, 1982). (*Actes*)

— *Les deux Actes des Apôtres* (EBib, NS, 6; Paris: J. Gabalda, 1986). (*Les deux Actes*)

Freedman, D.N. (ed.), *Anchor Bible Dictionary* (6 vols.; New York: Doubleday, 1992). (*ABD*)

Haenchen, E., *The Acts of the Apostles: A Commentary* (trans. B. Noble, G. Shinn and R. McL. Wilson; Oxford: B. Blackwells, 1981).

Johnson, L.T., *The Acts of the Apostles* (Sacra Pagina, 5: Collegeville, MN: The Liturgical Press, 1992).

Levinsohn, S.H., *Textual Connections in Acts* (Atlanta: Scholars Press, 1987). (*Textual Connections*)

Liddell, H.G., R.J. Scott and H.S. Jones, *A Greek-English Lexicon: A New Edition* (Oxford: Clarendon Press, 1940). (L-S-J)

Louw, J.P., and E.A. Nida, *Greek-English Lexicon of the New Testament Based on Semantic Domains* (2 vols.; New York: United Bible Societies, 2nd edn, 1989). (Louw and Nida)

Marshall, I.H., *The Acts of the Apostles* (Tyndale New Testament Commentaries; Leicester: IVP, 1980).

Metzger, B.M., *A Textual Commentary on the Greek New Testament* (Stuttgartt: Deutsche Bibelgesellschaft, 2nd edn, 1994). (*Commentary*)

Moulton, J.H., *A Grammar of New Testament Greek.* I. *Prolegomena* (Edinburgh: T.&T. Clark, 1908). (Moulton)

Moulton, J.H., and W.F. Howard, *A Grammar of New Testament Greek.* II. *Accidence and Word-Formation* (Edinburgh: T.&T. Clark, 1929). (Moulton and Howard)

Parker, D.C., *Codex Bezae: An Early Christian Manuscript* (Cambridge: Cambridge University Press, 1994). (*Codex Bezae*)

Read-Heimerdinger, J., *The Bezan Text of Acts. A Contribution of Discourse Analysis to Textual Criticism* (JSNTSup, 236; Sheffield: Sheffield Academic Press, 2002). (*The Bezan Text*)

Robertson, A.T., *A Grammar of the Greek New Testament in the Light of Historical Research* (Nasville, TN: Broadman, 4th edn, 1934). (*Grammar*)

Ropes, J.H., *The Text of Acts*, in Foakes-Jackson and Lake (eds.); III. *The Beginnings of Christianity*. Part I. *The Acts of the Apostles*. (*Text*)

Roth C. (ed.), *Encyclopaedia Judaica* (16 vols.; 3rd edn; Jerusalem: Ketev Publishing House, 1974). (*Enc. Jud.*)

Schneider, G., *Die Apostelgeschichte* (2 vols.; Herders Theologische Kommentar zum Neuen Testament; Freiburg: Herder, 1980, 1982).

Strack, H.L., and P. Billerbeck, *Kommentar zum Neuen Testament aus Talmud und Midrasch* (6 vols.; München: C.H. Beck, 6th edn, 1974–75). (Strack and Billerbeck)

Scrivener, F.H., *Bezae Codex Cantabrigiensis* (repr.; Pittsburgh, Pennsylvania: Pickwick Press, 1978). (*Bezae Codex*)

Singer, I. (ed.), *The Jewish Encyclopaedia* (12 vols.; New York: KTAV Publishing House, 1901). (*Jew. Enc.*)

Turner, N., *A Grammar of New Testament Greek.* III. *Syntax*; IV. *Style* (Edinburgh: T.&T. Clark, 1963, 1976). (*Syntax*)

Winer, G.B., *A Treatise on the Grammar of New Testament Greek* (trans. W.F. Moulton; Edinburgh: T.&T. Clark, 1882). (*Grammar*)

Zerwick, M., *Biblical Greek* (trans., rev. and ed. J. Smith; Rome: Biblical Institute Press, 1963). (*Biblical Greek*)

Zerwick, M., and M. Grosvenor, *A Grammatical Analysis of the Greek New Testament* (Rome: Biblical Institute Press, 1981). (Zerwick and Grosvenor, *Analysis*).

II. *Other Works Referred to*

Abusch, T., J. Huehnergard and P. Steinkeller (eds.), *Lingering Over Words* (Atlanta: Scholars Press, 1990).

Aland, B., 'Entstehung, Charakter und Herkunft des sog. westlichen Textes untersucht an der Apostelgeschichte', *EThL* 62 (1986), pp. 5–65.

Aland, K., *Text und Textwert der griechischen Handschriften des Neuen Testaments.* III. *Apostelgeschichte* (2 vols.; ANTF, 20–21; Berlin: Walter de Gruyter, 1993).

Alexander, L.C.A., *The Preface to Luke's Gospel* (Cambridge: Cambridge University Press, 1993).

Ammassari, A. (ed.), *Bezae Codex Cantabrigiensis* (Città del Vaticano: Libreria Editrice Vaticana, 1996).

Amphoux, C.-B., 'Le chapitre 24 de Luc et l'origine de la tradition textuelle du Codex de Bèze (D.05 du NT)', *FN* 4 (1991), pp. 21–49.

— *La parole qui devient évangile* (Paris: Seuil, 1993).

— 'Schéma d'histoire du texte grec du Nouveau Testament', *New Testament Update* 3 (1995), pp. 41–46.

— *L'Évangile selon Matthieu. Codex de Bèze* (L'Isle-sur-la-Sorgue: Le Bois d'Orion, 1996).

Amphoux, C.-B., and J.K. Elliott (eds.), *The New Testament Text in Early Christianity: Proceedings of the Lille Colloquium, July 2000 / Le texte du Nouveau Testament au début du christianisme: Actes du colloque de Lille, juillet 2000* (forthcoming).

Anderson, R., 'À la recherche de Théophile', in *Saint Luc, évangéliste et historien* (*Dossiers d'Archéologie* 279 [2002–3]), pp. 64–71.

Bailey, K.E., *Poet and Peasant* and *Through Peasant Eyes* (Grand Rapids: Eerdmans, combined edn, 1983).

Barc, B., 'Le texte de la Torah a-t-il été récrit?', in Tardieu (ed.), *Les règles de l'interprétation*, pp. 69–88.

— *Les arpenteurs du temps: Essai sur l'histoire religieuse de la Judée à la période héllenistique* (Lausanne: Éditions du Zèbre, 2000).

Barrett, C.K., 'Is there a Theological Tendency in Codex Bezae?', in Best and Wilson (eds.), *Text and Interpretation*, pp. 15–27.

Baruk, H., *Tsedek, droit hébraïque, et science de la paix* (Paris: Zikaron, 1970).

Bauckham, R., 'Kerygmatic Summaries in the Speeches of Acts', in Witherington (ed.), *History, Literature and Society*, pp. 185–217.

— 'The Restoration of Israel in Luke-Acts', in Scott (ed.), *Restoration*, pp. 435–87.

Beardslee, W.A., 'The Casting of Lots at Qumran', *NovT* 4 (1960), pp. 245–52.

Beattie, D.R.G., and M.J. McNamara, *The Aramaic Bible: Targums in their Historical Context* (JSOTSup, 166; Sheffield: Sheffield Academic Press, 1994).

Bernheim, P.-A., *James, Brother of Jesus* (London: SCM Press, 1997).

Best, E., and R. McL. Wilson (eds.), *Text and Interpretation* (Cambridge: Cambridge University Press, 1979).

Black, D., and S.H. Levinsohn, *Linguistics and New Testament Interpretation* (Nashville, TN: Broadman Press, 1992).

Black, M., *An Aramaic Approach to the Gospels and Acts* (Oxford: Clarendon, 3rd edn, 1967).

Blass, F., *Acta Apostolorum sive Lucae ad Theophilum liber alter: Editio philologica apparatu critico* (Göttingen: Vandenhoeck & Ruprecht, 1895).

Bock, D.L., *Proclamation from Prophecy and Pattern: Lucan Old Testament Christology* (JSNTSup, 12; Sheffield: JSOT Press, 1987).

Boismard, M-.É., and A. Lamouille, *Les Actes des deux Apôtres*. I. *Le texte*; II. *Le sens des récits*; III. *Analyses littéraires* (EBib, NS, 12–14; Paris: J. Gabalda, 1990).

—*Le texte occidental des Actes des Apôtres: Édition nouvelle entièrement refondue* (EBib, NS, 40; Paris: J. Gabalda, 2000).

Borrell, A., A. de la Fuente and A. Puig (eds.), *La Bíblia i el Mediterrani* (2 vols.; Montserrat, Barcelona: Publicacions de l'Abadia de Montserrat, 1997).

Bossuyt, P., and J. Radermakers, *Témoins de la parole de grâce: Lecture des Actes des Apôtres* (2 vols.; Brussels: Institut d'Études Théologiques, 1995).

Bovon, F., 'Studies in Luke-Acts: Retrospect and Prospect', *HTR* 85 (1992), pp. 175–96.

Brawley, R.L., *Luke-Acts and the Jews* (Atlanta: Scholars Press, 1987).

— *Text to Text Pours Forth Speech* (Bloomington, Ind.: Indiana University Press, 1995).
Brock, S., 'ΒΑΡΝΑΒΑΣ ΥΙΟΣ ΠΑΡΑΚΛΗΣΕΩΣ', *JTS* 25 (1974), pp. 93–98.
Brosend, W.F., 'The Means of Absent Ends', in Witherington (ed.), *History, Literature and Society*, pp. 348–62.
Brown, G., and G. Yule, *Discourse Analysis* (Cambridge: Cambridge University Press, 1983).
Bruce, F.F., 'The Acts of the Apostles Today', *BJRL* 65 (1982), pp. 36–56.
Cadbury, H.J., *The Book of Acts in History* (London: A&C Black, 1955).
— *The Making of Luke-Acts* (London: SPCK, 1958, repr. 1968).
Charlesworth, J.H. (ed.), *The Old Testament Pseudepigrapha*. I. *Apocalyptic Literature and Testaments* (London: Dartman, Longman and Todd, 1983).
Charlesworth, J.H., and C.A. Evans (eds.), *The Pseudepigrapha and Early Biblical Interpretation* (JSP 14; Studies in Scriptures in Early Judaism and Christianity 2; Sheffield: JSOT, 1993).
Chilton, B.D., *God in Strength* (Freistadt: Verlag F. Plöchl, 1979).
— *The Glory of Israel: The Theology and Provenience of the Isaiah Targum* (JSOTSup, 23; Sheffield: JSOT Press, 1982).
— *A Galilean Rabbi and his Bible* (London: SPCK, 1984).
— *The Isaiah Targum: Introduction, Translation, Apparatus, Notes* (Edinburgh: T.&T. Clark, 1987).
Chilton, B.D., and J. Neusner, *Judaism in the New Testament: Practices and Beliefs* (London: Routledge, 1995).
Colwell, E.C., *Studies in Methodology in Textual Criticism of the New Testament* (Leiden: E.J. Brill, 1969).
Cosgrove, C.H., 'The Divine δεῖ in Luke-Acts', *NovT* 26 (1984), pp. 168–90.
Daube, D., *The Exodus Pattern in the Bible* (London: Faber and Faber, 1963).
Davies, J.G., 'Pentecost and Glossolalia', *JTS*, NS, 3 (1952), pp. 228–31.
Del Agua Pérez, A., *El método midrásico y la exégesis del Nuevo Testamento* (Valencia: Institución San Jerónimo, 1985).
Delebecque, É., 'Trois simples mots, chargés d'une lumière neuve (Actes des Apôtres, II, 47b)', *RevThom* 80 (1980), pp. 75–85.
— 'Les deux prologues des Actes des Apôtres', *RevThom* 80 (1980), pp. 628–34.
— 'Ascension et Pentecôte dans les Actes des Apôtres selon le Codex Bezae', *RevThom*.82 (1982), pp. 79–83.
— *Études sur le grec du Nouveau Testament* (Aix-en-Provence: Publications de l'Université de Provence, 1995).
De Waard, J., *A Comparative Study of the Old Testament Text in the Dead Sea Scrolls and the New Testament* (Studies on the Texts of the Desert of Judah, 4; Leiden: E.J. Brill, 1966).
Dibelius, M., *Studies in the Acts of the Apostles* (trans. M. Ling; London: SCM, 1956).
Dunn, J.D.G., *The Partings of the Ways Between Christianity and Judaism and their Significance for the Character of Christianity* (London: SCM Press, 1991, repr. 1996).
Dupont, J., '᾿ΑΝΕΛΗΜΦΘΗ (Actes 1,2)', *NTS* 8 (1962), pp. 154–57.
— 'La prière des apôtres persécutés', in *idem*, *Études sur les Actes des Apôtres* (Lectio Divina, 45; Paris: Cerf, 1967), pp. 521–22.
— 'Le douzième apôtre (Actes 1,15–26). À propos d'une explication récente', *Bibbia e Oriente* 24 (1982), pp. 193–98.
Eckart, R., *Pseudo-Philo und Lukas* (Tübingen: J.C.B. Mohr [Paul Siebeck], 1994).
Ehrman, B.D., and M.W. Holmes (eds.), *The Text of the New Testament in Contemporary Research* (Grand Rapids: Eerdmans, 1995).

Eisenman, R., *James, the Brother of Jesus. Recovering the True History of Early Christianity* (London: Faber and Faber, 1997).
Elliott, J.K., *Essays and Studies in New Testament Textual Criticism* (Córdoba: El Almendro, 1992).
— 'Codex Bezae and the Earliest Greek Papyri', in Parker and Amphoux (eds.), *Lunel Colloquium*, pp. 161–82.
— 'A Comparison of Two Recent Greek New Testaments', *ExpT* 107 (1996), pp. 105–106.
— 'Thoroughgoing Eclecticism in New Testament Textual Criticism', in Ehrman and Holmes (eds.), *Contemporary Research*, pp. 321–35.
— 'The Manuscript Heritage of the Book of Acts', in Amphoux and Elliott (eds.), *Lille Colloquium*, forthcoming.
— 'An Eclectic Textual Study of the Book of Acts', in Nicklas and Tilly (eds.), *Apostelgeschichte als Kirchengeschichte*, pp. 9–30.
Enns, P., *Exodus Retold: Ancient Exegesis of the Departure from Egypt in Wis 10:15–21 and 19:1–9* (Harvard Semitic Museum Monographs, 57; Atlanta, Georgia: Scholars Press, 1997).
Epp, E.J., *The Theological Tendency of Codex Bezae Cantabrigiensis in Acts* (Cambridge: Cambridge University Press, 1966).
— 'Coptic Manuscript G^{67} and the Role of Codex Bezae as a Western Witness in Acts', *JBL* 85 (1966), pp. 197–212.
— 'The Ascension in the Textual Tradition of Luke-Acts', in Epp and Fee (eds.), *New Testament Textual Criticism,* pp.131–46.
— 'Textual Criticism: New Testament', *ABD*, VI, pp. 412–35.
Evans, C.A., 'Luke and the Rewritten Bible: Aspects of Lukan Hagiography', in Charlesworth and Evans (eds.), *The Pseudepigrapha and Early Biblical Interpretation*, pp. 170–201.
Feldman, L.H., 'Palestinian and Diaspora Judaism in the First Century', in Shanks (ed.), *Christianity and Rabbinic Judaism*, pp. 1–40.
Fishbane, M., *Biblical Interpretation in Ancient Israel* (Oxford: Clarendon Press, 1987).
Fitzgerald, J.T. (ed.), *Friendship, Flattery, and Frankness of Speech: Studies on Friendship in the New Testament World* (Leiden: E.J. Brill, 1996).
Foakes-Jackson, F.J., and K. Lake (eds.), *The Beginnings of Christianity.* I. *The Acts of the Apostles* (5 vols.; London: Macmillan, 1920–33).
Freyne, S., *Galilee from Alexander the Great to Hadrian, 323 BCE to 135 CE* (Wilmington: Michael Glazier, Inc./Notre Dame: University of Notre Dame Press, 1980).
— 'The Geography of Restoration: Galilee-Jerusalem Relations in Early Christian and Jewish Experience', in Scott, *Restoration*, pp. 405–33.
Fuller, R.H., 'The Choice of Matthias', *SE* 6 (1973), pp. 140–46.
Fusco, V., 'Luke-Acts and the Future of Israel', *NovT* 38 (1996), pp. 1–17.
Garrard, A., *The Splendour of the Temple* (Eye, Suffolk: Moat Farm Publications, 1997).
Gasque, W.W., *A History of the Criticism of the Acts of the Apostles* (Tübingen: J.C.B. Mohr [Paul Siebeck], 1975).
— 'A Fruitful Field. Recent Study of the Acts of the Apostles', *Interpretation* 42 (1988), pp. 117–31.
Ginzberg, L., *The Legends of the Jews* (7 vols.; Philadelphia: The Jewish Publication Society of America, 11th edn, 1982).
Grabbe, L.L., *Judaism from Cyrus to Hadrian* (London: SCM Press, 1994).
Grant, M., *The Jews in the Roman World* (London: Weidenfeld and Nicolson, 1973).
Grässer, E., 'Acta-Forschung seit 1960'. I, *TR* 41 (1976), pp. 141–94; II, *TR* 41 (1976), pp. 259–90; III, *TR* 42 (1977), pp. 1–68.

Green, J.B., 'The Demise of the Temple as "Cultural Center" in Luke-Acts: An Exploration of the Rending of the Temple Veil', *RB* 101 (1994), pp. 495–515.

— 'Internal Repetition in Luke-Acts: Contemporary Narratology and Lukan Historiography', in Witherington (ed.), *History, Literature and Society*, pp. 283–99.

Haenchen, E., and P. Weigandt, 'The Original Text of Acts?', *NTS* 14 (1968), pp. 469–81.

Hahn, F., 'Die Himmelfarht Jesus. Ein Gespräch mit Gerhard Lohfink', *Bib* 55 (1974), pp. 418–26.

— 'Der gegenwärtige Stand der Erforschung der Apostelgeschichte: Kommentare und Aufsatzbände 1980–1985', *Theologische Revue* 82 (1986), pp. 180–200.

Heimerdinger, J. (see also Read-Heimerdinger, J.), 'Actes 8:37. La foi de l'eunuque éthiopien', *ETR* (1988), pp. 521–28.

— 'Acts 8:37: A Textual and Exegetical Study', *The Bulletin of the Institute for Reformation Biblical Studies* 2 (1991), pp. 8–13.

— 'Unintentional Sins in Peter's Speech: Acts 3:12–26', *RCatT* 20 (1995), pp. 269–76.

— 'The Seven Steps of Codex Bezae: A Prophetic Interpretation of Acts 12', in Parker and Amphoux (eds.), *Codex Bezae*, pp. 303–310.

— 'La tradition targumique et le Codex de Bèze. Ac 1:15–26', in Borrell, De la Fuente and Puig (eds.), *La Bíblia i el Mediterrani*, II, pp. 171–80.

Heimerdinger, J., and S.H. Levinsohn, 'The Use of the Definite Article before Names of People in the Greek Text of Acts with Particular Reference to Codex Bezae', *FN* 5 (1992), pp. 15–44.

Hemer, C.J., *The Book of Acts in the Setting of Hellenistic History* (ed. C.H. Gempf; Tübingen: J.C.B. Mohr, 1989).

Hengel, M., *Acts and the History of Earliest Christianity* (London: SCM 1979).

— *Jews, Greeks and Barbarians: Aspects of Judaism in the Pre-Christian Period* (London: SCM, 1980).

Hill, C.C., *Hellenists and Hebrews: Reappraising Division within the Earliest Church* (Minneapolis: Augsburg, 1992).

Holmes, M.W., 'Reasoned Eclecticism in New Testament Textual Criticism', in Ehrman and Holmes (eds.), *Contemporary Research*, pp. 336–60.

Horbury, W., 'Herod's Temple and "Herod's Days"', in *idem* (ed.), *Templum Amicitiae* (JSNTSup, 48; Sheffield: JSOT Press, 1991).

Instone Brewer, D., *Techniques and Assumptions in Jewish Exegesis before 70 CE* (Tübingen: J.C.B. Mohr [Paul Siebeck], 1992).

Jacobs, I., *The Midrashic Process* (Cambridge: Cambridge University Press, 1995).

Jaubert, A., 'L'élection de Matthias et le tirage au sort', *SE* 6 (1973), pp. 274–80.

Jáuregui, J.A., *Testimonio-apostolado-misión. Justificación teológica del concepto lucano Apóstol-Testigo de la Resurrección. Análisis exegético de Act 1,15–26* (Bilbao: Universidad de Deusto, 1973).

Jervell, J., *Luke and the People of God* (Minneapolis: Augsburg, 1972).

— *The Unknown Paul* (Minneapolis: Augsburg, 1984).

— 'Retrospect and Prospect in Luke-Acts Interpretation' (SBL Seminar Papers 1991, ed. E.H. Lovering, Atlanta: Scholars Press, 1991), pp. 383–404.

— 'The Future of the Past: Luke's Vision of Salvation History and its Bearing on his Writing of History', in Witherington (ed.), *History, Literature and Society*, pp. 104–26.

Keck, L.E., and J.L. Martyn (eds.), *Studies in Luke-Acts* (London: SPCK, 1968).

Kee, H.C., '*Testaments of the Twelve Patriarchs.* Introduction', in Charlesworth (ed.), *The Old Testament Pseudepigrapha,* I, pp. 775–81.

Kepler, T.S., 'Sabbath Day's Journey', in *Interpreter's Dictionary of the Bible* (G.A. Buttrick [ed.], Nasville, TN: Abingdon, 1962), p. 141.
Kilgallen, J., *The Stephen Speech* (Rome: Biblical Institute Press, 1976).
Kilpatrick, G.D., 'The Two Texts of Acts', in Schrage (ed.), *Studien zum Text und zur Ethik des Neuen Testaments*, pp. 188–99.
— *The Principles and Practice of New Testament Textual Criticism: Collected Essays of G.D. Kilpatrick* (ed. J.K. Elliott; Leuven: Leuven University Press, 1990).
Klassen, W., *Judas. Betrayer or Friend of Jesus?* (London: SCM Press, 1996).
Klawans, J., *Impurity and Sin in Ancient Judaism* (Oxford: Oxford University Press, 2000).
Klijn, A.J., *A Survey of the Researches into the Western Text of the Gospels and Acts*, Part I (Utrecht: Kemink, 1949); Part II (Leiden: E.J. Brill, 1969).
— 'In Search of the Original Text of Acts', in Keck and Martyn (eds.), *Studies in Luke-Acts*, pp. 103–10.
Kremer, J., *Les Actes des Apôtres. Traditions, rédaction, théologie* (Paris/Gembloux: Duculot/Leuven: Leuven University Press, 1979).
Kugel, J.L., *Poetry and Prophecy* (Ithaca and London: Cornell University Press, 1990).
— 'The Case Against Joseph', in Abusch, Huehnergard and Steinkeller (eds.), *Lingering Over Words*, pp. 271–87.
— *In Potiphar's House. The Interpretative Life of Biblical Texts* (Cambridge, MA.: Harvard University Press, 2nd edn, 1994).
— *Traditions of the Bible. A Guide to the Bible as it was at the Start of the Common Era* (Cambridge, MA.: Harvard University Press, 1998).
Kurz, W.S., 'Narrative Approaches to Luke-Acts', *Bib* 68 (1987), pp. 195–220.
— *Reading Luke-Acts: Dynamics of Biblical Narrative* (Louisville, KY: Westminster/John Knox Press, 1993).
Lake, K., *English Translation and Commentary*, in Foakes-Jackson and Lake (eds.), IV. *The Beginnings of Christianity*. Part I. *The Acts of the Apostles*.
Le Déaut, R., *La nuit pascale* (Rome: Biblical Institute Press, 1963).
— *Liturgie juive et Nouveau Testament* (Rome: Biblical Institute Press, 1965).
Lentz, J.C., *Luke's Portrait of Paul* (Cambridge: Cambridge University Press, 1996).
Levinsohn, S.H., *Discourse Features of New Testament Greek* (Dallas: Summer Institute of Linguistics, 1992).
Lohfink, G., *Die Himmelfahrt Jesu. Untersuchungen zu den Himmelfahrts – und Erhöhungstexten bei Lukas* (Munich, 1971).
McNamara, M., *New Testament and Palestinian Targum to the Pentateuch* (Rome: Biblical Institute Press, 1966).
Malina, B.J., *Windows on the World of Jesus: Time Travel to Ancient Judea* (Louisville: Westminster/John Knox, 1993).
Mann, J., *The Bible as Read and Preached in the Old Synagogue*. I (New York: KTAV, 1940); II (ed. I. Sonne; Ohio: Hebrew Union College, 1966).
Marguerat, D., *The First Christian Historian. Writing the 'Acts of the Apostles'* (trans. K. McKinney, G.J. Laughery and R. Bauckham; SNTS, 121; Cambridge: Cambridge University Press, 2002).
Marshall, I.H., *The Gospel of Luke* (New International Greek Testament Commentary; Paternoster: Exeter, 1978).
Mateos, J., *El aspecto verbal en el Nuevo Testamento* (Madrid: Cristiandad, 1977).
— 'Σάββατα, σάββατον, προσάββατον, παρασκευή', *FN* 3 (1990), pp. 19–38.
— *Los "Doce" y otros seguidores de Jesús en el Evangelio de Marcos* (Madrid: Cristiandad 1982).

Metzger, B.M., *The Text of the New Testament* (Oxford: Clarendon Press, 1964).
— *The Canon of the New Testament* (Oxford: Clarendon Press, 1987).
Moessner, D.P., 'The "Script" of the Scriptures in Acts: Suffering as God's "Plan" (βουλή) for the World for the "Release of Sins"', in Witherington (ed.) *History, Literature and Society*, pp. 218–50.
Nellessen, E., 'Tradition und Schrift in der Perikope der Erwählung des Matthias (Apg 1:15–26)', *BZ* 19 (1975), pp. 205–18.
Neusner, J., *The Rabbinic Traditions about the Pharisees before AD 70* (Leiden: E.J. Brill, 1971).
— *Judaism in the Beginning of Christianity* (London: SPCK, 1984).
— (ed.), *Genesis Rabbah: The Judaic Commentary to the Book of Genesis* (Atlanta: Scholars Press, 1985).
Neusner, J., *et al.* (eds.), *The Social World of Formative Christianity and Judasim* (Philadelphia: Fortress, 1988).
Nicklas, T., and M. Tilly (eds.), *Apostelgeschichte als Kirchengeschichte. Text, Traditionen und antike Auslegungen* (BZNW, 122: Berlin-New York: Walter de Gruyter, 2003).
O'Toole, R.F., *The Christological Climax of Paul's Defense (Ac 22:1–26:32)*, (Rome: Biblical Institute Press, 1978).
Osburn, C.D., 'The Search for the Original Text of Acts: The International Project on the Text of Acts', *JSNT* 44 (1991), pp. 39–55.
Parker, D.C., 'Professor Amphoux's History of the New Testament Text: A Response', *New Testament Update* 4 (1996), pp. 41–45.
Parker, D.C, and C.-B. Amphoux (eds.), *Codex Bezae: Studies from the Lunel Colloquium June 1994* (Leiden: E.J. Brill, 1996).
Parsons, M.C., 'The Text of Acts 1:2 Reconsidered', *CBQ* 50 (1988), pp. 58–71.
— *The Departure of Jesus in Luke-Acts. The Ascension Narratives in Context* (JSNTSup, 21; Sheffield: Sheffield Academic Press, 1987).
Parsons, M.C., and R.I. Pervo, *Rethinking the Unity of Luke and Acts* (Minneapolis: Augsburg, 1993).
Perrot, C., 'Un fragment christo-palestinien découvert à Khirbet-Mird', *RB* 70 (1963), pp. 506–55.
— *La lecture de la Bible* (Hildesheim: Verlag Dr. H.A. Gerstenberg, 1973).
Petersen, T.C., 'An Early Coptic Manuscript of Acts: An Unrevised Version of the Ancient So-Called Western Text', *CBQ* 26 (1964), pp. 225–41.
Plümacher, E., 'Acta-Forschung 1974–1982', *TR* 48 (1983), pp. 1–56.
Poorthuis, M., and C. Safrai (eds.), *The Centrality of Jerusalem: Historical Perspectives* (Kampen: Kok Pharos, 1996).
Pope, R. (ed.), *Remembering the Past and Shaping the Future: Religious and Biblical Studies in Wales* (Leominster: Gracewing, 2003).
Porter, S.E., *Verbal Aspect in the Greek of New Testament, with Reference to Sense and Mood* (Studies in Biblical Greek, I; New York: Peter Lang, 1989).
— *Idioms of New Testament Greek* (Biblical Languages: Greek, 2; Sheffield: JSOT Press, 1992).
— 'Discourse Analysis and New Testament Studies: An Introductory Survey', in Porter and Carson (eds.), *Discourse Analysis and Other Topics in Biblical Greek*, pp. 14–35.
Porter, S.E., and D.A. Carson (eds.), *Biblical Greek Language and Linguistics* (JSNTSup, 80; Sheffield: Sheffield Academic Press, 1993).
— *Discourse Analysis and Other Topics in Biblical Greek* (JSNTSup, 113; Sheffield: Sheffield Academic Press, 1995).

Potin, J., *La fête juive de la Pentecôte. Études des textes liturgiques* (2 vols.; Lectio Divina, 65; Paris: Cerf, 1971).

Prader, S.M., 'Jesus-Paul, Peter-Paul, and Jesus-Peter Parallelisms in Luke-Acts: A History of Reader Response' (SBL Seminar Papers 1984, ed. K.H. Richards, Atlanta: Scholars Press, 1984), pp. 23–39.

Rahlfs, A. (ed.), *Septuaginta* (Stuttgart: Deutsche Bibelstiftung, 1985).

Ravens, D., *Luke and the Restoration of Israel* (JSNT Sup, 119; Sheffield: Sheffield Academic Press, 1995).

Read-Heimerdinger, J. (see also Heimerdinger, J.), 'Barnabas in Acts: A Study of his Role in the Text of Codex Bezae', *JSNT* 72 (1998), pp. 23–66.

— Review of Taylor, *Les Actes des deux Apôtres*. V. *Commentaire historique* (EBib, NS, 23; Paris: J. Gabalda, 1994), *JTS* 47 (1996), pp. 239–45.

— Review of B.D. Ehrman and M.W. Holmes (eds.), *The Text of the New Testament in Contemporary Research* (Grand Rapids: Eerdmans, 1995), *NovT* 38 (1996), pp. 300–304.

— 'Where is Emmaus? Clues in the Text of Luke 24 in Codex Bezae' in Taylor (ed.), *Studies in the Early Text of the Gospels and Acts*, pp. 229–44.

— 'The Re-enactment of the History of Israel: Exodus Traditions in the Bezan Text of Acts', in Pope (ed.), *Remembering the Past and Shaping the Future*, pp. 81–96.

— 'The Apostles in the Bezan Text of Acts', in Nicklas and Tilly (eds.), *Apostelgeschichte als Kirchengeschichte*, pp. 263–80.

Read-Heimerdinger, J., and J. Rius-Camps, 'Emmaous or Oulammaous? Luke's Use of the Jewish Scriptures in the Text of Luke 24 in Codex Bezae', *RCatT* 27 (2002), pp. 23–42.

Rendel Harris, J., *Codex Bezae. A Study of the So-Called Western Text of the New Testament* (Text and Studies, 2.1; Cambridge: Cambridge University Press, 1891).

Rengstorf, K.H., 'Die Zuwahl des Matthias (Apg 1,15ff)', *ST* 15 (1961), pp. 53–56.

— 'The Election of Matthias', in W. Klassen and G.F. Snyder (eds.), *Current Issues in New Testament Interpretation* (New York: Scribner, 1962), pp. 178–92.

Richards (ed.), *Society of Biblical Literature 1984 Seminar Papers* (Chico: Scholars Press, 1984).

Richardson, P., *Herod: King of the Jews and Friend of the Romans* (Colombia, S. Carolina: University of South Carolina, 1996).

Rius-Camps, J., 'L'aparició/desaparició del "nosaltres" en el llibre dels Fets: un simple procediment teològico-literari?', *RCatT* 6 (1981), pp. 35–75.

— 'Lk 10,25–18,30: Una perfecta estructura concèntrica dins la Secció del Viatge (9,51–19,46)', *RCatT* 8 (1983), pp. 283–358.

— 'Estructura i funció significativa del tercer cicle o Secció de les Recognicions (Lc 6,12–9,50)', *RCatT* 9 (1984), pp. 269–329.

— '¿Constituye Lc 3,21–38 un solo período? Propuesta de un cambio de puntuación', *Bib* 65 (1984), pp. 189–208.

— *El camino de Pablo a la misión de los paganos. Comentario lingüístico y exegético a Hch 13–28* (Madrid: Cristiandad, 1984).

— *De Jerusalén a Antioquía: Génesis de la iglesia cristiana. Comentario lingüístico y exegético a Hch 1–12* (Córdoba: El Almendro, 1989).

— *Comentari als Fets dels Apòstols* (4 vols.; Barcelona: Facultat de Teologia de Catalunya/Herder, 1991–2000).

— 'Las variantes de la recensión occidental de los Hechos de los Apóstoles (I-XII)', *FN* 6–13 (1993–2000): (I): (Hch 1,1–3), *FN* 6 (1993), pp. 59–68; (II): (Hch 1,4–14), *FN* 6 (1993), pp. 219–30; (III): (Hch 1,15–26), *FN* 7 (1994), pp. 53–64; (IV): (Hch 2,1–13), *FN* 7 (1994), pp. 197–208; (V): (Hch 2,14–40), *FN* 8 (1995), pp. 63–78; (VI): (Hch 2,41–46),

FN 8 (1995), pp. 199–208; (VII): (Hch 3,1–26), *FN* 9 (1996), pp. 61–76; (VIII): (Hch 4,1–22), *FN* 9 (1996), pp. 201–16; (IX): (Hch 4,23–31), *FN* 10 (1997), pp. 99–104; (X): (Hch 4,32–5,16), *FN* 11 (1998), pp. 107–22; (XI): (Hch 5,17–42), *FN* 12 (1999), pp. 107–21; (XII): (Hch 6,1–7,22), *FN* 13 (2000), pp. 89–109.

— 'El seguimiento de Jesús, el Señor, y de su Espíritu en los prolegómenos de la misión (Hch 1–12)', *Estudios Bíblicos* 51 (1993), pp. 73–116.

— 'María, la madre de Jesús, en los Hechos de los Apostoles', *Ephemerides Mariologicae* 43 (1993), pp. 263–75.

— 'Origen lucano de la perícopa de la mujer adúltera (Jn 7.53–8.11)', *FN* 6 (1993), pp. 149–76.

— 'Le substrat grec de la version latine des Actes dans le codex de Bèze', in Parker and Amphoux (eds.), *Codex Bezae*, pp. 271–95.

— 'La utilización del libro de Joel (Jl 2,28–32A LXX) en el discurso de Pedro (Hch 2,14–21): Estudio comparativo de dos tradiciones manuscritas', in Taylor (ed.), *Studies in the Early Text of the Gospel and Acts*, pp. 245–70.

— 'The Spelling of Jerusalem in the Gospel of John: The Significance of Two Forms in Codex Bezae', *NTS* 48 (2002), pp. 84–94.

— 'The Gradual Awakening of Paul's Awareness of his Mission to the Gentiles', in Nicklas and Tilly (eds.), *Apostelgeschichte als Kirchengeschichte*, pp. 281–296.

Sacks, J., *Crisis and Covenant* (Manchester: Manchester University Press, 1992).

Safrai, S., and M. Stern (eds.), *The Jewish People in the First Century* (2 vols.; I, Philadelphia: Fortress Press, 1974; II, Assen – Amsterdam: Van Gorcum, 1976).

Sanders, E.P., '*Testament of Abraham.* Introduction', in Charlesworth (ed.), *The Old Testament Pseudepigrapha*, I, pp. 871–81.

— *Jesus and Judaism* (London: SCM Press, 1985).

Sanders, J.T., *Schismatics, Sectarians, Dissidents, Deviants. The First One Hundred Years of Jewish-Christian Relations* (London: SCM, 1993).

Schiffman, L.H., *Who was a Jew?* (Huboken, N.J.: KTAV, 1985).

Schrage, W. (ed.), *Studien zum Text und zur Ethik des Neuen Testaments* (Berlin: Walter de Gruyter, 1986).

Schürer, E., *The History of the Jewish People in the Age of Jesus Christ* (3 vols.; rev. and ed. G. Vermes, F. Millar and M. Black; Edinburgh: T&T Clark, 1973).

Schwartz, D.R., 'The End of the γῆ (Acts 1.8): Beginning or End of the Christian Vision?', *JBL* 105 (1986), pp. 669–76.

— 'Temple or City?', in Poorthuis and Safrai (eds.), *The Centrality of Jerusalem*, pp. 114–27.

Scott, J.M. (ed.), *Restoration: Old Testament, Jewish, and Christian Perspectives* (Leiden: E.J. Brill, 2001).

Scrivener, F.H., *Bezae Codex Cantabrigiensis* (Pittsburgh, Pennsylvania: Pickwick Press, repr. 1978).

Serra Zanetti, P., *ΕΝΩΣΙΣ – ΕΠΙ ΤΟ ΑΥΤΟ*, I. *Un 'dossier' preliminare per lo studio dell'unità cristiana al'inizio del 2° secolo* (Bologna: Zanichelli, 1969).

Shanks, H. (ed.), *Christianity and Rabbinic Judaism* (London: SPCK, 1993).

Silva, M., 'Modern Critical Editions and Apparatuses of the Greek New Testament', in Ehrman and Holmes (eds.), *Contemporary Research*, pp. 283–96.

Smallwood, E.M., *The Jews under Roman Rule: From Pompey to Diocletian* (Leiden: E.J. Brill, 1976).

Spencer, F.S., 'Neglected Widows in Acts 6:1–7', *CBQ* 56 (1994), pp. 715–33.

Stanton G.N., and G.G. Strousma (eds.), *Tolerance and its Limits in Early Judaism and Christianity* (Cambridge: Cambridge University Press, 1998).

Stauffer, E., 'Jüdisches Erbe im urchristlichen Kirchenrecht', *TLZ* 77 (1952), pp. 201–206.
Stenger, W., 'Beobachtungen zur sogenannten Völkerliste des Pfingstwunders (Apg. 2,7–11)', *Kairos* 21 (1979), pp. 211–12.
Strange, W.A., *The Problem of the Text of Acts* (Cambridge: Cambridge University Press, 1992).
Strauss, M.L., *The Davidic Messiah in Luke-Acts: The Promise and its Fulfillment in Lukan Christology* (JSNTSup, 110; Sheffield: Sheffield Academic Press, 1995).
Swanson, R., *New Testament Greek Manuscripts: Variant Readings Arranged in Horizontal Lines against Codex Vaticanus. The Acts of the Apostles* (Sheffield: Sheffield Academic Press, 1998).
Talbert, C.H., *Literary Patterns, Theological Themes and the Genre of Luke-Acts* (Missoula: Scholars Press, 1974).
Tannehill, R.C., 'Israel in Luke-Acts: A Tragic Story', *JBL* 104 (1995), pp. 69–85.
— *The Narrative Unity of Luke-Acts. A Literary Interpretation*, I. *Luke*; II, *Acts* (Philadelphia: Fortress Press, 1986, 1990).
Tardieu, M. (ed.), *Les règles de l'interprétation* (Paris: Cerf, 1987).
Tavardon, P., *Le texte alexandrin et le texte occidental des Actes des Apôtres. Doublets et variantes de structure* (Cahiers de la Revue Biblique, 37; Paris: J. Gabalda, 1997).
Taylor D.G.K. (ed.), *Studies in the Early Text of the Gospels and Acts* (Text and Studies, 3/I; Birmingham: University Press, 1999).
Taylor, J., *Les Actes des deux Apôtres*. V. *Commentaire historique* (EBib, NS, 23; Paris: J. Gabalda, 1994).
— *Les Actes des deux Apôtres*. VI. *Commentaire historique* (EBib, NS, 30; Paris: J. Gabalda, 1996).
— *Les Actes des deux Apôtres*. IV. *Commentaire historique* (EBib, NS, 41; Paris: J. Gabalda, 2000).
Thiele, W., 'Eine Bemerkung zu Act 1,14', in *ZNW* 53 (1962), pp. 110–11.
Thornton, T.C.G., 'To the end of the earth: Acts 1[8]', *ExpT* 89 (1977–8), pp. 374–75.
Thurston, B.B., 'Τὸ ὑπερῷον in Acts i.13', *ExpT* 80 (1968–9), pp. 21–22.
Tiede, D.L., 'The Exaltation of Jesus and the Restoration of Israel in Acts 1', *HTR* 79 (1986), pp. 278–86.
— '"Glory to Thy People, Israel": Luke-Acts and the Jews', in Neusner *et al.* (eds.), *The Social World of Formative Christianity and Judaism*, pp. 327–41.
Tromp, J., 'The Davidic Messiah in Jewish Eschatology of the First Century BCE', in Scott (ed.), *Restoration*, pp. 179–201.
Tyson, J.B., *Images of Judaism in Luke-Acts* (Colombia, S. Carolina: University of S. Carolina Press, 1992).
Vaganay, L., and C.-B. Amphoux, *An Introduction to New Testament Textual Criticism* (Cambridge: Cambridge University Press, 1992).
Van Unnik, W.C., 'Der Ausdruck ῾ΕΩΣ᾽ΕΣΞΑΤΟΥ ΤΗΣ ΓΗΣ (Apostelgeschichte 1.8) und sein alttestamentlicher Hintergrund', in *Studia Biblica et Semitica,* Wageningen, 1966, pp. 335–49.
Weatherly, J.A., *Jewish Responsibility for the Death of Jesus in Luke-Acts* (JSNTSup, 106; Sheffield: Sheffield Academic Press, 1994).
Wiener, A., *The Prophet Elijah in the Development of Judaism* (London: Routledge and Kegan Paul, 1978).
Wilcox, M., *The Semitisms of Acts* (Oxford: Clarendon Press, 1965).
— 'The Judas-Tradition in Acts 1.15–26', *NTS* 19 (1973), pp. 438–52.

Winter, B. (series ed.), *The Book of Acts in its First Century Setting* (6 vols.; Grand Rapids: Eerdmans, 1994–98).

Winter, S.C., 'ΠΑΡΡΗΣΙΑ in Acts', in Fitzgerald (ed.), *Friendship, Flattery, and Frankness of Speech*, pp. 185–202.

Witherington, B., *The Acts of the Apostles: A Socio-Rhetorical Commentary* (Grand Rapids: Eerdmans/Carlisle: Paternoster, 1998).

— (ed.), *History, Literature and Society in the Book of Acts* (Cambridge: Cambridge University Press, 1996).

Young, R.A., *Intermediate New Testament Greek* (Nashville, TN: Broadman & Holman, 1994).